ESSENTIALS OF ENTREPRENEURSHIP AND SMALL BUSINESS MANAGEMENT

Second Edition

THOMAS W. ZIMMERER

EAST TENNESSEE STATE UNIVERSITY

NORMAN M. SCARBOROUGH

PRESBYTERIAN COLLEGE

Prentice Hall

PRENTICE HALL
UPPER SADDLE RIVER, N.J. 07458

Associate Editor: Lisamarie Brassini
Editorial Assistant: Crissy Statuto
Editor-in-Chief: Natalie Anderson
Marketing Manager: Stephanie Johnson
Senior Production Editor: Cynthia Regan
Managing Editor: Dee Josephson
Manufacturing Buyer: Diane Peirano
Manufacturing Supervisor: Arnold Vila
Manufacturing Manager: Vincent Scelta
Senior Designer: Ann France
Interior Design: Nicole Leong/Jill Little
Cover Director: Jayne Conte
Illustrator (Interior): Electra Graphics, Inc.
Composition: East End Publishing Services

Library of Congress Cataloging-in-Publication Data
Zimmerer, Thomas.
    Essentials of entrepreneurship and small business management /
Thomas W. Zimmerer, Norman M. Scarborough.—2nd ed.
        p.   cm.
    Previous ed. published under title: The essentials of small
business management. 1994.
    Includes bibliographical references and index.
    ISBN 0-13-727298-7 (pbk.)
    1. Small business—Management. 2. New business enterprises—
Management. I. Scarborough, Norman M. II. Zimmerer, Thomas.
Essentials of small business management. III. Title.
HD62.7.Z55   1998
    658.02'2—DC21   97-10751

Prentice-Hall International (UK) Limited, *London*
Prentice-Hall of Australia Pty. Limited, *Sydney*
Prentice-Hall of Canada, Inc., *Toronto*
Prentice-Hall Hispanoamericana, S. A., *Mexico*
Prentice-Hall of India Private Limited, *New Delhi*
Prentice-Hall of Japan, Inc., *Tokyo*
Prentice-Hall Asia Pte. Ltd., *Singapore*
Editora Prentice-Hall do Brasil, Ltda., *Rio de Janeiro*

Printed in the United States of America

10   9   8   7

*We dedicate this book to the women whose love, support,
and encouragement helped make this project a reality.*

Linda Williams Zimmerer
— T.W.Z.

Cindy Scarborough
— N.M.S.

May your own dreams be your only boundaries.
—The Reverend Purlie Victorious

BRIEF CONTENTS

CONTENTS

SECTION IV PUTTING THE PLAN TO WORK: BUILDING A COMPETITIVE EDGE 301

PREFACE

Today, increasing numbers of students are choosing to become entrepreneurs, starting businesses that spring from their dreams of freedom and independence and their hopes for meaningful careers. Entrepreneurship is now the driving force behind economic growth and rejuvenation all across the globe—from the United States to the countries of the former Soviet Union. At the same time, teaching small business and entrepreneurship has become one of the most challenging tasks in colleges and universities today. Like most practicing entrepreneurs, entrepreneurial students expect to maximize the amount of practical, "hands-on" knowledge they get from a course in the shortest possible time. This book allows students to do exactly that.

The second edition of *Essentials of Entrepreneurship and Small Business Management* is designed to provide future entrepreneurs with a learning tool that allows them to quickly master the most essential issues involved in starting and managing a successful new business venture. This book uses a variety of tools to stimulate student interest and to promote learning:

 "You Be the Consultant." These short vignettes, drawn from actual small businesses, develop students' critical thinking skills by allowing them to apply the knowledge they gain to actual business problems. The best way for students to learn is to put their knowledge into practice; these exercises give them the opportunity to do just that.

 "Surfing the Net." At end of every chapter, several exercises appear that lead students into cyberspace, where they discover the fascinating power and dimensions of the World Wide Web (WWW). These exercises encourage students to explore the wealth of information and knowledge that is only a keystroke away. Preparing to run a business in the 21st century begins at our Website: **http://www.prenhall.com/scarbzim.**

 "Learning Objectives." Every chapter begins with a set of learning objectives, but it doesn't end there! The learning objectives are integrated into the chapters as "markers" that appear at the beginning of the appropriate section of the chapter. The chapter summaries also are built around these learning objectives, reinforcing the key concepts covered in every chapter.

 **Lots of real-world examples.** Every chapter is loaded with many examples of small companies that are living proof that the concepts and techniques covered in the text actually do work! These examples are easy to spot; they are identified in the margin.

☆ **High-quality tables, charts, and figures.** Thanks to computers, television, and movies, today's students are very visually oriented, and modern textbooks should recognize this. Every chapter contains helpful tables, charts, and figures designed to help students capture and retain meaningful concepts and information. We believe that learning should be fun and include many quality cartoons that are relevant to each chapter.

☆ **A sample business plan.** We have included a new sample business plan for an entrepreneurial venture ("Septic Sense") which was developed by a team of real student entrepreneurs. It offers a good example of how a team of entrepreneurs can convert an idea into a business. (See the Appendix.)

☆ **Comprehensive teaching package.** Supplements to accompany this text include: an instructor's manual, a printed test bank containing approximately 4,000 test questions (also available on disk), 275 Powerpoint electronic transparencies (in both color and black-and-white versions), and transparency masters. There are also ABC/*Wall Street Journal Report* videos and a video guide available to qualified faculty members. A business planning package titled, *A Business Plan for Small Business*, provides a series of computerized templates. Please contact your Prentice Hall sales representative for more information.

Essentials of Entrepreneurship and Small Business Management includes topics that are vital to any entrepreneur considering launching a business—all in a manageable 15 chapters. There is a right way—and wrong way—to launch a business. This book teaches entrepreneurs and entrepreneurs-to-be the *right way* to launch their companies so they can maximize their probability of success. It progresses in a logical fashion that reflects the input of dozens of experienced, successful small business professionals. It provides a map for building a business plan to guide a business down the road to success.

This book provides valuable guidance in the critical areas entrepreneurs face as they evaluate the potential of their business ideas. Its major strengths include in-depth, practical coverage of strategic management, choosing a form of ownership or a franchise, buying an existing business, developing a marketing strategy, managing cash flow, building a financial plan, and assembling a useful business plan. Once established, a business must maintain its competitive advantage. *Essentials of Entrepreneurship and Small Business Management* addresses this need with strong chapters on advertising and pricing; purchasing, quality, and inventory control; leading and managing a growing business; the ethical, legal, and regulatory environment; and others.

Students and faculty also have access to our World Wide Web (WWW) page at **http://www. prenhall.com/scarbzim** that serves as a valuable resource to those interested in learning more about the exciting world of small business entrepreneurship.

As you can see, we have used our combined 48 years of teaching experience (and our 42 years of experience writing textbooks) to produce a book that contains a multitude of both student- and professor-friendly features. We trust that this edition of *Essentials of Entrepreneurship and Small Business Management* will help the next generation of entrepreneurs reach their full potential and achieve their dreams of success as independent business owners. It is their dedication, perseverance, and creativity that keep the world's economy moving forward.

Acknowledgments

We thank the many people who played a vital role in creating this edition of *Essentials of Entrepreneurship and Small Business Management*. The contributions of the following reviewers were extremely valuable in helping us develop the features and the content of this edition: Dick LaBarre, *Ferris State University*; Deborah Streeter, *Cornell University*; and Jim Walker, *Moorhead State University*.

In addition, we thank members of the production team at Prentice Hall, all genuine professionals in every sense of the word. Their superb work lies at the core of the top-quality book you see before you. Creating a book is a team effort, and we could not have asked for a more cooperative, helpful group with which to work. Specifically, we thank:

Cynthia Regan, our outstanding production editor and one of the best we ever worked with.

Lisamarie Brassini, who did an excellent job coordinating all of our ancillaries and the Web site.

Crissy Statuto, editorial assistant, who handled what must have been hundreds of details masterfully and always with a smile in her voice.

We also thank Vernell Smith and Nancy Casteel for their phenomenal typing skills, which they graciously applied to both the manuscript and the ancillaries that accompany this book.

Finally, we thank Natalie Anderson, management editor, whose vision and dedication transformed the idea for this project into reality. Her experience and support have helped make this book the success that it is. Many thanks!!!

Thomas W. Zimmerer
Phone: (423) 929-6486
fax: (423) 929-6671

Norman M. Scarborough
Phone: (864) 833-8273
fax: (864) 833-8481
e-mail: nmscarb@csl.presby.edu

CHAPTER

ONE

The Foundations of Entrepreneurship

When work is a pleasure, life is a joy. When work is duty, life is slavery.
- Maxim Gorky

People ask me when I'm going to retire. I tell them I'm retired now.
I don't consider what I'm doing to be work. Mowing the lawn—that's work.
- Norman Brodsky, founder of Perfect
Courier, his sixth startup company.

Being defeated is often a temporary condition. Giving up is what makes it permanent.
- Marilyn vos Savant

Every great improvement has come after repeated failure . . . Failures, repeated failures,
are posts on the road to achievement.
- Charles F. Kettering

LEARNING OBJECTIVES

Upon completion of this chapter, you will be able to:

1. **Define** the role of the entrepreneur in business—in the United States and across the world.
2. **Describe** the entrepreneurial profile and evaluate your potential as an entrepreneur.
3. **Describe** the benefits and drawbacks of entrepreneurship.
4. **Explain** the forces that are driving the growth of entrepreneurship.
5. **Identify** the groups that are leading the nation's boom in entrepreneurship.
6. **Describe** the important role small businesses play in our nation's economy.
7. **Describe** the causes of small business failures and explain how small business owners can avoid them.

The World of the Entrepreneur

Welcome to the world of the entrepreneur! Never before have more people been realizing that Great American Dream of owning and operating their own business. Studies indicate that more people are working to start their own business than are getting married or having babies![1] Currently, one out of every 25 adults is actively involved in trying to start a new business.[2] This resurgence of the entrepreneurial spirit is the most significant economic development in recent business history. These heroes of the new economy are rekindling an intensely competitive business environment that had all but disappeared from the landscape of U.S. business. With amazing vigor, their businesses have introduced innovative products and services, pushed back technological frontiers, created new jobs, opened foreign markets, and, in the process, sparked the U.S. economy into regaining its competitive edge in the world. Congressman John J. LaFalce recently paid tribute to the vital role these small businesses play:

> We are at a crossroads in the economic history of this nation . . . . We can no longer rely on big business and big government to solve our problems. More than ever, small business is the key to our nation's future prosperity and competitiveness.[3]

The past two decades have seen record numbers of entrepreneurs launching businesses (see Figure 1.1), and current trends suggest that we may be on the crest of a new wave of entrepreneurial activity—not only in the United States but across the globe as well. America's largest companies have engaged in massive downsizing campaigns, dramatically cutting the number of managers and workers on their payrolls. This flurry of "pink slips" has spawned a new population of entrepreneurs: "castoffs" from large corporations (in which many of these individuals thought they would spend a lifetime climbing the corporate ladder) with solid management experience and many productive years left before retirement. This downsizing has all but destroyed the longstanding notion of job security in large corporations. As a result, people who once saw launching a business as being too risky now see it as the ideal way to create their own job security!

This downsizing trend among large companies has created a more significant philosophical change. It has ushered in an age in which "small is beautiful." Twenty-five years

Figure 1.1
Number of New Incorporations

Source: Copyright 1996, Dun & Bradstreet, a company of The Dun & Bradstreet Corporation.

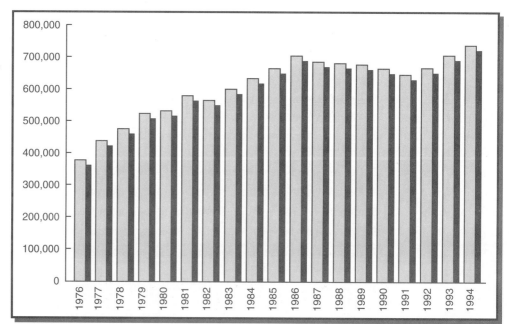

ago, competitive conditions favored large companies with their hierarchies and layers of management; today, with the pace of change constantly accelerating, fleet-footed, agile, small companies have the competitive advantage. These nimble competitors can dart into and out of niche markets as they emerge and recede; they can move faster to exploit market opportunities; and they can use modern technology to create within a matter of weeks or months products and services that once took years and all of the resources a giant corporation could muster. The balance has tipped in favor of small, entrepreneurial companies. Howard Stevenson, Harvard's chaired professor of entrepreneurship, says, "Why is it so easy [for small companies] to compete against giant corporations? Because while they [the giants] are studying the consequences, [entrepreneurs] are changing the world."[4]

The United States is not the only nation to benefit from the surge in entrepreneurship; Eastern European countries, China, Vietnam, Russia, and many others whose economies were state controlled and centrally planned are now fertile ground for growing small businesses.

When the government in the former Soviet Union crumbled in 1990, Alexander Gordin and David Veitsman, two Russian émigrés, saw a unique business opportunity in their former homeland. "The conditions were beginning to emerge for small businesses to take root," says Gordin. "We looked at the market and saw a once-in-a-lifetime opportunity." At first, the partners considered selling advertising on the Moscow subway system, a standard practice in the United States but unheard of in the Eastern bloc. However, their market research quickly led them to abandon that idea. Next Gordin and Veitsman approached Motorola, then Gordin's employer, about establishing a distributorship for two-way radios in the former Soviet Union countries. Because they tapped the Russian market so early, their first six months were lean. "We came in about a year and a half before any commercial entities were really running and capitalized," recalls Veitsman. Soon, the demand for communication equipment grew, and their company, Radio Communications International Corporation (RCI) was already well established. By combining their fluency of the Russian language and their knowledge of Russian business customs with their entrepreneurial zeal, Gordin and Veitsman expanded RCI from a radio distributorship into a full-service communications company. Within five years, they had built RCI into a company with $10 million in annual sales, 40 employees, and nine offices in three countries![5]

Wherever they may choose to launch their companies, these business builders continue to embark on one of the most exhilarating—and one of the most frightening—adventures ever known: launching a business. It's never easy, but it can be incredibly rewarding, both financially and emotionally. One writer calls it "life without a safety net—thrilling and dangerous."[6] Still, true entrepreneurs see owning a business as the real measure of success. Indeed, entrepreneurship often provides the only avenue for success to those who otherwise might have been denied the opportunity.

Who are these entrepreneurs, and what drives them to work so hard with no guarantee of success? What forces lead them to risk so much and to make so many sacrifices in an attempt to achieve an ideal? Why are they willing to give up the security of a steady paycheck working for someone else to become the last person to be paid in their own companies? This chapter will examine the entrepreneur, the driving force behind the American economy.

> **Radio Communications International Corporation**

What Is an Entrepreneur?

2. Describe the entrepreneurial profile.

An **entrepreneur** is one who creates a new business in the face of risk and uncertainty for the purpose of achieving profit and growth by identifying opportunities and assembling the necessary resources to capitalize on them. Researchers have invested a great deal of time and effort over the last decade trying to paint a clear picture of the entrepreneurial personality. While these studies have identified several characteristics entrepreneurs tend to exhib-

entrepreneur—*one who creates a new business in the face of risk and uncertainty for the purpose of achieving profit and growth by identifying opportunities and assembling the necessary resources to capitalize on them.*

it, none of them has isolated a set of traits required for success. We now turn to a brief summary of the entrepreneurial profile.[7]

1. *Desire for responsibility.* Entrepreneurs feel a personal responsibility for the outcome of ventures with which they are associated. They prefer to be in control of their resources, and use those resources to achieve self-determined goals.

2. *Preference for moderate risk.* Entrepreneurs are not wild risk takers but are instead calculating risk takers. Unlike "high-rolling, riverboat" gamblers, they rarely gamble. Entrepreneurs look at a venture in terms of some personal level of perceived risk. The goal may appear to be high—even impossible—in others' perceptions, but entrepreneurs see the situation from a different perspective and believe that their goals are realistic and attainable. They usually spot opportunities in areas that reflect their knowledge, backgrounds, and experiences, which increase their probability of success. Paul Hawken, cofounder of Smith & Hawken, a highly successful mail-order garden tool company, explains:

   Good entrepreneurs are risk avoiders, not risk takers. They appear to be risk takers because they see the market differently than the rest of us do; they see a product or service that will converge with how the culture is changing. Once they create it, they methodically eliminate all the factors that will prevent them from getting to market. They become risk eliminators.[8]

3. *Confidence in their ability to succeed.* Entrepreneurs typically have an abundance of confidence in their ability to succeed. They tend to be optimistic about their chances for success, and usually their optimism is based in reality. One recent study by the National Federation of Independent Businesses (NFIB) found that one-third of the entrepreneurs rated their chances of success to be 100 percent![9] This high level of optimism may explain why some of the most successful entrepreneurs have failed in business—often more than once—before finally succeeding.

4. *Desire for immediate feedback.* Entrepreneurs like to know how they are doing and are constantly looking for reinforcement. Tricia Fox, founder of Fox Day Schools, Inc., claims, "I like being independent and successful. Nothing gives you feedback like your own business."[10]

5. *High level of energy.* Entrepreneurs are more energetic than the average person. That energy may be a critical factor given the incredible effort required to launch a startup company. Long hours and hard work are the rule rather than the exception.

"Actually, son, whether the glass is half full or empty isn't important it's who *owns* the glass."

Source: Reprinted by permission of Cartoon Features Syndicate.

6. *Future orientation*. Entrepreneurs have a well-defined sense of searching for opportunities. They look ahead and are less concerned with what was done yesterday than with what might be done tomorrow. While traditional managers are concerned with managing available *resources*, entrepreneurs are more interested in spotting and capitalizing on *opportunities*.

    Sometimes opportunities—and ideas—arise when least expected. For instance, when Alan and Joann Zucker were required by law to send out certified letters informing their neighbors that they were requesting a zoning variance to remodel their house, Joann sighed, "I wish we could do this with certified phone calls instead of letters." Alan, semiretired at 65, immediately saw potential in his wife's idea. The Zuckers contacted an attorney, who helped them create a ten-page patent application with the U.S. Patent Office that included an outline of how a certified phone call could work with existing technology. Patent now in hand, the Zuckers plan to license nationwide rights to the certified phone call to a single company and collect the royalties. Noting that the U.S. Postal Service handles 200 million certified letters each year, the Zuckers estimate that annual revenues for certified phone calls would be $200 million. Twenty-three companies worldwide have already requested licensing agreements from the Zuckers. "It's been an amazing journey," says Alan.[11]

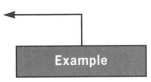

Example

7. *Skill at organizing*. Building a company "from scratch" is much like piecing together a giant jigsaw puzzle. Entrepreneurs know how to put the right people together to accomplish a task. Effectively combining people and jobs enables entrepreneurs to transform their visions into reality.

YOU BE THE CONSULTANT...

A One-of-a-Kind Business

As far as he knows, Gay Balfour has a one-of-a-kind business; his company, Dog Gone, vacuums up prairie dogs from ranches, farms, Indian reservations, and towns for relocation to other less bothersome locations! Balfour got into this unique business after he lost his machine welding company because he did not have the cash to repay a bank loan. "[The bank] couldn't wait any longer [for payment], so they took the welding business, worth about $500,000," recalls Balfour.

Two years later, Balfour got the inspiration for Dog Gone in a dream. "I woke up early one Friday morning in the spring of 1991, turned to my wife and said, 'Honey, I had this crazy dream last night; I learned how to catch prairie dogs with a giant vacuum!'" he recalls. Later that morning, Balfour heard about a welding job on a nearby Indian reservation. When he finished the job, Balfour says he "looked around and saw prairie dogs everywhere. I told the Indians I was working on an idea to catch prairie dogs. I talked it over with the farm manager, and he agreed to a test."

Balfour went straight to the district sanitation department, which he knew had a truck with the basic equipment he would need: a truck with a vacuum attachment that was powerful enough to do the job. When the department superintendent, unsolicited, offered to sell him the truck, Balfour couldn't believe it! Before he struck a deal with the sanitation department, Balfour arranged a test with the truck. The principle was simple: He would use suction hose attachments to suck the prairie dogs from their holes using air conveyance, which transfers high air volume with low pressure, so that the prairie dogs would not be injured. Back at the Indian reservation, Balfour successfully caught 23 prairie dogs in 45 minutes. The test was a complete success!

Balfour then borrowed $30,000 from friends and a bank, bought the truck, and launched Dog Gone, the world's first prairie dog sucker-upper business! He invested another $30,000 to refine the process to make it more effective and safer for the prairie dogs. Today, Balfour's company is growing. He has vacuumed prairie dogs from Durango, Colorado to Columbus, Ohio. Naturally, he says that his company's uniqueness is its greatest asset. "We have a tornado painted on the side of our yellow truck that's got hold of a prairie dog's tail," he says. "Wherever we go, people pull up, honk, and take our picture."

1. What would you consider Dog Gone's strengths to be? Weaknesses?

2. Assume that you were the banker that Balfour approached with his idea for a prairie dog vacuuming business. What questions would you have asked him? Would you have approved the loan?

3. How might Balfour have convinced skeptical lenders and investors that his idea could become a profitable business?

Source: Haidee Jezek, "Hot Diggity Dog," *Business Start-Ups,* May 1996, p. 100.

8. *Value of achievement over money.* One of the most common misconceptions about entrepreneurs is that they are driven wholly by the desire to make money. To the contrary, *achievement* seems to be entrepreneurs' primary motivating force; money is simply a way of "keeping score" of accomplishments—a symbol of achievement. One business researcher says, "What keeps the entrepreneur moving forward is more complex—and more profound—than mere cash. It's about running your own show. It's about doing what is virtually impossible."[12]

Table 1.1 summarizes the nine characteristics that successful entrepreneurs demonstrated overall. Other characteristics frequently exhibited by entrepreneurs include:

High degree of commitment. Launching a company successfully requires total commitment from the entrepreneur. Business founders often immerse themselves completely in their businesses. "The average entrepreneur has to hurdle discouraging barriers in the beginning," explains one expert.[13] That requires commitment. "I equate commitment with survival," claims one consultant."[14]

Tolerance for ambiguity. Entrepreneurs tend to have a high tolerance for ambiguous, ever changing situations, the environment in which they most often operate. This ability to handle uncertainty is critical since these business builders constantly make decisions using new, sometimes conflicting information gleaned from a variety of unfamiliar sources.

Flexibility. One hallmark of true entrepreneurs is their ability to adapt to the changing demands of their customers and their businesses. In this rapidly changing world economy, rigidity often leads to failure. As our society, its people, and their tastes change, entrepreneurs also must be willing to adapt their businesses to meet those changes.

> *When Bill Hewlett and Dave Packard founded their company in the late 1930s, they had no clear idea of what to make. They knew that they wanted to create a business in the vaguely defined field of electronic engineering. Their company, Hewlett-Packard, which is now one of the most successful electronics companies in the world, probably survived because of the founders' flexibility. Some of their early product ideas included a clock drive for a telescope, a bowling foul-line indicator, a device to make urinals flush automatically, and a shock machine to make people lose weight!*[15]

Hewlett-Packard

Table 1.1

Competencies That Are Characteristic of Successful Entrepreneurs

Source: Entrepreneurship and Small Enterprise Development, second annual report by McBer and Co. to the United States Agency for International Development, March 25, 1986.

Proactivity	
1. Initiative	Does things before being asked or forced by events.
2. Assertiveness	Confronts problems with others directly. Tells others what they have to do.
Achievement Orientation	
3. Sees and acts on opportunities	Seizes unusual opportunities to start a new business, obtain financing, land, work space, or assistance.
4. Efficiency orientation	Looks for and finds ways to do things faster or at less cost.
5. Concern for high quality work	States a desire to produce or sell a top- or better-quality product or service.
6. Systematic planning	Breaks a large task down into subtasks or subgoals. Anticipates obstacles. Evaluates alternatives.
7. Monitoring	Develops or uses procedures to ensure that work is completed or that work meets standards of quality.
Commitment to Others	
8. Commitment to work	Makes a personal sacrifice or expends extraordinary effort to complete a job. Pitches in with workers or works in their place to get a job done.
9. Recognizes the importance of fundamental business relationships	Acts to build rapport or friendly relationships with customers. Sees interpersonal relationships as a business resource. Places long-term goodwill over short-term gain.

In *The Journal of Creative Behavior*, researchers Erik K. Winslow and George T. Solomon compare the profile of successful entrepreneurs to that of the typical manager, revealing some unusual characteristics. The psychological profile of the successful entrepreneur actually resembles in some ways that of criminally insane sociopaths who commit crimes without feeling any remorse! Entrepreneurs, whom the researchers describe as "mildly sociopathic," are "charming, spontaneous, and likable on first meetings and ambivalent about close personal relationships . . . They are opportunistic . . . [and] are uncomfortable with rules, conventional wisdom, and others' expectations." The researchers go on to report that the entrepreneurial culture that came to light in the 1980s and continues today has many of the same core beliefs and assumptions that the antiestablishment "hippie" culture of the 1960s held. According to their research, Winslow and Solomon conclude that the psychic opposite of the entrepreneur is the conventional manager.

Table 1.2
The Differences Between Managers and Entrepreneurs
Source: Adapted from *The Journal of Creative Behavior*, Vol. 21, no. 3, 1995.

Conventional Manager	Entrepreneur
• Very conscious of rules and taboos.	• Views rules as guidelines only.
• Sensitive to the future and willing to postpone rewards.	• Concept of the future based on personal fantasy. Low threshold of frustration.
• Has a powerful need for acceptance.	• Ambivalent toward control, success, and responsibility. Can be manipulative and exploitative of others.
• Able to identify problems in any course of action. Makes detailed plans.	• Impatient with discussions and theories. Is prone to action and seems impulsive.

Tenacity. Obstacles, obstructions, and defeat typically do not dissuade entrepreneurs from doggedly pursuing their visions. "The ones who make it relish the game and never give up—no matter how tough things get," says one researcher.[16]

What conclusion can we draw from the volumes of research conducted on the entrepreneurial personality? Entrepreneurs are not of one mold; no one set of characteristics can predict who will become entrepreneurs and whether or not they will succeed. Indeed, *diversity* seems to be a central characteristic of entrepreneurs. One researcher of the entrepreneurial personality explains, "Entrepreneurs don't fit any statistical norm... Most are aberrant or a bit odd by nature."[17] Table 1.2 summarizes research contrasting entrepreneurs and conventional managers.

As you can see from the examples in this chapter, anyone—regardless of age, race, sex, color, national origin, or any other characteristic—can become an entrepreneur. There are no limitations on this form of economic expression. Entrepreneurship is not a genetic trait; it is a learned skill. The editors of *Inc.* magazine claim, "Entrepreneurship is more mundane than it's sometimes portrayed. . . . You don't need to be a person of mythical proportions to be very, very successful in building a company."[18]

The Benefits of Entrepreneurship

3–A. Describe the benefits of entrepreneurship.

Surveys show that owners of small businesses believe they work harder, earn more money, and are happier than if they worked for a large company. Before launching any business venture, every potential entrepreneur should consider the benefits of small business ownership.

Opportunity to gain control over your own destiny. Owning a business provides entrepreneurs with the independence and the opportunity to achieve what is important to them. Christopher Good, who at age 28 founded Good Food Systems, a maker of bar-code scanners for school cafeterias, explains, "I knew I'd be OK if I did something I was happy doing and was in control of my life."[19] Like Good, entrepreneurs want to "call the shots" in their lives, and they use their businesses to bring this desire to life. They reap the intrinsic rewards of knowing they are the driving forces behind their businesses.

Opportunity to make a difference. Increasingly, entrepreneurs are starting businesses because they see an opportunity to make a difference in a cause that is important to them. Whether it is providing low-cost, sturdy housing for families in developing countries or establishing a recycling program to preserve the earth's limited resources, entrepreneurs are finding ways to combine their concerns for social issues and their desire to earn a good living.

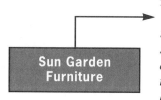

While living in the suburbs, Steve Row watched builders put up house after house in rapid succession. What disturbed him was not the new neighbors, but the large amounts of scrap wood the builders wasted. "It struck me that this wood was still in its original condition and could be usable for other things—like furniture," recalls Row. He approached the contractors who told him to help himself to all of the scrap lumber he wanted. Today, his company, Sun Garden Furniture, produces and sells a variety of unique furnishings across northern California, ranging from tables and chairs to picket-fence benches and seed cabinets—all made from scrap lumber recycled from building sites.[20]

Opportunity to reach your full potential. Too many people find their work boring, unchallenging, and unexciting. But to most entrepreneurs, there is little difference between work and play; the two are synonymous. Entrepreneurs' businesses become the instrument for self-expression and self-actualization. Tim McDonald, who at 31 has already launched several startups, explains, "I want to be in a situation where your growth is limited only by your own talent, your own energy—and that ...means an entrepreneurial situation.[21]

Opportunity to reap unlimited profits. Although money is not the primary force driving most entrepreneurs, the profits their businesses can earn are an important motivating factor in their decisions to launch companies. Most of the 64 entries for those with more than $1 billion in net worth on the *Forbes* 400 list of wealthiest Americans are entrepreneurs who started their own companies. One venture capitalist who has financed many small companies says, "Starting your own company has always been the best way to create wealth. And even if you don't get rich doing it, you'll still have more fun."[22]

Opportunity to contribute to society and be recognized for your efforts. Often, small business owners are among the most respected and most trusted members of their communities. Business deals based on trust and mutual respect are the hallmark of many established small companies. These owners enjoy the trust and recognition they receive from the customers whom they have served faithfully over the years. Playing a vital role in their local business systems and knowing that their work has a significant impact on how smoothly the nation's economy functions is yet another reward for small business managers. Says one young entrepreneur, "I want to be a person who 20 years down the road can look back and say, 'I was instrumental in creating something. I left a mark.'"[23]

Opportunity to do what you enjoy. A common sentiment among small business owners is that their work really isn't work. Most successful entrepreneurs choose to enter their particular business fields because they have an interest in them and enjoy those lines of work. They have made their avocations (hobbies) their vocations (work) and are glad they did! These entrepreneurs are living Harvey McKay's advice: "Find a job doing what you love, and you'll never have to work a day in your life."

Jim Haggard, founder of Builders in Scale, did just that and has never regretted it! His company makes kits for the buildings that go with scale-model railroads. After graduating from college, Haggard took a job as a mortgage banker and was miserable for eight years in it. He dreamed of owning his own business, and fondly remembered the many happy hours he had spent as a kid constructing miniature buildings. One day, he picked up Model Railroader *magazine and saw ads for such miniature buildings. "I remember thinking," he says, "Wow! This is not only a hobby but also a vocation." For the next two years Haggard worked nights and weekends, teaching himself the intricacies of metal-casting techniques.*

As disenchantment with his bank job set in, he began developing a business plan to test the viability of his idea for a company. Haggard's wife Jan kept her full-time job, enabling him to quit his banking job and launch Builders in Scale, which he ran from his backyard shop. First-year sales were just $40,000, but Haggard was patient. Within six years, the business was strong enough for Jan to quit her job and work full time with Jim in the home-based business.[24] Not only has Haggard found a way to make a living, but he also is doing something he loves!

The Potential Drawbacks of Entrepreneurship

Although owning a business has many benefits and provides many opportunities, anyone planning to enter the world of entrepreneurship should be aware of its potential drawbacks. "If you aren't 100 percent sure you want to own a business," says one business consultant, "there are plenty of demands and mishaps along the way to dissuade you."[25]

Uncertainty of income. Opening and running a business provides no guarantees that an entrepreneur will earn enough money to survive. Some small businesses barely earn enough to provide the owner-manager with an adequate income. In a business's early days the owner often has trouble meeting financial obligations and may have to live on savings. The steady income that comes with working for someone else is absent. The owner is always the last one to be paid.

Risk of losing your entire investment. The small business failure rate is relatively high. According to recent research, 24 percent of new businesses fail within two years, and 51 percent shut down within four years. Within six years, 63 percent of new businesses will have folded. Studies also show that when a company creates at least one job in its early years, the probability of failure after six years plummets to 35 percent!

Before "reaching for the golden ring," entrepreneurs should ask themselves if they can cope psychologically with the consequences of failure:

- ✯ What is the worst that could happen if I open my business and it fails?
- ✯ How likely is it for the worst to happen? (Am I truly prepared to launch my business?)
- ✯ What can I do to lower the risk of my business failing?
- ✯ If my business were to fail, what is my contingency plan for coping?

Long hours and hard work. Business startups often demand that owners keep nightmarish schedules. Figure 1.2 on page ten shows that the majority of new business owners work more than 60 hours per week, and one-fourth put in more than 70 hours per week! In many startups, six- or seven-day workweeks with no paid vacations are the norm. When the business closes, the revenue stops coming in and the customers go elsewhere. "Even when you own your own business," says Jil Stenn, cofounder of a business that designs edible landscapes, "you still always are working for someone else—your customers and clients."[26]

Lower quality of life until the business gets established. The long hours and hard work needed to launch a company can take their toll on the rest of the entrepreneur's life. Business owners often find that their roles as husbands or wives and fathers or mothers take a back seat to their roles as company founders. Part of the problem is that most entrepreneurs launch their businesses between the ages of 25 and 39, just when they start their families (see Figure 1.3 on page ten). Jim Katzman, cofounder of Tandem Computers, says, "It's very tough to give the amount of work that's required to build a company without slighting your family."[27] As a result, marriages and friendships are too often casualties of small business ownership.

High levels of stress. Starting and managing a business can be an incredibly rewarding experience, but it also can be a highly stressful one. Entrepreneurs often have made significant investments in their companies, have left behind the safety and security of a steady

Figure 1.2
**Number of Hours
New Business Owners
Work Per Week**
Source: Copyright 1996,
Dun & Bradstreet, a company of
The Dun & Bradstreet Corporation.

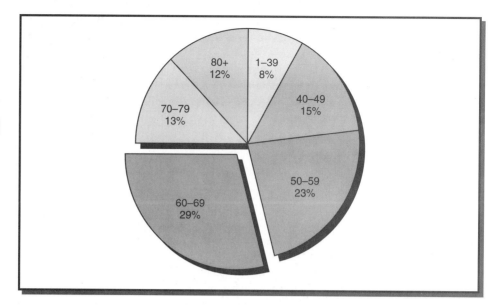

paycheck, and have mortgaged everything they own to get into business. Failure may mean total financial ruin, and that creates intense levels of stress and anxiety! After launching an advertising agency with a partner, one entrepreneur recalls their struggle to survive their early years: "We had envisioned ourselves smiling, closing sales, and making deals, but stress headaches, pains in the neck, and unreturned phone calls marked our first year-and-a-half in business."[28]

Complete responsibility. It's great to be the boss, but many entrepreneurs find that they must make decisions on issues about which they are not really knowledgeable. When there is no one to ask, the pressure can build quickly. The realization that the decisions they make are the cause of success or failure has a devastating effect on some people. Small business owners discover quickly that *they* are the business.

Figure 1.3
**Owner Age When
Business Formed**
Source: Adapted from
National Federation of
Independent Businesses,
Washington, D.C.

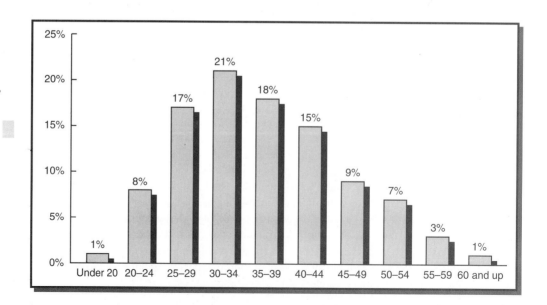

It's Never Too Soon

Disenchanted with their prospects in corporate America and willing to take a chance to control their own destinies, scores of young people are choosing entrepreneurship as their primary career path. A recent study by Paul Reynolds of Babson College suggests that 10 percent of Americans aged 25 to 34 are actively working to create businesses. That's nearly three times higher than any other age group. "Because opportunities are limited for us, a lot of us ... have gone out and started our own companies," explains one twenty-something entrepreneur.

Increasingly, students at America's colleges are getting a head start on their entrepreneurial careers by launching their companies while still in school. Buoyed by more course offerings in entrepreneurship and inspired by those who have done it before them, many so-called "Generation Xers" are using their knowledge, technological skills, enthusiasm, and creativity to transform their class assignments into real businesses. "Things are changing faster, and you have people that grew up using technology and computers," explains Michael Dell, who founded Austin, Texas-based Dell Computer Corporation from his college dormitory room in the 1980s. "They have open ways of thinking, and they're less rigid in their thoughts about how things ought to be." College entrepreneurs find that they have a captive audience for market research—their fellow students. The friendships and relationships they forge in college also prove to be beneficial to these young entrepreneurs. "Once you leave school, many of these people go on to careers and positions that make them valuable contacts," says Joey Yaffe, who started his software development company while in college. Another benefit is that these entrepreneurs have access to the consulting services of their professors—without having to pay high-priced consulting fees.

Some young people don't wait to get into college to launch their businesses. A recent survey by the Center for Entrepreneurial Research found that 69 percent of high school students want to start their own companies. Most of them said their primary motivation behind their entrepreneurial aspirations was not to earn large sums of money but to "be their own bosses." Michael Simmons started his own business when he was just 12 years old, operating a computer bulletin board out of his grandmother's home in Palm Springs, California. By age 16, his company, Dataport Computer Services, had five employees and annual sales of $800,000.

Michael Rubin also started his entrepreneurial exploits at an early age. At nine, he created personalized stationery on his computer and sold it door-to-door in his neighborhood. By age 13, he had launched a ski-repair business from his basement with $2,500 in bar mitzvah money. Business was so brisk that he soon outgrew the location and moved into a strip mall. He got special permission to leave school every day at 11:00 a.m. to run his business as part of a cooperative education program. At age 17, Rubin discovered the closeout business, in which distributors purchase overruns and discontinued items of manufacturers' stock and then resell them to retailers. He stumbled onto $200,000 worth of overstocked ski equipment that the manufacturer was selling for $17,000. He bought it and within a month sold it at a profit.

Today, Rubin is an established figure in the world of closeout sporting goods. His company, KPR Sports International, specializes in finding closeouts on athletic shoes and reselling them to retailers. KPR generates some $50 million in annual revenues. Rubin also has purchased a controlling interest in Ryka, a publicly held manufacturer of women's athletic shoes, and is chairman of its board.

After such a terrific start in business at such an early age, where does Rubin plan to go from here? "Owning a $2 or $3 billion business would be the most awesome thing in the world," he says.

1. What advantages does a young person have when it comes to launching a business? Disadvantages?

2. What barriers does a young person face when trying to start a business? How would you recommend overcoming them?

3. What advice would you offer a fellow college student about to start a business?

Sources: Adapted from Tom Stein, "No Experience Required," *Success*, March 1996, pp. 33-42; Stephanie N. Mehta, "Man in a Hurry: A Mogul in Sporting Goods at Age 22," *Wall Street Journal*, June 5, 1995, pp. B1-B7; Kurt Dowdle, "Burning the Corporate Ladder," *In Business*, November/December 1994, pp. 35-36; Stephanie N. Mehta, "More Students Start Businesses While in School," *Wall Street Journal*, May 6, 1996, pp. B1-B5; Stephanie N. Mehta, "Young Entrepreneurs Turn Age to Advantage," *Wall Street Journal*, September 1, 1995, pp. B1-B2; Susan Hightower, "Young Adults Make Their Mark," *The State*, May 30, 1995, pp. B7-B8; George Gendron, "The Next Generation," *Inc.*, March 1995, p.13.

Behind the Boom: What's Feeding the Entrepreneurial Fire?

What forces are driving this entrepreneurial trend in our economy? Which factors have led to this age of entrepreneurship? Some of the most significant ones include the following:

Entrepreneurs as heroes. An intangible but very important factor is the attitude that Americans have toward entrepreneurs. As a nation we have raised them to hero status and have held out their accomplishments as models to follow. Business founders such as Fred Smith (Federal Express), Sandra Kurtzig (ASK Computer Systems), Mary Kay Ash (Mary Kay Cosmetics), and Richard Thalheimer (The Sharper Image) are to entrepreneurship what Shaquille O'Neal and Emmit Smith are to sports.

Entrepreneurial education. Colleges and universities have discovered that entrepreneurship is an extremely popular course of study. Disillusioned with corporate America's downsized job offerings and less promising career paths, a rapidly growing number of students sees owning a business as an attractive career option. Today more than 1,500 colleges and universities offer courses in entrepreneurship and small business to some 15,000 students. Many colleges and universities have difficulty meeting the demand for courses in entrepreneurship and small business.

Economic and demographic factors. Most entrepreneurs start their businesses between the ages of 30 and 40, and our nation's baby-boomer generation is well into that age range. Plus, more people are discovering that there are no limits on their entrepreneurial aspirations. *Anyone*, regardless of age, gender, race, national origin, social status, economic background, or anything else, can achieve success by owning a business!

Shift to a service economy. By the year 2000, the service sector will produce 92 percent of the jobs and 85 percent of the gross domestic product (GDP) in the United States, compared with just 70 percent of the jobs and 60 percent of the GDP today. Because of their relatively low startup costs, service businesses have been very popular with entrepreneurs. The booming service sector continues to provide many business opportunities.

Technological advancements. With the help of modern business machines such as personal computers, laptop computers, fax machines, copiers, color printers, answering machines, and voice mail, even one person working at home can look like a big business. At one time, the high cost of such technological wizardry made it impossible for small businesses to compete with larger companies who could afford the hardware. Today, however, powerful computers and communication equipment are priced within the budgets of even the smallest businesses. Although entrepreneurs may not be able to manufacture heavy equipment in their spare bedrooms, they can run a service- or information-based company from their homes very effectively and look like any *Fortune* 500 company to customers and clients.

Independent lifestyle. Entrepreneurship fits the way Americans want to live—independent and self-sustaining. People want the freedom to choose where they live, the hours they work, and what they do. Although financial security remains an important goal for most entrepreneurs, many place top priority on lifestyle issues such as more time with family and friends, more leisure time, and more control over work-related stress. In a recent study by Hilton Hotels, 77 percent of adults surveyed listed spending more time with family and friends as their top priority; 66 percent wanted more free time. Making money ranked a lowly fifth place, and spending money on material possessions came in last.[29]

International opportunities. No longer are small businesses limited to pursuing customers within their own borders. The dramatic shift to a global economy has opened the door to tremendous business opportunities for these entrepreneurs willing to reach across the globe. While the United States is an attractive market for entrepreneurs, approximately 95 percent of the world's population lives outside its borders. Recent world events such as the crumbling of the Berlin Wall, the revolt of the Soviet Union's Baltic states, and the breaking down of trade barriers as a result of the European Community agreement have opened much of that world market to entrepreneurs. Still, only 8.5 percent of U.S. firms with fewer than 100 employees currently export; however, those small companies account for 20 percent of total exports.[30] International opportunities will continue to grow rapidly into the twenty-first century. "Going global is the theme now, even for small companies," says one small business consultant.[31]

Trends in Entrepreneurship

5. Identify the groups that are leading the nation's boom in entrepreneurship.

As we have seen, virtually anyone has the potential to become an entrepreneur. Certain groups, however, are leading the surge in entrepreneurial activity. We turn our attention to these.

Women Entrepreneurs

Despite years of legislative effort, women still face discrimination in the work force. However, small business has been a leader in offering women opportunities for economic expression through employment and entrepreneurship. One writer says, "Entrepreneurship has become as unisex as blue jeans, a place where women can fulfill their largest dreams and entrepreneurial expectations."[32] Increasing numbers of women are discovering that the best way to break the "glass ceiling" that prevents them from rising to the top of many organizations is to start their own companies. In fact, women are opening businesses at a rate 2.4 times that of men. Women entrepreneurs have even broken through the comic strip barrier. Blondie Bumstead, long a typical suburban housewife married to Dagwood, now owns her own catering business with her best friend and neighbor Tootsie Woodly! Dean Young, Blondie cartoonist and son of the strip's creator, says, "Blondie has come a long way. She's a very confident, intelligent woman who has great ability in what she's doing."[33]

Although the businesses women start tend to be smaller than those men start, their impact is anything but small. Women-owned companies employ more than 15.5 million workers, 35 percent more than all of the *Fortune* 500 companies employ worldwide! Women own about 36 percent of all businesses—some 7.7 million—in the United States (see Figure 1.4 on page 14), generating some $1.4 trillion in annual sales.[34] Although their businesses tend to grow more slowly than those owned by men, women-owned businesses have a higher survival rate than U.S. businesses overall. One recent study found that their three-year survival rate was 72.2 percent, compared to 66.6 percent for all businesses.[35]

Although about 72 percent of women-owned businesses are concentrated in retailing and services (as are most businesses), female entrepreneurs are branching out into previously male-dominated industries such as manufacturing, construction, transportation, and agriculture.

Sally Fox, founder of Natural Cotton Colours, is one entrepreneur who has entered the traditionally male-dominated agricultural industry and has achieved success. In 1982, while working for a California cotton breeder, Fox came across a paper bag of brown cotton seeds. The breeder had planned to investigate the insect resistance of the plants, which produced naturally colored brown bolls. Fox, herself an accomplished cotton spinner and weaver, took some of the seeds the breeder offered her and planted them in six plastic pots in her mother's backyard. At the time, she had no idea that from those seeds would sprout not only naturally colored cotton but also a thriving business.

Natural Cotton Colours

By 1986 she was growing brown and green cotton with 1-inch fibers, long enough to sell to hand-spinning hobbyists like herself. First-year sales of her mail-order company totaled less than $1,000. She quickly realized that to build a viable business she would have to go

Figure 1.4
**Women-Owned
Businesses**
Source: Adapted from
National Association of
Women Business Owners,
Washington, D.C.

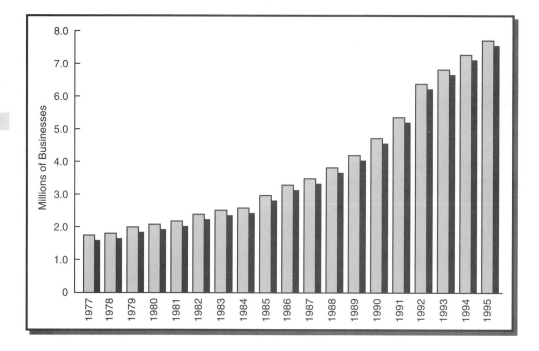

after the commercial market. In 1988, Fox sold her 12-acre crop to a Japanese textile mill. The winning bid was $5 per pound for 2,000 pounds of brown and green cotton, an attractive price for Fox since white cotton was selling for just 70 cents a pound!

The transaction gave Fox the incentive to quit her regular job and run her business full-time. The next year she harvested 100,000 pounds of cotton, which the same Japanese mill bought for $279,000. Fox also earned plant variety protection for some of her seeds and a trademark for "Fox Fibre." In 1990, Natural Cotton Colours earned its first profit on sales of $600,000, and Fox began selling her colored cotton to jeans maker Levi Strauss. The appeal of Fox Fibre is not so much its earth-tone colors as its lack of chemical pesticides and dyes, a major selling point for environmentally correct shoppers. Today, Fox's business, now located in Arizona, is thriving, and Sally Fox is busy developing new varieties of cotton plants as well as new customers and new markets. Her next project: fire-resistant cotton textiles.[36]

Minority Enterprises

Like women, minorities are choosing entrepreneurship more often than ever before. Asians, Hispanics, and African-Americans, are the minority groups most likely to become entrepreneurs, but minority business ownership remains low. African-Americans, for example, make up 12.4 percent of the U.S. population; yet they own just 3.1 percent of the nation's businesses, and those businesses account for only 1 percent of total U.S. commercial revenues.[37] Like women, minorities cite discrimination as a principal reason for their limited access to the world of entrepreneurship.

Minority-owned businesses have come a long way in the past decade, and their success rate is climbing. Increasingly, minorities are finding ways to overcome the barriers to business ownership. For instance, the U.S. Census Bureau's latest statistics show that the number of companies owned by African-Americans grew 2.5 times faster than the total number of new business formations.[38] The new generation of African-American entrepreneurs is better educated, has more business experience, and is better prepared for business ownership than its predecessors.

A Genuine Sister Act

As children, the Yee sisters grew up in their parents' Chinese restaurant in Columbus, Ohio, learning everything from running the cash register to making egg rolls. That exposure to business from an early age helped the Yees make the decision to launch Zhen Cosmetics with $50,000 of their own money and $50,000 from their parents. Their business idea came from their inability to find makeup suitable for the skin tones of Asian women. Most foundation makeup has a pink undertone for Caucasians, whereas yellow-toned foundations are more common among Asian women. Existing makeup manufacturers were ignoring the needs of a huge potential market; there are 3.8 million Asian women in the United States, and their numbers are growing rapidly. These women also have ample purchasing power; the median Asian-American family income is 18 percent higher than the U.S. average.

Sisters Susan, Elaine, Jane, and Leigh saw their opportunity and launched Zhen (which means "genuine" or "true" in Chinese). They immediately began contacting contract makeup manufacturers that would produce small batch orders. They got samples from several, testing their formulas on themselves and on their friends. Through trial and error, they developed a line of 20 cosmetic products specifically designed for Asian women, including foundation, lipstick, and eye shadow. All of their products are hypoallergenic and fragrance-free.

Although their development costs were minimal, the Yees soon had to tap their $100,000 capital base. They used $20,000 to produce 50,000 copies of a mail-order catalog, which a friend designed for free. Another $10,500 went to install a toll-free telephone system and to buy ads in Asian-American magazines such as *Filipnas* and *Face*. They also bought $10,000 worth of inventory.

The ads worked, and requests for catalogs came pouring in. Susan Yee says that one in four women who request a catalog purchases makeup. Zhen's 25 percent response rate is far higher than the 10% mail-order industry average. Soon, upscale department chain Nordstrom signed on to test demand for Zhen Cosmetics' products in its stores. If the test is successful, Nordstrom will allot more counter space to Zhen products.

Susan Yee, president of Zhen, has 15 years of management experience in the retail industry and knows how tough the business can be. Elaine is in charge of product distribution; Jane manages the sales function and doubles as a model with Leigh.

Explaining why they were chosen as the company's models, Jane and Leigh explain, "We were free!"

If the Nordstrom test doesn't work out, the Yees have a backup plan. In addition to their direct-mail catalog, they are considering using direct sales techniques similar to those Avon used so successfully. "The Asian community is so tight-knit that if you have women holding parties, having seminars—well, it could be huge," says Susan. Although the Yees are not guaranteed success, they are confident. They have built their company, attracted some impressive customers, generated sales of more than $100,000 within a year, and still have $35,000 of their original capital!

1. What factors have attributed to Zhen's success so far?
2. What did the Yee sisters do right as they launched their business? What should they have done differently?
3. On scale of 0 to 100, how would you assess the Yees' chances of business success? Explain.

Sources: Adapted from Holly Celeste Fisk, "Face Value," *Entrepreneur*, May 1996, p. 220; Marcia Berss, "The Zhen-uine Article," *Forbes*, June 5, 1995, pp. 104-105.

Immigrant Entrepreneurs

The United States has always been a "melting pot" of diverse cultures, and many immigrants have been drawn to this nation by its economic freedom. Unlike the unskilled "huddled masses" of the past, today's immigrants arrive with more education and experience. Although many of them come to the United States with few assets, their dedication and desire to succeed enable them to achieve their entrepreneurial dreams.

Mohamed Diop was born in Senegal and worked for Citicorp in West Africa for 13 years before he came to the United States to start his own company, Homeland Fashions. Homeland imports textiles from Senegal and Ghana and transforms them into more than 300 types of Afrocentric items—from $8 kente baseball caps to $200 evening suits. Diop's company generates more than $6 million in annual sales.[39]

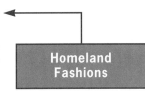

Homeland Fashions

Part-Time Entrepreneurs

Starting a part-time business is a popular gateway to entrepreneurship. Part-time entrepreneurs have the best of both worlds: They can ease into business for themselves without sacrificing the security of a steady paycheck and benefits. Approximately 13 million Americans are self-employed part-time.[40] A major advantage of going into business part-time is the lower risk in case the venture flops. Many part-timers are "testing the entrepreneurial waters" to see whether their business ideas will work and whether they enjoy being self-employed. As they grow, many part-time enterprises absorb more of the entrepreneur's time until they become full-time businesses.

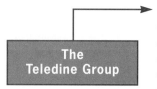

The Teledine Group

Adam Rodell, a sales representative for AT&T, and Frank Capristo, an engineer for a construction firm, decided that the best way to test their business idea was to become self-employed in their spare time. During evenings and weekends, the two entrepreneurs operate The Teledine Group, an interactive dining guide which customers can call up free of charge and access information about a variety of local restaurants. Operating from an office in Rodell's home, the two have managed to sign up more than 300 restaurants for listing on their service. Although running the business part-time has produced a slower growth rate than Capristo and Rodell wanted, the partners had little choice. "From a financial standpoint," says Rodell, "there was no way we could have done it without keeping our jobs."[41]

Home-Based Businesses

Home-based businesses are booming! Entrepreneurs operate 27.1 million businesses from their homes (a trend dubbed "HomeComing" by marketing experts), and their ranks are growing rapidly; on average, a new home-based business pops up every 11 seconds! These companies generate $383 billion in annual revenues and create an estimated 8,219 new jobs each day.[42] Currently, 44 percent of all U.S. households support some form of home office activity. Figure 1.5 illustrates the growth in the number of home-based entrepreneurs in recent years.

Figure 1.5
The Growth of Home-Based Businesses
Source: Adapted from Link Resources, Inc., Marietta, Georgia.

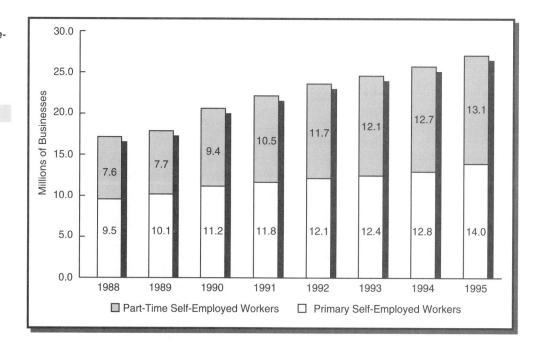

In the past, home-based businesses tended to be rather unexciting cottage industries such as crafts or sewing. Today's home-based businesses are more diverse; modern home-based entrepreneurs are more likely to be running high-tech or service companies with millions of dollars in sales.

For example, entrepreneur Jill Shtulman runs her creative services agency, which sells creative ad designs to a wide variety of firms, from her Chicago high-rise apartment. Shtulman, who earns more than $130,000 per year, once conducted a highly technical brainstorming session with a client on an unexpected conference call while she luxuriated in a bubble bath![43]

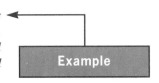

Example

About 57 percent of home-based businesses involve white-collar work. They produce attractive incomes for their owners. The average home-based business earns $50,250 in annual income; 20 percent earn more than $75,000 a year.[44] Home-based companies are an important entrepreneurial outlet for women, who own two-thirds of all home-based businesses. The increasing number of women and part-time entrepreneurs will continue to feed the growth of these home-based businesses, as will technological advances (computers and communication devices), which are transforming many ordinary homes into "electronic cottages." Esther Schindler, who operates a computer software company out of her home, says, "Clients care about the product, the results. It's becoming less relevant whether or not your office is within 30 feet of your kitchen."[45] Studies by Link Resources Corporation, a research and consulting firm, suggest that the success rate for home-based businesses is high: 85 percent of such businesses are still in operation after three years.[46] Table 1.3 on page 18 offers 18 "rules" home-based entrepreneurs should follow to be successful.

Family Businesses

A **family business** is one that includes two or more members of a family with financial control of the company. Family businesses are an integral part of our economy. Of the 21 million businesses in the United States, 90 percent are family owned and managed. These companies employ more than 50 million people and generate 55 percent of the U.S. GDP. Not all of them are small; one-third of the *Fortune* 500 companies are family businesses.[47]

family business—*one that includes two or more members of a family with financial control of the company.*

"When it works right," says one writer, "nothing succeeds like a family firm. The roots run deep, embedded in family values. The flash of the fast buck is replaced with long-term plans. Tradition counts."[48] Despite their magnitude, family businesses face a major threat, a threat from within: management succession. Only 30 percent of family businesses survive to the second generation, and just 10 percent make it to the third generation. Business periodicals are full of stories describing bitter disputes among family members that have crippled or destroyed once thriving businesses.

To avoid such senseless destruction of valuable assets, founders of family businesses should develop plans for management succession long before retirement looms before them.

For example, when Jim Henson, founder of Jim Henson Productions and creator of The Muppets, died unexpectedly in 1990, his 26-year-old son Brian was able to step in to run the $50 million company and keep it moving forward. "I . . . couldn't have anticipated how the transition to second-generation leadership would be smoothed in a number of ways by groundwork my father laid . . . ," Henson says. The creative spark within the company could have died with Jim Henson, but it did not because he took the time to pave the way for the next generation of family management. Brian Henson explains, "I . . . was more prepared by my father for succession than I knew . . . I'm suddenly very aware of all the teaching my father was doing when we worked together—the conversations . . . about how to treat people, how people should work together, how you can't hold a grudge. He thought about what his philosophies were and about how people should live and talked with me a lot about those things over the last nine years. Now I use those ideas every day, and . . . they've turned out to be the main reason we've all been able to carry on here so well."[49]

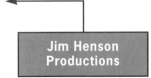

Jim Henson Productions

Table 1.3

Follow These Rules to a Successful Home-Based Business

Sources: Lynn Beresford, Janean Chun, Cynthia E. Griffin, Heather Page, and Debra Phillips, "Homeward Bound," *Entrepreneur,* September 1995, pp. 116-118; Jenean Huber, "House Rules," *Entrepreneur,* March 1993, pp. 89-95; Hal Morris, "Home-Based Businesses Need Extra Insurance," *AARP Bulletin,* November 1994, p. 16; Stephanie N. Mehta, "What You Need," *Wall Street Journal,* October 14, 1994, p. R10.

Rule 1. Do your homework. Much of a home-based business's potential for success depends on how much preparation an entrepreneur makes *before* ever opening for business. The library is an excellent source for research on customers, industries, competitors, and the like.

Rule 2. Find out what your zoning restrictions are. In some areas local zoning laws make running a business from home illegal. Avoid headaches by checking these laws first. You can always request a variance.

Rule 3. Choose the most efficient location for your office. About half of all home-based entrepreneurs operate out of spare bedrooms. The best way to determine the ideal office location is to examine the nature of your business and your clients. Avoid locating your business in your bedroom or your family room.

Rule 4. Focus your home-based business idea. Avoid the tendency to be "all things to all people." Most successful home-based businesses focus on a particular customer group or in some specialty.

Rule 5. Discuss your business rules with your family. Running a business from your home means you can spend more time with your family . . . and that your family can spend more time with you. Establish the rules for interruptions up front.

Rule 6. Select an appropriate business name. Your first marketing decision is your company's name, so make it a good one! Using your own name is convenient, but it's not likely to help you sell your product or service.

Rule 7. Buy the right equipment. Modern technology allows a home-based entrepreneur to give the appearance of any *Fortune* 500 company—but only if you buy the right equipment. A well-equipped home office should have a separate telephone line, a computer, a laser or inkjet printer, a fax machine (or board), a copier, a scanner, and an answering machine (or voice mail), but realize that you don't have to have everything from Day One.

Rule 8. Dress appropriately. Being an "open-collar worker" is one of the joys of working at home. But, when you need to dress up (to meet a client, make a sale, meet your banker, close a deal), do it! Avoid the tendency to lounge around in your bathrobe all day.

Rule 9. Learn to deal with distractions. The best way to fend off the distractions of working at home is to create a business that truly interests you. Budget your time wisely. Your productivity determines your company's success.

Rule 10. Realize that your phone can be your best friend . . . or your worst enemy. As a home-based entrepreneur, you'll spend lots of time on the phone. Be sure you use it productively.

Rule 11. Be firm with friends and neighbors. Sometimes friends and neighbors get the mistaken impression that because you're at home, you're not working. If one drops by to chat while you're working, tactfully ask your visitor to come back "after work."

Rule 12. Take advantage of tax breaks. Although a 1993 Supreme Court decision tightened considerably the standards for business deductions for an office at home, many home-based entrepreneurs still qualify for special tax deductions on everything from computers to cars. Check with your accountant.

Rule 13. Make sure you have adequate insurance coverage. Some homeowner's policies provide adequate coverage for business-related equipment, but many home-based entrepreneurs have inadequate coverage on their business assets. Ask your agent about a business owner's policy (BOP), which may cost as little as $300 to $500 per year.

Rule 14. Understand the special circumstances under which you can hire outside employees. Sometimes zoning laws allow in-home businesses, but they prohibit hiring employees. Check zoning laws carefully.

Rule 15. Be prepared if your business requires clients to come to your home. Dress appropriately. (No pajamas!) Make sure your office presents a professional image.

Rule 16. Get a post office box. With burglaries and robberies on the rise, you're better off using a "P.O. Box" address rather than your specific home address. Otherwise you may be inviting crime.

Rule 17. Network, network, network. Isolation can be a problem for home-based entrepreneurs, and one of the best ways to combat it is to network. It's also a great way to market your business.

Rule 18. Be proud of your home-based business. Merely a decade ago there was a stigma attached to working from home. Today, home-based entrepreneurs and their businesses command respect. Be proud of your company!

Copreneurs

Copreneurs are entrepreneurial couples who work together as co-owners of their business. Unlike the traditional "Mom and Pop" (Pop as "boss" and Mom as "subordinate"), copreneurs "are creating a division of labor that is based on expertise as opposed to gender," says one expert.[50] Studies suggest that companies co-owned by spouses represent one of the fastest-growing business sectors, up by 90 percent from 1980. Managing a small business with a spouse may appear to be a recipe for divorce, but most copreneurs say not. "There is nothing more exciting than nurturing a business and watching it grow with someone you love," says Marcia Sherrill, who, with her husband, William Kleinberg, runs Kleinberg Sherrill, a leather goods and accessories business.[51] Successful copreneurs learn to build the foundation for a successful working relationship before they ever launch their companies. Some of the characteristics they rely on include:

copreneurs—*entrepreneurial couples who work together as co-owners of a business.*

- ☆ an assessment of whether their personalities will mesh—or conflict—in a business setting.
- ☆ mutual respect for each other and one another's talents.
- ☆ compatible business and life goals—a common "vision"—a view that they are full and equal partners, not a superior and a subordinate.
- ☆ complementary business skills that each acknowledges and appreciates and that lead to a unique business identity for each spouse.
- ☆ the ability to keep lines of communication open, talking and listening to each other about personal as well as business issues.
- ☆ a clear division of roles and authority, ideally based on each partner's skills and abilities, to minimize conflict and power struggles.
- ☆ the ability to encourage each other and to "lift up" a disillusioned partner.
- ☆ separate work spaces that allow them to "escape" when the need arises.
- ☆ boundaries between their business life and their personal life so that one doesn't consume the other.
- ☆ a sense of humor.

Although copreneuring isn't for everyone, it works extremely well for many couples and often leads to successful businesses. "Both spouses are working for a common purpose but also focusing on their unique talents," says a family business counselor. "With all these skills put together, one plus one equals more than two."[52]

For instance, Laura and Chip Goode have worked hard for nearly a decade to build both a successful marriage and a successful business, Kiradjieff and Goode, a Boston-based executive search firm. The Goodes say they owe their copreneuring success to careful planning in both their personal and business lives. They chose to launch their company in a market niche they both knew and were excited about, and they developed a detailed business plan, outlining each partner's areas of responsibility. Chip is the company strategist and visionary, spending his time developing clients; Laura is better at finding and cultivating relationships with executive candidates. The Goodes agree that their shared passion for and dedication to their business are the nucleus for making their company a success.[53]

Kiradjieff and Goode

Corporate Castoffs

Concentrating on shedding the excess bulk they took on during the 1970s and 1980s, American corporations have been downsizing in an attempt to remain competitive. During the 1990s, large companies have reduced their employment roles by an estimated 5 million workers. One major corporation after another has announced layoffs—and not just among blue-collar workers. Companies are cutting back their executive ranks as well. "[Downsizing] is turning legions of blue- and white-collar workers into dislocated refugees, the boat people of economic upheaval. Neither they nor the survivors and witnesses are likely to put their loyalties into a corporation that deals with people as interchangeable digits," says one business writer.[54]

These corporate castoffs have become an important source of entrepreneurial activity. Some 20 percent of these discharged corporate managers have become entrepreneurs, and many of those left behind in corporate America would like to join them. A recent study by Accountemps found that nearly half of the executives surveyed believed their peers would take the entrepreneurial plunge—if they only had the money to do so. Four years before, just one-third of corporate executives were inclined to start their own companies.[55]

Many corporate castoffs are deciding that the best defense against future job insecurity is an entrepreneurial offense.

IBM, which has shed more than 180,000 employees in recent years, has a reputation for creating entrepreneurs. Former IBM employees have launched a multitude of businesses, ranging from Topsy Tail Company, which makes hair gadgets, and Finally Finished, a furniture restoration company, to Bob Soto's Diving Ltd. in Grand Cayman Island and Holt Brothers Barbeque. "One of the things you learn at IBM is how to run a business," says Bill Holt, whose restaurant recently won an award for the best barbecue in Atlanta. "The rules and principles apply to any business you go into."[56]

Corporate Dropouts

The dramatic downsizing of corporate America has created another effect among the employees left after restructuring: a trust gap. The result of this trust gap is a growing number of dropouts from the corporate structure who then become entrepreneurs. Although their workdays may grow longer and their incomes may shrink, those who strike out on their own often find their work more rewarding and more satisfying because they are doing what they want. For corporate dropouts, "there's a sense that you won't make a lot of money, but you'll have more security, and you're part of the action," says the head of one research company. "It's part of a big structural change in how people work, and . . . it will continue."[57] When one dropout left his corporate post, he invited his former coworkers to a bonfire in the parking lot—fueled by a pile of his expensive business suits! He happily passed out marshmallows to everyone who came. Today he and his wife run an artists' gallery in California's wine country.[58]

Because they have college degrees, a working knowledge of business, and years of management experience, both corporate dropouts and castoffs may ultimately increase the small business survival rate. A recent survey by Richard O'Sullivan found that 64 percent of people starting businesses have some college education, and 16 percent have advanced degrees.[59] Better-trained, more experienced entrepreneurs are less likely to fail. The National Federation of Independent Businesses reports that 77 percent of new companies formed since the mid-eighties were still in operation three years later.[60]

YOU BE THE CONSULTANT...

Coed Naked Entrepreneurship

Mark Lane and Scott MacHardy, co-owners of Coed Sportswear Inc., a company selling a unique line of T-shirts and sportswear popular with students, worked extremely hard to get their company where it is today. Coed Sportswear now generates $25 million in annual sales and is growing at a rate of between 200 and 300 percent per year.

It didn't start out that way.

While attending the University of New Hampshire, both Lane and MacHardy worked part-time on marketing projects at Riefer Sportswear, the small company that owned a trademark called Coed Naked. Riefer sold T-shirts with its design to college bookstores and clothing stores throughout the state. Unfortunately, the company was on the verge of bankruptcy. Lane and MacHardy recognized the value of the trademark, and with the help of a silent partner and a bank loan, they purchased the Coed Naked name and Riefer's customer list. "It had a powerful identity . . . with untold marketing potential," recalls Lane.

Their first order of business was to build a customer base for Coed Sportswear. After talking with some of their inherited customer base, the partners decided they would use superb customer service to differentiate their company from the pack. Because their existing accounts were small stores reluctant to place large orders, the two decided to eliminate the minimum-order requirement, which virtually all of their competitors required. That shifted all of the risk of buying Coed's T-shirts away from their customers and went a long way toward building a relationship of trust with them. In addition, Coed guaranteed order processing and shipping within 24 hours—something unheard of in their industry. The move increased their costs, but it also made their company unique in the market, and customers responded. Lane and MacHardy also hired experienced sales representatives to comb the country for new accounts.

For the next five years, Lane and MacHardy dedicated themselves to their business, setting aggressive performance targets and developing detailed plans for reaching them. Gradually, they built their original 40 accounts into a customer base of 10,000, which today includes national chains such as Foot Locker and The Sports Authority, among others. They also have developed strong relationships with textile mills in both Pennsylvania and North Carolina, where their high-quality T-shirts are made.

Realizing that to achieve their performance targets would require more than just a line of T-shirts, Lane and MacHardy began to extend their product line, adding such items as boxer shorts, caps, sweatsuits, turtlenecks, and athletic shorts. "Clothing buyers are fickle," says one longtime Coed customer. "They demand fresh products every year. Coed gives it to them." The company also broadened its customer base by adding to its line products that are designed for older buyers.

Coed Sportswear now employs 45 people, and Lane and MacHardy have hired experienced managers in manufacturing, finance, and marketing to help them run their fast-growing company. Lane oversees the company's operations as "the number cruncher"; MacHardy is in charge of sales and marketing—the creative end of the business. Their complementary skills have proved to be a major strength for Coed. MacHardy explains, "We're a good mix because we share the same philosophy—that the customer is number one—which allows us to meet in the middle to make things happen."

1. What factors have enabled Lane and MacHardy to achieve the success that they have with Coed Sportswear?

2. What weaknesses and potential threats do you see facing Coed in the future? How should Lane and MacHardy deal with them?

3. Why do so many entrepreneurs have difficulty making the "entrepreneurial transition" once their companies reach a certain level? How have Lane and MacHardy handled this transition?

Source: Adapted from Bob Weinstein, "Ready to Wear," *Business Start-Ups,* May 1995, pp. 58-62.

The Power of "Small" Business

6. *Describe* the important role small businesses play in our nation's economy.

Of the 22 million businesses in the United States today, approximately 21.75 million, or 99 percent, can be considered "small." They thrive in virtually every industry, although the majority of small companies are concentrated in the retail and service industries (see Figure 1.6 on page 22). Their contributions to the economy are as numerous as the businesses themselves. For example, small companies employ more than 50 percent of the nation's private-sector work force, even though they possess less than one-fourth of total business assets. Almost 90 percent of all businesses employ fewer than 20 workers.[61] And, because they are primarily labor intensive, small businesses actually create more jobs than do big businesses. In fact, small companies have created two-thirds of all the 20-plus million net new jobs in the U.S. economy since the early 1970s.[62]

David Birch, president of the research firm Cognetics, says that the ability to create jobs is not distributed evenly across the small business sector, however. His research shows that just 4 percent of these small companies created 70 percent of the new jobs, and they did so across all industry sectors, not just in "hot" industries. Birch calls these job-creating small companies "gazelles," those growing at 20 percent or more per year with at least $100,000 in annual sales. His research also identified "mice," small companies that never grow much and don't create many jobs. The majority of small companies are mice. Birch tabbed the country's largest job-shedding businesses "elephants," which continue to lose jobs in the 1990s.[63]

Figure 1.6

***A Profile of Small
Business by Industry***

Source: Adapted from
Small Business Administration,
Washington, D.C.

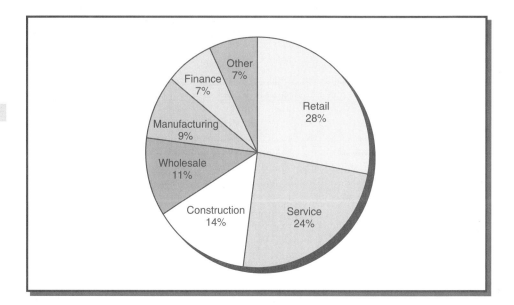

Not only do small companies lead the way in creating jobs, but they also bear the brunt of training workers for them. A recent study by the Small Business Administration concluded that small businesses are the leaders in offering training and advancement opportunities to workers. Small companies offer more general skills instruction and training than large ones, and their employees receive more benefits from the training than do those in larger firms. Although their training programs tend to be informal, in-house, and on-the-job, small companies teach employees valuable skills, from written communication to computer literacy.[64]

Small businesses also produce 48 percent of the country's GDP and account for 53 percent of business sales.[65] Overall, small firms provide directly or indirectly the livelihoods of more than 100 million Americans. Research conducted for the National Science Foundation concluded that small firms create four times more innovations per research and development (R&D) dollar than medium-sized firms and 24 times as many as large companies. In another study of the most important technological innovations introduced into the U.S. market, researchers found that, on average, smaller companies contributed 20 per-

Source: B.C. Cartoon. Reprinted by permission of Johnny Hart and Creators Syndicate, Inc. ©1993, Creators Syndicate, Inc.

cent more of these innovations per employee than did large companies.[66] Many important inventions trace their roots to an entrepreneur—including the zipper, the FM radio, air conditioning, the escalator, the light bulb, and the automatic transmission. An analysis of government economic forecasts shows that the trend of small business success will continue. Bureau of Labor Statistics projections call for the small business sector to grow by 25 percent over the next 15 years, creating another 13.5 million jobs. Large companies, however, are expected to grow by just 10.5 percent over the same period.[67] Currently, between 800,000 and 900,000 new companies with employees come into existence each year.[68]

Why Small Businesses Fail— and How to Beat the Odds

7-A. Describe the causes of small business failure.

Because of their limited resources, inexperienced management, and lack of financial stability, small businesses suffer a mortality rate significantly higher than that of larger, established businesses. Figure 1.7 illustrates the small business survival rate over a ten-year period. Figure 1.8 on page 24 shows the business failure rate per 10,000 listed concerns since 1927. Exploring the circumstances surrounding failure may help you to avoid it.

Management Incompetence

In most small businesses, management inexperience or poor decision-making ability is the chief problem of the failing enterprise. Sometimes the manager of the small business does not have the capacity to operate it successfully. The owner lacks the leadership ability and knowledge necessary to make the business work. Many managers simply do not have what it takes to run a small enterprise. "What kills companies usually has less to do with insufficient money, talent, or information than with something more basic: a shortage of good judgment and understanding at the very top," says one business researcher.[69]

Lack of Experience

Small business managers need to have experience in the field they want to enter. For example, if a person wants to open a retail clothing business, she should first work in a retail clothing store. This will provide practical experience as well as knowledge about the nature of the business. This type of experience can spell the difference between failure and success.

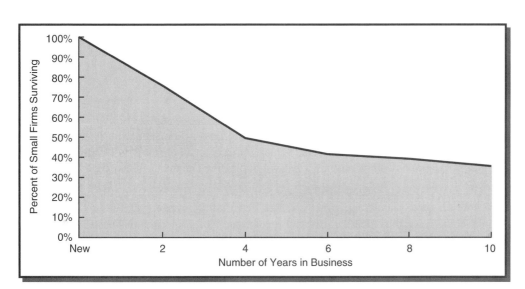

Figure 1.7
Small Business Survival Rate
Source: Adapted from NFIB Foundation/VISA Business Card Primer, Washington, D.C.

Figure 1.8
The Business Failure Rate
Source: Copyright 1996, Dun & Bradstreet, a company of The Dun & Bradstreet Corporation.

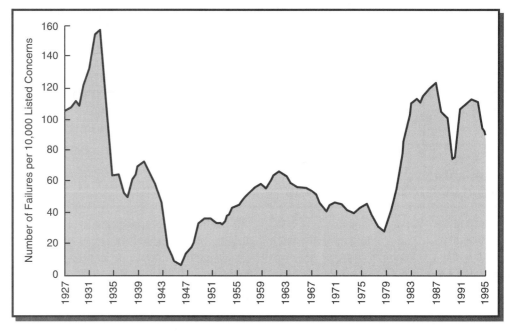

Example

One West Coast entrepreneur had always wanted to own a restaurant, but he had no experience in the restaurant business. He later admitted that he thought that running a restaurant consisted primarily of dressing up in black tie, greeting his regular customers at the door, and showing them to his best tables. He invested $150,000 of his own money and found a partner to put up more capital and to help manage the restaurant. They opened and immediately ran into trouble because they knew nothing about running a restaurant. In desperation, the restaurateurs came up with an idea to attract business: Why not become the first topless restaurant in the area? The gimmick worked for a while, and then business dropped off. Then they decided to become the first bottomless restaurant. Again, business picked up briefly, but the novelty soon wore off, and sales slipped. Eventually the restaurant closed, and the partners lost their original investments, their homes, and their cars; they also spent the next several years paying off back taxes.[70]

Ideally, the prospective entrepreneur should have adequate technical ability (a working knowledge of the physical operations of the business and sufficient conceptual ability); the power to visualize, coordinate, and integrate the various operations of the business into a synergistic whole; and the skill to manage the people in the organization and motivate them to higher levels of performance.

Poor Financial Control

Sound management is the key to a small company's success, and effective managers realize that any successful business venture requires proper financial control. The margin for error in managing finances is especially small for most small businesses. Two financial pitfalls are common in small business: undercapitalization and lax customer credit policies.

LACK OF CAPITAL. Many small business owners make the mistake of beginning their businesses on a "shoestring," which is a fatal error. Entrepreneurs tend to be overly optimistic and often misjudge the financial requirements of going into business. As a result, they start off undercapitalized and can never seem to catch up financially as their companies consume increasing amounts of cash to fuel their growth. "A little bit of cash is a dangerous thing," says one consultant."[71]

Harvey Harris's Grandmother Calendar Company, which made personalized calendars from customers' photos, failed because it was undercapitalized. Demand for its elaborate calendars skyrocketed, but Grandmother's thin capital base couldn't support the rapid growth. As the company strained under a load of orders, quality slipped, orders went unfilled, and cash became even more scarce until finally there was no more cash. "I made mistakes, and did not track receivables, payables, [or our] funding," says Harris.[72]

Grandmother Calendar Company

LAX CUSTOMER CREDIT. The pressure for a small business to sell on credit is intense. Some managers see an opportunity to gain a competitive edge over rivals by granting credit; others feel forced to keep up with competitors who already offer their customers credit sales. Whatever the case, the small business owner must control credit sales carefully as failure to do so can devastate a small company's financial health. Poor credit and collection practices are common to many small business bankruptcies.

After 5 years, Liz Rich's costume jewelry business failed because of cash flow problems associated with credit sales. The company, Maison de Fou, Inc., was "an artistic success and a financial failure," she says. Sales for her jewelry were brisk, but customers took 120 days to pay and suppliers demanded immediate payment. "We were always behind," says Rich.[73]

Maison de Fou, Inc.

Failure to Develop a Strategic Plan

Too many small business managers neglect the process of strategic planning because they think that it is something that only benefits large companies. "I don't have the time" or "We're too small to develop a strategic plan," they rationalize. Failure to plan, however, usually results in failure to survive. Without a clearly defined strategy, a business has no sustainable basis for creating and maintaining a competitive edge in the marketplace. Building a strategic plan forces an entrepreneur to assess *realistically* the proposed business's potential. Is it something customers are willing and able to purchase? Who is the target customer? How will the business attract and keep those customers? What is the company's basis for serving customers' needs better than existing companies? We will explore these and other vital issues in Chapter 2, "Strategic Management and the Entrepreneur."

Uncontrolled Growth

Growth is a natural, healthy, and desirable part of any business enterprise, but it must be planned and controlled. Management expert Peter Drucker says that startup companies can expect to outgrow their capital bases each time sales increase 40 to 50 percent.[74] Ideally, expansion should be financed by retained earnings or by capital contributions from the owner, but most businesses wind up borrowing at least a portion of the capital investment.

Expansion usually requires major changes in organizational structure, business practices such as inventory and financial control procedures, personnel assignments, and other areas. But the most important change occurs in managerial expertise. As the business increases in size and complexity, problems tend to increase in proportion, and the manager must learn to deal with this. Sometimes entrepreneurs encourage rapid growth only to have the business outstrip their ability to manage it.

Poor Location

For any business, choosing the right location is partly an art—and partly a science. Too often, business locations are selected without proper study, investigation, and planning. Some beginning owners choose a particular location just because they noticed a vacant building. But the location question is much too critical to leave to chance. Especially for retailers, the lifeblood of the business—sales—is influenced heavily by choice of location. One small merchandiser located in a rural area depended heavily on the customers of a nearby restaurant for her clientele. Because of the inconvenience of this location, sales suffered and the business failed.

Another factor to consider in selecting location is the amount of rent to be paid. Although it is prudent not to pay an excessive amount for rent, business owners should weigh the cost against the location's effect on sales. Location has two important features: what it costs and what it generates in sales volume.

Improper Inventory Control

Normally, the largest investment the small business manager must make is in inventory, yet inventory control is one of the most neglected managerial responsibilities. Insufficient inventory levels result in shortages and stockouts, causing customers to become disillusioned and leave. A more common situation is that the manager has not only too much inventory but also too much of the *wrong type* of inventory. Many small firms have an excessive amount of cash tied up in an accumulation of useless inventory. We will discuss both purchasing and inventory control techniques in Chapter 12.

Inability to Make the Entrepreneurial Transition

Making it over the "entrepreneurial startup hump" is no guarantee of business success. After the startup, growth usually requires a radically different style of management. The very abilities that make an entrepreneur successful often lead to managerial ineffectiveness. Growth requires entrepreneurs to delegate authority and to relinquish hands-on control of daily operations—something many entrepreneurs simply can't do. Growth pushes them "into areas where most entrepreneurs aren't good," says one expert.[75]

Table 1.4 explains some of the most common mistakes entrepreneurs must avoid.

Table 1.4
Avoid These
Common Mistakes
Sources: Mel Mandell, "Fifteen Start-Up Mistakes," *Business Start-Ups,* December 1995, p. 22; Kenneth Labich, "Why Companies Fail," *Fortune,* November 14, 1994, pp. 52-68; Sharon Nelton, "Ten Key Threats to Success," *Nation's Business,* June 1992, pp. 22-30; Bruce G. Posner, "Why Companies Fail," *Inc.,* June 1993, pp. 102-106; Robert J. Cook, "Famous Last Words," *Entrepreneur,* June 1994, pp. 122-128.

Entrepreneurs whose businesses fail usually can look back on their experiences and see what they did wrong, vowing never to make the same mistake again. If you find yourself making any of the following statements as you launch your business, look out! You may be heading for trouble.

☆ *"We've got a great product (or service)! It will sell itself."* Don't get so caught up in your product or service that you forget to evaluate whether real live customers are willing and able to pay for it. Oh . . . and no product or service has ever "sold itself."

☆ *"With a market this big, we only need a tiny share of it to become rich."* Entrepreneurs tend to be overly optimistic in their sales, profits, and cash flow estimates, especially in the beginning. Most don't realize until they get into business how tough it really is to capture even a tiny share of the market.

☆ *"Strategic plan?! We don't need a strategic plan. That's only for big corporations."* One of the quickest and surest paths to failure is neglecting to build a strategic plan that defines some point of distinction for your company. A plan helps you focus on what you can do for your customers that your competitors cannot.

☆ *"What a great business idea! It's cheap, easy to start, and it's the current rage."* Because a business idea is so cheap and easy to start does not necessarily make it attractive. Too many entrepreneurs get clobbered in such businesses once the market matures and the competition gets stiff or the fad passes.

☆ *"We may not know what we're doing yet, but we've got enough capital to last us until we do. We'll figure it out as we go."* Everything—especially launching a business—takes longer and costs more than you think. Experienced entrepreneurs call it "the rule of two and three": Startups take either twice as long or need three times as much money (or both) to get off the ground as the founders forecast. Plan accordingly.

☆ *"Our forecast shows that we'll be making profits within three months, and that's very conservative...really."* Everyone expects entrepreneurs to be optimistic about their ventures' future, but you have to temper your optimism with reality. Launching a business on the basis of one set of forecasts is asking for trouble. Make sure you develop at least three sets of forecasts—pessimistic, most likely, and optimistic—and have contingency plans for all three.

☆ *"It's a good thing that we've got enough capital to last us the few months until we hit our break-even point."* Attracting adequate startup financing is essential to launching your business, but you also have to have access to *continuing* sources of funding. Growing businesses consume cash, and fast-growing businesses consume cash even faster. Don't become a victim of your own success; make sure you establish reliable sources of capital once your business is up and running.

★ *"We'll make it easy for customers to buy from us. We'll extend credit to almost anyone to make a sale."* One of the shortest routes to cash flow problems is failing to manage customer credit. It's easy to make a sale, but remember: Sales don't count unless you actually collect the payments from them. Watch for slow-paying customers.

★ *"We're in the big time now. Our largest customer is [insert name of large customer here]."* Landing a big customer is great, but it's dangerous to become overly dependent on a single customer for most of your sales. What happens if the customer decides to squeeze you for price concessions or to go to a competitor?

★ *Let's have our annual meeting in the Cayman Islands. We're the only 'stockholders,' and, besides, we deserve it. We've worked hard."* Avoid the tendency to drain cash out of your business unnecessarily. A good rule of thumb: Don't start your business unless you have enough savings to support yourself (without taking cash from it) until the business breaks even.

★ *"Let's go with this location. I know it's 'off the beaten path,' but it's so much cheaper!"* For some businesses, choice of location is not a crucial issue. However, if your company relies on customers coming into your place of business to make sales, do not settle for the cheapest location. There's a reason such places are cheap! It's better to pay a higher price for a location that produces adequate sales volume.

★ *Computer?! I don't know anything about computers. A legal pad and an adding machine are all I need to manage my business!"* These days almost any business—no matter how small—can benefit from a computer. First, find the software that will help you maintain control over your business; then buy the computer that will run it. Don't forget to budget both time and money for training and support.

★ *We're so small here. Everybody knows what our goals and objectives are."* Just because a business is small doesn't necessarily mean that everyone who works there understands where you are trying to take the company. Do not assume that people will read your mind concerning your company's mission, goals, and objectives. You must communicate your vision for the business to everyone involved in it.

★ *This business is so easy it can run itself."* Don't fool yourself. The only place a business will run itself is downhill! You must manage your company, and one of the most important jobs you have as the leader is to prioritize your business's objectives.

★ *"Of course our customers are satisfied! I never hear them complain."* Most customers never complain about poor service or bad quality. They simply refuse to do business with you again. More often than not, the service and level of personal treatment that customers receive is what allows many small businesses to gain an edge over their larger rivals. Unfortunately, it's also one of the most overlooked aspects of a business. Set up a system to get regular feedback from your customers.

★ *"What do you mean we're out of cash? We've been making a profit for months now, and sales are growing."* Don't confuse cash and profits. You cannot spend profits—just cash. Many businesses fail because their founders mistakenly assume that if profits are rising, so is the company's cash balance. To be successful, you must manage both profits and cash!

Table 1.4
Avoid These Common Mistakes

Continued

How to Avoid the Pitfalls

We have seen the most common reasons behind many small business failures. Now we must examine the ways to avoid becoming another failure statistic and gain insight into what makes a successful business. The suggestions for success follow naturally from the causes of business failure.

7-B. Explain how entrepreneurs can avoid business failure.

Know Your Business in Depth

We have already emphasized the need for the right type of experience in the business you plan to start. "If you get into something you don't really know, you are going to fail," says one small business consultant.[76] Get the best education in your business area you possibly can *before* you set out on your own. Read everything you can—trade journals, business periodicals, books—relating to your industry. Personal contact with suppliers, customers, trade associations, and others in the same industry is another excellent way to get that knowledge.

Before she launched Executive Temporaries, Suzanne Clifton contacted other entrepreneurs in the temporary personnel services business (far enough away from her home base to avoid competitors) to find out "what it takes to operate this kind of business." She picked up many valuable tips and identified the key factors required for success. Today her company has achieved sales exceeding $4 million.[77]

Successful entrepreneurs are like sponges, soaking up as much knowledge as they can from a variety of sources.

Develop a Solid Business Plan

For the new entrepreneur, a well-written business plan is a crucial ingredient in preparing for business success. Without a sound business plan, a firm merely drifts along without any real direction. Yet entrepreneurs, who tend to be people of action, too often jump right into a business venture without taking time to prepare a written plan outlining the essence of the business. "Most entrepreneurs don't have a solid business plan," says one business owner. "But a thorough business plan and timely financial information are critical. They help you make the important decisions about your business; you constantly have to monitor what you're doing against your plan."[78]

Planning allows you to replace "I think" with "I know." In many cases businesses are built on faulty assumptions like "I think there are enough customers in town to support a health food shop." The experienced entrepreneur investigates these assumptions and replaces them with facts before making the decision to go into business. We will discuss the process of developing a business plan in Chapter 9, "Crafting a Winning Business Plan."

Manage Financial Resources

The best defense against financial problems is developing a practical information system and then using this information to make business decisions. No entrepreneur can maintain control over a business unless she is able to judge its financial health.

The first step in managing financial resources effectively is to have adequate startup capital. Too many entrepreneurs begin their businesses with too little capital. One experienced business owner advises, "Estimate how much capital you need to get the business going and then double that figure."[79] His point is well taken; it almost always costs more to launch a business than any entrepreneur expects.

The most valuable financial resource to any small business is *cash*. While earning a profit is essential to its long-term survival, a business must have an adequate supply of cash to pay its bills and obligations. Some entrepreneurs count on growing sales to supply their company's cash needs, but it almost never happens. Growing companies usually consume more cash than they generate; and the faster they grow, the more cash they gobble up! We will discuss cash management techniques in Chapter 7, "Managing Cash Flow."

Understand Financial Statements

Every business owner must depend on records and financial statements to know the condition of her business. All too often these records are used only for tax purposes and are not employed as vital control devices. To truly understand what is going on in the business, an owner must have at least a basic understanding of accounting and finance.

When analyzed and interpreted properly, these financial statements are reliable indicators of a small firm's health. They can be quite helpful in signaling potential problems. For example, declining sales, slipping profits, rising debt, and deteriorating working capital are all symptoms of potentially lethal problems that require immediate attention. We will discuss financial statement analysis in Chapter 8, "Creating a Successful Financial Plan."

Learn to Manage People Effectively

No matter what kind of business you launch, you must learn to manage people. Every business depends on a foundation of well-trained, motivated employees. No business owner can do everything alone. The people an entrepreneur hires ultimately determine the heights to which the company can climb—or the depths to which it can plunge. Attracting and retaining a corps of quality employees is no easy task, however. It remains a challenge for every small business owner. "In the end, your most dominant sustainable resource is the quality of the people you have," says one small business expert.[80] We will discuss the techniques of managing and motivating people effectively in Chapter 13, "Leading the Growing Company and Planning for Management Succession."

YOU BE THE CONSULTANT...

Three Strikes, But You're Not Out

Debbie Nigro knows what it's like to taste business failure. In fact, three of the first four businesses she has started have ended in failure, which caused her to lose her entire life savings. Yet, that has not dimmed her entrepreneurial enthusiasm. Nigro recently launched Sweet Talk Productions, Inc., which produces a syndicated radio talk show, "The Working Mom on the Run," which she hosts. Obviously targeted at working mothers trying to juggle a variety of demands, the show is a fast-paced combination of entertainment, news, and information. "I knew I had it in me," says Nigro of her latest business startup, "and I would use my last breath to make it happen. This had to work, period."

Nigro started her first business, a tiny advertising agency, while only a sophomore in college. After that business closed, she went to work as a radio news director and on-air personality. However, she still yearned for an entrepreneurial lifestyle. So, she launched a doomed television cable news venture. Shortly after recovering from that setback, Nigro started a company to produce a talent show for cable television, which was booming at that time. When the talent show venture folded in 1990, her third strikeout, Nigro recalls "everyone had lost faith in me."

Everyone except Nigro herself. She had piled up $15,000 in credit card debt to get the talent show venture up and running. To pay the bills, she decided to find a job working for someone else. Unfortunately, not many companies were interested in hiring a failed entrepreneur. Nigro took a job selling clothing at a New York men's store for $300 per week. Soon she had the idea for the company that would produce the talk radio show aimed at working mothers. But getting the financing to start Sweet Talk Productions after three failures proved to be a daunting task. She had just $200, and that wouldn't go very far. In late 1992, Nigro moved with her daughter into her mother's house and managed to borrow a few hundred dollars from relatives to launch Sweet Talk Productions.

Nigro produced her first show and then started calling on radio stations to sell it. She convinced two stations to broadcast the show and share the advertising revenue it generated. Then she went out and sold advertising spots. One radio station manager let her use a spare conference room as her office, which she had to vacate whenever anyone wanted to have lunch there. "She was absolutely broke," recalls the station manager. "But I listened to her idea, and I thought, 'This will be a home run.'"

Nigro then convinced customers to help finance her business, a common technique among entrepreneurs searching for startup capital. She was able to convince Avon Products, a company highly interested in reaching Nigro's target audience, to invest $3,000 in the show in exchange for the lead sponsorship and ground-floor advertising rates. Three years later, Sweet Talk Productions is still struggling to survive. Cash flow has been a constant problem. In the early days, "I used to make $1 purchases at the local deli so I could cash checks for $25 that I didn't yet have in the bank," Nigro recalls. "I still wake up with nightmares about work," she admits. Sweet Talk Productions has come a long way in just a short time, however. Today, more than 130 radio stations carry her weekly show, which has attracted advertising from other big advertisers, including Procter & Gamble. The company now has five employees, and Nigro has taken on a business partner. Sweet Talk Productions' annual sales currently exceed $1 million.

1. On a scale of 0 to 100, how would you assess Sweet Talk Productions' chances of survival? Explain.

2. Does Debbie Nigro exhibit the entrepreneurial spirit? If so, in what ways?

3. Looking back at how Nigro started Sweet Talk Productions, what would you have advised her to do differently?

4. What advice would you offer Debbie Nigro today? What pitfalls would you warn her about?

Source: Adapted from Roger Rickleffs, "More Failed Entrepreneurs Give Success Another Shot," *Wall Street Journal*," February 13, 1996, pp. B1-B2.

Keep in Tune with Yourself

"Starting a business is like running a marathon. If you're not physically and mentally in shape, you'd better do something else," says one business consultant.[81] Your business's success will depend on your constant presence and attention, so it is critical to monitor your health closely. Stress is a primary problem, especially if it is not kept in check. Employees may also suffer health problems. Some small businesses have found it cost-effective to create company-sponsored fitness programs.

> "I had the courage to start my own business, but I realized that it takes more than guts and a good product or service to succeed. An entrepreneur must also have the skills of a salesman, secretary, bookkeeper, manager, analyst, and errand boy. Neglect one area too long, and—zap—you're out of business."
>
> *Rafael J. Gerena, cofounder of an advertising agency*

CHAPTER SUMMARY

1. Define the role of the entrepreneur in business in the United States and around the world.
- Record numbers of people have launched companies over the past decade. The entrepreneurship boom is not limited to the United States; many nations across the globe are seeing similar growth in their small business sectors. A variety of competitive, economic, and demographic shifts has created a world in which "small is beautiful."
- Capitalist societies depend on entrepreneurs to provide the drive and risk taking necessary for the system to supply people with the goods and services they need.

2. Describe the entrepreneurial profile.
- Entrepreneurs have some common characteristics, including a desire for responsibility, a preference for moderate risk, confidence in their ability to succeed, desire for immediate feedback, a high energy level, a future orientation, skill at organizing, and a value of achievement over money. In a phrase, they are tenacious high achievers.

3-A. Describe the benefits of entrepreneurship.
- Driven by these personal characteristics, entrepreneurs establish and manage small businesses to gain control over their lives, make a difference in the world, become self-fulfilled, reap unlimited profits, contribute to society, and do what they enjoy doing.

3-B. Describe the drawbacks of entrepreneurship.
- Entrepreneurs also face certain disadvantages, including uncertainty of income, the risk of losing their investments (and more), long hours and hard work, a lower quality of life until the business gets established, high stress levels, and complete decision-making responsibility.

4. Explain the forces that are driving the growth of entrepreneurship.
- Several factors are driving the boom in entrepreneurship, including entrepreneurs portrayed as heroes, better entrepreneurial education, economic and demographic factors, a shift to a service economy, technological advancements, more independent lifestyles, and increased international opportunities.

5. Identify the groups that are leading the nation's boom in entrepreneurship.
- Several groups are leading the nation's drive toward entrepreneurship: women, minorities, immigrants, part-timers, home-based business owners, family business owners, copreneurs, corporate castoffs, and corporate dropouts.

6. Describe the important role small businesses play in our economy.
- Small business's contributions are many. They make up 99 percent of all U.S. businesses; they employ 50 percent of the private-sector work force; they have created two-thirds of all the net new jobs over the past two decades; they constantly create new products and services; and they account for 53 percent of all business sales and 48 percent of the U.S. GDP.

7-A. Describe the causes of small business failure.
- There are no guarantees that the business will make a profit or even survive. Small Business Administration (SBA) statistics show that 63 percent of new businesses will fail within six years. The primary cause of business failure is incompetent management. Other reasons include lack of experience, poor financial control, lack of strategic planning, uncontrolled growth, inappropriate location, lack of inventory control, and inability to make the entrepreneurial transition.

7-B. Explain how entrepreneurs can avoid business failure.
- Entrepreneurs can employ several general tactics to avoid these pitfalls. Entrepreneurs should know their businesses in depth, prepare a solid business plan, manage financial resources effectively, understand financial statements, learn to manage people, and try to stay healthy.

1. What forces have led to the boom in entrepreneurship in the United States and across the globe?
2. What is an entrepreneur? Give a brief description of the entrepreneurial profile.
3. *Inc.* magazine claims, "Entrepreneurship is more mundane than it's sometimes portrayed . . . you don't need to be a person of mythical proportions to be very, very successful in building a company." Do you agree? Explain.
4. What are the major benefits of business ownership?
5. Which of the potential drawbacks to business ownership are most critical?
6. Briefly describe the role of the following groups in entrepreneurship: women, minorities, immigrants, part-timers, home-based business owners, family business owners, copreneurs, corporate castoffs, and corporate dropouts.
7. What is a small business? What contributions do small businesses make to our economy?
8. Describe the small business failure rate.
9. Outline the causes of business failure. Which problems cause most business failures?
10. How can the small business owner avoid the common pitfalls that often lead to business failures?
11. Why is it important to study the small business failure rate and the causes of business failures?
12. Explain the typical entrepreneur's attitude toward risk.
13. Are you interested in one day launching a small business? If so, when? What kind of business? Describe it. What can you do to ensure its success?

Beyond the Classroom...

1. Choose an entrepreneur in your community and interview him or her. What's the "story" behind the business? How well does the entrepreneur fit the entrepreneurial profile described in this chapter? What advantages and disadvantages does the owner see in owning a business? What advice would he or she offer to someone considering launching a business?

2. Select one of the categories under the section "Entrepreneurial Profiles" in this chapter and research it in more detail. Find examples of that category. Prepare a brief report for your class.

3. Search through recent business publications (especially those focusing on small companies) and find an example of an entrepreneur, past or present, who exhibits the entrepreneurial spirit of striving for success in the face of failure. Prepare a brief report for your class.

SURFING THE NET

1. Using one of the search engines on the World Wide Web (WWW) such as Lycos, Magellan, Yahoo!, or others, conduct a search on the word entrepreneur. Select one of the sites you find and prepare a one-page report on its contents.

2. Access the home page for the Association of Collegiate Entrepreneurs (ACE) at:

http://www/cuspomona.edu/ace/

What is the purpose of ACE? What upcoming events is it sponsoring? What resources are available to entrepreneurs wanting to start a business?

3. Access the home page of Entrepreneurs on the Web (EOTW) at:

http://www/eotw.com

Prepare a report on the information you find there. How might an entrepreneur about to start a company use some of the information on the WWW?

CHAPTER

TWO

Strategic Management and the Entrepreneur

If you don't know where you're going, you'll end up somewhere else.
- Yogi Berra

A danger foreseen is half avoided.
- Italian proverb

Lack of opportunity is often nothing more than lack of purpose or direction.
- Anonymous

Whether your goal is business growth or winning a ball game, strategy should be your framework. Strategy is not defined by which tactics you use on a day-to-day basis but by an overarching plan to reach your objective.
- Jan Freeman

LEARNING OBJECTIVES

Upon completion of this chapter, you will be able to:

1. **Understand** why and how a small business must build a competitive advantage in the market.

2. **Create** a strategic plan using the ten steps in the strategic planning process.

3. **Know** why and how to write a meaningful mission statement.

4. **Understand** how to identify a company's SWOT—strengths, weaknesses, opportunities, and threats.

5. **Establish** meaningful goals and objectives.

6. **Understand** the three basic strategic alternatives a small company has—low cost, differentiation, and focus—and know when and how to employ them.

Building and maintaining a competitive advantage in the markets any business serves is essential for survival. Firms must continually strive to achieve both strategic and operational excellence. In simple terms, a business must create a strategy for delivering its goods and services in a way that creates greater value for its customers. The company must have the capacity to constantly reinvent itself through organizational learning and dedication to continuous improvement. Not only does such learning produce improvements in products and services, but it also enhances the way a business evolves into the supplier of choice for its customers.

Competition has become increasingly dynamic and global in scope. Failing to think strategically about the business is inviting disaster. Technology, demographics, globalization, and the economy are each individual forces that interact to produce our rapidly changing business environment. Approximately half of the technological changes on Earth have taken place since 1900. Furthermore, the last 15 years of this century will produce as much technological change as the first 85 years![1] Small businesses are not immune from these forces. To the contrary, many exceptional small businesses realize the competitive advantage they possess in their ability to respond quickly to the forces of change. Nimbleness and agility are organizational traits that allow for rapid strategic change in response to market conditions. Small business owners are quick to learn the need to read and understand the trends that affect their businesses. Entrepreneurs must focus strategic actions on achieving specific objectives and must implement them with a high degree of commitment. Small businesses do not possess depth in financial resources, and consequently, every strategic initiative must be well planned, highly focused, and efficiently implemented.

To cope with such rapid change and intense competitive conditions requires a new way of managing a business. To be successful, entrepreneurs need a powerful weapon: strategic management. **Strategic management** involves developing a game plan to guide a company as it strives to accomplish its mission, goals, and objectives, and to keep it on its desired course. The basic premise is to create a blueprint that allows business owners to match their companies' strengths and weaknesses to the environment's opportunities and threats. One recent study of 500 small businesses found that one of the biggest distinguishing factors between growing companies and those in decline was the use of a written business plan. Unfortunately, only 42 percent of the small businesses used such a plan.[2] Too many small business owners still run their companies "by the seat of their pants."

strategic management—*the process of developing a game plan to guide the company as it strives to accomplish its mission, goals, and objectives, and to keep it on its desired course.*

The Search for a Competitive Advantage

Developing a strategic plan is crucial to creating a small company's **competitive advantage**—that aggregation of factors that sets a company apart from its competitors and gives it a unique position in the market. Building a competitive advantage is the result of strategic thinking, and successful entrepreneurs are masters of strategic thinking. They know what is takes to be successful in the markets in which they compete. They know that they must invest their scarce resources wisely. These entrepreneurs think out every strategic move they make to ensure that it reinforces the firm's fundamental strategic focus.

Gaining a competitive advantage is a moving target and is not necessarily permanent. The details making up a company's advantage require continuous modification and adaptation to meet ever evolving requirements. One business may sustain such an advantage for decades, while another loses its advantage to a competitor in one season. To thrive, a small company must establish a plan for creating a unique image in the minds of its potential customers. No business can be everything to everyone. Drawing up a strategic plan prevents a

1. Understand why and how a small business must build a competitive advantage in the market.

competitive advantage—*the aggregation of factors that sets a company apart from its competitors and gives it a unique position in the market.*

small business from stumbling into the pitfall of failing to differentiate itself from its competitors.

Sashco Sealants, Inc.

For instance, Les Burch, president of Sashco Sealants, Inc., says that most of the products in his company's line were "me-too items made because the competition had them first, not because we had something better." In a bold strategic move, Sashco dropped 80 percent of its product line and concentrated on selling its unique specialty sealants and adhesives to independent dealers and distributors rather than through large chain stores. The move paid off; sales continue to climb. "Entrepreneurs are constantly tempted to expand into markets and products in which their company has no uniqueness," says Burch. "It is a siren song that rarely works."[3]

Another avenue for small businesses seeking a competitive advantage is one specifically tailored to the skills and resources of small business—customer intimacy, which involves focusing on the goods and services customers want and value. The goal is to build long-term customer relationships through providing goods and services that create value for the customer. Businesses that excel at this strategy are always looking one step ahead of what customers say they need today toward what these customers will need tomorrow. They strive to exceed their customers' expectations by being the first in meeting tomorrow's needs. This strategy is extremely well suited to smaller firms that concentrate on niches in the market and can afford to invest to ensure that they retain their leadership positions.

When it comes to developing a strategic plan, small companies actually have many natural advantages over their larger rivals. The typical small business has fewer product lines, a more clearly defined (and usually smaller) customer base, and a specific geographic market area. Small business owners also maintain close contact with their customers, enabling them to detect shifts in customers' needs and wants. Therefore, strategic planning should come more naturally to small business than to large businesses.

Strategic management can increase a small firm's effectiveness, but owners must rely on a procedure designed to meet their needs and their business's special characteristics. A small business's strategic management procedure should include the following features:

- Use a relatively short planning horizon—two years or less for most small companies.
- Be informal and not overly structured; a shirt-sleeve approach is ideal.
- Encourage the participation of employees and outside parties to improve the reliability and creativity of the resulting plan.
- Do not begin with setting objectives, as extensive objective setting early on may interfere with the creative process of strategic management.
- Focus on strategic *thinking*, not just planning, by linking long-range goals to day-to-day operations.

YOU BE THE CONSULTANT...

A Business on a Roll

At age 30, Chris Zane has built a very successful small business. His bicycle shop, Zane's Cycles, is the largest independent bicycle dealer in New Haven, Connecticut, an impressive accomplishment given that sports superstores and chains now account for three out of every four bikes sold. In New Haven alone, three bike shops all closed within a year. "The smaller guys are fading away because they won't get into the game and compete at a higher level," says one bike manufacturer.

Zane's Cycles is not fading away, however, because Chris Zane not only is willing to compete at a higher level, but he is usually the first one to reach that higher plane. His business has actually gained market share over the years, and sales are growing at about 25 percent a year. Zane does it by trying not just to sell bikes to customers but to *own* his customers. He has read all of the latest management best-sellers, conducted focus groups, studied customer behavior in his own store, and picked his suppliers brains for new ideas.

The mechanically gifted Zane started in the bicycle business at age 12, fixing bikes in his East Haven neighborhood.

Word about the quality of his work spread quickly, and soon the youngster was pulling in $300 to $400 a week. At age 16, he took a job at a local bike shop, but shortly after he started, the owner told him the shop was going out of business. Showing his entrepreneurial flair, Zane convinced his parents to help him buy the shop's inventory and take over its lease. With a $20,000 loan from his grandfather, Zane took over the business and rang up sales of $56,000 the first year. Zane recalls learning a valuable principle that has guided his business ever since: "The customer *is* your job," he says.

Zane is the master of hard-nose competition. Over the years he has taken market share from his competitors by constantly offering his customers more value for their dollars, giving him a powerful competitive advantage. For instance, Zane was the first in the market to introduce free lifetime service on all the bikes he sells, or has ever sold! Making the policy retroactive really captured customers' attention. "We wanted to make our existing customers our apostles," he explains. Most of the business strategies Zane has used to differentiate his business look expensive on the surface, but, in reality, usually cost him very little. Some of the strategies which have shaped the success and growth of the business include:

• *Never charging for any item that cost less than a dollar.* This inexpensive expression of goodwill brings a lot of customers back for their next major bike or accessory purchase. Annual cost: less than $150.
• *Becoming highly visible in the community through involvement in public projects.* Zane started the Zane Foundation which awards $1,000 college scholarships to graduates of his high school alma mater. The foundation is supported from revenues generated by 50 candy machines located in his market area. Each machine, as well as the scholarships, is a positive reminder to potential customers of the community support Zane's Cycles provides.
• *Creating goodwill by sponsoring programs for children.* Zane sponsors bike safety programs and, in cooperation with the New Haven police, a bike registration program. In addi-

tion, when Connecticut passed a mandatory bicycle helmet law, Zane's Cycles began offering kids bike helmets at cost.
• *Looking bigger than you really are.* Zane has a slick, 32-page catalog which features both merchandise and biking trips. Although the catalog appears to be customized, it is really the result of a cooperative advertising effort. He also has a toll-free phone number for customer convenience.
• *Appealing to adults by taking care of the kids.* When he relocated his shop, Zane built a play area for children. He would give them a free Snapple and sit them in front of a video while Mom and Dad shopped. He also added a 14-foot mahogany coffee bar serving free gourmet coffee. These additions help to create the warm atmosphere that encourage customers to relax and shop in a leisurely fashion. "People fell in love with it," says Zane.
• *Taking away customers' uncertainty by offering a price guarantee.* Zane knows that his prices are competitive, but to convince customers of that, he began offering a 90-day price guarantee on all merchandise. If a customer finds a product anywhere in the state of Connecticut for less, Zane's will refund the difference, plus 10 percent.

Zane's business philosophy and the strategies he has spun off of it have worked well. However, Wal*Mart is about to open a store nearby, as is Ski Market a "category-killer" sporting goods store. Discussing his upcoming competitors, Zane says, "You have to have all your programs in place. You have to work to be as strong as they are and kill them where they're weak. And customer service is where they're weakest."

1. What factors have accounted for Zane's Cycles' success so far? What threats do you see for this bike retailer?

2. How has Zane been able to build a competitive advantage? Do you agree with Zane's assessment of his upcoming competition? Explain.

3. What strategic recommendations would you make for Zane's Cycles?

Source: Adopted from Donna Fenn, "Leader of the Pack," *Inc.,* February 1996, pp. 31–38.

The Strategic Management Process

Strategic planning is not a result or an outcome but an ongoing process. Strategic thinking does not have an endpoint, and, consequently, the planning process itself is continuous. The strategic management process consists of ten steps (see Figure 2.1 on page 36):

Step 1 Develop a clear vision and translate it into a meaningful mission statement.
Step 2 Define the firm's core competencies and the market segment, and position the business to compete effectively.
Step 3 Assess the company's strengths and weaknesses.
Step 4 Scan the environment for significant opportunities and threats facing the business.
Step 5 Identify the key factors for success in the business.

2. Create a strategic plan using the ten steps in the strategic planning process.

Step 6 Analyze the competition.

Step 7 Create company goals and objectives.

Step 8 Formulate strategic options and select the appropriate strategies.

Step 9 Translate strategic plans into action plans.

Step 10 Establish accurate controls.

3. Know why and how to write a meaningful mission statement.

Step 1: Develop a clear vision and translate it into a meaningful mission statement

VISION. Throughout history, the greatest political and business leaders have been visionaries. Whether the vision is as grand as Martin Luther King, Jr.'s "I have a dream" speech or as simple as Ray Kroc's devotion to quality, service, cleanliness, and value at McDonald's, the purpose is the same: to focus everyone's attention and efforts on the same target. The vision touches everyone associated with the company—employees, investors, lenders, customers, the community. It is an expression of what the owner (and therefore the company) stands for and believes in. One manager says that vision is "the picture that leaps into your mind when you close your eyes and dream about what you want your organization to become. It's just over the horizon."[4] Highly successful entrepreneurs are able to communicate their vision and their enthusiasm about the vision to those around them.

Vision is based on values. One of the most valuable exercises an entrepreneur can perform is to write down her values and share them with employees. "Values are like organizational DNA," says one consultant. "They tell people how to act."[5] Successful entrepre-

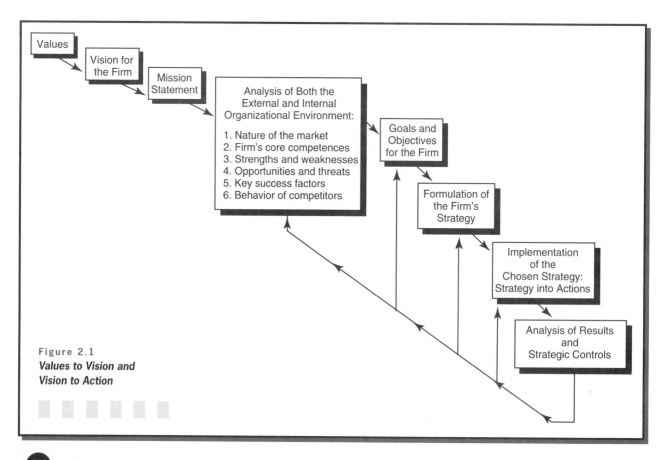

Figure 2.1
Values to Vision and Vision to Action

neurs build their ventures around a set of three to six core values, which might range from respect for the individual and innovation to creating satisfied customers and making the world a better place. Indeed, truly visionary entrepreneurs see their company's primary purpose as more than just "making money."

For instance, Anne Beiler, founder of Auntie Anne's, believes her work-filled upbringing and strong religious values helped her to create her thriving soft pretzel franchise. Beiler learned the value of hard work and honesty and the importance of family and faith as a child growing up in a traditional Amish-Mennonite community in rural Pennsylvania. Those same core values—rather than money—drive her business today. "One of the harder things about growing a business is transmitting your values because they're not tangible."[6]

 **Auntie Anne's**

The most effective way to communicate the values of the company to everyone it touches is by formulating a written mission statement.

MISSION. The mission statement addresses the first question of any business venture: What business am I in? Establishing the business's purpose in writing must come first to give the company a sense of direction. The mission is the mechanism for making it clear to everyone a company touches "why we are here" and "where we are going." Without a concise, meaningful mission statement, the small business risks wandering aimlessly in the marketplace, with no idea of where to go or how to get there. The mission statement essentially sets the tone for the entire company. "A mission statement defines what an organization is, why it exists, its reason for being," says one expert.[7]

At Zytec Corporation, a maker of electronic components and winner of the Malcolm Baldrige National Quality Award, every new employee attends a 16-hour seminar called "Zytec-Involved People." Presented by top managers, it introduces employees to Zytec's values, mission, and culture. Employees learn the keys to the company's success: its commitment to quality, service, value, continuous improvement, and ethical business practices.[8]

Zytec Corporation

ELEMENTS OF A MISSION STATEMENT. A sound mission statement need not be lengthy to be effective. It should, however, answer certain key questions:

- ✩ What are our organization's basic beliefs and values? What do we stand for?
- ✩ Who are our target customers?
- ✩ What are our basic products and services? What customer needs or wants do they satisfy?
- ✩ How can we better satisfy these needs and wants?
- ✩ Why should customers do business with us rather than the competitor down the street (or across town, on the other coast, or on the other side of the globe)?
- ✩ What constitutes value to our customers? How can we offer them better value?
- ✩ What is our competitive advantage? What is its source?
- ✩ In which markets (or market segments) will we choose to compete?
- ✩ Who are the key stakeholders in our company and what effect do they have on it?
- ✩ What benefits should we be providing to our customers five years from now?

By answering such basic questions, the company will have a much clearer picture of what it is and what it wants to be. Table 2.1 offers some useful tips on writing a mission statement.

> *Haworth, Inc. of Holland, Michigan, places a great deal of value on its mission development process. The mission statement sets forth "the kind of company we are, what our principles are, what our objectives are, and how we want to work," says Haworth's president. Managers believe that regularly reviewing the mission statement forces them to think strategically and has been a key component in the company's success. In less than two decades, Haworth has grown from 250 employees and $14 million in sales to 7,000 employees worldwide and sales in excess of $800 million.*[9]

Haworth, Inc.

A firm's mission statement may be the most essential and basic communication it puts forward. If the people on the plant, shop, retail, or warehouse floor don't know what a company's mission is, then, for all practical purposes, it does not have one! The mission statement expresses the firm's character, identity, and scope of operation, but writing it is only half the battle, at best. *The most difficult part is living that mission every day.* For instance, a business owner may *say* that quality is important, but deciding to ship what he knows is a substandard order just to meet a deadline tells employees (and the customer) what *really* counts! To be effective, a mission statement must become a living, breathing document that is embodied in the minds, habits, and attitudes of everyone in the company every day. Consider the mission statement of Blazing Graphics of Cranston, Rhode Island, which illustrates its identity and scope of operation:

> Blazing Graphics will provide you with the most effective visual communication attainable. We will help you achieve all of your goals while providing you with the greatest value both seen and unseen.
>
> Here at Blazing Graphics we will take the time to do things right. We do this by controlling the entire graphic arts process. This enables us to better coordinate each job while providing a higher level of service.
>
> Our mission is to ensure exceptional quality by opening up communication between crafts normally separated and at times adverse to one another.
>
> Here at Blazing Graphics we have committed ourselves and our resources to being on the forefront of technology.
>
> Creative technical know-how is the single most critical determinant of economic competitiveness.
>
> It's our real belief that together we can create an environment that will be both personally and professionally fulfilling for all the people who make up the Blazing Community.[10]

A mission statement is a useful tool for getting everyone in a company fired up and heading in the same direction, but writing one is not as easy as it may first appear. Here are some tips for writing a powerful mission statement:

* ✩ Keep it short. The best mission statements are just a few sentences long. If they are short, people will tend to remember them better.

* ✩ Keep it simple. Avoid using fancy jargon just to impress outsiders such as customers or suppliers. The first and most important use of a mission statement is inside a company.

* ✩ Get everyone involved. If the boss writes the mission statement, who is going to criticize it? Although the entrepreneur has to be the driving force behind the mission statement, everyone in the company needs the opportunity to have a voice in writing it. Expect to write several drafts before you arrive at a finished product.

* ✩ Keep it current. Mission statements can get stale over time. As business and competitive conditions change, so should your mission statement. Make a habit of evaluating your mission periodically so that it stays fresh.

* ✩ Make sure your mission statement reflects the values and beliefs you hold dear. They are the foundation on which your company is built.

* ✩ Make sure your mission includes values that are worthy of your employees' best efforts. One entrepreneur says that a mission statement should "send a message to employees, suppliers, and customers as to what the purpose of the company is aside from just making profits."

* ✩ Make sure your statement reflects a concern for the future. Business owners can get so focused on the present that they forget about the future. A mission statement should be the first link to the company's future.

* ✩ Keep the tone of the statement positive and upbeat. No one wants to work for a business with a pessimistic outlook of the world.

* ✩ Consider using your mission statement to lay an ethical foundation for your company. This is the ideal time to let employees know what your company stands for—and what it won't stand for.

* ✩ Look at other company's mission statements to generate ideas for your own. Two books, *Say It and Live It: The 50 Corporate Mission Statements That Hit the Mark* (Currency/Doubleday) and *Mission Statements: A Guide to the Corporate and Nonprofit Sectors* (Garland Publishing), are useful resources.

* ✩ Make sure that your mission statement is appropriate for your company's culture. Although you should look at other companies' missions, do *not* make the mistake of trying to copy them. Your company's mission statement is unique to you and your company!

* ✩ Use it. Don't go to all of the trouble of writing a mission statement just to let it collect dust. Post it on bulletin boards, print it on buttons and business cards, stuff it into employees' pay envelopes. Talk about your mission often, and use it as you develop your strategic plan. That's what it's for!

Table 2.1.

Tips on Writing a Powerful Mission Statement

Sources: Adapted from Alan Farnham, "Brushing Up Your Vision Thing," *Fortune*, May 1, 1995, p. 129; Sharon Nelton, "Put Your Purpose in Writing," *Nation's Business*, February 1994, pp. 61–64; Jacquelyn Lynn, "Single-Minded," *Entrepreneur*, January 1996, p. 97.

A company may have a powerful competitive advantage, but it is wasted unless (1) the owner has communicated that advantage to workers, who, in turn, are working hard to communicate it to customers and potential customers, and (2) customers are recommending the company to their friends because they understand the benefits they are getting from it that they cannot get elsewhere. *That's* the real power of a mission statement! Although many of the benefits of developing a meaningful mission and using it to guide a company are difficult to assess, the ultimate result is more tangible. "There's a definite business logic for it," says one consultant. "The company becomes more profitable and more competitive."[11]

Step 2: Define the company's core competencies, its targeted market segment(s), and position the company to compete effectively

CORE COMPETENCIES. In the long term, what sets apart companies that thrive from those that struggle to survive is the ability to develop a set of core competencies that enables it to

core competencies—a unique set of capabilities that a company develops in key operational areas that allow it to vault past competitors.

serve customers better. **Core competencies** are a unique set of capabilities that a company develops in key operational areas, such as quality, service, innovation, team building, flexibility, responsiveness, and others, that allow it to vault past competitors. These core competencies become the nucleus of a company's competitive advantage and are usually quite enduring over time. Small companies' core competencies often have to do with the benefits of their size—agility, speed, closeness to their customers, ability to innovate. In short, their smallness allows them to do things that larger companies cannot!

Successful small businesses know the market segment(s) in which they compete and build and retain core competencies that directly contribute to their long-term effectiveness. The answers to the following questions allow entrepreneurs to focus their resources on creating or reinforcing their companies' core competencies:

☆ Who are the customers for our product or service?

☆ What are our customers' characteristics (e.g., age, income, buying habits, location)?

☆ Why do they buy our goods or use our service?

☆ How loyal are they to their present supplier?

☆ What factors cause them to increase or decrease purchases?

☆ Are there major customers in the market? If so, who are they?

☆ What portion of total sales do major customers represent?

☆ How many competitors will we have?

☆ How broad will our customer base be?

☆ How vulnerable would our business be to sudden changes in economic, social, or political conditions?

☆ To what extent does focusing on this segment build on skills that we already have? How will this focus affect our financial structure?

MARKET SEGMENTATION. Market segmentation simply means carving up the mass market into smaller, more homogeneous units and then attacking each segment with a specific marking strategy designed to appeal to its members. This requires information—knowing the firm's customers and their characteristics. To segment a market successfully, a small business owner must first identify the characteristics of two or more groups of customers with similar needs or wants. The owner must develop a basis for segmenting the market, such as benefits sought, product usage, brand preference, purchase patterns, and so on, and use this basis to identify the various submarkets to enter. Then the owner must verify that the segments are large enough and have enough purchasing power to generate a profit for the firm because segmentation is useless if the firm cannot earn a profit serving its segments. Finally, the owner must reach the market. To be profitable, a segment must be accessible. Typical market segments might be college students, retired people, young singles, ethnic groups, or high-income individuals. We will discuss this strategy in more detail in Chapter 5.

POSITIONING. Positioning the company in the market involves influencing customers' perceptions to create the desired image for the business and its goods and services. Most often a business attempts to position its products by differentiating them from those of competitors using some characteristic important to the customer, such as price, quality, service, or performance.

For example, Debbie Owens, owner of High Adventure Sports and Travel, sets her travel agency apart from its traditional competitors by targeting vacationers looking for high adventure or unique, out-of-the-way travel adventures. Using contacts cultivated over the years, she has sent clients on biking marathons in Norway, dog-sledding trips through the Yukon, and fly-fishing excursions in Russia. Owens decided to position her agency in this unique niche while developing her business plan because she saw there was very little com-

High Adventure Sports and Travel

petition there and the demand for such trips was growing. "Adventure vacations are becoming more popular because they're exciting, and people are doing something out of the ordinary," she says.[12]

Proper positioning gives the small business a foundation for developing a competitive advantage—some way of setting itself apart from the competition. Lower prices are a common method of establishing a competitive advantage, but this can be especially dangerous for small businesses that cannot rely on the economies of scale that larger businesses can. A smarter tactic for the small business owner is to rely on a natural advantage, such as the small firm's flexibility in reaching the market, a wider variety of customer services, or special knowledge of the good or service. For example, small independently owned drugstores cannot offer lower prices than the chain drugstores, which can take advantage of high-volume purchases to get quantity discounts. However, local drugstores can develop a competitive advantage by offering such extras as more convenient hours, customer credit, delivery services, or some special feature like an old-fashioned soda fountain. In customers' eyes, these features set independent drugstores apart from their larger competitors.

Step 3: Assess the company's strengths and weaknesses

4. Understand how to identify a company's SWOT—strengths, weaknesses, opportunities, and threats.

Having identified the firm's core competencies and its desired position in the market, the entrepreneur can turn her attention to assessing company strengths and weaknesses. Building a successful competitive strategy demands that a business magnify its strengths and overcome or compensate for its weaknesses. **Strengths** are positive internal factors that contribute to a company's ability to accomplish its mission, goals, and objectives; **weaknesses** are negative internal factors that inhibit its ability to accomplish its mission, goals, and objectives. Identifying strengths and weaknesses helps the owner understand her business as it exists (or will exist). The organization's strengths should support the core competencies that are essential for remaining competitive in each of the market segments in which the firm competes. "Choose the areas where you can gain a competitive advantage, one based on your business's strengths against your competitors' weaknesses," says one strategy expert.[13]

strengths—*positive internal factors that contribute to a company's ability to accomplish its mission, goals, and objectives.*

weaknesses—*negative internal factors that inhibit a company's ability to accomplish its mission, goals, and objectives.*

One effective technique for taking this strategic inventory is to prepare a "balance sheet" of the company's strengths and weaknesses (see Table 2.2 on page 42). The left side should reflect important skills, knowledge, or resources that contribute to achieving the company's overall mission. The right side should record honestly any limitations that detract from the company's ability to compete. This strategic balance sheet should include all key performance areas of the business: personnel, finance, production, marketing, product development, organization, and others. Subsequent analysis should give owners a more realistic perspective of their businesses, pointing out foundations on which they can build future strengths and obstacles that they must remove for business progress. This exercise can help owners move from their current position to future actions.

Step 4: Scan the environment for significant opportunities and threats facing the business

OPPORTUNITIES. Once entrepreneurs have taken an internal inventory of company strengths and weaknesses, they must turn to the external environment to identify any opportunities and threats that might have a significant impact on the business. **Opportunities** are positive external options that a business could exploit to accomplish its mission, goals, and objectives. The number of potential opportunities is limitless, so managers need to analyze only those most significant to the company's future success (probably two or three at most).

When identifying opportunities, the owner must pay close attention to new potential markets. Are competitors overlooking a niche in the market?

opportunities—*positive external options that a business could exploit to accomplish its mission, goals, and objectives.*

Table 2.2
Strengths and Weaknesses

List the specific skills, unique knowledge, and special resources of your business.	List any areas where your business lacks skills, knowledge, or resources.
Strengths	**Weaknesses**

Wo Kee Hong, Ltd.

While conducting a survey in China as part of an MBA class, Richard Lee discovered a tremendous opportunity for his father's export company, Wo Kee Hong Ltd. Although 90 percent of the Chinese he surveyed enjoyed listening to music, less than 10 percent of them owned stereo equipment. Lee soon joined the company and began exporting stereo equipment to China. He also saw the tremendous popularity of karaoke in both China and Hong Kong and began exporting laser disk players designed for that use. Since then, Lee has added other products to his export list, all of them consistent with his basic strategy: to sell products with the potential to improve the life of the Chinese people. Although just 1 percent of China's population—some 12 million people—can afford his products today, Lee estimates that within five years 5 percent—nearly 65 million people—will be able to buy them. The strategy has been a tremendous success. Wo Kee Hong's sales and profits have grown an average of 30 percent per year over the past five years! [14]

threats—*negative external forces that inhibit a company's ability to accomplish its mission, goals, and objectives.*

THREATS. **Threats** are negative external forces that inhibit a company's ability to achieve its mission, goals, and objectives. These external shocks to a business can take a variety of forms, such as new competitors entering the local market, a government mandate regulating a business activity, an economic recession, rising interest rates, technological advances making a company's product obsolete, and many others.

For instance, business owners in downtown Baltimore enjoy the millions of dollars the 3.6 million Baltimore Orioles fans spend during baseball season. However, the baseball strike during the 1994 season eliminated six weeks of baseball (25 home games) and reduced the number of downtown customers by more than 1 million. Bill Grauel, owner of Balls Sports Bar, which caters specifically to Orioles fans, was especially hard hit. He lost more than $200,000 and was forced to terminate 39 of his 45 employees just to survive. "No baseball meant no business," he says. [15]

Balls Sports Bar

Table 2.3
Opportunities and Threats

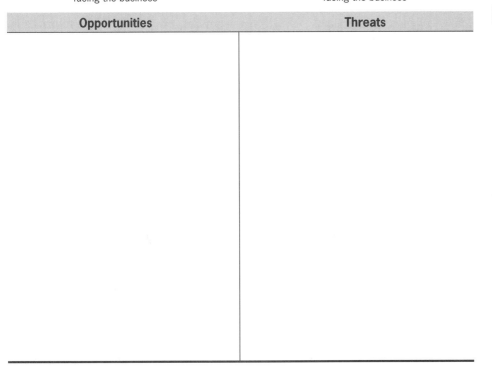

Opportunities	Threats
List the two or three best opportunities facing the business	List the top five threats facing the business

Entrepreneurs must prepare a plan for shielding their businesses from such threats. Table 2.3 presents a balance sheet designed to help business owners take a strategic inventory of the opportunities and threats facing their companies.

Figure 2.2 illustrates that opportunities and threats are the products of the interacting forces, trends, and events outside the entrepreneur's direct control. These external forces will affect the behavior of the markets in which the business operates, the behavior of competitors, and the behavior of customers.

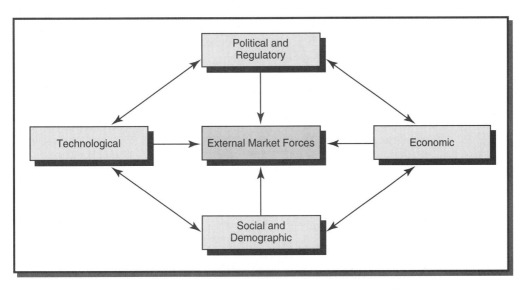

Figure 2.2
The Power of External Forces

Step 5: Identify the key factors for success in the business

Every business is characterized by controllable variables that determine the relative success of market participants. Identifying and manipulating these variables is how a small business gains a competitive advantage. Through focusing efforts on maximizing performance in these key success factors, effective business management can result in achieving dramatic market advantages over competitors. Companies that understand the specific key success factors for their market segment(s) tend to be leaders of the pack, whereas those who fail to recognize them become also-rans.

key success factors—
relationships between a controllable variable and a critical factor influencing a company's ability to compete in the market.

Key success factors come in a variety of patterns depending on the industry. Simply stated, they are relationships between a controllable variable (e.g., plant size, size of sales force, advertising expenditures, product packaging) and a critical factor influencing a company's ability to compete in the market. Many of these sources of competitive advantages are based on cost factors such as manufacturing cost per unit, distribution cost per unit, or development cost per unit. Some are less tangible and less obvious but are just as important, such as product quality, services offered, store location, and the availability of customer credit. Table 2.4 presents a form designed to help an owner identify the most important key success factors in the industry and their implications for the company.

Owners must use this information to analyze their businesses, the competition, and the industry to isolate the most appropriate sources of competitive advantage. Highly successful companies understand these key success factors and how they affect competition in the market, but marginal companies are mystified by which factors determine success in their particular industry.

Step 6: Analyze the competition

Another vital strategic activity is keeping tabs on the competition through a competitive intelligence program. The primary goals of competitive intelligence programs include the following:

☆ Avoiding surprises from existing competitors' new strategies and tactics.

☆ Identifying potential new competitors and the threats they pose.

☆ Improving reaction time to competitors' actions.

☆ Outmaneuvering competitors on key strategic fronts by knowing what they are up to and staying one step ahead.

Unfortunately, many small companies fail to gather competitive intelligence because their owners mistakenly assume that it is too costly or that it will require them to do something unethical or illegal. In reality, the cost of collecting information about competitors typically is minimal, but it does require discipline. Also, performing competitive intelligence does *not* mean that entrepreneurs must engage in illicit espionage activities such as telephone bugging or spying. "Almost all competitive intelligence is based on publicly available sources," says the head of one research firm. "The real trick is setting up a system to collect, store, and use the data."[16] Setting up an effective system involves first deciding what information a company needs to know about its competitors, then creating a centralized database or filing system to store what is collected, and finally assigning a person or a committee to coordinate the effort.

COMPETITOR ANALYSIS. Sizing up the competition gives owners a more realistic view of the market and their position in it. A competitor intelligence exercise enables entrepreneurs to update their knowledge of competitors by answering the following questions:

☆ Who are your major competitors?

☆ What distinctive competencies have they developed?

List the specific skills, characteristics, and competencies that your business must possess if it is to be successful.

Table 2.4
Key Success Factors

Key Success Factors	How your company rates
1.	Low 1 2 3 4 5 6 7 8 9 10 high
2.	Low 1 2 3 4 5 6 7 8 9 10 high
3.	Low 1 2 3 4 5 6 7 8 9 10 high
4.	Low 1 2 3 4 5 6 7 8 9 10 high
5.	Low 1 2 3 4 5 6 7 8 9 10 high
Conclusions:	

★ How do their cost structures compare with yours?

★ Are new competitors entering the business?

★ Can you identify your major competitors' key strategies?

★ What are their strengths and weaknesses?

★ How do customers view the market leaders? How do customers describe their products or services; their way of doing business, and the additional services they might supply?

★ Can your business match or exceed your competitors' high profitability on their behavior or performance?

A small business owner can collect a great deal of information about competitors ethically and inexpensively using low-cost methods including the following:

★ Read trade publications for announcements competitors make.

★ Ask customers and suppliers what competitors are doing. In many cases this information is easy to gather because some people love to gossip.

★ Talk to employees, especially sales representatives and purchasing agents. Experts estimate that 70 to 90 percent of the competitive information a company needs already resides with employees who collect it in their routine dealings with suppliers, customers, and other industry contacts.[17]

★ Attend trade shows and collect the competitors' sales literature.

★ If appropriate, buy competitors' products and assess their quality and features.

★ Benchmark their products against yours.

★ Obtain credit reports from firms such as Dun & Bradstreet on each of your major competitors to evaluate their financial condition.

☆ Check out the resources of your local library, including articles, computerized databases, and on-line searches.

☆ Use the vast resources available on the World Wide Web to learn more about your competitors.

Using the information gathered, a business owner can set up management committees to evaluate each competitor and make recommendations on specific strategic actions that will improve the firm's competitive position against each.

The owner can use the results of the competitive intelligence analysis to create a competitive profile matrix for each market segment in which the firm operates. A **competitive profile matrix** allows a business owner to evaluate his company against major competitors on the key success factors for that market segment (refer to Table 2.4). The first step is to list the key success factors identified in step 5 of the strategic planning process and to attach weights to them reflecting their relative importance. (For simplicity, the weights in this matrix add up to 1.00.) In this example, notice that product quality is weighted twice as heavily (twice as important) as price competitiveness.

The next step is to identify the company's major competitors and to rate each one (and your company) on each of the key success factors:

If factor is a:	Rating is:
Major weakness	1
Minor weakness	2
Minor strength	3
Major strength	4

Upon completing the rating, the owner simply multiplies the weight by the rating for each factor to get a weighted score, and then adds up each competitor's weighted scores to get a total weighted score. Table 2.5 shows a sample competitive profile matrix. The results should show which company is strongest, which is weakest, and which of the key success factors each one is best and worst at meeting. By carefully studying and interpreting the results, the small business owner can begin to envision the ideal strategy for building a competitive edge in his market segment. By this stage of the planning, the owner has begun to

competitive profile matrix—*a tool that allows a business owner to evaluate his company against major competitors on the key success factors for that market.*

Table 2.5
Sample Competitive Profile Matrix

Key Success Factors (from step 5)	Your Business			Competitor 1		Competitor 2	
	Weight x	Rating =	Weighted Score	Rating	Weighted Score	Rating	Weighted Score
Market Share	0.10	3	0.30	2	0.20	3	0.30
Price Competitiveness	0.20	1	0.20	3	0.60	4	0.80
Financial Strength	0.10	2	0.20	3	0.30	2	0.20
Product Quality	0.40	4	1.60	2	0.80	1	0.40
Customer Loyalty	0.20	3	0.60	3	0.60	2	0.40
Total	1.00		2.90		2.50		2.10

How to Compete?

When Shy Oogav, a 29-year-old immigrant from Israel, visited Texas's South Padre Island in 1989, he thought he had found paradise and decided to move there. He got a job at one of the ten T-shirt shops on the island, and in 1992, he and a partner bought their own T-shirt shop. They paid $20,000 in cash, signed a note for another $20,000, and purchased the store's existing inventory, a press for imprinting decals, and the lease. Within a year, Oogav used the cash the shop generated to buy out his partner. Now, however, his paradise is threatened. More than 40 T-shirt shops operate on the tiny island, and the competition among them is fierce. "Every day you have to compete with other shops," he says. "And if you invent something new, they will copy you." Oogav worries about the future of his business, Too Cool.

T-shirt retailing is "the quintessential small business," says one expert. "It's also one of the most volatile. It's seasonal . . . and they compete with the guy right next door." Oogav knows firsthand the impact that has on a small business. When he bought out his partner, he did not anticipate the explosion in the number of competitors, which meant *lots* of guys right next door. Other external factors have created business problems for South Padre Island T-shirt retailers. Recently, cold, rainy weather has hit at crucial times, such as spring break, when sales normally peak. A weak peso has driven away tourists from Mexico. "The business fluctuates up and down like a roller coaster," says one of Oogav's competitors.

Too Cool is packed with $35,000 of inventory, ranging from $150 jackets made of hemp to $34 pairs of sunglasses. But the majority of the stock is T-shirts, which Oogav sells for $8.99 each, or three for $24. "There are two routes you can go in this business," he explains. "Either the low end— three shirts for 10 bucks—or the high end." Oogav has chosen the high end. He pays $34 for a dozen first-quality, all-cotton T-shirts, dismissing the lower-quality shirts as junk "that fall apart after one wash." He uses his $15,000 computer system to design and produce his own T-shirt decals. After watching a competitor steal one of his most popular designs several years ago, Oogav now copyrights all of his designs.

South Padre Island merchants have two selling seasons in which to make a living: spring break, when Too Cool is open almost around-the-clock to serve the 100,000-plus college students who invade the island, and summer, when the tourists flock there. In the spring sales can hit $3,000 per day, and in the summer, $700 a day. In the most recent selling season, however, Too Cool's sales were off 33 percent. In its best year, Too Cool grossed $160,000. In a more typical year, sales are $110,000. Out of that, Oogav must pay $60,000 to suppliers and about $24,000 for rent and overhead. With the increased competition and difficult external conditions, Oogav says he's lucky if he can gross $70,000.

Oogav cannot afford to advertise, but he does use some special promotions during spring break for college students. During busy seasons, he hires part-time workers. The shop closes in October when everyone leaves the island and reopens after Christmas as a sweatshirt shop when the "snow-birds" descend on the island from the North. Oogav recently borrowed $15,000 from a bank to pay bills and to make improvements in his business. He worries about the thin winter months that lie ahead. "I don't sleep at night," he says.

1. Conduct a SWOT analysis for Too Cool.

2. Can Oogav create a competitive advantage for Too Cool in the face of such intense competition? How?

3. What advice would you offer Oogav about surviving the upcoming winter months? What advice would you offer him for competing successfully in the next peak sales season?

Source: Adapted from Mark Pawlosky, "T-Shirt Shop Owner's Lament: Too Many T-Shirt Shops," *Wall Street Journal,* July 31, 1995, p. B1.

---

compare the firm's strengths to those of competitors and to formulate ways of magnifying the firm's strengths and exploiting competitors' weaknesses. In other words, the owner is looking forward to the future and planning ahead.

Step 7: Create company goals and objectives

Before the small business manager can build a comprehensive set of strategies, he must first establish business goals and objectives, which provide targets as a basis for evaluating the company's performance. Without goals and objectives, the owner cannot know where the business is going or how well it is performing. The following conversation between Alice and the Cheshire Cat, taken from Lewis Carroll's *Alice in Wonderland,* illustrates the importance of creating meaningful targets for performance:

5. Establish meaningful goals and objectives.

"Would you tell me please, which way I ought to go from here?" asked Alice.

"That depends a good deal on where you want to get to," said the Cat.

"I don't much care where. . . ," said Alice.

"Then it doesn't matter which way you go," said the Cat.

A small business that "doesn't much care where" it wants to go (i.e. has no goals and objectives) will find that "it really doesn't matter which way" it chooses to go (i.e., strategy is irrelevant.)

---

goals—*the broad, long-range attributes that a business seeks to accomplish; they tend to be general and sometimes even abstract.*

GOALS. **Goals** are the broad, long-range attributes that a business seeks to accomplish; they tend to be general and sometimes even abstract. Goals are not intended to be specific enough for a manager to act on, but simply to state the general level of desired accomplishment. Do you want to boost your market share? Does your cash balance need strengthening? Would you like to enter a new market or increase sales in a current one? What return on your investment do you seek? Addressing these broad issues will help you focus on the next phase—developing specific, realistic objectives.

---

objectives—*more specific targets of performance, commonly addressing such areas as profitability, productivity, growth, and other key aspects of a business.*

OBJECTIVES. **Objectives** are more specific targets of performance. Common objectives concern profitability, productivity, growth, efficiency, market share, financial resources, physical facilities, organizational structure, employee welfare, and social responsibility. Because some of these objectives might conflict with one another, the manager must establish priorities. Which objectives are most important? Which are least important? Arranging objectives in a hierarchy according to their priorities can help the small business manager resolve conflicts when they arise. Well-written objectives have the following characteristics:

They are specific. Objectives should be quantifiable and precise. For example, "to achieve a healthy growth in sales" is not a meaningful objective; whereas "to increase retail sales by 12 percent and wholesale sales by 10 percent in the next fiscal year" is precise and spells out exactly what management wants to accomplish.

They are measurable. Managers should be able to plot the organization's progress toward its objectives; this requires a well-defined reference point from which to start and a scale for measuring progress.

They are attainable. To motivate managers and employees, objectives must be attainable; otherwise, people will see only futility and stop striving for them. This does not mean, however, that objectives should be easy to accomplish.

They are realistic and challenging. Objectives must be within the organization's reach or motivation will disappear. In any case, managerial expectations must remain high. In other words, the more challenging an objective is (within realistic limits), the higher the performance will be. Set objectives that will challenge your business and its employees.

They are timely. Objectives must specify not only what is to be accomplished but also when it is to be accomplished. A time frame for achievement is important.

They are written down. This writing process does not have to be complex; in fact, the manager should make the number of objectives relatively small, from five to fifteen.

The process works best when managers and employees are actively and jointly involved in setting objectives. Developing a plan is top management's responsibility, but encouraging other managers and employees to participate broadens the plan's perspective and increases the motivation to make the plan work. In addition, managers and employees know about the organization and are usually willing to share this knowledge.

Step 8: Formulate strategic options and select the appropriate strategies

By now, the small business owner should have a clear picture of what her business does best and what its competitive advantages are. Similarly, the owner should know her firm's weaknesses and limitations as well as those of its competitors. The next step is to evaluate strategic options and then prepare a game plan designed to achieve the business's objectives.

STRATEGY. A **strategy** is a road map of the tactics and actions an entrepreneur draws up to fulfill the firm's mission, goals, and objectives. In other words, the mission, goals, and objectives spell out the ends the company wants to achieve, and the strategy defines the means for reaching them. The strategy is the master plan that covers all of the organization's major parts and ties them together into a unified whole. The plan must be action oriented—that is, it should breathe life into the entire organization. The manager must build a sound strategy from the preceding steps that focuses on those areas outlined in analyzing the business.

A successful strategy is comprehensive and well integrated. It must focus on establishing for the company the key success factors identified in step 5. For instance, if maximum shelf space is a key success factor for a small manufacturer's product, the strategy must identify techniques for gaining more in-store shelf space (e.g., offering higher margins to distributors and brokers than competitors do, assisting retailers with in-store displays, or designing a wider, more attractive package).

Obviously, the number of strategies from which the small business owner can choose is infinite. When all the glitter is stripped away, however, three broad-based, generic strategies remain (See Figure 2.3). In *Competitive Strategy,* Michael Porter defined these strategies:[18]

1. cost leadership
2. differentiation
3. focus

COST LEADERSHIP. A company pursuing a **cost leadership strategy** strives to be the lowest-cost producer relative to its competitors in the industry. Low-cost leaders have a competitive advantage in reaching buyers whose primary purchase criterion is price, and they have the power to set the industry's price floor. Such a strategy works well when buyers are sensitive to price changes, when competing firms sell the same commodity products, and when companies can benefit from economies of scale. Not only is a low-cost leader in the best position to defend itself in a price war, but it can also use its power to attack competitors with the lowest price in the industry.

6. Understand the three basic strategic alternatives a small company has—low cost, differentiation, and focus—and know when and how to employ them.

strategy—*a road map of the tactics and actions an entrepreneur draws up to fulfill the firm's mission, goals, and objectives.*

cost leadership strategy—*a strategy in which a company strives to be the lowest-cost producer relative to its competitors in the industry.*

	Source of Competitive Advantage	
Target Market	Uniqueness as Perceived by the Customer	Low-Cost Position
Industry	Differentiation	Low-Cost
Niche	Focus—Differentiation	Focus—Low-Cost

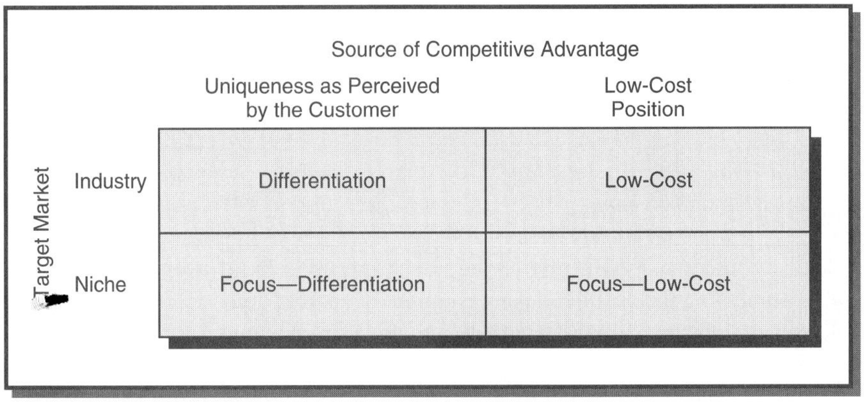

Figure 2.3
Three Business Strategies
Source: Adapted from Michael Porter, *Competitive Strategy* (New York: The Free Press, 1980).

Regal Cinemas, Inc., a Knoxville, Tennessee–based theater chain, successfully uses a low-cost strategy to generate profit margins that are twice those of its larger competitors. CEO Michael Campbell learned how to make a low-cost strategy work running a grocery store, a business characterized by razor-thin profit margins, and he applies many of the same principles at Regal Cinemas. Company headquarters is in a suburban warehouse rather than an upscale high-rise in a major city. A computer system monitors every aspect of the chain's concession stand yields, including how much popcorn goes into a container and how much syrup goes into a soft drink. As a result, the cost of supplying and running Regal's concession stands is just 13 percent of sales, compared to most movie chains' 21 percent. Regal also shaves its costs by multiplexing, putting multiple screens (usually at least ten) under one roof.[19]

There are many ways to build a low-cost strategy, but the most successful cost leaders know where they have cost advantages over their competitors, and they use this information as the foundation for their strategies. For example, a small nonunion airline is likely to have a significant advantage in labor costs, but not in fuel costs, over those of its larger, unionized competitors.

One small clothing manufacturer was able to lower its production costs substantially by constantly introducing the most modern, state-of-the-art equipment into its process. Computer-aided design, lasers, and other automation techniques applied to traditionally high-cost activities permitted the company to produce clothing at a cost well below that of competitors.

Of course, there are dangers in following a cost leadership strategy. Sometimes a company focuses exclusively on lowering *manufacturing* costs, without considering the impact the strategy will have on purchasing, distribution, or overhead costs. Another danger is misunderstanding the firm's true cost drivers. For instance, one food processor drastically underestimated its overhead costs and, as a result, was selling its products at a loss. Finally, a firm may pursue a low-cost leadership strategy so zealously that it essentially locks itself out of other strategic choices.

differentiation strategy—*a strategy in which a company seeks to build customer loyalty by positioning its goods or services in a unique or different fashion.*

DIFFERENTIATION. A company following a **differentiation strategy** seeks to build customer loyalty by positioning its goods or services in a unique or different fashion. In other words, the firm strives to be better than its competitors at something that customers value. There are many ways to create a differentiation strategy, but the key concept is to be special at something that is important to the customer. If a small company can improve the product's (or service's) performance, reduce the customer's cost and risk of purchasing it, or both, it has the potential to differentiate.

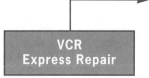

For example, when Eldridge Helwick saw competitors eroding his market share in the stereo sales and services business, he began to consider a new strategy. He realized that the problem was that he had failed to differentiate his company from its competition. "We all offered the same service—slow, late, or next week at best," he says. He also saw a new opportunity for his business: VCR repair. As VCRs became more common in households, there was greater demand for servicing them. Helwick began offering VCR repair services, but this time, he found a way to differentiate his company: He offered guaranteed repairs within 48 hours! Business exploded. "Within six months, I closed my stereo store and [developed] my new company, VCR Express Repair," he says. Within a year, he had expanded into camcorder service as well.[20]

The key to a successful differentiation strategy is to build it on a *distinctive competence*—something the small company is uniquely good at doing in comparison to its competitors. Common bases for differentiation include superior customer service, special product features, complete product lines, instantaneous parts availability, absolute product reliability, supreme product quality, and extensive produce knowledge. Figure 2.4 shows

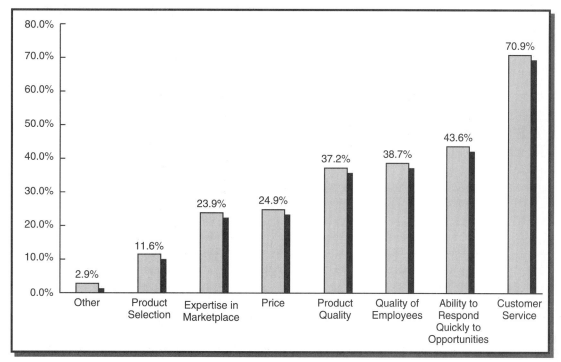

Figure 2.4

Competitive Advantage

Areas in which small companies believe they have a competitive advantage over their larger rivals.

Source: Adapted with permission *Inc.* magazine, (July, 1990). Copyright 1990 by Goldhirsh Group, Inc., 38 Commercial Wharf, Boston, MA 02110.

the areas in which small business owners believe they have an advantage over their larger rivals. To be successful, a differentiation strategy must create the perception of *value* in the customer's eyes. No customer will purchase a good or service that fails to produce its perceived value, no matter how real its value may be.

There are risks in pursing a differentiation strategy. One danger is trying to differentiate a product or service on the basis of something that does not boost its performance or lower its cost to the buyer. Another pitfall is overdifferentiating and charging so much that the company prices its products out of the market. The final risk is focusing only on the physical characteristics of a product or service and ignoring important psychological factors, such as status, prestige, image, and customer service.

FOCUS   A **focus strategy** recognizes that not all markets are homogeneous. In fact, in any given market there are many different customer segments, each having different needs, wants, and characteristics. The principal idea of this strategy is to select one (or more) segment(s), identify customers' special needs, wants, and interests, and approach them with a good or service specifically designed to excel in meeting these needs, wants, and interests. Focus strategies build on *differences* among market segments.

A successful focus strategy depends on a small company's ability to identify the changing needs of its targeted customer group and to develop the skills required to serve them. That means the owner and *everyone* in the organization must have a clear understanding of how to add value to the product or service for the customer. How does the product or service meet the customer's needs at each stage, from raw material to final sale? What can the company do to enhance the value the product or service offers customers?

focus strategy—*a strategy in which a company selects one (or more) segments of a market, identifies their special needs, wants, and interests, and offers them a good or service designed to excel in meeting those needs, wants, and interests.*

Rather than attempting to serve the total market, the focusing firm specializes in serving a specific target segment or niche. A focus strategy is ideally suited to many small businesses, which often lack the resources to reach a national market. Their goal is to serve their narrow target markets more effectively and efficiently than do competitors that pound away at the broad market.

Friedman's Shoes

For instance, Friedman's Shoes, a downtown Atlanta retail store, targets a highly profitable niche that has special shoe needs. Friedman's stocks a huge inventory of high-quality, premium shoes in exotic leathers (ranging from crocodile to anteater) in really hard-to-find sizes—say, 23 EEE. Not surprisingly, many of Friedman's customers are professional athletes, who, with their multimillion-dollar salaries, are not price sensitive. Shaquille O'Neal recently purchased a pair of crocodile loafers there. ("They must have used the whole crocodile for these suckers," teased one of his professional colleagues.) Pitcher Dwight Gooden once tried on 57 pairs of shoes before purchasing 53 of them. Fight promoter Don King once bought 110 pairs for a total bill of $64,100![21]

The most successful focusers build a competitive edge by concentrating on specific market niches and serving them better than any other competitors can. Essentially, this strategy depends on creating value for the customer, either by being the lowest-cost producer or by differentiating the product or service in a unique fashion, but doing it in a narrow target segment.

Baby Superstore, Inc.

Jack Tate founded Baby Superstore, Inc. on a retail focus strategy. Today, the stores have 40,000-plus square feet of cribs, strollers, bedding, and clothing, all aimed at capturing the business of Baby Superstore's primary target customer: first-time mothers . To fully equip for a new infant can easily mean parents buying $2,000 in equipment, plus those indispensable items of diapers and clothes. Tate's target: the estimated $13 billion a year spent in America on infants, newborn through age 1. To make his stores more appealing to this audience, Tate sponsors educational seminars featuring health care specialists, publishes a newsletter, and makes its stores "mother-to-be friendly." In 25 years, Tate has built the business from a single-store startup to a national chain grossing in excess of $300 million.[22]

An effective strategy identifies a complete set of success factors—financial, operating, and marketing—that, taken together, yield a competitive advantage for the small business. The resulting action plan distinguishes the firm from its competitors by exploiting its competitive advantage. The focal point of this entire strategy is the *customer.* The customer is the nucleus of the business, so a competitive strategy will succeed only if it is aimed at serving the customers better than the competition does. An effective strategy draws out the competitive advantage in a small company by building on its strengths and by making the customers its focal point. It also designates methods of overcoming the firm's weaknesses and identifies opportunities and threats that demand action.

The strategies a small business selects will be related to the assessment of its competitive advantage in the market segments in which it competes. In some cases, the business will be implementing more than one strategy. When a business has a well-defined strategic advantage, it may act highly aggressively in an attempt to deepen its market penetration. This is especially true when the business has achieved "first mover" advantages (being the first company to enter a market segment) with little direct or immediate competition. A company does not have to be large to be a strong and aggressive competitor. In many cases the old adage of being the "big frog in a small pond" allows a relatively small firm to pursue a highly aggressive strategy.

In other circumstances, a small business is best served by avoiding a high-profile strategy, seeking instead to gain a smaller number of highly profitable customers, while never achieving a substantial share of the market. Some firms will achieve this through a "specialist" strategy, where they build a highly defensible market position through product uniqueness, service, or knowledge that competitors cannot easily duplicate. An example of this strategy would be Red Adair, the world-famous fighter of oil well fires. His is not a large company, but it certainly is the specialist in one very unique service requiring years of knowledge learned the hard way.

To compete successfully, small businesses must be able to exploit all the competitive advantages of their size by:

- ★ Responding quickly to customers' needs.
- ★ Remaining flexible and willing to change.
- ★ Constantly searching for new, emerging market segments.
- ★ Building and defending market niches.
- ★ Erecting "switching costs" (the cost associated with switching from your company's product or service to a competitor's product or service) through personal service and loyalty.
- ★ Remaining entrepreneurial and willing to take risks and acting with lightning speed.
- ★ Continuously innovating.

YOU BE THE CONSULTANT...

A Fading Dream?

Ed and Nancy Greenberg, both retired school teachers, did what thousands of Americans dream of doing every time they stay at a quaint bed and breakfast (B&B) inn: They took their pensions and bought an inn of their own. The Greenbergs own and operate the Admiral Peary House, once the residence of the man who first trekked to the North Pole and now a charming five-bedroom bed and breakfast inn located in Fryeburg, Maine (population 1,580). Each newly remodeled room in the circa 1865 house is spacious, with an adjoining sitting room and a private bath. Amenities include a basket of toiletries, a journal for guests to write in, a free homemade breakfast, and lots of individual attention. "People want B&Bs to be personal," says Nancy. "Otherwise, they'd choose a hotel." Outside, guests can enjoy an outdoor hot tub, clay tennis courts, nearby lakes and snow skiing, and a golf course just 15 minutes away. Room rates vary from $70 to $118 per night, depending on the season. (Rates are highest in the fall foliage season and are lowest in the winter.)

Although sales have grown steadily since the inn opened, its occupancy rate averages just 20 percent. By comparison, the typical New England inn's occupancy rate is twice that of the Admiral Peary. During a recent winter, business was so slow (nonexistent) that the Greenbergs closed the inn and took a five-week Florida vacation. Annual revenues for the inn have never exceeded $31,000; the average inn of this size produces revenues of $75,000 a year. The largest profit the Greenbergs have earned is just $3,100, although industry studies suggest that a B&B the size of the Admiral Peary should be able to produce an annual profit of about $37,000, more than ten times greater. The Greenbergs continue to live off of their savings. "But we're pretty confident we'll make it," says Ed. "We're getting very positive feedback from our guests, and we already have 34 reservations booked for next summer and fall." Customer satisfaction appears to be high; about 40 per-

cent of the Greenberg's business is from repeat customers, compared to an average of just 17 percent for inns this size. For the past three years, the Admiral Peary House has earned an "A+ Excellent" rating from the American Bed and Breakfast Association, which grants such status to only 15 percent of its 470 members. The Greenbergs, who run the B&B without any employees, are surprised by the low sales but admit that they did no research before moving to Fryeburg to open the inn.

To attract customers, the Greenbergs rely on word-of-mouth referrals from existing customers, brochures placed in six tourist information booths throughout Maine, and ads touting their inn as a country oasis for travelers to Boston or Portland who want to explore New England. Recently, the couple teamed up in a cooperative advertising campaign with seven other inns to run an ad in an annual tourist publication that drew about 20 reservations, they think. "We're not very careful about keeping track of how our guests find us," Ed admits.

As their savings dwindle, the Greenbergs fear that they will be forced to close the inn unless sales pick up within the next two years. "For now," says Ed, "we're hanging on and hoping that the inn continues to grow slowly as word spreads."

1. What strengths and weaknesses do you identify in the Admiral Peary House bed and breakfast?

2. Which of the three strategies described in the previous section would be best suited for this inn? Explain.

3. What kind of strategy would you recommend for the Admiral Peary House? What recommendations would you make to the Greenbergs?

Source: Adapted from Barbara B. Bucholz and Margaret Crane, "Turning a Dream into a Money Maker," *Your Company*, February/March 1996, pp. 26–30.

Step 9: Translate strategic plans into action plans

No strategic plan is complete until it is put into action. The small business manager must convert strategic plans into operating plans that guide the company on a daily basis and become a visible, active part of the business. The small business cannot benefit from a strategic plan sitting on a shelf collecting dust.

IMPLEMENT THE STRATEGY. To make the strategic plan workable, a business owner should divide it into projects, carefully defining each one by the following criteria.[23]

- ☆ *Purpose.* What is the project designed to accomplish?
- ☆ *Scope.* Which areas of the company will be involved in the project?
- ☆ *Contribution.* How does the project relate to other projects and to the overall strategic plan?
- ☆ *Resource requirements.* What human and financial resources are needed to complete the project successfully?
- ☆ *Timing.* Which schedule and deadline will ensure project completion?

Once the relevant people assign a priority to these projects, they can begin to implement the strategic plan. Involving employees and delegating adequate authority to them is essential, since these projects affect them most directly.

If the organization's people have been involved in the strategic management process to this point, they will have a better grasp of the steps they must take to achieve the organization's goals. Early involvement of the total work force is a luxury that larger businesses cannot achieve. Commitment to achieving the firm's objectives is a powerful force for success. Involvement is a prerequisite for the achievement of total employee commitment. It is important to remember that without a commitment by the employees, the organization's strategies will almost inevitably fail.

Step 10: Establish accurate controls

So far, the planning process has created company objectives and has developed a strategy for reaching them, but rarely, if ever, will the company's actual performance match stated objectives. The manager quickly realizes the need to control actual results that deviate from plans.

CONTROLLING THE STRATEGY. Planning without control has little operational value, so a sound planning program requires a practical control process. The plans created in this process become the standards against which actual performance is measured. It is important for everyone in the organization to understand—and to be involved in—the planning and controlling process.

Controlling projects and keeping them on schedule mean that the owner must identify and track key performance indicators. The source of these indicators is the operating data from the company's normal business activity; they are the guideposts for detecting deviations from established standards. Accounting, production, sales, inventory, and other operating records are primary sources of data the manager can use for controlling activities. For example, for a customer service project, performance indicators might include customer complaints, orders returned, on-time shipments, and order accuracy.

As conditions change, the manager must make corrections in performance, policies, strategies, and objectives to get performance back on track. A practical control system is also economical to operate. Most small businesses have no need for a sophisticated, expensive control system. The system should be so practical that it becomes a natural part of the management process.

1. Understand why and how a small business must build a competitive advantage in the market.

- Strategic planning, often ignored by small companies, is crucial for business success. Empirical studies have concluded that strategic planning is a key determinant of small companies' ultimate survival. Developing a plan also gives the firm a way to create a competitive edge—the factors that set the small business apart from its competitors.

2. Create a strategic plan using the ten steps in the strategic planning process.

- Small businesses need a strategic planning process designed to suite their particular needs. It should be relatively short, be informal and unstructured, encourage outsiders' participation, and not begin with extensive objective setting. The strategic planning process should follow a bottom-up approach, placing special emphasis on the customer and following these steps:

Step 1. Develop a clear vision and translate it into a meaningful mission statement.

Step 2. Define the company's core competencies and identify its market position. Core competencies are what the company does best; they are the focal point of the strategy. The owner must identify some way to differentiate his business from competitors.

Step 3. Assess the company's strengths and weaknesses.

Step 4. Scan the environment for significant opportunities and threats facing the business.

Step 5. Identify the key factors for success in the business. Every business has key factors that determine a firm's success, and they must be an integral part of a company's strategy.

Step 6. Analyze the competition. Know your competitors as well as you know yourself.

Step 7. Create company goals and objectives.

Step 8. Formulate strategic options and select the appropriate strategies.

Step 9. Translate strategic plans into action plans. No strategic plan is complete until the owner puts it into action.

Step 10. Establish accurate controls. Actual performance rarely, if ever, matches plans exactly. Operating data from the business serve as guideposts for detecting deviations from plans. Such information is helpful when plotting future strategies.

3. Know why and how to write a meaningful mission statement.

- Highly successful entrepreneurs are able to communicate their vision to those around them. The firm's mission statement answers the first question of any venture: What business am I in?

4. Understand how to identify a company's SWOT—strengths, weaknesses, opportunities, and threats.

- Developing a sound mission statement requires quality information. Strengths are positive internal factors; weaknesses are negative internal factors. Opportunities are positive external options; threats are negative external forces. Five environments are significant: macro, industry, competitive, customer, and internal.

5. Establish meaningful goals and objectives.

- Goals are the broad, long-range attributes that the firm seeks to accomplish. Objectives are quantifiable and more precise; they should be specific, measurable, attainable, realistic, timely, and written down. The process works best when subordinate managers and employees are actively involved.

6. Understand the three basic strategic alternatives a small company has—low cost, differentiation, and focus—and know when and how to employ them.

- A strategy is the game plan the firm plans to use to achieve its objectives and mission. It must center on establishing for the firm the key success factors identified earlier. Three basic strategies exist: low cost, differentiation, and focus.

1. What is a competitive advantage? Why is it important for a small company to establish one?
2. What are the steps involved in the strategic management process?
3. What are strengths, weaknesses, opportunities, and threats? Give an example of each.
4. Explain the characteristics of effective objectives. Why is setting objectives important?
5. What are business strategies?
6. Describe the three strategies available to small companies. Under what conditions is each most successful?
7. What are the advantages of involving operative employees in the planning process?
8. How is the controlling process related to the planning process?

1. Choose an entrepreneur in your community and interview him or her. Does the company have a strategic plan? A mission statement? Why or why not? What does the owner consider the company's strengths and weaknesses to be? What opportunities and threats does the owner perceive? What image is the owner trying to create for the business? Has the effort been successful? (Do you agree?) Which of the generic competitive strategies is the company following? Who are the company's primary competitors? When you have completed the interview, use the following evaluation questionnaire to rank the firm. Compare your evaluation with those of other classmates. What, if any, generalizations can be drawn from the interviews? Use the following questions to rate the company's strategic orientation.

Is the Owner Managing the Business Strategically?

Rate the present managerial actions on each of the following questions:

a. In the past two years have the owners written or reviewed their firm's mission statement?

_____ Yes (10 pts.)

_____ No (0 pts.)   Q.1. _____

b. Are the owners confident that the employees are aware of the key underlying values that drive the business?

_____ Absolutely (10 pts.)

_____ Generally (7 pts.)

_____ Not sure (3 pts.)

_____ I have never shared my values with them (0 pts.)   Q.2. _____

c. Does each manager have a clear set of performance objectives for his or her area of responsibility?

_____ Yes (10 pts.)

_____ Some do (5 pts.)

_____ No (0 pts.)   Q.3. _____

d. Do the owners regularly meet with key managers and employees to discuss their competitors' behavior?

_____ Regularly and often (10 pts.)

_____ Informally, but not a scheduled event (5 pts.)

_____ Never have done so (0 pts.)   Q.4. _____

e. Would employees be able to describe accurately the strategies their firm is attempting to employ?

_____ Definitely (10 pts.)

_____ Most of them (5 pts.)

_____ The firm's strategies have never been explained

to them (0 pts.)   Q.5. _____

f. Does each employee understand that through the achievement of success for the organization they enhance the opportunity to achieve their own personal goals?

_____ Definitely (10 pts.)
_____ Most do (7 pts.)
_____ A few do (4 pts.)
_____ It has never been explained to them (0 pts.)   Q.6. _____

g. Does the firm annually conduct an environmental scanning exercise with its managers in an attempt to identify future opportunities for the firm?

_____ Yes (10 pts.)
_____ Informally (5 pts.)
_____ No (0 pts.)   Q.7. _____

h. Can each of the managers explain the impact of their performance, and that of their people, on the performance of the total organization?

_____ Absolutely (10 pts.)
_____ Generally (7 pts.)
_____ Not sure (3 pts.)
_____ No (0 pts.)   Q.8. _____

i. Has the business been moving in a clear and positive direction over the past three years?

_____ Definitely (10 pts.)
_____ Generally (7 pts.)
_____ Not sure (3 pts.)
_____ No (0 pts.)   Q.9. _____

j. Do the key managers think and behave strategically?

_____ Always (10 pts.)
_____ Generally (7 pts.)
_____ Not sure (4 pts.)
_____ Seldom (0 pts.)   Q.10. _____

**Total points**   _____
**Maximum Score: 100**
**Minimum Score: 0**

Grading the Firm:

_A+_ =	_95-100 pts._	_B_ =	_80-84 pts._	_D+_ =	_65-69 pts._
_A_ =	_90-94 pts._	_C+_ =	_75-79 pts._	_D_ =	_60-64 pts._
_B+_ =	_85-89 pts._	_C_ =	_70-74 pts._	_F_ =	_below 60 pts._

Your recommendations:

2. Interview two local business owners and ask them how the following trends are affecting their businesses. How are they responding to them? What future do you predict for these companies?

- ☆ an increasingly older, more skeptical, more educated population.
- ☆ the increasing cultural diversity of the population.
- ☆ the trend toward cheaper, faster, easier-to-use technology.
- ☆ the shift from a manufacturing-based economy to a service-based economy.
- ☆ the trend toward a "borderless economy," a truly global market.
- ☆ the division of mass markets into many small market niches.
- ☆ the growing number of women entering the work force, many choosing to launch their own companies.
- ☆ the "green revolution," focusing attention on preserving our planet and its delicate environment.
- ☆ the growing appeal to customers of quality and convenience.
- ☆ the decreasing number of people in the group aged 18 to 24.
- ☆ the emergence of the Pacific Rim nations as a major trade center.

3. Contact a small business owner who must compete against an industry giant (such as Wal*Mart, Kmart, Target, Best Buy, etc.). What does the owner see as his or her firm's competitive advantage? How does the business communicate this advantage to its customers? What competitive strategy is the owner using ? How successful is it? What changes would you suggest the owner make?

SURFING THE NET

1. Using one of the search engines on the World Wide Web (WWW) such as Lycos, Magellan, Yahoo!, or others, conduct a search on the words *strategy* or *strategic management.* Select one of the sites you find and prepare a one-page report on its contents.

2. Access the following Websites. What information relating to the topics discussed in this chapter material can you find?

http://www.netmarquee.com/

http://www.smartbiz.com/sbs/cats/startup.htm

3. Access the home page for the Covey Leadership Center at the following Website:

http://www.covey.com/

Use the mission statement builder at this site to create a personal mission statement. Compare the process of creating a personal mission statement with that of building one for a company. How can a personal mission statement benefit you?

CHAPTER

THREE

Forms of Ownership and Franchising

Before you run in double harness, look well to the other horse.
- Ovid

The big print giveth, and the fine print taketh away.
- Bishop Fulton J. Sheen

Ignorance per se is not nearly as dangerous as ignorance of ignorance.
- Sydney Harris

LEARNING OBJECTIVES

Upon completion of this chapter, you will be able to:

1. **Explain** the advantages and the disadvantages of the three major forms of ownership: the sole proprietorship, the partnership, and the corporation.
2. **Discuss** the advantages and the disadvantages of the S corporation, the limited liability company, the professional corporation, and the joint venture.
3. **Describe** the three types of franchising: trade name, product distribution, and pure.
4. **Explain** the benefits and the drawbacks of buying a franchise.
5. **Understand** the laws covering franchise purchases.
6. **Discuss** the right way to buy a franchise.
7. **Outline** the major trends shaping franchising.

One of the first decisions an entrepreneur faces when starting a new business is selecting the form of ownership for the new business venture. Too often, entrepreneurs give little thought to choosing a form of ownership and simply select the form that is most popular, even though it may not suit their needs best. Although the decision is not irreversible, changing from one form of ownership to another once a business is up and running can be difficult, expensive, and complicated. That's why it is so important for an entrepreneur to make the right choice at the outset. This seemingly mundane decision can have a significant impact on almost every aspect of a business and its owner(s)—from the taxes the company pays and how it raises money to the owner's liability for the company's debts and her ability to transfer the business to the next generation. Each form of ownership has its own unique set of advantages and disadvantages. The key to choosing the "right" form of ownership is understanding the characteristics of each one and knowing how they affect an entrepreneur's business and personal circumstances. Although there is no best form of ownership, there may be a form of ownership that is best for each entrepreneur's circumstances.

The following are a few considerations that every entrepreneur should review prior to making the final form of ownership choice:

Tax considerations. The graduated tax rates under each form of ownership, the government's constant tinkering with the tax code, and the year-to-year fluctuations in a company's income mean that an entrepreneur must calculate the firm's tax bill under each ownership option every year.

Liability exposure. Certain forms of ownership offer business owners greater protection from personal liability due to financial problems, faulty products, and a host of other difficulties. Entrepreneurs must decide the extent to which they are willing to assume personal responsibility for their companies' obligations.

Startup capital requirements. Forms of ownership differ in their ability to raise startup capital. Depending upon how much capital an entrepreneur needs and where she plans to get it, some forms are superior to others.

Control. By choosing certain forms of ownership, an entrepreneur automatically gives up some control of the company. Entrepreneurs must decide early how much control they are willing to sacrifice in exchange for help from other people in building a successful business.

Business goals. How big and how profitable an entrepreneur plans for the business to become will influence the form of ownership chosen. Businesses often switch forms of ownership as they grow, but moving from some formats to others can be extremely complex and expensive.

Management succession plans. When choosing a form of ownership, business owners must look ahead to the day when they will pass their companies on to the next generation or to a buyer. Some forms of ownership make this transition much smoother than others.

Cost of formation. Some forms of ownership are more costly and involved to create. An entrepreneur must weigh the benefits and the costs of the particular form she chooses.

Entrepreneurs have a wide choice of forms of ownership. In recent years, various hybrid forms of business ownership have emerged. This chapter will outline the key features of the most common forms of ownership, beginning with the sole proprietorship, the partnership, and the corporation.

1-A. Explain the advantages and disadvantages of the sole proprietorship.

The Sole Proprietorship

The **sole proprietorship** is a business owned and managed by one individual. This form of ownership is by far the most popular. Approximately 73 percent of all businesses in the United States are proprietorships.

The Advantages of a Proprietorship

SIMPLE TO CREATE. One of the most attractive features of a proprietorship is how fast and simple it is to begin operations. If an entrepreneur wants to operate a business under his own name (e.g., Bob's Bait and Tackle), he simply obtains the necessary licenses from state, county, and/or local governments and begins operation! For most entrepreneurs, it would not be impossible to start a proprietorship in a single day.

LEAST COSTLY FORM OF OWNERSHIP TO BEGIN. In addition to being easy to begin, the proprietorship is generally the least expensive form of ownership to establish. There is no need to create and file legal documents that are recommended for partnerships and required for corporations. An entrepreneur simply goes to the city or county government, states the nature of the business he will start, and pays the appropriate fees and license costs. Paying these fees and license costs gives the entrepreneur the right to conduct business in that particular jurisdiction.

Someone planning to conduct business under a trade name is usually required to acquire a certificate of doing business under an assumed name from the secretary of state. Filing this certificate also notifies the state whom the owner of the business is. In a proprietorship, the owner *is* the business.

PROFIT INCENTIVE. One major advantage of the proprietorship is that once the owner pays all of the company's expenses, she can keep the remaining profits (less taxes, of course). The profit incentive is a powerful one, and profits represent an excellent way of "keeping score" in the game of the business.

TOTAL DECISION-MAKING AUTHORITY. Because the sole proprietor is in total control of operations, she can respond quickly to changes, which is an asset in a rapidly shifting market. The freedom to set the company's course of action is a major motivational force. For the individual who thrives on the enjoyment of seeking new opportunities in business, the freedom of fast, flexible decision making is vital. Sole proprietor Max Gouge of Industrial Propane & Petroleum says, "I like the feeling of being on my own . . . I make this company work."[1]

NO SPECIAL LEGAL RESTRICTIONS. The proprietorship is the least regulated form of business ownership. In a time when government requests for information seem never ending, this feature has much merit.

EASY TO DISCONTINUE. If the entrepreneur decides to discontinue operations, he can terminate the business quickly, even though he will still be liable for all of the business's outstanding debts and obligations.

The Disadvantages of a Proprietorship

UNLIMITED PERSONAL LIABILITY. Probably the greatest disadvantage of a sole proprietorship is the **unlimited personal liability** of the owner, which means that the sole proprietor is personally liable for all of the business's debts. Remember: In a proprietorship, the owner *is* the business. The proprietor owns all of the business's assets, and if the business fails, creditors can force the sale of these assets to cover its debts. If unpaid business debts remain, creditors can also force the sale of the proprietor's personal assets to recover

sole proprietorship— *a business owned and managed by one individual.*

unlimited personal liability—*a situation in which the sole proprietor is personally liable for all of the business's debts.*

payment. In short, the company's debts are the owner's debts. Laws vary from one state to another, but most states require creditors to leave the failed business owner a minimum amount of equity in a home, a car, and some personal items. The reality: *Failure of the business can ruin the owner financially.*

LIMITED SKILLS AND CAPABILITIES. A sole proprietor may not have the wide range of skills that running a successful business requires. Each of us has areas in which our education, training, and work experiences have taught us a great deal; yet there are other areas where our decision-making ability is weak. Many business failures occur because owners lack the skills, knowledge, and experience in areas that are vital to business success. Owners tend to push aside problems they don't understand or don't feel comfortable with in favor of those they can solve more easily. Unfortunately, the problems they set aside seldom solve themselves. By the time an owner decides to ask for help in addressing these problems, it may be too late to save the company.

FEELINGS OF ISOLATION. Running a business alone allows an entrepreneur maximum flexibility, but it also creates feelings of isolation that there is no one else to turn to for help in solving problems or getting feedback on a new idea. Lee Gardner, the sole proprietor of a company that arranges sponsorships for sporting events, says, "After I set up my company, I realized I was all by myself and responsible for everything. Building a business brick by brick, alone, is not easy.[2]

LIMITED ACCESS TO CAPITAL. If the business is to grow and expand, a sole proprietor generally needs additional financial resources. However, many proprietors have already put all they have into their businesses and have used their personal resources as collateral on existing loans, making it difficult to borrow additional funds. A sole proprietorship is limited to whatever capital the owner can contribute and whatever money can be borrowed. In short, proprietors, unless they have great personal wealth, find it difficult to raise additional money while maintaining sole ownership. Most banks and other lending institutions have well-defined formulas for determining borrowers' eligibility. Unfortunately, many sole proprietorships cannot meet those borrowing requirements, especially in the early days of business.

LACK OF CONTINUITY FOR THE BUSINESS. Lack of continuity is inherent in a sole proprietorship. If the proprietor dies, retires, or becomes incapacitated, the business automatically terminates. Unless a family member or employee can take over, the business could be in jeopardy. Because people look for secure employment and an opportunity for advancement, proprietorships, being small, often have trouble recruiting and retaining good employees. If no one is trained to run the business, creditors can petition the courts to liquidate the assets of the dissolved business to pay outstanding debts.

Some entrepreneurs find that forming partnerships is one way to overcome the disadvantages of the sole proprietorship. For instance, when one person lacks specific managerial skills or has insufficient access to needed capital, he can compensate for these weaknesses by forming a partnership with someone who has complementary management skills or money to invest.

1-B. Explain the advantages and the disadvantages of the partnership.

The Partnership

A **partnership** is an association of two or more people who co-own a business for the purpose of making a profit. In a partnership the co-owners (partners) share the business's assets, liabilities, and profits according to the terms of a previously established partnership agreement.

The law does not require a partnership agreement (also known as the articles of partnership), but it is wise to work with an attorney to develop one that spells out the exact status and responsibility of each partner. All too often the parties think they know what they are agreeing to, only to find later that no real meeting of the minds took place. The **partnership agreement** is a document that states in writing all of the terms of operating the partnership for the protection of each partner involved. Every partnership should be based on a written agreement. "When two entrepreneurial personalities are combined, there is a tremendous amount of strength and energy—but it must be focused in the same direction, or it will tear the relationship apart," explains one business writer. "A good partnership agreement will guide you through the good times, provide you with a method for handling problems, and serve as the infrastructure for a successful operation."[3]

When no partnership agreement exists, the Uniform Partnership Act governs the partnership, but its provisions may not be as favorable as a specific agreement hammered out among the partners. Creating a partnership agreement is not costly. In most cases the partners can discuss each of the provisions in advance. Once they have reached an agreement, an attorney can draft the formal document. Banks will often want to see a copy of the partnership agreement before lending the business money. Probably the most important feature of the partnership agreement is that it resolves potential sources of conflict that, if not addressed in advance, could later result in partnership battles and the dissolution of an otherwise successful business. Spelling out details—especially sticky ones such as profit splits, contributions, workloads, decision-making authority, dispute resolution, dissolution, and others—in a written agreement at the outset will help avoid damaging tension in a partnership that could lead to a business "divorce." Business divorces, like marital ones, are almost always costly and unpleasant for everyone involved.

Unfortunately, the tendency for partners just starting out is to ignore writing a partnership agreement as they ride the emotional high of launching a company together. According to one writer, "In the eager, hectic days of startup, when two people come together with a 'brilliant idea,' they never imagine that someday they may not want to be partners anymore. Instead, their thoughts race to marketing strategies, product development, sales pitches, and customer service."[4] The result? Every year, thousands of partners find themselves mired in irreconcilable disputes that damage their businesses because they failed to establish a partnership agreement.

Generally, a partnership agreement can include any terms the partners want (unless they are illegal). The standard partnership agreement will likely include the following:

1. *Name of the partnership.*
2. *Purpose of the business.* What is the reason the business was brought into being?
3. *Domicile of the business.* Where will the principal business be located?
4. *Duration of the partnership.* How long will the partnership last?
5. *Names of the partners and their legal addresses.*
6. *Contributions of each partner to the business,* at the creation of the partnership and later. This would include each partner's investment in the business. In some situations a partner may contribute assets that are not likely to appear on a balance sheet. Experience, sales contacts, or a good reputation in the community may be reasons for asking a person to join in partnership.
7. Agreement on *how the profits or losses will be distributed.*
8. Agreement on *salaries or drawing rights* against profits for each partner.
9. Procedure for *expansion through the addition of new partners.*
10. If the partners *voluntarily dissolve the partnership how will the partnership's assets be distributed?*
11. *Sale of partnership interest.* The articles of partnership should include terms defining how a partner can sell her interest in the business.

partnership—an association of two or more people who co-own a business for the purpose of making a profit.

partnership agreement—a document that states in writing all of the terms of operating the partnership for the protection of each partner involved.

12. *Absence or disability of one of the partners.* If a partner is absent or disabled for an extended period of time, should the partnership continue? Will the absent or disabled partner receive the same share of profits as she did prior to her absence or disability? Should the absent or disabled partner be held responsible for debts incurred while unable to participate?

13. *Alternations or modifications of the partnership agreement.* No document is written to last forever. Partnership agreements should contain provisions for alternations or modifications.

The Uniform Partnership Act

The Uniform Partnership Act (UPA) codifies the body of law dealing with partnerships in the United States. Under the UPA the three key elements of any partnership are common ownership interest in a business, sharing the business's profits and losses, and the right to participate in managing the operation of the partnership. Under the act each partner has the *right* to:

1. share in the management and operations of the business
2. share in any profits the business might earn from operations
3. receive interest on additional advances made to the business
4. be compensated for expenses incurred in the name of the partnership
5. have access to the business's books and records
6. receive a formal accounting of the partnership's business affairs

The UPA also sets forth the partners' general obligations. Each partner is *obligated* to:

1. share in any losses sustained by the business
2. work for the partnership without salary
3. submit differences that may arise in the conduct of the business to majority vote or arbitration
4. give the other partner complete information about all business affairs
5. give a formal accounting of the partnership's business affairs

Beyond what the law prescribes, a partnership is based above all else on mutual trust and respect. Any partnership missing these elements is destined to fail.

The Advantages of the Partnership

EASY TO ESTABLISH. Like the proprietorship, the partnership is easy and inexpensive to establish. The owner must obtain the necessary business licenses and submit a minimal number of forms. In most states, partners must file a certificate for conducting business as partners, if the business is run under a trade name.

COMPLEMENTARY SKILLS. In a sole proprietorship, the owner must wear lots of different hats, and not all of them will fit well. In successful partnerships, the parties' skills and abilities usually complement one another, strengthening the company's managerial foundation.

DIVISION OF PROFITS. There are no restrictions on how partners distribute the company's profits as long as they are consistent with the partnership agreement and do not violate the rights of any partner. The partnership agreement should articulate the nature of each partner's contribution and proportional share of the profits. If the partners fail to create an agreement, the UPA says that the partners share equally in the partnership's profits, even if their original capital contributions are unequal.

LARGER POOL OF CAPITAL. The partnership form of ownership can significantly broaden the pool of capital available to a business. Each partner's asset base improves the business's ability to borrow needed funds; together the partners' personal assets will support a larger borrowing capacity.

ABILITY TO ATTRACT LIMITED PARTNERS. When partners share in owning, operating, and managing a business, they are **general partners.** General partners have unlimited liability and usually take an active role in managing the business. **Limited partners** do not participate in the day-to-day management of a company; they typically are only financial investors in the business. A partnership can have any number of limited partners, but there *must* be at least one general partner. A limited partnership can attract investors by offering them limited liability and the potential to realize a substantial return on their investments if the business is successful. Many individuals find it very profitable to invest in high-potential small businesses, but only if they avoid the disadvantages of unlimited liability while doing so.

LITTLE GOVERNMENTAL REGULATION. Like the proprietorship, the partnership form of operation is not burdened with red tape.

FLEXIBILITY. Although not as flexible as sole ownership, the partnership can generally react quickly to changing market conditions because no giant organization stifles quick and creative responses to new opportunities.

TAXATION. The partnership itself is not subject to federal taxation. It serves as a conduit for the profit or losses it earns or incurs; its net income or losses are passed along to the partners as personal income, and the partners pay income tax on their distributive shares. The partnership, like the proprietorship, avoids the double-taxation disadvantage associated with the corporate form of ownership.

general partners—
partners who share in owning, operating, and managing a business and who have unlimited liability for the partnership's debts.

limited partners—
partners who do not take an active role in managing the business and whose liability for the partnership's debts is limited to the amount they have invested.

The Disadvantages of the Partnership

UNLIMITED LIABILITY OF AT LEAST ONE PARTNER. At least one member of every partnership must be a general partner. The general partner has unlimited personal liability, even though he is often the partner with the least personal resources.

CAPITAL ACCUMULATION. Although the partnership form of ownership is superior to the proprietorship in its ability to attract capital, it is generally not as effective as the corporate form of ownership.

DIFFICULTY IN DISPOSING OF PARTNERSHIP INTEREST WITHOUT DISSOLVING THE PARTNERSHIP. Most partnership agreements restrict how a partner can dispose of his share of the business. It is common to find that a partner is required to sell his interest to the remaining partners. Even if the original agreement contains such a requirement and clearly delineates how the value of each partner's ownership will be determined, there is no guarantee that the other partner(s) will have the financial resources to buy the seller's interest. When the money is not available to purchase a partner's interest, the other partner(s) may be forced either to accept a new partner, or to dissolve the partnership, distribute the remaining assets, and begin again. When a partner withdraws from the partnership, the partnership ceases to exist unless there are specific provisions in the partnership agreement for a smooth transition. When a general partner dies, becomes incompetent, or withdraws from the business, the partnership automatically dissolves, although it may not terminate. Even when there are numerous partners, if one wishes to disassociate her name from the business, the remaining partners will probably form a new partnership.

LACK OF CONTINUITY. If one partner dies, complications arise. Partnership interest is often nontransferable through inheritance because the remaining partner(s) may not want to be in a partnership with the person who inherits the deceased partner's interest. Partners can make provisions in the partnership agreement to avoid dissolution due to death if all parties agree to accept as partners those who inherit the deceased's interest.

POTENTIAL FOR PERSONALITY AND AUTHORITY CONFLICTS. Being in a partnership is much like being in a marriage. Making sure partners' work habits, goals, ethics, and general business philosophy are compatible is an important step in avoiding a nasty business divorce. Still, as in a marriage, friction among partners is inevitable. The key is having a mechanism such as a partnership agreement and open lines of communication for controlling it. The demise of many partnerships can often be traced to interpersonal conflicts and the lack of a procedure to resolve those conflicts.

YOU BE THE CONSULTANT...

I Love My Brother, But!

Mary Ellen and James McGregor were the only two children of successful parents. Both children had the advantage of excellent educations, and, after graduating from college, Mary Ellen had spent six years in retailing. She had been fortunate in being selected for an intensive two-year training program that was designed to provide hands-on learning in each of the major functional areas of the business. Her next four years took Mary Ellen deeper into the inner workings of the business. Those around her commented about how quickly she seemed to learn complex concepts, some of which the "old-timers" in the business say it takes most years to learn, and that others never understand.

James McGregor was four years younger than his sister and was a well-rounded young man (the "B" student in school, athletically gifted and well liked by almost everyone). Upon graduation, James went directly into sales for a large manufacturer of industrial equipment. He enjoyed traveling and was willing to work as long as it took to ensure he made every possible sale. Like his sister, James's peers and managers considered him to be a "rising star" with exceptional potential.

With the untimely death of their grandmother came an unforeseen opportunity. Grandmother McGregor had been true to her Scottish heritage and had quietly amassed almost $800,000 through several wise investments. Grandmother McGregor loved her only two grandchildren and, knowing her son and his wife were financially secure, left the entire estate to Mary Ellen and James. In addition to the money was her request that they go into business to, as she put it, "make the money grow."

The opportunity to open a business appealed to both Mary Ellen and James. Their parents strongly supported the idea and expressed confidence in the their abilities. Mary Ellen had been investigating the competitive practices of specialty retailers and was confident that she had a good handle on the strategies and practices of the most successful ones. James

had no experience in retail business but was confident in his ability to sell. Mary Ellen began to focus all of her extra time and energies on identifying a retail niche that was underserved or poorly served in the immediate geographic market. In addition, she continued to study the practices of specialty retailers in an attempt to improve the likelihood of success for their new venture. James continued in his job and did not interfere with the research his sister was conducting.

Two years ago last February, Mary Ellen made her final decision regarding the business with the highest potential for becoming a new startup considering her experience. A new mall was four months from opening in an upper-income section of the city. Based on her research, Mary Ellen believed that an intimate apparel shop would have the highest success potential. The three anchor retailers in the mall were large stores but had never focused on upscale young women shoppers. The lingerie departments in these stores were traditional, focusing more on the older woman. Consequently, although these competitors had excellent products, they were staffed by personnel accustomed to selling to a more mature customer. The products in these department stores appealed to their traditional, mature customers.

Mary Ellen and James had enough money to get the venture off the ground. Although James was absolutely "in the dark" about the products the store was to sell, he went along with his big sister's idea. James had a great deal of respect for Mary Ellen's ability. The two formed a partnership with each contributing equally from their inheritance. The fifty-fifty partnership seemed like the right thing to do; after all, they were family. Mary Ellen took the lead when it came to designing the store's layout and purchasing inventory. After she left her job, Mary Ellen put every ounce of her energy into the business. James saw no need to quit his job because he wasn't sure what contribution he could make at that stage in the business.

Within nine months of the opening of the new store, Mary Ellen had proof that her plan was solid. Sales were running 17 percent ahead of her most optimistic projections. The younger professional women whom she had targeted turned out to be even larger in number and more loyal than she had expected. In fact, analysis of sales data revealed that 20 percent of the customers drove more than 12 miles to shop at the store. Mary Ellen concentrated on listening to her customers to insure that the store would have the inventory that matched their needs and wants.

Throughout this period James was supportive but seldom came by the store. He told Mary Ellen that he "felt funny" standing around in "that kind of store." He was concerned that his presence would be a deterrent to shoppers. "What woman wants to shop for garments like that with a man standing around?" he said.

The situation didn't change much over the next year. The business is successful, but Mary Ellen is putting in 60- to 70-hour weeks while James meets with her on weekends when he is "off the road" from his sales job. Finally, the day comes when Mary Ellen has "had enough." At Sunday dinner at her parents' home, she puts the whole problem on the table: James has earned 50 percent of all profits for the past two years but has not spent a full day in the store since it opened. "I love my brother, but it just doesn't seem fair," she says.

1. Does simply investing an equal amount of money in a partnership entitle one to an equal share of the profits?
2. What steps should Mary Ellen and James have taken to have avoided this problem?
3. What role should James play in this business?
4. What recommendations would you make to preserve this successful business and resolve Mary Ellen's concern?

Limited Partnerships

A **limited partnership,** which is a modification of a general partnership, is composed of at least one general partner and at least one limited partner. In a limited partnership the general partner is treated, under the law, exactly as in a general partnership. The limited partner(s) is treated more as an investor in the business venture; limited partners have limited liability. They can lose only the amount invested in the business.

Most states have ratified the Revised Uniform Limited Partnership Act. The formation of a limited partnership requires its founder to file a certificate of limited partnership in the state in which the limited partnership plans to conduct business. The certificate of limited partnership should include the following information:

> **limited partnership**—a partnership composed of at least one general partner and at least one limited partner.

1. the name of the limited partnership
2. the general character of its business
3. the address of the office of the firm's agent authorized to receive summonses or other legal notices
4. the name and business address of each partner, specifying which ones are general partners and which are limited partners
5. the amount of cash contributions actually made, and agreed to be made in the future, by each partner
6. a description of the value of noncash contributions made or to be made by each partner
7. the times at which additional contributions are to be made by any of the partners
8. whether and under what conditions a limited partner has the right to grant limited partner status to an assignee of his or her interest in the partnership
9. if agreed upon, the time or the circumstances when a partner may withdraw from the firm (unlike the withdrawal of a general partner, the withdrawal of a limited partner does *not* automatically dissolve a limited partnership)
10. if agreed upon, the amount of, or the method of determining, the funds to be received by a withdrawing partner
11. any right of a partner to receive distributions of cash or other property from the firm, and the times and circumstances for such distributions
12. the time or circumstances when the limited partnership is to be dissolved
13. the rights of the remaining partners to continue the business after withdrawal of a general partner
14. any other matters the partners want to include

The general partner has the same rights and duties as under a general partnership: the right to make decisions for the business, to act as an agent for the partnership, to use the property of the partnership for normal business, and to share in the business's profits. The limited partner does not have the right to manage the business in any way. In fact, if he takes part in managing the business, a limited partner may actually forfeit limited liability, taking on the liability status of a general partner. Limited partners can, however, make management suggestions to the general partners, inspect the business, and make copies of business records. A limited partner is, of course, entitled to a share of the business's profits as agreed on and specified in the certificate of limited partnership. The primary disadvantage of limited partnerships is the complexity and the cost of establishing them.

Master Limited Partnership

master limited partnership—
a partnership whose shares are traded on stock exchanges, just like a corporation's.

A relatively new form of business structure, the **master limited partnership (MLP),** is just like regular limited partnerships, except its shares are traded on stock exchanges. The master limited partnership provides most of the same advantages to investors as a corporation—including limited liability. One analyst says that a master limited partnership "looks like a corporation, acts like a corporation, and trades on major stock exchanges like a corporation."[5] Congress originally allowed MLPs to be taxed as partnerships. However, in 1987 it ruled that any MLP not involved in natural resources or real estate would be taxed as a corporation, eliminating its ability to avoid the double-taxation disadvantages. MLP profits typically must be divided among thousands of partners.

1-C. Explain the advantages and the disadvantages of the corporation.

Corporations

corporation—*a separate legal entity apart from its owners which receives its right to exist from the state in which it is incorporated.*

domestic corporation— *a corporation doing business in the state in which it is incorporated.*

foreign corporation— *a corporation doing business in a state other than the one in which it is incorporated.*

alien corporation—*a corporation formed in another country but doing business in the United States.*

The corporation is the most complex of the three major forms of business ownership. It is a separate entity apart from its owners and may engage in business, make contracts, sue and be sued, and pay taxes. The Supreme Court has defined the **corporation** as "an artificial being, invisible, intangible, and existing only in contemplation of the law."[6] Because the life of the corporation is independent of its owners, the shareholders can sell their interests in the business without affecting its continuation.

Corporations (also known as "C corporation") are creations of the state. When a corporation is founded, it accepts the regulations and restrictions of the state in which it is incorporated and any other state in which it chooses to do business. A corporation doing business in the state in which it is incorporated is a **domestic corporation**. When a corporation conducts business in another state, that state considers it to be a **foreign corporation**. Corporations that are formed in other countries but do business in the United States are **alien corporations**.

Generally, the corporation must report annually its financial operations to its home state's attorney general. These financial reports become public record. If the corporation's stock is sold in more than one state, the corporation must comply with federal regulations governing the sale of corporate securities. There are substantially more reporting requirements for a corporation than for the other forms of ownership.

How to Incorporate

Most states allow entrepreneurs to incorporate without the assistance of an attorney. Some states even provide incorporation kits to help in the incorporation process. Although it is cheaper for entrepreneurs to complete the process themselves, it is not always the best idea. In some states, the application process is complex, and the required forms are confusing. The price for filing incorrectly can be high. "If you [complete the incorporation process] yourself and you do it improperly, it's generally invalid," explains one attorney.[7]

Once the owners decide to form a corporation, they must choose the state in which to incorporate. If the business will operate within a single state, it is probably most logical to incorporate in that state. States differ—sometimes rather dramatically—in the requirements they place on the corporations they charter and how they treat corporations chartered in other states. They also differ in the tax rate they impose on corporations, the restrictions placed on their activities, the capital required to incorporate, and the fees or organization tax charged to incorporate.

Every state requires a certificate of incorporation or charter to be filed with the secretary of state. The following information is generally required to be in the certificate of incorporation:

The corporation's name. The corporation must choose a name that is not so similar to that of another firm in that state that it causes confusion or lends itself to deception. It must also include a term such as *corporation, incorporated, company,* or *limited* to notify the public that it is dealing with a corporation.

The corporation's statement of purpose. The incorporators must state in general terms the intended nature of the business. The purpose must, of course, be lawful. An illustration might be "to engage in the sale of office furniture and fixtures." The purpose should be broad enough to allow for some expansion in the activities of the business as it develops.

The corporation's time horizon. In most cases corporations are formed with no specific termination date; they are formed "for perpetuity." However, it is possible to incorporate for a specific duration (e.g., 50 years).

Names and addresses of the incorporators. The incorporators must be identified in the articles of incorporation and are liable under the law to attest that all information in the articles of incorporation is correct. In some states one or more of the incorporators must reside in the state in which the corporation is being created.

Place of business. The post office address of the corporation's principal office must be listed. This address, for a domestic corporation, must be in the state in which incorporation takes place.

"There's a stockholder here to see you, sir."

Source: Reprinted by permission of Cartoon Features Syndicate.

Capital stock authorization. The articles of incorporation must include the amount and class (or type) of capital stock the corporation wants to be authorized to issue. This is not the number of shares it must issue; a corporation can issue any number of shares up to the amount authorized. This section must also define the different classifications of stock and any special rights, preferences, or limits each class has.

Capital required at the time of incorporation. Some states require a newly formed corporation to deposit in a bank a specific percentage of the stock's par value prior to incorporating.

Provisions for preemptive rights, if any, that are granted to stockholders.

Restrictions on transferring shares. Many closely held corporations—those owned by a few shareholders, often family members—require shareholders interested in selling their stock to offer it first to the corporation. (Shares the corporation itself owns are called **treasury stock.**) To maintain control over their ownership, many closely held corporations exercise their right, known as the **right of first refusal**.

Names and addresses of the officers and directors of the corporation.

Rules under which the corporation will operate. **Bylaws** are the rules and regulations the officers and directors establish for the corporation's internal management and operation.

Once the attorney general of the incorporating state has approved a request for incorporation and the corporation has paid its fees, the approved articles of incorporation become its charter. With the charter in hand, the next order of business is to hold an organizational meeting for the stockholders to formally elect directors who in turn, will appoint the corporate officers.

The Advantages of the Corporation

LIMITED LIABILITY OF STOCKHOLDERS. The corporation allows investors to limit their liability to the total amount of their investment. This legal protection of personal assets beyond the business is of critical concern to many potential investors.

This shield of limited liability may not be impenetrable, however. Because startup companies are so risky, lenders and other creditors require the owners to personally guarantee loans made to the corporation. Robert Morris Associates, a national organization of bank loan officers, estimates that 95 percent of small business owners have to sign personal guarantees to get the financing they need. By making these guarantees, owners are putting their personal assets at risk (just as in a proprietorship) despite choosing the corporate form of ownership. Recent court decisions have extended the personal liability of small corporation owners beyond the financial guarantees that banks and other lenders require, "piercing the corporate veil" much more than ever before. More courts are holding entrepreneurs personally liable for environmental, pension, and legal claims against their corporations—much to the surprise of the owners, who chose the corporate form of ownership to shield themselves from such liability.[8]

ABILITY TO ATTRACT CAPITAL. Based on the protection of limited liability, corporations have proved to be the most effective form of ownership for accumulating large amounts of capital. Limited only by the number of shares authorized in its charter (which can be amended), the corporation can raise money to begin business and expand as opportunity dictates by selling shares of its stock to investors. A corporation can sell its stock to a limited number of private investors (a private placement) or to the public (a public offering).

ABILITY TO CONTINUE INDEFINITELY. Unless limited by its charter, the corporation as a separate legal entity theoretically can continue indefinitely. The corporation's existence does not depend on the fate of any single individual. Unlike a proprietorship or partnership

treasury stock—*the shares a corporation owns in itself.*

right of first refusal— *a provision requiring shareholders who want to sell their stock to offer it first to the corporation.*

bylaws—*the rules and regulations the officers and directors establish for the corporation's internal management and operation.*

in which the death of a founder ends the business, the corporation lives beyond the lives of those who gave it life. This perpetual life gives rise to the next major advantage—transferable ownership.

TRANSFERABLE OWNERSHIP. If stockholders in a corporation are displeased with the business's progress, they can sell their shares to someone else. Millions of shares of stock representing ownership in companies are traded daily on the world's stock exchanges. Shareholders can also transfer their stock through inheritance to a new generation of owners. During all of these transfers of ownership, the corporation continues to conduct business as usual.

Unlike that of large corporations whose shares are traded on organized stock exchanges, the stock of many small corporations is held by a small number of people ("closely held"), often company founders, family members, or employees. The small number of people holding the stock means that the resale market for shares is limited, which could make the transfer of ownership more difficult.

The Disadvantages of Corporations

COST AND TIME INVOLVED IN THE INCORPORATION PROCESS. Corporations can be costly and time-consuming to establish. The owners are giving birth to an artificial legal entity—and the gestation period can be prolonged for the novice. In some states an attorney must handle an incorporation, but in most states entrepreneurs can complete all of the required forms alone. However, an owner must exercise great caution when incorporating without the help of an attorney. Also, incorporating a business requires a variety of fees that is not applicable to proprietorships or partnerships. Creating a corporation can cost between $500 and $2,500, typically averaging around $1,000.

DOUBLE TAXATION. Because a corporation is a separate legal entity, it must pay taxes on its net income at the federal level, in most states, and to some local governments as well. Before stockholders receive a penny of its net income as dividends, a corporation must pay these taxes at the corporate tax rate. Then stockholders must pay taxes on the dividends they receive from these same profits at the *individual* tax rate. Thus, a corporation's profits are taxed twice. This **double taxation** is a distinct disadvantage of the corporate form of ownership.

double taxation—*a disadvantage of the corporate form of ownership in which a corporation's profits are taxed twice: at the corporate rate and at the individual rate (on the portion of profits distributed as dividends).*

POTENTIAL FOR DIMINISHED MANAGERIAL INCENTIVES. As corporations grow, they often require additional managerial expertise beyond that which the founder can provide. Because the founder created the company and often has most of her personal wealth tied up in it, the entrepreneur has an intense interest in making it a success and is willing to make sacrifices for it. Professional managers the entrepreneur brings in to help run the business as it grows do not always have the same degree of interest in or loyalty to the company. As a result, the business may suffer without the founder's energy, care, and devotion. One way to minimize this potential problem is to link managers' (and even employees') compensation to the company's financial performance through a profit-sharing or bonus plan. Corporations can also stimulate managers' and employees' incentive on the job by creating an employee stock ownership plan (ESOP) in which managers and employees become part or whole owners in the company.

LEGAL REQUIREMENTS AND REGULATORY RED TAPE. Corporations are subject to more legal and financial requirements than other forms of ownership. Entrepreneurs must resist the temptation to commingle their personal funds with those of the corporation and must meet more stringent requirements for recording and reporting business transactions. They must also hold annual meetings and consult the board of directors about major decisions that are beyond day-to-day operations. Managers may be required to submit some major decisions to the stockholders for approval. Corporations that are publicly held must file quarterly and annual reports with the Securities and Exchange Commission (SEC).

POTENTIAL LOSS OF CONTROL BY THE FOUNDER(S). When entrepreneurs sell shares of ownership in their companies, they relinquish some control. Especially when they need large capital infusions for startup or growth, entrepreneurs may have to give up *significant* amounts of control, so much, in fact, that the founder becomes a minority shareholder. Losing majority ownership—and therefore control—in her company leaves the founder in a precarious position. She no longer has the power to determine the company's direction; "outsiders" do. In some cases, founders' shares have been so diluted that majority shareholders actually vote them out of their jobs!

2. Discuss the advantages and the disadvantages of the S corporation, the limited liability company, the professional corporation, and the joint venture.

Other Forms of Ownership

In addition to the sole proprietorship, the partnership, and the corporation, entrepreneurs can choose from other forms of ownership, including the S corporation, the limited liability company, the professional corporation, and the joint venture.

The S Corporation

S corporation—*a corporation that retains the legal characteristics of a regular (C) corporation, but has the advantage of being taxed as a partnership if it meets certain criteria.*

In 1954 the Internal Revenue Service Code created the subchapter S corporation. In recent years the IRS has changed the title to S corporation and has made a few modifications in its qualifications. An **S corporation** is only a distinction that is made for federal income tax purposes, and is, in terms of legal characteristics, no different from any other corporation. Although Congress is considering legislation that would simplify or eliminate some of the rules and requirements for S corporations, currently a business seeking "S" status must meet the following criteria:

1. It must be a domestic corporation.
2. It cannot have a nonresident alien as a shareholder.
3. It can issue only one class of common stock, which means that all shares must carry the same rights (e.g., the right to dividends or liquidation rights). The exception is voting rights, which may differ. In other words, an S corporation can issue voting and nonvoting common stock.
4. It must limit its shareholders to individuals, estates, and certain trusts.
5. It cannot have more than 75 shareholders.

Violating any of these terms *automatically* terminates a company's "S" status. If a corporation satisfies the definition for an S corporation, the owners must actually elect to be treated as one. The election is made by filing IRS Form 2553 (within the first 75 days of the tax year), and *all* shareholders must consent to have the corporation treated as an S corporation.

THE ADVANTAGES OF AN S CORPORATION. The S corporation retains all of the advantages of a regular corporation, such as continuity of existence, transferability of ownership, and limited personal liability for its owners. The most notable provision of the S corporation is that it passes all of its profits or losses through to the individual shareholders, and its income is taxed only once at the individual tax rate. Thus, electing S corporation status avoids a primary disadvantage of the regular (or "C") corporation—double taxation. In essence, the tax treatment of an S corporation is exactly like that of a partnership; its owners report their proportional shares of the company's profits on their individual income tax returns and pay taxes on those profits at the individual rate (even if they never take the money out of the business).

Another advantage the S corporation offers is avoiding the tax C corporations pay on assets that have appreciated in value and are sold. Also, owners of S corporations enjoy the ability to make year-end payouts to themselves if profits are high. In a C corporation, owners have no such luxury because the IRS watches for excessive compensation to owners/managers.

DISADVANTAGES OF AN S CORPORATION. When the Tax Reform Act (TRA) of 1986 restructured individual and corporate tax rates, many business owners switched to S corporations to lower their tax bills. For the first time since Congress enacted the federal income tax in 1913, the maximum individual rate was lower than the maximum corporate rate. However, in 1993 Congress realigned the tax structure by raising the maximum personal tax rate to 39.6 percent from 31 percent. This new rate is 4.6 percent *higher* than the maximum corporate tax rate of 35 percent. Although these changes make S corporation status much less attractive than before, entrepreneurs considering switching to C corporation status must consider the total impact of such a change on their companies, especially if they pay out a significant amount of earnings to owners. In addition to the tax implications of making the switch from an S corporation, owners should consider the size of the company's net profits, the tax rates of its shareholders, plans (and their timing) to sell the company, and the impact of the C corporation's double-taxation penalty on income distributed as dividends.

Another disadvantage of the S corporation is that the costs of many fringe benefits such as insurance, meals, and lodging, paid to shareholders with 2 percent or more of stock cannot be deducted as business expenses for tax purposes; these benefits are then considered to be taxable income. In addition, S corporations offer shareholders only a limited range of retirement benefits, while regular corporations make a wide range of retirement plans available.

WHEN IS AN S CORPORATION A WISE CHOICE? Choosing S corporation status is usually beneficial to startup companies anticipating net losses and to highly profitable firms with substantial dividends to pay out to shareholders. In these cases the owner can use the loss to offset other income or is in a lower tax bracket than the corporation, thus saving money in the long run. Companies that plan to reinvest most of their earnings to finance growth also find S corporation status favorable. Small business owners who intend to sell their companies in the near future will prefer "S" over "C" status because the taxable gains on the sale of an S corporation are generally lower than those of a C corporation.

On the other hand, small companies with the following characteristics are not likely to benefit from S corporation status:

- ☆ highly profitable personal service companies with large numbers of shareholders, in which most of the profits are passed on to shareholders as compensation or retirement benefits.
- ☆ fast-growing companies that must retain most of their earnings to finance growth and capital spending.
- ☆ corporations in which the loss of fringe benefits to shareholders exceeds tax savings.
- ☆ corporations in which the income before any compensation to shareholders is less than $100,000 per year.
- ☆ corporations with sizable net operating losses that cannot be used against S corporation earnings.

Figure 3.1 on page 74 shows the number of sole proprietorships, partnerships, corporations, and S corporations in operation today versus 1980.

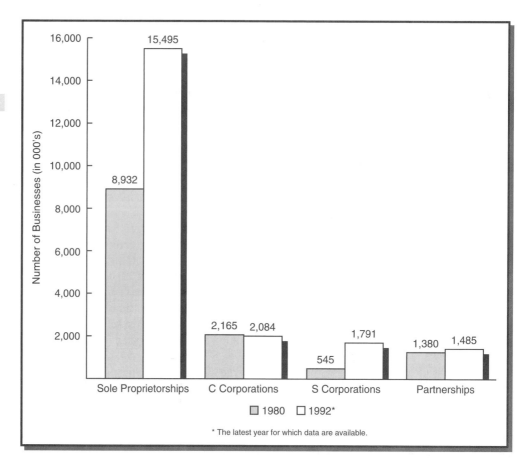

* The latest year for which data are available.

The Limited Liability Company (LLC)

**limited liability
company (LLC)—**

*a relatively new form of
ownership that, like an
S corporation, is a cross
between a partnership
and a corporation; it is
not subject to many of
the restrictions currently
imposed on S
corporations.*

A relatively new creation, the **limited liability company (LLC)**, is like an S corporation, a cross between a partnership and a corporation. LLCs however, are not subject to many of the restrictions currently imposed on S corporations. For example, S corporations cannot have more than 75 shareholders, none of whom can be foreigners or corporations. S corporations are also limited to only one class of stock. LLCs eliminate those restrictions. An LLC must have at least two owners (called "members"), but it offers its owners limited liability without imposing any requirements on their characteristics or any ceiling on their numbers. Unlike a limited partnership, which prohibits limited partners from participating in the day-to-day management of the business, an LLC does not restrict its members' ability to become involved in managing the company.

In addition to offering its members the advantage of limited liability, LLCs also avoid the double taxation imposed on C corporations. Like an S corporation, an LLC does not pay income taxes; its income flows through to the members, who are responsible for paying income taxes on their shares of the LLC's net income. Because they are not subject to the many restrictions imposed on other forms of ownership, LLCs offer entrepreneurs another significant advantage: flexibility. Like a partnership, an LLC permits its members to divide income (and thus tax liability) as they see fit.

These advantages make the LLC an ideal form of ownership for small companies in virtually any industry—retail, wholesale, manufacturing, real estate, or service. Because they offer the tax advantage of a partnership, the legal protection of a corporation, and maximum flexibility, LLCs have become an extremely popular form of ownership among entrepreneurs.

For example, Marian Fletcher launched a profitable party-planning and catering service in 1995 as a sole proprietorship. Her company, Let's Go Party, grew quickly, and Fletcher wanted to bring her daughter into the business as an owner. Reviewing the advantages and disadvantages of each form of ownership led Fletcher to create an LLC. "We decided this was the best way to go for us," she says. "In case anything happens, my daughter and I won't be liable for anything more than what we have invested in the company already." Fletcher, who set up her LLC without the help of an attorney for just $50, also found the LLC's tax treatment to be a major advantage for her and her daughter.[9]

Creating an LLC is much like creating a corporation. Forming an LLC requires an entrepreneur to file two documents with the secretary of state: the articles of organization and the operating agreement. The LLC's **articles of organization**, similar to the corporation's articles of incorporation, establish the company's name, its method of management (board managed or member managed), its duration, and the names and addresses of each organizer. In most states the company's name must contain the words "limited liability company," "limited company," or the letters "L.L.C." or "L.C." Unlike a corporation, an LLC does not have perpetual life; in most states an LLC's charter may not exceed 30 years. However, the same factors that would cause a partnership to dissolve would also cause the dissolution of an LLC before its charter expires.

The **operating agreement**, similar to a corporation's bylaws, outlines the provisions governing the way the LLC will conduct business. To ensure that their LLCs are classified as a partnership for tax purposes, entrepreneurs must draft the operating agreement carefully. The operating agreement must create an LLC that has more characteristics of a partnership than of a corporation to maintain this favorable tax treatment. Specifically, an LLC cannot have any more than *two* of the following four corporate characteristics:

1. *Limited liability.* Limited liability exists if no member of the LLC is personally liable for the debts or claims against the company. Because entrepreneurs choosing this form of ownership usually do so to get limited liability protection, the operating agreement almost always contains this characteristic.

2. *Continuity of life.* Continuity of life exists if the company continues to exist in spite of changes in stock ownership. To avoid continuity of life, any LLC member must have the power to dissolve the company. Most entrepreneurs choose to omit this characteristic from their LLC's operating agreements.

3. *Free transferability of interest.* Free transferability of interest exists if each LLC member has the power to transfer his ownership to another person without the consent of other members. To avoid this characteristic, the operating agreement must state that a recipient of a member's LLC stock cannot become a substitute member without the consent of the remaining members.

4. *Centralized management.* Centralized management exists if a group that does not include all LLC members has the authority to make management decisions and to conduct company business. To avoid this characteristic, the operating agreement must state that the company elects to be "member managed."

Despite their universal appeal to entrepreneurs, LLCs suffer some disadvantages. They can be expensive to create, often costing between $1,500 and $5,000. Although an LLC may be ideally suited for an entrepreneur launching a new company, it may pose problems for business owners considering converting an existing business to an LLC. Switching to an LLC from a general partnership, a limited partnership, or a sole proprietorship and reorganizing to bring in new owners are usually not a problem. However, owners of corporations and S corporations would incur large tax obligations if they converted their companies to LLCs.

To date, the biggest disadvantage of the LLC stems from its newness. As yet, no uniform legislation for LLCs exists (although a Uniform Limited Liability Act is pending at the fed-

> Let's Go Party

articles of organization—*the document that establishes for an LLC its name, method of management, its duration, and other details.*

operating agreement—*the document that establishes for an LLC the provisions governing the way it will conduct business.*

Which Form Is Best?

Watoma Kinsey and her daughter Katrina are about to launch a business that specializes in children's parties. Their target audience is upscale families who want to throw unique, memorable parties to celebrate special occasions for their children between the ages of 5 and 15. The Kinseys have leased a large building and have renovated it to include many features designed to appeal to kids, including special gym equipment, a skating rink, an obstacle course, a mockup of a pirate ship, a ball crawl, and even a moveable haunted house. They can offer simple birthday parties (cake and ice cream included) or special theme parties as elaborate as the customer wants. Their company will provide magicians, clowns, comedians, jugglers, tumblers, and a variety of other entertainers.

Watoma and Katrina have invested $45,000 each to get the business ready to launch. Based on the quality of their business plan and their preparation, the Kinseys have negotiated a $40,000 bank loan. Because they both have families, the Kinseys want to minimize their exposure to potential legal and financial problems. A large portion of their startup costs went

to purchase a liability insurance policy to cover the Kinseys in case a child is injured at a party. If their business plan is accurate, the Kinseys will earn a small profit in their first year (about $1,500), and a more attractive profit of $16,000 in their second year of operation. Within five years, they expect their company to generate as much as $50,000 in profits. The Kinseys have agreed to split the profits and the workload equally.

If the business is as successful as they think it will be, the Kinseys eventually want to franchise their company. That, however, is part of their long-range plan. For now, they want to perfect their business system and prove that it can be profitable before they try to duplicate it in the form of franchises.

As they move closer to the launch date for their business, the Kinseys are reviewing the different forms of ownership.

1. Which form(s) of ownership would you recommend to the Kinseys? Explain.

2. Which form(s) of ownership would you recommend the Kinseys *avoid*? Explain.

3. What factors should the Kinseys consider as they try to choose the form of ownership that is best for them?

---

eral level). Two states (Vermont and Hawaii) still do not recognize LLCs as a legal form of ownership, but that could change soon.

The Professional Corporation

Professional corporations are designed to offer professionals—lawyers, doctors, dentists, accountants, and others—the advantages of the corporate form of ownership. They are ideally suited for professionals, who must always be concerned about malpractice lawsuits, because they offer limited liability. For example, if three doctors formed a professional corporation, none of them would be liable for the others' malpractice. (Of course, each would be liable for her own actions.) Owners create a professional corporation in the same way as a regular corporation. Such corporations are often identified by the abbreviations P.C. (professional corporation), P.A. (professional association), or S.C. (service corporation).

The Joint Venture

A joint venture is very much like a partnership, except that it is formed for a specific, limited purpose. For instance, assume you have a 500-acre tract of land 60 miles from Chicago. This land has been cleared and is normally used in agricultural production. You have a friend who has solid contacts among major musical groups and would like to put on a concert. You expect prices for your agricultural products to be low this summer, so you and your friend form a joint venture for the specific purpose of staging a three-day concert. Your contribution will be the exclusive use of the land for one month, and your friend will provide all the performers as well as technicians, facilities, and equipment. All costs will be paid out of receipts and the net profits will be split, with you receiving 20 percent for the use of your land. When the concert is over, the facilities removed, and the accounting for all costs completed, you and your friend split the profits 20–80, and the joint venture terminates.

In any endeavor where neither party can effectively achieve the purpose alone, a joint venture becomes a common form of ownership. The "partners" form a new joint venture for each new project they undertake. The income derived from a joint venture is taxed as if it arose from a partnership.

Table 3.1 provides a summary of the key features of the major forms of ownership discussed in this chapter.

Table 3.1
Characteristics of the Major Forms of Ownership

Feature	Sole Proprietorship	Partnership	C Corporation	S Corporation	Limited Liability Company
Owner's Personal Liability	Unlimited	Unlimited for general partners; Limited for limited partners	Limited	Limited	Limited
Number of Owners	1	2 or more (at least 1 general partner required)	Any number	Maximum of 35 (with restrictions on who they are)	2 or more
Tax Liability	Single tax; proprietor pays at individual rate	Single tax; partners pay on their proportional shares at individual rate	Double tax; corporation pays tax and shareholders pay tax on dividends distributed	Single tax; owners pay on their proportional shares at individual rate	Single tax; members pay on their proportional shares at individual rate
Maximum Tax Rate	39.6%	39.6%	35% (39.6% on dividends distributed)	39.6%	39.6%
Transferability of Ownership	Fully transferable through sale or transfer of company assets	May require consent of all partners	Fully transferable	Transferable (but may affect "S" status)	Usually requires consent of all members
Continuity of Business	Ends on death or insanity of proprietor or upon termination by proprietor	Dissolves upon death, insanity, or retirement of a general partner (business may continue)	Perpetual Life	Perpetual Life	Perpetual Life
Cost of Formation	Low	Moderate	High	High	High
Liquidity of Owner's Investment in Business	Poor to average	Poor to average	High	Average (Transfer may be restricted)	Average

Continued

Table 3.1
Characteristics of the Major Forms of Ownership, Continued

Feature	Sole Proprietorship	Partnership	C Corporation	S Corporation	Limited Liability Company
Complexity of Formation	Extremely low	Moderate	High	High	High
Ability to Raise Capital	Low	Moderate	Very high	Moderate to high	High
Formation Procedure	No special steps required other than buying necessary licenses	Now written partnership agreements (but highly advisable)	Must meet formal requirements specified by state law	Must follow same procedure as C corporation, then elect "S" status with IRS	Must meet formal requirements specified by state law

Franchising

Franchising is booming! Since 1990, sales by franchised businesses have grown ten times faster than the U.S. economy as a whole.[10] Much of its popularity arises from its ability to offer those who lack business experience the chance to own and operate a business with a high probability of success. Today, more than 4,500 franchisers operate some 570,000 franchise outlets throughout the world, and more are opening at an incredible pace. A new franchise opens somewhere in the world every six-and-a-half minutes![11] Franchises account for 42 percent of all retail sales, totaling more than $810 billion. Franchises also employ more than 8 million people in more than 70 major industries.[12]

Franchising's impressive growth will continue into the next century. Experts predict that, by 2004, franchises will be ringing up sales of $2.5 *trillion* worldwide![13] By then, franchising will account for 50 percent of all retail sales. An International Franchise Association spokesperson says that franchising "will become the dominant form of retailing in most of the developed countries around the world."[14]

In **franchising**, semi-independent business owners (franchisees) pay fees and royalties to a parent company (franchiser) in return for the right to sell its products or services and often to use its business format and system. Franchisees do not establish their own autonomous businesses; instead, they buy a "success package" from the franchiser, who shows them how to use it. Franchisees, unlike independent business owners, don't have the freedom to change the way they run their businesses—for example, shifting advertising strategies or adjusting product lines—but they do have a formula for success that the franchiser has worked out. "In fact," says one writer, "the secret to success in franchising is following the formula precisely... Successful franchisers claim that neglecting to follow the formula is one of the chief reasons that franchisees fail."[15]

Steve Gaffney, a highly successful MAACO (automotive services) franchisee, is convinced that the system the franchiser taught him is the key to his company's progress and growth to date. "You have to follow the plan every day," he says. "The [franchiser's] operations manuals are my road map. They explain the business in terms anyone can understand. And I follow every detail to make the system work."[16]

franchising—*a system of distribution in which semi-independent business owners (franchisees) pay fees and royalties to a parent company (franchiser) in return for the right to sell its products or services and often to use its business format and system.*

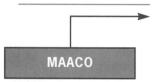

MAACO

Franchising is based on a continuing relationship between a franchiser and a franchisee. The franchiser provides valuable services such as market research, a proven business system, name recognition, and many others; in return, the franchisee pays a percentage of sales to the franchiser as royalties and agrees to operate the outlet according to the franchiser's system. Because franchisers develop the business systems their franchisees use and direct their distribution methods, they maintain substantial control over their franchisees. Yet, this standardization lies at the core of franchising's success as a method of distribution.

Types Of Franchising

3. Describe the three types of franchising: tradename, product distribution, and pure.

There are three basic types of franchising: tradename franchising, product distribution franchising, and pure franchising. **Tradename franchising** involves a brand name such as True Value Hardware or Western Auto. Here, the franchisee purchases the right to use the franchiser's tradename without distributing particular products exclusively under the franchiser's name. **Product distribution franchising** involves a franchiser licensing a franchisee to sell specific products under the franchiser's brand name and trademark through a selective, limited distribution network. This system is commonly used to market automobiles (Chevrolet, Oldsmobile, Chrysler), gasoline products (Exxon, Sunoco, Texaco), soft drinks (Pepsi-Cola, Coca-Cola), bicycles (Schwinn), appliances, cosmetics, and other products. These two methods of franchising allow franchisees to acquire some of the parent company's identity.

tradename franchising—*a system of franchising in which a franchisee purchases the right to use the franchiser's tradename without distributing particular products exclusively under the franchiser's name.*

Pure (or **comprehensive** or **business format) franchising** involves providing the franchisee with a complete business format, including a license for a tradename, the products or services to be sold, the physical plant, the methods of operation, a marketing strategy plan, a quality control process, a two-way communications system, and the necessary business services. The franchisee purchases the right to use all of the elements of a fully integrated business operation. Pure franchising is the most rapidly growing of all types of franchising and is common among fast-food restaurants, hotels, business service firms, car rental agencies, educational institutions, beauty aid retailers, and many others. Although product and tradename franchises annually ring up more sales than pure franchises, pure franchising outlets' sales are growing much faster.

product distribution franchising—*a system of franchising in which a franchiser licenses a franchisee to sell its products under the franchiser's brand name and trademark through a selective, limited distribution network.*

pure franchising—*a system of franchising in which a franchiser sells a franchisee a complete business format and system.*

The Benefits of Buying a Franchise

A franchisee gets the opportunity to own a small business relatively quickly, and, because of the identification with an established product and brand name, a franchise often reaches the breakeven point faster than an independent business would. Still, most new franchise outlets don't break even for at least six to eighteen months.

Franchisees also benefit from the franchiser's business experience. In fact, experience is the essence of what a franchisee is buying from a franchiser. Many entrepreneurs go into business by themselves and make many costly mistakes. Given the thin margin for error in the typical startup, a new business owner cannot afford to make many mistakes. In a franchising arrangement, the franchiser already has worked out the kinks in the system by trial and error, and franchisees benefit from that experience. Gary Mandichak, owner of a successful Petland franchise, says, "[Franchisers] have the experience, they know what works and what doesn't, and they know what's happening in the market."[17]

4-A. Explain the benefits of buying a franchise.

Franchisees also derive a great deal of satisfaction from their work. According to a recent Gallup survey of franchise owners, 82 percent of franchisees said they were "somewhat satisfied" to "very satisfied" with their work. Plus, 75 percent said they would purchase their franchises again if given the opportunity (compared to just 39 percent of Americans who say they would choose the same job or business again).[18] Another survey reported that 94 percent of franchise owners rated their operations as "very successful" or "successful."[19]

Before jumping at a franchise opportunity, an entrepreneur should consider carefully the question "What can a franchise do for me that I cannot do for myself?" The answer to the question will depend on the particular situation and is just as important as the systematic evaluation of an individual franchise opportunity. After careful deliberation, a franchisee may conclude that the franchise offers nothing that she could not do independently; on the other hand, it may turn out that the franchise is the key to success as a business owner. Franchisees often cite the following advantages.

MANAGEMENT TRAINING AND SUPPORT. Recall from Chapter 1 that the leading cause of business failure is incompetent management. Franchisers are well aware of this and, in an attempt to reduce the number of franchise casualties, offer managerial training programs to franchisees prior to opening a new outlet. Many franchisers, especially the well-established ones, also provide follow-up training and counseling services. This service is vital since most franchisers do not require a franchisee to have experience in the business. These programs teach franchisees the details they need to know for day-to-day operations as well as the nuances of running their businesses successfully.

Training programs often involve both classroom and on-site instruction to teach franchisees the basic operations of the business. Before beginning operations, McDonald's franchisees spend 14 days in Illinois at Hamburger University where they learn everything from how to scrape the grill correctly to "how to manage a $1.6 million business."[20] MAACO franchisees spend four weeks at the company's headquarters delving into a five-volume set of operations manuals and learning to run an auto services shop. H & R Block trains its franchisees to unravel the mysteries of tax preparation, while Dunkin' Donuts trains a franchisee for as long as five weeks in everything from accounting to doughnut-making.

To ensure franchisees' continued success, many franchisers supplement their startup training programs with ongoing instruction and support. For instance, Ponderosa Steak House provides continuing support to franchisees in customer service, quality control, and general restaurant management. Franchisers offer these training programs because they realize that their ultimate success depends on the franchisee's success.

Despite the positive features of training, inherent dangers exist in the trainer/trainee relationship. Every would-be franchisee should be aware that, in some cases, "assistance" from the franchiser tends to drift into "control" over the franchisee's business. Also, some franchisers charge fees for their training services, so the franchisee should know exactly what she is agreeing to, and what it costs.

BRAND-NAME APPEAL. A licensed franchisee purchases the right to use a nationally known and advertised brand name for a product or service. Thus, the franchisee has the advantage of identifying his business with a widely recognized name, which usually provides a great deal of drawing power. Customers recognize the identifying trademark, the standard symbols, the store design, and the products of an established franchise. Indeed, one of franchising's basic tenets is cloning the franchiser's success. For example, nearly everyone is familiar with the golden arches of McDonald's or the red roof of the Red Roof Inn and the standard products and quality offered at each. A customer is confident that the quality and content of a meal at McDonald's in Fort Lauderdale will be consistent with a meal at a San Francisco McDonald's. One franchising expert explains, "The day you open a McDonald's franchise, you have instant customers. If you choose to open [an independent] hamburger restaurant, . . . you'd have to spend a fortune on advertising and promotion before you'd attract customers."[21]

STANDARDIZED QUALITY OF GOODS AND SERVICES. Because a franchisee purchases a license to sell the franchiser's product or service and the privilege of using the associated brand name, the quality of the goods or service sold determines the franchiser's reputation. Building a sound reputation in business is not achieved quickly, although destroying a good reputation takes no time at all. If some franchisees were allowed to operate at substandard levels, the entire chain's image would suffer irreparable damage; therefore, franchisers normally demand compliance with uniform standards of quality and service throughout the entire chain. In many cases, the franchiser conducts periodic inspections of local facilities to assist in maintaining acceptable levels of performance. Maintaining quality is so important that most franchisers retain the right to terminate the franchise contract and to repurchase the outlet if the franchisee fails to comply with established standards.

NATIONAL ADVERTISING PROGRAMS. An effective advertising program is essential to the success of virtually all franchise operations. Marketing a brand-name product or service over a wide geographic area requires a far-reaching advertising campaign. A regional or national advertising program benefits all franchisees. Normally, such an advertising campaign is organized and controlled by the franchiser. It is financed by each franchisee's percentage of monthly sales contribution, usually 1 to 5 percent, or a flat monthly fee. For example, Kentucky Fried Chicken franchisees must pay 1.5 percent of gross revenues to the KFC national advertising program. These funds are pooled and used for a cooperative advertising program, which has more impact than if the franchisees spent the same amount of money separately. "The name recognition that comes from this coordinated effort has a tremendously positive impact on each store," says one franchisee of his franchiser's advertising campaign.[22]

Many franchisers also require franchisees to spend a minimum amount on local advertising. To supplement their national advertising efforts, both Wendy's and Burger King require franchisees to spend at least 3 percent of gross sales on local advertising. Some franchisers assist each franchisee in designing and producing its local ads. Many companies help franchisees create promotional plans and provide press releases and advertisements for grand openings.

FINANCIAL ASSISTANCE. Because they rely on their franchisees' money to grow their businesses, franchisers typically do not provide any extensive financial help for franchisees. Franchisers rarely make loans to enable franchisees to pay the initial franchise fee. However, once franchisers locate a suitable prospective franchisee, they may offer the qualified candidate direct financial assistance in specific areas, such as purchasing equipment, inventory, or even the franchise fee. Since the startup costs of some franchises are already at breathtaking levels, some franchisers find that they must offer direct financial assistance.

For example, US Franchise Systems, franchiser of Microtel Inn and Hawthorn Suites hotels, has set up a subsidiary, US Funding Corporation, which makes available to its franchisees $200 million in construction and mortgage financing. Not only has the in-house financing program cut the time required to open a new hotel franchise, but it also has accelerated the franchise's growth rate.[23]

US Franchise Systems

Nearly half of the International Franchise Association's members indicate that they offer some type of financial assistance to their franchises; however, only one-fourth offer direct financial assistance. In most instances, financial assistance takes a form other than direct loans, leases, or short-term credit.

Franchisers usually are willing to assist the qualified franchisee in establishing relationships with banks, private investors, and other sources of funds. Such relationships can be critical since, according to one financing expert, "The market for franchise financing is capital starved."[24]

Brakes, ETC

Dan Rhode, founder of Brakes ETC., helps qualified franchisees locate likely lenders if they have trouble coming up with the $219,000 startup money. "We make a presentation to the bank as though the bank itself were buying the franchise," says Rhode.[25] Such support from the franchiser may enhance the franchisee's credit standing because lenders recognize the lower failure rate among established franchises.

PROVEN PRODUCTS AND BUSINESS FORMATS. What a franchisee essentially is purchasing is the franchiser's experience, expertise, and products. A franchise owner does not have to build the business from scratch. Instead of being forced to rely solely on personal ability to establish a business and attract a clientele, the franchisee can depend on the methods and techniques of an established business. These standardized procedures and operations greatly enhance the franchisee's chances of success and avoid the most inefficient type of learning—trial and error.

With a franchise, a franchisee does not have to struggle for recognition in the local marketplace as much as an independent owner might.

West Coast Video

Kenneth Gabler's independent video rental store had the largest share of the local market when his landlord leased space in the same shopping center to a nationally known video franchise, West Coast Video. When he discovered that the unit was company owned, Gabler offered to buy it. "I figured that if I stayed an independent and tried to compete, West Coast would take away 30 percent of my business anyway. So it was cheaper for me to pay the $15,000 initial fee and a 7 percent royalty every month," he says. West Coast Video's broader tape selection, marketing techniques, and recognized name "have helped tremendously," according to Gabler. Since he converted his business to a franchise, Gabler's sales have tripled!

CENTRALIZED BUYING POWER. A significant advantage a franchisee has over an independent small business owner is participation in the franchiser's centralized and large-volume buying power. If franchisers sell goods and materials to franchisees, they may pass on to franchisees any cost savings from quantity discounts they earn by buying in volume. For example, it is unlikely that a small, independent ice-cream parlor could match the buying power of Baskin-Robbins with its 3,000-plus retail ice-cream stores. In many instances, economies of scale simply preclude the independent owner from competing head-to-head with a franchise operation.

TERRITORIAL PROTECTION. A proper location is critical to the success of any small business, and franchises are no exception. In fact, franchise experts consider the three most important factors in franchising to be *location, location,* and *location.* Becoming affiliated with a franchiser may be the best way to get into prime locations. Many franchisers will make an extensive location analysis for each new outlet, including researching traffic patterns, zoning ordinances, accessibility, and population density. McDonald's, for example, is well known for its ability to obtain prime locations in high-traffic areas.

Some franchisers offer franchisees territorial protection, which gives existing franchisees the right to exclusive distribution of brand-name goods or services within a particular geographic area. A clause establishing such a protective zone that bars other outlets from the same franchise gives franchisees significant protection and security. The size of a franchisee's territory varies from industry to industry. For example, one national fast-food restaurant agrees not to license another franchisee within 1.5 miles of existing locations. But one soft-serve ice cream franchiser defines its franchisees' territories on the basis of Zip code designations. The purpose of such protection is to prevent an invasion of the existing franchisee's territory and the accompanying dilution of sales.

GREATER CHANCE FOR SUCCESS. Investing in a franchise is not risk free. Between 200 and 300 new franchise companies enter the market each year, and not all of them survive. But available statistics suggest that franchising is less risky than building a business from the ground up. One expert says that "becoming a franchisee can be the safest way to scratch the entrepreneurial itch."[26] Approximately 24 percent of new businesses fail by the second year of operation; in contrast, only about 7 percent of all franchises will fail by the second year. After six years, 84 percent of franchises are still in business compared to just 63 percent of independent businesses. This impressive success rate for franchises is attributed to the broad range of services, assistance, and guidelines the franchiser provides. These statistics must be interpreted carefully, however, because when a franchise is in danger of failing, the franchiser often repurchases or relocates the outlet and does not report it as a failure. As a result, some franchisers boast of never experiencing a failure.

The risk of purchasing a franchise is two-pronged: Success—or failure—depends on the entrepreneur's managerial skills and motivation and on the franchiser's business experience and system. Many owners are convinced that franchising has been a crucial part of their success. Says one franchiser, "It's the opportunity to be in business for yourself but not by yourself."[27]

The Drawbacks of Buying a Franchise

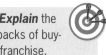

4-B. Explain the drawbacks of buying a franchise.

Obviously, the benefits of franchising can mean the difference between success and failure for a small business. However, the franchisee must sacrifice some freedom to the franchiser. The prospective franchisee must explore other limitations of franchising before undertaking this form of ownership.

FRANCHISE FEES AND PROFIT SHARING. Virtually all franchisers impose some type of fees and demand a share of the franchisee's sales revenues in return for the use of the franchiser's name, products or services, and business system. The fees and the initial capital requirements vary among the different franchisers. The Commerce Department reports that total investments for franchises range from $1,000 for business services up to $10 million for hotel and motel franchises. For example, H & R Block requires a capital investment of $2,000 to $3,000; I Can't Believe It's Yogurt requires $55,000 to $60,000 in equity capital; and McDonald's requires an investment of $350,000 to $450,000 (but McDonald's owns the land and the building).

Startup costs for franchises often include numerous additional fees. Most franchises impose a franchise fee up front for the right to use the company name. Wendy's International, for example, charges a $20,000 technical assistance fee for each restaurant a franchisee opens. Other additional startup costs might include site purchase and preparation, construction, signs, fixtures, equipment, management assistance, and training. Some franchise fees include these costs, while others do not. Before signing any contract, a prospective franchisee should determine the total cost of a franchise. For example, Table 3.2 on page 84 shows the estimated startup costs for a 100-room, two-story hotel.

Franchisers also impose continuing royalty fees as profit-sharing devices. The royalty usually involves a percentage of gross sales with a required minimum, or a flat fee levied on the franchise. Royalty fees typically range from 1 percent to 11 percent and can increase the franchisee's overhead expenses significantly. Because the franchiser's royalties and fees are calculated as a percentage of a franchisee's sales, they get paid—even if the franchisee fails to earn a profit. Sometimes unprepared franchisees discover (too late) that the franchiser's royalties and fees are about what the normal profit margin is for a franchise. To avoid such problems, a prospective franchisee should find out which fees are required (some are merely recommended) and then determine what services and benefits the fees cover. One of the best ways to do this is to itemize what you are getting for your money, and then determine whether the cost corresponds to the benefits provided. Be sure to get the details on all expenses—amount, time of payment, and financing arrangements; find out which items, if any, are included in the initial franchise fee and which ones are "extra."

Item	Amount	Payment
Initial franchise application fee (varies with contract term)	$10,000–$30,000	Lump Sum due with application
Building	$3,000,000–$4,500,000	As required by third parties
Furniture, fixtures, and equipment	$800,000–$1,050,000	As required by suppliers
Opening inventory	$100,000–$200,000	As required by suppliers
Working capital	$75,000–$200,000	—
Freestanding sign	$24,000–$45,000	As supplied by suppliers
Training expense	$15,500–$22,500	Lump sum due prior to attending
Property management and multimedia	$24,500–$32,500	Lump-sum cost at shipment
Holidex reservation system	$14,100–$22,300	Lump-sum cost at shipment
Total	$4,076,000–$6,088,800 + real estate, licesnses and permits, and professional fees	

STRICT ADHERENCE TO STANDARDIZED OPERATIONS. Although the franchisee owns the business, she does not have the autonomy of an independent owner. To protect its public image, the franchiser requires that the franchisee maintain certain operating standards. If a franchise constantly fails to meet the minimum standards established for the business, the franchiser may terminate its license. Determining compliance with standards is usually accomplished by periodic inspections. At times, strict adherence to franchise standards may become a burden to the franchisee. The owner may believe that the written reports the franchiser demands require an excessive amount of time. In other instances, the owner may be required to enforce specific rules she believes are inappropriate or unfair.

RESTRICTIONS ON PURCHASING. In the interest of maintaining quality standards, franchisees may be required to purchase products, special equipment, or other items from the franchiser or from an approved supplier. For example, Kentucky Fried Chicken requires that franchisees use only seasonings blended by a particular company because a poor image could result from franchisees using inferior products to cut costs. Under some conditions, such purchase arrangements may be challenged in court as a violation of antitrust laws, but generally the franchiser has a legal right to see that franchisees maintain acceptable quality standards. Franchisees at several chains have filed antitrust suits alleging that franchisers overcharge their outlets for supplies and equipment and eliminate competition by failing to approve alternative suppliers.[28] Generally, a franchiser may set the prices paid for the products it sells but may not establish the retail prices to be charged on products sold by the franchisee. A franchiser legally can suggest retail prices but cannot force the franchisee to abide by them.

LIMITED PRODUCT LINE. In most cases, the franchise agreement stipulates that the franchise can sell only those products approved by the franchiser. Unless willing to risk license cancellation, a franchisee must avoid selling any unapproved products through the franchise.

A franchise may be required to carry an unpopular product or be prevented from introducing a desirable one by the franchise agreement. A franchisee's freedom to adapt a product line to local market conditions is restricted. But some franchisers solicit product suggestions from their franchisees.

In fact, a McDonald's franchisee, Herb Peterson, created the highly successful Egg McMuffin while experimenting with a Teflon-coated egg ring that gave fried eggs rounded corners and a poached appearance. Peterson put his round eggs on English muffins, adorned them with Canadian bacon and melted cheese, and showed his creation to McDonald's chief, Ray Kroc. Kroc devoured two of them and was sold on the idea when Peterson's wife suggested the catchy name. In 1975, McDonald's became the first fast-food franchise to open its doors for breakfast, and the Egg McMuffin became a staple on the breakfast menu." [29]

McDonald's

UNSATISFACTORY TRAINING PROGRAMS. Every would-be franchisee must be wary of the unscrupulous franchiser who promises extensive services, advice, and assistance but delivers nothing. For example, one owner relied on the franchiser to provide what had been described as an "extensive, rigorous training program" after paying a handsome technical assistance fee. The program was nothing but a set of pamphlets and do-it-yourself study guides. Other examples include those impatient entrepreneurs who paid initial franchise fees without investigating the business and never heard from the franchiser again. Although disclosure rules have reduced the severity of the problem, dishonest characters still thrive on unprepared prospective franchisees.

MARKET SATURATION. As the owners of many fast-food and yogurt and ice-cream franchises have discovered, market saturation is a very real danger. Although some franchisers offer franchisees territorial protection, others do not. Territorial encroachment has become a hotly contested issue in franchising as growth-seeking franchisers have exhausted most of the prime locations and are now setting up new franchises in close proximity to existing ones. In some areas of the country, franchisees are upset, claiming that their markets are oversaturated and their sales are suffering.

LESS FREEDOM. When a franchisee signs a contract, he agrees to sell the franchiser's product or service by following its prescribed formula. When McDonald's rolls out a new national product, for instance, all franchisees put it on their menus. Franchisers want to ensure success, and most monitor their franchisees' performances closely. Strict uniformity is the rule rather than the exception. "There is no independence. Successful franchisees are happy prisoners," says one writer.[30] Entrepreneurs who want to be their own bosses may be disappointed with a franchise. Highly independent, "go-my-own-way" individuals probably should *not* choose the franchise route to business ownership. Table 3.3 offers a quiz to help you determine whether or not you have what it takes to be a franchisee.

Of those people who set out to buy a franchise, only 15 percent actually buy one. Some of that 15 percent make the wrong decision. They discover too late that they are not cut out to be franchisees. Do you have what it takes to be a successful franchisee? The following quiz will help you determine your "franchise quotient."

1. You own a company. How much operational detail are you comfortable with?
   a. I want direct control over all operations.
   b. I delegate less than half.
   c. I delegate more than half.

2. You have three job offers with comparable salary and benefits. Choose one.
   a. Small company but high management responsibility and exposure.
   b. Mid-sized company with less personal exposure but more prestigious name.
   c. Large company with least personal exposure but very well-known name.

Continued

Table 3.3

What Is Your Franchise Quotient?

Sources: Adapted from Erika Kotite, "Is Franchising for You?" *Franchise & Business Opportunities* 1995, pp. 14-18; Heather Page, "True Confessions," *Entrepreneur*, January 1996, pp. 184-186; Franchise Solutions.

Table 3.3
**What Is Your Franchise
Quotient?
Continued**

3. You reach a major stumbling block on a project. You:

  a. Seek help from others immediately.

  b. Think it through and then present possible solutions to your superior.

  c. Keep working until you resolve it on your own.

4. Which investment sounds most appealing?

  a. Five percent fixed return over a period of time.

  b. From -20 percent to +50 percent loss or return over a period of time, depending on changing economic situations.

5. Which business arrangement is most appealing?

  a. You're the sole owner.

  b. You're in a partnership and own a majority of the stock.

  c. You're in an equal partnership.

6. Your company's sales technique increases sales 10 percent per year. You used a technique elsewhere you feel will result in 15 percent to 20 percent annual increases, but it requires extra time and capital. You:

  a. Avoid the risk and stay with the present plan.

  b. Suggest your new method, showing previous results.

  c. Privately use your system, and show the results later.

7. You suggest your system to your boss, and he says, "Don't rock the boat." You:

  a. Drop your different approach.

  b. Approach your boss at a later time.

  c. Go to your boss's boss with your suggestion.

  d. Use your own system anyway.

8. Which would mean the most to you?

  a. Becoming the president of a company.

  b. Becoming the highest-paid employee of a company.

  c. Winning the highest award for achievement in your profession.

9. What three activities do you find most appealing?

  a. Sales and marketing.

  b. Administration.

  c. Payroll.

  d. Training.

  e. Customer service.

  f. Credit and collections.

  g. Management.

10. What work pace do you generally prefer?

  a. Working on one project until it is completed.

  b. Working on several projects at one time.

Scoring: 1. a=5, b=3, c=1; 2. a=3, b=2, c=1; 3. a=1, b=5, c=7; 4. a=2, b=6;
5. a=7, b=5, c=2; 6. a=1, b=6, c=10; 7. a=1, b=5, c=8, d=10; 8. a=8, b=2, c=5;
9. a=10, b=1, c=3, d=3, e=8, f=2, g=5; 10. a=3, b=6.

Total Score:

20–33   You're a corporate player and are happiest in a structured environment. Franchising suits you.

34–71   You're a potentially good franchisee.

72–85   You're an entrepreneur who prefers total independence.

Franchising and the Law

5. Understand the laws covering franchise purchases

The franchising boom spearheaded by McDonald's in the late 1950s brought with it many prime investment opportunities. However, the explosion of legitimate franchises also ushered in with it several fly-by-night franchisers who defrauded their franchisees. In response to these specific incidents and to the potential for deception inherent in a franchise relationship, California in 1971 enacted the first Franchise Investment Law. The law (and those of sixteen other states which have since passed similar laws) requires franchisers to register a Uniform Franchise Offering Circular (UFOC) and deliver a copy to prospective franchisees before any offer or sale of a franchise. The UFOC establishes full-disclosure guidelines for the franchising company.

In October 1979, the Federal Trade Commission (FTC) enacted the Trade Regulation Rule, requiring all franchisers to disclose detailed information on their operations at the first personal meeting or at least ten days before a franchise contract is signed, or before any money is paid. The FTC rule covers all franchisers, even those in the 33 states lacking franchise disclosure laws. The purpose of the regulation is to assist the potential franchisee's investigation of the franchise deal and to introduce consistency into the franchiser's disclosure statements. In 1994, the FTC modified the requirements for the UFOC, making more information available to prospective franchisees and making the document shorter and easier to read and understand. The FTC's philosophy is not so much to prosecute abusers as to provide information to prospective franchisees and help them to make intelligent decisions. Although the FTC requires each franchiser to provide a potential franchisee with this information, it does not verify its accuracy. Prospective franchisees should use these data only as a starting point for the investigation. The Trade Regulation Rule requires a franchiser to include 23 major topics in its disclosure statement:

1. Information identifying the franchiser and its affiliates, and describing their business experience and the franchises being sold.

2 Information identifying and describing the business experience of each of the franchiser's officers, directors, and management personnel responsible for the franchise program.

3. A description of the lawsuits in which the franchiser and its officers, directors, and managers have been involved.

4. Information about any bankruptcies in which the franchiser and its officers, directors, and managers have been involved.

5. Information about the initial franchise fee and other payments required to obtain the franchise, including the intended use of the fees.

6. A description of any other continuing payments franchisees are required to make after startup, including royalties, service fees, training fees, lease payments, advertising charges, and others.

7. A detailed description of the payments a franchisee must make to fulfill the initial investment requirement and how and to whom they are made. The categories covered are initial franchise fee, equipment, opening inventory, initial advertising fee, signs, training, real estate, working capital, legal, accounting and utilities.

8. Information about quality restrictions on goods and services used in the franchise and where they may be purchased, including restricted purchases from the franchises.

9. Information covering requirements to purchase goods, services, equipment, supplies, inventory, and other items from approved suppliers (including the franchiser).

10. A description of any financial assistance available from the franchiser in the purchase of the franchise.

11. A description of all obligations the franchiser must fulfill in helping a franchisee prepare to open,and operate a unit, plus information covering location selection methods and the training program provided to franchisees.

12. A description of any territorial protection that will be granted to the franchise and a statement as to whether the franchiser may locate a company-owned store or other outlet in that territory.

13. All relevant information about the franchiser's trademarks, service marks, trade names, logos, and commercial symbols, including where they are registered.

14. Similar information on any patents and copyrights the franchiser owns, and the rights to these transferred to franchisees.

15. A description of the extent to which franchisees must participate personally in the operation of the franchise.

16. A description of any restrictions on the goods or services franchises are permitted to sell and with whom franchisees may deal.

17. A description of the conditions under which the franchise may be repurchased or refused renewal by the franchiser, transferred to a third party by the franchisee, and terminated or modified by either party.

18. A description of the involvement of celebrities and public figures in the franchise.

19. A complete statement of the basis for any earnings claims made to the franchisee, including the percentage of existing franchises that have actually achieved the results that are claimed. New rules put two requirements on franchisers making earnings claims: (a) Any earnings claim must be included in the UFOC, and (b) the claim must "have a reasonable basis at the time it is made." However, franchisers are *not* required to make any earnings claims at all; in fact, 86 percent of franchisers don't make earnings claims in their circulars, primarily because of liability concerns about committing such numbers to paper.[31]

20. Statistical information about the present number of franchises; the number of franchises projected for the future; the number of franchises terminated; the number the franchiser has not renewed; the number repurchased in the past; and a list of the names and addresses of other franchises.

21. The financial statements of the franchisers.

22. A copy of all franchise and other contracts (leases, purchase agreements, etc.) the franchisee will be required to sign.

23. A standardized, detachable "receipt" to prove that the prospective franchisee received a copy of the UFOC.[32]

The information contained in the UFOC does not fully protect a potential franchisee from deception, nor does it guarantee success. It does, however, provide enough information to begin a thorough investigation of the franchiser and the franchise deal.

6. Discuss the right way to buy a franchise

How to Buy a Franchise

The UFOC is a powerful tool designed to help would-be franchisers avoid dishonest franchisers. The best defenses a prospective entrepreneur has against unscrupulous franchisers are preparation, common sense, and patience. By investigating thoroughly before investing in a franchise, a potential franchisee eliminates the risk of being hoodwinked into a nonexistent business. Asking the right questions and resisting the urge to rush into an investment decision helps a potential franchisee avoid being taken.

The president of a franchise consulting firm estimates that 5 to 10 percent of franchisers are dishonest,"the rogue elephants of franchising." Potential franchisees must beware. Because dishonest franchisers tend to follow certain patterns, well-prepared franchisees can avoid trouble. The following clues should arouse the suspicion of an entrepreneur about to invest in a franchise:

☆ Claims that the franchise contract is a standard one and that "you don't need to read it."

☆ A franchiser that fails to give you a copy of the required disclosure document at your first face-to-face meeting.

- ☆ A marginally successful prototype store or no prototype at all.
- ☆ A poorly prepared operations manual outlining the franchise system or no manual (or system) at all.
- ☆ Oral promises of future earnings without written documentation.
- ☆ A high-franchisee turnover rate or a high-termination rate.
- ☆ An unusual amount of litigation brought against the franchiser.
- ☆ Attempts to discourage you from allowing an attorney to evaluate the franchise contract before you sign it.
- ☆ No written documentation to support claims and promises.
- ☆ A high-pressure sale—sign the contract now or lose the opportunity.
- ☆ Claiming to be exempt from federal laws requiring complete disclosure of franchise details.
- ☆ "Get-rich-quick schemes," promises of huge profits with only minimum effort.
- ☆ Reluctance to provide a list of present franchisees for you to interview.
- ☆ Evasive, vague answers to your questions about the franchise and its operation.

Not every franchise "horror story" is the result of dishonest franchisers. More often than not, the problems that arise in franchising have more to do with franchisees who buy legitimate franchises without proper research and analysis. They end up in businesses they don't enjoy and that they are not well suited to operate. How can you avoid this mistake? The following steps will help you make the right choice.

EVALUATE YOURSELF. Before looking at any franchise, an entrepreneur should study her own traits, goals, experience, likes, dislikes, risk orientation, income requirements, time and family commitments, and other characteristics. Will you be comfortable working in a structured environment? What kinds of franchises fit your desired lifestyle? Knowing what you enjoy doing (and what you don't want to do) will help you narrow your search. The goal is to find the franchise that is right for you!

RESEARCH YOUR MARKET. Before shopping for a franchise, research the market in the area you plan to serve. How fast is the overall area growing? In which areas is that growth occurring fastest? Investing some time at the library developing a profile of the customers in your target area is essential; otherwise, you will be flying blind. Who are your potential customers? What are their characteristics? Their income and education levels? What kinds of products and services do they buy? What gaps exist in the market? These gaps represent potential franchise opportunities for you.

CONSIDER YOUR FRANCHISE OPTIONS. The International Franchise Association publishes the Franchise Opportunities Guide, which lists its members and some basic information about them. Many cities host franchise trade shows throughout the year, where hundreds of franchisers gather to sell their franchises. The Franchising and Licensing World Center in Chicago is a year-round showcase of franchise opportunities. Many business magazines such as *Entrepreneur, Inc., Business Start-Ups, Success,* and others devote at least one issue to franchising, where they often lists hundreds of franchises. These guides can help you find a suitable franchise within your price range.

GET A COPY OF THE FRANCHISER'S UFOC. Once you narrow down your franchise choices, you should contact each franchise and get a copy of its UFOC. Then read it! This document is an important tool in your search for the right franchise, and you should make the most of it. Not only does the UFOC cover the 23 items discussed in the previous section, but it also includes a copy of the company's franchise agreement and any contracts accompanying it. It is best to have an attorney experienced in franchising review the UFOC and discuss it with you. The franchise contract summarizes the details that will govern the franchiser-franchisee relationship over its life. It outlines *exactly* the rights and the obligations of each party and sets the guidelines which govern the franchise relationship. Still, a recent study by the FTC suggests that 40 percent of new franchisees sign contracts without reading them![33] Franchise contracts typically are long term; 50 percent run for 15 years or more, so it is extremely important for prospective franchisees to understand their terms before they sign a contract.

TALK TO EXISTING FRANCHISEES. One of the best ways to evaluate the reputation of a franchiser is to interview (in person) several franchise owners who have been in business at least one year about the positive and the negative features of the agreement and whether or not the franchiser delivered what was promised. Knowing what they know now, would they buy the franchise again? It also helps to interview past franchisees to get their perspectives on the franchiser-franchisee relationship. Why did they leave? Franchisees of some companies have formed associations, which might provide prospective franchisees with valuable information. Other sources of information include the American Association of Franchisees and Dealers, the American Franchise Association, and the International Franchise Association.

ASK THE FRANCHISER SOME TOUGH QUESTIONS. Take the time to ask the franchiser questions about the company and its relationship with its franchisees. You will be in this relationship a long time (half of all franchise contracts run for 15 years or more), and you need to know as much about it as you possibly can beforehand. What is its philosophy concerning the relationship? What is the company culture like? How much input do franchisees have into the system? What are the franchise's future expansion plans? How will they affect your franchise? What kind of profits can you expect? (If the franchiser made no earnings claims in item 19 of the UFOC, why not?) Does the franchiser have a well-formulated strategic plan?

MAKE YOUR CHOICE. The first lesson in franchising is "Do your homework *before* you get out your checkbook." Once you have done your research, you can make an informed choice about which franchise is right for you. Then it is time to put together a solid business plan that will serve as your road map to success in the franchise you have selected. The plan is also a valuable tool to use as you arrange the financing for your franchise. We will discuss the components of a business plan in Chapter 9.

Table 3.4 offers a checklist of questions a potential franchisee should ask before entering into any franchise agreement.

Table 3.4
A Franchise Evaluation Checklist

The Franchiser and the Franchise
1. Is the potential market for the product or service adequate to support your franchise? Will the prices you charge be in line with the market?
2. Is the market's population growing, remaining static, or shrinking? Is the demand for your product or service growing, remaining static, or shrinking?
3. Is the product or service safe and reputable?
4. Is the product or service a fad, or is it a durable business idea?
5. What will the competition, direct or indirect, be in your sales territory? Do any other franchisees operate in this general area?
6. Is the franchise international, national, regional, or local in scope? Does it involve full-time or part-time involvement?
7. How many years has the franchiser been in operation? Does it have a sound reputation for honest dealings with franchisees?

8. How many franchise outlets now exist? How many will there be a year from now? How many outlets are company owned?

9. How many franchises have failed? Why?

10. What service and assistance will the franchiser provide? Training programs? Continuous in nature?

11. Will the franchiser perform a location analysis to help you find a suitable site?

12. Will the franchiser offer you exclusive distribution rights for the length of the agreement, or may it sell to other franchises in this area?

13. What facilities and equipment are required for the franchise? Who pays for construction? Is there a lease agreement?

14. What is the total cost of the franchise? What are the initial capital requirements? Will the franchiser provide financial assistance? Of what nature? What is the interest rate? Is the franchiser financially sound enough to fulfill all its promises?

15. How much is the franchise fee? Exactly what does it cover? Are there any continuing fees? What additional fees are there?

16. Does the franchiser provide an estimate of expenses and income? Are they reasonable for your particular area? Are they sufficiently documented?

17. How risky is the franchise opportunity? Is the return on the investment consistent with the risks?

18. Does the franchiser offer a written contract which covers all the details of the agreement? Have your attorney and your accountant studied its terms and approved it? Do you understand the implications of the contract?

19. What is the length of the franchise agreement? Under what circumstances can it be terminated? If you terminate the contract, what are the costs to you? What are the terms and costs of renewal?

20. Are you allowed to sell the franchise to a third party? If so, will you receive the proceeds?

21. Is there a national advertising program? How is it financed? What media are used? What help is provided for local advertising?

22. Once you open for business, *exactly* what support will the franchiser offer you?

23. How does the franchise handle complaints from and disputes with franchisees? How well has the system worked?

The Franchisees

1. Are you pleased with your investment in this franchise?

2. Has the franchiser lived up to its promises?

3. What was your greatest disappointment after getting into this business?

4. How effective was the training you received in helping you to run the franchise?

5. What are your biggest challenges and problems?

6. What is your franchise's cash flow like?

7. How much money are you making on your investment?

8. What do you like most about being a franchisee? Least?

9. Is there a franchisee advisory council that represents franchisees?

10. Knowing what you know now, would you buy this franchise again?

Yourself

1. Are you qualified to operate a franchise successfully? Do you have adequate drive, skills, experience, education, patience, and financial capacity? Are you prepared to work hard?

2. Are you willing to sacrifice some autonomy in operating a business to own a franchise?

3. Can you tolerate the financial risk?

Continued

Table 3.4

**A Franchise Evaluation
Checklist,
Continued**

4. Are you genuinely interested in the product or service you will be selling? Do you enjoy this kind of business?

5. Will the business generate enough profit to suit you?

6. Has the franchiser investigated your background thoroughly enough to decide if you are qualified to operate the franchise?

7. What can this franchiser do for you that you cannot do for yourself?

YOU BE THE CONSULTANT...

The Opportunity of a Lifetime

"Honey, I think I've found it!" said Joe Willingham to his wife Allie. "This is just what I've been looking for, and just in time, too. My severance package from the company runs out next month. The man said that if we invested in this franchise now, we could be bringing in good money by then. It's that easy!"

Allie knew that Joe had been working hard at finding another job since he had been a victim of his company's latest downsizing, but jobs were scarce even for someone with his managerial experience and background in manufacturing. "Nobody wants to hire a 51-year-old man with experience when they can hire 23-year-old college graduates at less than half the salary and teach them what they need to know," Joe told her after months of fruitless job hunting. That's when Joe got the idea of setting up his own business. Rather than start an independent business from scratch, Joe felt more comfortable, given his 26-year corporate career, opening a franchise. "A franchiser can give me the support I need," he told Allie.

"Tell me about this franchise," Allie said.

"It's a phenomenal opportunity for us," Joe said, barely able to contain his excitement. "I saw this booth for American Speedy Print at the Business Expo this morning. There were all kinds of franchises there, but this one really caught my eye," Joe said as he pulled a rather plain-looking photocopy of a brochure from his briefcase.

"Is that their brochure?" asked Allie.

"Well, the company is growing so fast that they have temporarily run out of their normal literature. This is just temporary."

"Oh . . . You would think that a printing franchise could print flashier brochures even on short notice, but I guess . . .," said Allie.

"The main thing is the profit potential this business has," said Joe. "I met one of their franchisees. I tell you the guy was wearing a $2,000 suit if ever there was one, and he had expensive jewelry dripping from his fingers. He's making a mint with this franchise, and he said we could too!"

Joe continued, "With the severance package I have from the company, we could pay the $10,000 franchise fee and

lease most of the equipment we need to get started. It'll take every penny of my package, but, hey, it's an investment in our future. The representative said the company would help us with our grand opening, and would help us compile a list of potential customers."

"What would you print?" asked Allie.

"Anything!" said Joe. "The franchisee I talked to does fliers, posters, booklets, newsletters, advertising pieces . . . you name it!"

"Wow! It seems like you'd need lots of specialized equipment to do all of that. How much does the total franchise package cost?" asked Allie.

"Well, I'm not exactly sure. He never gave me an exact figure, but we can lease all the equipment we need from the franchiser!"

"Is this all of the material they gave you? I thought franchisers were supposed to have some kind of information packet to give to people," said Allie.

"Yeah, I asked him about that," said Joe. "He said that American Speedy Print is just a small franchise. They'd rather put their money into building a business and helping their franchisees succeed than into useless paperwork that nobody reads anyway. It makes sense to me."

"I guess . . .," Allie said reluctantly.

"I think we need to take this opportunity, hon," Joe said, with a look that spoke of determination and enthusiasm. "Besides, he said that there was another couple in this county that is already looking at this franchise, and that the company will license only one franchisee in this area. They don't want to saturate the market. He thinks they may take it. I think we have to move on this now, or we'll lose the opportunity of a lifetime."

Allie had not seen Joe exhibit this much enthusiasm and excitement for anything since he had lost his job at the plant. Piles of rejection letters from his job search had sapped Joe's zest for living. Allie was glad to see "the old Joe" return, but she still had her doubts about the franchise opportunity Joe was describing.

"It might just be the opportunity of a lifetime, Joe," she said. "But don't you think we need to find out a little more about this franchise before we invest that much money? I mean . . ."

"Hon, I'd love to do that, but like the man said, we may miss out on the opportunity of a lifetime if we don't sign today. I think we've got to move on this thing now!"

1. What advice would you offer Joe about investing in this franchise?

2. Map out a plan for Joe to use in finding the right franchise for him. What can Joe do to protect himself from making a bad franchise investment?

3. Summarize the advantages and disadvantages Joe can expect if he buys a franchise.

Trends Shaping Franchising

7. Outline the major trends shaping franchising.

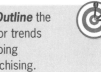

Franchising has experienced three major growth waves since its beginning. The first wave occurred in the early 1970s when fast-food restaurants used the concept to grow rapidly. The fast-food industry was one of the first to discover the power of franchising, but other businesses soon took notice and adapted the franchising concept to their industries. The second wave took place in the mid-1980s as our nation's economy shifted heavily toward the service sector. Franchises followed suit, springing up in every service business imaginable—from maid services and copy centers to mailing services and real estate. The third wave began in the early 1990s and continues today. It is characterized by new, low-cost franchises that focus on specific market niches. In the wake of major corporate downsizing and the burgeoning costs of traditional franchises, these new franchises allow would-be entrepreneurs to get into proven businesses faster and at lower costs. These companies feature startup costs in the $2,000 to $250,000 range and span a variety of industries—from leak detection in homes and auto detailing to day care and tile glazing. Other significant trends affecting franchising include the following:

INTERNATIONAL OPPORTUNITIES. One of the biggest trends in franchising is the internationalization of American franchise systems. Increasingly, franchising is becoming a major export industry for the United States. Over the past decade, a growing number of franchises were attracted to international markets to boost sales and profits. About 11 percent of U.S. franchisers have outlets in other countries, and another 28 percent expect to establish franchises abroad by 2000.[34] Canada is the primary market for U.S. franchisers, with Mexico, Japan, and Europe following (see Table 3.5). These markets are most attractive to franchisers because they are similar to the U.S. market with rising personal incomes, strong demand for consumer goods, growing service economies, and spreading urbanization.

Country	Total Value of Goods and Services Sold by U.S. Franchisers (in millions of $)
1. Canada	$40,749
2. Mexico	3,500
3. Japan	1,890
4. United Kingdom	975
5. Germany	900
6. Switzerland	870
7. Brazil	640
8. France	580
9. Singapore	440
10. Spain and Italy	350

Table 3.5
The Top International Franchise Markets

Source: International Trade Administration and the U.S. Department of Commerce.

Future growth is likely to occur in other countries as well. Because of its growing middle class, favorable economic trends, and a recent free trade agreement with the United States, Mexico will become a popular target for franchisers. The Pacific Rim is another area with high-growth potential.

Countries that recently have thrown off the chains of communism are turning to franchising to help them move toward a market economy. "Nothing better suits the startup of a free market economy than franchising," says a franchising attorney.[35] Some countries of Eastern Europe, including Hungary, Poland, and Yugoslavia, already have attracted franchises. Even Russia is fertile ground for franchising. McDonald's scored a hit with its 700-seat restaurant in Moscow. Despite being one of the largest McDonald's outlets in the world, "the waiting line winds along busy Pushkin Square for well over 500 yards," reports one Soviet magazine."[36] Franchisers in these countries must have patience, however. Lack of capital, archaic infrastructure, and a shortage of hard currencies mean that profits will be slow in coming. Despite such difficulties, the trend toward international franchising will continue.

SMALLER, NONTRADITIONAL LOCATIONS. As the high cost of building full-scale locations continues to climb, more franchisers are searching out nontraditional locations in which to build smaller, less expensive outlets. Based on the principle of **intercept marketing**, the idea is to put a franchise's products or services directly in the paths of potential customers, wherever that may be. Franchises are putting scaled-down outlets on college campuses, in sports arenas, in hospitals, on airline flights, and in zoos. Taco Bell has plans to put more than 200,000 carts and kiosks in convenience stores, gas stations, grocery stores, theaters, airports, and other retail locations by 2000.[37] Many franchisees have discovered that smaller outlets in these nontraditional locations generate nearly the same sales volume as full-sized outlets at just a fraction of the cost! Such locations will be a key to continued franchise growth in the domestic market.

CONVERSION FRANCHISING. The recent trend toward **conversion franchising**, where owners of independent businesses become franchisees to gain the advantage of name recognition, will continue. Approximately 40 percent of all franchisers now offer conversion franchises, up from just 10 percent in 1989.[38] "[Existing] business owners realize they need a competitive edge, and the best way to get it is by joining a franchise," says one expert.[39] The biggest force in conversion franchising has been Century 21, the real estate sales company.

MULTIPLE-UNIT FRANCHISING. **Multiple-unit franchising (MUF)** became extremely popular in the early 1990s. In multiple-unit franchising, a franchisee opens more than one unit in a broad territory within a specific time period. A recent survey shows that 54.7 percent of franchisers use multiple-unit franchising, up from just 17.9 percent in 1989.[40] "Multiple ownership of units by franchisees has exploded," says one franchise expert. "Twenty or 30 years ago, it would have been rare for any one franchisee to own 10 or 20 units. Now it's not uncommon . . . for one franchisee to own 60, 70, or even 200 units. Franchisers are finding it's far more efficient in the long run to have one well-trained franchisee operate a number of units than to train many franchisees."[41]

For franchisers, multiple-unit franchising is an efficient way to expand into either domestic or international markets quickly. Multiple-unit franchising is an extremely effective strategy for franchisers targeting foreign markets, where having a local representative who knows the territory is essential. For franchisees, multiple-unit franchising offers the opportunity for rapid growth without leaving the safety net of the franchise. Also, because franchisers usually offer discounts of about 25 percent off their standard fees on multiple units, franchisees can get fast-growing companies for a bargain.

---

intercept marketing—the principle of putting a franchise's products or services directly in the paths of potential customers, wherever they may be.

conversion franchising—a franchising trend in which owners of independent businesses become franchisees to gain the advantage of name recognition.

multiple-unit franchising—a method of franchising in which a franchisee opens more than one unit in a broad territory within a specific time period.

MASTER FRANCHISING. A **master franchise** (or **subfranchise**) gives a franchisee the right to create a semi-independent organization in a particular territory to recruit, sell, and support other franchisees. A master franchisee buys the right to develop subfranchises within a broad geographic area or, sometimes, within an entire country. Subfranchising "turbocharges" a franchiser's growth. Many franchisers use it to open outlets in international markets more quickly and efficiently because the master franchisees understand local laws and the nuances of selling in local markets.

For instance, a master franchisee with TCBY International, a yogurt franchise, has opened 21 stores in China and in Hong Kong. Based on his success in these markets, the company has sold him the master franchise in India.[42]

PIGGYBACKING (OR COMBINATION FRANCHISING). Some franchisers also are discovering new ways to reach customers by teaming up with other franchisers selling complementary products or services. A growing number of companies are **piggybacking** outlets—combining two or more distinct franchises under one roof. This "buddy system" approach works best when the two franchise ideas are compatible and appeal to similar customers. For example, ActionFax, a franchise that sells completely equipped fax booths, has found its way into many existing franchises, including print shops, drugstores, and convenience stores. "We fit in with many other preexisting franchises where the facility and manpower are already in place, and we offer an added-value service to customers," says one ActionFax executive.[43] At one location, a Texaco gasoline station, a Pizza Hut restaurant, and a Dunkin' Donuts—all owned by one franchisee—work together in a piggyback arrangement to draw customers.[44] Doughnut franchiser Dunkin' Donuts and ice-cream franchiser Baskin-Robbins are working together to build hundreds of combination outlets, a concept that has proved to be highly successful.[45] Properly planned, piggy-backed franchises can magnify many times over the sales and profits of individual, self-standing outlets.

master franchising—*a method of franchising that gives a franchisee the right to develop subfranchises within a broad geographic area or, sometimes, within an entire country.*

TCBY International

piggybacking—*a method of franchising in which two or more franchisers team up to sell complementary products or services under one roof.*

Conclusion

Franchising has proved its viability in the U.S. economy and has become a key part of the small business sector because it offers many would-be entrepreneurs the opportunity to own and operate a business with a greater chance for success. Despite its impressive growth rate to date, the franchising industry still has a great deal of room to grow. Describing the future of franchising, one expert says, "Franchising has not yet come close to reaching its full potential in the American marketplace."[46]

CHAPTER SUMMARY

1-A. Explain the advantages and the disadvantages of the sole proprietorship.
- A sole proprietorship is a business owned and managed by one individual and is the most popular form of ownership.
- Sole proprietorships offer these *advantages*: They are simple to create; they are the least costly form to begin; the owner has total decision-making authority; there are no special legal restrictions; and they are easy to discontinue.

- They also suffer from these *disadvantages*: unlimited personal liability of owner; limited managerial skills and capabilities; limited access to capital; lack of continuity.

1-B. Explain the advantages and the disadvantages of the partnership.
- A partnership is an association of two or more people who co-own a business for the purpose of making a profit. Partnerships offer these *advantages*: ease of establishing; complementary skills of partners; division of profits or losses; larger pool of capital available; abili-

ty to attract limited partners; little government regulation flexibility; and tax advantages.

- Partnerships suffer from these *disadvantages*: unlimited liability of at least one partner; difficulty in disposing of partnership interest; lack of continuity; potential for personality and authority conflicts; and partners bound by the law of agency.

1-C. Explain the advantages and the disadvantages of the corporation.

- A corporation, the most complex of the three basic forms of ownership, is a separate legal entity. To form a corporation, an entrepreneur must file the articles of incorporation with the state in which the company will incorporate. Corporations offer these *advantages*: limited liability of stockholders; ability to attract capital; ability to continue indefinitely; and transferable ownership.
- Corporations suffer from these *disadvantages*: cost and time involved in incorporating; double taxation; potential for diminished managerial incentives; legal requirements and regulatory red tape; and potential loss of control by the founder(s).

2. Discuss the advantages and the disadvantages of the S corporation, the limited liability company, the professional corporation, and the joint venture.

- Entrepreneurs can also choose from several other forms of ownership, including S corporations and limited liability companies. An S corporation offers its owners limited liability protection but avoids the double taxation of C corporations.
- A limited liability company, like an S corporation, is a cross between a partnership and a corporation, yet it operates without the restrictions imposed on an S corporation. To create an LLC, an entrepreneur must file the articles of organization and the operating agreement with the secretary of state.
- A professional corporation offers professionals the benefits of the corporate form of ownership.
- A joint venture is like a partnership except that it is formed for a specific purpose.

3. Describe the three types of franchising: tradename, product distribution, and pure.

- Trade-name franchising involves a franchisee purchasing the right to become affiliatedwith a franchiser's tradename without distributing its products exclusively.

- Product distribution franchising involves licensing a franchisee to sell products or services under the franchiser's brand name through a selective, limited distribution network.
- Pure franchising involves selling a franchisee a complete business format.

4. Explain the benefits and the drawbacks of buying a franchise.

- Franchises offer many benefits: management training and support; brand-name appeal; standardized quality of goods and services; national advertising programs; financial assistance; proven products and business formats; centralized buying power; territorial protection; and a greater chance of success.
- Franchising also suffers from certain drawbacks: franchise fees and profit sharing; strict adherence to standardized operations; restrictions on purchasing; limited product lines; unsatisfactory training programs; market saturation; and less freedom.

5. Understand the laws covering franchise purchases.

- The Federal Trade Commission (FTC) enacted the Trade Regulation Rule in 1979, which requires all franchisers to disclose detailed information on their operations at the first personal meeting or at least ten days before a franchise contract is signed, or before any money is paid. The FTC rule covers *all* franchisers. The Trade Regulation Rule requires franchisers to provide information on 23 topics in their disclosure statements.
- Seventeen states have passed their own franchise laws requiring franchisers to provide prospective franchisees with a Uniform Franchise Offering Circular (UFOC).

6. Discuss the right way to buy a franchise.

- The following steps will help you make the right franchise choice: Evaluate yourself; research your market; consider your franchise options; get a copy of the franchiser's UFOC; talk to existing franchisees; ask the franchiser some tough questions; make your choice.

7. Outline the major trends shaping franchising.

- Several trends are shaping a changing franchising environment, including: international franchise opportunities; smaller, nontraditional locations using the principle of intercept marketing; conversion franchising, multiple-unit franchising; master franchising; and piggybacking (or combination franchising).

DISCUSSION QUESTIONS

1. What factors should an entrepreneur consider before choosing a form of ownership?
2. Why are sole proprietorships so popular as a form of ownership?
3. How does personal conflict affect partnerships?

4. What issues should the articles of partnership address? Why are the articles important to a successful partnership?
5. Can one partner commit another to a business deal without the other's consent? Why?

6. What issues should the certificate of incorporation cover?

7. How does an S corporation differ from a regular corporation?

8. What role do limited partners play in a partnership? What happens if a limited partner takes an active role in managing the business?

9. What advantages does a limited liability company offer over an S corporation? A partnership?

10. How is an LLC created? What criteria must an LLC meet to avoid double taxation?

11. Briefly outline the advantages and disadvantages of the major forms of ownership.

12. What is franchising?

13. Describe the three types of franchising and give an example of each.

14. Discuss the advantages and the limitations of franchising for the franchisee.

15. Why might an independent entrepreneur be dissatisfied with a franchising arrangement?

16. What kinds of clues should tip off a prospective franchisee that he is dealing with a disreputable franchiser?

17. Should a prospective franchisee investigate before investing in a franchise? If so, how and in what areas?

18. What is the function of the FTC's Trade Regulation Rule? Outline the protection the Trade Regulation Rule gives all prospective franchisees.

19. Describe the current trends in franchising.

20. One franchisee says, "Franchising is helpful because it gives you somebody [the franchiser] to get you going, nurture you, and shove you along a little. But, the franchiser won't make you successful. That depends on what you bring to the business, how hard you are prepared to work, and how committed you are to finding the right franchise for you." Do you agree? Explain.

Beyond the Classroom...

1. Interview five local small business owners. What form of ownership did each choose? Why? Prepare a brief report summarizing your findings, and explain advantages and disadvantages those owners face because of their choices.

2. Invite entrepreneurs who operate as partners to your classroom. Do they have a written partnership agreement? Are their skills complementary? How do they divide responsibility for running their company? How do they handle decision making? What do they do when disputes and disagreements arise?

4. Visit a local franchise operation. Is it a tradename, product distribution, or pure franchise? To what extent did the franchisee investigate before investing? What assistance does the franchiser provide? How does the franchisee feel about the franchise contract he or she signed? What would he or she do differently now?

5a. Consult a copy of the International Franchise Association publication *Franchise Opportunities Handbook* (the library should have a copy). Write several franchisers in a particular business category and ask for their franchise packages. Write a report comparing their treatment of the topics covered by the Trade Regulation Rule.
   b. Analyze the terms of their franchise contracts. What are the major differences? Are some terms more favorable than others? If you were about to invest in the franchise, which terms would you want to change?

6. Ask a local franchisee to approach his or her regional franchise representative about leading a class discussion on franchising.

7. Contact the International Franchise Association (1350 New York Avenue, N.W., Suite 900, Washington, D.C., 20005-4709, tel. [202] 628-8000) for a copy of *Investigate Before Investing*. Prepare a report outlining what a prospective franchisee should do before buying a franchise.

1. Using one of the search engines on the World Wide Web, (WWW), such as Lycos, Magellan, Yahoo!, or others, conduct a search on the words *proprietorship, partnership, limited partnership, corporation, S corporation,* and *limited liability company.* Prepare a one-page report on what you learned about any two topics.

2. Access the Web site for FranInfo at the following address:

http://www.frannet.com/

Take the self-tests ("Franchise Suitability" and "Are You a Good Candidate to Own a Franchise?"). Prepare a brief report on what you learn at this Web site.

3. Access the Web site for *Successful Franchising* at the following address:

http://www.entremkt.com/sf/

Summarize in one page or less one of the articles you find there. What topics are people discussing on the Bulletin Board feature of this site?

4. Access the Web site for the International Franchise Association (IFA) at the following address:

http://www.entremkt.com/ifa/

a. Choose one of the articles making the franchise news list and prepare a summary of it.

b. Use the IFA's Franchise Guide On-Line to search the franchise options available in a category of interest to you. Write a brief report on what you find.

5. Access the Web site for *The Virtual Entrepreneur* at the following address:

http://emporium.turnpike.net/B/bizopp/articles.html

Use the resources available here (e.g., "How to Succeed in Franchising" and the "Franchising Workshop") to determine if you have what it takes to become a successful franchisee. Prepare a brief report on what you learn at this site.

CHAPTER

FOUR

Buying an Existing Business

Experience is a hard teacher because she gives the test first, the lesson afterwards.
                                                    - Vernon Sanders Law

You can't buy experience on the easy payment plan.
                                                    - fortune cookie

Sometimes when you get into a fight with a skunk, you can't tell who started it.
                                                    - Lloyd Dogget

LEARNING OBJECTIVES

Upon completion of this chapter, you will be able to:

1. **Understand** the advantages and disadvantages of buying an existing business.
2. **Define** the steps involved in the *right* way to buy a business.
3. **Explain** the process of evaluating an existing business.
4. **Describe** the various methods of determining the value of a business.
5. **Understand** the seller's side of the buyout decision and how to structure the deal.
6. **Understand** how the negotiation process works and identify the factors that affect the negotiation process.

Starting a business "from scratch" or buying a franchise are not the only options available to an entrepreneur. Every year, more than 500,000 existing businesses are sold, 90 percent of which are valued at under $5 million. Because of the ongoing boom in entrepreneurship, purchasing an existing small business has become a hot trend in the 1990s. Buying a business is not (and probably should not be) something to be done quickly or easily, however. There is seldom a need to "rush into the deal." Each purchase is unique because each business is unique. In almost every situation, it takes weeks or months to analyze and evaluate the positive and negative aspects of a potential purchase candidate. It may take longer to complete the final negotiations. Be patient, and do your homework. Be sure that you have answers to all of the following questions:

- ⭐ Is the right type of business for sale in the market in which you want to operate?
- ⭐ What experience do you have in this particular business and the industry in which it operates?
- ⭐ How critical is experience in the business to your ultimate success? Where should such a business be located?
- ⭐ What price and payment method are reasonable for you and acceptable to the seller?
- ⭐ Should you start the business and build it from the ground up or should you shop around to buy an existing company?
- ⭐ What is this company's potential for success?
- ⭐ What kind of changes will you have to make—and how extensive will they be—to realize the business's full potential?

Buying an Existing Business

1-A. Understand the advantages of buying an existing business

Advantages of Buying an Existing Business

A SUCCESSFUL EXISTING BUSINESS MAY CONTINUE TO BE SUCCESSFUL. Purchasing a thriving business at an acceptable price increases the likelihood of success. The previous management already has established a customer base, built supplier relationships, and set up a business system. The new owner's objective should be to make those modifications that will attract new customers while retaining the firm's existing customers. Maintaining the proper balance of old and new is not an easy task, however. The customer base that you inherit through purchasing an established business can carry you while you study how the business has become successful and why customers want to buy from you. The time you spend learning about the business and its customers before introducing changes will increase the probability that the changes you do make will be successful.

AN EXISTING BUSINESS MAY ALREADY HAVE THE BEST LOCATION. When the location of the business is critical to its success, it may be wise to purchase a business that is already in the right place. Opening in a second-choice location and hoping to draw customers may prove fruitless. In fact, the existing business's biggest asset may be its location. If this advantage cannot be matched by other locations, an entrepreneur may have little choice but to buy instead of build.

EMPLOYEES AND SUPPLIERS ARE ESTABLISHED. An existing business already has experienced employees, so there are fewer problems associated with the shakedown phase of getting started. Experienced employees can help the company earn money while a new owner learns the business.

For example, when Bob Hammer and Sue Crowe, two former executives at major corporations, purchased a small mail-order model-ship-kit manufacturer, BlueJacket Ship Crafters, as a "retirement business," they knew they had a lot to learn about running a small business. Just how much they had to learn, however, was a surprise. Fortunately, the experienced employees they inherited with the company kept it going while Hammer and Crowe got their sea legs. "The learning curve was intense," says Crowe. "We didn't know what we were doing, so we had to keep asking employees how things worked."[1]

BlueJacket Ship Crafters

In addition, an existing business has an established set of suppliers with a history of business dealings. Those vendors can continue to supply the business while the new owner investigates the products and services of other suppliers. Thus, the new owner is not pressured to choose a supplier quickly without thorough investigation.

EQUIPMENT IS INSTALLED AND PRODUCTIVE CAPACITY IS KNOWN. Acquiring and installing new equipment exerts a tremendous strain on a fledgling company's financial resources. In an existing business, a potential buyer can determine the condition of the plant and equipment and its capacity before buying. The previous owner may have established an efficient production operation through trial and error, although the new owner may need to make modifications to improve it. In many cases, the entrepreneur can purchase physical facilities and equipment at prices significantly below replacement costs.

INVENTORY IS IN PLACE AND TRADE CREDIT IS ESTABLISHED. The proper amount of inventory is essential to both cost control and sales volume. If a business has too little inventory, it will not have the quantity and variety of products to satisfy customer demand. But if a business has too much inventory, it is tying up excessive capital, thereby increasing costs and reducing profitability. Owners of successful, established businesses have learned to balance these extremes. Previous owners have established trade credit relationships of which the new owner can take advantage. The business's proven track record gives the new owner leverage in negotiating for trade credit concessions. No supplier wants to lose a good customer.

THE NEW BUSINESS OWNER HITS THE GROUND RUNNING. The entrepreneur who purchases an existing business saves the time, costs, and energy required to plan and launch a new business. The day the new owner takes over the ongoing business is the day his revenues begin. In this way, the new owner earns while he learns.

THE NEW OWNER CAN USE THE EXPERIENCE OF THE PREVIOUS OWNER. Even if the previous owner is not around after the sale, the new owner will have access to all of the business's records, which can be a guide until he becomes acclimated to the business and the local market. The new owner can trace the impact on costs and revenues of the major decisions that the previous owner made and can learn from those mistakes and profit from those achievements. In many cases, the previous owner spends time in an orientation period with the new owner, which gives the new manager the opportunity to question the previous owner about the policies and procedures he developed and the reasons for them. Previous owners also can be extremely helpful in unmasking the unwritten rules of business in the area—what types of behavior are acceptable, whom to trust or not, and other important intangibles. After all, most owners who sell out want to see the buyer succeed in carrying on their businesses.

IT'S A BARGAIN. Some existing businesses may be real bargains. The current owners may wish to sell on short notice, which may lead them to sell the business at a low price. The more specialized the business is, the greater the likelihood is that a bargain might be found. If special skill or training is required to operate the business, the number of potential buyers will be significantly smaller. If the owner wants a substantial down payment or the entire selling price in cash, few buyers may qualify; however, those who do may be able to negotiate a good deal.

1-B. Understand the disadvantages of buying an existing business.

Disadvantages of Buying an Existing Business

"IT'S A DOG." A business may be for sale because it has never been profitable. Such a situation may be disguised; owners can employ various creative accounting techniques that make the firm's financial picture appear much brighter than it really is. The reason that a business is for sale will seldom be stated honestly as "it's losing money." If there is an area of business where the maxim "let the buyer beware" still prevails, it is in the sale of a business. Any buyer unprepared to do a complete and thorough analysis of the business may be stuck with a real dog.

Although buying a money-losing business is risky, it is not necessarily taboo. If your analysis of a company shows that it is poorly managed or suffering from neglect, you may be able to turn it around. However, if you do not have a well-defined plan for improving a struggling business, do *not* consider buying it!

B.J.'s Professional Business Center

When Kay Austin-Holmes found a word processing/print shop that she was interested in buying, she did not rule it out because it was losing money and relied on outdated computers. "The owner had been losing money ever since she turned the day-to-day operations over to a manager [instead of overseeing the shop herself], had gotten involved in other projects, and just wanted to get out," says Austin-Holmes. "She'd had the business up for sale for a year, but all anybody saw was . . . these old, out-of-date word processors. . . and that after two years in business she was more than $20,000 in debt." Austin-Holmes, however, saw more: a business with potential—a long list of clients, low operating expenses, and the power to grow. She and the seller negotiated a deal in which the seller kept responsibility for the company's debts and Austin-Holmes purchased the company's assets. The business, now called B.J.'s Professional Business Center, turns out résumés, brochures, scripts, and other documents for a growing list of clients. It also turns a profit for Austin-Holmes. "There was nothing wrong with the business," she says. "It just needed to be watched over every day by someone who had a direct interest in its success."[2]

THE PREVIOUS OWNER MAY HAVE CREATED ILL WILL. Just as ethical, socially responsible business dealings create goodwill for a company, improper business behavior creates ill will. The business may look great on the surface, but customers, suppliers, creditors, or employees may have extremely negative feelings about it. Business relations may have begun to deteriorate but their long-term effects may not yet be reflected in the business's financial statements. Ill will can permeate a business for years.

EMPLOYEES INHERITED WITH THE BUSINESS MAY NOT BE SUITABLE. If the new owner plans to make changes in the business, the present employees may not suit her needs. Others may not be able to adapt to the new owner's management style.

BlueJacket Ship Crafters

For instance, when Bob Hammer and Sue Crowe bought BlueJacket Ship Crafters, they changed the management style in the company from an authoritarian one to one built around empowered work teams. Unfortunately, this new philosophy ran counter to the existing supervisor's management style. Within a year, the supervisor left the company. "She couldn't work with empowered people," recalls Crowe, who described her as "dictatorial."[3]

Previous managers may have kept marginal employees because they were close friends or because they started off with the company. The new owner, therefore, may have to make some very unpopular termination decisions. For this reason, employees often do not welcome a new owner because they feel threatened. Furthermore, employees who may have wanted to buy the business themselves but could not afford it are likely to see the new owner as the person who stole their opportunity. Bitter employees are not likely to be productive workers.

THE BUSINESS LOCATION MAY HAVE BECOME UNSATISFACTORY. What was once or is currently an ideal location may become obsolete as market and demographic trends change. Large shopping malls, new competitors, or highway reroutings can spell disaster for a small retail shop. Prospective buyers should always evaluate the existing market in the area surrounding an existing business as well as its potential for expansion.

EQUIPMENT AND FACILITIES MAY BE OBSOLETE OR INEFFICIENT. Potential buyers sometimes neglect to have an expert evaluate a firm's facilities and equipment before they purchase it. Only later do they discover that the equipment is obsolete and inefficient, and the business may suffer losses from excessively high costs. The equipment may have been well suited to the business they purchased, but not to the business they want to build. Modernizing equipment and facilities is seldom inexpensive.

CHANGE AND INNOVATION ARE DIFFICULT TO IMPLEMENT. It is easier to plan for change than it is to implement it. Methods previously used in a business may have established precedents that are hard to modify. For example, if the previous owner allowed a 10 percent discount to customers purchasing 100 or more units in a single order, it may be almost impossible to eliminate the discount practice without losing some of those customers. The previous owner's policies, even if proven unwise, still affect the changes a new owner can make. It is just as difficult to reverse a downward trend in sales. Implementing changes to bring in new business and convince former clients to return can be an expensive and laborious process.

INVENTORY MAY BE OUTDATED OR OBSOLETE. Inventory is valuable only if it is salable, or if it can be converted into salable products. Never trust the firm's balance sheet evaluation of inventory. Some of it may actually appreciate in value in periods of rapid inflation, but more likely it has depreciated. A prospective buyer must judge inventory on the basis of its market value, not its book value.

After Hendrix Neimann had already agreed in principle to purchase Automatic Door Specialists, a security company, from its founder, he and his team of advisers discovered that much of the inventory reported in the company's books was useless scrap and junk. After taking into account the worthless inventory and past-due accounts receivable, Neimann ultimately offered the owner 50 percent of the amount in the original preliminary agreement.[4]

Automatic Door Specialists

Potential buyers should check the status of a company's inventory to see whether or not it is outdated and obsolete. They should make sure it is still salable and, if so, at what price.

ACCOUNTS RECEIVABLE MAY BE WORTH LESS THAN FACE VALUE. Like inventory, accounts receivable rarely are worth their face value. The prospective buyer should age the accounts receivable to determine their collectibility. The older the receivables are, the less likely they are to be collected, and, consequently, the lower their value is. Table 4.1 on page 104 shows a simple but effective method of evaluating accounts receivable once they have been aged.

THE BUSINESS MAY BE OVERPRICED. Each year, many people purchase businesses at prices far in excess of their value. If a buyer accurately values a business's accounts receivable, inventories, and other assets, she will be in a better position to negotiate a price that will allow the business to be profitable. Making payments on a business that was overpriced is a millstone around the new owner's neck, making it difficult to carry this excess weight and keep the business afloat.

Table 4.1
**Valuing Accounts
Receivable**

A prospective buyer asked the current owner of a business about the value of her accounts receivable. The owner's business records showed $101,000 in receivables. But when the prospective buyer aged them and then multiplied the resulting totals by his estimated collection probabilities, he discovered their *real* value:

Age of Accounts	Amount	Collection Probability	Value
0–30 days	$40,000	.95	$38,000
31–60 days	$25,000	.88	$22,000
61–90 days	$14,000	.70	$9,800
91–120 days	$10,000	.40	$4,000
121–150 days	$7,000	.25	$1,750
151+ days	$5,000	.10	$500
Total	$101,000		$76,050

Had he blindly accepted the seller's value of these accounts receivable, this prospective buyer would have overpaid nearly $25,000 for them!

Although most buyers do not realize it, the price they pay for a company typically is not as crucial to its continued success as the terms on which they make the purchase. Of course, wise business buyers will try to negotiate a reasonable price, but they are much more interested in the deal's terms—how much cash they must pay out and when, how much of the price the seller is willing to finance and for how long, the interest rate at which the deal is financed, and other such terms. Their primary concern is making sure that the deal does not endanger the company's future financial health and that it preserves the company's cash flow.

Source: FRANK & ERNEST reprinted by permission of Newspaper Enterprise Association, Inc.

The Steps in Acquiring a Business

2. Define the steps involved in the *right* way to buy a business.

Buying an existing business can be risky if approached haphazardly. Studies show that more than 50 percent of all business acquisitions fail to meet the buyer's expectations. To avoid costly mistakes, an entrepreneur-to-be should follow a logical, methodical approach:[5]

- ✰ Analyze your skills, abilities, and interests to determine what kind(s) of businesses you should consider.
- ✰ Prepare a list of potential candidates.
- ✰ Investigate those candidates and evaluate the best one(s).
- ✰ Explore financing options.
- ✰ Ensure a smooth transition.

Analyze Your Skills, Abilities, and Interests

The first step in buying a business is conducting a self-audit to determine the ideal business for you. At this point, you should not be concerned about what kinds of businesses are available to buy. Your primary focus is to identify the type of business *you* will be happiest and most successful owning. Consider, for example, the following questions:

- ✰ What business activities do you enjoy most? Least? Why?
- ✰ Which industries interest you most? Least? Why?
- ✰ What kind of business do you want to buy?
- ✰ What kinds of businesses do you want to avoid?
- ✰ What do you expect to get out of the business?
- ✰ How much time, energy, and money can you put into the business?
- ✰ What business skills and experience do you have? Which ones do you lack?
- ✰ How easily can you transfer your skills and experience to other types of businesses? In what kinds of businesses would that transfer be easiest?
- ✰ How much risk are you willing to take?
- ✰ What size company do you want to buy?
- ✰ Is there a particular geographic location you desire?

Answering these and other questions beforehand will allow you to develop a list of precise criteria a company must meet before it becomes a purchase candidate. Addressing these issues early in the process will also save a great deal of time, trouble, and confusion as you wade through a multitude of business opportunities.

Prepare a List of Potential Candidates

Once you know what your goals are for acquiring a business, you can begin your search. Do *not* limit yourself to only those businesses that are advertised as being "for sale." In fact, the **hidden market** of companies that might be for sale but are not advertised as such is one of the richest sources of top-quality businesses. "About 85 percent of [purchase] opportunities are tucked away within the unadvertised hidden market," says one business broker.[6] Although they maintain a low profile, these hidden businesses represent some of the most attractive purchase targets a prospective buyer may find. How can you tap into this hidden market of potential acquisitions? Typical sources include the following:

hidden market—
low-profile companies that might be for sale but are not advertised as such.

- ✰ business brokers
- ✰ bankers

- ★ accountants
- ★ investment bankers
- ★ industry contacts—suppliers, distributors, customers, insurance brokers, and others
- ★ networking—social and business contacts with friends and relatives
- ★ knocking on the doors of businesses you'd like to buy (even if they're not advertised for sale)
- ★ trade associations
- ★ newspapers and trade journals listing businesses for sale

Investigate and Evaluate Candidate Businesses and Evaluate the Best One

Once you have a list of prospective candidates, it is time to do your homework. The next step is to investigate the candidates in more detail:

- ★ What are the company's strengths? Weaknesses?
- ★ Is the company profitable? What is its overall financial condition?
- ★ What is its cash flow cycle? How much cash will the company generate?
- ★ Who are its major competitors?
- ★ How large is the customer base? Is it growing or shrinking?
- ★ Are the current employees suitable? Will they stay?
- ★ What is the physical condition of the business, its equipment, and its inventory?
- ★ What new skills must you learn to be able to manage this business successfully?

Determining the answers to these questions (and others addressed in this chapter) will allow a prospective buyer to develop a list of the most attractive prospects and to prioritize them in descending order of attractiveness. This process also will make the task of valuing the business much easier.

Explore Financing Options

Placing a value on an existing business represents a major hurdle for many would-be entrepreneurs. The next challenging task in closing a successful deal is financing the purchase. Although financing the purchase of an existing business usually is easier than financing a new one, some traditional lenders shy away from deals involving the purchase of an existing business. Those that are willing to finance business purchases normally lend only a portion of the value of the assets, so buyers often find themselves searching for alternative sources of funds. Fortunately, most business buyers have access to a ready source of financing: the seller. Once a seller finds a suitable buyer, she typically will agree to finance anywhere from 30 percent to 80 percent of the purchase price. Usually, a deal is structured so that the buyer makes a down payment to the seller, who then finances a note for the balance. The buyer makes regular principal and interest payments over time—perhaps with a larger balloon payment at the end—until the note is paid off. The terms and conditions of such a loan are a vital concern to both buyer and seller. They cannot be so burdensome that they threaten the company's continued existence; that is, the buyer must be able to make the payments to the seller out of the company's cash flow. At the same time, the deal must give the seller the financial security she is seeking from the sale. Defining reasonable terms is the result of the negotiation process between the buyer and the seller.

Ensure a Smooth Transition

Once the parties strike a deal, the challenge of making a smooth transition immediately arises. No matter how well planned the sale is, there are *always* surprises. For instance, the new owner may have ideas for changing the business—sometimes radically—that cause a great deal of stress and anxiety among employees and the previous owner. Charged with such emotion and uncertainty, the transition phase is always difficult and frustrating—and sometimes painful. To avoid a bumpy transition, a business buyer should do the following:

⭐ Concentrate on communicating with employees. Business sales are fraught with uncertainty and anxiety, and employees need reassurance.

⭐ Be honest with employees. Avoid telling them only what they want to hear. "Be frank, open, and honest" with existing employees, advises one business broker.[7]

⭐ Listen to employees. They have intimate knowledge of the business and its strengths and weaknesses and usually can offer valuable suggestions.

⭐ Consider asking the seller to serve as a consultant until the transition is complete. The previous owner can be a valuable resource.

Table 4.2 describes 15 steps potential buyers should take to increase the probability that the businesses they buy are the right ones for them.

Table 4.2
15 Steps to Buying the Company That's Right for You

Source: Adapted from: Jay Finegan, "The Insider's Guide," *Inc.*, October 1991, pp. 26–36.

1. *Make sure you shouldn't be starting a company instead.* You should have solid reasons for buying a company rather than starting one—and you should know what they are.

2. *Determine the kind of business you want—and whether you're capable of running it.* This requires an unflinching assessment of your own strengths, weaknesses, personality, and goals.

3. *Consider the lifestyle you want.* What are you expecting from the business? Money? Freedom? Flexibility?

4. *Consider the location you want.* What part of the country (or world) do you want to live in?

5. *Reconsider lifestyle again.* You may own this business for a long, long time; it had better be one you enjoy.

6. *Cozy up to lenders in advance.* Go visit potential lenders long before you need to borrow any money. Develop a rapport with them.

7. *Prepare to sell yourself to the sellers.* You're buying their "baby," and they'll want to make sure you're the right person for the job!

8. *Once you've defined the kind of business you're after, find the right company.* Three major sources of potential candidates are: (1) the network of businesspeople and advisers in the area, (2) business brokers specializing in companies of the size or type you want to buy, and (3) businesses that technically are not for sale (but are very attractive).

9. *Choose the right seller.* Is he honest? What's the *real* reason she's selling the business?

10. *Do your research before agreeing to a price.* Ask lots of questions and get the facts to help you estimate the company's value.

11. *Make sure your letter of intent is specific.* It should establish deadlines, escape clauses, payment terms, confidentiality, and many other key issues.

12. *Don't skimp on due diligence.* Don't believe everything you see and hear; a relentless investigation will show whether or not the seller is telling the truth. Not all of them will.

13. *Be skeptical.* Don't fall in love with the deal; look for reasons *not* to buy the company.

14. *Don't forget to assess the employees.* You're not just buying a company; you're also buying the services of people who go with it.

15. *Make sure the final price reflects the company's real value.* Don't lower your chances of success by paying too much for the business.

"Fishing" for the Right Company to Buy

After graduating with an MBA from Wharton in 1987, K.C. Walsh took a job as a management consultant in Los Angeles with Deloitte and Touche. His wife, Karen, was an account executive with the advertising agency Chiat/Day. They settled into what K.C. calls a comfortable "yuppie life," although in the back of his mind was a yearning to enjoy the pleasures of life in a safe, friendly, small town. K.C. and Karen, however, were so busy making a living that they pushed their small-town dream aside.

In 1991 and 1992, a series of events changed the Walshes' outlook on life. A promotion K.C. believed he deserved never materialized. The couple learned that they were expecting their first baby, and the L.A. riots had destroyed buildings within a mile of their home. "I felt I had to make something happen *now*," recalls K.C.

For years, K.C.'s father, himself an entrepreneur, had been encouraging K.C. to abandon the hassles of corporate life and start his own business. In his consulting work at Deloitte and Touche, K.C. was seeing, almost daily, how profitable successful small businesses could be. He and Karen decided to buy a business, using the money they had been saving for a down payment on a house. What kind of business and where it would be he didn't know yet, but K.C. got busy with his search to find the right company for him. He worked nights and weekends and even used his vacation time to search for possible target companies.

He looked at a sausage company, a business that made bowling accessories, and one that made huge wooden beams. At that point K.C. said, "Wait a minute—I'm not really that interested in wooden beams." What he *was* interested in, however, was fishing. An avid fly fisherman since the age of seven, K.C. decided to make his favorite avocation his new vocation. "It took me a year and a half to zero in on the kind of company I wanted," he says.

He soon found a fly-rod manufacturer for sale, but he lost the deal because he couldn't get enough time away from his job to negotiate with the seller. "I missed buying [the company] because I couldn't act quickly enough," says K.C. To avoid losing out again, he took the bold step of quitting his job so he could devote himself to his search for the ideal company. After several months, K.C. found a likely candidate: Simms, a small maker of fishing accessories in Boseman, Montana. Negotiations crept along, and virtually stalled when the ski season set in, which made it difficult to get all of Simmses' managers together at once.

The negotiations tested K.C.'s patience, but he didn't give up. "You've got to stay positive and be persistent," he says. "Twice the deal looked dead; then it would revive, and I'd hop on a plane. It was just such an attractive thing." The Walshes began vacationing in Boseman to see if they would enjoy living there. They did.

A year and a half after he had first contacted the company, K.C. finally became the sole owner of Simms. To make the purchase, he used $150,000 of the family's savings, plus some money borrowed from his family. A local bank extended K.C a $150,000 line of credit "pretty much on the strength of a handshake" says K.C. The seller also agreed to finance a portion of the sale.

Today, the Walshes live five minutes away from Simmses' new 15,000-square-foot factory. Under K.C.'s leadership, the company has more than doubled its work force and its sales. Simmses' products have won several awards and were featured in the popular Neiman Marcus Christmas catalogue. Still, Walsh works as many hours as he did but earns only half of what he made at the peak of his corporate career as a consultant. That doesn't seem to bother him much, however. The cost of living is much lower in Boseman than in L.A., and, besides, says K.C., "Right now I'm building up a business."

1. Evaluate the way in which K.C. Walsh went about finding a business to buy. What did he do right? What did he do wrong?

2. What should he have done differently?

Source: Adapted from Alan Farnheim, "Casting Off: Three Who Did It Right," *Fortune*, January 15, 1996, pp. 60–64.

---

3. Explain the process of evaluating an existing business.

Evaluating an Existing Business

When evaluating an existing business, a lone buyer quickly feels overwhelmed by the tremendous number and complexity of the issues involved. Therefore, a clever buyer will assemble a team of specialists to help in investigating the potential business opportunity. This team is usually composed of a banker, an accountant familiar with the particular industry, an attorney, and perhaps a small business consultant or a business broker. The cost of such a team can range from $3,000 to $20,000, but most buyers agree that using a team significantly lowers the likelihood of making a bad buy. Because making a bad purchase will cost many times the cost of a team of experts, most buyers see it as a wise investment. It is important for a buyer to trust the members of the business evaluation team. With this team assembled, the potential buyer is ready to explore the business opportunity by examining five critical areas.

1. Why does the owner want to sell?
2. What is the physical condition of the business?
3. What is the potential for the company's products or services?
4. What legal aspects should you consider?
5. Is the business financially sound?

Why Is the Business for Sale?

WHY DOES THE OWNER WANT TO SELL? Every prospective business buyer should investigate the *real* reason the business owner wants to sell. A recent study by the Geneva Corporation found that the most common reasons that owners of small- and medium-sized businesses gave for selling were boredom and burnout.[8] Others decided to cash in their business investments and diversify into other types of assets.

Smart business buyers know that the biggest and most unpleasant surprises can crop up outside the company's financial records and may never appear on the spreadsheets designed to analyze a company's financial position. For instance, a business owner might be looking to sell his business because a powerful new competitor is about to move into the market, a major highway rerouting will cause customer traffic to evaporate, the lease agreement on the ideal location is about to expire, or the primary customer base is declining. Every prospective buyer should investigate thoroughly any reason a seller gives for wanting to sell a business.

Businesses do not last forever, and most owners know when the time has come to sell. Some owners consider their behavior ethical only if they do not make false or misleading statements, but they may not disclose the whole story. In most business sales, the buyer bears the responsibility of determining whether or not the business is a good value. The best way to do that is to get out into the local community, talk to people, and ask a lot of questions. Visiting local business owners may reveal general patterns about the area and its overall vitality. The local chamber of commerce also may have useful information. Suppliers, customers, and even competitors may be able to shed light on why a business is up for sale. By combining this information with an analysis of the company's financial records, the potential buyer should be able to develop a clearer picture of the business and its real value.

The Condition of the Business

WHAT IS THE PHYSICAL CONDITION OF THE BUSINESS? A prospective buyer should evaluate the business's assets to determine their value. Are they reasonably priced? Are they obsolete? Will they need to be replaced soon? Do they operate efficiently? The potential buyer should check the condition of both the equipment and the building. It may be necessary to hire a professional to evaluate the major components of the building—its structure and its plumbing, electrical, and heating and cooling systems. Renovations are rarely inexpensive or simple. Unexpected renovations can punch a gaping hole in a buyer's financial plan.

How fresh is the firm's inventory? Is it consistent with the image the new owner wants to project? How much of it would the buyer have to sell at a loss? A potential buyer may need to get an independent appraisal to determine the value of the firm's inventory and other assets because the current owner may have priced them far above their actual value.

These items typically comprise the largest portion of a business's value, and a potential buyer should not accept the seller's asking price blindly. Remember: *Book value is not the same as market value*. Usually, a buyer can purchase equipment and fixtures at substantially lower prices than book value. Value is determined in the market, not on a balance sheet. Other important factors that the potential buyer should investigate follow.

Accounts Receivable. If the sale includes accounts receivable, the buyer should check their quality before purchasing them. How creditworthy are the accounts? What portion of them are past due? How likely are you to be able to collect them? By aging the accounts receivable, the buyer can judge their quality and determine their value. (Refer to Table 4.1.)

Lease Arrangements. Is the lease included in the sale? When does it expire? What restrictions does it have on renovation or expansion? The buyer should determine *beforehand* what restrictions the landlord has placed on the lease and negotiate any change prior to purchasing the business.

Business Records. Well-kept business records can be a valuable source of information and can tell a prospective buyer a lot about the company's pattern of success (or lack of it). Unfortunately, many business owners are sloppy recordkeepers. Consequently, the potential buyer and his team may have to reconstruct some critical records. It is important to verify as much information about the business as possible. For instance, does the owner have customer or mailing lists? These can be a valuable marketing tool for a new business owner.

Intangible Assets. Does the sale include any intangible assets like trademarks, patents, copyrights, or goodwill? How long do patents have left to run? Is the trademark threatened by lawsuits for infringement? Does the company have logos or slogans that are unique or widely recognized? Determining the value of such intangibles is much more difficult than computing the value of the tangible assets.

Location and Appearance. The location and the overall appearance of the building are important factors for a prospective buyer to consider. What had been an outstanding location in the past may be totally unacceptable today. Even if the building and equipment are in good condition and are fairly priced, the business may be located in a declining area. What kinds of businesses are in the area? Every buyer should consider the location's suitability several years into the future.

The potential buyer should also check local zoning laws to ensure that any changes he wants to make are legal. In some areas, zoning laws are very difficult to change and, as a result, can restrict the business's growth.

Products and Services

WHAT IS THE POTENTIAL FOR THE COMPANY'S PRODUCTS OR SERVICES? No one wants to buy a business with a dying market. A thorough market analysis can lead to a more accurate and more realistic sales forecast for an existing business. This research will tell a buyer whether or not he should consider buying a particular business and will help spot trends in the business's sales and customer base.

CUSTOMER CHARACTERISTICS AND COMPOSITION. Before purchasing an existing business, a buyer should analyze both existing and potential customers. Discovering why customers buy from the business and developing a profile of the entire customer base can help the buyer identify a company's strengths and weaknesses. The entrepreneur should determine the answers to the following questions:

☆ Who are my customers in terms of race, age, gender, and income level? What is their demographic profile?

- ☆ Why do they buy?
- ☆ What do the customers want the business to do for them? What needs are they satisfying?
- ☆ How often do customers buy? Do they buy in seasonal patterns?
- ☆ How loyal are my present customers?
- ☆ Is it practical or even possible to attract new customers? If so, are the new customers significantly different from my existing customers?
- ☆ Does the business have a well-defined customer base? Is it growing? Do these customers come from a large geographical area or do they all live near the business?

Analyzing the answers to these questions can help the potential owner create and implement a more powerful marketing plan. Most likely he will try to keep the business attractive to existing customers while changing some features of its marketing plan to attract new customers.

COMPETITOR ANALYSIS. A potential buyer must identify the company's direct competition—those businesses in the immediate area that sell similar products or services. The potential profitability and survival of the business may well depend on the behavior of these competitors.

In addition to analyzing direct competitors, the buyer should identify businesses that compete indirectly. For example, supermarkets and chain retail stores often carry a basic product line of automobile supplies (oil, spark plugs, and tune-up kits), competing with full-line auto parts stores. These chains often purchase bulk quantities at significant price reductions and do not incur the expense of carrying a full line of parts and supplies. As a result, they may be able to sell such basic products at lower prices. Even though these chains are not direct competitors, they may have a significant impact on local auto parts stores' sales and profitability. Indirect competitors frequently limit their product lines to the most profitable segments of the market, and by concentrating on high-volume or high-profit items, they can pose a serious threat to other businesses.

A potential buyer should also evaluate the trends in the competition. How many competitors have opened in recent years? How many have closed in the past five years? What caused these failures? Has the market already reached the saturation point? Being a latecomer in an already saturated market is not the path to long-term success.

When evaluating the competitive environment, a prospective buyer should address other questions:

- ☆ Which competitors have survived and what characteristics have led to their success?
- ☆ How do the competitors' sales volumes compare with those of the business the entrepreneur is considering?
- ☆ What unique services do the competitors offer?
- ☆ How well organized and coordinated are the marketing efforts of competitors?
- ☆ What are the competitors' reputations?
- ☆ What are the strengths and weaknesses of the firm's competitors?
- ☆ What competitive edge does each competitor have?
- ☆ How can you gain market share in this competitive environment?

Legal Aspects

WHAT LEGAL ASPECTS SHOULD YOU CONSIDER? Business buyers must be careful to avoid several legal pitfalls as they negotiate the final deal. The biggest potential traps include liens, bulk transfers, contract assignments, covenants not to compete, and ongoing legal liabilities.

Liens. The key legal issue in the sale of any asset is typically the proper transfer of good title from seller to buyer. However, because most business sales involve a collection of assorted assets, the transfer of a good title is more complex. Some business assets may have **liens** (creditors' claims) against them and unless they are satisfied before the sale, the buyer must assume them and is financially responsible for them. One way to reduce this potential problem is to include a clause in the sales contract stating that any liability not shown on the balance sheet at the time of sale remains the responsibility of the seller. A prospective buyer should have an attorney thoroughly investigate all of the assets for sale and their lien status before buying any business.

lien—*a creditor's claim against an asset.*

Bulk Transfers. To protect against surprise claims from the seller's creditors after purchasing a business, the buyer should meet the requirements of a **bulk transfer** under Section 6 of the Uniform Commercial Code. Suppose that an owner owing many creditors sells his business to a buyer. The seller, however, does not use the proceeds of the sale to pay his debts to business creditors. Instead, he pockets them to use for his own benefit. Without the protection of a bulk transfer, those creditors could make claim to the assets that the buyer purchased in order to satisfy the previous owner's debts (within six months).

bulk transfer—*protects a buyer of a business's assets from the claims unpaid creditors might have against those assets.*

To be effective, a bulk transfer must meet the following criteria:

- ✯ The seller must give the buyer a signed, sworn list of existing creditors.
- ✯ The buyer and the seller must prepare a list of the property included in the sale.
- ✯ The buyer must keep the list of creditors and the list of property for six months.
- ✯ The buyer must give written notice of the sale to each creditor at least ten days before the buyer takes possession of the goods or pays for them (whichever is first).

By meeting these criteria, a buyer acquires free and clear title to the assets purchased, which are not subject to prior claims from the seller's creditors.

Contract Assignments. A buyer must investigate the rights and the obligations he would assume under existing contracts with suppliers, customers, employees, lessors, and others. To continue the smooth operation of the business, the buyer must assume the rights of the seller under many existing contracts. Assuming these rights and obligations means having the seller assign existing contracts to the new owner. For example, the current owner may have four years left on a ten-year lease and will need to assign this contract to the buyer. To protect her interest, the buyer (who is the assignee) should notify the other party involved in the contract of the assignment. In the previous example, the business buyer should notify the landlord promptly of the lease assignment from the previous owner.

Generally, the seller can assign any contractual right to the buyer, unless the contract specifically prohibits the assignment or the contract is personal in nature. For instance, loan contracts sometimes prohibit assignments with **due-on-sale clauses.** These clauses require the buyer to pay the full amount of the remaining loan balance or to finance the balance at prevailing interest rates. Thus, the buyer cannot assume the seller's loan (at a lower interest rate). Also, a seller usually cannot assign his credit arrangements with suppliers to the buyer because they are based on the seller's business reputation and are personal in nature. If such contracts are crucial to the business operation and cannot be assigned, the buyer must renegotiate new contracts.

due-on-sale clause— *loan contract provision that prohibits a seller from assigning a loan arrangement to the buyer. Instead, the buyer is required to finance the remaining loan balance at prevailing interest rates.*

The prospective buyer also should evaluate the terms of any other contracts the seller has, including the following:

- ✯ patent, trademark, or copyright registrations
- ✯ exclusive agent or distributor contracts
- ✯ real estate leases

☆ financing and loan arrangements

☆ union contracts

Covenants Not to Compete. One of the most important and most often overlooked legal considerations for a prospective buyer is negotiating a **covenant not to compete** (or a **restrictive covenant**) with the seller. Under a restrictive covenant, the seller agrees not to open a new competing store within a specific time period and geographic area of the existing one. (The covenant should be negotiated with the *owner*, not the corporation, because if the corporation signs the agreement, the owner may not be bound.) However, the covenant must be a part of a business sale and must be reasonable in scope in order to be enforceable. Without such protection, a buyer may find his new business eroding beneath his feet. For example, Bob purchases a tire business from Alexandra, whose reputation in town for selling tires is unequaled. If Bob fails to negotiate a restrictive covenant, nothing can stop Alexandra from opening a new shop next to her old one and keeping all of her customers, thereby driving Bob out of business. A reasonable covenant in this case might restrict Alexandra from opening a tire store within a three-mile radius for three years. Every business buyer should negotiate a covenant not to compete with the seller.

covenant not to compete—*an agreement between a buyer and a seller in which the seller agrees not to compete with the buyer within a specific time and geographic area.*

Ongoing Legal Liabilities. Finally, the potential buyer must look for any potential legal liabilities the purchase might expose. These typically arise from three sources: (1) physical premises, (2) product liability claims, and (3) labor relations. First, the buyer must examine the physical premises for safety. Are employees at risk because of asbestos or some other hazardous material? If a manufacturing environment is involved, does it meet Occupational Safety and Health Administration (OSHA) and other regulatory agency requirements?

One entrepreneur who purchased a retail business located in a building that once housed a gasoline service station was quite surprised when the Environmental Protection Agency informed him that he would have to pay for cleaning up the results of an old, leaking gas tank that still sat beneath the property. Even though he had no part in running the old gas station and did not know the leaking tank was there, he was responsible for the cost of the cleanup! Removing the tank and cleaning up the site cost him several thousand dollars, for which he had not budgeted.

Example

Second, the buyer must consider whether or not existing products contain defects that could result in **product liability** lawsuits, which claim that a company is liable for damages and injuries caused by the products or services they sell. Existing lawsuits might be an omen of more to follow. In addition, the buyer must explore products that the company has discontinued, since a new owner might be liable for them if they prove to be defective. The final bargain between the parties should require the seller to guarantee that the company is not involved in any product liability lawsuits.

product liability— *lawsuits that claim that a company is liable for damages and injuries caused by the products or services they sell.*

Third, what is the relationship between management and employees? Does a union contract exist? The time to discover sour management-labor relations is before the purchase, not after.

If the buyer's investigation reveals such potential liabilities, it does not necessarily eliminate the business from consideration. Insurance coverage can shift such risks from the potential buyer, but the buyer should check to see whether or not the insurance will cover lawsuits resulting from actions predating the purchase.

Financial Soundness of the Business

IS THE BUSINESS FINANCIALLY SOUND? A prospective buyer must analyze the financial records of a target business to determine its health. The buyer shouldn't be afraid to ask an accountant for help. Accounting systems and methods can vary tremendously from one type of business to another and can be quite confusing to a novice. Current profits can be inflated by changes in the accounting procedure or in the method for recording sales. For the buyer, the most dependable financial records are audited statements, those prepared by a CPA firm in accordance with generally accepted accounting principles (GAAP). Unfortunately, audited records do not exist in many small companies that are for sale. In some cases, a potential buyer has to hire an accountant to construct reliable financial statements because the owner's accounting and recordkeeping are so sloppy.

When evaluating the financial status of any business prospect, a buyer must remember that any investment in a company should produce a reasonable salary for the owner and a healthy return on the money invested. Otherwise, it makes no sense to purchase the business.

A buyer also must remember that she is purchasing the future profit potential of an existing business. To evaluate the firm's profit potential, she should review past sales, operating expenses, and profits as well as the assets used to generate those profits. A buyer must compare current balance sheets and income statements with previous ones and then develop pro forma statements for the next two or three years. Sales tax records, income tax returns, and financial statements are valuable sources of information.

Are profits consistent over the years, or are they erratic? Is this pattern typical in the industry, or is it a result of unique circumstances or poor management? Can the business survive with such a serious fluctuation in revenues, costs, and profits? If these fluctuations are caused by poor management, can a new manager turn the business around? Some of the financial records that a potential buyer should examine follow.

Income statements and balance sheets for the past three to five years. It is important to review data from several years because creative accounting techniques can distort financial data in any single year. Even though buyers are purchasing the future profits of a business, they must remember that many businesses intentionally show low profits in order to minimize the owners' tax bills. Low profits should prompt a buyer to investigate their causes.

Income tax returns for the past three to five years. Comparing basic financial statements with tax returns can reveal discrepancies of which the buyer should be aware. Some small business owners **skim** from their businesses, that is, they take money from sales without reporting it as income. Owners who skim will claim their businesses are more profitable than their tax returns show. Although such underreporting is illegal and unethical, it is surprisingly common. Do *not* pay for undocumented, "phantom" profits the seller claims exist. In fact, you should consider whether or not you want to buy a business from someone who admits to doing business unethically. "If [the seller] is lying to the IRS, he may be lying to [you] about plenty of other things," cautions one consultant.[9]

Skimming—*taking money from sales without reporting it as income.*

Owner's compensation (and that of relatives). The owner's compensation is especially important in small companies; and the smaller the company is, the more important it will be. Although many companies do not pay their owners what they are worth, others compensate their owners lavishly. The buyer must consider the impact of fringe benefits such as company cars, insurance contracts, country club memberships, and the like. It is important to adjust the company's income statements for the salary and fringe benefits that the seller and others have been paid.

Cash Flow. Most buyers understand the importance of evaluating a company's profitability, but few recognize the necessity of analyzing its cash flow. They assume that if profits are adequate, there will be sufficient cash to pay all of the bills and to fund an attractive salary for themselves. *That is not necessarily the case!* Before you agree to a deal, you should sit down with an accountant and convert the target company's financial statements into a cash flow forecast. Not only must this forecast take into account existing debts and obligations but also any modifications the buyer would make in the business. It must also reflect the repayment of any financing the buyer arranges to purchase the company. Will the company generate enough cash to be self-supporting? How much cash will it generate for you?

A potential buyer must look for suspicious deviations from the norm (in either direction) for sales, expenses, profits, cash flow, assets, and liabilities. Have sales been increasing or decreasing? Is the equipment really as valuable as it is listed on the balance sheet? Is advertising expense unusually high? How is depreciation reflected in the financial statements?

This financial information gives the buyer the opportunity to verify the seller's claims about the business's performance. Sometimes, however, an owner will take short-term actions that produce a healthy financial statement but will weaken the firm's long-term health and profit potential. For example, a seller might lower costs by gradually eliminating equipment maintenance or boost sales by selling to marginal businesses that will never pay their bills. Such techniques can artificially inflate assets and profits, but a well-prepared buyer should be able to see through them.

Finally, a potential buyer should walk away from a deal—no matter how good it may appear on the surface—if the present owner refuses to disclose the company's financial records.

Table 4.3 lists some of the records a potential buyer should study before committing to a deal.

Buying an existing business is a process filled with potential missteps along the way. The expression "Let the buyer beware" should govern your thoughts and actions throughout the entire process. However, by following the preceding procedure, a buyer can dramatically lower the probability of getting "burned" with a business that does not suit her personality or one that is in on the verge of failure. Figure 4.1 on page 116 illustrates the sequence of events leading up to a successful negotiation with a seller.

1. Balance sheets and income statements from the previous three to five years.
2. Income tax returns for the previous three to five years.
3. Cash flow analysis and forecasts.
4. Records of accounts receivable (preferably aged).
5. Records of accounts payable.
6. Loan agreements with banks and other lenders.
7. Existing contracts with major suppliers or customers.
8. Contracts or leases on real estate, fixtures, or equipment.
9. Repair and maintenance records on equipment, machinery, and fixtures.
10. Insurance policies, including workers' compensation coverage.
11. Documentation on existing patents, trademarks, or copyrights.
12. Individual employees' labor contracts or union (collective bargaining) contracts.
13. Copies of appropriate business licenses.
14. Articles of incorporation (if incorporated) or articles of organization and operating agreement (if a limited liability company).
15. Any lawsuits the company is currently involved in.

Table 4.3
The Records a Business Buyer Should Review Before Committing to a Deal

Source: Adapted from Joseph Anthony, "Maybe You Should *Buy* a Business," *Kiplinger's Personal Finance Magazine,* May 1993, p. 84.

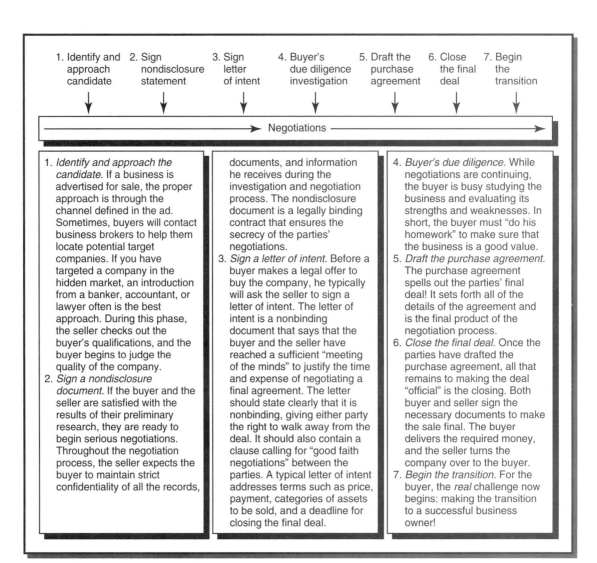

1. Identify and approach candidate 2. Sign nondisclosure statement 3. Sign letter of intent 4. Buyer's due diligence investigation 5. Draft the purchase agreement 6. Close the final deal 7. Begin the transition

← Negotiations →

1. *Identify and approach the candidate.* If a business is advertised for sale, the proper approach is through the channel defined in the ad. Sometimes, buyers will contact business brokers to help them locate potential target companies. If you have targeted a company in the hidden market, an introduction from a banker, accountant, or lawyer often is the best approach. During this phase, the seller checks out the buyer's qualifications, and the buyer begins to judge the quality of the company.

2. *Sign a nondisclosure document.* If the buyer and the seller are satisfied with the results of their preliminary research, they are ready to begin serious negotiations. Throughout the negotiation process, the seller expects the buyer to maintain strict confidentiality of all the records,

documents, and information he receives during the investigation and negotiation process. The nondisclosure document is a legally binding contract that ensures the secrecy of the parties' negotiations.

3. *Sign a letter of intent.* Before a buyer makes a legal offer to buy the company, he typically will ask the seller to sign a letter of intent. The letter of intent is a nonbinding document that says that the buyer and the seller have reached a sufficient "meeting of the minds" to justify the time and expense of negotiating a final agreement. The letter should state clearly that it is nonbinding, giving either party the right to walk away from the deal. It should also contain a clause calling for "good faith negotiations" between the parties. A typical letter of intent addresses terms such as price, payment, categories of assets to be sold, and a deadline for closing the final deal.

4. *Buyer's due diligence.* While negotiations are continuing, the buyer is busy studying the business and evaluating its strengths and weaknesses. In short, the buyer must "do his homework" to make sure that the business is a good value.

5. *Draft the purchase agreement.* The purchase agreement spells out the parties' final deal! It sets forth all of the details of the agreement and is the final product of the negotiation process.

6. *Close the final deal.* Once the parties have drafted the purchase agreement, all that remains to making the deal "official" is the closing. Both buyer and seller sign the necessary documents to make the sale final. The buyer delivers the required money, and the seller turns the company over to the buyer.

7. *Begin the transition.* For the buyer, the *real* challenge now begins: making the transition to a successful business owner!

Figure 4.1
The Acquisition Process
Source: Adapted from Price Waterhouse *Buying and Selling: A Company Handbook* (New York: 1993), pp. 38–42; Charles F. Claeys, "The Intent to Buy," *Small Business Reports*, May 1994, pp. 4–47.

YOU BE THE CONSULTANT...

There's a Right Way and a Wrong Way

Grant Beck, president of BaseLine Inc., a Kent, Washington, manufacturer of products used in the printing industry, saw an opportunity to expand into the Northeast by purchasing a troubled business whose product line was similar to his company's. The problem was that creditors were closing in

on the company fast. Beck had to move quickly, before the creditors forced the company into bankruptcy. Within just two weeks, Beck purchased the entire company at a "fire sale price" of $150,000 without the help of a business broker. Nor did he have the time to complete the due diligence process of the company.

It soon became apparent that Beck had not gotten the bargain he had originally thought. The financial statements he had relied on dramatically inflated the company's sales volume. The acquisition created a host of headaches for Beck, running up total losses of $250,000. A wiser Beck says, "I learned that if the time line is that tight, you walk away."

Unfortunately, Beck's story is all too common in the world of business buyouts. According to one consultant, "Part of the problem is that entrepreneurs...tend to fall in love with deals rather than analyze them." Done properly, however, buying a business can accomplish all that an entrepreneur envisions. It all depends on how you go about it.

Before he bought Rational Technology, Inc., a contract-engineer placement firm, with the help of a business broker, Larry Hammons studied the company's status, position in the market, customer base, and its financial statements. He signed a letter of intent, which was contingent on a more thorough analysis of the company. Then he hired an attorney and two CPAs to comb through Rational's financial statements and contracts, looking for what he might have missed. The research cost him nearly $20,000, which Hammons considered money well spent. Before closing the deal, Hammons also spent time analyzing the company's computer system and interviewing all nine employees. "This is a service business," he explains. "It's the employees who ultimately make or break the business."

Rational Technology was the third company Hammons had bought—and by far the best. He got well-trained employees, a smoothly functioning computer system, and a fair price. Hammons also convinced the former owner to stay on after the purchase to teach him about running the company. Sales and profits are rising 40 percent a year, and Hammons is convinced that he made a good bargain. "Buying a business can be a treacherous affair," he says. "But if you do your homework, thoroughly understand the basics of the business, and get some breaks, it can be a tremendously satisfying experience."

1. Why did Grant Beck's business purchase go awry? List some of the errors Beck committed. How could he have avoided them? If Beck had come to you for advice on buying the company, what would you have told him?

2. Why did Larry Hammons's purchase of Rational Technology work out so well? What did he do that Grant Beck did not? What conclusions can you draw from comparing the experiences of these two business buyers?

Source: Adapted from Steven B. Kaufman, "Before You Buy, Be Careful," *Nation's Business*, March 1996, pp. 45-46.

Methods for Determining the Value of a Business

2. Describe the various ways of determining the value of a business.

Business valuation is partly an art and partly a science. Part of what makes establishing a reasonable price for a privately held business so difficult is the wide variety of factors that influence its value: the nature of the business itself, its position in the market or industry, the outlook for the market or industry, the company's financial status, its earning capacity, any intangible assets it may own (e.g., patents, trademarks, or copyrights), the value of other similar publicly held companies, and many other factors.

Computing the value of the company's tangible assets normally poses no major problem, but assigning a price to the intangibles, such as goodwill, almost always creates controversy. The seller expects goodwill to reflect the hard work and long hours invested in building the business. The buyer, however, is willing to pay extra only for those intangible assets that produce exceptional income. So, how can the buyer and the seller arrive at a fair price? There are few hard-and-fast rules in establishing the value of a business, but the following guidelines are helpful:

⭐ There is no single best method for determining a business's worth, since each business sale is different. The wisest approach is to compute a company's value using several techniques and then to choose the one that makes the most sense.

⭐ The deal must be financially feasible for both parties. The seller must be satisfied with the price received for the business, but the buyer cannot pay an excessively high price that would require heavy borrowing and would strain his cash flows from the outset.

⭐ Both the buyer and the seller should have access to the business records.

⭐ Valuations should be based on facts, not fiction.

⭐ No surprise is the best surprise. Both parties should deal with one another honestly and in good faith.[10]

The main reason that buyers purchase existing businesses is to get their future earning potential. The second most common reason is to obtain an established asset base. It is much easier to buy assets than to build them. Although evaluation methods should take these characteristics into consideration, too many business sellers and buyers depend on rules of thumb that ignore the unique features of small companies. Often, these rules of thumb are based on multiples of a company's net earnings and vary by industry. For instance, computer service companies are valued at 25 times their earnings, restaurants at 15 times earnings, and life insurance companies at 9 times earnings.[11] One recent study of small business sales across the United States conducted by Bizcomps found the average sales price was 2.7 times a company's earnings.[12] The problem is that such "one-size-fits-all" approaches seldom work because no two businesses are alike. The best rule of thumb to use when valuing businesses is "Don't use rules of thumb to value businesses." One expert warns, "Rules of thumb usually do not recognize the unique qualities of businesses or their economic value."[13]

This next section describes three basic techniques and several variations on them for determining the value of a hypothetical business, Lewis Electronics.

Basic Balance Sheet Methods: Net Worth = Assets − Liabilities

balance sheet technique—*a method of valuing a business based on the value of the company's net worth (net worth = total assets − total liabilities).*

BALANCE SHEET TECHNIQUE. The **balance sheet technique** is one of the most commonly used methods of evaluating a business, although it is not highly recommended because it oversimplifies the valuation process. This method computes the company's net worth or owner's equity (net worth = total assets − total liabilities) and uses this figure as the value. The problem with this technique is that it fails to recognize reality: Most small businesses have market values that exceed their reported book values.

The first step is to determine which assets are included in the sale. In most cases, the owner has some personal assets that he does not want to sell. Professional business brokers can help the buyer and the seller arrive at a reasonable value for the collection of assets included in the deal. Remember that net worth on a financial statement will likely differ significantly from actual net worth in the market. Figure 4.2 shows the balance sheet for Lewis Electronics. Based on this balance sheet, the company's net worth is $266,091 − $114,325 = $151,766.

adjusted balance sheet technique—*a method of valuing a business based on the market value of the company's net worth (net worth = total assets − total liabilities).*

VARIATION: ADJUSTED BALANCE SHEET TECHNIQUE. A more realistic method for determining a company's value is to adjust the book value of net worth to reflect *actual* market value. The values reported on a company's books may either overstate or understate the true value of assets and liabilities. Typical assets in a business sale include notes and accounts receivable, inventories, supplies, and fixtures. If a buyer purchases notes and accounts receivable, he should estimate the likelihood of their collection and adjust their value accordingly (refer to Table 4.1).

In manufacturing, wholesale, and retail businesses, inventory is usually the largest single asset in the sale. Taking a physical inventory count is the best way to determine accurately the quantity of goods to be transferred. The sale may include three types of inventory, each having its own method of valuation: raw materials, work-in-process, and finished goods.

The buyer and the seller must arrive at a method for evaluating the inventory. First-in, first-out (FIFO), last-in, first-out (LIFO), and average costing are three frequently used techniques, but the most common methods use the cost of last purchase and the replacement value of the inventory. Before accepting any inventory value, the buyer should evaluate the condition of the goods.

Figure 4.2
*Balance Sheet for
Lewis Electronics*

Lewis Electronics
Balance Sheet
June 30, 199X

Assets

Current Assets:

Cash	$11,655	
Accounts Receivable	15,876	
Inventory	56,523	
Supplies	8,574	
Prepaid Insurance	5,587	
Total Current Assets		$98,215

Fixed Assets:

Land		$24,000	
Buildings	$141,000		
less accumulated depreciation	51,500	89,500	
Office Equipment	$12,760		
less accumulated depreciation	7,159	5,601	
Factory Equipment	$59,085		
less accumulated depreciation	27,850	31,235	
Trucks and Autos	$28,730		
less accumulated depreciation	11,190	17,540	
Total Fixed Assets			$167,876
Total Assets			$266,091

Liabilities

Current Liabilities:

Accounts Payable	$19,497	
Mortgage Payable (current portion)	5,215	
Salaries Payable	3,671	
Note Payable	10,000	
Total Current Liabilities		$38,383

Long-term Liabilities:

Mortgage Payable	$54,542	
Note Payable	21,400	
Total Long-term Liabilities		$75,942
Total Liabilities		$114,325

Owners' Equity

Owners' Equity	$151,766
Total Liabilities and Owners' Equity	$266,091

Example

One young couple purchased a lumber yard without sufficiently examining the inventory. After completing the sale, they discovered that most of the lumber in a warehouse they had neglected to inspect was warped and was of little value as building material. The bargain price they paid for the business turned out not to be the good deal they had expected.

To avoid such problems, some buyers insist on having a knowledgeable representative on an inventory team to count the inventory and check its condition. Nearly every sale involves merchandise that cannot be sold, but by taking this precaution, a buyer minimizes the chance of being stuck with worthless inventory. Fixed assets transferred in a sale might include land, buildings, equipment, and fixtures. Business owners frequently carry real estate and buildings at prices well below their actual market value. Equipment and fixtures, depending on their condition and usefulness, may increase or decrease the true value of the business. Appraisals of these assets on insurance policies are helpful guidelines for establishing market value. Also, business brokers can be useful in determining the current market value of fixed assets. Some brokers use an estimate of what it would cost to replace a company's physical assets (less a reasonable allowance for depreciation) to determine value. For Lewis Electronics, the adjusted net worth is $274,638 − $114,325 = $160,313 (see the adjusted balance sheet in Figure 4.3), indicating that some of the entries in its books did not accurately reflect true market value.

Business evaluations based on balance sheet methods suffer one major drawback: they do not consider the future earning potential of the business. These techniques value assets at current prices and do not consider them as tools for creating future profits. The next method for computing the value of a business is based on its expected future earnings.

EARNINGS APPROACH. The buyer of an existing business is essentially purchasing its future income. The **earnings approach** is more refined because it considers the future income potential of the business. There are three variations of the earnings approach.

earnings approach— *a method of valuing a business that recognizes that a buyer is purchasing the future income (earnings) potential of a business.*

VARIATION 1: EXCESS EARNINGS METHOD. This method combines both the value of a business's existing assets (minus its liabilities) and an estimate of its future earnings potential to determine its selling price. One advantage of this technique is that it offers an estimate of goodwill. **Goodwill** is an intangible asset that often creates problems in a business sale. In fact, the most common method of valuing a business is to compute its tangible net worth and then to add an often arbitrary adjustment for goodwill. In essence, goodwill is the difference between an established, successful business and one that has yet to prove itself. It is based on the company's reputation and its ability to attract customers. A buyer should not accept blindly the seller's arbitrary adjustment for goodwill because it is likely to be inflated.

goodwill—*an intangible asset that reflects the value of a company's reputation, its established customer and supplier contacts, name recognition, and other factors.*

The excess earnings method provides a more consistent and realistic approach for determining the value of goodwill. It measures goodwill by the amount of profit the business earns above that of the average firm in the same industry. It also assumes that the owner is entitled to a reasonable return on the firm's adjusted tangible net worth.

Step 1: Compute Adjusted Tangible Net Worth. Using the previous method of valuation, the buyer should compute the firm's adjusted tangible net worth. Total tangible assets (adjusted for market value) minus total liabilities yields adjusted tangible net worth. In the Lewis Electronics example, adjusted tangible net worth is $274,638 − $114,325 = $160,313 (refer to Figure 4.3).

opportunity cost—*the cost of the next best alternative choice; the cost of giving up one alternative to get another.*

Step 2: Calculate the Opportunity Costs of Investing in the Business. Opportunity costs represent the cost of forgoing a choice. If the buyer chooses to purchase the assets of a business, he cannot invest his money elsewhere. Therefore, the opportunity cost of the purchase would be the amount that the buyer could earn by investing the same amount *in a similar risk investment.*

Lewis Electronics
Adjusted Balance Sheet
June 30, 199X

Assets

Current Assets:

Cash	$11,655	
Accounts Receivable	10,051	
Inventory	39,261	
Supplies	7,492	
Prepaid Insurance	5,587	
Total Current Assets		$74,046

Fixed Assets:

Land		$36,900	
Buildings	$177,000		
less accumulated depreciation	51,500	125,500	
Office Equipment	$11,645		
less accumulated depreciation	7,159	4,486	
Factory Equipment	$50,196		
less accumulated depreciation	27,850	22,346	
Trucks and Autos	$22,550		
less accumulated depreciation	11,190	11,360	
Total Fixed Assets			$200,592
Total Assets			$274,638

Liabilities

Current Liabilities:

Accounts Payable	$19,497	
Mortgage Payable (current portion)	5,215	
Salaries Payable	3,671	
Note Payable	10,000	
Total Current Liabilities		$38,383

Long-term Liabilities:

Mortgage Payable	$54,542	
Note Payable	21,400	
Total Long-term Liabilities		$75,942
Total Liabilities		$114,325

Owners' Equity

Owners' Equity	$160,313
Total Liabilities and Owners' Equity	$274,638

There are three components in the rate of return used to value a business: (1) the basic, risk-free return, (2) an inflation premium, and (3) the risk allowance for investing in the particular business. The basic, risk-free return and the inflation premium are reflected in investments like treasury bonds. To determine the appropriate rate of return for investing in a business, the buyer must add to this base rate a factor reflecting the risk of purchasing the company. The greater the risk is, the higher the rate of return will be. A normal-risk business typically indicates a 25 percent rate of return. In the Lewis Electronics example, the opportunity cost of the investment is $160,313 \times 25$ percent $= \$40,078$.

The second part of the buyer's opportunity cost is the salary that she could earn working for someone else. For the Lewis Electronics example, if the buyer purchases the business, she must forgo the $25,000 that she could earn working elsewhere. Adding these amounts together yields a total opportunity cost of $65,078.

Step 3: Project Net Earnings. The buyer must estimate the company's net earnings for the upcoming year before subtracting the owner's salary. Averages can be misleading, so the buyer must be sure to investigate the trend of net earnings. Have they risen steadily over the past five years, dropped significantly, remained relatively constant, or fluctuated wildly? Past income statements provide useful guidelines for estimating earnings. In the Lewis Electronics example, the buyer and an accountant project net earnings to be $74,000.

Step 4: Compute Extra Earning Power. A company's extra earning power is the difference between forecasted earnings (step 3) and total opportunity costs (step 2). Many small businesses that are for sale do not have extra earning power (i.e., excess earnings), and they show marginal or no profits. The extra earning power of Lewis Electronics is $74,000 - \$65,000 = \$8,922$.

Step 5: Estimate the Value of Intangibles. The owner can use the extra earning power of the business to estimate the value of its intangible assets, that is, its goodwill. Multiplying the extra earning power by a years-of-profit figure yields an estimate of the intangible assets' value. The years-of-profit figure for a normal-risk business ranges from 3 to 4. A very high risk business may have a years-of-profit figure of 1, whereas a well-established firm might use a figure of 7. For Lewis Electronics, the value of intangibles (assuming normal risk) would be $8,922 \times 3 = \$26,766$.

Step 6: Determine the Value of the Business. To determine the value of the business, the buyer simply adds together the adjusted tangible net worth (step 1) and the value of the intangibles (step 5). Using this method, the value of Lewis Electronics is $160,313 + \$26,766 = \$187,079$.

Both the buyer and seller should consider the tax implications of transferring goodwill. The amount that the seller receives for goodwill is taxed as ordinary income. The buyer cannot count this amount as a deduction because goodwill is a capital asset that cannot be depreciated or amortized for tax purposes. Instead, the buyer would be better off paying the seller for signing a covenant not to compete because its value is fully tax deductible. The success of this approach depends on the accuracy of the buyer's estimates of net earnings and risk, but it does offer a systematic method for assigning a value to goodwill.

VARIATION 2: CAPITALIZED EARNINGS APPROACH. Another earnings approach capitalizes expected net profits to determine the value of a business. The buyer should prepare his own pro forma income statement and should ask the seller to prepare one also. Many appraisers use a five-year weighted average of past sales (with the greatest weights assigned to the most recent years) to estimate sales for the upcoming year.

Once again, the buyer must evaluate the risk of purchasing the business to determine the appropriate rate of return on the investment. The greater the perceived risk, the higher the return that the buyer requires. Risk determination is always somewhat subjective, but it is necessary for proper evaluation.

The **capitalized earnings approach** divides estimated net earnings (after subtracting the owner's reasonable salary) by the rate of return that reflects the risk level. For Lewis Electronics, the capitalized value (assuming a reasonable salary of $25,000) is:

$$\frac{\text{Net earnings (after deducting owner's salary)}}{\text{Rate of return}} = \frac{\$74,000 - \$25,000}{25\%} = \$196,000$$

Clearly, firms with lower risk factors are more valuable (e.g., a 10 percent rate of return would yield a value of $499,000) than are those with higher risk factors (e.g., a 50 percent rate of return would yield a value of $99,800). Most normal-risk businesses use a rate-of-return factor ranging from 25 to 33 percent. The lowest risk factor that most buyers would accept for any business ranges from 15 to 20 percent.

VARIATION 3: DISCOUNTED FUTURE EARNINGS APPROACH. This variation of the earnings approach assumes that a dollar earned in the future will be worth less than that same dollar today. Therefore, using this approach, the buyer estimates the company's net income for several years into the future and then discounts these future earnings back to their present value. The resulting present value is an estimate of the company's worth.

The reduced value of future dollars has nothing to do with inflation. Instead, present value represents the cost of the buyers' giving up the opportunity to earn a reasonable rate of return by receiving income in the future instead of today. To illustrate the importance of the time value of money, consider two $1 million sweepstake winners. Rob wins $1 million in a sweepstakes, but he receives it in $50,000 installments over 20 years. If Rob invested every installment at 15 percent interest, he would have accumulated $5,890,505.98 at the end of 20 years. Lisa wins $1 million in another sweepstakes, but she collects her winnings in one lump sum. If Lisa invested her $1 million today at 15 percent, she would have accumulated $16,366,537.39 at the end of 20 years. The difference in their wealth is the result of the time value of money.

DISCOUNTED FUTURE EARNINGS APPROACH. The **discounted future earnings approach** has five steps.

Step 1: Project future earnings for five years into the future. One way is to assume that earnings will grow by a constant amount over the next five years. Perhaps a better method is to develop three forecasts—an optimistic, a pessimistic, and a most likely—for each year and then find a weighted average using the following:

$$\text{Forecasted earnings for year } i = \frac{\begin{pmatrix}\text{Optimistic earnings for year } i\end{pmatrix} + \begin{pmatrix}\text{Most likely forecast for year } i \times 4\end{pmatrix} + \begin{pmatrix}\text{Pessimistic forecast for year } i\end{pmatrix}}{6}$$

For Lewis Electronics, the buyer's forecasts are:

Year	Pessimistic	Most Likely	Optimistic	Weighted Average
XXX1	$65,000	$74,000	$92,000	$75,500
XXX2	$74,000	$90,000	$101,000	$89,167
XXX3	$82,000	$100,000	$112,000	$99,000
XXX4	$88,000	$109,000	$120,000	$107,333
XXX5	$88,000	$115,000	$122,000	$111,667

The buyer must remember that the farther into the future one forecasts, the less reliable the estimates will be.

capitalized earnings approach—*a method of valuing a business that divides estimated (earnings) by the rate of return that the buyer could earn on a similar-risk investment.*

discounted future earnings approach—*a method of valuing a business that forecasts a company's earnings several years into the future and then discounts them back to their present value.*

Step 2: Discount these future earnings at the appropriate present value rate. The rate that the buyer selects should reflect the rate that he could earn on a similar risk investment. Because Lewis Electronics is a normal-risk business, the buyer chooses a present value rate of 25 percent.

Year	Income Forecast (Weighted Average)	Present Value Factor (at 25 percent)*	Net Present Value
XXX1	$75,500	.8000	$60,400
XXX2	$89,167	.6400	$57,067
XXX3	$99,000	.5120	$50,688
XXX4	$107,333	.4096	$43,964
XXX5	$111,667	.3277	$36,593
		Total	$248,712

*the appropriate present value factor can be found by looking in published present value tables, by using modern calculators or computers, or by solving this formula:

$$\text{Present value factor} = \frac{1}{(1 + k)^t}$$

where k = rate of return
t = year (t = 1,2,3 ..., n).

Step 3: Estimate the income stream beyond five years. One technique suggests multiplying the fifth year income by 1/rate of return. For Lewis Electronics, the estimate is:

$$\text{Income beyond year 5} = \$111,667 \times \frac{1}{25\%} = \$446,668$$

Step 4: Discount the income estimate beyond five years using the present value factor for the sixth year. For Lewis Electronics:

$$\text{Present value of income beyond year 5} = \$446,668 \times 0.2622 = \$117,116$$

Step 5: Compute the total value of the business.

$$\text{Total value} = \$248,712 + \$117,116 = \$365,828$$

The primary advantage of this technique is that it evaluates a business solely on the basis of its future earning potential, but its reliability depends on making forecasts of future earnings and on choosing a realistic present value rate. In other words, a company's present value is tied to its future performance, which is not always easy to project. The discounted cash flow technique is especially well suited for valuing service businesses (whose asset bases are often small) and for companies experiencing high growth rates.

market approach—
a method of valuing a business that uses the price/earnings (P/E) ratio of similar, publicly-held companies to determine value.

MARKET APPROACH. The **market (or price/earnings) approach** uses the price/earnings ratios of similar businesses to establish the value of a company. The buyer must use businesses whose stocks are publicly traded in order to get a meaningful comparison. A company's price/earnings ratio (or P/E ratio) is the price of one share of its common stock in the market divided by its earnings per share (after deducting preferred stock dividends). To get a representative P/E ratio, the buyer should average the P/Es of as many similar businesses as possible.

To compute the company's value, the buyer multiplies the average price/earnings ratio by the private company's estimated earnings. For example, suppose that the buyer found four companies comparable to Lewis Electronics, but whose stock is publicly traded.

Their price/earnings ratios are:

Company 1	3.3
Company 2	3.8
Company 3	4.7
Company 4	4.1
Average	3.975

Using this average P/E ratio produces a value of $294,150:

Value = Average P/E ratio × Estimated net earnings = 3.975 × $74,000 = $294,150

The biggest advantage of the market approach is its simplicity, but this method does have several disadvantages, including the following:[14]

Necessary comparisons between publicly traded and privately owned companies. Because the stock of privately owned companies is illiquid, the P/E ratio used is often subjective and lower than that of publicly held companies.

Unrepresented earnings estimates. The private company's net earnings may not realistically reflect its true earning potential. To minimize taxes, owners usually attempt to keep profits low and rely on fringe benefits to make up the difference.

Finding similar companies for comparison. Often, it is extremely difficult for a buyer to find comparable publicly held companies when estimating the appropriate P/E ratio.

Applying the after-tax earnings of a private company to determine its value. If a prospective buyer is using an after-tax P/E ratio from a public company, he also must use the after-tax earnings from the private company.

Despite its drawbacks, the market approach is useful as a general guideline to establish a company's value.

Which of these methods is best for determining the value of a small business? Simply stated, there is no single best method. Valuing a business is partly an art and partly a science. Using these techniques, a range of values will emerge. Buyers should look for values that might cluster together and then use their best judgment to determine their offering price.

Figure 4.4 on page 127 shows how small business owners, business brokers, and financial consultants differ in the business valuation methods they prefer to use. Table 4.4 summarizes the valuation techniques covered in this chapter.

Table 4.4
What's It Worth? A Summary of Business Valuation Techniques

Balance Sheet Technique

Book value of net worth = Total assets − Total liabilities
= $266,091 − $114,325
= $151,766

Variation: Adjusted Balance Sheet Technique

Net worth adjusted to reflect market value = $274,638 − $114,325
= $160,313

Earnings Approach

Variation: Excess Earnings Method

Step 1: Adjusted tangible net worth = $274,638 − $114,325 = $160,313

Step 2: Opportunity costs = Opportunity cost of investing + Salary forgone
= $160,313 x 25% + 25,000 = $65,078

Step 3: Estimated net earnings = $74,000

Continued

Step 4: Extra earning power = Estimated net earnings − Total opportunity costs
= $74,000 − $65,078
= $8,922

Step 5: Value of intangibles (goodwill) = Extra earning power × Years of profit figure
= $8,922 × 3
= $26,766

Step 6: Value of business = Tangible net worth + Value of intangibles
= $160,313 + 26,766
= $187,079

Variation 2: Capitalized Earnings Approach

$$\text{Value} = \frac{\text{Net earnings (after deducting owner's salary)}}{\text{Rate of return on a similar-risk investment}}$$

$$= \frac{\$74,000 - \$25,000}{25\%} = \$196,000$$

Variation 3: Discounted Future Earnings Approach

Step 1. Project future earnings

Year	Pessimistic	Most Likely	Optimistic	Weighted Average*
XXX1	$65,000	$74,000	$94,000	$75,500
XXX2	$74,000	$90,000	$101,000	$89,167
XXX3	$82,000	$100,000	$112,000	$99,000
XXX4	$88,000	$109,000	120,000	$107,333
XXX5	$88,000	$115,000	$122,000	$111,667

$$^*\text{Weighted average} = \frac{P + 4 \times ML + O}{6}$$

Step 2. Discount future earnings using the appropriate present value factor

Year	Forecasted Earnings	Present Value Factor	Net Present Value
XXX1	$75,500	.8000	$60,400
XXX2	$89,167	.6400	$57,067
XXX3	$99,000	.5120	$50,688
XXX4	$107,333	.4096	$43,964
XXX5	$111,667	.3277	$36,593
		Total	$248,712

Step 3. Estimate income stream beyond 5 years.

$$\text{Income Stream} = \text{Fifth Year Forecasted Income} \times \frac{1}{\text{Rate of Return}}$$

$$= \$111,667 \times \frac{1}{25\%}$$

$$= \$446,668$$

Step 4. Discount income stream beyond 5 years (using sixth year present value factor).
Present value of income stream = $446,668 × .2622 = $117,116

Continued

Step 5. Compute total value.

    Total value = $248,712 + $117,116 = $365,828

Market Approach

Value = Estimated earnings × Average Price/Earnings ratio of representative companies
    = $74,000 × 3.975 = $294,150

Which value is correct? Remember: There is no best method of valuing a business. These techniques provide only estimates of a company's worth. The particular method used depends on the unique qualities of the business and the special circumstances surrounding the sale.

Figure 4.4
Preferred Methods of Business Valuation
Source: Small Business Reports, July 1992, p. 7.

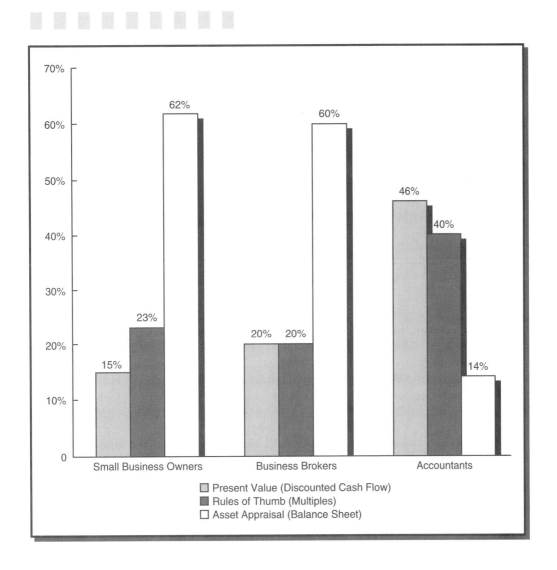

5. Understand
the seller's side
of the buyout
decision and how to
structure the deal

Understanding the Seller's Side

Few events are more anticipated—and more emotional—for entrepreneurs than selling a business. It often produces vast personal wealth and a completely new lifestyle, and this newly gained wealth offers freedom and the opportunity to catch up on all the things the owners missed out on while building the business. Yet, many entrepreneurs who sell out experience a tremendous void in their lives. One entrepreneur who sold out regretfully explains, "I never realized the role of my business in my life. More than the focal point of my life, it was my very identity."[15].

Selling a business is no simple task. Done properly, it takes time, patience, and preparation to locate a suitable buyer, strike a deal, and make the transition. Too often, business owners put off the selling process until the last minute—at retirement age or when a business crisis looms. One entrepreneur who sold his business says, "Entrepreneurs always think their businesses will be worth more later on. Mistakenly, they hold on [until] it's too late. Know when to walk away, and don't get greedy."[16] Such a "fire sale" approach rarely yields the maximum price for a business. Advance planning and maintaining accurate financial records are keys to a successful sale.

Before selling the business, an entrepreneur must ask some important questions: Do I want to walk away from the business completely, or do I plan to stay on after the sale? If I decide to stay on, how involved do I want to be in running the company? How much can I realistically expect to get for the business? Is this amount of money sufficient to maintain my desired lifestyle? Rather than sell the business to an outsider, should I be transferring ownership to my kids or to my employees? Who are the professionals (business brokers, accountants, attorneys, tax advisers) I will need to help me close the sale successfully? How do I expect the buyer to pay for the company? Am I willing to finance at least some of the purchase price?

Structuring the Deal

Next to picking the right buyer, planning the structure of the deal is one of the most important decisions a seller can make. Entrepreneurs who sell their companies without considering the tax implications of the deal can wind up paying the IRS as much as 70 percent of the proceeds in the form of capital gains and other taxes![17] A skilled tax adviser or financial planner can help business sellers legally minimize the bite various taxes take out of the proceeds of the sale.

Exit Strategy Options

STRAIGHT BUSINESS SALE. A straight business sale may be best for those entrepreneurs who want to step down and turn over the reins of the company to someone else. A recent study of small business sales in 60 different categories found that 94 percent were asset sales; the remaining 6 percent involved the sale of stock. About 22 percent were for cash, and 75 percent included a down payment with a note carried by the seller. The remaining 3 percent relied on a note from the seller with no down payment. When the deal included a down payment, it averaged 33 percent of the purchase price. Only 40 percent of the business sales studied included covenants not to compete.[18]

Although selling a business outright is often the safest exit path for an entrepreneur, it usually is the most expensive one. Sellers who cash out and take the money "up front" face an oppressive tax burden. They must pay a 28 percent capital gains tax on the sale price less their investments in the company. Neither is a straight sale an attractive exit strategy for those who want to stay on with the company or for those who want to surrender control of the company gradually rather than all at once.

FORM A FAMILY LIMITED PARTNERSHIP. An entrepreneur could transfer her business to her children but still maintain control over it by forming a family limited partnership. The entrepreneur would take the role of the general partner with the children becoming limited partners in the business. The general partner keeps just 1 percent of the company, but the partnership agreement gives the entrepreneur total control over the business. The children own 99 percent of the company but have little or no say over how to run the business. Until the founder decides to step down and turn over the reins of the company to the next generation, she continues to run the business and sets up significant tax savings for the ultimate transfer of power.

SELL A CONTROLLING INTEREST. Sometimes business owners sell the majority interest in their companies to investors, competitors, suppliers, or large companies with an agreement that they will stay on after the sale as managers or consultants.

For instance, Leon and Pam Seidman sold 55 percent of Cosmic Pet Products, a catnip business Leon started while in college, to Four Paws Pet Products, a much larger company. Four Paws gives the Seidmans the autonomy to run the business as they did before the sale, although the Seidmans do work with Four Paws on strategic planning and pricing issues. For both the Seidmans and Four Paws, the sale has produced positive outcomes. The Seidmans still get to run the day-to-day operations of the business they love without having to worry about the financial struggles of keeping a small company going. With the Seidman's help, Four Paws has improved Cosmic Pet Products' distribution and pricing and built it into the largest catnip company in the country, commanding 60 percent of the market! [19]

| Cosmic Pet Products |

RESTRUCTURE THE COMPANY. Another way for business owners to cash out gradually is to replace the existing corporation with a new one, formed with other investors. The owner essentially is performing a leveraged buyout of his own company. For example, assume that you own a company worth $15 million. You form a new corporation with $12 million borrowed from a bank and $3 million in equity: $1.5 million of your own equity and $1.5 million in equity from an investor who wants you to stay on with the business. The new company buys your company for $15 million. You net $13.5 in cash ($15 million − your $1.5 million equity investment) and still own 50 percent of the new leveraged business (see Figure 4.5).[20]

SELL TO AN INTERNATIONAL BUYER. In an increasingly global marketplace, small U.S. businesses have become attractive buyout targets for foreign companies. Foreign buyers— mostly European—buy more than 1,000 U.S. businesses each year. Despite the publicity that Japanese buyouts get, England leads the list of nations acquiring U.S. companies.

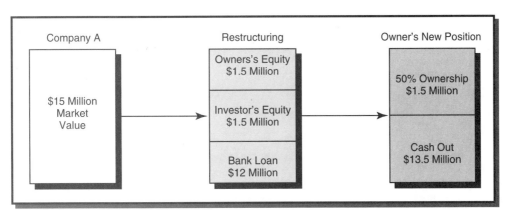

Figure 4.5
Restructuring a Business for Sale
Source: Peter Collins, "Cashing Out and Maintaining Control," *Small Business Reports,* December 1989, p. 28

Small business owners are receptive to international offers. According to one survey, of the entrepreneurs considering selling their businesses, 69 percent said they would sell to a foreign investor.[21]

In most instances, foreign companies buy U.S. businesses to gain access to a lucrative, growing market. They look for a team of capable managers, whom they typically retain for a given time period. They also want companies that are profitable, stable, and growing.

Selling to foreign buyers can have disadvantages, however. They typically purchase 100 percent of a company, thereby making the previous owner merely an employee. Relationships with foreign owners also can be difficult to manage. In a recent survey, executives at foreign-owned small businesses stated that they don't understand what drives their bosses, and that their relationships generally get worse over time .[22]

USE A TWO-STEP SALE. For owners wanting the security of a sales contract now but not wanting to step down from the company's helm for several years, a two-step sale may be ideal. The buyer purchases the business in two phases—getting 20 to 70 percent today and agreeing to buy the remainder within a specific time period. Until the final transaction takes place, the entrepreneur retains at least partial control of the company.

ESTABLISH AN EMPLOYEE STOCK OWNERSHIP PLAN (ESOP). Some owners cash out by selling to their employees through an **employee stock ownership plan (ESOP).** An ESOP is a form of employee benefit plan in which a trust created for employees purchases their employer's stock. Here's how an ESOP works: The company transfers shares of its stock to the ESOP trust, and the trust uses the stock as collateral to borrow enough money to purchase the shares from the company. The company guarantees payment of the loan principal and interest and makes tax-deductible contributions to the trust to repay the loan (see Figure 4.6). The company then distributes the stock to employees' accounts based on a predetermined formula. In addition to the tax benefits an ESOP offers, the plan permits the owner to transfer all or part of the company to employees as gradually or as suddenly as preferred.

To use an ESOP successfully, a small business should be profitable (with pretax profits exceeding $100,000) and should have a payroll of more than $500,000 a year. Generally,

employee stock ownership plan (ESOP)—*an employee benefit plan in which a trust created for employees purchases stock in their employer's company.*

Figure 4.6
A Typical Employee Stock Ownership Plan (ESOP)
Source: Corey Rosen, "Sharing Ownership with Employees," *Small Business Reports,* December 1990, p.63.

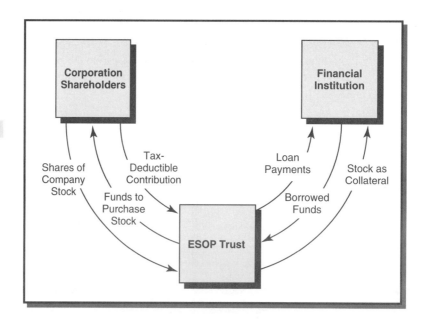

companies with fewer than 15 to 20 employees do not find ESOPs beneficial. For companies that prepare properly, however, ESOPs offer significant financial and managerial benefits. "The owner gets to sell off his stock at whatever annual pace appeals to him. There's no cost to the employees, who eventually get to take over the company. And for the company the cost of the buyout is fully deductible," says one consultant.[23]

YOU BE THE CONSULTANT...

A Seller's Tale

Joesph Grassadonia loves the ocean so much that he planned his life around it, including starting businesses that would allow him to have both the time and the money to enjoy the sun and surf of California's beaches. Over the years, Grassadonia launched six magazines, including his most recent, *Dive Travel*. He compares the thrill and challenge of starting and managing a magazine to surfing and catching the ultimate wave. "When you're surfing and you're totally in control of the wave, and the equipment is right and everything is working, it's exhilarating," he says. After five years of running *Dive Travel*, however, Grassadonia says he got to the point where it wasn't fun anymore. "That's when I knew I had to sell," he recalls.

Actually, Grassadonia knew he would eventually sell *Dive Travel* from the day he started it. Managing and growing a magazine is "not my forte," he says. He began shopping for a business broker, and settled on a local firm to help him sell the company. The first order of business was to put a price tag on *Dive Travel*, something that proved to be a more emotional experience for Grassadonia than he had imagined. Although he knew that a company's value depends on the cash it can generate, he couldn't help but recall all of the energy, time, and talent he had invested in building the magazine from nothing to its current level. "This business is a chunk of my life. How do you put a value on that?" he asks philosophically.

Grassadonia had built *Dive Travel* into a successful publication. "We do business with just about every major advertiser in the marketplace," he says. "It would be very expensive to try and [re]create that." Using *Dive Travel's* sales of $324,000 and earnings of $50,000, the broker suggested an asking price of $500,000. For the next year, the business attracted very few leads—not an unusual pattern in selling a business. Ads in industry trade journals produced only a few nibbles but no serious buyers. Waiting to sell was wearing on Grassadonia, so he and the broker reduced the price to $450,000. Several more months slipped by with no interest from buyers, and Grassadonia was beginning to wonder if *anyone* wanted to buy *Dive Travel*.

Finally, Susan Wilmink and Thomas Schneck contacted Grassadonia's broker about *Dive Travel*. The couple was living in Germany, where Wilmink worked for a large international magazine publisher and Schneck owned a software company. The only problem was that Wilmink and Schneck couldn't afford to buy *Dive Travel* outright. They proposed that Grassadonia sell them a controlling interest in the company and stay on as a consultant for three years. Grassadonia hesitated at first but then agreed to stay on as long as Wilmink and Schneck took over the day-to-day operations of running the business. A major factor in his decision was Wilmink's presentation on how she and Schneck planned to run the company—from adding a World Wide Web page to repositioning the magazine. "Susan came in with a vision," says Grassadonia.

Negotiating the final deal took another six months, and at times the discussions became heated. At one such emotional moment, Barkley, Grassadonia's 13-year-old golden retriever walked over to Wilmink's chair, jumped up, and licked her face. That broke the tension, everyone started laughing, and Wilmink decided to name the new business Barkley Publishing. The final price the parties agreed on was $215,000 for the 51 percent controlling interest Wilmink and Schneck got. Wilmink became the new president and publisher, and Grassadonia agreed to stay on as a paid consultant for three years. At the end of that time, he would sell his stock, with Wilmink and Schneck getting the right of first refusal. In addition, Grassadonia got a percentage of the company's revenues over the three years.

The deal has worked to everyone's satisfaction. Grassadonia has the freedom to surf whenever he pleases, and Wilmink and Schneck have the company they wanted. *Dive Travel's* circulation has more than doubled, revenues have nearly doubled, and profits are up.

1. Why is the process of valuing a business so difficult for the entrepreneur who founded it?
2. Which method(s) of valuing a business do you think would be most appropriate in placing a realistic value on *Dive Travel*? Explain.
3. Evaluate the final deal the parties struck from both the buyers' and the seller's perspectives. Do you think the deal was "fair"?

Source: Adapted from Christopher Caggiano, "The Seller," *Inc.*, June 1996, pp. 54–56.

Negotiating the Deal

Although determining the value of a business for sale is an important step in the buying process, it is not the final one. The buyer must sit down with the seller to negotiate the actual selling price for the business and, more importantly, the terms of the deal. The final deal the buyer strikes depends, in large part, on her negotiating skills. The first rule of negotiating a deal is never confuse price with value. Value is what the business is actually worth; price is what the buyer agrees to pay. In a business sale, the party who is the better bargainer usually comes out on top. The seller is looking to:

- ☆ get the highest price possible for the business.
- ☆ sever all responsibility for the company's liabilities.
- ☆ avoid unreasonable contract terms that might limit her future opportunities.
- ☆ maximize the cash she gets from the deal.
- ☆ minimize the tax burden from the sale.
- ☆ make sure the buyer will be able to make all future payments.

The buyer seeks to:

- ☆ get the business at the lowest possible price.
- ☆ negotiate favorable payment terms, preferably over time.
- ☆ get assurances that he is buying the business he thinks he is getting.
- ☆ avoid putting the seller in a position to open a competing business.
- ☆ minimize the amount of cash paid "up front."

FACTORS AFFECTING THE NEGOTIATION PROCESS. Before beginning negotiations, a buyer should take stock of some basic issues. How strong is the seller's desire to sell? Is the seller willing to finance part of the purchase price? What terms does the buyer suggest? Which ones are most important to the buyer? Is it urgent that the seller close the deal quickly? What deal structure best suits the buyer's needs? What are the tax consequences for both parties? Will the seller sign a restrictive covenant? Is the seller willing to stay on with the company for a time as a consultant? What general economic conditions exist in the industry at the time of the sale? Sellers tend to have the upper hand in good economic times, and buyers will have an advantage during recessionary periods in an industry.

THE NEGOTIATION PROCESS. On the surface, the negotiation process appears to be strictly adversarial. Although each party may be trying to accomplish objectives that are at odds with those of the opposing party, the negotiation process does not have to turn into a nasty battle of wits with overtones of "If you win, then I lose." The negotiation process will go much more smoothly and much faster if both parties work to establish a cooperative relationship based on honesty and trust from the outset. A successful deal requires both parties to examine and articulate their respective positions while trying to understand the other party's position. Recognizing that neither of them will benefit without a deal, both parties must work to achieve their objectives while making certain concessions to keep the negotiations alive. To avoid a stalled deal, both buyer and seller should go into the negotiation with a list of objectives ranked in order of priority. This increases the likelihood of both parties getting most of what they want from the bargain. Knowing which terms are most important (and which are least important) to them allows the parties to make concessions without "giving away the farm" and without getting bogged down in "nit-picking." If, for instance, the seller insists on a term that the buyer cannot agree to, he can explain why and then offer to give up something in exchange.

Figure 4.7 offers five tips on making the negotiation process a successful one.

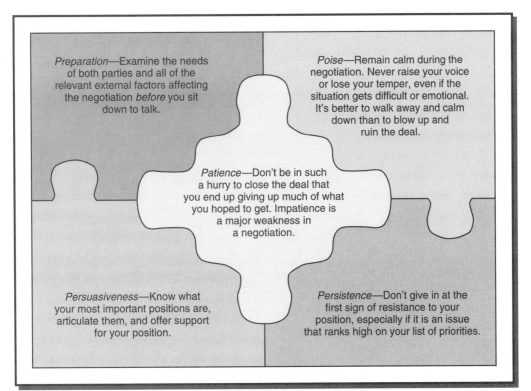

Figure 4.7
The Five Ps of Negotiating
Source: Adapted from Right Associates, Philadelphia, PA.

Preparation—Examine the needs of both parties and all of the relevant external factors affecting the negotiation *before* you sit down to talk.

Poise—Remain calm during the negotiation. Never raise your voice or lose your temper, even if the situation gets difficult or emotional. It's better to walk away and calm down than to blow up and ruin the deal.

Patience—Don't be in such a hurry to close the deal that you end up giving up much of what you hoped to get. Impatience is a major weakness in a negotiation.

Persuasiveness—Know what your most important positions are, articulate them, and offer support for your position.

Persistence—Don't give in at the first sign of resistance to your position, especially if it is an issue that ranks high on your list of priorities.

CHAPTER SUMMARY

1. Understand the advantages and disadvantages of buying an existing business.
- The *advantages* of buying an existing business include: A successful business may continue to be successful; the business may already have the best location; employees and suppliers are already established; equipment is installed and its productive capacity known; inventory is in place and trade credit established; the owner hits the ground running; the buyer can use the expertise of the previous owner; and the business may be a bargain.
- The *disadvantages* of buying an existing business include: An existing business may be for sale because it is deteriorating; the previous owner may have created ill will; employees inherited with the business may not be suitable; its location may have become unsuitable; equipment and facilities may be obsolete; change and innovation are hard to implement; inventory may be outdated; accounts receivable may be worth less than face value; and, the business may be overpriced.

2. Define the steps involved in the right way to buy a business.
- Buying a business can be a treacherous experience unless the buyer is well prepared. The right way to buy a business is: Analyze your skills, abilities, and interests to determine the ideal business for you; prepare a list of potential candidates, including those that might be in the hidden market; investigate and evaluate candidate businesses and evaluate the best one; explore financing options before you actually need the money; and, finally, ensure a smooth transition.

3. Explain the process of evaluating an existing business.
- Rushing into a deal can be the biggest mistake a business buyer can make. Before closing a deal, every business buyer should investigate five critical areas: **a.** Why does the owner wish to sell? Look for the *real* reason. **b.** Determine the physical condition of the business. Consider both the building and its location. **c.** Conduct a thorough analysis of the market for your products or services. Who are the present and potential customers? Conduct an equally thorough analysis of competitors, both direct and indirect. How do they operate and why do customers prefer them? **d.** Consider all of the legal aspects which might constrain the expansion and growth of the business: Did you comply with the provisions of a bulk transfer? Negotiate a restrictive covenant? Consider ongoing legal liabilities? **e.** Analyze the financial condition of the business, looking at financial statements, income tax returns, and especially cash flow.

4. Describe the various ways of determining the value of a business.

- Placing a value on a business is partly an art and partly a science. There is no single "best" method for determining the value of a business. The following techniques (with several variations) are useful: the balance sheet technique (adjusted balance sheet technique); the earnings approach (excess earnings method, capitalized earnings approach, and discounted future earnings approach); and the market approach.

5. Understand the seller's side of the buyout decision and how to structure the deal.

- Selling a business takes time, patience, and preparation to locate a suitable buyer, strike a deal, and make the transition. Sellers must always structure the deal with tax consequences in mind. Common exit strategies include: a straight business sale, forming a family limited partnership, selling a controlling interest in the business, restructuring the company, selling to an international buyer, using a two-step sale, and establishing an employee stock ownership plan (ESOP).

6. Understand how the negotiation process works and identify the factors that affect the negotiation process.

- The first rule of negotiating is never confuse price with value. In a business sale, the party who is the better negotiator usually comes out on top. Before beginning negotiations, a buyer should identify the factors that are affecting the negotiations and then develop a negotiating strategy. The best deals are the result of a cooperative relationship between the parties based on trust.

DISCUSSION QUESTIONS

1. What advantages can an entrepreneur who buys a business gain over one who starts a business "from scratch"?
2. How would you go about determining the value of the assets of a business if you were unfamiliar with them?
3. Why do so many entrepreneurs run into trouble when they buy an existing business? Outline the steps involved in the *right* way to buy a business.
4. When evaluating an existing business that is for sale, what areas should an entrepreneur consider? Briefly summarize the key elements of each area.
5. How should a buyer evaluate a business's goodwill?
6. What is a restrictive covenant? Is it fair to ask the seller of a travel agency located in a small town to sign a restrictive covenant for one year covering a 20-square-mile area? Explain.
7. How much negative information can you expect the seller to give you about the business? How can a prospective buyer find out such information?
8. Why is it so difficult for buyers and sellers to agree on a price for a business?
9. Which method of valuing a business is best? Why?
10. Outline the different exit strategy options available to a seller.
11. What are the five Ps of a successful negotiation process?

Beyond the Classroom...

1. Ask several new owners who purchased existing businesses the following questions:
   a. How did you determine the value of the business?
   b. How close was the price paid for the business to the value assessed prior to purchase?
   c. What percentage of the accounts receivable was collectible?
   d. How accurate have their projections been concerning customers (sales volume and number of customers, especially)?
2. Visit a business broker and ask how he or she brings a buyer and seller together. What does a broker do to facilitate the sale? What methods does the broker use to determine the value of a business?
3. Invite an attorney to speak to your class about the legal aspects of buying a business. How does he or she recommend a business buyer be protected legally in a business purchase?

1. Access the home page for BizQuest at:

http://www.bizquest.com/

Register as a "visitor" (follow instructions on-screen) and enter the "Businesses for Sale Database." Pick an industry category and conduct a search of the businesses available for sale. Prepare a brief report on the companies you found. Enter the "Database of Buyers" and conduct a similar search of potential buyers. Search the list of brokers who are members of the International Business Brokers Association. Print the list of brokers in your state. What other resources does BizQuest offer for business buyers or sellers?

2. Access the home page for the Net Marquee Family Business Net Center at:

http://199.103.128.199/fambiznc/default.htm

Once there, click "Search Topics" and search through the articles on "Valuation" and "Transfer of Ownership." Choose one article and prepare a brief summary of it.

CHAPTER

FIVE

Building a Powerful Marketing Plan

There is only one boss—the customer. Customers can fire everybody in the company from the chairman on down, simply by spending their money somewhere else.
- Sam Walton

This fishing lure manufacturer I know had all these flashy green and purple lures. I asked, "Do fish take these?" "Charlie," he said, "I don't sell these lures to fish."
- Charles Munger

LEARNING OBJECTIVES

Upon completion of this chapter, you will be able to:

1. **Describe** the components of a marketing plan and explain the benefits of preparing one.

2. **Discuss** the role of market research and outline the market research process.

3. **Explain** how small businesses can pinpoint their target markets.

4. **Describe** the factors on which a small business can build a competitive edge in the marketplace: customer focus, quality, convenience, innovation, service, and speed.

5. **Discuss** the marketing opportunities the World Wide Web (WWW) offers entrepreneurs and how to best take advantage of them.

6. **Explain** the various marketing strategies available to business owners.

7. **Discuss** the "four Ps" of marketing—product, place, price, and promotion—and their role in building a successful marketing strategy.

The culmination of the next five chapters is the creation of a valuable business tool—the *business plan*. This document is a statement of *what* the entrepreneur plans to accomplish in both quantitative and qualitative terms and of *how* she plans to accomplish it. The business plan consolidates many of the topics we have discussed in preceding chapters with those of the next four chapters to produce a concise statement of how the entrepreneur plans to achieve success in the marketplace.

Too often, business plans describe in great detail what the entrepreneur intends to accomplish (e.g., "the financials") and pay little, if any, attention to the strategies to achieve those targets. Too many entrepreneurs squander enormous effort pulling together capital, people, and other resources to sell their products and services because they fail to determine what it will take to attract and keep a profitable customer base. To be effective, a solid business plan must contain both a financial plan and a marketing plan. Like the financial plan, an effective marketing plan projects numbers and analyzes them, but from a different perspective. Rather than focus on cash flow, net profits, and owner's equity, the marketing plan concentrates on the *customer*.

This chapter is devoted to creating an effective marketing plan, which must support the total business plan. Before producing reams of computer-generated spreadsheets of financial projections, an entrepreneur must determine what to sell, to whom and how often, on what terms and at what price, and how to get the product or service to the customer. In short, a marketing plan identifies a company's target customers and describes how that business will attract and keep them. Its primary focus is capturing and maintaining a competitive edge for a small business.

Market-Driven Companies and the Marketing Plan

Marketing is the process of creating and delivering desired goods and services to customers and involves all of the activities associated with winning and retaining loyal customers. The "secret" to successful marketing is to understand what your target customers' needs, demands, and wants are before your competitors can; to offer them the products and services that will satisfy those needs, demands, and wants; and to provide customers with service, convenience, and value so that they will keep coming back. The marketing function cuts across the entire organization, affecting every aspect of its operation from finance and production to hiring and purchasing. As the global business environment becomes more turbulent, small business owners must understand the importance of developing relevant marketing strategies; they are *not* just for megacorporations competing in international markets. Though they may be small in size and cannot match their larger rivals' marketing budgets, entrepreneurial companies are not powerless when it comes to developing effective marketing strategies. By using guerrilla marketing strategies—unconventional, low-cost, creative techniques—small companies can wring as much or more "bang" from their marketing bucks. For instance, facing the power of discount giants such as Wal*Mart, Kmart, and sports superstores determined to increase their market shares, small retail shops are turning to guerrilla marketing tactics to lure new customers and to keep existing ones. One small retailer explains, "If the chains are the steamships plowing through the ocean, then we have to be the cigarette [racing] boats zipping around and through them, changing direction on a dime. That must be our advantage when going up against the tremendous cash and resources of the biggies."[1]

Although his Just Books bookstore in Greenwich, Connecticut is very small (just 650 square feet of store space with one-and-a-half employees), Warren Cassell says he competes "very effectively" with the giant chain bookstores. Cassell uses a variety of guerrilla marketing techniques and doting customer service to differentiate his store and to keep his customers coming back. Cassell knows his customers so well that he is able to call them

1. Describe the components of a marketing plan and explain the benefits of preparing one.

marketing—*the process of creating and delivering desired goods and services to customers; it involves all of the activities associated with winning and retaining loyal customers.*

Just Books

when Just Books gets a title by a favorite author. He also offers special orders at no extra charge, provides free gift wrapping, a toll-free number with multiple lines, a newsletter devoted to books, worldwide "no-hassle" shipping, autographed copies of books, out-of-print book searches, and many other extras customers cannot get at large chain stores. Using relationships he has developed over the years in the publishing industry, Cassell has hosted many "Meet the Author" breakfasts, which have included authors Margaret Thatcher and Henry Kissinger, among others. The result of Cassell's marketing strategy: an impressive 6,000-plus name mailing list of loyal customers who don't mind paying full price for the books they buy and $1,500 in sales per square foot—a number most big chains can only envy.[2]

The marketing plan focuses the company's attention on the *customer* and recognizes that satisfying the customer is the foundation of every business. Its purpose is to build a strategy of success for a business—but *from the customer's point of view*. Indeed, the customer is the central player in the cast of every business venture. According to marketing expert Theodore Levitt, the primary purpose of a business is not to earn a profit; instead, it is "to create and keep a customer. The rest, given reasonable good sense, will take care of itself."[3] Every area of the business must practice putting the customer first in planning and actions. Tom Melohn, CEO of the highly successful North American Tool & Die, Inc., explains his company's customer focus, "You know why we're such an enormously customer-driven company? 'Cause we like to eat, that's why. If the customer wants the product packed in a paper bag and shipped at midnight during a full moon, then baby, that's the way we deliver it."[4]

A marketing plan should accomplish four objectives:

1. It should determine customer needs and wants through market research.
2. It should pinpoint the specific target markets the small company will serve.

"I'm not sure, but I think it's a marketing problem."

Source: Farcus® is reprinted with permission from Farcus Cartoons Inc., Ottawa, Canada.

3. It should analyze the firm's competitive advantages and build a marketing strategy around them.

4. It should help to create a marketing mix that meets customer needs and wants.

The rest of this chapter focuses on building a customer orientation into these four objectives of the small company's marketing plan.

Determining Customer Needs and Wants Through Market Research

2-A. Discuss the role of market research

The changing nature of the U.S. population is a potent force altering the landscape of business. Shifting patterns in age, income, education, race, and other population characteristics (which are the subject of **demographics**) will have a major impact on companies, their customers, and the way they do business with those customers. Businesses that ignore demographic trends and fail to adjust their strategies accordingly run the risk of becoming competitively obsolete.

demographics—*the study of important population characteristics such as age, income, education, race, and others.*

A demographic trend is like a train; a business owner must find out early on where it's going and decide whether or not to get on board. Waiting until the train is roaring down the tracks and gaining speed means it's too late to get on board. However, by checking the schedule early and planning ahead, an entrepreneur may find himself at the train's controls wearing the engineer's hat! Similarly, small companies that spot demographic trends early and act on them can gain a distinctive edge in the market. "A company has to . . . know what it's about, and it has to have a vision of the future to match what it's about with where the world is going, " says one trend tracker.[5]

For example, observing basic demographic trends such as aging baby boomers, burgeoning numbers of busy dual-career couples, and rising income levels led Don Hay to create a business that converged with all of these trends: Maid Brigade, which provides in-home maid services. Recognizing that working couples placed a premium on the value of their time (and that cleaning their houses after work or on weekends wasn't the way they wanted to spend it), Hay designed his company to appeal to them. His market research proved to be accurate: today, about 17 percent of U.S. households have hired a maid, up from just 10 percent a decade ago. Maid Brigades' current market research shows that two of the fastest-growing segments of the maid market are people aged 60 and over and young single professionals.[6]

Maid Brigade

The Value of Market Research

By performing some basic market research, small business owners can detect key demographic and market trends. Indeed, *every* business can benefit from a better understanding of its market, customers, and competitors. "Market information is just as much a business asset and just as important as your inventory or the machine you have in the back room," says one marketing consultant.[7] **Market research** is the vehicle for gathering the information that serves as the foundation for the marketing plan. It involves systematically collecting, analyzing, and interpreting data pertaining to the small company's market, customers, and competitors. It answers questions such as: Who are my customers and potential customers? What are they looking for? What kind of people are they? Where do they live? How often do they buy these products or services? What models, styles, colors, or flavors do they prefer? Why do or don't they buy from my store? How do the strengths of my product or service serve their needs and wants? What hours do they prefer to shop? How do they perceive my business? Which advertising media are likely to reach them? How do customers

market research—*the vehicle for gathering information that serves as the foundation of the marketing plan; it involves systematically collecting, analyzing, and interpreting data pertaining to a company's market, customers, and competitors.*

perceive my business versus competitors? Such information is an integral part of developing a productive marketing plan.

When marketing its goods and services, a small company must avoid marketing mistakes because there is no margin for error when funds are scarce and budgets are tight.

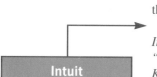

"The big guys have bigger budgets," says Tim Tinoteo, founder of a highly successful restaurant chain, R.J. Gator's. "We have fewer dollars, so when we fire the bullet, we have to hit our target. We can't afford to miss."[8] Every year, R.J. Gator's conducts extensive surveys of its guests and uses the information to focus its marketing efforts. The company also collects valuable information on its customers through its frequent-diner club that issues $10 gift certificates for every $150 spent. Learning about customers' favorite dishes, their birthdays, favorite sports teams, and other tidbits allows R.J. Gator's to increase the payoff it gets from its marketing efforts. If, for instance, the restaurant runs a stone-crab special, a direct-mail ad goes first to those who are stone-crab enthusiasts. The company's computer also combs the club's database for members who have not dined in the past six months and prompts them with a coupon.

Although most small businesses are closer to their customers than their larger rivals, many owners who use market research are surprised when they learn something new about their markets or see their customers from a new angle.

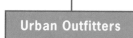

All companies, no matter what size should do research," says Scott Cook, founder of Intuit, the company that sells the world's most popular personal finance software, Quicken. "If you can't afford to hire an outside research firm, have employees collect information. Knowing the customer should be part of their job description."[9] Intuit encourages customers to drive the way it does business—from the products it develops to the way it markets them. In the company's Follow Me Home program, company representatives visit customers in their homes to observe them using the software, listen to their suggestions, and answer their questions. Every two weeks, Intuit conducts customer surveys, and the company routinely conducts focus groups with both customers and noncustomers. Every employee in the company, including Cook, spends several hours each month taking customers' calls. The result is greater understanding of and sensitivity to customers' needs. Upgrades of Intuit's software products reflect what employees learn in their encounters with customers, which explains the company's 65 to 70 percent market share!

Market research does *not* have to be time consuming, complex, or expensive to be useful.

Urban Outfitters, a fast-growing clothing chain that targets young people with its trendy, chic styles, uses cheap market research techniques to stay on the cutting edge of its customers' fashion tastes. Rather than rely on traditional market research techniques such as focus groups and customer surveys, Urban Outfitters gauges its customers' rapidly changing fashion preferences by videotaping and taking snapshots of them in the stores as well as in their own neighborhoods. These "customer profiles" give company merchandisers a clear sense of what its target audience is wearing and allow them to adjust their merchandise mix quickly as tastes change.[10]

Meaningful market research for a small business can be informal; it does not have to be highly sophisticated nor expensive to be valuable.

Faith Popcorn, a marketing consultant, encourages small business owners to be their own "trend-tracking sleuths." Merely by observing their customers' attitudes and actions, small business owners can shift their product lines and services to meet changing tastes in the market. To spot significant trends, Popcorn suggests the following:

☆ Read as many current publications as possible.

☆ Watch the top ten TV shows. ("They're indicators of consumers' attitudes and values and what they're going to be buying.")

☆ See the top ten movies. They also influence consumer behavior.

- ✩ Talk to at least 150 customers a year about what they're buying and why.
- ✩ Talk with the ten smartest people you know. They can offer valuable insights and fresh perspectives.
- ✩ Listen to your children. ("They can be tremendous guides for you.")[11]

Next, the owner should make a list of the major trends spotted and should briefly describe how well the company's products or services match the trends. "If you see your product falling away from too many trends, you've got to either change your product or dump it because you know you're going to have a failure," Popcorn says.[12]

Owners whose businesses are diverging from major social, demographic, and economic trends, rather than converging with them, run the risk of their markets evaporating before their eyes.

A.J. Cohen's business, Lady Jane, Inc., a fourth-generation women's apparel store with four locations in downtown Savannah, Georgia, recently closed because it failed to keep pace with fundamental market changes. Over the years, Cohen's customers moved away from the downtown district to shop in the suburbs. Before long, he was competing—unsuccessfully—with suburban shopping malls for his former customers' business. "Our customers' habits changed because of where they were living," says Cohen. "Shopping malls were just more convenient for them than coming back into town to shop at my stores."[13]

Table 5.1 describes several key trends that are driving the marketing strategies of successful small companies into the next millennium. These trends will be reshaping the nature of marketing for decades to come, and successful business owners will reformulate their marketing strategies to capitalize on them. How can the typical small business owner find the right match between her product or service and the appropriate market segments? Market research!

Lady Jane, Inc.

The United States in the twenty-first century will be a profoundly different place than the one we know today. Technology will change the lives of the average American in ways we cannot fathom today. Even the "average American" in the year 2050 will look very different from that of the 1990s (see the accompanying figure). The following are some key trends that will account for significant changes in the makeup of the U.S. population.

Increasing Population Diversity. The United States is becoming a bipolar society: a predominantly white older population and a growing nonwhite younger one. In 1980, minorities comprised just 20 percent of the U.S. population; by 2027, they will make up more than 36 percent! Through the early twenty-first century, minorities will account for 80 percent of the nation's population growth. By 2050, Hispanics will be the largest minority group. The growth of such groups is proof that our nation's "melting pot" is thriving. Selling to such a diverse group of customers offers special challenges to business owners, however. To be successful, "entrepreneurs have to target a specific group and make sure they understand that culture completely," says one business owner.

Changing Family Patterns. The typical household of the 1950s—a working father, a homemaker mother, and two kids—represented 53 percent of all households. Today, this "Leave It To Beaver" family accounts for just 7 percent of all households! Changes in basic family structure have forced marketers to rethink their strategies. More divorces, longer life spans, the trend toward marrying later, and lower birthrates have altered dramatically companies' definitions of the "typical family."

Greater Environmental and Health Concerns. Thirty years ago, very few customers considered themselves to be environmentalists. Today, nearly 40 percent of the population would label themselves that way. Today's customers consider the environmental impact of the products and services they buy. They'll likely pass up cosmetics tested on animals, tuna caught in nets that endanger dolphins, and aerosol cans with

Continued

Table 5.1
Key Trends Driving Marketing Strategies into the Next Millennium

Sources: Roberta Maynard, "New Directions in Marketing," *Nation's Business*, July 1995, pp. 25–26; Alecia Swasy, "Changing Times," *Wall Street Journal*, March 22, 1991, p. B6; Bob Jones, "Black Gold," *Entrepreneur*, July 1994, p. 62; "Marketing to the Melting Pot," *Entrepreneur*, June 1990, p. 50; Faye Rice, "How to Deal with Tougher Customers," *Fortune*, December 3, 1990, p. 40; Erika Kotite, "Face of the '90s," *Entrepreneur*, August 1991, p. 97; Les Rager, "The Future Grows Older," *Nation's Business*, March 1991, pp. 48-49; "Marketing with a Cause," *Small Business Reports*, August 1994, p. 5.

Table 5.1
*Key Trends
Driving Marketing
Strategies into the
Next Millennium,
Continued*

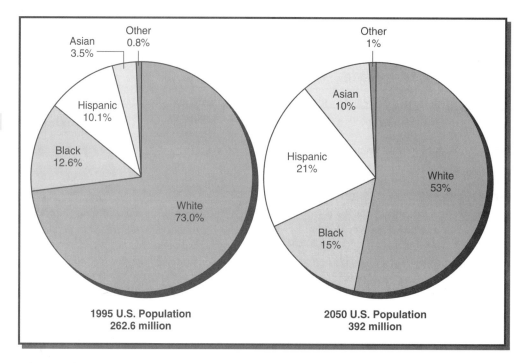

Other
0.8%

Asian
3.5%

Hispanic
10.1%

Black
12.6%

White
73.0%

**1995 U.S. Population
262.6 million**

Other
1%

Asian
10%

Hispanic
21%

Black
15%

White
53%

**2050 U.S. Population
392 million**

chlorofluorocarbons (CFCs) that erode the ozone layer. Consumers also are more concerned about health and nutrition and shop accordingly.

Emergence of Premium and Discount Niches. In many markets, two distinct—and rapidly growing—segments are emerging: the *premium* niche and the *discount* niche. The premium segment is seeking high quality, customized products and services, fast response and delivery times, and personalized service—and is willing to pay for it. Companies selling in this niche can get premium prices for products and services that meet or exceed customer expectations. The discount segment, on the other hand, considers low price to be the primary purchase criteria. By 2000, 36 percent of all households will have annual incomes of $15,000 or less—a significant number of bargain seekers.

Surge in Baby Boomers and the Elderly. Often described as a "pig in a python," the baby boomers (those born between 1946 and 1964) represent a population bulge moving through our economy. They now make up 31 percent of the U.S. population. As the front edge of the boomers reaches middle age, they are entering their prime spending years, when they put their money into their children's education, retirement planning, health care for themselves, care for their elderly parents, and sprucing up their homes (often converting them into "electronic castles" with a variety of gadgets). Baby boomers will hit their peak spending years between 1992 and 2010.

Well into the next century, the elderly will offer businesses a major marketing opportunity. Today, 21 percent of the U.S. population are 55 or older; by 2010, 26 percent—some 75 million people—will be in that age bracket. Moreover, the number of people age 85 and over will double by 2020. Those 55 or older control more than 50 percent of the nation's discretionary income and account for 40 percent of total consumption expenditures. Marketing to the elderly can be tricky, however, since "old age" is relative.

Greater Emphasis on Social Responsibility. Growing numbers of people are interested in buying from businesses that have a sense of social responsibility. In a recent survey, 78 percent of adults said they would be more likely to buy a product that is associated with a cause they care about.

Slower Growing Markets. Although the nation's population continues to grow, the rate of growth is slowing. Over the next six decades, experts expect the rate of population growth to decrease by about 50 percent. A slower-growing population means a slower-growing consumer market. To be successful, businesses will have to focus on narrow niches, understand their customers' needs and wants, and give them value.

How To Conduct Market Research

2-B. Outline the market research process.

The goal of market research is to reduce the risks associated with making business decisions. It can replace misinformation and assumptions with facts. Opinion and hearsay are not viable foundations on which to build a solid marketing strategy. Successful market research consists of four steps: define the problem, collect the data, analyze and interpret the data, and draw conclusions.

Step 1: Define the Problem

The first, and most crucial step in market research is defining the research problem clearly and concisely. A common error at this stage is to confuse a symptom with the true problem. For example, dwindling sales is not a problem but rather a symptom. To get to the heart of the matter, the owner must list all the possible factors that could have caused it. Is there new competition? Are the firm's sales representatives impolite or unknowledgeable? Have customer tastes changed? Is the product line too narrow? Do customers have trouble finding what they want? In other cases, an owner may be interested in researching a specific type of question. What are the characteristics of my customers? What are their income levels? What radio stations do they listen to? Why do they shop here? What factors are most important in their buying decisions?

Business owners also can use market research to uncover new market opportunities as well.

For example, after Gary Hirshberg, founder of Stoneyfield Farm, Inc., a small yogurt manufacturer, set up a computerized database to track customers' responses, he noted a significant number of requests for chocolate-flavored yogurt. Within months, the new flavor was on store shelves, and sales were running well ahead of projections.[14]

Stoneyfield Farm, Inc.

Step 2: Collect the data

The marketing approach that dominates today is **individualized (or one-to-one) marketing**, gathering data on individual customers and then developing a marketing program designed specifically to appeal to their needs, tastes, and preferences. In a society where people feel so isolated and interactions are so impersonal, one-to-one marketing gives a business a competitive edge. Companies following this approach know their customers, understand how to give them the value they want, and perhaps most important, know how to make them feel special and important. Such a marketing approach requires business owners to gather and to assimilate detailed information about their target customers, however. Fortunately, even owners of the smallest businesses can collect and use such information relatively easily with the help of a little creativity and a computerized database.

individualized marketing—*a system based on gathering data on individual customers and then developing a marketing program designed specifically to appeal to their needs, tastes, and preferences.*

For an effective individualized marketing campaign to be successful, business owners must collect three types of information:

1. *Geographic.* Where are my customers located? Do they tend to be concentrated in one geographic region?
2. *Demographic.* What are the characteristics of my customers (age, education levels, income, sex, marital status, and many other features)?
3. *Psychographic.* What drives my customers' buying behavior? Are they receptive to new products or are they among the last to accept them? What values are most important to them?

For most business owners, collecting valuable information about their target customers is simply a matter of noting and organizing data that are already floating around somewhere in their companies.

Silverman's

For example, at Silverman's, a men's clothing chain in the Dakotas, owner Stephen Silverman and a salesperson recently were reviewing a customer's purchasing history on a computer that doubles as a cash register. The flowchart revealed that he has spent more than $2,000 to date and had shopped four times in the previous six months. Looking at the average time between his visits, they noted that he should be coming in soon. Examining the profile more closely, they saw that this customer prefers double-breasted suits, likes Perry Ellis and Christian Dior suits in gray or blue, and has one shoulder slightly lower than the other. He also was among the customers who received a direct-mail ad featuring the upcoming season's new suits. Then, as if on cue, the customer walked in the door! The salesperson greeted him enthusiastically, personally, and knowledgeably. Within 15 minutes, he completed the sale, and the customer raved about how much he enjoys shopping at Silverman's because they know just what he likes and make it so easy to buy! Silverman's chalks up another sale to a satisfied, loyal customer thanks to its "segment of one" marketing strategy.[15]

Figure 5.1 shows how to conduct one-to-one marketing, and Figure 5.2 summarizes the advantages of an individualized marketing strategy.

Table 5.2 offers suggestions for collecting valuable market and customer information.

Step 3: Analyze and interpret the data

The results of market research alone do not provide a solution to the problem; the owner must attach some meaning to them. What do the facts mean? Is there a common thread running through the responses? Do the results suggest any changes needed in the way the business operates? Are there new opportunities the owner can take advantage of? There are no hard-and-fast rules for interpreting market research results; the owner must use judgment and common sense to determine what the numbers mean.

Step 4: Draw conclusions and act

The market research process is not complete until the business owner acts upon the information collected. In many cases, the conclusion is obvious once a small business owner

Figure 5.1
How to Become an Effective One-to-One Marketer
Source: Adapted with permission, *Inc.* magazine, (October 1995). Copyright 1995 by Goldhirsh Group, Inc. 38 Commercial Wharf, Boston, MA 02110.

Identify your best customers, never passing up the opportunity to get their names.

Enhance your products and services by giving customers information about them and how to use them.

Collect information on these customers, linking their identities to their transactions.

See customer complaints for what they are—a chance to improve your service and quality. Encourage complaints and then fix them!

Successful One-to-One Marketing

Calculate the long-term value of customers so you know which ones are most desirable (and most profitable).

Make sure your company's product and service quality will astonish your customers.

Know what your customers' buying cycle is and time your marketing efforts to coincide with it—"just-in-time marketing."

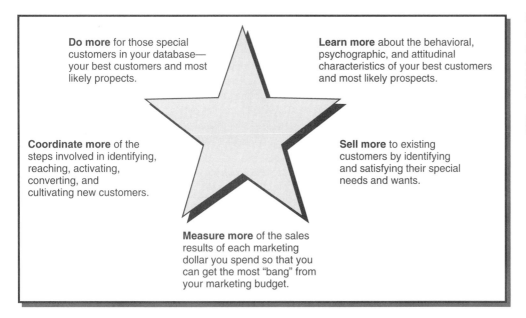

Figure 5.2
Benefits of One-to-One Marketing
Source: Adapted from Harry S. Dent, "Individualized Marketing," *Small Business Reports*, April 1991, p. 45.

Do more for those special customers in your database—your best customers and most likely propects.

Learn more about the behavioral, psychographic, and attitudinal characteristics of your best customers and most likely prospects.

Coordinate more of the steps involved in identifying, reaching, activating, converting, and cultivating new customers.

Sell more to existing customers by identifying and satisfying their special needs and wants.

Measure more of the sales results of each marketing dollar you spend so that you can get the most "bang" from your marketing budget.

interprets the results of the market research. Based on her understanding of what the facts really mean, the owner must then decide how to use the information in the business. For example, the owner of a retail shop discovered from a survey that her customers preferred evening shopping hours over early morning hours. She made the schedule adjustment, and sales began to climb.

Table 5.2
How to Collect Valuable Market and Customer Research

Thorough market research is the foundation of any successful marketing plan. Where can an entrepreneur go to get this information? The following are just a few of the sources of valuable marketing information:

Primary Research—data you collect yourself.

☆ *Customer surveys and questionnaires.* Keep them short; word your questions carefully so that you do not bias the results; use a simple ranking system (e.g., a 1 to 5 scale, with 1 representing "unacceptable" and 5 representing "excellent"); and test your survey for problems on a small number of people before putting it to use.

☆ *Focus groups.* Enlist a small number of customers to give you feedback on specific issues in your business—quality, convenience, hours of operation, service, and so on. Listen carefully for new marketing opportunities as customers or potential customers tell you what is on their minds.

☆ *Daily transactions.* Sift as much data as possible from existing company records and daily transactions—customer warranty cards, personal checks, frequent-buyer clubs, credit applications, and so on.

☆ *Other ideas.* Set up a suggestion system (for customers and employees) and use it. Establish a customer advisory panel to determine how well your company is meeting needs. Talk with suppliers about trends they have spotted in the industry. Contact customers who have not bought anything in a long time and find out why. Contact people who are not customers and find out why. Teach employees to be good listeners and then ask them what they hear.

Secondary Research—data that are already compiled for you. Less expensive to collect than primary data. The key is knowing where to look! The library is a good place to begin.

☆ *Business directories.* To locate a trade association, use *Business Information Sources* (University of California Press) or the *Encyclopedia of Associations* (Gale Research). To find suppliers, use *The Thomas Register of American Manufacturers* (Thomas Publishing Company) or *Standard and Poor's Register of Corporations, Executives, and Industries* (Standard and Poor Corporation). *The American Wholesalers and Distributors Directory* includes details on more than 18,000 wholesalers and distributors.

Continued

✯ *Direct-mail lists.* You can buy mailing lists for practically any type of business. *The Standard Rates and Data Service (SRDS) Directory of Mailing Lists* (Standard Rates and Data) is a good place to start looking.

✯ *Demographic data.* To learn more about the demographic characteristics of customers in general, use *The Statistical Abstract of the United States* (Government Printing Office). Profiles of more specific regions are available in *The State and Metropolitan Data Book* (Government Printing Office). *The Sourcebook of Zip Code Demographics* (CACI, Inc.) provides detailed breakdowns of the population in every zip code in the country. *Sales and Marketing Management's Survey of Buying Power* (Bill Communications) has statistics on consumer, retail, and industrial buying.

✯ *Census data.* The Bureau of the Census publishes a wide variety of reports that summarize the wealth of data found in its census database. Contact the government librarian at your local library for details.

✯ *Forecasts.* The *U.S. Global Outlook* traces the growth of 200 industries and gives a five-year forecast for each one. Many government agencies including the Department of Commerce offer forecasts on everything from interest rates to the number of housing starts. Again, a government librarian can help you find what you need.

✯ *Market research.* Someone may already have compiled the market research you need. *The FINDex Worldwide Directory of Market Research Reports, Studies, and Surveys* (Cambridge Information Group) lists more than 10,600 studies available for purchase. Other directories of business research include *Simmons Study of Media and Markets* (Simmons Market Research Bureau Inc.) and the *A.C. Neilsen Retail Index* (A.C. Neilsen Company).

✯ *Articles.* Magazine and journal articles pertinent to your business are a great source of information. Use the *Reader's Guide to Periodical Literature*, the *Business Periodicals Index* (similar to the Reader's Guide but focuses on business periodicals), and *Ulrich's Guide to International Periodicals* to locate the ones you need.

✯ *Local data.* Your state Department of Commerce and your local chamber of commerce will very likely have useful data on the local market of interest to you. Call to find out what is available.

✯ *World Wide Web.* Most entrepreneurs are astounded at the marketing information that is available on the World Wide Web (WWW). Using one of the search engines such as Yahoo!, Lycos, Magellan, and others, you can gain access to a world of information—literally!

Why try to build your business on guesses and unknowns when you can increase your probability of hitting the target market you want most efficiently with the help of some basic market research?

3. Explain how small businesses can pinpoint their target markets.

target market— *the specific group of customers at whom a company aims its goods or services.*

Pinpointing the Target Market

One of the primary objectives of market research is to identify the small business's **target market**, the specific group of customers at whom the company aims its goods or services. Most marketing experts contend that the greatest marketing mistake small businesses make is failing to define clearly the target market to be served. In other words, most small businesses follow a "shotgun approach" to marketing, firing marketing blasts at every customer that they see, hoping to capture just some of them. Although this approach can work to get a small business established, it can lead to serious problems for a company using it to try to grow. Most small companies simply cannot use shotgun marketing to compete successfully with larger rivals and their deep pockets. These small businesses develop new products that do not sell because they were not targeted at a specific audience's needs; they broadcast ads that attempt to reach everyone and end up reaching no one; they spend precious time and money trying to reach customers who are not the most profitable; and, many of the customers they attract leave because they don't know what the company stands for. "You have limited resources to deliver 100% [customer] satisfaction, so you have to target customers and aim your service better than ever," explains one marketing consultant.[16]

Failing to pinpoint their target markets is especially ironic since small firms are ideally suited to reaching market segments that their larger rivals overlook or consider too small to be profitable. Why, then, is the shotgun approach so popular? Because it is easy and does not require market research or a marketing plan! The problem is that the shotgun approach is a sales-driven rather than a customer-driven strategy.[17] To be customer driven, an effective marketing program must be based on a clear, concise definition of the firm's target customers.

Meg Felton, owner of Software Sportswear, has focused her company on serving upscale women who have trouble finding just the right fit in swimsuits. Her company uses a video camera and specially designed computer software to record customers' measurements and to design perfectly fitting swimsuits for them. The camera-computer hookup enables Felton to show thousands of modifications (such as bows, a higher cut in the leg, a longer torso), and 150 fabric choices. Once the customer chooses a design, the computer generates an individually tailored pattern. It takes about a week to make a customized swimsuit that sells for $110 to $170, about 30 to 50 percent more than off-the-rack suits in department stores.[18]

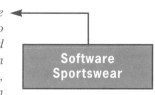

Like Software Sportswear, the most successful businesses have well-defined portraits of the customers they are seeking to attract. From market research, they know their customers' income levels, lifestyles, buying patterns, likes and dislikes, and even psychological profiles. The target customer permeates the entire business from the merchandise purchased to the layout and decor of the store. They have an advantage over their larger rivals because the images they have created for their companies appeal to their target customers, and that's why they prosper.

The West Point Market in Akron, Ohio is a specialty food store that conveys the image of an upscale department store. Founder Russ Vernon does not compete on the basis of price because that is not what is most important to his customers. Instead, he uses a broad selection of products, high-quality, innovative displays, unique merchandising, and extra services to gain an edge over his rivals. Vernon explains, "Our [target] market is the business and professional clientele looking for product convenience and service not found in conventional stores. We are a cook's resource. We set the stage for the product... We are theatrical with our lighting, with our special events, with classical music. We do not want to look like a supermarket."[19]

Without such a clear picture of its target market and the image it must create to attract those customers, a small company will try to reach almost everyone and usually ends up appealing to almost no one.

The nation's increasingly diverse population offers businesses of all sizes tremendous marketing opportunities if they target specific customers, learn how to reach them, and offer goods and services designed specifically for them.

Judy George, founder of the high-fashion furniture chain Domain, has developed a unique marketing approach in the core baby-boomer target segment. Her market research told her that these customers were as concerned about self-improvement as they were about decorating their homes properly. George launched two series of in-store seminars, one focusing on design and furnishings and the other on women's issues (including starting a business). The seminars are packed , and Domain's repeat business among these upscale customers has nearly doubled.[20]

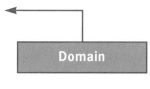

Sometimes new target markets emerge on their own, much to the surprise of the small business owner.

When Roger Dunavant took over Straight Arrow, Inc., a tiny maker of horse care products in 1988, he heard grooms and horse owners talk about how the company's hoof strengthener made their own fingernails stronger. He also heard stories of how Straight Arrow's horse shampoo, Mane & Tail, made their hair softer and fuller. Dunavant recognized a marketing opportunity when he saw one. Acting on his informal market research, he began selling products, once available only in feed stores, pet shops, and veterinarians' offices, through beauty salons, drugstores, and supermarkets. Within five years, annual sales shot up from $500,000 to more than $30 million. Straight Arrow estimates that two-thirds of

its sales are for human use rather than for horses. One feed store owner admits that she and her entire family shampoo with Mane & Tail, but, she adds, "We do use it on the horses.[21]

YOU BE THE CONSULTANT...

"X" Marks the Spot

Jamal Bantry operates a small clothing store, Ladies and Gents, in a town of about 27,000 people that is home to an upscale private college with an enrollment of about 6,800 students. His current store offers traditional, classic clothing for both men and women at moderate prices. His target audience is professional men and women who are buying "business suits and buttondowns." As fashion preferences have become more casual in recent years and as more companies allow workers to "dress down" at work, Bantry has shifted the focus of his inventory somewhat to reflect a more casual look. He also sells very casual, "weekend" clothes and has watched sales of this line climb steadily over the past five years. Still, the majority of his sales come from business and professional garments.

Ladies and Gents has a reputation for providing good-quality garments at reasonable prices, and Bantry takes pride in his customer-oriented salespeople. Most of them have been with the company for years, and they treat their customers with respect and are genuinely interested in helping them pick out just the right garment and then seeing that it fits perfectly. Ladies and Gents is a popular destination for college seniors in need of an "interview suit," but otherwise, Bantry sees very few college students in the store.

Recently, Bantry has thought a great deal about this untapped market. Some of his best part-time workers have been students from the local college, and many of them have encouraged him over the years to carry merchandise that would appeal to the college market. "I can't keep up with the fashion whims of you young people," Bantry would always reply jokingly. "I've read about Generation X! You guys change your fashion minds on the average...what? Every two weeks!" Still, he realizes that with the right approach, a business could serve the clothing needs of the local college students and young people in town and make a good profit. "But what is the right approach?" Bantry wondered.

In some of his small business magazines, Bantry had read about the so-called "Generation Xers." He discovered that they are the most diverse population ever: 70 percent white, 13 percent African-American, 12 percent Hispanic, 4 percent Asian, and 1 percent Native American. One article described the results of an extensive study that identified four key segments of Generation X: the "cynical disdainers," the most pessimistic and skeptical group; the "traditional materialists," the group most like the baby boomers before them, who are positive, optimistic, and striving for the Great American Dream; the "hippies revisited," who are replaying the lifestyle of the '60s and express themselves through music, fashion, and spirituality; and the "fifties machos," the young, very conservative group that still believes in traditional gender roles and is least tolerant of multiculturalism.

After an evening trip to the college library, Bantry was able to learn more about this sizable market. These young people are hardly the "slackers" with no money and only a bleak future facing them that much of the press has made them out to be. They are well educated, have substantial purchasing power, and are postponing getting married and having children. They also love to shop! One study Bantry discovered reported that people ages 17 to 30 are more likely than other shoppers to spend time in retail stores. Plus, 56 percent of this group said that they feel the need to keep up with new fashion styles (compared to just 35 percent of other consumers). However, when shopping, they tend to be turned off by what they consider to be "pushy" salespeople and "hard" selling approaches. Instead, they want lots of information about the products and services they buy because they want to make informed decisions. Having lots of options is also important. Bantry's research also showed that Generation X shoppers are four times more likely than other customers to shop by computer. More than 35 percent of all college students own their own computers; even more have access to them through college computer labs.

Bantry learned that undergraduate students at four-year universities spend more than $7 billion a year on discretionary purchases. "I'd love to tap into this market," he thought, "but I'm not sure of the best way to reach these young people. Should I use some of the extra space we have at Ladies and Gents to add new clothing lines to what I currently sell, or should I rent that retail space near the campus and set up a new shop there? How could I keep in touch with the shifts in the fashion trends of this market? How should I reach these customers? What sales approach will work best? How can I encourage the students at the local college to become customers? What kind of environment do they want to shop in?"

1. Help Jamal Bantry answer the questions he has posed.

2. What advice would you offer Bantry before he attempts to reach this target audience?

3. What pitfalls would you warn Bantry to avoid as he tries to move into this market?

Sources: Adapted from Laura Radloff, "The X Factor," *Entrepreneur*, October 1995, pp. 190-194; Faye Rice,[11] Making Generational Marketing Come of Age," *Fortune*, June 26, 1995, pp. 110-114; Jeff Giles, "Generalizations X," *Business Week,* June 6, 1994, pp.62-72; Laura M. Litvan, "X Marks the Spot for Low-Key Sales," *Nation's Business*, May 1996, pp. 32-35.

Plotting a Marketing Strategy: How to Build a Competitive Edge

4. Describe the factors on which a small business can build a competitive edge in the marketplace.

A competitive edge is crucial for business success. A small company has a competitive edge when customers perceive that its products or services are superior to those of its competitors. A business owner can create this perception in a variety of ways. Small companies sometimes try to create a competitive edge by offering the lowest prices. This approach may work for many products and services—especially those that customers see as being commodities—but price can be a dangerous criterion upon which to build a competitive edge. Independent hardware stores have discovered that large chains can use their buying power to get volume discounts and undercut the independents' prices. Individual store owners are finding new ways, such as hands-on assistance and advice, individual attention, charge accounts, and convenience to differentiate themselves and to retain customer loyalty. "Instead of being forced out of business by the 'category killers,'" says a retail expert, "small retailers are thriving by providing the services and products that larger stores are not able to.[22]

Karen Adler's Pig Out Publications thrives in the same market as publishing giants Simon and Schuster and Random House. Pig Out publishes barbecue cookbooks and offbeat travel guides in what Adler calls the "barbecue belt" of the South. As the publishing industry's giants turn out thousands of titles in a year, Pig Out publishes an average of seven books per year. " I don't compete with the large publishers," she declares. "My books are for a certain geographic area, and we always find a local author to write them." To avoid going head-to-head with the industry giants, Adler chooses an alternative distribution channel. Rather than sell through chain bookstores where her titles would get lost, she instead targets gourmet shops, specialty stores, and mail order, "places where they'll stand out to the customer," she says. Her niche strategy is very successful. Pig Out Publications earns a healthy profit , and only six of the 30 books the company has published are out of print.[23]

Pig Out Publications

Like Karen Adler, successful entrepreneurs often use the special advantages they have to build a competitive edge over their larger rivals. Their close contact with the customer, personal attention, focus on service, and organizational and managerial flexibility provide a solid foundation from which to build a towering competitive edge in the market. Small companies are more effective than their larger rivals at **relationship marketing**—developing and maintaining long-term relationship with customers so that they will keep coming back to make repeat purchases. "It's like running your business the way the old-fashioned greengrocer did in the nineteenth century," says one marketing consultant. "We try to create a circle of friends, with the customer at the center."[24]

relationship marketing—*the process of developing and maintaining long-term relationships with customers so they will keep coming back to make repeat purchases.*

To make relationship marketing work, a small business must achieve the highest of the following four levels of customer involvement .[25]

Level 1: Customer Awareness. The prevailing attitude in the company is "There's a customer out there." Managers and employees know little about the company's customers and view them only in the most general terms. No one understands the benefits of a close customer-supplier relationship.

Level 2: Customer Sensitivity. A wall stands between the company and its customers. Employees know more about their customers' characteristics, but they have not begun to share much information with them. Similarly, the company doesn't solicit feedback from its customers.

Level 3: Customer Alignment. Managers and employees understand the customer's central role in the business. They spend considerable time talking with, and about, customers. They also seek out customer feedback through surveys, focus groups, customer interviews, and visits.

Level 4: Customer Partnership. The company has refined its customer service attitude from mere techniques to an all-encompassing part of its culture. Customers are part of all major issues. Employees at every level of the organization receive intelligence reports on customers and interact with them whenever possible. Customers play an important role in product development and in other aspects of the business. Managers and employees focus on building lasting relationships with customers.

Table 5.3 describes the differences between relationship marketing and its polar opposite, transaction selling.

Because it is knowledge based, relationship marketing usually requires an investment in technology (e.g., a computer database to track customer preferences) and a commitment from the business owner to make it work, but the payoff can be a powerful competitive edge. "You create and add value to a transaction—to a relationship—that a big company can't match," explains one business owner who relies on relationship marketing.[26] To achieve the highest level of customer satisfaction, many small businesses rely on six important sources to develop a competitive edge: a focus on the customer; devotion to quality, attention to convenience, concentration on innovation; dedication to service, and emphasis on speed.

Focus on the Customer

Too many businesses have lost sight of the important component of every business: the customer. Wooing these disillusioned customers back will require businesses to focus on them as never before. Businesses must realize that everything in the business—even the business itself—depends on the satisfied customer. One entrepreneur says, "If you're not taking care of your customers and nurturing that relationship, you can bet there's someone else out there who will."[27]

Businesses are just beginning to discover the true costs of poor customer relations. For instance:

- ✮ Sixty-seven percent of customers who stop patronizing a particular store do so because an indifferent employee treated them poorly.[28]
- ✮ Ninety-six percent of dissatisfied customers never complain about rude or discourteous service, but . . .
- ✮ Ninety-one percent will not buy from the business again.
- ✮ One hundred percent of those unhappy customers will tell their "horror stories" to at least nine other people.
- ✮ Thirteen percent of those unhappy customers will tell their stories to at least twenty other people.[29]

According to the authors of *Keeping Customers for Life*, "The nasty result of this customer indifference costs the average company from 15 to 30 percent of gross sales."[30] Because 70 percent of the average company's sales come from present customers, few can afford to alienate any shoppers. In fact, the typical business loses 20 percent of its customers each year. But a recent study by the consulting firm Bain & Co. shows that companies that retain just 5 percent more customers experience profit increases of at least 25 percent and, in some cases, as much as 95 percent![31] Studies by the Boston Consulting Group also show that customer retention results in above-average profits and superior growth in market share.[32]

Because about 20 percent of a typical company's customers account for about 80 percent of its sales, it makes more sense to focus resources on keeping the best (and most profitable) customers than to spend them trying to chase "fair weather" customers who will defect to any better deal that comes along. Suppose that a company increases its customer base by 20 percent each year, but it retains only 85 percent of its existing customers. Its

Table 5.3
The Differences Between Relationship Marketing and Transaction Selling

Source: Adapted from Timothy M. Baye, "Relationship Marketing: A Six-Step Guide for the Business Start-Up," *Small Business Forum*, Spring 1995, pp. 26–41.

Feature	Relationship Marketing	Transaction Selling
Duration	Ongoing	Distinct beginning and end; one-transaction attitude
Key Concepts	Collaborate and cooperate	Negotiate
Driven by	Commitment and trust	Making profitable short-term transactions
Style	Mutual dependence	Independence
Business Plan Implications	Building a network of relationships with dependable suppliers and customers that will lead to long-term profitability	Maximize short-term profits; make the bottom line look good, whatever the long-term costs
Primary Advantage	Intimate knowledge of customers' needs, wants, and preferences developed over time	Cash in hand
Primary Disadvantage	Dependence on other partners in the web of relationships	Losing the sale if a competitor makes the customer a better offer
Foundation	Knowledge based	Bottom-line oriented
Outlook	Increasing in popularity	On the decline

effective growth rate is just 5 percent per year [20% − (100% − 85%) = 5%]. If this same company can raise its customer retention rate to 95 percent, its net growth rate *triples* to 15 percent [20% − (100% − 95%) = 15%].[33]

Michael J. Stineman, president of Citation Homes, Inc., a custom-home manufacturer, uses a seven-member customer advisory council to boost customer retention rates. Each member represents a different target market or geographic region. Stineman meets regularly with the council to get feedback about Citation's performance in the market, to get ideas about how to serve customers better, and to generate new product ideas. The meetings are a rich source of valuable customer information and have helped Citation improve its customer retention rate to an impressive 90 percent.[34]

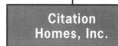

Citation Homes, Inc.

Although winning new customers keeps a company growing, keeping existing ones is essential to success. Attracting a new customer actually costs *five times* as much as keeping an existing one. Therefore, small business owners would be better off asking, "How can we improve customer value and service to encourage our existing customers to do more business with us?" rather than "How can we increase our market share by 10 percent?"

The most successful small businesses have developed a customer orientation and have instilled a customer satisfaction attitude *throughout* the company. Companies with world-class customer attitudes set themselves apart by paying attention to "little things." For example, at one dentist's office, staff members take photos on a patient's first visit. The photo, placed in the patient's file, allows everyone in the office to call him by name on subsequent visits. When McDonald's opened stores in the financial districts of Los Angeles and New York, it installed stock "ticker boards" and telephones on the tables.[35] A small flower shop offers a special service for customers who forget that special event. The shop will insert a card reading, "Please forgive us! Being short-handed this week, we were unable to deliver this gift on time. We hope the sender's thoughtfulness will not be less appreciated because of our error. Again, we apologize."[36]

"It's our way of saying, 'Thank you for shopping at Wilson's.'"

Source: Drawing by M. Twohy; © 1995 The New Yorker Magazine, Inc.

How do these companies focus so intently on their customers? They constantly ask customers four basic questions and then act on what they hear:

1. What are we doing right?
2. How can we do that even better?
3. What have we done wrong?
4. What can we do in the future?

Table 5.4 offers some basic strategies for developing and retaining loyal customers.

Devotion to Quality

In this intensely competitive global business environment, quality goods and services are a prerequisite for success—and even survival. According to one marketing axiom, the worst of all marketing catastrophes is to have great advertising and a poor-quality product. Customers have come to expect and demand quality goods and services, and those businesses that provide them consistently have a distinct competitive advantage.

Today, quality is more than just a slogan posted on the company bulletin board; world-class companies treat quality as a strategic objective—an integral part of the company culture. "The real difference comes when you decide [quality is] no longer a program; it's a business strategy," says one top manager." This philosophy is called **total quality management (TQM)**—quality not just in the product or service itself but in *every* aspect of the business and its relationship with the customer and *continuous improvement* in the quality delivered to customers.

Companies on the cutting edge of the quality movement are developing new ways to measure quality. Manufacturers were the first to apply TQM techniques, but retail, wholesale, and service organizations have seen the benefits of becoming champions of quality.

total quality management (TQM)—*the philosophy of producing a high-quality product or service and achieving quality in every aspect of the business and its relationship with the customer; the focus is on continuous improvement in the quality delivered to customers.*

- ☆ Identify your best customers and give them incentives to return. Focus resources on the 20 percent of customers that account for 80 percent of sales.

- ☆ When you create a dissatisfied customer, fix the problem fast. One study found that, given the chance to complain, 95 percent of customers will buy again if a business handles their complaints promptly and effectively. The worst way to handle a complaint is to ignore it, to pass it off to a subordinate, or to let a lot of time slip by before dealing with it.

- ☆ Make sure your business system makes it easy for customers to buy from you. Eliminate unnecessary procedures that challenge customers' patience.

- ☆ *Encourage* customer complaints. You can't fix something if you don't know it's broken. Find out what solution the customer wants and try to come as close to that as possible.

- ☆ Ask employees for feedback on improving customer service. A study by Technical Assistance Research Programs (TARP), a customer service research firm, found that front-line service workers can predict nearly 90 percent of the cases which produce customer complaints. Emphasize that *everyone* is part of the customer satisfaction team.

- ☆ Get total commitment to superior customer service from top managers and allocate resources appropriately.

- ☆ Allow managers to wait on customers occasionally. It's a great dose of reality. The founder of a small robot manufacturer credits such a strategy with saving his company. "We now require every officer of this company—including myself—to meet with customers at least four times a month," he says.

- ☆ Carefully select and train *everyone* who will deal with customers. Never let rude employees work with customers.

- ☆ Develop a service theme that communicates your attitude toward customers. Customers want to feel they are getting something special.

- ☆ Reward employees "caught" providing exceptional service to the customer.

- ☆ Remember: The customer pays the bills. Special treatment wins customers and keeps them coming back.

Table 5.4

Strategies for Developing and Retaining Loyal Customers

Sources: Adapted from: Laura M. Litvan, "Increasing Revenue with Repeat Sales," *Nation's Business*, January 1996, pp. 36–37. "Encourage Customers to Complain," *Small Business Reports*, June 1990, p. 7; Dave Zielinski, "Improving Service Doesn't Require a Big Investment," *Small Business Reports*, February 1991, p. 20; John H. Sheridan, "Out of the Isolation Booth," *Industry Week*, June 19, 1989, pp. 18-19; Lin Grensing-Pophal, "At Your Service," *Business Start-Ups*, May 1995, pp. 72-74.

They are tracking customer complaints, contacting "lost" customers, and finding new ways to track the cost of quality (COQ) and their return on quality (ROQ).

The key to developing a successful TQM philosophy is seeing the world from the customer's point of view. In other words, quality must reflect the needs and wants of the customer. How do customers define quality? According to a recent poll, Americans rank quality components in this order: reliability (average time between failures), durability (how long it lasts), ease of use, a known or trusted brand name, and, last, a low price.[37] In services, customers are likely to look for similar characteristics: tangibles (equipment, facilities, and people), reliability (doing what you say you will do), responsiveness (promptness in helping customers), and assurance and empathy (conveying a caring attitude). For example, the owner of a very successful pest-control company offered his customers a unique unconditional guarantee: If the company fails to eliminate all roach and rodent breeding and nesting areas on the client's premises, it will refund the customer's last 12 monthly payments and will pay for one-full-year's service by another exterminator. The company has had to honor its guarantee only once in 17 years.

The benefits of a successful TQM philosophy can be substantial, sometimes making the difference in success and failure.

In 1986, Globe Metallurgical, a small maker of ferroalloy and silicon metals, was facing extinction because of quality problems with its products and its employee relations. To save itself, Globe adopted the TQM philosophy, rewrote workers' job descriptions, flattened its management structure, created worker teams, and focused on customer satisfaction. The changes literally saved the company. Globe turns out 1,100 tons of product per worker-hour

Globe Metallurgical

compared to an industry average of 500 tons. Productivity is up 50 percent, and sales and profits are hitting record levels. Exports have climbed from 2 percent to 20 percent of sales.[38]

Companies successful in capturing a reputation for top-quality products and services follow certain guidelines to "get it right the first time":

☆ Build quality into the process; don't rely on inspection to obtain quality.

☆ Foster teamwork and dismantle the barriers that divide disparate departments.

☆ Establish long-term ties with select suppliers; don't award contracts on low price alone.

☆ Provide managers and employees the training needed to participate fully in the quality improvement program.

☆ Empower workers at all levels of the organization; give them authority and responsibility for making decisions that determine quality.

☆ Get managers' commitment to the quality philosophy. Otherwise, the program is doomed. Describing his role in his company's TQM philosophy, one CEO says, "People look to see if you just talk about it or actually do it."[39]

☆ Rethink the processes the company uses now to get its products or services to its customers. Employees at Analog Devices redesigned its production process and significantly lowered the defect rate on its silicon chips, saving $1.2 million a year.[40]

☆ Reward employees for quality work. Ideally, workers' compensation is linked clearly and directly to key measures of quality and customer satisfaction.

☆ Develop a companywide strategy for constant improvement of product and service quality.

Attention to Convenience

Ask customers what they want from the businesses they deal with and one of the most common responses is "convenience." In this busy, fast-paced world of dual-career couples and lengthy commutes to and from work, customers increasingly are looking for convenience. Several studies have found that customers rank easy access to goods and services at the top of their purchase criteria. Unfortunately, too few businesses deliver adequate levels of convenience, and they fail to attract and retain customers. One print and framing shop, for instance, alienated many potential customers with its abbreviated business hours: 9 to 5 daily, except for Wednesday afternoons, Saturdays, and Sundays when the shop was closed. Other companies make it a chore to do business with them. In an effort to defend themselves against unscrupulous customers, these businesses have created elaborate procedures for exchanges, refunds, writing checks, and other basic transactions. One researcher claims, "What they're doing is treating the 98 percent of honest customers like crooks to catch the 2 percent who are crooks."[41]

HomeBased Warehouse

Successful companies go out of their way to make sure that it is easy for customers to do business with them. The HomeBased Warehouse in San Bernadino, California, has borrowed an idea from fast-food restaurants to make buying lumber more convenient for its customers: drive-in windows. More than 200 cars a day pull in and load up with lumber before driving to the cashier's booth to pay. The drive-thru "has increased [sales] volume and enhanced contractor business. They like the time-saving [convenience] of being able to drive in, load up, and cash out at the outside register," says one manager. In Las Vegas, a couple can pull up at the Wedding Window, and an ordained minister in the drive-thru window will marry them![42]

How can a business owner boost the convenience level of her business? By conducting a "convenience audit" from the customer's point of view to get an idea of its ETDBW ("Easy To Do Business With") index:

☆ Is your business located near your customers? Does it provide easy access?

☆ Are your business hours suitable to your customers? Should you be open evenings and weekends to serve them better?

✮ Would customers appreciate pickup and delivery service? The owner of a restaurant located near a major office complex installed a fax machine to receive orders from busy workers; a crew of workers would deliver lunches to office workers at their desks!

✮ Does your company make it easy for customers to make purchases on credit or with credit cards?

✮ Are your employees trained to handle business transactions quickly, efficiently, and politely? Waiting while rude, incompetent employees fumble through routine transactions destroys customer goodwill.

✮ Does your company handle telephone calls quickly and efficiently? Long waits "on hold," transfers from one office to another, and too many rings before answering signal customers that they are not important.

The Scruba Dub Auto Wash in Natick, Massachusetts, makes sure that it scores high on an ETDBW index. Not only do carefully trained employees sweat the details of cleaning their customers' cars, but this family business also backs up its work with several guarantees, tracks customers' buying habits to boost sales, and measures customers' satisfaction. Customers drive through an attractive entrance, where a well-groomed employee wearing a tie greets them. They get free snacks while the car is in the cleaning tunnel. Members of the Scruba Dub Club get special amenities such as a pass that entitles them to specials such as a free wash after ten paid cleanings. To keep its customers happy, the company backs up all of its work with guarantees of satisfaction. If a customer believes the car wash has damaged his car, managers are authorized to spend up to $150 to fix the problem—no questions asked. Club members get extra protection; Scruba Dub offers them free replacement washes if it rains or snows within 24 hours of them leaving the lot. Employees go through various training programs to ensure consistent quality of service from location to location. In addition, up to half of employees' pay is linked to service and quality goals. This customer-oriented strategy is a success. Scuba Dub has become the largest car-wash chain in the Boston area and is growing consistently at 10 percent a year.[43]*

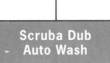

Scruba Dub Auto Wash

Concentration on Innovation

Innovation is the key to future success. Markets change too quickly and competitors move too fast for a small company to stand still and remain competitive. Because they cannot outspend their larger rivals, small companies often turn to superior innovation as the way to gain a competitive edge. Thanks to their organizational and managerial flexibility, small businesses often can detect and act on new opportunities faster than large companies. Innovation is one of the greatest strengths of the entrepreneur, and it shows up in the new products, unique techniques, and unusual marketing approaches they introduce. Despite their limited resources, small businesses frequently are leaders in innovation. For instance, in the hotly competitive pharmaceutical industry, the dominant drugs in most markets were discovered by small companies rather than the industry giants like Merck or Glaxos with their multimillion-dollar R&D budgets.

Obviously, there is more to innovation than spending megadollars on research and development. "It takes money to fund a business," says one small business advisor, "but it's continuous creativity that keeps the venture running smoothly and profitably."[44] How do small businesses manage to maintain their leadership role in innovating new products and services? They use their size to their advantage, maintaining their speed and flexibility much like a martial arts expert does against a larger opponent. Their closeness to their customers enables them to read subtle shifts in the market and to anticipate trends as they unfold. Their ability to concentrate their efforts and attention in one area also gives small businesses an edge in innovation. "The small companies have an advantage: a dedicated management team totally focused on a new product or market," says one venture capitalist.[45]

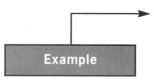

Example

New York high school chemistry teacher Bob Black was angry about the graffiti scrawled all over city buildings and the cost to taxpayers to remove it. Rather than merely complain, he decided to do something about it. After four years of experimenting, Black invented G-Pro, a powerful chemical that prevents graffiti paint from sticking to surfaces. He received a patent for his chemical concoction and then began selling it to cities all across the country. Demand for G-Pro has been so strong that Black has had difficulty keeping up with it![46]

Dedication to Service and Customer Satisfaction

In the new economy, companies are discovering that unexpected innovative, customized service can be a powerful strategic weapon. Providing incomparable service—not necessarily a low price—is one of the most effective ways to attract and maintain a growing customer base. In fact, a recent study of consumer behavior reported that 73 percent of customers buy for reasons other than price![47] One business writer explains, "It matters not whether a company creates something you can touch . . . or something you can only experience . . . What counts most is the service built into that something—the way the product is designed and delivered, billed and bundled, explained and installed, repaired and renewed."[48]

Although more companies than ever before are preaching customer service to employees, the reality is that most Americans still rate U.S. companies low on customer service. In a recent survey of 200 companies, 57 percent of the managers said that "customer service" is their top priority. However, 73 percent said that the only way to survive is with "price competition."[49] Such a short-run philosophy short-circuits real progress toward superior customer service. "Sales starts a customer relationship," says one customer service expert. "Service turns it into a profitable or unprofitable relationship."[50]

Successful businesses recognize that superior customer service is only an intermediate step toward the goal of customer *satisfaction*. These companies seek to go beyond customer satisfaction, striving for *customer astonishment!* They concentrate on providing customers with quality, convenience, and service *as their customers define those terms.*

Peabody Hotel

At the famous Peabody Hotel in Memphis, Tennessee, customer service holds a hallowed place among the attentive, doting staff. This historic 468-room hotel is as famous for astonishing its guests as it is for the ducks who march to the impressive lobby fountain to a lively John Philip Sousa tune, escorted by Duckmaster James Means. The five mallards, the most famous animal act in the South, spend the day splashing in the fountain, eating cracked corn, and napping. The only thing more pampered than the Peabody ducks are the Peabody guests! From its impressive ice carvings and beautiful Italian Renaissance Revival architecture to its always gleaming brass and marble features, the Peabody strives to get everything about a guest's stay right the first time . . . plus some. When actor Robert Duvall wanted to practice a dance scene for a movie he was filming in Memphis, the hotel installed a parquet floor in his room. "The ducks are truly the ambassadors of the hotel," says marketing director Phil Yankovich, "but if the Peabody didn't have quality and terrific service, the ducks wouldn't mean anything."[51]

Certainly the least expensive and the most effective way to achieve customer satisfaction is through friendly, personal service. Numerous surveys of customers in a wide diversity of industries, from manufacturing and services to banking and high tech, conclude that the most important element of service is "the personal touch." Calling customers by name, making attentive, friendly contact, and truly caring about customers' needs and wants are much more essential than any other factor, even convenience, quality, and speed! One entrepreneur explains, "In our society, everything has become so automated that we're starved for personal attention. True customer service means reaching across that automation, recognizing that each person is an individual with needs and doing what it takes to meet those needs."[52]

How can a company achieve stellar customer service and satisfaction?

LISTEN TO CUSTOMERS. The best companies constantly listen to their customers and respond to what they hear! This allows them to keep up with customers' changing needs and expectations. The best way to find out what customers really want and value is to ask them. Businesses rely on a number of techniques including surveys, focus groups, telephone interviews, comment cards, suggestion boxes, toll-free hot lines, and regular one-on-one conversations (perhaps the best technique).

Price's Market

When business slowed at Price's Market, a Richmond, Virginia convenience store, owners Bob and Candy Kocher started asking their neighborhood customers, "What are you always looking for but can't get?" The overwhelming answer surprised them: imported beer. They began stocking it, and now their small convenience store is the hottest spot in town. Not only has neighborhood traffic picked up, but the store also attracts customers from all over town to buy its imported brews.[53]

DEFINE SUPERIOR SERVICE. Based on what customers say, managers and employees must decide exactly what "superior service" means in the company. Such a statement should: (1) be a strong statement of intent, (2) differentiate the company from others, and (3) have value to customers. Deluxe Corporation, a printer of personal checks, defines superior service quite simply: "Forty-eight hour turnaround; zero defects."[54]

SET STANDARDS AND MEASURE PERFORMANCE. To be able to deliver on its promise of superior service, a business must establish specific standards and measure overall performance against them. Satisfied customers should exhibit at least one of three behaviors: loyalty (increased customer retention rate), increased purchases (climbing sales and sales per customer), and resistance to rivals' attempts to lure them away with lower prices (market share and price tolerance).[55] Companies must track performance on these and other service standards and reward employees accordingly.

EXAMINE YOUR COMPANY'S SERVICE CYCLE. What steps must a customer go through to get your product or service? Business owners often are surprised at the complexity that has seeped into their customer service systems as they have evolved over time. One of the most effective techniques is to work with employees to flowchart each component in the company's service cycle, including *everything* a customer has to do to get your product or service. The goal is to look for steps and procedures that are unnecessary, redundant, or unreasonable and then to eliminate them.

HIRE THE RIGHT EMPLOYEES. The key ingredient in the superior service equation is *people*. There is no substitute for friendly, courteous sales/service representatives. The new service attitude "demands a new breed of service worker, folks who are empathetic, flexible, informed, articulate, inventive, and able to work with minimal levels of supervision," says one writer.[56]

TRAIN EMPLOYEES TO DELIVER SUPERIOR SERVICE. Successful businesses train *every* employee who deals directly with customers; they don't leave customer service to chance. Superior service companies devote 1 to 5 percent of their employees' work hours to training, concentrating on how to meet, greet, and serve customers. Leading mail-order companies such as Lands' End and L.L. Bean spend *many* hours training the employees who handle telephone orders before they deal with their first customer.

EMPOWER EMPLOYEES TO OFFER SUPERIOR SERVICE. One of the biggest single variables determining whether or not employees deliver superior service is whether or not they perceive they have permission to do so. The goal is to push decision making down the organization to the employees who have contact with customers. This includes giving them the freedom to circumvent "company policy" if it means improving customer satisfaction. If front-line workers don't have the power to solve disgruntled customers' problems, they quickly become frustrated and the superior service cycle breaks down. To be empowered, employees need knowledge and information, adequate resources, and managerial support.

USE TECHNOLOGY TO PROVIDE IMPROVED SERVICE. The role of technology is not to create a rigid bureaucracy but to free employees from routine clerical tasks, giving them more time and better tools to serve customers more effectively. Ideally, technology gives workers the information they need to help their customers and the time to serve them.

To use technology effectively, entrepreneurs must ask: "What is the best technology for our strategy?" This question leads to four key service issues: (1) What is our primary service strategy? (i.e., What do we want customers to think of when they hear our name?) (2) What barriers are preventing our company from fully implementing this strategy now? (3) What, if anything, can technology do to overcome these barriers? (4) What is our strategy for encouraging our customers to adopt the new technology?[57]

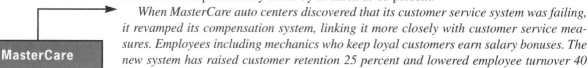

Roger Kao, owner of the Golden Wok, a four-store chain of Chinese restaurants in California, uses technology to provide superior customer service and to maximize his company's efficiency. Using PCs linked through a local area network and an order-and-inventory management system (total cost = $70,000), employees can compare customers' orders with past orders, access instantly maps and directions for take-out orders, and call up details of customers' dining preferences. The system automatically routes incoming orders to the Golden Wok location closest to the customer's address, sends the order to the appropriate person in the kitchen (all equipped with their own terminals), and deducts the appropriate ingredients used to prepare each dish from the company's inventory. Kao generates hourly sales reports, which allow him to begin to prepare some dishes before the orders actually arrive to better serve customers! The result: a growing base of satisfied, loyal customers who get quality food delivered quickly.[58]

REWARD SUPERIOR SERVICE. What gets rewarded gets done. Companies that want employees to provide stellar service must offer rewards for doing so. A recent National Science Foundation study concluded that when pay is linked to performance, employees' motivation and productivity climb by as much as 63 percent.[59]

When MasterCare auto centers discovered that its customer service system was failing, it revamped its compensation system, linking it more closely with customer service measures. Employees including mechanics who keep loyal customers earn salary bonuses. The new system has raised customer retention 25 percent and lowered employee turnover 40 percent.[60]

GET TOP MANAGERS' SUPPORT. The drive toward superior customer service will fall far short of its target unless top managers support it fully. Success requires more than just a verbal commitment; it calls for managers' involvement and dedication. Achieving customer satisfaction must become part of the strategic planning process and work its way into every nook and cranny of the organization.

Emphasis On Speed

Speed has become a major competitive weapon. World-class companies recognize that reducing the time it takes to develop, design, manufacture, and distribute a product reduces costs, increases quality, and boosts market share. One study by McKinsey and Company found that high-tech products that come to market on budget but six months late will earn 33 percent less profit over five years. Bringing the product out on time but 50 percent over budget cuts profits just 4 percent![61] Service companies also know that they must build speed into their business systems if they are to satisfy their impatient, time-pressured customers.

This philosophy of speed is called time compression management (TCM), and it involves three aspects: (1) speeding new products to market, (2) shortening customer response time in manufacturing and delivery, and (3) reducing the administrative time required to fill an order. Studies show plenty of room for improvement; most businesses waste 85 to 99 percent of the time it takes to produce products or services without ever realizing it! [62]

For example, when managers and employees at United Electric Controls, a family-owned maker of temperature and pressure controls and sensors, studied their production process, they were amazed at what they found. In their 50,000-square-foot factory, "We had one product that traveled 12 miles just in our plant," says one manager. Rearranging the plant's layout around products rather than processes solved the problem. "The product that once traveled 12 miles now travels 40 feet," he says. "The outcome was a reduction in lead time from 10 or 12 weeks to just a couple of days."[63]

United Electric Controls

Although speeding up the manufacturing process is a common goal, companies using TCM have learned that manufacturing takes only 5 percent to 10 percent of the total time between an order and getting the product into the customer's hands. The rest is consumed by clerical and administrative tasks. "The primary opportunity for TCM lies in its application to the administrative process," says one manager.

Companies relying on TCM to help them turn speed into a competitive edge should:

- ☆ Reengineer the entire process rather than attempt to do the same things in the same way— only faster.

- ☆ Create cross-functional teams of workers and give them the power to attack and solve problems. In world-class companies, product teams include engineers, manufacturers, salespeople, quality experts—even customers.

- ☆ Set aggressive goals for time reduction and stick to the schedule. Some companies using TCM have been able to reduce cycle time from several weeks to just a few hours!

- ☆ Instill speed in the culture. At Domino's Pizza, kitchen workers watch videos of the fastest pizza makers in the country.

- ☆ Use technology to find shortcuts wherever possible. Rather than build costly, time-consuming prototypes, many time-sensitive businesses use computer-aided design and computer-assisted manufacturing (CAD/CAM) to speed product design and testing.

YOU BE THE CONSULTANT...

In the Shadow of the Giants

- As managed-care health insurance plans increasingly favored large drugstore chains over smaller independent drugstores, Tom Young, owner of Foley Rexall Drugs in Foley, Minnesota, has watched the number of prescriptions he fills decline dramatically. The threat is a serious one; prescriptions represent a major profit center for his independent drugstore. Chain drugstores in the area are siphoning off a significant part of Young's sales.

- The King Group, a family-owned office supply store founded in 1956, watches glumly as Staples, a large, national office supply chain, opens a superstore just one block from its location in New York City. With its volume buying power and advertisements touting its low prices on basic office supplies, Staples represents the most serious threat the company has faced in its history.

- When Don and Gloria Connell heard that Wal-Mart would be opening a store less than a block away from their independent hardware store, they immediately began to focus on making sure their business would survive. Their store, Mr. D's Ace Hardware, carries a wide selection of housewares, appliances, gifts, sporting goods, and automotive products in addition to a small range of traditional hardware. After studying the products at a Wal-Mart in another town, the Connells discovered that their mix of merchandise was very similar to the giant retailer's. "The trip back was very depressing," says Don. "We saw what they were doing in our best departments and knew that we didn't stand a chance." It will be impossible for Mr. D's to match Wal-Mart's low prices, and Wal-mart spends as much on marketing in an hour as Mr. D's does in a year.

1. What chance of survival would you give each of these small companies if they continue to rely on their existing

1. strategies to compete with their larger, more powerful rivals?

2. What suggestions would you make to the owners of these three businesses in the face of their new competitive conditions?

3. Working on your own, develop a new marketing strategy for each of these three companies. After you complete your own plan, form a team with several of your classmates to brainstorm a team-generated set of strategies.

Sources: Adapted from Dale D. Buss, "The Little Guys Strike Back," *Nation's Business*, July 1996, pp. 18-24; Meg Whittemore, "Retailing Looks to a New Century," *Nation's Business*, December 1994, pp. 18-24.

Tiny JTECH, Inc., a manufacturer of on-premises pagers, uses speed as a potent competitive weapon in its David-and-Goliath battle for market share against giants such as Motorola. Drawing on his restaurant experience, cofounder David Miller targeted the restaurant industry with a vibrating pager that quietly alerted customers when their tables were ready. To further differentiate the company, JTECH began offering a guarantee to replace faulty pagers within 24 hours. "The larger you are, the harder it is to respond to customers," explains cofounder Jeff Graham. JTECH had the restaurant niche all to itself until Motorola introduced its own pager called the Diner Delight. JTECH responded by expanding its product line and focusing on responding to customers even faster. One winter, for instance, a restaurant manager complained that customers wearing heavy jackets could not feel the vibrating pagers. "Two days later, we modified the pagers so they beeped as well," says Graham. "In a big company, that problem wouldn't even get back to the engineers within 48 hours."[64]

5. Discuss the marketing opportunities the World Wide Web (WWW) offers entrepreneurs and how to best take advantage of them.

World Wide Web—*the vast network that links computers around the globe via the Internet and opens up endless oceans of information to its users.*

Website—*the "electronic storefront" for a company on the World Wide Web; its exact location on the Web is defined by the site's Universal Resource Locator (URL).*

Marketing on the World Wide Web (WWW)

Much like the telephone, the fax machine, and home shopping networks, the World Wide Web (WWW, or the Web) promises to become a revolutionary business tool. Although most entrepreneurs have heard about the **World Wide Web**, the vast network that links computers around the globe via the Internet and opens up endless oceans of information to its users, the majority of them are still struggling to understand what it is, how it can work for them, and how they can establish a presence on it. Businesses get on the Web by using one of thousands of "electronic gateways" to set up an address (called a Universal Resource Locator, or URL) there. By establishing a creative, attractive **Website**, the "electronic storefront" for a company on the Web, even the smallest companies can market their products and services to customers across the globe. With its ability to display colorful graphics, sound, animation, and video as well as text, the Web allows small companies to equal—even surpass—their larger rivals' Web presence. Although small companies cannot match the marketing efforts of their larger competitors, a creative Web page can be "the great equalizer" in a small company's marketing program. "It's like advertising your product in the world's largest directory," says the president of the Internet Society. "The [World Wide Web] lets small companies expand far beyond their immediate region. [It is] a phenomenal commercial opportunity that offers businesses a worldwide marketing and distribution system"[65]

Well-designed Websites, commonly called *home pages,* include interactive features that allow customers to access information about a company, its products and services, its history, and other features such as question-and-answer sessions with experts or the ability to conduct electronic conversations with company officials. The Web also allows business owners to link their companies' home pages to other related Websites, something advertisements in other media cannot offer. For instance, the home page of a company selling cookware might include hypertext links to Web pages containing recipes, cookbooks, foods, and other cooking resources. This allows small business owners to engage in cross-marketing with companies on the Web selling complementary products or services.

The Web gives small businesses the power to broaden their scope to unbelievable proportions. Do you know where the best-stocked music and video store on the planet is? On the Web!

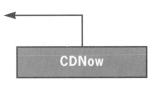

A cyber-company called CDNow carries a selection of 165,000 music titles and 30,000 videotapes, making it one of the hottest sights on the Web. Within two years of launching CDNow, twin brothers Jason and Matthew Olim built it into a company generating $6 million in annual revenues! It took the Olims just six months and $2,500 to build their Website and set up shop on the Web. The key to the success of CDNow's Website is that is offers a wide array of features that draw music lovers and that competing retail stores such as Tower Records and Best Buy cannot provide: free reviews of new releases, in-depth biographies of musicians, and an on-line juke box for previewing selections before you purchase. The site also allows customers to find exactly what they are looking for within a matter of seconds by clicking on a particular type of music or by entering an artist or a title into CDNow's search engine, which instantly returns every title that meets the specified criteria. Convenience is a major advantage; placing an order is as simple as entering your credit card information into the computer. "You can order on-line and have your items the next day," says Jason.[66]

Small companies have plenty of incentive to set up shop on the World Wide Web. More than 50 million people have access to the Internet, and the number is growing rapidly. Plus, the demographic profile of the typical Web user is very attractive to plenty of entrepreneurs: young, educated, and wealthy. According to a recent study of Web users:[67]

- ☆ The average age is 35, and 53 percent are between the ages of 16 and 34.
- ☆ Sixty-four percent have college degrees.
- ☆ Average annual household income is $69,000, and 25 percent earn more than $80,000 per year.
- ☆ Seventy percent are male.
- ☆ Seventy-seven percent browse the Web at least once a day.

Despite all of the hoopla about the marketing potential of the Web, not every business owner should rush out and establish a Website. In fact, many of those currently trying to sell on the Web are not making any money at it! However, they are looking to the future, using the Web to connect with their existing customers and, eventually, to attract new ones.

For instance, Richard Burton, owner of Flying Pictures, Inc., a company that rents camera equipment to the movie industry, says his bare-bones Website has generated no new business—yet. Still, Burton is pleased with his Web presence and recognizes its importance to his company's future. "Because we're in the motion picture industry, our customers are very tuned into the digital revolution . . . A lot of people are looking . . . It's ongoing exposure," he says.[68]

Just as in any marketing venture, the key to successful marketing on the World Wide Web is selling the right product or service at the right price to the right target audience. Entrepreneurs on the Web, however, also have two additional challenges: attracting Web users to their Websites and converting them into paying customers. That requires setting up an electronic storefront that is inviting, easy to navigate, interactive, and offers more than a monotonous laundry list of items. Companies that do can—and are—selling everything from wine and vacations to jewelry and electronics successfully on the Web. So far, the top-selling items on the Web are computers and accessories, software, travel and financial services, and consumer electronics.[69] "As time goes on," says one entrepreneur selling wine on the Web, "this medium will have a major impact on how people get information and buy products."[70]

Harvesting a Customer Base

Rachael and Richard Close bottled their first wine vintage in 1991. As a small winery in California's Sonoma Valley, their company, Buena Vista Winery, had few resources for marketing their excellent wines. Despite its reputation for producing high-quality wines, Buena Vista's vintages had gained little exposure outside a small circle of customers along the West Coast. The company scored a major marketing strike when one of its Chardonnays received an excellent rating in the *Wine Spectator*, a magazine widely read by wine enthusiasts.

The winery's $520,000 in sales generated a small profit for the Closes, but both Rachael and Richard know that they could generate more sales and profits if they could build on the publicity generated by the review in *Wine Spectator*. Thanks to favorable weather conditions and timely harvesting, the current crop of grapes is one of the best in years. The Closes know that this crop will produce the largest wine vintage in Buena Vista's short existence. The question they face is how to best market the wines those grapes will produce.

The Closes have some information about their customers. With the help of a computer they purchased the year they launched Buena Vista, Rachael has been building a database of existing customers. The database includes the usual address information and a brief demographic profile for most but not all of their customers. Analyzing these data, the Closes are not surprised to find that their typical customer is well educated,

wealthy, and well traveled. Forty-eight percent live in California, and another 36 percent are residents of adjoining West Coast states. The remaining 16 percent of Buena Vista's customers are scattered about the rest of the United States and the world. Many of these customers discovered this unique little winery while on vacation and have remained loyal customers via mail order. Rachael has developed a small mailing list using this database, but she would like to expand it. "Remember the speaker at that marketing seminar we attended a few months ago?" she asked Richard. "He talked about buying mailing lists for practically any niche a small business wanted. Perhaps we should look into that."

Two weeks earlier, Richard was reading a computer magazine and saw a demographic profile of the typical World Wide Web user. "These Web cruisers sound a lot like our customers," he told Rachael, "but I'm not sure what is the best way to reach them. What do you think?"

1. What recommendations would you make to the Closes concerning the foundation for building Buena Vista's competitive advantage?

2. How should Buena Vista market its new wine vintage? What channel(s) should the company use to reach customers?

3. Should Buena Vista establish a presence on the World Wide Web? Explain. If so, what advice would you offer the Closes about building their Website?

---

6. Explain the various marketing strategies available to business owners.

marketing strategy— *the result of an owner blending together meaningful market research with a plan to develop a competitive edge in a particular target market(s) to create a successful marketing mix.*

Choosing a Marketing Strategy

A **marketing strategy** results when a small business owner blends together the results of meaningful market research with a plan to develop a competitive advantage in a particular target market(s) to create a successful marketing mix. There are several basic marketing strategies an entrepreneur can use to establish a competitive edge. A **market penetration strategy** seeks to increase sales of existing products in current markets (or in current locations) through greater selling and advertising efforts, and is quite feasible for many small businesses. On the other hand, a **market development strategy** attempts to increase sales by introducing existing products or services into new markets. For example, a small accounting firm may boost sales by opening a satellite office in a nearby town. Introducing its services to this new market increases the firm's sales. A **product development strategy** tries to increase sales by adding new goods or services in existing markets. These new products may be modifications of existing items or entirely new ones. For instance, a small fast-food restaurant whose menu is built primarily around hamburgers might increase sales by adding pork, fish, and chicken dishes.

Market segmentation is another popular marketing strategy. Here, the small business manager segments the mass market, that is, carves it up into smaller, more homogenous segments (niches) and then attacks one or more of them with a unique marketing strategy designed to appeal to that segment's members. Usually, such a "rifle approach" in specific niches is more successful than the "shotgun approach" used to appeal to the general market. One marketing expert explains, "The essence of marketing is narrowing your focus. You become stronger when you reduce the scope of your operations."[71] The specific approach comes down to knowing who the firm's customers are and how to serve their particular needs and wants most effectively.

Rather than compete head-to-head with larger rivals, many successful small companies choose their niches carefully and defend them fiercely. A niche strategy allows a small company to maximize the advantages of its smallness and to compete effectively even in industries dominated by giants. Focusing on niches that are too small to be attractive to large companies is a common recipe for success among small companies. "Finding such unserved niches is an excellent way to begin 'whupping' the big guys, if not in their own back yard, at least on the same street," says one marketing expert.[72]

As the name of her business implies, Phyllis Stoller, owner of the Women's Travel Club, has targeted that portion of the market that accounts for 41 percent of all travel. Market research told Stoller that women travelers are more interested in safety and sanitary conditions than are men. She plans every club trip with these factors in mind. Stoller also discovered that women are more interested in experiencing everyday life than typical tourist activities when traveling to foreign lands. Rather than offer the traditional vacation getaways her competitors sell, Stoller specializes in tours that offer plenty of opportunities for cultural exchanges. Because she knows that women want more information than men do before they make a significant purchase, Stoller publishes a monthly newsletter describing upcoming trips in rich detail, focusing on historical attractions, unusual tourist destinations, and local shopping and dining options.[73]

"Small business is uniquely positioned for niche marketing," says marketing expert Philip Kotler. "If a small business sits down and follows the principles of targeting, segmenting, and differentiating, it doesn't have to collapse to larger companies."[74]

Table 5.5 describes several low-cost, highly effective guerrilla marketing strategies small businesses have used to outperform their larger rivals.

marketing penetration strategy—*seeks to increase sales of existing products in current markets through greater selling and advertising efforts.*

marketing development strategy—*attempts to increase sales by introducing existing products or services into new markets.*

Women's Travel Club

product development strategy—*attempts to increase sales by adding new goods or services in existing markets.*

market segmentation strategy—*carves up the mass market into smaller, more homogenous segments and then attacks one or more of them with a unique, "tailored" marketing strategy.*

- ✰ Help organize and sponsor a service- or community-oriented project.
- ✰ Sponsor offbeat, memorable events. Build a giant banana split, rent a theater for a morning and invite kids for a free viewing.
- ✰ Always be on the lookout for new niches to enter. Try to develop multiple niches.
- ✰ Offer to speak about your business, industry, product, or service to local organizations.
- ✰ Ask present customers for referrals.
- ✰ Develop a sales "script" that asks customers a series of questions to hone in on what they are looking for and that will lead them to the conclusion that your product or service is IT!
- ✰ Offer customers gift certificates. They really boost your cash flow.
- ✰ Create samples of your product and give them to customers. You'll increase sales later.
- ✰ Offer a 100 percent, money-back, no-hassles guarantee. By removing the customer's risk of buying, you increase your product's attractiveness.

Table 5.5
Guerrilla Marketing Strategies

Sources: Adapted from Lynn Beresford, Janean Chun, Cynthia E. Griffin, Heather Page, and Debra Phillips, "Marketing 101," *Entrepreneur*, May 1996, pp. 104-114; Guen Sublette, "Marketing 101," *Entrepreneur*, May 1995, pp. 86-98; Denise Osburn, "Bringing Them Back for More," *Nation's Business*, August 1995, p. 31R; Jay Conrad Levinson, "Survival Tactics, *Entrepreneur*, March 1996, p. 84; Tom Stein, Outselling the Giants," *Success*, May 1996, pp. 38-41.

Continued

Table 5.5
*Guerrilla Marketing
Strategies, Continued*

☆ Create a "frequent buyer" program. Remember how valuable existing customers are. Work hard to keep the customers you have! One coffee shop kept its customers coming back with a punch-card promotion that gave a free pound of coffee after a customer purchased nine pounds.

☆ Clip articles that feature your business and send reprints to customers and potential customers. Keep reminding them of who you are and why you're valuable to them.

☆ Test how well your ads "pull" with coded coupons that customers bring in. Focus your ad expenditures on those media that produce the best results for you.

☆ Create "tip sheets" to pass out to customers and potential customers, e.g., landscape tips on lawn maintenance.

☆ Create an award for your community, e.g., a landscape company presented a "best yard" award each season.

☆ Conduct a contest in the community, e.g., a photographer sponsored a juried photo contest for different age groups.

☆ Collect testimonials from satisfied customers and use them in ads, brochures, etc. Testimonials are one of the most effective forms of advertising!

☆ Get a former journalist to help you write a story "pitch" for local media.

☆ Show an interest in your customers' needs. If you spot a seminar that would be of interest to them, tell them! Become a valuable resource for them.

☆ Find unique ways to thank customers (especially first-time buyers) for their business—a note, a lunch, a gift basket . . .

☆ Give loyal customers a "freebie" occasionally. You might be surprised at how long they will remember it.

☆ Create a newsletter that features your customers or clients and their businesses—e.g., photo of client using your product in his business.

☆ Cooperate with other businesses selling complementary products and services in marketing efforts and campaigns, a process called fusion marketing. Share mailing lists and advertising time or space, or work together on a special promotion.

☆ Use major competitors' coupons against them. The owner of an independent sandwich shop routinely pulled business from a nearby national chain store by advertising that he would accept its coupons.

☆ Market your company's uniqueness. Many customers enjoy buying from small companies that are different and unique. The owners of the only tea plantation in the United States used that fact to their advantage in establishing a customer base.

---

7. Discuss the "four Ps" of marketing—product, place, price, and promotion—and their role in building a successful marketing strategy.

The Marketing Mix

The major elements of a marketing strategy are the four Ps of marketing—**p**roduct, **p**lace, **p**rice, and **p**romotion. These four elements are self-reinforcing, and when coordinated, increase the sales appeal of a product or service. Small business managers must integrate these elements to maximize the impact of their product or service on the consumer. All four Ps must reinforce the image of the product or service the company presents to the potential customer. One long-time retailer claims, "None of the modern marvels of computerized inventory control and point-of-sale telecommunications have replaced the need for the entrepreneur who understands the customer and can translate that into the appropriate merchandise mix."[75]

product life cycle—
measures the stages of development, growth, and decline in a product's life.

Product

The product itself is an essential element in marketing. A product is any item or service that satisfies the need of a consumer. Products can have form and shape, or they can be services with no physical form. Products travel through various stages of development. The **product life cycle** (see Figure 5.3) measures these stages of growth, and these measurements

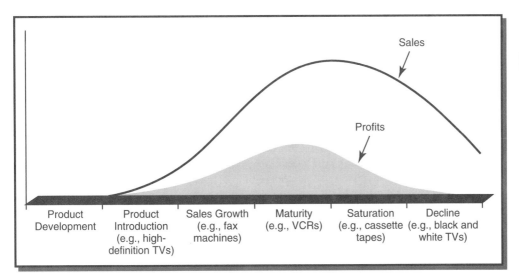

Figure 5.3
Product Life Cycle

Sales

Profits

| Product Development | Product Introduction (e.g., high-definition TVs) | Sales Growth (e.g., fax machines) | Maturity (e.g., VCRs) | Saturation (e.g., cassette tapes) | Decline (e.g., black and white TVs) |

enable the company's management to make decisions about whether or not to continue selling the product and when to introduce new follow-up products.

In the **introductory stage**, the marketers present their product to the potential consumers. Initial high levels of acceptance are rare. Generally, new products must break into existing markets and compete with established products. Advertising and promotion help the new product become more quickly recognized. Potential customers must get information about the product and the needs it can satisfy. The cost of marketing a product at this level of the life cycle is usually high. The small company must overcome customer resistance and inertia. Thus, profits are generally low, or even negative, at the introductory stage.

After the introductory stage, the product enters the **growth and acceptance stage**. In the growth stage, consumers begin to compare the product in large enough numbers for sales to rise and profits to materialize. Products that reach this stage, however, do not necessarily become successful. If in the introductory or the growth stage the product fails to meet consumer needs, it does not sell and eventually disappears from the marketplace. For successful products, sales and profit margins continue to rise through the growth stage.

In the **maturity and competition stage**, sales volume continues to rise, but profit margins peak and then begin to fall as competitors enter the market. Normally, this causes reduction in the product's selling price to meet competition and to hold its share of the market.

Sales peak in the **market saturation stage** of the product life cycle and give the marketer fair warning that it is time to introduce the next generation product.

The final stage of the product life cycle is the **product decline stage**. Sales continue to drop, and profit margins fall drastically. However, when a product reaches this stage of the cycle, it does not mean that it is doomed to failure. Products that have remained popular are always being revised. No firm can maintain its sales position without product innovation and change. Even the maker of Silly Putty, first introduced at the 1950 International Toy Fair (with lifetime sales of more than 200 million "eggs") recently introduced new Day-Glo and glow-in-the-dark colors. These innovations have caused the classic toy's sales to surge by more than 60 percent.[76]

The time span of the stages in the product life cycle depends on the type of products involved. High-fashion and fad clothing have a short product life cycle, lasting for only four to six weeks. Products that are more stable may take years to complete a life cycle. Research conducted by MIT suggests that the typical product's life cycle lasts ten to fourteen years.

introductory stage—*stage in which the product or service must break into the market and overcome customer inertia.*

growth and acceptance stage—*stage in which sales rise and profits materialize.*

maturity and competition stage—*stage in which sales rise, but profits peak and then fall as competitors enter the market.*

market saturation stage—*stage in which sales peak, indicating the time to introduce the next generation product.*

product decline stage—*stage in which sales continue to fall and profit margins decline drastically.*

Zebra Technologies

For example, when Edward Kaplan and Gary Cless launched a company in 1969, they sold a product they had developed that used punch cards to help merchants collect data on their customers' buying patterns. Using the same technology, they also created a machine to program machine tools. By 1982, their company was the market leader in the paper-tape-punching machine industry. Kaplan and Cless saw that the rapidly advancing computer revolution would render all of their products obsolete, so they looked for new products and markets. Soon they had come up with a line of specialized printers that could print bar codes on almost any surface. Their new company, Zebra Technologies, sold its first bar-code printer in 1982; today, bar-code tags printed by Zebra printers appear on everything from grocery products and park admission tickets to airline baggage and laying hens![77]

Thomas Venable, owner of Spectrum Control, Inc., uses the concept of the product life cycle to plan the introduction of new products to the company's product line. Too often, companies wait until too late into the life cycle of one product to introduce another. The result is that they are totally unprepared when a competitor produces "a better mousetrap" and their sales decline. "If you are not developing something new early in the current product's life cycle, you're living on borrowed time," says Venable. "If you wait until your line is mature, you're dead."

In Venable's industry, a 12-year life cycle is common. His company's strategy is to begin turning out prototypes of sequel products two to three years before the maturity phase of the original product (see Figure 5.4). "The whole idea behind the process is to avoid crises," Venable says. "You want to be ready to go with the second product, just as the first one is about to die off ."[78]

Place

Place (or method of distribution) has grown in importance as customers expect greater service and more convenience from businesses. Because of this trend, mail-order houses offering the ultimate in convenience—shop at home—have experienced booming sales in the last decade. In addition, many traditionally stationary businesses have added wheels, becoming mobile animal clinics, computer shops, and dentist offices.

Any activity involving movement of goods to the point of consumer purchase provides place utility. Place utility is directly affected by the marketing channels of distribution, the path that goods or services and their titles take in moving from producer to consumer. Channels typically involve a number of intermediaries who perform specialized functions that add valuable utility to the goods or service. Specifically, these intermediaries provide

Figure 5.4
Time Between Introduction of Products

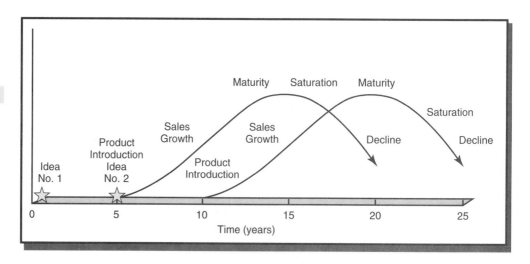

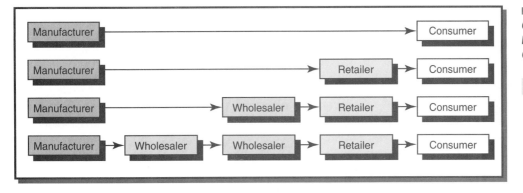

Figure 5.5
*Channels of
Distribution—
Consumer Goods*

time utility (making the product available when customers want to buy it) and place utility (making the product available where customers want to buy it).

For consumer goods, there are four common channels of distribution (see Figure 5.5).

1. *Manufacturer to Consumer.* In some markets, producers sell their goods or services directly to consumers. Services, by nature, follow this channel of distribution. Dental care and haircuts, for example, go directly from creator to consumer.

2. *Manufacturer to Retailer to Consumer.* Another common channel involves a retailer as an intermediary. Many clothing items, books, shoes, and other consumer products are distributed in this manner.

3. *Manufacturer to Wholesaler to Retailer to Consumer.* This is the most common channel of distribution. Prepackaged food products, hardware, toys, and other items are commonly distributed through this channel.

4. *Manufacturer to Wholesaler to Wholesaler to Consumer.* A few consumer goods (e.g., agricultural goods and electrical components) follow this pattern of distribution.

Two channels of distribution are common for industrial goods (see Figure 5.6).

1. *Manufacturer to Industrial User.* The majority of industrial goods are distributed directly from manufacturers to users. In some cases, the goods or services are designed to meet the user's specifications.

2. *Manufacturer to Wholesaler to Industrial* User. Most expense items (paper clips, paper, rubber bands, cleaning fluids) that firms commonly use are distributed through wholesalers. For most small manufacturers, distributing goods through established wholesalers and agents is often the most effective route.

Price

Almost everyone agrees that the price of the product or service is a key factor in the decision to buy. Price affects both sales volume and profits, and without the right price, both sales and profits will suffer. As we will see in Chapter 6, the right price for a product or service, depends on three factors: (1) a small company's cost structure, (2) an assessment of

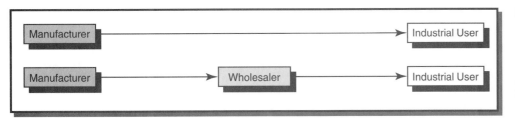

Figure 5.6
*Channels of
Distribution—
Industrial Goods*

what the market will bear, and (3) the desired image the company wants to create in its customers' minds.

Price can be a powerful tool for changing a company's image relatively quickly.

D.G. Yuengling & Sons

In the 1980s, D.G. Yuengling & Sons, the nation's oldest brewery, was "considered a cheap, coal-region beer," says president Dick Yuengling. But the brewery changed its image to appeal to upscale beer drinkers intrigued by the mystique of nostalgic microbreweries. After a price-cutting campaign failed to slow sliding sales, Yuengling managers reversed their marketing strategy, raising the price of their beer to above-premium levels, focusing promotions on the brewery's rich history, and getting their brew into upscale restaurants and pubs. Within a few years, Yuengling became the drink of choice in its northeastern territory, and the brewery couldn't make enough beer to keep it on the local shelves.[79]

For many small businesses, nonprice competition—focusing on factors other than price—is a more effective strategy than trying to beat larger competitors in a price war. Nonprice competition, such as free trial offers, free delivery, lengthy warranties, and money-back guarantees, intends to play down the product's price and stress its durability, quality, reputation, or special features.

Promotion

Promotion involves both advertising and personal selling. Its goal is to inform and persuade consumers. Advertising communicates to potential customers through some mass medium the benefits of a good or service. Personal selling involves the art of persuasive sales on a one-to-one basis. A small company's promotional program can play a significant role in creating a specific image in its customers' minds—whether it is upscale, discount, or somewhere in between. "Marketing is not a battle of products; it's a battle of perceptions," says one marketing expert.[80]

CHAPTER SUMMARY

1. Describe the components of a marketing plan and explain the benefits of preparing one. A major part of the entrepreneur's business plan is the marketing plan, which focuses on a company's target customers and how best to satisfy their needs and wants. A solid marketing plan should:
- determine customer needs and wants through market research.
- pinpoint the specific target markets the company will serve.
- analyze the firm's competitive advantages and build a marketing strategy around them.
- create a marketing mix that meets customer needs and wants.

2. Discuss the role of market research and outline the market research process. Market research is the vehicle for gathering the information that serves as the foundation of the marketing plan. Good research does *not* have to be complex and expensive to be useful. The steps in conducting market research include:
- defining the problem: "What do you want to know?"
- collecting the data from either primary or secondary sources.
- analyzing and interpreting the data.

- drawing conclusions and acting on them.

3. Explain how small businesses can pinpoint their target markets. Sound market research helps the owner pinpoint a target market. The most successful businesses have well-defined portraits of the customers they are seeking to attract.

4. Describe the factors on which a small business can build a competitive edge in the marketplace: customer focus, quality, convenience, innovation, service, and speed. When plotting a marketing strategy, owners must strive to achieve a competitive advantage—some way to make their companies different from and better than the competition. Successful small businesses rely on six sources to develop a competitive edge:
- a focus on the customer
- devotion to quality
- attention to convenience
- concentration on innovation
- dedication to service
- emphasis on speed

5. Discuss the marketing opportunities the World Wide Web (WWW) offers entrepreneurs and how to best take advantage of them. The Web offers small business owners tremendous marketing potential on a par with their larger rivals.

Entrepreneurs are just beginning to uncover the Web's profit potential, which is growing rapidly. Establishing a presence on the Web is important for companies targeting educated, wealthy, young customers. Successful Websites are attractive, inviting, easy to navigate, interactive, and offers users something of value.

6. Explain the various marketing strategies available to business owners. A marketing strategy results when a small business owner blends together the results of meaningful market research with a plan to develop a competitive advantage in a particular target market(s) to develop a successful marketing mix. Common marketing strategies include:

- market penetration
- market development
- product development
- market segmentation

7. Discuss the "four Ps" of marketing—product, place, price, and promotion—and their role in building a successful marketing strategy. The marketing mix consists of the " four Ps":

- Product. Entrepreneurs should understand where in the product life cycle their products are.
- Place. The focus here is on choosing the appropriate channel of distribution and using it most efficiently.
- Price. Setting the right price for a product or service is partly an art and partly a science.
- Promotion. Promotion involves both advertising and personal selling.

DISCUSSION QUESTIONS

1. Define the marketing plan. What lies at its center?

2. What objectives should a marketing plan accomplish?

3. How can market research benefit a small business owner? List some possible sources of market information.

4. Does market research have to be expensive and sophisticated to be valuable? Explain.

5. Describe several market trends that are driving markets into the next millennium and their impact on small businesses.

6. Why is it important for small business owners to define their target markets as part of their marketing strategies?

7. What is a competitive advantage? Why is it important for a small business owner to create a plan for establishing one?

8. Describe how a small business owner could use the following sources of a competitive advantage:

- a focus on the customer
- devotion to quality

- attention to convenience
- concentration on innovation
- dedication to service
- emphasis on speed

9. What is the World Wide Web? What marketing potential does it offer small businesses?

10. Explain the concept of the marketing mix. What are the four Ps?

11. List and explain the stages in the product life cycle. How can a small firm extend its product's life?

12. With a 70 percent customer retention rate (average for most U.S. firms, according to the American Management Association) every $1 million of business in 1995 will grow to more than $4 million by the year 2005. If you retain 80 percent of your customers, the $1 million will grow to a little over $6 million. If you can keep 90 percent of your customers, that $1 million will grow to more than $9.5 million. What can the typical small business do to increase its customer retention rate?

Beyond the Classroom...

1. Interview the owner of a local restaurant about its marketing strategy. From how large a geographic region does the restaurant draw its clientele? What is the firm's target market? What are its characteristics? Does the restaurant have a competitive edge?

2. Select a local small manufacturing operation and evaluate its primary product. What stage of the product life cycle is it in? What channels of distribution does the product follow after leaving the manufacturer?

3. Obtain a copy of Management Aid #4.012, *Marketing Checklist for Small Retailers*, from the Small Business Administration. Interview a local business owner, using the checklist as a guide. What sources for developing a competitive edge did you find? What weaknesses do you see? How do you recommend overcoming them?

4. Contact three local small business owners and ask them about their marketing strategies. How have they achieved a competitive edge? Develop a series of questions to judge the sources of their competitive edge:a focus on the customer: devotion to quality,attention to convenience, concentration on innovation, dedication to service, and emphasis on speed. How do the businesses compare?

5. Select three local businesses (one large and two small) and play the role of "mystery shopper." How easy was it to do business with each company? How would you rate their service, quality, and convenience? Were salespeople helpful and friendly? How would you rate the business's appearance? How would you describe each company's competitive advantage? What future would you predict for each company? Prepare a brief report for your class on your findings and conclusions.

SURFING THE NET

1. Access the home pages for CDNow, Amazon Books, and CyberShop at:

http://cdnow.com

http://www.amazon.com

http://www.cybershop.com

Evaluate the quality of Websites. What do they offer that traditional retail stores do not? Can you offer any suggestions for improving these Websites?

2. Using one of the search engines on the World Wide Web (WWW) such as Lycos, Magellan, Yahoo!, or others, conduct a search of a product category you are interested in (e.g., T-shirts, baseball cards, antiques, etc.). Visit several retail sites and prepare a report on them. Did they attract attention? Were they interactive? Did they offer you something of value or interest? Which Website do you consider most effective? Least effective? Why?

3. Visit the following Websites offering resources on building a Website and using it as an effective marketing tool:

Internet Business Center.

http://internetbusinesscenter.com/

Internet Commercial Use Strategies.

http://pass.wayne.edu.business.html

The Do's and Don'ts of On-Line Marketing.

http://pass.wayne.edu/dosdonts.html

Internet Statistics and Demographics.

**http://www.yahoo.com/Computers/
Internet/Statistics_and_Demographics**

Use these resources to develop a guide to launching and doing business on the World Wide Web.

CHAPTER
SIX

Advertising and Pricing for Profit

Half the money I spend on advertising is wasted, and the trouble is I don't know which half.
- John Wannamaker

A salesman is one who sells goods that won't come back to customers who will.
- Arnold H. Glasgow

Doing business without advertising is like winking at a girl in the dark.
You know what you're doing, but nobody else does.
- Stewart Britt

If your price isn't right, you can't sell it regardless of fit, quality, or style.
- Bud Konheim

LEARNING OBJECTIVES

Upon completion of this chapter, you will be able to:

1. **Explain** the differences among promotion, publicity, personal selling, and advertising.

2. **Describe** the advantages and disadvantages of the various advertising media.

3. **Present** the steps in developing an advertising plan.

4. **Identify** four basic methods for preparing an advertising budget.

5. **Explain** practical methods for stretching the small business owner's advertising budget.

6. **Describe** effective pricing techniques for introducing new goods or services and for existing ones.

7. **Explain** the pricing methods and strategies for retailers, manufacturers, and service firms.

8. **Describe** the impact of credit on pricing.

Some small business owners believe that because of limited budgets they cannot afford the "luxury" of advertising. In their view, advertising is an expense they undertake only when their budgets permit—a leftover expense, something to spend if anything remains after paying the other bills. These owners discover, often after it's too late, that advertising is not just an expense; it is an *investment* in a company's future. Without a steady advertising and promotional campaign, a small business's customer base will soon dry up. Advertising can be an effective means of increasing sales by informing customers of the business and its goods or services, by improving the image of the firm and its products, or by persuading customers to purchase the firm's goods or services. A megabudget is *not* a prerequisite for building an effective advertising campaign. With a little creativity and ingenuity, a small company can make its voice heard above the clamor of its larger competitors—and stay within a limited budget!

> *For example, Elaine Petrocelli, co-owner of Book Passage, a small bookstore in Corte Madera, California, keeps her company's name in front of customers by staging some 400 promotional events of all types each year. In addition to her regular advertising, Petrocelli publishes a customer newsletter, has a World Wide Web site, and regularly offers classes and workshops at her store. One of her most popular promotions is a call-in radio show when she evaluates the best and worst books of the season. Petrocelli also organizes an annual travel writer's conference, teaming up with British Airways as a cosponsor. Book Passage has boosted sales of its cookbooks by having a well-known local chef prepare meals while authors are on hand to talk with customers. Petrocelli says Book Passage's promotional efforts are not only fun for both her and her customers, but they also create interest in her store's books and keep her business thriving in the face of competition from giant chains—and for very little money!*[1]

Book Passage

Developing an effective advertising program has become more of a challenge for business owners in recent years. Because of media overflow, overwhelming ad clutter, increasingly fragmented audiences, and more skeptical consumers, companies have had to become more innovative and creative in their promotional campaigns. Rather than merely turning up the advertising volume on their campaigns, companies are learning to change their frequencies, trying out new approaches in different advertising media.

1. Explain the differences among promotion, advertising, publicity, and personal selling.

What Is Promotion?

The terms *advertising* and *promotion* are often confused. **Promotion** is any form of persuasive communication designed to inform consumers about a product or service and to influence them to purchase these goods or services. It includes publicity, personal selling, and advertising.

promotion—*any form of persuasive communication designed to inform customers about a product or service and to influence them to purchase these goods or services; it includes publicity, personal selling, and advertising.*

Publicity

Publicity is any commercial news covered by the media that boosts sales but for which the small business does not pay. "[Publicity] is telling your story to the people you want to reach—namely, the news media, potential customers, and community leaders," says the head of a public relations firm. "It is not . . . haphazard . . . It requires regular and steady attention."[2] Publicity has power; a national survey found that a news feature about a company or a product appearing in a newspaper or magazine would have more impact on people's buying decisions than an advertisement would.[3] The following tactics can help any small business owner stimulate publicity for her firm:

> *Write an article that will interest your customers or potential customers.* One investment advisor writes a monthly column for the local newspaper on timely topics such as "retirement planning," "minimizing your tax bill," and "investing strategies for the next century." Not

only do the articles help build her credibility as an expert, they have attracted new customers to her business.

Contact local TV and radio stations and offer to be interviewed. Many local news or talk shows are looking for guests to talk about topics of interest to their audiences (especially in January and February). Even local shows can reach new customers.

Publish a newsletter. With a personal computer and desktop publishing software, any entrepreneur can publish a professional-looking newsletter. Freelancers can offer design and editing advice. Use the newsletter to reach present and potential customers.

Contact local business and civic organizations and offer to speak to them. A powerful, informative presentation can win new business. (Be sure your public speaking skills are up to par first! If not, consider joining Toastmasters.)

Offer or sponsor a seminar. Teaching people about a subject about which you know a great deal builds confidence and goodwill among potential customers. The owner of a landscaping service and nursery offers a short course in landscape architecture and always sees sales climb afterwards!

Write news releases and fax them to the media. The key to having a news release picked up and printed is finding a unique angle on your business or industry that would interest an editor. Keep it short, simple, and interesting.

Volunteer to serve on community and industry boards and committees. You can make your town a better place to live and work and raise your company's visibility at the same time.

Sponsor a community project or support a nonprofit organization or charity. Not only will you be giving something back to the community, but you will also gain recognition, goodwill, and, perhaps, customers for your business.

The owner of a dry cleaning business received the equivalent of thousands of dollars worth of advertising from the publicity generated by a program called "Give the gift of warmth." Customers donated winter coats, which the company cleaned for free and then distributed to the needy.

Promote a cause. Joseph Crilley, owner of Crilley's Circle Tavern, was concerned about the dangers of drinking and driving, so he renovated an old school bus and began offering his customers a free shuttle service. Not only has his service made the roads safer, but it also has boosted his business. During off-peak hours, Crilley uses the bus to shuttle school kids on field trips and senior citizens around town to run errands.[4]

What started out as a socially responsible act has turned into a successful public relations campaign.

Publicity—any commercial news covered by the media that boosts sales but for which the small business does not pay.

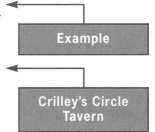

Personal Selling

Personal selling is the personal contact between salespeople and potential customers resulting from sales efforts. Effective personal selling can give the small company a definite advantage over its larger competitors by creating a feeling of personal attention. Personal selling deals with the salesperson's ability to match customer needs to the firm's goods and services. A recent study of top salespeople found that they:

personal selling— the personal contact between salespeople and customers resulting from sales efforts.

- ☆ Are enthusiastic and are alert to opportunities. Star sales representatives demonstrate deep concentration, high energy, and drive.
- ☆ Concentrate on select accounts. They focus on customers with the greatest sales potential.
- ☆ Plan thoroughly. On every sales call, the best representatives act with a purpose to close the sale.
- ☆ Use a direct approach. They get right to the point with customers.
- ☆ Work from the customer's perspective. They know their customers' businesses and their needs.

★ Use "past success stories." They encourage customers to express their problems and then present solutions using examples of past successes.

★ Leave sales material with clients. The material gives customers the opportunity to study company and product literature in more detail.[5]

★ See themselves as problem solvers, not just vendors.

★ Measure their success not just by sales volume but by customer satisfaction.[6]

One extensive study of salespeople found that just 20 percent of all salespeople have the ability to sell and are selling the "right" product or service. That 20 percent makes 80 percent of all sales. The study also concluded that 55 percent of sales representatives have "absolutely no ability to sell"; the remaining 25 percent have sales ability but are selling the wrong product or service.[7]

A recent study by Dartnell Corporation found that it takes an average of 3.9 sales calls to close a deal.[8] Common causes of sales rejections include the representative's failure to determine customers' needs, talking too much, and neglecting to ask for the order. (Studies show that 60 percent of the time, salespeople never ask the customer to buy!)[9] Unfortunately, the cost of making a sales call exceeds $225, making those "missed opportunities" quite costly.[10] Figure 6.1 shows how sales representatives spend their time in an average 45.5-hour workweek.

Small business owners can improve their sales representatives' "batting averages" by following some basic guidelines:

Develop a selling system. One sales consultant recommends a six-step process to increase the likelihood of closing a sale:[11]

1. *Approach.* Establish rapport with the prospect. Customers seldom buy from salespeople they dislike or distrust.

2. *Interview.* Get the prospect to do most of the talking; the goal is to identify his or her needs, preferences, and problems.

Figure 6.1
How Salespeople Spend Their Time (Breakdown of an Average 45.5-hour Workweek)
Source: Adapted from Dartnell Corporation, Chicago, Illinois.

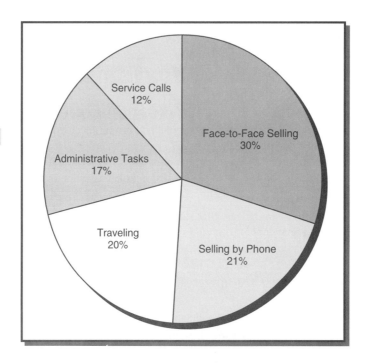

Service Calls 12%

Face-to-Face Selling 30%

Administrative Tasks 17%

Traveling 20%

Selling by Phone 21%

3. *Demonstrate, explain, and show.* Make clear the features and benefits of your product or service and point out how they meet the prospect's needs or solve his problems.

4. *Validate.* Prove the claims about your product or service. If possible, offer the prospect names and numbers of other satisfied customers (with their permission, of course). Testimonials really work.

5. *Negotiate.* Listen for objections from the prospect. Try to determine the *real* objection and confront it. Work to overcome it. Objections can be the salesperson's best friend; they tell a salesperson what must be "fixed" before the prospect will commit to an order. Work out the prospect's problems.

6. *Close.* Ask for a decision. Good sales representatives know when the prospect flashes the green light on a sale. They stop talking and ask for the order.

   Be empathetic. The best salespeople look at the sale from the customer's viewpoint, not their own! Doing so encourages the sales representative to stress *value* to the customer.

   Set multiple objectives. Before making a sales call, salespeople should set three objectives:

1. *The primary objective*—the most reasonable outcome expected from the meeting. It may be to get an order or to learn more about a prospect's needs.

2. *The minimum objective*—the very least the salesperson will leave with. It may be to set another meeting or to identify the prospect's primary objections.

3. *The visionary objective*—the most optimistic outcome of the meeting. This objective forces the salesperson to be open-minded and to shoot for the top.

   Monitor sales efforts and results. Selling is just like any other business activity and must be controlled. At a minimum, the small business manager should know:

1. Actual sales versus projected sales.

2. Sales generated per call made.

3. Total sales costs.

4. Sales by product, salesperson, territory, customer, and so on.

5. Profit contribution by product, sales person, territory, customer, and so on.

Advertising

Advertising is any sales presentation that is nonpersonal in nature and is paid for by an identified sponsor. One recent study on the effectiveness of advertising concluded that ads influence purchases of some products for six to nine months. "Advertising can develop long-term brand equity," says the study's author.[12] The remainder of this chapter will focus on selecting advertising media, developing an advertising plan, and creating an advertising budget.

advertising—*any sales presentation that is nonpersonal in nature and is paid for by an identified sponsor.*

Selecting Advertising Media

One of the most important decisions a small business manager must make is which media to use in disseminating the advertising message. The medium used to transmit the message influences the consumer's perception—and reception—of it. By choosing the proper advertising means, a small business owner can reach his target audience effectively at minimum cost. One promotion expert says, "There are literally thousands of conduits for reaching your potential customer. And there's not a person managing a business who can afford not to be concerned with reaching, precisely, his or her target audience."[13] While no single formula exists for determining the ideal medium to use, there are several important character-

2. Describe the advantages and disadvantages of the various advertising media.

istics that make some media better suited to certain business than others. Understanding the qualities of the various media available can simplify an owner's decision. Before selecting the vehicle for the message, the owner should consider several questions:

How large is my firm's trading area? How big is the geographical region from which the firm will draw its customers? The size of this area clearly influences the choice of media.

Who are my target customers and what are their characteristics? Determining a customer profile often points to the appropriate medium to use to get the message across most effectively.

Which media are my target customers most likely to watch, listen to, or read? Until a business owner knows who his target audience is, he cannot select the proper advertising media to reach it.

What budget limitations do I face? Every business owner must direct the firm's advertising program within the restrictions of its operating budget. Certain advertising media cost more than others.

What media do my competitors use? It is helpful for the small business manager to know the media that competitors use, although he should *not* automatically assume that these media are the best. An approach that differs from the traditional one may produce better results.

How important are repetition and continuity of my advertising message? Generally, an ad becomes effective only after it is repeated several times, and many ads must be continued for some time before they produce results. Some experts suggest that an ad must be run at least six times in most mass media before it becomes effective.

What does the advertising medium cost? There are two types of advertising costs the small business manager must consider: the absolute cost and the relative cost. **Absolute cost** is the actual dollar outlay a business owner must make to place an ad in a particular medium for a specific time period. An even more important measure is an ad's **relative cost,** the ad's cost per potential customer reached. Suppose a manager decides to advertise his product in one of two newspapers in town. The *Sentinel* has a circulation of 21,000 and charges $1,200 for a quarter-page ad. The *Democrat* has a circulation of 18,000 and charges $1,300 for the same space. Reader profiles of the two papers suggest that 25 percent of Sentinel readers and 37 percent of the *Democrat* readers are potential customers. Using this information, the manager computes the following relative costs:

absolute cost—*the actual dollar outlay a business owner must make to place an ad in a particular medium for a specific time period.*

relative cost—*the cost of an ad per potential customer reached.*

	Sentinel	Democrat
Circulation	21,000	18,000
Percent of readers that are potential customers	× 37%	× 25%
Potential customers reached	5,250	6,660
Absolute cost of ad	$1,200	$1,300
Relative cost of ad (per potential customer reached)	$\frac{\$1,200}{5,250} = 22.86$ cents per potential customer	$\frac{\$1,300}{6,660} = 19.52$ cents per potential customer

Although the *Sentinel* has a larger circulation and a lower absolute cost for running the ad, the *Democrat* will serve the small business owner better because it offers a lower cost per potential customer reached. It is important to note that this technique does not give a reliable comparison across media; it is a meaningful comparison only within a single medium. Differences among the format, presentation, and coverage of ads in different media are so vast that such comparisons are not meaningful.

Media Options

Figure 6.2 gives a breakdown of U.S. business advertising expenditures by medium. Choosing advertising media is no easy task since each has distinctive advantages, disadvantages, and cost. The "right" message in the "wrong" medium will miss its mark.

NEWSPAPERS. Traditionally, the local newspaper has been the medium that most advertisers rely on to get their messages across to customers. Although the number of newspapers in the United States has declined 19 percent since 1960, this medium attracts nearly 27 percent of all advertising dollars nationwide, establishing it as the leader among all media.

Newspapers provide several *advantages* to the small business advertiser:

Selected geographical coverage. Newspapers are geared to a specific geographic region, and they reach potential customers across all demographic classes.

Flexibility. Newspaper advertisements can be changed readily on very short notice. The owner can select the size of the ad and its location in the paper.

Timeliness. Papers almost always have very short closing times, the publication deadline prior to which the advertising copy must be submitted.

Communication potential. Newspaper ads can convey a great deal of information by employing attractive graphics and copy.

Low costs. Newspapers normally offer advertising space at low absolute cost and, because of their blanket coverage of a geographic area, at low relative cost as well.

Prompt responses. Newspaper ads typically produce relatively quick customer responses. A newspaper ad is likely to generate sales the very next day.

Of course, newspaper advertisements also have *disadvantages:*

Wasted readership. Since newspapers reach such a variety of people, at least a portion of an ad's coverage will be wasted on those who are not potential customers.

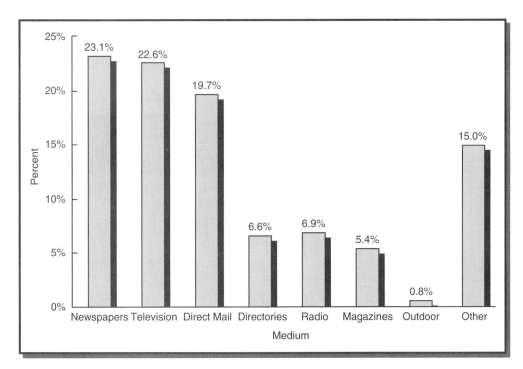

Figure 6.2
Advertising Expenditures by Medium
Source: Statistical Abstract of the United States, 1995, p. 584.

Reproduction limitations. The quality of reproduction in newspapers is limited, especially when it is compared to that of magazines and direct mail.

Lack of prominence. One frequently cited drawback of newspapers is that they carry so many ads that a small company's message might be lost in the crowd. The typical newspaper is 65 percent advertising.

Declining readership. Newspaper circulation as a percentage of U.S. households has dropped from 98 percent in 1970 to 70 percent today. Newspaper ads would be least effective for small businesses targeting young people, who are least likely to read newspapers.

Short ad life. The typical newspaper is soon discarded and, as a result, an ad's life is extremely short. Business owners can increase the effectiveness of their ads by giving them greater continuity. Spot ads can produce results, but maintaining a steady flow of business requires some degree of continuity in advertising.

Buying Newspaper Space. Newspapers typically sell ad space by lines and columns or inches and columns. For instance, a 4-column x 100-line ad occupies four columns and 100 lines of space (14 lines are equal to 1 column inch). For this ad, the small business owner would pay the rate for 400 lines. Most papers offer discounts for bulk, long-term, and frequency contracts and for full-page ads. Advertising rates vary from one paper to another, depending on such factors as circulation and focus. A small business owner would do well to investigate the circulation statements, advertising rates, and reader profiles of the various newspapers available before selecting one.

RADIO. Newspapers offer blanket advertising coverage of a region, but radio permits advertisers to appeal to specific audiences over large geographic areas. By choosing the appropriate station, program, and time for an ad, a small company can reach virtually *any* target market.

Radio advertising offers several *advantages:*

Universal infiltration. The radio's nearly universal presence gives advertisements in this medium a major advantage. Virtually every home and car in the United States is equipped with a radio, which means that these advertising messages receive a tremendous amount of exposure in the target market.

Market segmentation. Radio advertising is flexible and efficient because advertisers can choose stations directed toward a specific market within a broad geographic region.

Flexibility and timeliness. Radio commercials have short closing times and can be changed quickly.

Friendliness. Radio ads are more "active" than ads in printed media since they use the spoken word to influence customers. Vocal subtleties used in radio ads are impossible to convey through printed media. Table 6.1 offers a guide to producing effective radio copy.

Radio advertisements also have a number of *disadvantages:*

Poor listening. Radio's intrusiveness into the public life almost guarantees that customers will hear ads, but they may not listen to them.

Need for repetition. Radio ads must be broadcast repeatedly to be effective.

Limited message. Since radio ads are limited to one minute or less, the message must be brief.

Buying Radio Time. The small business owner can zero in on a specific advertising target by using the appropriate radio station. Stations follow various formats—from rap to rhapsodies—to appeal to specific audiences. Radio advertising time usually sells in 10-second, 20-second, 30-second, and 60-second increments, with the latter being the most common. Fixed spots are guaranteed to be broadcast at the times specified in the owner's contract with the station. Preemptible spots are cheaper than fixed spots, but the advertiser risks being preempted by an advertiser willing to pay the fixed rate for a time slot. Floating spots are the

Table 6.1

Guidelines for Effective Radio Copy

Source: *Radio Basics*, Radio Advertising Bureau.

☆ Stress the benefit to the listener. Don't say "Bryson's has new fall fashions." Say "Bryson's fall fashions make you look fabulous."

☆ Use attention-getters. Radio has a whole battery—music, sound effects, unusual voices. Crack the barrier with sound.

☆ Zero in on your audience. Radio's selectivity attracts the right audience. It's up to you to communicate in the right language.

☆ Keep the copy simple and to the point. Don't try to impress listeners with vocabulary. "To be or not to be" may be the best-known phrase in the language . . . and the longest word has just three letters.

☆ Sell early and often. Don't back into the selling message. At most, you've got 60 seconds. Make the most of them. Don't be subtle.

☆ Write for the ear. Write conversationally.

☆ Prepare your copy. Underline words you want to emphasize.

☆ Triple space. Type clean, legible copy. Make the announcer rehearse.

☆ Use positive action words. Use words such as *now* and *today*, particularly when you're writing copy for a sale. Radio has qualities of urgency and immediacy. Take advantage of them by including a time limit or the date the sale ends.

☆ Put the listener in the picture. Radio's theater of the mind means you don't have to talk about a new car. With sounds and music, you can put the listener behind the wheel.

☆ Mention the business often. This is the single most important and inflexible rule in radio advertising. Also make sure listeners know how to find your business. If the address is complicated, use landmarks.

☆ Focus the spot on getting a response. Make it clear what you want the listener to do. Don't try to get a mail response. Use phone numbers only, and repeat the number three times. End the spot with the phone number.

☆ Don't stay with a loser. Direct-response ads produce results right away—or not at all. Don't stick with a radio spot that is not generating sales. Change it.

least expensive, but the advertiser has no control over broadcast times. Many stations offer package plans, using flexible combinations of fixed, preemptible, and floating spots.

Radio rates vary depending on the time of day the ads are broadcast, and, like television, there are prime-time slots known as drive-time spots. While exact hours may differ from station to station, the following classifications are common:

Class AA: Morning drive time—6 A.M. to 10 A.M.

Class A: Evening drive time—4 P.M. to 7 P.M.

Class B: Home worker time—10 A.M. to 4 P.M.

Class C: Evening time—7 P.M. to Midnight

Class D: Nighttime—Midnight to 6 A.M.

Some stations may also have different rates for weekend time slots.

TELEVISION. In advertising dollars spent, television ranks second in popularity of all media. Although the cost of national TV ads precludes their use by most small businesses, local spots can be an extremely effective means of broadcasting a small company's message. A 30-second commercial on network television may cost over $500,000, but a 30-second spot on a local cable station may go for $200 or less.

Television offers a number of distinct *advantages*:

Broad coverage. Television ads provide extensive coverage of a sizable region, and they reach a significant portion of the population. About 97 percent of the homes in any area will have a television, and those sets are switched on an average of 7 hours and 8 minutes each day.

Visual advantage. The primary benefit of television is its capacity to present the advertiser's product or service in a graphic, vivid manner. Research shows that 46 percent of television ads result in long-term sales increases and that 70 percent of campaigns boost sales immediately.[14]

Flexibility. Television ads can be modified quickly to meet the rapidly changing conditions in the marketplace. Advertising on TV is the closest substitute for personal selling.

Design assistance. Few small business owners have the skills to prepare an effective television commercial. Although professional production firms might easily charge $50,000 for a commercial production, the television station from which the manager purchases the air time may be willing to offer design assistance very inexpensively.

Television advertising also has several *disadvantages:*

Brief exposure. Most television ads are on the screen for only a short time and require substantial repetition to achieve the desired effect.

Clutter. The typical person sees 1,500 advertising messages a day, and more ads are on the way. With so many ads beaming across the airwaves, a small business's advertising message could easily become lost in the shuffle.

"Zapping." **Zappers**, television viewers who flash from one channel to another, especially during commercials, pose a real threat to TV advertisers. Zapping means TV advertisers are not reaching the audiences they hope to reach.

Costs. Television commercials can be expensive to create. A 30-second ad can cost several thousand dollars to develop, even before the owner purchases air time. Table 6.2 offers some suggestions for developing creative television commercials.

MAGAZINES. Another advertising medium available to the small business owner is magazines. Some 1,800 nontrade magazines are in circulation across the United States. Magazines have a wide reach; today, nearly nine out of ten adults read an average of seven different magazines per month. The average magazine attracts 6 hours and 3 minutes of total adult reading time, and studies show that the reader is exposed to 89 percent of the ads in the average copy.[15]

Magazines offer several *advantages* for advertisers:

Long life spans. Magazines have a long reading life because readers tend to keep them longer than other printed media. The result is that each magazine ad has a good chance of being seen several times.

Table 6.2
Guidelines for Creative TV Ads

Source: Adapted from *How to Make a Creative Television Commercial,* Television Bureau of Advertising, Inc.

- ☆ *Keep it simple.* Avoid confusing the viewer by sticking to a simple concept.
- ☆ *Have one basic idea.* The message should focus on a single, important benefit to the customer. Why should people by from your business?
- ☆ *Make your point clear.* The customer benefit should be obvious and easy to understand.
- ☆ *Make it unique . . . different.* To be effective, a television ad must reach out and grab the viewer's attention. Take advantage of television's visual experience.
- ☆ *Get viewer attention.* Unless viewers watch the ad, its effect is lost.
- ☆ *Involve the viewer.* To be most effective, an ad should portray a situation to which the viewer can relate. Common, everyday experiences are easiest for people to identify with.
- ☆ *Use emotion.* The most effective ads evoke an emotion from the viewer—a laugh, a tear, or a pleasant memory.
- ☆ *Consider production values.* Television offers vivid sights, colors, motions, and sounds. Use them!
- ☆ *Prove the benefit.* Television allows an advertiser to prove a product's or service's customer benefit by actually demonstrating it.
- ☆ *Identify your company well and often.* Make sure your store's name, location, and product line stand out. The ad should portray your company's image.

Multiple readership. The average magazine has a readership of 3.9 adult readers, and each reader spends about 1 hour and 33 minutes with each copy. Many magazines have a high "passalong" rate—they are handed down from reader to reader.

Target marketing. By selecting the appropriate special-interest periodical, a small business owner can reach those customers with a high degree of interest in his goods or service.

Ad quality. Magazine ads usually are of high quality. Photographs and drawings can be reproduced very effectively, and color ads are readily available.

Magazines also have several *disadvantages*:

Costs. Magazine advertising rates vary according to their circulation rates; the higher the circulation, the higher the rate. Thus, local magazines, whose rates are often comparable to newspaper rates, may be the best bargain for small businesses.

Long closing times. Another disadvantage of magazines is the relatively long closing times they require. For a weekly periodical, the closing date for an ad may be several weeks before the actual publication date.

Lack of prominence. Another disadvantage of magazine ads arises from their popularity as an advertising vehicle. The effectiveness of a single ad may be reduced because of a lack of prominence. Proper ad positioning, therefore, is critical to an ad's success. Research show that readers "tune out" right-hand pages and look mainly at left-hand pages.

DIRECT MAIL. Direct mail has long been a popular method of small business advertising and includes such tools as letters, postcards, catalogs, discount coupons, brochures, computer disks, and videotapes mailed to homes or businesses. The earliest known catalogs were printed by fifteenth-century printers. Today, direct-mail marketers sell virtually every kind of product imaginable from Christmas trees and lobsters to furniture and clothing (the most popular mail-order purchase). Responding to the convenience of "shopping at home," customers purchase more than $306 billion worth of goods and services through mail order each year![16]

Direct mail offers a number of distinct *advantages* to the small business owner:

Selectivity. The greatest strength of direct-mail advertising is its ability to target a specific audience to receive the message. Depending on mailing list quality, an owner can select an audience with virtually any set of characteristics. Small business owners can develop, rent, or purchase a mailing list of prospective residential, commercial, or industrial customers.

When Sandy and Tom Callahan launched their mail-order company, Grand River Toy Company, which markets toys made from environmentally safe materials, they placed newspaper ads and mailed their brief catalog to those who responded. Their list grew, albeit slowly, by word of mouth. In their third year of business, the Callahans purchased mailing lists of upscale, educated buyers concerned about the environment and education from list brokers. Their home-based company has doubled its sales every year since.[17]

Grand River Toy Company

Flexibility. Another advantage of direct mail is its capacity to tailor the message to the target. The advertiser's presentation to the customer can be as simple or as elaborate as necessary. In addition, the advertiser controls the timing of the campaign by sending the ad when it is most appropriate.

Reader attention. With direct-mail, the advertiser's message does not have to compete with other ads for the reader's attention. People enjoy getting mail, and a recent study found that recipients opened and read 48 percent of their direct mail.[18]

Rapid feedback. Direct-mail advertisements produce quick results. In most cases the ad will generate sales within three to four days after customers receive it.

Measurable results and testable strategies. Because they control their mailing lists, direct marketers can readily measure the results their ads produce. Also, direct mail allows advertisers to test different ad layouts, designs, and strategies (often within the same "run") to see which one "pulls" the greatest response. Table 6.3 on page 182 offers guidelines for creating direct-mail ads that really work.

Table 6.3

Guidelines for Creating Direct Mail Ads that Really Work

Sources: Adapted from Paul Hughes, "Profits Due," *Entrepreneur*, February 1994, pp. 74-78; "Why They Open Direct Mail," *Communications Briefings*, December 1993, p. 5; Teri Lammers, "The Elements of Perfect Pitch," *Inc.*, March 1992, pp. 53-55; "Special Delivery," *Small Business Reports*, February 1993, p. 6; Gloria Green and James W. Peltier, "How to Develop a Direct Mail Program," *Small Business Forum*, Winter 1993/1994, pp. 30-45.

"Mail order means trend watching, meticulous planning, and devouring news and information on the industry, your niche, technology, politics, and the world—and that's just for starters," says one observer. "You'll have to deal with the laws of a vast federal bureaucracy and 50 states (plus a couple hundred countries if you go international), the intricacies of designing and mailing a catalog, and the fickle nature of a demanding public."

You'll also have to write copy that will get results. Try these proven techniques:

★ Promise readers your most important benefit in the headline or first paragraph.

★ Use short "action" words and paragraphs.

★ Make the copy look easy to read—lots of "white space."

★ Use eye-catching words such as *free, you, save, guarantee, new, profit, benefit, improve,* and others.

★ Forget grammatical rules; write as if you were speaking to the reader.

★ Repeat the offer three or more times in various ways.

★ Back up claims and statements with proof and endorsements whenever possible.

★ Ask for the order or a response.

★ Ask questions such as "Would you like to lower your home's energy costs?" in the copy.

★ Use high-quality paper and envelopes (those with windows are best) because they stand a better chance of being opened and read.

★ Envelopes that resemble bills almost always get opened.

★ Address the envelope to an individual, not "Occupant."

★ Use a postscript (P.S.) always—they are the most often read part of a printed page.

Direct-mail ads also suffer from several *disadvantages*:

Inaccurate mailing lists. The key to the success of the entire mailing is the accuracy of the customer list. The Direct Marketing Association estimates that 60 percent of the success of direct marketing is based on the quality of the mailing list.[19]

High relative costs. Relative to the size of the audience reached, the cost of designing, producing, and mailing an advertisement via direct mail is high. But if the mailing is well planned and properly executed, it can produce a high percentage of returns, making direct mail one of the least expensive advertising methods in terms of results.

High throwaway rate. Often called junk mail, direct-mail ads become "junk" when an advertiser selects the wrong audience or broadcasts the wrong message. To boost returns small business owners can supplement their traditional direct-mail pieces with toll-free (800 or 888) numbers (an increase of 1 to 2 percent) and carefully timed follow-up phone calls (an increase of 2 to 14 percent).[20]

For instance, Marc Kaner, owner of Fitness Connection, a retailer of vitamin supplements, estimates that his 800 number has increased his sales by 15 percent.[21]

"High-Tech" Direct Mail. Sending out ads on computer diskettes is an excellent way to reach upscale households and businesses. Not only do computer-based ads give advertisers the power to create flashy, attention-grabbing designs, but they also hold the audience's attention. "Customized diskettes are rarely thrown away," says the founder of one diskette advertising firm. "Human curiosity practically guarantees they will be reviewed." Studies show that recipients of a computer diskette ad spend an average of 26 to 30 minutes interacting with it and that their retention rate is twice that of other ads.[22]

Compact disks (CDs) offer advertisers the same benefits as computer disks with one extra—more space to do it in. Companies are using CDs with interactive ads to sell everything from cars to computers. The ads usually contain videos, computer games, quizzes, animation, music, graphics, and other features to engage more of their audience's senses. In a world where U.S. households receive *3.7 million tons* of paper each year in the form of direct-mail ads, multimedia ads can offer a distinct advantage: They get noticed. One expert explains the appeal of multimedia ads, "You remember 20 percent of what you see, 30 percent of what you see and hear, and 60 percent of what you interact with."[23]

How to Use Direct Mail. The key to a direct mailing's success is the right mailing list. Even the best direct-mail ad will fail if sent to the "wrong" customers. Owners can develop lists themselves, using customer accounts, telephone books, city and trade directories, and other sources. Other sources for mailing lists include companies selling complementary but not competing products, professional organizations' membership lists, business or professional magazines' subscription lists, and mailing lists brokers who sell lists for practically any need.

THE WORLD WIDE WEB. Increasingly, small businesses are turning to the World Wide Web as a valuable tool in reaching their customers and building an awareness of their products and services. A recent Nielsen survey found that 37 million people in North America have access to the Internet, and they spend an average of 5.5 hours per week on-line.[24] In addition, the World Wide Web generated more than $46 billion in sales in 1998 (an amount growing at about 10 percent per year).[25]

The Web's multimedia capabilities make it an ideal medium for companies to demonstrate their products and services with full motion, color, and sound and to get customers involved in the demonstrations. Businesses that normally use direct mail can bring the two-dimensional photos and product descriptions in their print catalogs to life and avoid the expense of mailing them at the same time.

When Dan Sullivan started Faucet Outlet, a discounter of plumbing fixtures, he advertised his products solely in catalogs that cost $2 each to print and mail. Four years later, Sullivan established a Web site for Faucet Outlet (http://www.faucet.com/faucet/), which allowed him to display more products in a more interesting way and lower his catalog costs. Soon after the site went on-line, it received a few thousand "hits" (visits) per month. Within a few months, however, the site's traffic had grown to 17,000 shoppers per month! "The results have been fantastic," says Sullivan. "It costs just pennies for me to get leads on the Internet, and I can show so much more . . . with an Internet catalog versus my paper catalog." The number of Internet orders Faucet Outlet receives has reached 5 percent of its total orders and continues to grow.[26]

Faucet Outlet

OUTDOOR ADVERTISING. National advertisers have long used outdoor ads, and small firms (especially retailers) are now using this medium. Very few small businesses rely solely on outdoor advertising; instead, they supplement other advertising media with billboards. With a creative outdoor campaign, a small company can make a big impact—even on a small budget.

Frank Cipriani, owner of Garcia's Irish Pub, created an incredibly successful outdoor campaign over several months to promote his business. The whimsical "boy meets girl at Garcia's" campaign featured a series of messages exchanged among "William," his "Angel in Red," and other characters. The ads had the entire town waiting to see what would happen next! "It really took on a life of its own," says one of the designers. "I wanted something inconspicuous, something that didn't seem like advertising," adds Cipriani.[27]

Garcia's Irish Pub

Outdoor advertising offers certain *advantages* to the small business:

High exposure. Outdoor advertising offers a high-frequency exposure; studies suggest that the typical billboard reaches an adult 29 to 31 times each month. Most people tend to follow the same routes in their daily traveling, and billboards are there waiting for them when they pass by.

Broad reach. The nature of outdoor ads makes them effective devices for reaching a large number of potential customers within a specific area. The people outdoor ads reach tend to be younger, wealthier, and better educated than the average person.

Flexibility. Advertisers can buy outdoor advertising units separately or in a number of packages. Through its variety of graphics, design, and unique features, outdoor advertising enables the small advertiser to match her message to the particular audience.

Cost efficiency. Outdoor advertising offers one of the lowest costs per thousand customers reached of all the advertising media.

Outdoor ads also have several *disadvantages*:

Brief exposure. Because billboards are immobile, the reader is exposed to the advertiser's message for only a short time—typically no more than five seconds. As a result, the message must be short and to the point.

Legal restrictions. Outdoor billboards are subject to strict regulations and to a high degree of standardization. Many cities place limitations on the number and type of signs and billboards allowed along the roadside.

Lack of prominence. A clutter of billboards and signs along a heavily traveled route tends to reduce the effectiveness of a single ad that loses its prominence among the crowd of billboards.

Using Outdoor Ads. Because the outdoor ad is stationary and the viewer is in motion, the small business owner must pay special attention to its design. An outdoor ad should:

★ Identify the product and the company clearly and quickly.

★ Use a simple background. The background should not compete with the message.

★ Rely on large illustrations that jump out at the viewer.

★ Include clear, legible type. All lowercase or a combination of uppercase and lowercase letters are best. Very bold or very thin typefaces become illegible at a distance.

★ Use black-and-white designs. Research shows that black-and-white outdoor ads are more effective than color ads. If color is important to the message, pick color combinations that contrast both in hue and brightness (e.g., black on yellow).

★ Emphasize simplicity; short copy and short words are best. Don't try to cram too much onto a billboard. One study found that ads with fewer than eight words were most effective, and those containing more than ten words were least effective.

★ Be located on the right-hand side of the highway. Studies show that ads located there draw higher recall scores than those located on the left-hand side.[28]

TRANSIT ADVERTISING. Transit advertising includes advertising signs inside and outside some 70,000 public transportation vehicles throughout the country's urban areas. The medium is likely to grow as more cities look to public transit systems to relieve transportation problems. Transit ads offer a number of *advantages*:

Wide coverage. Transit advertising offers advertisers mass exposure to a variety of customers. The message literally goes to where the people are. This medium also reaches people with a wide variety of demographic characteristics.

Repeat exposure. Transit ads provide repeated exposure to a message. The typical transit rider averages 24 rides per month and spends 61 minutes per day riding.

Low cost. Even small business owners with limited budgets can afford transit advertising. One study shows that transit advertising costs an average of only $0.30 per thousand.[29]

Flexibility. Transit ads come in a wide range of sizes, numbers, and durations. With transit ads, an owner can select an individual market or any combination of markets across the country.

Transit ads also have several *disadvantages*:

Generality. Even though a small business can choose the specific transit routes on which to advertise, it cannot target a particular segment of the market through transit advertising. The effectiveness of transit ads depends on the routes that public vehicles travel and on the people they reach, which, unfortunately, the advertiser cannot control.

Limited appeal. Unlike many media, transit ads are not beamed into the potential customer's residence or business. The result is that customers cannot keep them for future reference. Also, these ads do not reach with great frequency the upper-income, highly educated portion of the market.

Brief message. Transit ads do not permit the small advertiser to present a detailed description or a demonstration of the product or service for sale. Although inside ads have a relatively long exposure (the average ride lasts 22.5 minutes), outside ads must be brief and to the point.

DIRECTORIES. Directories are an important advertising medium for reaching those customers who have already made purchase decisions. The directory simply helps these customers locate the specific product or service they have decided to buy. Directories include telephone books, industrial or trade guides, buyer guides, annuals, catalog files, and yearbooks that list various businesses and the products they sell.

Directories offer *advantages* to advertisers:

Prime prospects. Directory listings reach customers who are prime prospects, since they have already decided to purchase an item. The directory just helps them find what they are looking for.

Long life. Directory listings usually have long lives. A typical directory may be published annually.

However, there are certain *disadvantages* to using directories:

Lack of flexibility. Listings and ads in many directories offer only a limited variety of design features. Business owners may not be as free to create unique ads as in other printed media.

Obsolescence. Because directories are commonly updated only annually, some of their listings become obsolete. This is a problem for a small firm that changes its name, location, or phone number.

When choosing a directory, the small business owner should evaluate several criteria:

- ★ Completeness. Does the directory include enough listings that customers will use it?
- ★ Convenience. Are the listings well organized and convenient? Are they cross-referenced?
- ★ Evidence of use. To what extent do customers actually use the directory? What evidence of use does the publisher offer?
- ★ Age. Is the directory well established and does it have a good reputation?
- ★ Circulation. Do users pay for the directory or do they receive complimentary copies? Is there an audited circulation statement?

TRADE SHOWS. Trade shows provide manufacturers and distributors with a unique opportunity to advertise to a preselected audience of potential customers who are inclined to buy. Literally thousands of trade shows are sponsored each year, and carefully evaluating and selecting a few shows can produce profitable results for a small business owner.

The owner of a small tool shop attends 40 trade shows a year across the nation to promote his line of high-quality, specialty tools. The shows produce sales at minimal costs. "I can buy a booth for a weekend show for $600, and pay another $600 for hotels and meals. For this $1200 expense, I often sell $20,000 in merchandise, and generate 10 times more leads than I receive from a space advertisement," he says.[30]

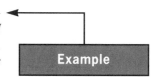

Trade shows offer the following *advantages:*

A natural market. Trade shows bring together buyers and sellers in a setting where products can be explained, demonstrated, and handled. Comparative shopping is easy, and the buying process is more efficient.

Preselected audience. Trade exhibits attract potential customers with a specific interest in the goods or services being displayed. There is a high probability that these prospects will make a purchase.

New customer market. Trade shows offer exhibitors a prime opportunity to reach new customers and to contact people who are not accessible to sales representatives.

Cost advantage. As the cost of making a field sales call continues to escalate, more companies are realizing that trade shows are an economical method for making sales contacts and presentations.

There are, however, certain *disadvantages* associated with trade shows:

Increasing costs. The cost of exhibiting at trade shows is rising quickly. Registration fees, travel and set-up costs, sales salaries, and other expenditures may be a barrier to some small firms.

Wasted effort. A poorly planned exhibit ultimately costs the small business more than its benefits are worth. Too many firms enter exhibits in trade shows without proper preparation, and they end up wasting their time, energy, and money on unproductive activities.

To avoid these disadvantages, business owners should:

☆ Communicate with key potential customers *before* the show; send them invitations.

☆ Have knowledgeable salespeople staffing the booth.

☆ Demonstrate your product or service; let customers see it in action.

☆ Learn to distinguish between serious customers and "tirekickers."

☆ Distribute literature that clearly communicates the product or service sold.

☆ Project a professional image at all times.

☆ Follow up promptly on sales leads.

SPECIALTY ADVERTISING. As advertisers have shifted their focus to "narrow casting" their messages to target audiences and away from "broadcasting," specialty advertising has grown in popularity. Advertisers now spend more than $3 billion annually on specialty items. This category includes all customer gift items imprinted with the company's name, address, telephone number, and slogan. Specialty items are best used as reminder ads to supplement other forms of advertising and help to create goodwill among existing and potential customers.

Specialty advertising offers several *advantages*:

Reaching select audiences. Advertisers have the ability to reach specific audiences with well-planned specialty items.

For instance, Corhart Refractories Corporation wanted to increase the number of steel executives reached at a trade show. The company mailed the executives invitations in a box containing a set of radio earphones. To get the radio (without which the earphones were useless), the executives had to stop by the Corhart's booth. An overflow crowd stopped to get their radios, imprinted with Corhart's logo.[31]

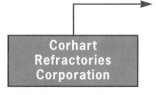

Corhart Refractories Corporation

Personalized nature. By carefully choosing a specialty item, a business owner can "personalize" an advertisement. When choosing advertising specialties, a small business owner should use items that are unusual and related to the nature of the business and are meaningful to customers.

Versatility. The rich versatility of specialty advertising is limited only by the business owner's imagination. Advertisers print their logos on everything from pens and scarves to wallets and caps.

There are *disadvantages* to specialty advertising:

Potential for waste. Unless owners choose the appropriate specialty item, they will be wasting their time and money. The options are virtually infinite.

Costs. Some specialty items can be quite expensive. Plus, some owners have a tendency to give advertising materials to anyone—even to those who are not potential customers.

SPECIAL EVENTS AND PROMOTIONS. A growing number of small companies are finding that special events and promotions attract a great deal of interest and provide a lasting impression of the company. As customers become increasingly harder to reach through any single advertising medium, companies of all sizes are finding that sponsoring special events and promotions—from wine tastings and beach volleyball tournaments to fitness walks and rock climbs—is an excellent way to reach their target audiences.

In Japan, one maker of pork products generates millions of dollars of publicity and recognition by sponsoring a baseball team—the Nippon Ham Fighters![32]

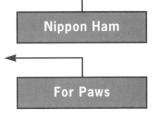

Nippon Ham

For Paws

Creativity and uniqueness are essential ingredients in any special event promotion, and most entrepreneurs excel at those.

For example, the owner of For Paws, a California pet boutique, sponsors free "doggy brunches" each week, complete with "kibble quiche" and "wheat-germ woofies." The shop also caters birthday parties, beach parties (picture a dog with a whistle around his neck, a muscle T-shirt, and a dab of Noxzema on his nose), and other gala events for its four-legged customers and their owners.[33]

POINT-OF-PURCHASE ADS. In the last several years, in-store advertising has become more popular as a way of reaching the customer at a crucial moment—the point of purchase. Research suggests that consumers make two-thirds of all buying decisions at the point of sale. Self-service stores are especially well suited for in-store ads as they remind people of the products as they walk the aisles. These in-store ads are not just blasé signs or glossy photographs of the product in use. Some businesses use in-store music interspersed with household hints and, of course, ads. Another ploy involves tiny devices that sense when a customer passes by and triggers a prerecorded sales message. Other machines emit scents—chocolate chip cookies or pina coladas—to appeal to passing customers' sense of smell.[34]

In sum, small business owners have an endless array of advertising tools, techniques, and media available to them. Even postage stamps, bathroom walls, sides of cows, and parking meters offer advertising space! Table 6.4 on page 188 summarizes the different advertising media and their suitability for reaching particular customer groups.

Developing an Advertising Plan

3. Present the steps in developing an advertising plan.

Every small business needs an advertising plan to ensure that the money spent on ads is not wasted. A well-developed plan does not guarantee advertising success, but it does increase the likelihood of good results.

The first step is to define the purpose of the company's advertising program by creating specific, measurable objectives. In other words, the owner must decide, "What do I want to accomplish with my advertising?" Some ads are designed to stimulate immediate responses by encouraging customers to purchase a particular product in the immediate future. The object here is to trigger a purchase decision. Other ads seek to build the firm's image among its customers and the general public. These ads try to create goodwill by keeping the firm's name in the public's memory so that customers will recall the small firm's name when they decide to purchase a product or service. Still other ads strive to draw new customers, build

Table 6.4
*Advertising Media
Comparison Chart*

Media	Coverage	Special Characteristics
Newspapers	Selected geographic coverage. Entire city or metropolitan area with major newspapers. Single town with smaller, weekly papers.	Top advertising media; attracts about 23% of advertising expenditures.
Radio	Market area radio stations serves. Stations' formats range from country and easy listening to rap and golden oldies.	Ability to reach almost any market by choosing proper station. The average household has 5.6 radios, and 95% of the cars in the United States have radios.
Television	Market area TV station serves; could be local (cable) or national (major network).	Powerful medium; especially effective at reaching younger, less-educated audiences.
Magazines	Local magazines typically cover a particular city or region.	Magazines usually target specific audiences, from wealthy owners of country estates to low-income apartment dwellers.
Direct Mail	Advertiser chooses the audience.	An effective advertising medium for small companies in virtually *any* business.
World Wide Web (WWW)	Anyone in the world who is wired to the WWW.	Reaches upscale, well-educated consumers anywhere in the world; most WWW users are male.
Outdoor Advertising	Ranges from a neighborhood to an entire metropolitan area.	An excellent media to supplement other forms of advertising.
Transit Advertising	Urban areas.	Typically does not reach upper income, well-educated audience.
Directories	Customers who have already made a purchase decision.	Many directories available; the key is picking the right ones.
Trade Shows	Pre-selected audience.	Potential customers are inclined to buy.
Specialty Advertising	Advertiser chooses the audience.	Allows advertiser to "narrow cast" message rather than broadcast it.
Special Events and Promotions	Advertiser chooses the audience.	Allows advertiser maximum flexibility and creativity in ads.
Point-of-Purchase Ads	Existing customers.	Two-thirds of buying decisions are made at the point of sale.

Advantages	Disadvantages	Tips
Extensive coverage; low absolute and relative costs; timeliness.	Blanket coverage means some ads are wasted on those who are not potential customers; limited reproduction quality; significant ad "clutter"	Research newspaper's reader profile; focus on placing ads in proper sections.
Universal infiltration; radio ads are more "active" than print ads, giving advertisers the ability to be more creative with ads.	Need to repeat ads for effectiveness; no visual possibilities; brief ads mean limited message potential.	Make sure station's listener profile matches company's target audience. Keep ad copy simple.
Visual advantage—advertiser can *show* customers product or service benefits; cable stations bring TV ads into price ranges that small businesses can afford.	Brief exposure to ads, often because of "zapping"; creating TV commercials can be expensive.	Consider "infomercials." They may be obnoxious to many, but they work, if properly done. Try to evoke emotion in ads.
Long life spans for ads; most magazines have multiple readers; high ad quality.	Long closing times for ads requires advance planning; ad "clutter" can reduce ads' effectiveness.	As in newspaper advertising, proper placement is the key. Left-hand pages are best.
Ability to select a specific audience and tailor a message to it; captures reader's attention, at least for a moment.	Will become "junk mail" if improperly targeted; high relative cost because of low response rates.	Plan direct mail ads so that you can measure results; use catchy words—"Free," "Save," "New."
Attractive audience profile; rapid growth of the WWW as a marketing tool; ability to use full-color, sound, animation, etc.	Audience may bypass ads without ever seeing them; advertising "clutter" is a problem and will grow as WWW use grows.	Make site interactive, if possible; games, puzzles, and contests can be effective draws.
Multiple exposures; a bargain because of its low relative cost.	Brief exposure requires limited messages; lack of prominence.	Keep ads short and simple; use clear, legible type.
Wide coverage and repeat exposure to ads; low relative cost.	Difficulty in reaching specific target audiences; brief exposure requires limited message.	Use contrasting colors and designs that give ads a 2-D appearance.
Targets prime prospects; long ad life.	Danger of listing or directory becoming obsolete; ad "clutter."	Design ad so that it stands out from the crowd.
Ample time for personal selling; ability to demonstrate products.	High cost of traveling to show, setting up, and staffing booth.	Make the most of sales time and follow up leads.
Ability to reach specific audience and to personalize the message.	Potential for waste and high costs.	Specialty items should prompt customer recall.
Reaches some customers when all other attempts fail.	Requires time to plan and coordinate; can be expensive.	Creativity is a must if a specialty promotion is to be successful.
Reaches customer at a crucial moment—the point of purchase.	Requires customers to come into the business first.	Capture customer's attention first; then sell.

Source: B.C. Cartoon. Reprinted by permission of Johnny Hart and Creators Syndicate, Inc.

mailing lists, increase foot traffic in a store, or introduce a company or a product into a new territory.

The next step in developing an advertising plan is to analyze the firm and its target audience. A business owner who does not know who his advertising target is cannot reach it! The small business owner should address the following questions:

☆ What business am I in?

☆ What image do I want to project?

☆ Who are my target customers and what are their characteristics?

☆ Where can they best be reached?

☆ What do my customers *really* purchase from me?

* What benefits can the customer derive from my goods or services?
* How do I want to position my company in the market?
* What advertising approach do my competitors take?

Answering these questions will help the owner to define her business and profile its customers, which will help her to focus the advertising message on a specific target market and get more for her advertising dollar.

For instance, Dale Kesel, owner of a small photography studio specializing in portraits, defines his target customers as "parents, ages 25 to 45, with children under 14," but he designs his ads to appeal to the real decision maker in family portraits, "the woman in the household."[35]

Once the small business owner has defined her target audience, she can design an advertising message and choose the media for transmitting it. At this stage, the owner decides what to say and how to say it. One advertising expert claims, "You won't win customers by boring them into buying. You've got to create a desire." [36]

Owners should build their ads around a **unique selling proposition (USP)**, a key customer benefit of a product or service that sets it apart from its competition. To be effective, a USP must be unique—something the competition does not (or cannot) provide—and strong enough to encourage the customer to buy. A successful USP answers the critical question every customer asks: "What's in it for me?" The USP becomes the heart of the advertising message. Sometimes, the most powerful USPs are the *intangible or psychological* benefits a product or service offers customers, for example, safety, security, acceptance, status, and others. An advertiser must be careful, however, to avoid stressing minuscule differences that are irrelevant to customers. Table 6.5 describes a six-sentence advertising strategy designed to create powerful ads that focus on a USP.

The best way to identify a meaningful USP is to describe the primary benefit your product or service offers customers and then to list other secondary benefits it provides. "You are not likely to have more than three top benefits you can give someone," says one advertising expert.[37] It is also important to develop a brief list of the facts that support your company's USP, for example, 24-hour service, a fully trained staff, awards won, and others. By focusing ads on these top benefits and the facts supporting them, business owners can communicate their USPs to their target audiences in a meaningful, attention-getting way. Building an ad around a USP spells out for customers the specific benefit they get if they buy that product or service. "If your audience has to study your ad to figure out what you're trying to say, forget it!" says one expert.[38]

> **Dale Kesel Photography**

> **unique selling proposition (USP)—**
> *a key customer benefit of a product or service that sets it apart from the competition; it answers the customer's question: "What's in it for me?"*

Does your advertising deliver the message you want to the audience you are targeting? If not, try stating your strategy in six sentences:

* **Primary purpose.** What is the primary purpose of this ad? "The purpose of Rainbow Tours' ads is to get people to call or write for a free video brochure."
* **Primary benefit.** What USP can you offer customers? "We will stress the unique and exciting places our customers can visit."
* **Secondary benefits.** What other key benefits support your USP? "We will also stress the convenience and value of our tours and the skill of our tour guides."
* **Target audience.** At whom are we aiming the ad? "We will aim our ads at adventurous male and female singles and couples, 21 to 34, who can afford our tours."
* **Audience reaction**. What response do you want from your target audience? "We expect our audience to call or write to request our video brochure."
* **Company personality.** What image do we want to convey in our ads? "Our ads will reflect our innovation, excitement, conscientiousness—and our warm, caring attitude toward our customers."

Table 6.5
A Six-Sentence Advertising Strategy

Source: Adapted from Jay Conrad Levinson, "The Six-Sentence Strategy," *Communication Briefings*, December 1994, p. 4.

Kesel, for example, offers his customers enduring family memories in the form of high-quality portraits that capture the personalities of the children he photographs. His ads appeal to customers at an emotional level.

Figure 6.3 illustrates the characteristics of a successful ad.

A company's target audience and the nature of its message determine the advertising media it will use. As you learned in the previous section, some messages are much more powerful in some media than in others.

For instance, because Kesel uses samples of portraits in his ads, he relies heavily on ads in the community newspapers nearest his location, although he does supplement his campaign with radio spots.

The process does not end with creating and broadcasting an ad. The final step involves evaluating the ad campaign's effectiveness. Did it accomplish the objectives it was designed to accomplish? Immediate-response ads can be evaluated in a number of ways. For instance, a manager can include coupons that customers redeem to get price reductions on products and services. Dated coupons identify customer responses over certain time periods. Some firms use hidden offers—statements hidden somewhere in an ad that offer customers special deals if they make a special request. For example, one small firm offered a price reduction to any customer who mentioned that he heard the advertisement for the product on the radio.

The manager can also gauge an ad's effectiveness by measuring the volume of store traffic generated. Effective advertising should increase store traffic, which boosts sales of advertised and nonadvertised items. Of course, if an advertisement promotes a particular bargain item, the manager can judge its effectiveness by comparing sales of the items to preadvertising sales levels. Remember: the ultimate test of an ad is whether or not it increases sales!

Ad tests can help to determine the most effective methods of reaching potential customers. An owner can design two different ads (or use two different media or broadcast times) that are coded for identification and see which one produces more responses. For

Figure 6.3
Five Fundamentals of a Successful Advertisement
Source: Adapted from Jerry Fisher, "Fine Print," *Entrepreneur*, November 1994, pp. 145–147.

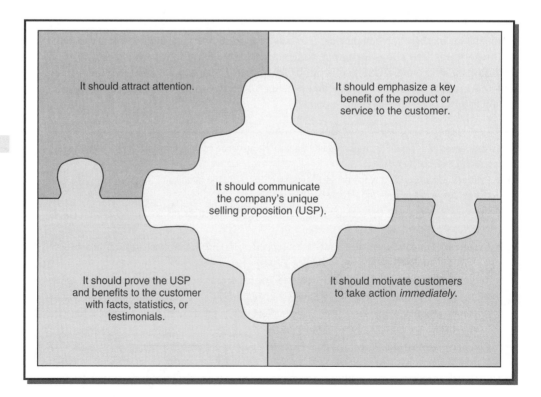

It should attract attention.

It should emphasize a key benefit of the product or service to the customer.

It should communicate the company's unique selling proposition (USP).

It should prove the USP and benefits to the customer with facts, statistics, or testimonials.

It should motivate customers to take action *immediately.*

example, the manager can use a split run of two different ads in a local newspaper. That is, he can place one ad in part of the paper's press run and another ad in the remainder of the run. Then the manager can measure the response level to each ad.

Table 6.6 offers 12 "don'ts" for creating an effective advertising campaign.

Table 6.6

12 "Don'ts" in Advertising

Sources: Adapted from Sue Clayton, "Advertising," *Business Start-Ups*, December 1995, pp. 6-7; *Marketing for Small Business*, The University of Georgia Small Business Development Center: Athens, Georgia, 1992, p. 69; "Advertising Leads to Sales," *Small Business Reports*, April 1988, p. 14; Shelly Meinhardt, "Put It in Print," *Entrepreneur*, January 1989, p. 54; adapted from Danny R. Arnold and Robert H. Solomon, "Ten 'Don'ts' in Bank Advertising," *Burroughs Clearing House*, Vol. 16, No. 12, September 1980, pp. 20-24, 42-43; Howard Dana Shaw, "Success with Ads," *In Business*, November/December 1991, pp. 48-49.

1. *Don't plan only one advertisement at a time.* An advertising campaign is likely to be more effective if it is developed from a comprehensive plan for a specific time period. A piecemeal approach produces ads that lack continuity and a unified theme.

2. *Don't fail to set any long-run advertising objectives.* One cause of inadequate planning is the failure to establish specific objectives for the advertising program. Without defining what is expected from advertising, the program lacks a sense of direction.

3. *Don't use only those advertisements, themes, and vehicles that have a personal appeal to you.* Although personal judgment influences every business decision, you cannot afford to let bias interfere with advertising decisions. For example, you should not use a particular radio station just because you like it.

4. *Don't view advertising expenditures as expenses.* In an accounting sense, advertising is a business expense, but money spent on ads tends to produce sales and profits over time that might not be possible without advertising. An effective advertising program generates more sales than it costs. You must ask, "Can I afford not to advertise?"

5. *Don't always use the same type of advertising as your competitors.* Some managers tend to "follow the advertising crowd" because they fear being different from their competitors. "Me-too" advertising frequently is ineffective because it fails to create a unique image for the firm. Don't be afraid to be different!

6. *Don't always go with the media vehicle that claims to be number one.* It is not uncommon for several media within the same geographic region to claim to be "number one." As you saw in this chapter, different media offer certain advantages and disadvantages. The manager should evaluate each according to its ability to reach his target audience effectively.

7. *Don't always be the spokesperson on your television and radio commercials.* Although this may lend a personal touch to your ads, the commercial may be seen as being nonprofessional or "homemade." The ad may detract from the firm's image rather than improve it.

8. *Don't cram as much as possible into every ad.* Some small business managers think that to get the most for their advertising dollar, they must pack their ads full of facts and illustrations. But overcrowded ads confuse customers and are often ignored. Simple, well-designed ads that focus on your USP are much more effective.

9. *Don't assume your ad is good if two or three customers mention it to you.* Measuring the effectiveness of advertising is an elusive art at best. But the opinions of a small sample of customers whose opinions may be biased are not a reliable gauge of an ad's effectiveness. The techniques described earlier offer a more objective measurement of an ad's ability to produce results.

10. *Don't drop the ad because something does not happen immediately.* Some ads are designed to produce immediate results, but many ads require more time because of the lag effect they experience. One of advertising's rules is: "It's not the size; it's the frequency."

11. *Don't emphasize only product or service features.* Too often, ads emphasize only the features of the products or services a company offers without mentioning the benefits they provide to customers. Customers really don't care about a product's or service's "bells and whistles"; they are much more interested in the *benefits* those features can give them! Their primary concern is: "How can this solve my problem?"

12. *Don't always choose the "cheapest" advertising medium.* Remember the difference between the absolute and relative cost of an ad. The medium that has a low absolute cost may actually offer a high relative cost if it does not reach your intended target audience. Evaluate the cost of different media by looking at the cost per thousand customers reached. Remember: No medium is a bargain if it fails to connect you with your intended customers.

You must be patient, giving the advertising campaign a reasonable time to produce results. One recent study concluded that sales increases are most noticeable four to six months after an advertising campaign begins. One advertising expert claims that successful advertisers "are not capricious ad-by-ad makers; they're consistent ad campaigners."

Advertising Naturally

When a tree limb crashed through the roof of his art studio, Bennett Abrams had no idea that it would be the beginning of a business. Abrams, who made "microcosms"—compositions of silk foliage, real flowers, and wax plants—added some of his creations to the limb, and "all of a sudden, the tree limb became a full-grown tree," he recalls. That triggered his interest in making trees as parts of residential interior design. Abrams and partner Gary Hanick launched California Country Trees and began making trees for residential customers and department stores such as Macy's.

Although their trees look like the real thing, they are "all handmade, hand-sculpted, and hand-painted" over a steel skeleton. Their "bark" is a proprietary substance that hardens more slowly than fiberglass and allows sculptors more carving time. California Country Trees' artisans strive to replicate the nuances and imperfections that exist on real trees. In fact, the company makes only reproductions of real trees, not fantasy trees. "We're known primarily for oaks, pines, and banyan," says Hanick. The appeal of the company's trees is their ability to go where real trees cannot—from hotel atriums to museum exhibits—because of a lack of natural light. "This gives [our customers] the opportunity to really expand what they can do indoors," says Hanick. The company's largest tree to date, a 50-foot oak, is housed in a Las Vegas casino.

"Our major market is architects and designers," most of whom hear about the company through word of mouth, says Abrams. California Country Trees also sells to upscale residential customers, too. Currently, about half of the company's work is with foreign clients. Because each tree is unique, California Country Trees has no standard price list to offer customers. Some of its trees sell for hundreds of thousands of dollars. Eight craftspeople currently sculpt each tree, while other workers build the steel frames and apply the leaves. Annual sales are about $4 million, and Abrams and Hanick take great pride in the artistic satisfaction they get from their work. "There isn't anything else in the world I'd rather be doing than what we're doing," says Abrams.

1. Design an advertising program for California Country Trees.
2. How would you define the company's target audience?
3. What unique selling proposition (USP) would you build the advertising program around?
4. What media would you recommend the company use to reach its target customers?

Source: Michael Barrier, "Competing With Nature," *Nation's Business,* May 1996, p.15.

---

4. Identify four basic methods for preparing an advertising budget.

Preparing an Advertising Budget

One of the most challenging decisions confronting a small business owner is how much money to invest in advertising. The amount the owner wants to spend and the amount the firm can afford to spend on advertising usually differ significantly. There are four methods of determining an advertising budget: what is affordable; matching competitors; percentage of sales; and objective and task.

Under the what-is-affordable method, the owner sees advertising as a luxury and views advertising completely as an expense, not as an investment that produces sales and profits in the future. Therefore, as the name implies, management spends whatever it can afford on advertising. Too often, the advertising budget is allocated funds after all other budget items have been financed. The result is an inadequate advertising budget. This method also fails to relate the advertising budget to the advertising objective.

Another approach is to match the advertising expenditures of the firm's competitors, either in a flat dollar amount or as a percentage of sales. This method assumes that a firm's advertising needs and strategies are the same as those of its competitors. While competitors' actions can be helpful in establishing a floor for advertising expenditures, relying on this technique can lead to blind imitation instead of a budget suited to the small firm's circumstances.

The most commonly used method of establishing an advertising budget is the simple percentage-of-sales approach. This method relates advertising expenditures to actual sales results. Tying advertising expenditures to sales is generally preferred to relating them to profits because sales tend to fluctuate less than profits. One expert suggests a useful rule of thumb when establishing an advertising budget: 10 percent of projected sales the first year in business; 7 percent the second year; and at least 5 percent each year after that.[39] Relying totally on such broad rules can be dangerous, however. They may not be representative of a small company's advertising needs.

The objective-and-task method is the most difficult and least used technique for establishing an advertising budget. It also is the method most often recommended by advertising experts. With this method, an owner links advertising expenditures to specific objectives. While the previous methods break down the total amount of funds allocated to advertising, the task method builds up the advertising funds by analyzing what it will cost to accomplish these objectives. For example, suppose that a manager wants to boost sales of a particular product 10 percent by attracting local college students. He may determine that a nearby rock radio station would be the best medium to use. Then he must decide on the number and frequency of the ads and estimate their costs.

The manager follows this same process for each advertising objective. A common problem with the method is the tendency for the manager to be overly ambitious in setting advertising objectives, which leads to unrealistically high advertising expenditures. The manager may be forced to alter objectives, or the plans to reach them, to bring the advertising budget back to a reasonable level. However, the plan can still be effective.

Most small companies find it useful to plan in advance their advertising expenditures on a weekly basis. This short-term planning ensures a more consistent advertising effort throughout the year. A calendar like the one pictured in Figure 6.4 can be one of the most valuable tools in planning a small company's advertising program. The calendar enables the owner to prepare for holidays and special events, to monitor actual and budgeted expenditures, and to ensure that ads are scheduled for the appropriate media at the proper times.

October

Sunday	Monday	Tuesday	Wednesday	Thursday	Friday	Saturday
Advertising Budget for October: 9% of Sales = $2,275 Co-op Ads = $ 550 Total $2,825		October Advertising Expenditures: $2845 Under/(Over) Budget = $ 20 Remaining Balance = $6400		1 WPCC Radio 5 spots - $125 Billboard - $350	2 *The Chronicle* 140 lines - $100	3
4	5	6	7	8	9 *The Chronicle* 140 lines - $100	10
11	12	13 Meet w/Leslie Re: November Ad Campaigns - 2pm	14	15 Envelope "Stuffer" in Invoices - Halloween Sale - $175	16 *The Chronicle* 140 lines - $100	17 WPCC Radio 5 Spots - $100
18	19	20 WPCC Radio 5 Spots - $125	21	22 Direct Mail Halloween Sale - Promo "Preferred Customers" - $120	23 *The Chronicle* 140 lines - $100	24 WPCC Radio 5 Spots - $100
25	26 WPCC Radio 5 Spots - $125	27 WPCC Radio 5 Spots - $125	28 WPCC Radio 5 Spots - $125	29 WPCC Radio 5 Spots - $125	30 *The Chronicle* Half-Page Spread Sale - $300	31 WPCC Radio Live Remote Broadcast - $425

Figure 6.4
A Calendar Can Be a Powerful Tool for Planning Advertising

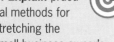

How to Advertise Big on a Small Budget

The typical small business does not have the luxury of an unlimited advertising budget. Most cannot afford to hire a professional ad agency. This does not mean, however, that the small company should assume a second-class advertising posture. Most advertising experts say that, unless a small company spends more than $10,000 a year on advertising, it probably doesn't need an ad agency. For most, hiring freelance copywriters and artists on a per-project basis is a much better bargain. With a little creativity and a dose of ingenuity, small business owners can stretch their advertising dollars and make the most of what they spend. Three useful techniques to do this are cooperative advertising, shared advertising, and publicity.

cooperative advertising—*an arrangement in which a manufacturing company shares the cost of advertising with a small retailer if the retailer features its products in those ads.*

Cooperative Advertising

In **cooperative advertising**, a manufacturing company shares the cost of advertising with a small retailer if the retailer features the manufacturer's products in those ads. Both the manufacturer and the retailer get more advertising per dollar by sharing expenses.

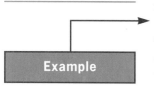

David Lang, owner of a small lawn equipment store, purchases his inventory from ten different manufacturers, nine of whom offer cooperative advertising programs. "Without [the manufacturers' help], we could only spend $20,000 a year [on advertising]," says Lang. "But now we can spend $40,000 because we're getting $20,000 back."[40]

Unlike Lang, who uses every dollar of cooperative advertising available to him, most small business owners fail to take advantage of manufacturers' cooperative advertising programs. Manufacturers, whose products cover the entire retail spectrum, make an estimated $15 billion of co-op ad dollars available each year; yet, more than two-thirds of it goes unused![41]

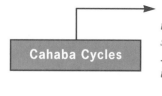

Barbara Malki, co-owner of Cahaba Cycles, is now a believer in the power of cooperative advertising, although she admits that she has not always been. "Two years ago," she says, "I was leaving co-op money on the table. I'm more aggressive about it now. [Now] I . . . use every co-op dollar." Cahaba Cycles recoups about 10 percent of its annual advertising budget through cooperative advertising.[42]

Manufacturers offer cooperative advertising programs in almost every medium.

For example, when a steep sales decline hit Bromby's Sport & Ski, Inc., owner Susan Fabbiano was forced to cut her advertising budget. Recognizing the importance of advertising to her business, Fabbiano was determined to maintain quality advertising despite a reduced budget. So, she began to pursue co-op ads with the manufacturers of her product line. One company split the costs of radio and outdoor ads with Fabbiano fifty-fifty. She claims, "Co-op advertising has allowed the store to keep its name before the public without increasing expenditures."[43]

Cooperative advertising not only helps small businesses stretch their advertising budgets, it also offers another source of savings: the free advertising packages that many manufacturers supply to retailers. These packages usually include photographs and illustrations of the product as well as professionally prepared ads to use in different media.

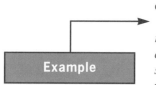

Once, when Fabbiano was preparing an outdoor ad featuring Solomon products, she requested "a good photograph," from a sales representative. The supplier sent her, free of charge, the artwork for a billboard that would have cost $700 to produce. On another occasion, Fabbiano found and used two 30-second radio spots that had been "professionally written by the manufacturer's agency." Her cost: only the air time.[44]

Shared Advertising

In **shared advertising**, a group of similar businesses forms a syndicate to produce generic ads that allow the individual businesses to dub in local information. The technique is especially useful for small businesses that sell relatively standardized products or services such as legal assistance, autos, and furniture. Because the small firms in the syndicate pool their funds, the result usually is higher-quality ads and significantly lower production costs.

Other cost-saving suggestions for advertising expenditures include the following:

★ *Repeating ads that have been successful.* In addition to reducing the cost of ad preparation, this may create a consistent image in a small firm's advertising program.

★ *Using identical ads in different media.* If a billboard has been an effective advertising tool, an owner should consider converting it to a newspaper or magazine ad or a direct-mail flier.

★ *Hiring the services of independent copywriters, graphic designers, photographers, and other media specialists.* Many small businesses that cannot afford a full-time advertising staff buy their advertising services à la carte. They work directly with independent specialists and usually receive high-quality work that compares favorably to that of advertising agencies without paying a fee for overhead.

★ *Concentrating advertising during times when customers are most likely to buy.* Some small business owners make the mistake of spreading an already small advertising budget evenly—and thinly—over a 12-month period. "Don't always look at your budget as having to be spent in equal installments," advises one media director. "Many times you're just throwing money away. What you need . . . is the most effective schedule for you."[45]

> **shared advertising—** *an arrangement in which a group of similar businesses forms a syndicate to produce generic ads that allow the individual businesses to dub in local information.*

Public Relations

The press can be either a valuable friend or a fearsome foe to a small business, depending on how well the owner handles her firm's public relations. Too often, entrepreneurs take the attitude, "My business is too small to be concerned about public relations." However, wise small business managers recognize that investing time and money in public relations benefits both the community and the company. The community gains the support of a good business citizen, and the company earns a positive image in the marketplace.

Many small businesses rely on media attention to get noticed, and getting that attention takes a coordinated effort. Public relations don't just happen; an owner must work at getting her company noticed by the media. While such publicity may not be free, it definitely can lower the company's advertising expenditures and still keep its name before the public. Because small companies' advertising budgets are limited, public relations take on significant importance.

Bob Mayberry, a car dealer in Monroe, North Carolina, recently bought a 1961 Ford squad car like the one used on the 1960s hit TV series, The Andy Griffith Show. *Not only does the car lure potential customers onto his lot, but it also has gotten the dealership into several newspaper articles. "We have sold a lot of cars from it," says Mayberry.*[46]

One successful public relations technique is **cause marketing**, in which a small business sponsors and promotes fund-raising activities of nonprofit groups and charities while raising its own visibility in the community.

For example, during the Muscular Dystrophy Association's annual telethon, a local shop, Cookies Cook'n, donated over 100 pounds of cookies and brownies to feed telephone volunteers. Several giant cookies were auctioned off during the telethon, and the small cookie shop's name was mentioned frequently. Cookies Cook'n got more television exposure for donating these cookies than it could have gotten spending its entire advertising budget on TV commercials.[47]

> **cause marketing—***an arrangement in which a small business sponsors and promotes fund-raising activities of nonprofit groups and charities while raising its own visibility in the community.*

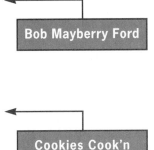

Bob Mayberry Ford

Cookies Cook'n

Pricing: A Creative Blend of Art and Science

Deciding how and where to advertise is not the only key to marketing success; small business owners also must determine prices for their goods and services that will draw customers and produce a profit. Unfortunately, too many small business owners set prices according to vague, poorly defined techniques, or even hunches. Price is an important factor in the relationship with customers, and haphazard pricing techniques can confuse and alienate customers and endanger a firm's profitability. Setting prices is not only one of the toughest decisions small business owners face, but it also is one of the most important. Improper pricing has destroyed countless businesses, where owners mistakenly thought their prices were sufficient to generate a profit.

Price is the monetary value of a product or service in the marketplace. It is a measure of what the customer must exchange in order to obtain various goods and services. As the media continuously reinforce, this is an era where shoppers seek value for their money. Price also is a signal of a product's or service's value to an individual, and so different customers assign different values to the same goods and services. From an owner's viewpoint, price must be compatible with the customer's definition of value. "Without an understanding of how customers perceive the value of your product or service, it's almost impossible to set a price they'll be willing—and able—to pay," says one business writer.[48]

Setting prices with a customer orientation is more important than trying to choose the ideal price for a product. In fact, for most products there is an acceptable price range, not a single ideal price. This price range is the area between the price ceiling defined by customers in the market and the price floor established by the firm's cost structure. The manager's goal should be to position the firm's prices within this acceptable price range. The final price that business owners set depends on the desired image they want to create for the business in the customer's mind—discount, middle of the road, or prestige (see Figure 6.5).

Setting appropriate prices requires more than just choosing a number based on intuition or gut feeling. Rather, proper pricing policies require information, facts, and analysis. The factors that small business owners must consider when determining the final price for goods and services include the following:

- ☆ Product/service costs
- ☆ Market factors—supply and demand
- ☆ Sales volume
- ☆ Competitors' prices
- ☆ The company's competitive advantage

Figure 6.5
What Determines Price?

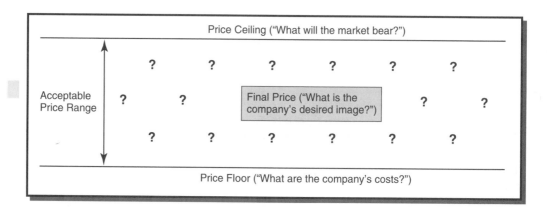

- ☆ Economic conditions
- ☆ Business location
- ☆ Seasonal fluctuations
- ☆ Psychological factors
- ☆ Credit terms and purchase discounts
- ☆ Customers' price sensitivity
- ☆ Desired image

Although the owner probably cannot get the ideal price for a product or service, she should set the price high enough to cover costs and earn a reasonable profit but low enough to attract customers and generate an adequate sales volume. Furthermore, the right price today may be completely inappropriate tomorrow because of changing market conditions.

Pricing Strategies and Tactics

6. Describe effective pricing techniques for introducing new goods or services and for existing ones.

There is no limit to the number of variations in pricing strategies and tactics. This wide variety of options is exactly what allows the small business manager to be so creative. This section will examine some of the more commonly used tactics under a variety of conditions. Pricing always plays a critical role in a firm's overall strategy; pricing policies must be compatible with a company's total marketing plan. "Your price must fit in with the goals and mission of your company," advises one small business owner.[49]

Introducing a New Product

Most small business managers approach setting the price of a new product with a great deal of apprehension because they have no precedent on which to base their decision. If the new product's price is excessively high, it is in danger of failing because of low sales volume. However, if its price is too low, the product's sales revenue might not cover costs. When pricing any new product, the owner should try to satisfy three objectives:

1. *Getting the product accepted.* No matter how unusual a product is, its price must be acceptable to the firm's potential customers.

2. *Maintaining market share as competition grows.* If a new product is successful, competitors will enter the market, and the small company must work to expand or at least maintain its market share. Continuously reappraising the product's price in conjunction with special advertising and promotion techniques helps the firm to acquire and retain a satisfactory market share.

3. *Earning a profit.* Obviously, the small firm must establish a price for the new product that is higher than its cost. The manager should not introduce a new product at a price below cost as it is much easier to lower the price than to increase it once the product is on the market.

Linda Calder, owner of Calder & Calder Promotions, a company that produces trade shows, knows how difficult it can be to raise prices. When she launched her company, Calder decided to set her price below the average price of competing trade show production companies because she thought that would give her a competitive edge. "My fee was so low. . . I sold out but did not make a profit," she says. Realizing her mistake, Calder raised prices in her second year, but her customers balked. Her sales fell by 50 percent.[50]

Calder & Calder Promotions

The small business manager has three basic strategies to choose from in establishing the new product's price: a penetration pricing strategy, a skimming pricing strategy, and a sliding down the demand curve strategy.

PENETRATION. If a small business introduces a product into a highly competitive market in which a large number of similar products are competing for acceptance, the product must penetrate the market to be successful. To gain quick acceptance and extensive distribution in the mass market, the firm should introduce the product with a low price. In other words, it should set the price just above total unit cost to develop a wedge in the market and quickly achieve a high volume of sales. The resulting low profit margins may discourage other competitors from entering the market with similar products.

In most cases, a penetration pricing strategy is used to introduce relatively low-priced goods into a market where no elite segment and little opportunity for differentiation exist. The introduction is usually accompanied by heavy advertising and promotional techniques, special sales, and discounts. The small firm must recognize that penetration pricing is a long-range strategy; until the firm achieves customer acceptance for the product, profits are likely to be small. But if the strategy works and the product achieves mass-market penetration, sales volume will increase, and the company will earn adequate profits. The objective of the penetration strategy is to achieve quick access to the market in order to realize high sales volume as soon as possible. Many consumer products, such as soap, shampoo, and light bulbs, are introduced through penetration pricing strategies.

SKIMMING. A skimming pricing strategy often is used when a company introduces a new product into a market with little or no competition. Sometimes the firm employs this tactic when introducing a product into a competitive market that contains an elite group that is able to pay a higher price. Here the firm uses a higher-than-normal price in an effort to quickly recover the initial developmental and promotional costs of the product. Startup costs usually are substantial due to intensive promotional expenses and high initial production costs. The idea is to set a price well above the total unit cost and to promote the product heavily in order to appeal to the segment of the market that is not sensitive to price. Such a pricing tactic often reinforces the unique, prestigious image of a store and projects a quality picture of the product. Another advantage of this technique is that the manager can correct pricing mistakes quickly and easily. If the firm sets a price that is too low under a penetration strategy, raising the price can be very difficult. But if a firm using a skimming strategy sets a price too high to generate sufficient volume, it can always lower the price.

SLIDING DOWN THE DEMAND CURVE. One variation of the skimming pricing strategy is called sliding down the demand curve. Using this tactic, the small company introduces a product at a high price. Then technological advancements enable the firm to lower its costs quickly and to reduce the product's price sooner than its competition can. By beating other businesses in a price decline, the small company discourages competitors and gradually, over time, becomes a high-volume producer. Computers are a prime example of a product introduced at a high price that quickly cascaded downward as companies forged important technological advances.

Sliding is a short-term pricing strategy that assumes that competition will eventually emerge. But even if no competition arises, the small business almost always lowers the product's price to attract a larger segment of the market. Yet, the initial high price contributes to a rapid return of startup costs and generates a pool of funds to finance expansion and technological advances.

Pricing Established Goods and Services

odd pricing—*establishing prices that end in odd numbers to create the psychological impression that prices are low.*

Each of the following pricing tactics or techniques can become part of the toolbox of pricing tactics entrepreneurs can use to set prices of established goods and services.

ODD PRICING. Although studies of consumer reactions to prices are mixed and generally inconclusive, many small business managers use the technique known as **odd pricing**. These managers prefer to establish prices that end in odd numbers (5, 7, 9) because they believe that merchandise selling for $12.95 appears to be much cheaper than the item priced at $13.00. Psychological techniques such as odd pricing are designed to appeal to certain customer interests, but their effectiveness remains to be proven.

PRICE LINING. **Price lining** is a technique that greatly simplifies the pricing function. Under this system, the manager stocks merchandise in several different price ranges or price lines. Each category of merchandise contains items that are similar in appearance, quality, cost, performance, or other features. For example, most music stores use price lines for their tapes and CDs to make it easier for customers to select items and to simplify stock planning. Most lined products appear in sets of three—good, better, and best—at prices designed to satisfy different market segment needs and incomes.

> **price lining**—*setting the same price for products that have similar features and appear within the same line.*

LEADER PRICING. **Leader pricing** is a technique in which the small retailer marks down the customary price (i.e., the price consumers are accustomed to paying) of a popular item in an attempt to attract more customers. The company earns a much smaller profit on each unit because the markup is lower, but purchases of other merchandise by customers seeking the leader item often boost sales and profits. In other words, the incidental purchases that consumers make when shopping for the leader item boost sales revenue enough to offset a lower profit margin on the leader. Grocery stores frequently use leader pricing.

> **leader pricing**—*marking down the normal price of a popular item in an attempt to attract more customers who make incidental purchases of other items at regular prices.*

GEOGRAPHICAL PRICING. Small businesses whose pricing decisions are greatly affected by the costs of shipping merchandise to customers across a wide range of geographical regions frequently employ one of the geographical pricing techniques. For these companies, freight expenses comprise a substantial portion of the cost of doing business and may cut deeply into already narrow profit margins. One type of geographical pricing is **zone pricing**, in which a small company sells its merchandise at different prices to customers located in different territories. For example, a manufacturer might sell at one price to customers east of the Mississippi and at another to those west of the Mississippi. The U.S. Postal Service's varying parcel post charges offer a good example of zone pricing. The small business must be able to show a legitimate basis (e.g., differences in selling or transportation costs) for the price discrimination or risk violating Section 2 of the Clayton Act.

> **zone pricing**—*setting different prices for customers located in different territories because of different transportation costs.*

Another variation of geographic pricing is uniform **delivered pricing**, a technique in which the firm charges all of its customers the same price regardless of their location, even though the cost of selling or transporting merchandise varies. The firm calculates the proper freight charges for each region and combines them into a uniform fee. The result is that local customers subsidize the firm's charges for shipping merchandise to distant customers.

> **delivered pricing**—*charging all customers the same price, regardless of their locations and different transportation costs.*

A final variation of geographical pricing is **FOB-Factory**, in which the small company sells its merchandise to customers on the condition that they pay all shipping costs. In this way, the company can set a uniform price for its product and let each customer cover the freight costs.

> **FOB-Factory**—*selling merchandise to customers on the condition that they pay all shipping costs.*

OPPORTUNISTIC PRICING. When products or services are in short supply, customers are willing to pay more for products they need. Some businesses use such circumstances to maximize short-term profits by engaging in price gouging. Many customers have little choice but to pay the higher prices. **Opportunistic pricing** may backfire, however, because customers know that unreasonably high prices mean that a company is exploiting them.

> **opportunistic pricing**—*charging customers unreasonably high prices when goods or services are in short supply.*

For example, after the devastating Los Angeles earthquake, one convenience store jacked up prices on virtually every item, selling small bottles of water for $8 each. Neighborhood residents had no choice but to pay the higher prices. After the incident, many customers remembered the store's unfair prices and began to shop elsewhere. The convenience store's sales slipped and never recovered.

discounts (or markdowns)—*reductions from normal list prices.*

DISCOUNTS. Many small business managers use **discounts or markdowns**—reductions from normal list prices—to move stale, outdated, damaged, or slow-moving merchandise. A seasonal discount is a price reduction designed to encourage shoppers to purchase merchandise before an upcoming season. For instance, many retail clothiers offer special sales on winter coats in midsummer. Some firms grant purchase discounts to special groups of customers, such as senior citizens or students, to establish a faithful clientele and to generate repeat business. For example, one small drugstore located near a state university offered a 10 percent student discount on all purchases and was quite successful in developing a large volume of student business.

multiple pricing—*a technique offering customers discounts if they purchase in quantity.*

MULTIPLE PRICING. **Multiple pricing** is a promotional technique that offers customers discounts if they purchase in quantity. Many products, especially those with relatively low unit value, are sold using multiple pricing. For example, instead of selling an item for 50 cents, a small company might offer 5 for $2.

SUGGESTED RETAIL PRICES. Many manufacturers print suggested retail prices on their products or include them on invoices or in wholesale catalogs. Small business owners frequently follow these suggested retail prices because this eliminates the need to make a pricing decision. Nonetheless, following prices established by a distant manufacturer may create problems for the small firm. For example, a haberdasher may try to create a high-quality, exclusive image through a prestige pricing policy, but manufacturers may suggest discount outlet prices that are incompatible with the small firm's image. Another danger of accepting the manufacturer's suggested price is that it does not take into consideration the small firm's cost structure or competitive situation. A manufacturer cannot force a business to accept a suggested retail price, or require a business to agree not to resell merchandise below a stated price because such practices violate the Sherman Antitrust Act and other legislation.

Two Potent Forces: Image and Competition

Price Conveys Image

A company's pricing policies offer important information about its overall image. For example, the prices charged by a posh men's clothing store reflect a completely different image from those charged by a factory outlet. Customers look at prices to determine what type of store they are dealing with. High prices frequently convey the idea of quality, prestige, and uniqueness to the customer. Accordingly, when developing a marketing approach to pricing, a small business manager must establish prices that are compatible with what its customers expect and are willing to pay. Too often, small business owners *underprice* their goods and services, believing that low prices are the only way they can achieve a competitive advantage. They fail to identify the extra value, convenience, service, and quality they give their customers—all things many customers are willing to pay for. These companies fall into the trap of trying to compete solely on the basis of price when they lack the sales volume—and hence, the lower costs—of their larger rivals. It is a recipe for failure. "People want quality," says one merchant selling upscale goods at upscale prices. "They want value. But if you lower prices, they think that you are lowering the value and lowering the quality."[51]

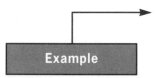
Example

Robin Golinski was selling hand-painted silk camisoles for just $22 on Boston Common, but many customers balked, believing the garments could not be authentic at that price. "I raised the price to $34, and sales doubled," says Golinski.[52]

The secret to setting prices properly is based on understanding the firm's target market, the customer groups at which the small company is aiming its goods or services. Target market, business image, and price are closely related.

"If we raise our prices high enough, people will think it's a luxury item and will have to have it."

Source: Reprinted with permission. Copyright by Harry Nelson.

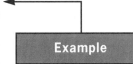

Example

For instance, as beers made by microbreweries have gained popularity, many of these tiny breweries now target upscale beer connoisseurs with brews at prices reminiscent of those for fine wines. For years, microbreweries have been selling all the beer they can produce at $4 to $7 per bottle, but now makers of "luxury beers" are selling their brews at 6 to 12 times that! Boon Marriage Parfait Gueze goes for $21.50 per bottle, and a three-liter bottle of Duvel goes for $75 (and is fermented three times and sold in corked, oversized bottles like champagne). Although they account for a small part of the total beer market, these microbreweries' sales are growing rapidly in an otherwise flat market.[53]

Competition and Prices

When setting prices, business owners should take into account their competitors' prices, but they should *not* automatically match or beat them. Two factors are vital to studying the effects of competition on the small firm's pricing policies: the location of the competitors and the nature of the competing goods. In most cases, unless a company can differentiate the quality and the quantity of extras it provides, it must match the prices charged by nearby competitors for identical items. For example, if a self-service station charges a nickel more per gallon for gasoline than does another self-service station across the street, customers would simply go across the street to buy. Without the advantage of a unique business image—quality of goods sold, value of services provided, convenient location, favorable credit terms—a small company must match local competitors' prices or lose sales. Although the prices that distant competitors charge are not nearly as critical to the small business as are those of local competitors, it can be helpful to know them and to use them as reference points. Before matching any competitor's price change, however, the small business owner should consider the rival's motives. The competition may be establishing its price structure based on a unique set of criteria and a totally different strategy.

The nature of the competitors' goods also influences the small firm's pricing policies. The manager must recognize which products are substitutes for those he sells and then strive to keep prices in line with them. For example, the local sandwich shop should consider the hamburger restaurant, the taco shop, and the roast beef shop as competitors because they all serve fast foods. Although none of them offers the identical menu of the sandwich shop, they're all competing for the same quick meal dollar. Of course, if the small firm can differentiate its product by creating a distinctive image in the consumer's mind, it can afford its own line of prices.

Because competitors' prices can have a dramatic impact on a small company's own prices, entrepreneurs should make it a habit to monitor their rivals' prices, especially on identical items.

Generally, the small business manager should avoid head-to-head price competition with other firms that can more easily achieve lower prices through lower cost structures. Most locally owned drugstores cannot compete with the prices of large national drug chains. However, many local drugstores operate successfully by using nonprice competition; these stores offer more personal service, free delivery, credit sales, and other extras that the chains have eliminated. Nonprice competition can be an effective strategy for a small business in the face of larger, more powerful enterprises, especially because there are many dangers in experimenting with price changes. For instance, price shifts cause fluctuations in sales volume that the small firm may not be able to tolerate. Also, frequent price changes may damage the company's image and its customer relations.

One of the most deadly games a small business can get into with competitors is a price war. Price wars can eradicate companies' profit margins and scar an entire industry for years. "Many entrepreneurs cut prices to the point of unprofitability just to compete," says one business writer. "In doing so, they open the door to catastrophe. Less revenue often translates into lower quality, poorer service, sloppier salesmanship, weaker customer loyalty, and financial disaster."[54] Price wars usually begin when one competitor thinks it can achieve higher volume instantaneously by lowering prices. Rather than sticking to their strategic guns, competitors believe they must follow suit.

Entrepreneurs usually overestimate the power of price cuts, however. Sales volume rarely rises enough to offset the lower profit margins of a lower price. "If you have a 25 percent gross [profit] margin, and . . . you cut your price 10 percent, you have to roughly triple your sales volume just to break even," says one management consultant.[55] In a price war, a company may cut its prices so severely that it is impossible to achieve the volume necessary to offset the lower profit margins. Even when price cuts work, their effects often are temporary. Customers lured by the lowest price usually have almost no loyalty to a business. The lesson: The best way to survive a price war is to stay out of it by emphasizing the unique features, benefits, and value your company offers its customers!

The underlying forces which dictate how a business prices its goods or services vary greatly across industries. In many instances, the specific nature of the business itself has a variety of unique factors which determines a firm's pricing strategy. The next four sections will investigate pricing techniques employed in retailing, manufacturing, service firms, and wholesalers.

7-A. Explain the pricing methods and strategies for retailers.

Pricing Concepts for Retailers

As retail customers have become more price conscious, retailers have changed their pricing strategies to emphasize value. This value/price relationship allows for a wide variety of highly creative pricing and marketing practices. Delivering high levels of recognized value in products and services is one key to retail customer loyalty.

Markup

The basic premise of a successful business operation is selling a good or service for more than it costs to produce it. The difference between the cost of a product or service and its selling price is called **markup** (or **markon**). Markup can be expressed in dollars or as a percentage of either cost or selling price:

$$\text{Dollar markup} = \text{retail price} - \text{cost of the merchandise}$$

$$\text{Percentage (of retail price) markup} = \frac{\text{dollar markup}}{\text{retail price}}$$

$$\text{Percentage (of cost) markup} = \frac{\text{dollar markup}}{\text{cost of unit}}$$

For example, if a man's shirt costs $15, and the manager plans to sell it for $25, markup would be as follows:

$$\text{Dollar markup} = \$25 - \$15 = \$10$$

$$\text{Percentage (of retail price) markup} = \frac{\$10}{\$25}$$

$$= 0.40$$

$$= 40\%$$

$$\text{Percentage (of cost) markup} = \frac{\$10}{\$15}$$

$$= 0.6667$$

$$= 66.67\%$$

Notice that the cost of merchandise used in computing markup includes not only the wholesale price of the merchandise but also any incidental costs (e.g., selling or transportation charges) that the retailer incurs and a profit minus any discounts (quantity, cash) that the wholesaler offers.

Once a business owner has a financial plan, including sales estimates and anticipated expenses, she can compute the firm's initial markup. The initial markup is the *average* markup required on all merchandise to cover the cost of the items, all incidental expenses, and a reasonable profit:

$$\text{Initial dollar markup} = \frac{\text{operating expenses} + \text{reductions} + \text{profits}}{\text{net sales} + \text{reductions}}$$

where operating expenses are the cost of doing business, such as rent, utilities, and depreciation; and reductions include employee and customer discounts, markdowns, special sales, and the cost of stockouts.

For example, if a small retailer forecasts sales of $380,000, expenses of $140,000, and $24,000 in reductions, and she expects a profit of $38,000, the initial markup percentage will be:

$$\text{Initial markup percentage} = \frac{\$140,000 + \$24,000 + \$38,000}{\$380,000 + \$24,000}$$

$$= 50\%$$

This retailer thus knows that an average markup of 50 percent is required to cover costs and generate an adequate profit.

Some businesses employ a standard markup on all of their merchandise. This technique, which is usually used in retail stores carrying related products, applies a standard percentage markup to all merchandise. Most stores find it much more practical to use a flexible markup, which assigns various markup percentages to different types of products. Because of the wide range of prices and types of merchandise they sell, department stores frequently rely on a flexible markup. It would be impractical for them to use a standard markup on all items because they have such a divergent cost and volume range. For instance, the markup percentage for socks is not likely to be suitable as a markup for washing machines.

Once the owner determines the desired markup percentage, she can compute the appropriate retail price. Knowing that the markup of a particular item represents 40 percent of the retail price:

$$
\begin{aligned}
\text{Cost} \;&=\; \text{retail price} - \text{markup} \\
&=\; 100\% - 40\% \\
&=\; 60\% \text{ of retail price}
\end{aligned}
$$

and assuming that the cost of the item is $18.00, the retailer can rearrange the percentage (of retail price) markup formula:

$$
\text{Retail price} \;=\; \frac{\text{dollar cost}}{\text{percentage cost}}
$$

Solving for retail price, the retailer computes a price of the following:

$$
\text{Retail price} \;=\; \frac{\$18.00}{0.60} \;=\; \$30.00
$$

Thus, the owner establishes a retail price of $30.00 for the item using a 40 percent markup.

Finally, the retailer must verify that the computed retail price is consistent with the planned initial markup percentage. Will it cover costs and generate the desired profit? Is it congruent with the firm's overall price image? Is the final price in line with the company's strategy? Is it within an acceptable price range? How does it compare with the prices charged by competitors? And, perhaps most important, are the customers willing and able to pay this price?

FOLLOW-THE-LEADER PRICING. Some small companies make no effort to be price leaders in their immediate geographic areas and simply follow the prices that their competitors establish. Managers wisely monitor their competitors' pricing policies and individual prices by reviewing their advertisements or by hiring part-time or full-time comparison shoppers. But then these retailers use this information to establish a "me-too" pricing policy, which eradicates any opportunity to create a special price image for their businesses. Although many retailers must match competitors' prices on identical items, maintaining a follow-the-leader pricing policy may not be healthy for a small business because it robs the company of the opportunity to create a distinctive image in its customers' eyes.

BELOW-MARKET PRICING. Some small businesses choose to create a discount image in the market by offering goods at below-market prices. By setting prices below those of their competitors, these firms hope to attract a sufficient level of volume to offset the lower profit margins. Many retailers using a below-market pricing strategy eliminate most of the extra services that their above-market pricing competitors offer. For instance, these businesses trim operating costs by cutting out services like delivery, installation, credit granting, and sales assistance. Below-market pricing strategies can be risky for small companies because they require small firms to constantly achieve high sales volume to remain competitive.

Pricing Concepts for Manufacturers

7-B. Explain the pricing methods and strategies for manufacturers.

For manufacturers, the pricing decision requires the support of accurate, timely accounting records. The most commonly used pricing technique for manufacturers is cost-plus pricing. Using this method, the manufacturer establishes a price composed of direct materials, direct labor, factory overhead, selling and administrative costs, plus the desired profit margin. Figure 6.6 illustrates the cost-plus pricing components.

The main advantage of the cost-plus pricing method is its simplicity. Given the proper cost accounting data, computing a product's final selling price is relatively easy. Also, because it adds a profit onto the top of the firm's costs, the manufacturer is guaranteed the desired profit margin. This process, however, does not encourage the manufacturer to use its resources efficiently. Even if the company fails to employ its resources in the most effective manner, it will still earn a reasonable profit, and thus, there is no motivation to conserve resources in the manufacturing process. Finally, because manufacturers' cost structures vary so greatly, cost-plus pricing fails to consider the competition sufficiently. But despite its drawbacks, the cost-plus method of establishing prices remains prominent in many industries such as construction and printing.

Direct Costing and Price Formulation

One requisite for a successful pricing policy in manufacturing is a reliable cost accounting system that can generate timely reports to determine the costs of processing raw materials into finished goods. The traditional method of product costing is called **absorption costing** because all manufacturing and overhead costs are absorbed into the finished product's total cost. Absorption costing includes direct materials and direct labor, plus a portion of fixed and variable factory overhead costs in each unit manufactured. Full-absorption financial statements are used in published annual reports and in tax reports and are very useful in per-

absorption costing—*the traditional method of product costing, in which all manufacturing and overhead costs are absorbed into the product's total cost.*

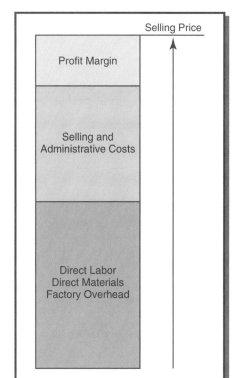

Figure 6.6
Cost-plus Pricing Components

forming financial analysis. But full-absorption statements are of little help to a manufacturer when determining prices or the impact of price changes.

variable (or direct) costing—*a method of product costing that includes only those costs that vary directly with the quantity produced in the product's total cost.*

A more useful technique for managerial decision making is **variable (or direct) costing**, in which the cost of the products manufactured includes only those costs that vary directly with the quantity produced. In other words, variable costing encompasses direct materials, direct labor, and factory overhead costs that vary with the level of the firm's output of finished goods. Those factory overhead costs that are fixed (for instance rent, depreciation, insurance) are *not* included in the costs of finished items. Instead, they are considered to be expenses of the period.

The manufacturer's goal in establishing prices is to discover the cost combination of selling price and sales volume that covers the variable costs of producing a product and contributes toward covering fixed costs and earning a profit. The problem with using full-absorption costing for this is that it clouds the true relationships among price, volume, and costs by including fixed expenses in unit cost. Using a direct-costing basis yields a constant unit cost for the product no matter what the volume of production is. The result is a clearer picture of the price–volume–costs relationship.

The starting point for establishing product prices is the direct-cost income statement. As Table 6.7 indicates, the direct-cost statement yields the same net profit as does the full-

Figure 6.7
A Full-Absorption Versus a Direct-Cost Income Statement

Full-Absorption Income Statement		
Revenues		$790,000
Cost of goods sold:		
Materials	250,500	
Direct labor	190,200	
Factory overhead	120,200	560,900
Gross Profit		229,100
Operating expenses:		
General and administrative	66,100	
Selling	112,000	
Other	11,000	
Total Expenses		189,100
Net Profit (before taxes)		$40,000
Direct-Cost Income Statement		
Revenues (100%)		$790,000
Variable costs:		
Materials	250,500	
Direct labor	190,200	
Variable factory overhead	13,200	
Variable selling expenses	48,100	
Total Variable Costs (63.54%)		502,000
Contribution Margin (36.46%)		288,000
Fixed Costs		
Fixed factory overhead	107,000	
Fixed selling expenses	63,900	
General and administrative	66,100	
Other	11,000	
Total Fixed Costs		248,000
Net Profit (before taxes)		$40,000

absorption income statement. The only difference between the two statements is the format. The full-absorption statement allocates costs such as advertising, rent, and utilities according to the activity that caused them, but the direct-cost income statement separates expenses into fixed and variable costs. Fixed expenses remain constant regardless of the production level, but variable expenses fluctuate according to production volume.

When variable costs are subtracted from total revenues, the result is the manufacturer's contribution margin—the amount remaining that contributes to covering fixed expenses and earning a profit. Expressing this contribution margin as a percentage of total revenue yields the firm's contribution percentage. Computing the contribution percentage is a critical step in establishing prices through the direct-costing method. This manufacturer's contribution percentage is 36.5 percent.

COMPUTING A BREAKEVEN SELLING PRICE. The manufacturer's contribution percentage tells what portion of total revenues remains after covering variable costs to contribute toward meeting fixed expenses and earning a profit. This manufacturer's contribution percentage is 36.5 percent, which means that variable costs absorb 63.5 percent of total revenues. In other words, variable costs should be 63.5 percent $(1.00 - 0.365 = 0.635)$ of the product's selling price. Suppose that this manufacturer's variable costs include the following:

Material	$2.08/unit
Direct labor	$4.12/unit
Variable factory overhead	$0.78/unit
Total variable cost	$6.98/unit

The minimum price at which the manufacturer would sell the item is $6.98. Any price below this would not cover variable costs. To compute the breakeven selling price for this product, find the selling price using the following equation:

$$\text{Profit} = \frac{\left(\begin{array}{c}\text{selling} \\ \text{price}\end{array} \times \begin{array}{c}\text{quantity} \\ \text{produced}\end{array}\right) + \left(\begin{array}{c}\text{variable cost} \\ \text{per unit}\end{array} \times \begin{array}{c}\text{quantity} \\ \text{produced}\end{array}\right) + \begin{array}{c}\text{total} \\ \text{fixed cost}\end{array}}{\text{quantity produced}}$$

which becomes:

$$\text{Breakeven selling price} = \frac{\text{profit} + \left(\begin{array}{c}\text{variable cost} \\ \text{per unit}\end{array} \times \begin{array}{c}\text{quantity} \\ \text{produced}\end{array}\right) + \begin{array}{c}\text{total} \\ \text{fixed cost}\end{array}}{\text{quantity produced}}$$

To break even, the manufacturer assumes $0 profit. Suppose that its plans are to produce 50,000 units of the product and that fixed costs will be $110,000. The breakeven selling price is as follows:

$$\text{Breakeven selling price} = \frac{\$0 + (\$6.98 \times 50{,}000 \text{ units}) + \$110{,}000}{50{,}000 \text{ units}}$$

$$= \frac{\$459{,}000}{50{,}000 \text{ units}}$$

$$= \$9.18/\text{unit}$$

Thus, $2.20 ($9.18/unit—$6.98/unit) of the $9.18 breakeven price contributes to meeting fixed production costs. But suppose the manufacturer wants to earn a $50,000 profit. Then the selling price is:

$$\text{Selling price} = \frac{\$50,000 + (\$6.98/\text{unit} \times 50,000 \text{ units}) + \$110,000}{50,000 \text{ units}}$$

$$= \frac{\$509,000}{50,000 \text{ units}}$$

$$= \$10.18/\text{unit}$$

Now the manufacturer must decide whether customers will purchase 50,000 units at $10.18. If not, it must decide either to produce a different, more profitable product or to lower the selling price. Any price above $9.18 will generate some profit, although less than that desired. In the short run, the manufacturer could sell the product for less than $9.18 if competitive factors so dictated, but not below $6.98 because this would not cover the variable costs of production.

Because the manufacturer's capacity in the short run is fixed, pricing decisions should be aimed at employing these resources most efficiently. The fixed costs of operating the plant cannot be avoided, and the variable costs can be eliminated only if the firm ceases to offer the product. Therefore, the selling price must be at least equal to the variable costs (per unit) of making the product. Any price above this amount contributes to covering fixed costs and providing a reasonable profit.

Of course, over the long run, the manufacturer cannot sell below total costs and continue to survive. So, selling price must cover total product cost—both fixed and variable—and generate a reasonable profit.

7-C. Explain the pricing methods and strategies for service firms.

Pricing Concepts for Service Firms

A service firm must establish a price based on the materials used to provide the service, the labor employed, an allowance for overhead, and a profit. As in the manufacturing operation, a service firm must have a reliable, accurate accounting system to keep a tally of the total costs of providing the service. Most service firms base their prices on an hourly rate, usually the actual number of hours required to perform the service. Some companies, however, base their fees on a standard number of hours, determined by the average number of hours needed to perform the service. For most firms, labor and materials comprise the largest portion of the cost of the service. To establish a reasonable, profitable price for service, the small business owner must know the cost of materials, direct labor, and overhead for each unit of service. Using these basic cost data and a desired profit margin, the owner of the small service firm can determine the appropriate price for the service.

Consider a simple example for pricing a common service—television repair. Ned's T.V. Repair Shop uses the direct-costing method to prepare an income statement for exercising managerial control (see Table 6.8). Ned estimates that he and his employees spent about 12,800 hours in the actual production of television service. So total cost per productive hour for Ned's T.V. Repair Shop comes to the following:

$$\frac{\$172,000}{12,800 \text{ hours}} = \$13.44/\text{hour}$$

Now Ned must add in an amount for his desired profit. He expects a net operating profit of 18 percent on sales. To compute the final price he uses this equation:

$$\text{Price per hour} = \text{total cost per productive hour} \times \frac{1.00}{(1.00 - \text{net profit target as \% of sales})}$$

$$= 13.44 \times 1.219$$

$$= \$16.38/\text{hour}$$

A price of $16.38 per hour will cover Ned's costs and generate the desired profit. The wise service shopowner computes the cost per production hour at regular intervals throughout the year. Rapidly rising labor costs and material prices dictate that the service firm's price per hour be computed even more frequently. As in the case of the retailer and the manufacturer, Ned must evaluate the pricing policies of competitors, and decide whether his price is consistent with his firm's image.

Of course, the price of $16.38 per hour assumes that each job requires the same amount of materials. If this is not a valid assumption, Ned must recompute the price per hour without including the cost of materials.

$$\text{Cost per productive hour} = \frac{\$172,000 - 40,500}{12,800 \text{ hours}}$$

$$= \$10.27/\text{hour}$$

Adding in the desired 18 percent net operating profit on sales:

$$\text{Price per hour} = \$10.27/\text{hour} \times \frac{1.00}{(1.00 - 0.18)}$$

$$= \$10.27/\text{hour} \times 1.219$$

$$= \$12.52/\text{hour}$$

Under these conditions Ned would charge $12.52 per hour plus the actual cost of materials used and any markup on the cost of materials. A repair job that takes four hours to complete would have the following price:

Cost of service (4 hours x 12.52/hour)	$50.08
Cost of materials	$21.00
Markup on material (10%)	$ 2.10
Total price	$73.18

Sales Revenue		$199,000
Variable Expenses:		
Labor	52,000	
Materials	40,500	
Variable factor overhead	11,500	
Total	104,000	
Fixed Expenses:		
Rent	2,500	
Salaries	38,500	
Fixed overhead	27,000	
Total	68,000	
Total Costs		172,000
Net Income		$27,000

Table 6.8
Direct-Cost Income Statement, Ned's T.V. Repair Shop

Pricing Web Services

Kerry Pinella, a recent business graduate of a small private college, started her career working for a large multinational computer software maker as a sales representative. After two years in sales, Kerry applied for a position on a development team that was working on software applications for the World Wide Web. Kerry thrived in the team atmosphere and learned the technical aspects of the new assignment very quickly. Not only did her team bring their project in on budget, but it also completed it slightly ahead of schedule. Team members give much of the credit for the project's success to Kerry's unofficial role as team leader. Her work ethic and relentless pursuit of quality inspired other team members.

After Kerry's team completed its project, however, Kerry had a hard time recapturing the thrill and excitement of developing the World Wide Web software. Subsequent projects simply could not measure up to the "magic" of that first assignment. After talking with several of the members of that software team, Kerry discovered that they felt the same way. Before long, Kerry and two of her former team members left the company to launch their own computer consulting company, Web Consultants. Having worked on the forefront of the Web's commercialization, Kerry and her partners saw the potential it had for revolutionizing business. Their company would specialize in developing, designing, and maintaining Web sites for clients. In their first year of business, Web Consultants accepted jobs from virtually anybody who wanted a Web site. Although they experienced some "growing pains," Web Consultants quickly earned a reputation for producing quality work on time and was more selective in the jobs it bid on.

Halfway into their second year of operation, the partners planned a weekend retreat at a nearby resort so they could get away, review their progress, and plan for the future. As they reviewed their latest financial statements, one of the questions that kept popping up dealt with pricing. Were Web Consultants' pricing policies appropriate? Its sales were growing twice as fast as the industry average, and the company's bid-winning ratio was well above that of practically all of its competitors. For the current year, sales were up, but Web Consultants' net profits were virtually the same as they had been in their first year.

Pulling the records from a computer database for each job they had completed since founding the company, the partners and their employees had spent 22,450 hours developing projects for their clients at a total cost of $951,207. "We were shooting for a net profit of 25 percent on sales," Kerry reminded her partners, "but so far, our net profit margin is just 7.7 percent, only one-third of our target."

"Maybe we could increase our profits if we increased our sales," offered one partner.

"We could," Kerry said, "but our margins wouldn't get any better. I think we need to re-evaluate our prices. One of our clients told me how pleased her company was to get such great work at such a great price. He mentioned that the other companies they talked to submitted higher bids—some *much* higher than ours!"

The partners began to wonder if their price of $45 per hour was appropriate. Admittedly, they had been so busy completing projects for clients that they had not kept up with what their competitors were charging. Nor had they been as diligent in analyzing their financial statements as they should have been.

As Kerry closed the cover on her laptop computer, she looked at her partners and asked, "What should Web Consultants' hourly price be?"

1. Help Kerry answer the question she has posed.
2. What factors should Kerry and her partners consider when determining Web Consultants' final price?
3. Is the company's current price too low? If so, what signals could have alerted Kerry and her partners?

---

8. *Describe* the impact of credit on pricing.

The Impact of Credit on Pricing

Credit Cards

Credit cards have become a popular method of payment among customers. Approximately 70 percent of the adult U.S. population uses credit cards to make purchases.[56] The number of credit cards in circulation in the United States exceeds 1 billion, an average of about four cards per person! Customers use credit cards to pay for $28 out of every $100 spent on consumable goods and services.[57] One recent study found that accepting credit cards increases the probability, speed, and magnitude of customer spending. In addition, surveys show that customers rate businesses offering credit options higher on key performance measures such as reputation, reliability, and service.[58] In short, accepting credit cards broadens a small company's customer base and closes sales it would normally lose if customers had to pay in cash.

The convenience of credit cards is not free to business owners, however. Companies must pay to use the system, typically 1 to 6 percent of the total credit card charges, which they must factor into the prices of their products or services. They also pay a transaction fee of 5 to 25 cents per charge. Given customer expectations, small businesses cannot drop major cards, even when the big card companies raise the fees that merchants must pay. Fees operate on a multistep process. On a $100 Visa or MasterCard purchase, a processing bank buys the credit card slip from the retailer for $97.44. Then, that bank sells the slip to the bank that issued the card for about $98.80. The remaining $1.20 discount is called the interchange fee, which is what the processing bank passes along to the issuing bank.

More small businesses also are equipping their stores to handle debit card transactions, which act as electronic checks, automatically deducting the purchase amount from a customer's checking account. The equipment is easy to install and to set up, and the cost to the company is negligible. The payoff can be big, however, in the form of increased sales. "How can you possibly lose when you're offering customers another avenue for purchasing merchandise?" says Mark Knauff, who recently installed a debitcard terminal in his guitar shop.[59]

Installment Credit

Small companies that sell big-ticket consumer durables—major appliances, cars, and boats—frequently rely on installment credit. Because very few customers can purchase such items in a single lump-sum payment, small businesses finance them over an extended time. The time horizon may range from just a few months up to 30 or more years. Most companies require the customer to make an initial down payment for the merchandise and then finance the balance for the life of the loan. The customer repays the loan principal plus interest on the loan. One advantage of installment loans for a small business is that the owner retains a security interest as collateral on the loan. If the customer defaults on the loan, the owner still holds the title to the merchandise. Because installment credit absorbs a small company's cash, many rely on financial institutions such as banks and credit unions to provide installment credit. When a firm has the financial strength to "carry their own paper," the interest income from the installment loan contract often yields more than the initial profit on the sale of the product. For some businesses, such as furniture stores, this has traditionally been a major source of income.

Trade Credit

Companies that sell small-ticket items frequently offer their customers trade credit, that is, they create customer charge accounts. The typical small business bills its credit customers each month. To speed collections, some offer cash discounts if customers pay their balances early; others impose penalties on late payers. Before deciding to use trade credit as a competitive weapon, the small business owner must make sure that the firm's cash position is strong enough to support the additional pressure.

CHAPTER SUMMARY

1. Explain the differences among promotion, publicity, personal selling, and advertising.
- Promotion is any form of persuasive communication designed to inform consumers about a product or service and to influence them to purchase these goods or services.
- Publicity is any commercial news covered by the media that boosts sales but for which the small business does not pay.

- Personal selling is the personal contact between salespeople and potential customers resulting from sales efforts.
- Advertising is any sales presentation that is nonpersonal in nature and is paid for by an identified sponsor.

2. Describe the advantages and disadvantages of the various advertising media.
- The medium used to transmit an advertising message influences the consumer's perception—and reception—of it.

- Media options include newspapers, radio, television, magazines, direct mail, the World Wide Web, outdoor advertising, transit advertising, directories, trade shows, special events and promotions, and point-of-purchase ads.
3. Present the steps in developing an advertising plan.
   - The first step is to define the purpose of the company's advertising program by creating specific, measurable objectives.
   - The next step is to analyze the firm and its target audience.
   - The next step involves deciding what to say and how to say it, making sure to build the message around the company's unique selling proposition (USP).
   - The final step involves evaluating the ad campaign's effectiveness.
4. Identify four basic methods for preparing an advertising budget.
   - Establishing an advertising budget presents a real challenge to the small business owner. There are four basic methods: what is affordable; matching competitors; percentage of sales; objective and task.
5. Explain practical methods for stretching the small business owner's advertising budget.
   - Despite their limited advertising budgets, small businesses do not have to take a second-class approach to advertising. Three techniques that can stretch small companies' advertising dollars are cooperative advertising, shared advertising, and publicity.
6. Describe effective pricing techniques for introducing new goods or services and for existing ones.
   - Pricing a new product is often difficult for the small business manager, but it should accomplish three objectives: getting the product accepted; maintaining market share as the competition grows; and earning a profit. Generally, there are three major pricing strategies used to introduce new products into the market: penetration, skimming, and sliding down the demand curve.
   - Pricing techniques for existing products and services include odd pricing, price lining, leader pricing, geographical pricing, opportunistic pricing, discounts, and suggested retail pricing.
7. Explain the pricing methods and strategies for retailers, manufacturers, andservice firms.
   - Pricing for the retailer means pricing to move merchandise. Markup is the difference between the cost of a product or service and its selling price. Most retailers compute their markup as a percentage of retail price, but some retailers put a standard markup on all their merchandise; more frequently, they use a flexible markup.
   - A manufacturer's pricing decision depends on the support of accurate cost accounting records. The most common technique is cost-plus pricing, in which the manufacturer charges a price that covers the cost of producing a product plus a reasonable profit. Every manufacturer should calculate a product's breakeven price, the price which produces neither a profit nor a loss.
   - Service firms often suffer from the effects of vague, unfounded pricing procedures, and frequently charge the going rate without any idea of their costs. A service firm must set a price based on the cost of materials used, labor involved, overhead, and a profit. The proper price reflects the total cost of providing a unit of service.
8. Describe the impact of credit on pricing.
   - Offering consumer credit enhances a small company's reputation and increases the probability, speed, and magnitude of customers' purchases. Small firms offer three types of consumer credit: credit cards, installment credit, and trade credit (charge accounts).

DISCUSSION QUESTIONS

1. What are the four elements of promotion? How do they support one another?
2. What factors should a small business manager consider when selecting advertising media?
3. Create a table to summarize the advantages and disadvantages of the following advertising media:

Newspapers	Direct mail
Radio	Outdoor advertising
Television	Transit advertising
Magazines	Directories
Specialty advertising	Trade shows

4. What are fixed spots, preemptible spots, and floating spots in radio advertising?
5. Describe the characteristics of an effective outdoor advertisement.
6. Briefly outline the steps in creating an advertising plan. What principles should the small business owner follow when creating an effective advertisement?
7. Describe the common methods of establishing an advertising budget. Which method is most often used? Which technique is most often recommended? Why?
8. How does pricing affect a small firm's image?
9. What competitive factors must the small firm consider when establishing prices?
10. Describe the strategies a small business could use in setting the price of a new product. What objectives should the strategy seek to achieve?
11. Define the following pricing techniques: odd pricing; price lining; leader pricing; geographical pricing; and discounts.
12. Why do many small businesses use the manufacturer's suggested retail price? What are the disadvantages of this technique?
13. What is a markup? How is it used to determine individual price?
14. What is a standard markup? A flexible markup?

15. What is cost-plus pricing? Why do so many manufacturers use it? What are the disadvantages of using it?

16. Explain the difference between full-absorption costing and direct costing. How does absorption costing help a manufacturer to determine a reasonable price?

17. Explain the techniques for a small service firm setting an hourly price.

18. What benefits does a small business get by offering customers credit? What costs does it incur?

Beyond the Classroom...

1. Contact a small retailer, manufacturer, and a service firm and interview each one about its advertising program.
   a. Are there specific advertising objectives?
   b. What media does the owner employ? Why?
   c. How does the manager evaluate an ad's effectiveness?
   d. What assistance does the manager receive in designing ads?

2. Contact several small business owners and determine how they establish their advertising budgets. Why do they use the method they do?

3. Collect two or three advertisements for local small businesses and evaluate them on a scale of 1 (low) to 10 (high) using the following criteria: attention getting, distinctive, interesting, brevity, personal appeal, credibility, USP focused, convincing, motivating, and effectiveness. How would you change the ads to make them more effective?

4. Browse through a magazine and find two ads that use sex to sell a good or service—one that you consider effective and one that you consider offensive. Compare your ads and reasoning with those of your classmates. What implications does your discussion have for advertisers?

5. Interview a successful small retailer and ask the following questions: Does it seek a specific image through its prices? What type of outlet would you consider the retailer to be? What role do its competitors play in the business owner's pricing? Does it use specific pricing techniques such as odd pricing, price lining, leader pricing, and geographical pricing? How are discounts calculated? What markup percentage does the firm use? How are prices derived? What are its cost structures?

6. Select an industry that has several competing small firms in your area. Contact these firms and compare their approaches to determining prices. Do prices on identical or similar items differ? Why?

SURFING THE NET

1. Access the Web site for *Advertising Age* at the following address:

http://www.adage.com/

As you explore this site, select one of the features that interests you (e.g., "The History of TV Advertising," "Advertising Age's 50 Best Commercials," or some of the articles about current advertising trends and issues). Prepare a short report on it.

2. Access the Web site for the Internet Ad Emporium, an electronic shopping mall with a multitude of virtual "storefronts" at:

http://mmink.cts.com/

Visit some of the stores in the mall and evaluate their advertisements on the Web. How well do they meet the criteria for successful ads described in this chapter? Which ones are most effective? Least effective? Why? What suggestions can you make for improving them?

3. Using one of the search engines on the World Wide Web (such as Lycos, Magellan, Yahoo!, and others), locate the on-line catalog of a company with which you are familiar. What advantages does an on-line catalog offer over a printed one? Disadvantages? Are you willing to send your credit card information over the World Wide Web? Are your classmates? What implications do your answers have for on-line merchants?

Managing Cash Flow

*Business is taking a pile of cash, doing something with it,
and ending up with a bigger pile of cash.*
- Leonard P. Shaykin

*Normalcy is when you run out of money; insolvency is when you run out of excuses;
bankruptcy is when you run out of town.*
- Current Comedy

A deficit is what you have when you haven't got as much as when you had nothing.
- Gerald F. Lieberman

LEARNING OBJECTIVES

Upon completion of this chapter, you will be able to:

1. **Explain** the importance of cash management to a small business's success.

2. **Differentiate** between cash and profits.

3. **Understand** the five steps in creating a cash budget and use them to create a cash budget.

4. **Describe** fundamental principles involved in managing the "Big Three" of cash management: accounts receivable, accounts payable, and inventory.

5. **Explain** the techniques for avoiding a cash crunch in a small company.

Cash is a four-letter word that has become a curse for many small businesses. Lack of this valuable asset has driven countless small companies into bankruptcy. Unfortunately, many more firms will become failure statistics because their owners have neglected the principles of cash management that can spell the difference between success and failure. One small business owner whose company barely survived a cash crisis explains simply, "Cash flow is everything, period."[1] Indeed, developing a cash forecast is essential for new businesses because early profit levels usually do not generate sufficient cash to keep the company afloat. A common cause of business failures is that owners neglect to forecast how much cash their companies will need until they reach the point of generating positive cash flow.

Controlling the financial aspects of a business using the traditional analysis of basic financial statements with ratios (the topic of Chapter 8) is immensely important; however, by themselves, these techniques are insufficient to achieve business success. Entrepreneurs are prone to focus on their companies' income statements—particularly sales and profits. The income statement, of course, shows only part of a company's financial picture. It is entirely possible for a business to earn a profit and still go out of business *by running out of cash*. Managing a company's financial performance effectively requires an entrepreneur to look beyond the "bottom line" and focus on what it takes to keep a company going—cash.

"This [monitoring your cash flow statement] is more important than watching your income statement or balance sheet," says Scott Trenner, owner of S.T. Lube, a company which operates six Jiffy Lube franchises. Trenner knows firsthand the importance of positive cash flow. His company ran into serious cash flow problems as he focused on rapid growth. "I was building a multimillion-dollar empire," he recalls, "but my revenues never caught up with my expenses." Cash was so tight that Trenner had trouble meeting the payroll for his company's 65 employees. "I once had to get a two-week, $30,000 loan from my father when we were struggling," he recalls. The turning point came when Trenner created a statement to track and analyze his company's cash flow. "We stopped focusing only on expansion and started paying attention to day-to-day management," he says. "By keeping a close eye on our cash flow statement, we went from a negative cash flow to a positive cash flow of $1,000 a week and turned around a $140,000 deficit in three years."[2]

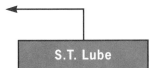

S.T. Lube

Cash Management

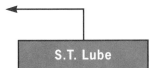

1. Explain the importance of cash management to a small business's success.

Cash is the most important yet least productive asset that a small business owns. The business must have enough cash to meet its obligations or it will be declared bankrupt. Creditors, employees, and lenders expect to be paid on time, and cash is the required medium of exchange. But some firms retain an excessive amount of cash to meet any unexpected circumstances that might arise. These dormant dollars have an income-earning potential that the owners are ignoring, and this restricts the firm's growth and lowers its profitability. Proper cash management permits the owner to adequately meet the cash demands of the business, to avoid retaining unnecessarily large cash balances, and to stretch the profit-generating power of each dollar the business owns.

Young companies, especially, are "cash sponges," soaking up every available dollar and always hungry for more. One recent Dun & Bradstreet survey found that 33 percent of small business owners say they have problems managing their cash flow as they build their businesses.[3] Managing cash flow is also an acute problem for rapidly growing businesses. In fact, fast-track companies are most likely to suffer cash shortages. Many successful, growing, and profitable businesses fail because they become insolvent; they do not have adequate cash to meet the needs of a growing business with a booming sales volume. If a company's sales are up, the owner also must hire more employees, expand plant capacity, increase the sales force, build inventory, and incur other drains on the firm's cash supply. During rapid growth, cash collections often fall behind, compounding the problem. The head of the National Federation of Independent Businesses says that many small business owners "wake up one day to find that the price of success is no cash on hand. They don't understand that if they're successful, inventory and receivables will increase faster than profits can fund them."[4] The resulting cash crisis may force the owner to lose equity control of the business or, ultimately, declare bankruptcy and close.

Table 7.1 describes the five key cash management roles every entrepreneur must fill.

The first step in managing cash more effectively is to understand the company's cash flow cycle—the time lag between paying suppliers for merchandise and receiving payment from customers (see Figure 7.1). The longer this cash flow cycle is, the more likely the business owner is to encounter a cash crisis. Preparing a cash forecast that recognizes this cycle, however, will help to avoid a crisis. "To develop a cash management strategy," says one small business owner, "you must understand [the] cash flow patterns [of your business]."[5]

The next step in effective cash management is to begin cutting down the length of the cash flow cycle. Reducing the cycle from 240 days to, say, 150 days would free up incredible amounts of cash that the company could use to finance growth and dramatically reduce its borrowing costs. What steps would you suggest the owner of the business whose cash flow cycle is illustrated in Figure 7.1 take to reduce its length?

Cash and Profits Are Not the Same

2. Differentiate between cash and profits.

In analyzing cash flow, a small business manager must understand that cash and profits are not the same. "Profit is not cash flow, and cash flow is not profit," says one entrepreneur. "Anyone who tries to glean something about one from looking at the other may be easily misled."[6] Profit (or net income) is the difference between a company's total revenue and its total expenses. It measures how efficiently the business is operating. Cash flow measures a company's liquidity, its ability to pay its bills and other financial obligations on time. Many

Table 7.1
Five Cash Management Roles of the Entrepreneur

Source: Adapted from Bruce J. Blechman, "Quick Change Artist," Entrepreneur, January 1994, pp. 18-21.

Role 1: Cash Finder. This is the entrepreneur's first and foremost responsibility. You must make sure there is enough capital to pay all present (and future) bills. This is not a one-time task; it is an ongoing job.

Role 2: Cash Planner. As cash planner, an entrepreneur makes sure the company's cash is used properly and efficiently. You must keep track of your cash, make sure it is available to pay bills, and plan for its future use. Planning requires you to forecast the company's cash inflows and outflows for the months ahead with the help of a cash budget (discussed later in this chapter).

Role 3: Cash Distributor. This role requires you to control the cash needed to pay the company's bills and the priority and the timing of those payments. Forecasting cash disbursements accurately and making sure the cash is available when payments come due are essential to keeping the business solvent.

Role 4: Cash Collector. As cash collector, your job is to make sure your customers pay *their* bills on time. Too often, entrepreneurs focus on pumping up sales, while neglecting to collect the cash from those sales. Having someone in your company responsible for collecting accounts receivable is essential. Uncollected accounts drain a small company's pool of cash very quickly.

Role 5: Cash Conserver. This role requires you to make sure your company gets maximum value for the dollars it spends. Whether you are buying inventory to resell or computers to keep track of what you sell, it is important to get the most for your money. Avoiding unnecessary expenditures is an important part of this task. The goal is to spend cash so it will produce a return for the company.

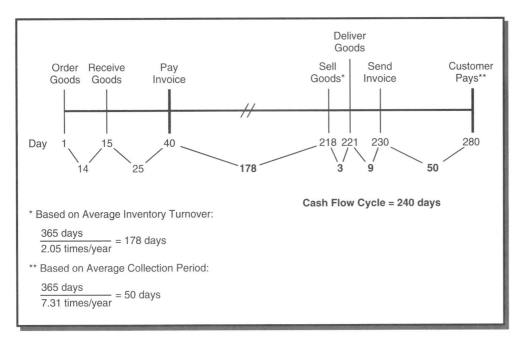

Figure 7.1
The Cash Flow Cycle

small business owners soon discover that profitability does not guarantee liquidity. As important as earning a profit is, no business owner can pay creditors, employees, the government, and lenders in profits; that requires *cash*! Although profits are tied up in many forms, such as inventory, computers, or machinery, cash is the money that flows through a business in a continuous cycle without being tied up in any other asset. "Businesses fail not because they are making or losing money," warns one financial expert, "but because they simply run out of cash."[7]

Figure 7.2 shows the flow of cash through a typical small business. Cash flow is the volume of actual cash that comes into and goes out of the business during an accounting peri-

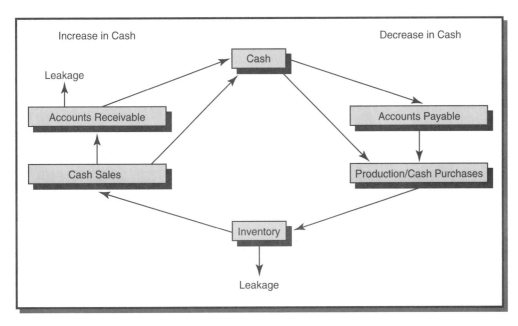

Figure 7.2
Cash Flow

od. Decreases in cash occur when the business purchases, on credit or with cash, goods for inventory or materials for use in production. The resulting inventory is sold either for cash or on credit. When cash is taken in or when accounts receivable are collected, the firm's cash balance increases. Notice that purchases for inventory and production lead sales; that is, these bills typically must be paid before sales are generated. However, collection of accounts receivable lags behind sales; that is customers who purchase goods on credit may not pay until next month.

YOU BE THE CONSULTANT...

The Price of Success

Rochelle Zabarkes is a classic entrepreneur. Before she opened her specialty food store in Manhattan in 1991, she put together a detailed business plan, lined up financing, and rented space on one of New York's busiest streets. With its universal mix of gourmet foods and spices from around the world, ethnic takeout food, and exotic gift items, Adriana's Bazaar was an instant hit with customers. *The New Yorker* magazine featured the store in an article, and *Gourmet* magazine frequently mentions it as a source of ingredients for its recipes. Daily sales revenues average $1,100, up 40 percent from the previous year. A newly installed coffee bar is drawing new customers, and Zabarkes has even started a mail-order business. She plans to open two more stores in New York City before going national. "My dream is to be as big as Body Shop," a fast-growing chain of shops selling skin- and hair-care items, says the entrepreneur.

What more could Zabarkes ask for?

C-A-S-H!!!

Despite her company's success, its rapid growth has devoured all of her startup capital and then some. When she launched Adriana's Bazaar, Zabarkes raised $245,000 through loans from a local bank and the National Association of Female Executives and in contributions from friends. She has since raised another $40,000 to keep the business going. Unfortunately, the rapid growth of the company pushed cash requirements closer to $350,000.

Failing to forecast cash requirements accurately during the volatile startup period almost cost Zabarkes her business. She defaulted on a $145,000 bank loan, which the Small Business Administration has taken over. She had to give up her 4,300 square foot loft apartment because she couldn't keep up the mortgage payments. Her desk is in a perpetual state of overflow—mostly past-due bills from suppliers and other creditors. The owner of the building housing her business is threatening eviction unless she comes up with the back rent—totaling nearly $20,000—pronto! Recently, she sent a check for $8,500 to a creditor by bicycle messenger to meet a court-ordered deadline.

At one point, Zabarkes was so desperate for cash that she used the proceeds of a check a state agency had made out to her for work a consultant did for her. Although the agency was furious at her for snagging the money, the consultant for whom the check was intended was not. "I don't hold it against her," he says. "I admire her for being aggressive." Ms. Zabarkes promises she will repay the money, but she claims she had no choice.

So far, her efforts to rescue her store from the cash crisis have been successful. Zabarkes has mollified most of her creditors with repeated phone calls and letters explaining her situation, asking for their patience, and promising eventual payment. She also has convinced the Small Business Administration into being flexible about her loan repayment schedule. "I called the SBA and asked: 'What is the worst that could happen?'" she recalls. The SBA official "said he could get a court order, auction off my assets, and close me down. I said, 'Are you crazy? I owe you $145,000, and you wouldn't get $2,500 in an auction.'" Zabarkes even threw a Depression-era "rent party" at her store to raise cash. "I'm absolutely dedicated to this store," she admits. "I'll do anything—beg, borrow, or steal—to keep it alive." And, she adds, "I will save it."

1. What factors caused the cash crises affecting Adriana's Bazaar?

2. Evaluate the manner in which Ms. Zabarkes has handled the cash crisis in her business.

3. What ethical dilemmas does Ms. Zabarkes face as a result of her company's cash crisis? How should she handle them?

4. What recommendations can you make to Ms. Zabarkes to avoid future cash flow problems?

Source: Adapted from Brent Bowers, "This Store Is a Hit But Somehow Cash Flow Is Missing," *Wall Street Journal,* April 13, 1993, p. B2.

The Cash Budget

Every small business manager should track the flow of cash through her business so she can project the cash balance available throughout the year. Many managers operate their businesses without knowing the pattern of their cash flows, believing that the process is too complex or time consuming. In reality, the small business manager simply cannot afford to disregard the process of cash management. The owner must ensure that an adequate, but not excessive, supply of cash is on hand to meet operating needs. "The aim of prudent cash-flow management," says one business writer, "is to make sure there'll be enough cash in the till to meet given demands for that cash at any given time."[8]

How much cash is enough? What is suitable for one business may be totally inadequate for another, depending on each firm's size, nature, and particular situation. The small business manager should prepare a **cash budget**, which is nothing more than a "cash map," showing the amount and timing of the cash receipts and the cash disbursements day by day, week by week, or month by month. It is used to predict the amount of cash the firm will need to operate smoothly over a specific period of time, and it is a valuable tool in managing a company successfully.

One consultant recalls how a cash budget helped salvage a once-successful service firm that had fallen on hard times. The five-year-old firm with $20 million in annual billings began to lose money and was having trouble paying its bills. After working with the consultant, the company began sending customer invoices much more promptly and implemented a much stricter collection policy. The new collection system involved employees in collecting overdue payments who took immediate action when an account became overdue. Managers set up a receivables report and reviewed it at weekly staff meetings. They also beefed up the company's financial reports, added a cash budget, and used it to make managerial decisions. Within six months, the company's cash balance had improved dramatically (a turnaround of $1.5 million), managers were able to pay down a line of credit at the bank, and the business was back on track again!

cash budget—*a "cash map," showing the amount and timing of cash receipts and cash disbursements on a daily, weekly, or monthly basis.*

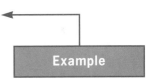

Example

Preparing a Cash Budget

Typically, a small business owner should prepare a projected monthly cash budget for at least one year into the future and a quarterly estimate several years in advance. It must cover all seasonal sales fluctuations. The more variable a firm's sales pattern, the shorter its planning horizon should be. For example, a firm whose sales fluctuate widely over a relatively short time frame might require a weekly cash budget. The key is to track cash flows over time. The timing of a company's cash flow is as important as the amounts. "An alert cash flow manager keeps an eye not on cash receipts or on cash demands as average quantities but on cash as a function of the *calendar*," says one business owner.[9]

Regardless of the time frame selected, the cash budget must be in writing for the small business manager to properly visualize the firm's cash position. Creating a written cash plan is not an excessively time-consuming task and can help the owner avoid unexpected cash shortages, a situation that can cause a business to fail. One financial consultant describes "a client who won't be able to make the payroll this month. His bank agreed to meet the payroll for him—but banks don't like to be surprised like that," he adds.[10] Preparing a cash budget will help business owners avoid such adverse surprises. It will also let owners know if they are keeping excessively large amounts of cash on hand.

The cash budget is based on the cash method of accounting, which means that cash receipts and cash disbursements are recorded in the forecast only when the cash transaction is expected to take place. For example, credit sales to customers are not reported until the company

3. Understand the five steps in creating a cash budget and use them to create a cash budget.

expects to receive the cash from them. Similarly, purchases made on credit are not recorded until the owner expects to pay them. Because depreciation, bad debt expense, and other non-cash items involve no cash transfers, they are omitted entirely from the cash budget.

The cash budget is nothing more than a forecast of the firm's cash inflows and outflows for a specific time period, and it will never be completely accurate. But it does give the small business manager a clear picture of the firm's estimated cash balance for the period, pointing out where external cash infusions may be required or where surplus cash balances may be available for investment. Also, by comparing actual cash flows with projections, the owner can revise his forecast so that future cash budgets will be more accurate.

Joseph Popper, CEO of Computer Gallery, knows how deadly running out of cash can be for a small company and does everything he can to make sure his business avoids that trap. Popper uses a computer spreadsheet to extract key sales, collection, and disbursement totals and to generate the resulting cash balance each day. Even when he is traveling, Popper keeps up with his company's daily cash balance. He has the spreadsheet results sent to an Internet service, which e-mails them to his alphanumeric pager every day he is out of the office. "We've been paranoid about cash from day one," Popper says. But his system keeps accounts receivable in control, ensures that the company's available cash is working hard, and improves his relationship with the company's banker.[11]

Formats for preparing a cash budget vary depending on the pattern of a company's cash flow. Table 7.2 shows a monthly cash budget for a small department store over a four-month period. Each monthly column should be divided into two sections—estimated and actual (not shown)—so that each succeeding cash forecast can be updated according to actual cash transactions. There are five basic steps in completing a cash budget:

1. Determining an adequate minimum cash balance.
2. Forecasting sales.
3. Forecasting cash receipts.
4. Forecasting cash disbursements.
5. Determining the end-of-month cash balance.

Step 1: Determining an Adequate Minimum Cash Balance

What is considered to be an excessive cash balance for one small business may be inadequate for another, even though the two firms are in the same trade. Some suggest that a firm's cash balance should equal at least one-fourth of its current debts, but this general rule clearly will not work for all small businesses. The most reliable method of determining an adequate cash balance is based on past experience. Past operating records should indicate the proper cash cushion needed to cover any unexpected expenses after all normal cash outlays are deducted from the month's cash receipts. For example, past records may indicate that it is desirable to maintain a cash balance equal to five days' sales. Seasonal fluctuations may cause the firm's minimum cash balance to change. For example, the desired cash balance for a retailer in December may be greater than in June.

Step 2: Forecasting Sales

The heart of the cash budget is the sales forecast. It is the central factor in creating an accurate picture of the firm's cash position because sales ultimately are transformed into cash receipts and cash disbursements. For most businesses, sales constitute the major source of the cash flowing into the business. Similarly, sales of merchandise require that cash be used to replenish inventory. As a result, the cash budget is only as accurate as the sales forecast from which it is derived.

For the established business, the sales forecast can be based on past sales, but the owner must be careful not to be excessively optimistic in projecting sales. Economic swings, increased competition, fluctuations in demand, and other factors can drastically alter sales patterns.

Several quantitative techniques, which are beyond the scope of this text (linear regression, multiple regression, time series analysis, exponential smoothing), are available to the owner of an existing business with an established sales pattern for forecasting sales. These methods enable the small business owner to extrapolate past and present sales trends to arrive at a fairly accurate sales forecast.

Table 7.2
Cash Budget For Small Department Store

Assumptions:

Cash balance on December 31 = $12,000.

Minimum cash balance desired = $10,000.

Sales are 75% credit and 25% cash.

Credit sales are collected in the following manner:
- ☆ 60% collected in the first month after the sale.
- ☆ 30% in the second month after the sale.
- ☆ 5% collected in the third month after the sale.
- ☆ 5% never collected.

Sales forecasts are as follows:	Most likely	Pessimistic	Optimistic
October (actual)	$300,000		
November (actual)	350,000		
December (actual)	400,000		
January	150,000	$120,000	$175,000
February	200,000	160,000	250,000
March	200,000	160,000	250,000
April	300,000	250,000	340,000
May	250,000	190,000	310,000

The store pays 70% of sales price for merchandies purchased, and pays for each month's anticipated sales in the preceding month.

Rent is $2,000 per month

An interest payment of $7,500 is due in March.

A tax prepayment of $50,000 must be made in March.

A capital addition payment of $130,000 is due in February.

Uilities expenses amount to $850 per month.

Miscellaneous expenses are $70 per month.

Interest income of $200 will be received in February.

Wages and salaries are estimated to be
January—$30,000
February—$40,000
March—$45,000
April—$50,000

Continued

Table 7.2
Cash Budget For Small Department Store Continued

		Cash Budget—		
		Oct.	Nov.	Dec.
Cash Receipts:				
Sales		$300,000	$350,000	$400,000
Credit Sales		225,000	262,500	300,000
Collections:				
60%—1st month after sale				
30%—2nd month after sale				
5%—3rd month after sale				
Cash Sales				
Interest				
Total Cash Receipts				
Cash Disbursements:				
Purchases				
Rent				
Utilities				
Interest				
Tax Prepayment				
Capital Addition				
Miscellaneous				
Wage/Salaries				
Total Cash Disbursements				
End-of-Month Balance:				
Cash (Beginning of month)				
+ Cash Receipts				
− Cash Disbursements				
Cash (end of month)				
Borrowing				
Cash (end of month [after borrowing])				

		Cash Budget—		
		Oct.	Nov.	Dec.
Cash Receipts:				
Sales		$300,000	$350,000	$400,000
Credit Sales		225,000	262,500	300,000
Collections:				
60%—1st month after sale				
30%—2nd month after sale				
5%—3rd month after sale				
Cash Sales				
Interest				
Total Cash Recipts				
Cash Disbursements:				
Purchases				
Rent				

Most Likely Sales Forecast

Jan.	Feb.	Mar.	Apr.	May
$150,000	$200,000	$200,000	$300,000	$250,000
112,000	150,000	150,000	225,000	187,500
$180,000	$67,500	$90,000	$90,000	$135,000
78,750	90,000	33,750	45,000	45,000
11,250	13,125	15,000	5,625	7,500
37,500	50,000	50,000	75,000	62,500
0	200	0	0	0
$307,500	$220,825	$188,750	$215,625	$250,000
$140,000	$140,000	$210,000	$175,000	—
2,000	2,000	2,000	2,000	
850	850	850	850	
0	0	7,500	0	
0	0	50,000	0	
0	130,000	0	0	
70	70	70	70	
30,000	40,000	45,000	50,000	—
$172,920	$312,920	$315,420	$227,920	
$12,000	$146,580	$54,485	$10,000	
307,500	220,825	188,750	215,625	
172,920	312,920	315,420	227,920	—
146,580	54,485	(72,185)	(2,295)	
0	0	82,185	12,295	—
$146,580	$54,485	$10,000	$10,000	

Pessimistic Sales Forecast

Jan.	Feb.	Mar.	Apr.	May
$120,000	$160,000	$160,000	$250,000	$190,000
90,000	120,000	120,000	187,500	142,500
180,000	54,000	72,000	72,000	112,500
78,750	90,000	27,000	36,000	36,000
11,250	13,125	15,000	4,500	6,000
30,000	40,000	40,000	62,500	47,500
0	200	0	0	0
$300,000	$197,325	$154,000	$175,000	$202,000
$112,000	$112,000	$175,000	$133,000	—
2,000	2,000	2,000	2,000	

Continued

Table 7.2
Cash Budget For Small Department Store Continued

	Cash Budget—		
	Oct.	Nov.	Dec.
Utilities			
Interest			
Tax Prepayment			
Capital Addition			
Miscellaneous			
Wage/Salaries			
Total Cash Disbursements			
End-of-Month Balance:			
Cash (Beginning of month)			
+ Cash Receipts			
− Cash Disbursements			
Cash (end of month)			
Borrowing			
Cash (end of month [after borrowing])			

	Cash Budget—		
	Oct.	Nov.	Dec.
Cash Receipts:			
Sales	$300,000	$350,000	$400,000
Credit Sales	225,000	262,500	300,000
Collections:			
60%—1st month after sale			
30%—2nd month after sale			
5%—3rd month after sale			
Cash Sales			
Interest			
Total Cash Receipts			
Cash Disbursements:			
Purchases			
Rent			
Utilities			
Interest			
Tax Prepayment			
Capital Addition			
Miscellaneous			
Wage/Salaries			
Total Cash Disbursements			
End-of-Month Balance:			
Cash (Beginning of month)			
+Cash Receipts			
- Cash Disbursements			
Cash (end of month)			
Borrowing			
Cash (end of month [after borrowing])			

Pessimistic Sales Forecast (continued)

Jan.	Feb.	Mar.	Apr.	May
850	850	850	850	
0	0	7,500	0	
0	0	50,000	0	
0	130,000	0	0	
70	70	70	70	
30,000	40,000	45,000	50,000	_____
$144,920	$284,920	$280,420	$185,920	

Jan.	Feb.	Mar.	Apr.	May
$12,000	$167,080	$79,485	$10,000	
300,000	197,325	154,000	175,000	
144,920	284,920	280,420	185,920	_____
167,080	79,485	(46,935)	(920)	
0	0	56,935	10,920	_____
$167,080	$79,485	$10,000	$10,000	

Optimistic Sales Forecast

Jan.	Feb.	Mar.	Apr.	May
$175,000	$250,000	$250,000	$340,000	$310,000
131,250	187,500	187,500	255,000	232,500

Jan.	Feb.	Mar.	Apr.	May
180,000	78,750	112,500	112,500	153,000
78,750	90,000	39,375	56,250	56,250
11,250	13,125	15,000	6,563	9,375
43,750	62,500	62,500	85,000	77,500
0	200	0	0	0
$313,750	$244,575	$229,375	$260,313	$296,125

Jan.	Feb.	Mar.	Apr.	May
$175,000	$175,000	$238,000	$217,000	—
2,000	2,000	2,000	2,000	
850	850	850	850	
0	0	7,500	0	
0	0	50,000	0	
0	130,000	0	0	
70	70	70	70	
30,000	40,000	45,000	50,000	_____
$207,920	$347,920	$343,420	$268,920	

Jan.	Feb.	Mar.	Apr.	May
$12,000	$117,830	$14,485	$10,000	
313,750	244,575	229,375	296,125	
207,920	347,920	343,420	269,920	_____
117,830	14,485	(99,560)	36,205	
0	0	109,560	0	_____
$117,830	$14,485	$10,000	$32,205	

The task of forecasting sales for the new firm is more difficult but not impossible. For example, the new owner might conduct research on similar firms and their sales patterns in the first year of operation to come up with a forecast. The local chamber of commerce and trade associations in the various industries also collect such information. Marketing research is another source of information that may be used to estimate annual sales for the fledgling firm. Other potential sources that may help predict sales include census reports, newspapers, radio and television customer profiles, polls and surveys, and local government statistics. Table 7.3 gives an example of how one entrepreneur used such marketing information to derive a sales forecast for his first year of operation.

No matter what techniques the small business manager employs, he must recognize even the best sales estimate will be wrong. Many financial analysts suggest that the owner create *three* estimates—an optimistic, a pessimistic, and a most likely sales estimate—and then make a separate cash budget for each forecast (a very simple task with a computer spreadsheet). This dynamic forecast enables the owner to determine the range within which company sales will likely be as the year progresses.

Step 3: Forecasting Cash Receipts

As noted earlier, sales constitute the major source of cash receipts. When a firm sells goods and services on credit, the cash budget must account for the delay between the sale and the actual collection of the proceeds. Remember: You cannot spend cash you haven't collected yet! For instance, an appliance store might not collect the cash from a refrigerator sold in February until April or May, and the cash budget must reflect this delay. To project accurately the firm's cash receipts, the owner must analyze the accounts receivable to determine the collection pattern. For example, past records may indicate that 20 percent of sales are for cash, 50 percent are paid in the month following the sale, 20 percent are paid two months after the sale, 5 percent after three months, and 5 percent are never collected. In

Table 7.3
Forecasting Sales for a Business Startup

Robert Adler wants to open a repair shop for imported cars. The trade association for automotive garages estimates that the owner of an imported car spends an average of $485 per year on repairs and maintenance. The typical garage attracts its clientele from a trading zone (the area from which a business draws its customers) with a 20-mile radius. Census reports show that the families within a 20-mile radius of Robert's proposed location own 84,000 cars, of which 24 percent are imports. Based on a local consultant's market research, Robert believes he can capture 9.9 percent of the market this year. Robert's estimate of his company's first year's sales are as follows:

Number of cars in trading zone	84,000 autos
× Percent of imports	× 24%
= Number of imported cars in trading zone	20,160 imports
Number of imports in trading zone	20,160 imports
× Average expenditure on repairs and maintenance	× $485
= Total import repair sales potential	$9,777,600
Total import repair sales potential	$9,777,600
× Estimated share of market	× 9.9%
= Sales estimate	$967,982

Now Robert Adler can convert this annual sales estimate of $967,982 into monthly sales estimates for use in his company's cash budget.

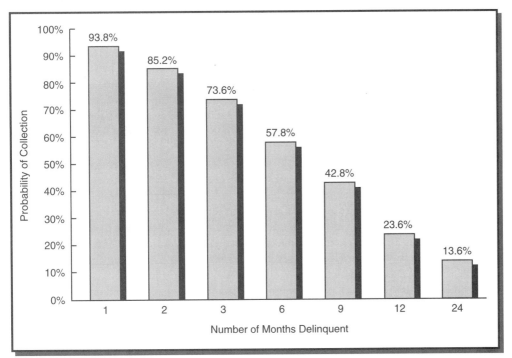

Figure 7.3
Collecting Delinquent Accounts
Source: Adapted from Commercial Collection Agency Section of the Commercial Law League of America, Chicago, Illinois.

addition to cash and credit sales, the small business may receive cash in a number of forms—interest income, rental income, dividends, and others.

Figure 7.3 demonstrates how vital it is to act promptly once an account becomes past due. Notice how the probability of collecting an outstanding account diminishes the longer the account is delinquent. Table 7.4 illustrates the high cost of failing to collect accounts receivable on time.

Table 7.4
Managing Accounts Receivable
Source: Adapted from "Financial Control," *Inc.,* Reprinted with permission of the publisher.

Are your customers who purchase on credit paying late? If so, these outstanding accounts receivable probably represent a significant leak in your company's profits. Regaining control of these late payers will likely improve the firm's profits and cash flow.

Slow-paying credit customers, in effect, are borrowing money from your business interest free. They are using your money without penalty while you forgo opportunities to place it in interest-earning investments. Exactly how much is poor credit control costing you? The answer may surprise you.

The first step is to compute the company's average collection period rate (see the "Operating Ratios" section in Chapter 8). The second step is to age the firm's accounts receivable to determine how many accounts are current and how many are overdue. The following example shows how to use these facts to compute the cost of the past due accounts for a company whose credit terms are "net 30":

Average collection period	65 days
Less: credit terms	-30 days
Excess in accounts receivable	35 days
Average daily sales of $21,500[a] x 35 days	$752,500
Normal rate of return on investments	x 8%
Annual cost of excess	$60,200

If your business is highly seasonal, quarterly or monthly figures may be more meaningful than annual ones.

[a] Average daily sales = $\dfrac{\text{Annual sales}}{\text{365 days}} = \dfrac{\$7,847,500}{365} = \$21,500$

Step 4: Forecasting Cash Disbursements

Most owners of established businesses have a clear picture of the firm's pattern of cash disbursements. In fact, many cash payments, such as rent, loan repayments, and interest, are fixed amounts due on specified dates. The key factor in forecasting disbursements for a cash budget is to record them in *the month in which they will be paid*, *not when the obligation is incurred*. Of course, the number of cash disbursements varies with each particular business, but the following disbursement categories are standard: purchase of inventory or raw materials; wages and salaries; rent, taxes, loans and interest; selling expenses; overhead expenses; and miscellaneous expenses.

Usually, an owner's tendency is to underestimate cash disbursements, which can result in a cash crisis. To prevent this, the wise owner cushions each cash disbursement account, assuming it will be higher than expected. This is particularly true of entrepreneurs opening new businesses. In fact, some financial analysts recommend that a new owner estimate cash disbursements as best he can and then add on another 10 to 25 percent of the total. Whatever forecasting technique is used, the small business manager must avoid underestimating cash disbursements, which may lead to severe cash shortages and possibly bankruptcy.

Sometimes, business owners have difficulty developing initial forecasts of cash receipts and cash disbursements. One of the most effective techniques for overcoming the "I don't know where to begin" hurdle is to make a *daily* list of the items that generated cash (receipts) and those which consumed it (disbursements).

For example, Susan Bowen, CEO of Champion Awards, a $9-million T-shirt screen printer, monitors cash flow by tracking the cash that flows into and out of her company every day. Focusing on keeping the process simple, Bowen sets aside a few minutes each morning to track updates from the previous day on four key numbers:

☆ *accounts receivable: 1. What was billed yesterday? 2. How much was actually collected?*

☆ *accounts payable: 3. What invoices were received yesterday? 4. How much in total was paid out?*

If Bowen observes the wrong trend—more new bills than new sales or more money going out than coming in—she makes immediate adjustments to protect her cash flow. The benefits produced (not the least of which is the peace of mind knowing no cash crisis is looming) more than outweigh the ten minutes she invests in the process every day. "I've tried to balance my books every single day since I started my company in 1970," says Bowen.[12]

Step 5: Estimating the End-of-Month Cash Balance

To estimate the firm's cash balance for each month, the small business manager first must determine the cash balance at the beginning of each month. The beginning cash balance includes cash on hand as well as cash in checking and savings accounts. As development of the cash budget progresses, the cash balance at the end of a month becomes the beginning balance for the following month. Next, the owner simply adds total cash receipts and subtracts total cash disbursements to obtain the end-of-month balance before any borrowing takes place. A positive amount indicates that the firm has a cash surplus for the month while a negative amount shows a cash shortage will occur unless the manager is able to collect or borrow additional funds.

Normally, a firm's cash balance fluctuates from month to month, reflecting seasonal sales patterns. Such fluctuations are normal, but the small business owner must watch closely for any increases and decreases in the cash balance over time. A trend of increases indicates that the small firm has ample cash that could be placed in some income-earning investment. On the other hand, a pattern of cash decreases should alert the owner that the business is approaching a cash crisis.

A cash budget not only illustrates the flow of cash into and out of the small business, but it also allows the owner to *anticipate* cash shortages and cash surpluses. "Then," explains a small business consultant, "you can go to the bank and get a 'seasonal' line of credit for six months instead of twelve. Right there you can cut your borrowing costs in half."[13] By planning cash needs ahead of time, the small business is able to do the following:

- ✩ Take advantage of money-saving opportunities, such as quantity and cash discounts.
- ✩ Make the most efficient use of available cash.
- ✩ Finance seasonal business needs.
- ✩ Develop a sound borrowing program.
- ✩ Develop a workable program of debt repayment.
- ✩ Provide funds for expansion.
- ✩ Plan for investing surplus cash.

"Cash flow spells survival for every business," claims one expert. "Manage cash flow effectively, and your business works. If your cash flow is not well managed, then sooner or later your business goes under. It's that simple."[14]

Unfortunately, most small business owners forgo these benefits because they fail to manage their cash properly. One recent study reported that just 26 percent of all small businesses used formal techniques for tracking the level of their cash balances.[15] Because cash flow problems usually sneak up on a business over time, improper cash management often proves to be a costly—and fatal—mistake.

YOU BE THE CONSULTANT...

In Search of a Cash Flow Forecast

"I'll never make that mistake again," Douglas Martinez said to himself as he got into his car. Martinez had just left a meeting with his banker, who had not been optimistic about the chances of Martinez's plumbing supply company getting the loan it needed. "I should have been better prepared for the meeting," he muttered, knowing that he could be angry only at himself. "That consultant at the Small Business Development Center was right. Bankers' primary concern when making loans is cash flow."

"At least I salvaged the meeting by telling him I wasn't ready to officially apply for a loan yet," Martinez thought. "But I've got a lot of work to do. I've got a week to figure out how to put together a cash budget to supplement my loan application. Maybe that consultant can help me."

When he returned to his office, Martinez gathered up the file folders containing all of his fast-growing company's financial reports and printed his projected revenues and expenses using his computer spreadsheet. Then he called the SBDC consultant he had worked with when he was launching his company and explained the situation. When he arrived at the consultant's office that afternoon, they started organizing the information. Here is what they came up with:

Current cash balance	$8,750
Sales pattern	71% on credit and 29% in cash
Collections of credit sales	68% in 1 to 30 days; 19% in 31 to 60 days; 7% in 61 to 90 days; 6% never collected (bad debts)

Sales forecasts:

	Pessimistic	Most Likely	Optimistic
July (actual)		$18,750	
August (actual)		19,200	
September (actual)		17,840	
October	$15,000	17,500	$19,750
November	14,000	16,500	18,500
December	11,200	13,000	14,000
January	9,900	12,500	14,900
February	10,500	13,800	15,800
March	13,500	17,500	19,900

Utilities expenses	$800	per month
Rent	1,200	per month
Truck loan	317	per month

Continued

The company's wages and salaries (including payroll taxes) estimates are:

October	$2,050
November	1,825
December	1,725
January	1,725
February	1,950
March	2,425

The company pays 63 percent of the sales price for the inventory it purchases, an amount that it actually pays in the following month. (Martinez has negotiated "net 30" credit terms with his suppliers.)

Other expenses include:

Insurance premiums	$1,200	payable in August and February
Office supplies	95	per month
Maintenance	75	per month

Computer supplies	75	per month
Advertising	550	per month
Legal and accounting fees	250	per month
Miscellaneous expenses	60	per month

A tax payment of $1,400 is due in December.

Martinez has established a minimum cash balance of $2,000.

"Well, what do you think?" Martinez asked the consultant.

1. Assume the role of the SBDC consultant and help Martinez put together a cash budget for the six months beginning in October.

2. What conclusions can you draw about Martinez's business from this cash budget?

3. What suggestions can you make to help Martinez improve his company's cash flow?

---

4. Describe fundamental principles involved in managing the "Big Three" of cash management: accounts receivable, accounts payable, and inventory.

The "Big Three" of Cash Management

It is unrealistic for business owners to expect to trace the flow of every dollar through their businesses. However, by concentrating on the three primary causes of cash flow problems, they can dramatically lower the likelihood of experiencing a devastating cash crisis. The "Big Three" of cash management are accounts receivable, accounts payable, and inventory. A firm should always try to accelerate a firm's receivables and to stretch out its payables. As one company's chief financial officer stated, the idea is to "get the cash in the door as fast as you can, cut costs, and pay people as late as possible."[16] Business owners also must monitor inventory carefully to avoid tying up valuable cash in an excessive stock of inventory.

Accounts Receivable

Selling merchandise and services on credit is a necessary evil for most small businesses. Many customers expect to buy on credit, so business owners extend it to avoid losing customers to competitors. However, selling to customers on credit is expensive; it requires more paperwork, more staff, and more cash to service accounts receivable. Also, because extending credit is, in essence, lending money, the risk involved is higher. Every business owner who sells on credit will encounter customers who pay late or, worst of all, who never pay at all.

Selling on credit is a common practice in business. Experts estimate that 90 percent of industrial and wholesale sales are on credit and that 40 percent of retail sales are on account.[17] One recent survey of small businesses across a variety of industries reported that 77 percent extend credit to their customers.[18] Because credit sales are so prevalent, an assertive collection program is essential to managing a company's cash flow. A credit policy that is too lenient can destroy a business's cash flow, attracting nothing but slow-paying and "deadbeat" customers. On the other hand, a carefully designed policy can be a powerful selling tool, attracting customers and boosting cash flow. "A sale is not a sale until you collect the money," warns the head of the National Association of Credit Management. "Receivables are the second most important item on the balance sheet. The first is cash. If you don't turn those receivables into cash, you're not going to be in business very long."[19]

Source: Reprinted by permission of Cartoon Features Syndicate.

HOW TO ESTABLISH A CREDIT AND COLLECTION POLICY. The first step in establishing a workable credit policy is to screen customers carefully *before* granting credit. Unfortunately, few small businesses conduct any kind of credit investigation before selling to a new customer. According to one survey, nearly 95 percent of small firms that sell on credit sell to *anyone* who wants to buy; most have no credit-checking procedure."[20] "One of the big problems we have had with . . . debt collection is that businesses open accounts without knowing whom they're dealing with," says one attorney specializing in debt collection. "It is a sad day when a business owner comes to me with a $10,000 bad debt claim and he doesn't have any information on the people he has been dealing with."[21]

The first line of defense against bad debt losses is a detailed credit application. Before selling to *any* customer on credit, a business owner should fill out a customized application designed to meet his company's specific needs. After collecting enough information to assemble a credit profile, the business owner should use it by checking the potential customer's credit references! The savings from lower bad debt expenses can more than offset the cost of using a credit-reporting service such as TRW or Dun & Bradstreet. The National Association of Credit Management (NACM) is another important source of credit information because it collects information on many small businesses that other reporting services ignore. The cost to check a potential customer's credit at reporting services such as these ranges from $10 to $35, a small price to pay when considering selling thousands of dollars worth of goods or services to a new customer. Unfortunately, few small businesses take the time to conduct a credit check; in one study, just one-third of the businesses protected themselves by checking potential customers' credit.[22]

The next step involves establishing a firm written credit policy and letting every customer know in advance the company's credit terms. The credit agreement must state clearly all the terms the business will enforce if the account goes bad—including interest, late charges, attorney's fees, and others. Failure to specify these terms in the contract means they *cannot* be added later after problems arise. When will you invoice? How soon is payment due: immediately, 30 days, 60 days? Will you add a late charge? If so, how much? The credit policies should be as tight as possible and within federal and state credit laws. According to the American Collectors Association, if a business is writing off more than 5 percent of sales as bad debts, the owner should tighten its credit and collection policy.

The third step in an effective credit policy is to send invoices promptly since customers rarely pay *before* they receive their bills. "The cornerstone of collecting accounts receivable on time is making sure you invoice your customers or send them their periodic billing statements promptly. The sooner you mail your invoice, the sooner the check will be in the mail," says one entrepreneur. "In the manufacturing environment, get the invoice en route to the customer as soon as the shipment goes out the door," he advises. "Likewise, service industries with billable hours should keep track of hours daily or weekly and bill as often as the contract or agreement with the client permits."[23]

Small business owners can take several steps to encourage prompt payment of invoices:

- ☆ Ensure that all invoices are clear, accurate, and timely.
- ☆ State clearly a description of the goods or services purchased and an account number, if possible.
- ☆ Make sure that prices on invoices agree with the price quotations on purchase orders or contracts.
- ☆ Highlight the terms of sale (e.g., "net 30") on all invoices and reinforce them, if necessary.
- ☆ Include a telephone number and a contact person in your organization in case the customer has a question or a dispute.

American Imaging, Inc.

Bob Dempster, cofounder of American Imaging, Inc., a distributor of x-ray tubes, once handled receivables the same way most entrepreneurs do: When customers ignored the "net 30" terms on invoices, he would call them around the 45th day to ask what the problem was. Payments usually would trickle in within the next two weeks, but by then 60 days had elapsed, and American Imaging's cash flow was always strained. Then Dempster decided to try a different approach. Today, he makes a "customer relations call" on the 20th day of the billing period to determine if the customer is satisfied with the company's performance on the order. Before closing, he reminds the customer of the invoice due date and asks if there will be any problems meeting it. Dempster's proactive approach to collecting receivables has cut his company's average collection period by at least 15 days, improved cash flow, and increased customer satisfaction![24]

When an account becomes overdue, the small business owner must take *immediate* action. The longer an account is past due, the lower is the probability of collecting it. As soon as an account becomes overdue, many business owners send a "second notice" letter requesting immediate payment. If that fails to produce results, the next step is a telephone call. "When you get on the phone, ask for payment in full," advises one expert who claims that a personal phone call "is ten times more productive than a letter."[25] If the customer still refuses to pay the bill after 30 days, collection experts recommend the following:

- ☆ Sending a letter from the company's attorney.
- ☆ Turning the account over to a collection attorney.
- ☆ As a last resort, hiring a collection agency. (The Commercial Law League can provide a list of reputable agencies.)

Although collection agencies and attorneys will take 25 to 50 percent of any accounts they collect, they are often worth the price paid. According to the American Collector's Association, only 5 percent of accounts more than 90 days delinquent will be paid voluntarily.

Lots of Growth, But Where's the Cash?

Douglas Roberson, president of Atlantic Network Systems (ANS), a data- and voice-systems integrating company, recalls the day he "woke up and realized we were out of cash." The company had grown so quickly—from $100,000 in sales its first year to $460,000 the next—that Roberson had never worried about managing cash flow. At the end of its second year of operation, ANS's "receivables had gone through the roof," recalls Roberson. "I actually believed that the more companies owed us, the better shape we were in." Then the company hit a long collection dry spell. Roberson watched "our money go out and *nothing* come in." ANS limped along with the help of a bank line of credit, waiting for customers to pay invoices.

It was a sobering lesson for Roberson on the difference between generating sales and managing cash flow. "If you don't do serious projections about how much cash you'll need to handle sales—and how long it takes to collect on invoices—you can wind up out of business, no matter how fast you're growing," he says. In fact, rapid growth usually compounds cash flow problems as a company spends increasing amounts of cash on inventory, supplies, payroll, and other expenses and waits 30 to 45 days or longer to collect its receivables. The result: a serious cash crisis that could destroy the company.

ANS's foreign customers pose a special problem for the company's cash flow because they often stretch out their payments to between 45 and 60 days. "I want to bring them in line with our other, faster-paying accounts," says Roberson.

1. Why does a small company's rapid growth often result in cash flow problems?

2. What can entrepreneurs do to avoid the cash flow perils associated with rapid growth?

3. What advice can you offer Douglas Roberson about his company's accounts receivable?

Source: "Running on Empty," *Inc.*, August 1994, p. 107.

Business owners must be sure to abide by the provisions of the federal Fair Debt Collection Practices Act, which prohibits any kind of harassment when collecting debts (e.g., telephoning repeatedly, issuing threats of violence, telling third parties about the debt, or using abusive language).

Table 7.5 on page 236 outlines ten collection blunders small business owners typically make and how to avoid them.

Other Techniques for Accelerating Accounts Receivable. Small business owners can rely on a variety of other techniques to speed cash inflow from accounts receivable:

- ☆ Speed up orders by having customers fax them to you.
- ☆ Send invoices when goods are shipped—not a day or a week later; consider faxing invoices to reduce "in transit" time to a minimum.
- ☆ Indicate in conspicuous print the invoice due date and any late payment penalties. (Check with an attorney to be sure all finance charges comply with state laws.)
- ☆ Restrict the customer's credit until past-due bills are paid.
- ☆ Deposit customer checks and credit card receipts *daily*.
- ☆ Identify the top 20 percent of your customers (by sales volume), create a separate file system for them, and monitor them closely. Twenty percent of the typical company's customers generate 80 percent of all accounts receivable.
- ☆ Ask customers to pay a portion of the purchase price up front.
- ☆ Consider using a bank's lockbox collection service (located near customers) to reduce mail time on collections. In a lockbox arrangement, customers send payments to a post office box the bank maintains. The bank collects the payments several times each day and deposits them immediately into the company account. The procedure sharply reduces processing and clearing times, especially if the lockboxes are located close to the firm's biggest customers' business addresses. The system can be expensive to operate and is most economical for companies with a high volume of large checks.

Table 7.5
**Ten Collection Blunders
and How to Avoid Them**

Source: Adapted from Bob
Weinstein, "Collect Calls,"
Entrepreneur, August 1995,
pp. 66-69.

Blunder 1: Delaying collection phone calls. Many entrepreneurs waste valuable time and resources sending four or five past-due letters to delinquent customers, usually with limited effectiveness.

Instead: Once a bill becomes past due, call the customer within a week to verify that he received the bill and that it is accurate. Ask for payment.

Blunder 2: Failing to ask for payment in clear terms. To avoid angering a customer, some entrepreneurs ask meekly, "Do you think you could take care of this bill soon?"

Instead: Firmly, but professionally, ask for payment (the full amount) by a specific date.

Blunder 3: Sounding desperate. Some entrepreneurs show weakness by saying that they must have payment or they "can't meet payroll" or "can't pay bills." That gives the customer more leverage to negotiate additional discounts or time.

Instead: Ask for payment simply because the invoice is past due—without any other explanation. Don't apologize for your request; it's *your* money.

Blunder 4: Talking tough. Getting nasty with delinquent customers does not make them pay any faster and may be a violation of the Fair Debt Collections Practices Act.

Instead: Remain polite and professional when dealing with past-due customers, even if you think they don't deserve it. *Never* lose your temper. Don't ruin your reputation by being rude.

Blunder 5: Trying to find out the customer's problem. Some entrepreneurs think it is necessary to find out why a delinquent customer has not paid a bill.

Instead: Don't waste time playing private investigator. Focus on the business at hand—collecting your money.

Blunder 6: Asking customers how much they can pay. When customers claim that they cannot pay the bill in full, inexperienced entrepreneurs ask, "Well, how much can you pay?" They don't realize that they have just turned control of the situation over to the delinquent customer.

Instead: Take charge of negotiations from the outset. Let the customer know that you expect full payment. If you cannot get full payment immediately, suggest a new deadline. Only as a last resort should you offer an extended payment plan.

Blunder 7: Continuing to talk after you get a promise to pay. Some entrepreneurs "blow the deal" by not knowing when to stop talking. They keep interrogating a customer after they have a promise to pay.

Instead: Wrap up the conversation as soon as you have a commitment. Summarize the agreement, thank the customer, and end the conversation on a positive note.

Blunder 8: Calling without being prepared. Some entrepreneurs call customers without knowing exactly which invoices are past due and what amounts are involved. The effort is usually fruitless.

Instead: Have all account details in front of you when you call and be specific in your requests.

Blunder 9: Trusting your memory: Some entrepreneurs think they can remember previous collection calls, conversations, and agreements.

Instead: Keep accurate records of all calls and conversations. Take notes about each customer contact and resulting agreements.

Blunder 10: Letting your computer control your collection efforts. Inexperienced entrepreneurs tend to think that their computers can manage debt collection for them.

Instead: Recognize that a computer is a valuable tool in collecting accounts but that you are in control. Past-due notices from a computer may collect some accounts, but your efforts will produce more results. Getting to know the people who handle the invoices at your customers' businesses can be a major advantage when collecting accounts.

Accounts Payable

The second element of the "Big Three" of cash management is accounts payable. The timing of payables is just as crucial to proper cash management as the timing of receivables, but the objective is exactly the opposite. An entrepreneur should strive to stretch out payables as long as possible *without damaging the company's credit rating*. Otherwise, suppliers may begin demanding prepayment or C.O.D. terms, which severely impair a company's cash flow, or they simply stop doing business with it. When one computer manufacturer ran into cash flow problems, it deferred payments to its suppliers for as long as 100 days (compared to an industry average of about 40 days). Because of the company's slow payments, many suppliers simply stopped selling to the computer maker.[26] One cash management consultant claims, "Some companies pay too early and wind up forgoing the interest they could have earned on their cash. Others pay too late and either wind up with late penalties or being forced to buy on a C.O.D. basis, which really kills them."[27] It is entirely reasonable for small business owners to regulate payments to their companies' advantage. Efficient cash managers set up a payment calendar each month that allows them to pay their bills on time and to take advantage of cash discounts for early payment.

Nancy Dunis, CEO of Dunis & Associates, a Portland, Oregon marketing firm, recognizes the importance of controlling accounts payable. "Our payables must be functioning just right to keep our cash flow running smoothly," says Dunis. She has set up a simple five-point accounts payable system:[28]

Dunis & Associates

1. Set scheduling goals. *Dunis strives to pay her company's bills 45 days after receiving them and to collect all her receivables within 30 days. Even though "it doesn't always work that way," her goal is to make the most of her cash flow.*

2. Keep paperwork organized. *Dunis dates every invoice she receives and carefully files it according to her payment plan. "This helps us remember when to cut the check," she says, and, "it helps us stagger our payments, over days or weeks," significantly improving the company's cash flow.*

3. Prioritize. *Dunis cannot stretch out all of her company's creditors for 45 days; some demand payment sooner. Those suppliers are at the top of the accounts payable list.*

4. Be consistent. *"Companies want consistent customers," says Dunis. "With a few exceptions," she explains, "most businesses will be happy to accept 45-day payments, so long as they know you'll always pay your full obligation at that point."*

5. Look for warning signs. *Dunis sees her accounts payable as an early warning system for cash flow problems. "The first indication I get that cash flow is in trouble is when I see I'm getting low on cash and could have trouble paying my bills according to my staggered filing system," she says.*

Business owners should verify all invoices before paying them. Some unscrupulous vendors will send out invoices for goods they never shipped, knowing that many business owners will simply pay the bill without checking its authenticity. Someone in the company—for instance, the accounts payable clerk—should have the responsibility of verifying every invoice received.

Generally, it is a good idea for owners to take advantage of cash discounts vendors offer. A cash discount (e.g., "2/10, net 30"—take a 2 percent discount if you pay the invoice within ten days; otherwise, total payment is due in 30 days) offers a price reduction if the owner pays an invoice early. A clever cash manager also will negotiate the best possible credit terms with suppliers. Almost all vendors grant their customers trade credit, and the small business owner should take advantage of it. However, because trade credit is so easy to get, the owner must be careful not to abuse it, putting the business in a precarious financial position.

Favorable credit terms can make a tremendous difference in a firm's cash flow. Table 7.6 on page 238 shows the same most likely cash budget (from Table 7.2) with one exception:

instead of purchasing on C.O.D. terms (Table 7.2), the owner has negotiated net 30 payment terms (Table 7.6). Notice the drastic improvement in the company's cash flow resulting from improved credit terms.

If owners do find themselves financially strapped when payment to a vendor is due, they should avoid making empty promises that "the check is in the mail" or sending unsigned checks. Instead, they should openly discuss the situation with the vendor. Most vendors will work out payment terms for extended credit. One small business owner who was experiencing a cash crisis claims:

> One day things got so bad I just called up a supplier and said, "I need your stuff, but I'm going through a tough period and simply can't pay you right now." They said they wanted to keep me as a customer, and they asked if it was okay to bill me in three months. I was dumbfounded: *They didn't even charge me interest.*[29]

The small business owner also can improve the firm's cash flow by scheduling controllable cash disbursements so that they do not come due at the same time. For example, paying employees every two weeks (or every month) rather than every week reduces adminis-

Table 7.6
Cash Budget,[a]
Most Likely Sales Forecast

	Jan.	Feb.	Mar.	Apr.
Cash Receipts:				
Sales	$150,000	$200,000	$200,000	$300,000
Credit Sales	112,500	150,000	150,000	225,000
Collections:				
60%—1st month after sale	$180,000	$67,500	$90,000	$90,000
30%—2nd month after sale	78,750	90,000	33,750	45,000
5%—3rd month after sale	11,250	13,125	15,000	5,625
Cash Sales	37,500	50,000	50,000	75,000
Interest	0	200	0	9
Total Cash Receipts	$307,500	$220,825	$188,750	$215,625
Cash Disbursements:				
Purchases[a]	$105,000	$140,000	$140,000	$210,000
Rent	2,000	2,000	2,000	2,000
Utilities	850	850	850	850
Interest	0	0	7,500	0
Tax Prepayment	0	0	50,000	0
Capital Addition	0	130,000	3	0
Miscellaneous	70	70	70	70
Wage/Salaries	30,000	40,000	45,000	50,000
Total Cash Disbursements[a]	$137,920	$312,920	$245,420	$262,920
End-of-Month Balance:				
Cash (Beginning of month)[a]	$12,000	$181,580	$89,485	$32,815
+ Cash Receipts	307,500	220,825	188,750	215,625
− Cash Disbursements[a]	137,920	312,920	245,420	262,920
Cash (end of month)[a]	181,580	89,485	32,815	(14,480)
Borrowing	0	0	0	24,480
Cash (end of month [after borrowing])[a]	$181,580	$89,485	$32,815	$10,000

[a]After negotiating "net 30" trade credit terms.

trative costs and gives the business more time to use its cash. Owners of fledgling businesses may be able to conserve cash by hiring part-time employees or by using freelance workers rather than full-time, permanent workers. Scheduling insurance premiums monthly or quarterly rather than annually also improves cash flows.

Wise use of business credit cards is another way to stretch the firm's cash balance. However, the owner should avoid cards that charge transaction fees. Credit cards differ in their interest-charging policies; many begin charging interest from the date of purchase, but some charge interest only from the invoice date.

Inventory

Inventory is a significant investment for many small businesses and can create a severe strain on cash flow. Although inventory represents the largest capital investment for most businesses, few owners use any formal methods for managing it. As a result, the typical small business not only has too much inventory but also too much of the *wrong* kind of inventory! Because inventory is illiquid, it can quickly siphon off a company's pool of available cash. "Small companies need cash to grow," says one consultant. "They've got to be able to turn [cash] over quickly. That's difficult to do if a lot of money is tied up in excess inventory."[30]

Surplus inventory yields a zero rate of return and unnecessarily ties up the firm's cash. "The cost of carrying inventory is expensive," says one small business consultant. "A typical manufacturing company pays 25 percent to 30 percent of the value of the inventory for the cost of borrowed money, warehouse space, materials handling, staff, lift-truck expenses, and fixed costs. This shocks a lot of people. Once they realize it, they look at inventory differently."[31] Marking down items that don't sell will keep inventory lean and allow it to turn over frequently. Even though volume discounts lower inventory costs, large purchases may tie up the company's valuable cash. Wise business owners avoid overbuying inventory, recognizing that excess inventory ties up valuable cash unproductively. In fact, only 20 percent of a typical business's inventory turns over quickly, so the owner must watch constantly for stale items.[32]

Carrying too much inventory increases the chances that a business will run out of cash. "The cash that pays for goods is channeled into inventory," says one business writer, "where its flow is dead-ended until the inventory is sold and the cash is set free again. The cash flow trick is to commit just enough cash to inventory to meet demand."[33] Scheduling inventory deliveries at the latest possible date will prevent premature payment of invoices. Finally, given goods of comparable quality and price, an entrepreneur should purchase goods from the fastest supplier to keep inventory levels low.

Monitoring the "Big Three" of cash management can help every business owner avoid a cash crisis while making the best use of available cash. According to one expert, maximizing cash flow involves "getting money from customers sooner; paying bills at the last moment possible; consolidating money in a single bank account; managing accounts payable, accounts receivable, and inventory more effectively; and squeezing every penny out of your daily business."[34]

Avoiding the Cash Crunch

5. *Explain* the techniques for avoiding a cash crunch in a small company.

Nearly every small business has the potential to improve its cash position with little or no investment. The key is to make an objective evaluation of the company's financial policies, searching for inefficiency in its cash flow. Young firms cannot afford to waste resources, especially one as vital as cash. By utilizing these tools, small business managers can get maximum benefit from their companies' pool of cash.

Bartering

Bartering, the exchange of goods and services for other goods and services rather than for cash, is an effective way to conserve cash. An ancient concept, bartering regained popularity during recent recessions. Over the last decade, more than 500 barter exchanges have cropped up, catering primarily to small- and medium-sized businesses. More than 350,000 companies—most of them small—engage in more than $1.2 billion worth of barter each year.[35] Every day, entrepreneurs across the nation use bartering to buy much needed materials, equipment, and supplies—*without using cash.* "Bartering is a great way to get the things your business needs without spending cash on them," says Sheri Smith, owner of Gourmet Catering, Inc.[36] The president of one barter exchange estimates that business owners can save "between $5,000 and $150,000 in yearly business costs."[37] In addition to conserving cash, companies that use barter also have the opportunity to transform slow-moving inventory into much-needed products and services.

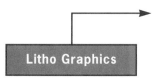

Litho Graphics

For instance, when Jerry Trombo relocated his printing business, Litho Graphics, he traded printing services for moving services, painting, carpeting, furnishings, a computer, and a newly paved driveway. For the year, Litho Graphics conducted more than $50,000 worth of bartering, an amount representing 8 percent of the company's sales— and no cash! "I don't buy anything unless I pick up the barter catalog," says Trombo, who has been bartering through an exchange for more than 11 years. "I'll do anything to avoid spending cash."[38]

Of course, there is a cost associated with bartering, but the real benefit is that the entrepreneur "pays" for products and services at her *wholesale* cost of doing business and gets credit for the *retail* price. In a typical arrangement, businesses accumulate trade credits when they offer goods or services through the exchange. Then they can use their trade credits to purchase other goods and services from other members of the exchange. The typical exchange charges a $500 membership fee and a 10 percent transaction fee (5 percent from the buyer and 5 percent from the seller) on every deal. The exchange tracks the balance in each member's account and typically sends a monthly statement summarizing account activity.

Trimming Overhead Costs

High overhead expenses can strain a small firm's cash supply to the breaking point. Frugal small business owners can trim their overhead in a number of ways.

WHEN PRACTICAL, LEASE INSTEAD OF BUY. By leasing automobiles, computers, office equipment, machinery, and other assets rather than buying them, an entrepreneur can conserve valuable cash. The value of such assets is not in owning them but in *using* them.

Approximately 80 percent of U.S. companies use leasing as a cash management strategy.[39] Although total lease payments typically are greater than those for a conventional loan, most leases offer 100 percent financing, which means the owner avoids the large capital outlays required as down payments on most loans. Also, leasing is an "off-the-balance-sheet" method of financing; the lease is considered an operating expense on the income statement, not a liability on the balance sheet. Thus, leasing conserves a company's borrowing capacity. Leasing companies typically allow businesses to stretch payments over a longer time period than those of a conventional loan. Lease agreements also are flexible. "There are so many ways to tailor a lease agreement to a company's individual equipment and financial needs that you might call it a personalized rental agreement," says the owner of a small construction firm.[40] Leasing gives entrepreneurs access to equipment even when they can't borrow the money to buy it. After his bank rejected his loan request for a $4,000 machine to straighten car frames, Roger Wolfanger decided to lease the equipment. He filled out a simple one-page application, and within two days the machine was in place.[41]

AVOID NONESSENTIAL OUTLAYS. By forgoing costly ego indulgences like ostentatious office equipment, first-class travel, and flashy company cars, an owner can make efficient use of the company's cash. "Entrepreneurs must first ask whether a purchase is critical to operations," explains a consultant.[42] Making across-the-board spending cuts to conserve cash is dangerous, however, because the owner runs the risk of cutting expenditures that literally drive the business. One common mistake during business slowdowns is cutting marketing and advertising expenditures. "As competitors pull back," says one advisor, "smart marketers will keep their ad budgets on an even keel, which is sufficient to bring increased attention to their products."[43] The secret to success is cutting *nonessential* expenditures. "If the lifeblood of your company is marketing, cut it less," advises one advertising executive. "If it is customer service, that is the last thing you want to cut back on. Cut from areas that are not essential to business growth."[44]

NEGOTIATE FIXED LOAN PAYMENTS TO COINCIDE WITH YOUR COMPANY'S CASH FLOW CYCLE. Many banks allow businesses to structure loans so that they can skip specific payments when their cash flow ebbs to its lowest point. Negotiating such terms gives businesses the opportunity to customize their loan repayments to their cash flow cycles.

For example, Ted Zoli, president of Torrington Industries, a construction-materials supplier and contracting business, consistently uses "skipped payment loans" in his highly seasonal business. "Every time we buy a piece of construction machinery," he says, "we set it up so that we're making payments for eight or nine months, and then skipping three or four months during the winter."[45]

Torrington Industries

BUY USED OR RECONDITIONED EQUIPMENT, ESPECIALLY IF IT IS "BEHIND-THE-SCENES" MACHINERY.

CONTROL EMPLOYEE ADVANCES AND LOANS. A manager should grant only those advances and loans that are necessary, and should keep accurate records on payments and balances.

ESTABLISH AN INTERNAL SECURITY AND CONTROL SYSTEM. Too many owners encourage employee theft by failing to establish a system of controls. Reconciling the bank statement monthly and requiring special approval for checks over a specific amount, say $1,000, will help to minimize losses. Separating recordkeeping and check-writing responsibilities, rather than assigning them to a single employee, offers more protection.

DEVELOP A SYSTEM TO BATTLE CHECK FRAUD. About 70 percent of all "bounced" checks occurs because nine out of ten customers fail to keep their checkbooks balanced; the remaining 30 percent of bad checks is the result of fraud.[46] The most effective way to battle bad checks is to subscribe to an electronic check approval service. The service works at the cash register, and approval takes about a minute. The fee a small business pays to use the service depends on the volume of checks. For most small companies, charges amount to 1 to 2 percent of the cleared checks' value.

CHANGE YOUR SHIPPING TERMS. Changing the firm's shipping terms from "F.O.B. (free on board) buyer," in which the *seller* pays the cost of freight, to "F.O.B. seller," in which the *buyer* absorbs all shipping costs, can improve cash flow.

SWITCH TO ZERO-BASED BUDGETING. Zero-based budgeting (ZBB) primarily is a shift in the philosophy of budgeting. Rather than build the current year budget on *increases* from the previous year's budget, ZBB starts from a budget of zero and evaluates the necessity of every item. "Start with zero and review all expenses, asking yourself whether each one is necessary," says one business consultant.[47]

Keeping Your Business Plan Current

Before approaching any potential lender or investor, a business owner must prepare a solid business plan. Smart owners keep their plans up-to-date in case an unexpected cash crisis forces them to seek emergency financing. Revising the plan annually also forces the owner to focus on managing the business more effectively.

Investing Surplus Cash

Because of the uneven flow of receipts and disbursements, a company will often temporarily have more cash than it needs—for a week, month, quarter, or longer. When this happens, most small business owners simply ignore the surplus because they are not sure how soon they will need it. They believe that relatively small amounts of cash sitting around for just a few days or weeks are not worth investing. However, this is not always the case. The small business manager who puts surplus cash to work *immediately* rather than allowing it to sit idle soon discovers that the yield adds up to a significant amount over time. This money can help ease the daily cash crunch during business troughs. "Your goal . . . should be to identify every dollar you don't need to pay today's bills and to keep that money invested to improve your cash flow," explains a consultant."[48]

However, when investing surplus cash, an owner's primary objective should *not* be to earn the maximum yield (which usually carries with it maximum risk); instead, the focus should be on the safety and the liquidity of the investments. The need to minimize risk and to have ready access to the cash restricts the small business owner's investment options to just a few.

Conclusion

Successful owners run their businesses "lean and mean." Trimming wasteful expenditures, investing surplus funds, and carefully planning and managing the company's cash flow enables them to compete effectively in a hostile market. The simple but effective techniques covered in this chapter can improve every small company's cash position. One business writer says, "In the day-to-day course of running a company, other people's capital flows past an imaginative CEO as opportunity. By looking forward and keeping an analytical eye on your cash account as events unfold (remembering that if there's no real cash there when you need it, you're history), you can generate leverage as surely as if that capital were yours to keep."[49]

CHAPTER SUMMARY

1. Explain the importance of cash management to a small business's success.
- Cash is the most important but least productive asset the small business has. The manager must maintain enough cash to meet the firm's normal requirements (plus a reserve for emergencies) without retaining excessively large, unproductive cash balances.
- Without adequate cash, a small business will fail.

2. Differentiate between cash and profits.
- Cash and profits are *not* the same. More businesses fail for lack of cash than for lack of profits.
- Profits, the difference between total revenue and total expenses, are an accounting concept. Cash flow represents the flow of actual cash (the only thing businesses

can use to pay bills) through a business in a continuous cycle. A business can be earning a profit and be forced out of business because it runs out of cash.

3. Understand the five steps in creating a cash budget and use them to create a cash budget.
- The cash budgeting procedure outlined in this chapter tracks the flow of cash through the business and enables the owner to project cash surpluses and cash deficits at specific intervals.
- The five steps in creating a cash budget are as follows: forecasting sales, forecasting cash receipts, forecasting cash disbursements, and determining the end-of-month cash balance.

4. Describe fundamental principles involved in managing the "Big Three" of cash management: accounts receivable, accounts payable, and inventory.

- Controlling accounts receivable requires business owners to establish clear, firm credit and collection policies and to screen customers *before* granting them credit. Sending invoices promptly and acting on past-due accounts quickly also improve cash flow. The goal is to collect cash from receivables as quickly as possible.
- When managing accounts payable, a manager's goal is to stretch out payables as long as possible without damaging the company's credit rating. Other techniques include verifying invoices before paying them, taking advantage of cash discounts, and negotiating the best possible credit terms.

- Inventory frequently causes cash headaches for small business managers. Excess inventory earns a zero rate of return and ties up a company's cash unnecessarily. Owners must watch for stale merchandise.

5. Explain the techniques for avoiding a cash crunch in a small company.

- Trimming overhead costs by bartering, leasing assets, avoiding nonessential outlays, using zero-based budgeting, and implementing an internal control system boost a firm's cash flow position.
- Also, investing surplus cash maximizes the firm's earning power. The primary criteria for investing surplus cash are security and liquidity.

DISCUSSION QUESTIONS

1. Why must small business owners concentrate on effective cash flow management?
2. Explain the difference between cash and profit.
3. Outline the steps involved in developing a cash budget.
4. How can an entrepreneur launching a new business forecast sales?
5. What are the "Big Three" of cash management? What effect do they have on a company's cash flow?

6. Outline the basic principles of managing a small firm's receivables, payables, and inventory.
7. How can bartering improve a company's cash position?
8. What steps can small business owners take to conserve the cash within their companies?
9. What should be a small business owner's primary concern when investing surplus cash?

Beyond the Classroom...

1. Interview several local small business owners about their cash management policies. Do they know how much cash their businesses have during the month? How do they track their cash flows? Do they use some type of cash budget? If not, ask if you can help the owner to develop one. Does the owner invest surplus cash?

2. Volunteer to help a small business owner develop a cash budget for his or her company. What patterns do you detect? What recommendations can you make for improving the company's cash management system?

3. Contact the International Reciprocal Trade Association (IRTA) at 6305 Hawaii Court, Alexandria, VA 22312 and get a list of the barter exchanges in your state. Interview the manager of one of the exchanges and prepare a report on how barter exchanges work and how they benefit small businesses. Ask the manager to refer you to a small business owner who benefits from the barter exchange and interview him or her. How does the owner use the exchange? How much cash has bartering saved? What other benefits has the owner discovered?

SURFING THE NET

1. Using one of the search engines on the World Wide Web (WWW) such as Lycos, Magellan, Yahoo!, or others, conduct a search on the words *cash flow, barter, accounts payable,* or *accounts receivable.* Select one of the sites you find and prepare a one-page report on it.

CHAPTER

EIGHT

Creating a Successful Financial Plan

Rule No. 1: Never lose money.
Rule No. 2: Never forget Rule No. 1.
- Warren Buffett

It is better to solve problems than crises.
- John Guinther

Financial ratios provide a report card. If you're doing a good job, you know it.
If you're not, you know that, too, and you can do something about it.
- Andy Bangs

 LEARNING OBJECTIVES

Upon completion of this chapter, you will be able to:

1. **Understand** the importance of preparing a financial plan.
2. **Describe** how to prepare the basic financial statements and use them to manage the small business.
3. **Create** pro forma financial statements.
4. **Understand** the basic financial statements through ratio analysis.
5. **Explain** how to interpret financial ratios.
6. **Conduct** a breakeven analysis for a small company.

One of the most important steps in launching a new business venture is fashioning a well-designed, logical financial plan. Potential investors demand such a plan before putting their money into a startup company. More importantly, a financial plan is a vital tool that helps entrepreneurs to manage their businesses more effectively, steering their way around the pitfalls that cause failures. Entrepreneurs who ignore the financial aspects of their businesses run the risk of becoming just another failure statistic. One financial expert says of small companies, "Those that don't establish sound controls at the start are setting themselves up to fail."[1] Still, according to one survey, one-third of all entrepreneurs run their companies *without any kind of financial plan*.[2] Another study found that only 11 percent of small business owners analyzed their financial statements as part of the managerial planning and decision-making process.[3] To reach profit objectives, small business managers must be aware of their firms' overall financial position and the changes in financial status that occur over time.

This chapter focuses on some very practical tools that will help the entrepreneur develop a workable financial plan, keep her aware of her company's financial plan, and enable her to plan for profit. The entrepreneur can use these tools to help anticipate changes and plot an appropriate profit strategy to meet them head on. These profit-planning techniques are not difficult to master, nor are they overly time consuming. We will discuss the techniques involved in preparing projected (pro forma) financial statements, conducting ratio analysis, and performing breakeven analysis.

1. Understand the importance of preparing a financial plan.

Basic Financial Statements

2. Describe how to prepare the basic financial statements and use them to manage the small business.

Before we begin building projected financial statements, it would be helpful to review the basic financial reports that measure a company's financial position: the balance sheet, the income statement, and the statement of cash flows. Studies show that the level of financial reporting among small businesses is high; some 81 percent of the companies in one survey regularly produced summary financial information, almost all of it in the form of these traditional financial statements.[4]

The Balance Sheet

The **balance sheet** takes a "snapshot" of a business, providing owners with an estimate of its worth on a given date. Its two major sections show what assets the business owns and what claims creditors and owners have against those assets. The balance sheet is usually prepared on the last day of the month. Figure 8.1 on page 246 shows the balance sheet for Sam's Appliance Shop for the year ended December 31, 199X.

The balance sheet is built on the fundamental accounting equation: Assets = liabilities + owner's equity. Any increase or decrease on one side of the equation must be offset by an equal increase or decrease on the other side; hence, the name *balance sheet*. It provides a baseline from which to measure future changes in assets, liabilities, and equity. The first section of the balance sheet lists the firm's assets (valued at cost, not actual market value) and shows the total value of everything the business owns. **Current assets** consist of cash and items to be converted into cash within one year or within the normal operating cycle of the company, whichever is longer, such as accounts receivable and inventory, and **fixed assets** are those acquired for long-term use in the business. Intangible assets include items that, although valuable, do not have tangible value, such as goodwill, copyrights, and patents.

The second section shows the business's **liabilities**—the creditors' claims against the firm's assets. **Current liabilities** are those debts that must be paid within one year or with-

balance sheet—
a financial statement that provides a snapshot of a business, estimating its worth on a given date; it is built on the fundamental accounting equation: Assets = liabilities + owner's equity.

current assets—*assets such as cash and other items to be converted into cash within one year, or within the company's normal operating cycle.*

fixed assets—*assets acquired for long-term use in the business.*

Figure 8.1
Balance Sheet,
Sam's Appliance Shop

Assets

Current Assets

Cash		$49,855
Accounts Receivable	$179,225	
Less Allowance for Doubtful Accounts	6,000	173,225
Inventory		455,455
Prepaid Expenses		8,450
Total Current Assets		$686,985

Fixed Assets

Land		$59,150
Buildings	$74,650	
Less Accumulated Depreciation	7,050	67,600
Equipment	22,375	
Less Accumulated Depreciation	1,250	21,125
Furniture and Fixtures	10,295	
Less Accumulated Depreciation	1,000	9,295
Total Fixed Assets		$157,170

Intangibles (Goodwill)		3,500
Total Assets		$847,655

Liabilities

Current Liabilites

Accounts Payable	$152,580
Notes Payable	83,920
Accrued Wages/Salaries Payable	38,150
Accrued Interest Payable	42,380
Accrued Taxes Payable	50,820
Total Current Liabilities	$367,850

Long-term Liabilities

Mortgage	$127,150
Note Payable	85,000
Total Long-term Liabilities	$212,150

Owner's Equity

Sam Lloyd, Capital	$267,655
Total Liabilities and Owner's Equity	$847,655

in the normal operating cycle of the company whichever is longer, and **long-term liabilities** are those that come due after one year. This section of the balance sheet also shows the **owner's equity**, the value of the owner's investment in the business. It is the balancing factor on the balance sheet, representing all of the owner's capital contributions to the business plus all accumulated earnings not distributed to the owner(s).

The Income Statement

The **income statement** (or **profit and loss statement** or **P&L**) compares expenses against revenue over a certain period of time to show the firm's net profit (or loss). The income statement is a "moving picture" of the firm's profitability over time. The annual P&L statement reports the bottom line of the business over the fiscal/calendar year. Figure 8.2 on page 248 shows the income statement for Sam's Appliance Shop for the year ended December 31, 199X.

To calculate net profit or loss, the owner records sales revenues for the year, which include all income that flows into the business from sales of goods and services. Income from other sources (rent, investments, interest) also must be included in the revenue section of the income statement. To determine net sales revenue, owners subtract the value of returned items and refunds from gross revenue. **Cost of goods** sold represents the total cost, including shipping, of the merchandise sold during the year. Most wholesalers and retailers calculate cost of goods sold by adding purchases to beginning inventory and subtracting ending inventory. Service companies typically have no cost of goods sold. Operating expenses include those costs that contribute directly to the manufacture and distribution of goods. General expenses are indirect costs incurred in operating the business. Other expenses is a catch-all category covering all other expenses that don't fit into the other two categories. Total revenue minus total expenses gives the net profit (or loss) for the year.

The Statement of Cash Flows

The **statement of cash flows** shows the changes in the firm's working capital since the beginning of the year by listing the sources of funds and the uses of these funds. Many small businesses never need to prepare such a statement, but in some cases creditors, investors, new owners, or the IRS may require this information.

To prepare the statement, the owner must assemble the balance sheets and the income statements summarizing the present year's operations. She begins with the company's net income for the period (from the income statement). Then she adds the sources of the company's funds—borrowed funds, owner contributions, decreases in accounts receivable, increases in accounts payable, decreases in inventory, depreciation, and any others. Depreciation is listed as a source of funds because it is a noncash expense that has already been deducted as a cost of doing business. But because the owner has already paid for the item being depreciated, its depreciation is a source of funds. Next the owner subtracts the uses of these funds—plant and equipment purchases, dividends to owners, repayment of debt, increases in accounts receivable, decreases in accounts payable, increases in inventory, and so on. The difference between the total sources and the total uses is the increase or decrease in working capital. By investigating the changes in the firm's working capital and the reasons for them, owners can create a more practical financial action plan for the future of the enterprise.

These statements are more than just complex documents used only by accountants and financial officers. When used in conjunction with the analytical tools described in the following sections, they can help small business managers map a firm's financial future and actively plan for profit. Mere preparation of these statement is not enough, however; owners and employees must *understand and use* the information contained in them to make the business more effective and efficient.

liabilities—*creditors' claims against the firm's assets.*

current liabilities—*those debts that must be paid within one year or within the normal operating cycle of a company.*

long-term liabilities—*liabilities that come due after one year.*

owner's equity—*the value of the owner's investment in the business.*

income statement—*a financial statement that represents a moving picture of a business, comparing its expenses against its revenue over a period of time to show its net profit (or loss).*

cost of goods sold—*the total cost, including shipping, of the merchandise sold during the year.*

statement of cash flows—*a financial statement showing the changes in a firm's working capital since the beginning of the year by listing the sources and the uses of those funds.*

Figure 8.2
Income Statement,
Sam's Appliance Shop

Net Sales Revenue		$1,870,841
Costs of Goods Sold		
Beginning Inventory, 1/1/xx	$805,745	
+ Purchases	939,827	
Goods Available for Sale	$1,745,572	
− Ending Inventory, 12/31/xx	455,455	
Costs of Goods Sold		$1,290,117
Gross Profit		$580,724
Operating Expenses		
Advertising	$139,670	
Insurance	46,125	
Depreciation		
Building	18,700	
Equipment	9,000	
Salaries	224,500	
Travel	4,000	
Entertainment	2,500	
Total Operating Expenses		$444,495
General Expenses		
Utilities	$5,300	
Telephone	2,500	
Postage	1,200	
Payroll Taxes	25,000	
Total General Expenses		$34,000
Other Expenses		
Interest Expense	$39,850	
Bad Check Expenses	1,750	
Total Other Expenses		$41,600
Total Expenses		$520,095
Net Income		$60,629

Creating Projected Financial Statements

Creating projected financial statements helps the small business owner transform business goals into reality. Budgets answer such questions as: What profit can the business expect to obtain? If the owner's profit objective is *x* dollars, what sales level must she achieve? What fixed and variable expenses can the owner expect at that level of sales? The answers to these and other questions are critical in formulating a successful financial plan for the small business.

This section will focus on creating projected income statements and balance sheets for the small business. These projected (or pro forma) statements estimate the profitability and the overall financial condition of the business for future months. They are an integral part of convincing potential lenders and investors to provide the financing needed to get the company off the ground. Also, because these statements project a firm's financial position through the end of the forecasted period, they help the owner plan the route to improved financial strength and healthy business growth.

Because the established business has a history of operating data from which to construct pro forma financial statements, the task is not nearly as difficult as it is for the beginning business. When creating pro forma financial statements for a brand-new business, an entrepreneur typically relies on published statistics summarizing the operation of similar-size companies in the same industry. These statistics are available from a number of sources (described later), but this section draws on information found in *Robert Morris Associates Annual Statement Studies*, a compilation of financial data on thousands of companies across hundreds of industries [organized by Standard Industrial Classification (SIC) Code].

Pro Forma Statements for the Small Business

One of the most important tasks confronting the entrepreneur launching a new enterprise is to determine the funds needed to begin operation as well as those required to keep going through the initial growth period. The amount of money needed to begin a business depends on the type of operation, its location, inventory requirements, sales volume, and other factors. But every new firm must have enough capital to cover all startup costs, including funds to rent or buy plant, equipment, and tools, as well as to pay for advertising, licenses, utilities, and other expenses. In addition, the owner must maintain a reserve of capital to carry the company until it begins to make a profit. Too often entrepreneurs are overly optimistic in their financial plans and fail to recognize that expenses initially exceed income for most small firms. This period of net losses is normal and may last from just a few months to several years. Owners must be able to meet payrolls, maintain adequate inventory, take advantage of cash discounts, grant customer credit, and meet personal obligations during this time.

THE PRO FORMA INCOME STATEMENT. In creating a projected income statement, an entrepreneur has two options: to develop a sales forecast and work down or set a profit target and work up. Most businesses employ the latter method—the owner targets a profit figure and then determines what sales level he must achieve to reach it. Of course, it is important to compare this sales target against the results of the marketing plan to determine whether or not it is realistic. Although they are projections, financial forecasts must be based in reality; otherwise, the resulting financial plan is nothing more than a hopeless dream. The next step is to estimate the expenses the business will incur in securing those sales. In any small business, the annual profit must be large enough to produce a return for time the owners spend operating the business, plus a return on their investment in the business.

Entrepreneurs who earn less in their own business than they could earn working for someone else must weigh carefully the advantages and disadvantages of choosing the path of entrepreneurship. Why be exposed to all of the risks, sacrifices, and hard work of beginning and operating a small business if the rewards are less than those of remaining in the secure employment of another? Ideally, the firm's net profit after taxes should be at least as much as the owner could earn by working for someone else.

An adequate profit must also include a reasonable return on the owner's total investment in the business. The owner's total investment is the amount contributed to the company at its inception plus any retained earnings (profits from previous years funneled back into the operation). If a would-be owner has $70,000 to invest and can invest it in securities and earn 10 percent, she should not consider investing it in a small business that would yield only 3 percent.

So, the owner's target income is the sum of a reasonable salary for the time spent running the business and a normal return on the amount invested in the firm. Determining how much this should be is the first step in creating the pro forma income statement.

The owner then must translate this target profit into a net sales figure for the forecasted period. To calculate net sales from a target profit, the owner needs published statistics for the particular type of business. Suppose an entrepreneur wants to launch a small retail bookstore and has determined that his target income is $29,000 annually. Statistics gathered from *Robert Morris Associates' Annual Statement Studies* show that the typical bookstore's net profit margin (net profit ÷ net sales) is 9.3 percent. Using this information, the owner can compute the sales level required to produce a net profit of $29,000:

$$\text{Net profit margin} = \frac{\text{net profit}}{\text{net sales (annual)}}$$

$$9.3\% = \frac{\$29,00}{\text{net sales (annual)}}$$

$$\text{Net sales} = \frac{\$29,000}{0.093}$$

$$= \$311,828$$

Now this entrepreneur knows that to make a net profit of $29,000 (before taxes), he must achieve annual sales of $311,828. To complete the projected income statement, the owner simply applies the appropriate statistics from *RMA Annual Statement Studies* to the annual sales figure. Because the statistics for each income statement item are expressed as percentages of net sales, he merely multiplies the proper statistic by the annual sales figure to obtain the desired value. For example, cost of goods sold usually comprises 61.4 percent of net sales for the typical small bookstore. So the owner of this new bookstore expects his cost of goods sold to be the following:

$$\text{Cost of goods sold} = \$311,828 \times 0.614 = \$191,462$$

The bookstore's complete projected income statement is shown as follows:

Net sales	(100%)	$311,828
− Cost of goods sold	(61.4%)	191,462
Gross profit margin	(38.6%)	$120,366
− Operating expenses	(29.3%)	$91,366
Net profit (before taxes)	(9.3%)	$29,000

At this point, the business appears to be a lucrative venture. But remember: This income statement represents a sales goal that the owner may not be able to reach. The next step is to determine whether or not this required sales volume is reasonable. One useful technique is to break down the required annual sales volume into daily sales figures. Assuming the store will be open six days per week for 50 weeks (300 days), the owner must average $1,039 per day in sales:

$$\text{Average daily sales} = \frac{\$311,828}{300 \text{ days}}$$

$$= \$1,039/\text{day}$$

This calculation gives the owner a better perspective of the sales required to yield an annual profit of $29,000.

To determine whether the profit expected from the business will meet or exceed the entrepreneur's target income, the prospective owner should also create an income statement based on a realistic sales estimate. The previous analysis showed the owner what sales level is needed to reach his desired profit. But what happens if sales are lower? Higher? The entrepreneur requires a reliable sales forecast using the market research techniques described in Chapter 5.

Suppose, for example, that after conducting a marketing survey of local customers and talking with nearby business owners, the prospective bookstore operator projects annual sales for the proposed business to be only $285,000. The entrepreneur must take this expected sales figure and develop a pro forma income statement.

Net sales	(100%)	$285,000
− Cost of goods sold	(61.4%)	174,990
Gross profit margin	(38.6%)	110,010
− Operating Expenses	(29.3%)	83,505
Net profit (before taxes)	(9.3%)	$ 26,505

Based on sales of $285,000, this entrepreneur should expect a net profit (before taxes) of $26,505. If this amount is acceptable as a return on the investment of time and money in the business, the owner should proceed with his planning.

At this stage in developing the financial plan, the owner should create a more detailed picture of the firm's expected operating expenses. One common method is to use the operating statistics data found in *Dun & Bradstreet's Cost of Doing Business* reports. These booklets document typical selected operating expenses (expressed as a percentage of net sales) for 190 different lines of businesses.

To ensure that no business expenses have been overlooked in the preparation of the business plan, the entrepreneur should list all of the initial expenses he will incur and have an accountant review the list. Figures 8.3 on page 252 and 8.4 on page 253 show two useful forms designed to help entrepreneurs estimate both monthly and startup expenses. Totals derived from this list of expenses should approximate the total expense figures calculated from published statistics. Naturally, entrepreneurs should be more confident of the total from their own lists of expenses since these reflect their particular set of circumstances.

THE PRO FORMA BALANCE SHEET. In addition to projecting the small firm's net profit or loss, the entrepreneur must develop a pro forma balance sheet outlining the fledgling firm's assets and liabilities. The owner primarily is concerned about the profitability, but the importance of the business assets is less obvious. In many cases, the small company begins its life on weak financial footing because the owner fails to determine the firm's total asset requirements. To prevent this major oversight, the owner should prepare a projected balance sheet listing every asset the business will need and all the claims against these assets.

Figure 8.3
Anticipated Expenses

Source: U.S. Small Business Administration, *Checklist for Going into Business*, Small Marketers Aid no. 71, Washington, DC, 1982, p. 6–7.

Worksheet No. 2
Estimated Monthly Expenses

Your estimate of monthly expenses based on sales of $_____ per year

Your estimate of how much cash you need to start your business (See column 3.)

What to put in column 2 (These figures are typical for one kind of business. You will have to decide how many months to allow for in your business.)

Item	Column 1	Column 2	Column 3
Salary of owner-manager	$	$	2 times column 1
All other salaries and wages			3 times column 1
Rent			3 times column 1
Advertising			3 times column 1
Delivery expense			3 times column 1
Supplies			3 times column 1
Telephone and telegraph			3 times column 1
Other utilities			3 times column 1
Insurance			Payment required by insurance company
Taxes, including Social Security			4 times column 1
Interest			3 times column 1
Maintenance			3 times column 1
Legal and other professional fees			3 times column 1
Miscellaneous			3 times column 1
Starting Costs You Have to Pay Only Once			Leave column 2 blank
Fixtures and equipment			Fill in worksheet 3 and put the total here
Decorating and remodeling			Talk it over with a contractor
Installation of fixtures and equipment			Talk to suppliers from who you buy these
Starting inventory			Suppliers will probably help you estimate this
Deposits with public utilities			Find out from utilities companies
Legal and other professional fees			Lawyer, accountant, and so on
Licenses and permits			Find out from city offices what you have to have
Advertising and promotion for opening			Estimate what you'll use
Accounts receivable			What you need to buy more stock until credit customers pay
Cash			For unexpected expenses or losses, special purchases, etc.
Other			Make a separate list and enter total
Total Estimated Cash You Need to Start		$	Add up all the numbers in column 2

Figure 8.4

Anticipated Expenditures For Fixtures and Equipment

Source: U.S. Small Business Administration, *Checklist for Going into Business,* Small Marketers Aid no. 71, Washington, DC, 1982, p. 12.

Worksheet No. 3

List of Furniture, Fixtures and Equipment

Leave out or add items to suit your business. Use separate sheets to list exactly what you need for each of the items below.	If you plan to pay cash in full, enter the full amount below and in the last column.	If you are going to pay by installments, fill out the columns below. Enter in the last column your downpayment plus at least one installment.			Estimate of the cash you need for furniture, fixtures and equipment
		Price	Downpayment	Amount of each installment	
Counters	$	$	$	$	$
Storage shelves, cabinets					
Display stands, shelves, tables					
Cash register					
Safe					
Window display fixtures					
Special lighting					
Outside sign					
Delivery equipment if needed					
Total Furniture, Fixtures, and Equipment (Enter this figure also in worksheet 2 under "Starting Costs You Have To Pay Only Once.")					$

Assets. Cash is one of the most useful assets the business owns; it is highly liquid and can quickly be converted into other tangible assets. But how much cash should a small business have at its inception? Obviously, there is no single dollar figure that fits the needs of every small firm. One practical rule of thumb, however, suggests that the company's cash balance should cover its operating expenses (less depreciation, a noncash expense) for one inventory turnover period. The cash balance for the small bookstore is calculated as follows:

Operating expenses = $83,505 (from projected income statement)

Less: depreciation (0.9% of annual sales*) of $2,565

Equals: cash expenses (annual) = $80,940

$$\text{Cash requirement} = \frac{\text{cash expenses}}{\text{average inventory turnover}}$$

$$= \frac{80,940}{3.5*}$$

$$= \$23,126$$

Notice the inverse relationship between the small firm's average turnover ratio and its cash requirements.

*From *RMA Annual Statement Studies.*

Another decision facing the entrepreneur is how much inventory the business should carry. A rough estimate of the inventory requirement can be calculated from the information found on the projected income statement and from published statistics:

Cost of goods sold = $174,990 (from projected income statement)

$$\text{Average inventory turnover} = \frac{\text{cost of goods sold}}{\text{inventory level}}$$

$$= 3.5 \text{ times/year}$$

Substituting,

$$3.5 \text{ times/year} = \frac{\$174,990}{\text{inventory level}}$$

Solving algebraically,

$$\text{Inventory level} = \$49,997$$

The owner can use the planning forms shown in Figures 8.3 and 8.4 to estimate fixed assets (land, building, equipment, and fixtures). Suppose the estimate of fixed assets is as follows:

Fixtures	$ 7,500
Office equipment	1,100
Cash register	1,200
Signs	300
Total	$10,100

LIABILITIES. To complete the projected balance sheet, the owner must record all of the small firm's liabilities—the claims against the assets. The bookstore owner was able to finance 50 percent of the inventory and fixtures through suppliers. The only other major claim against the firm's assets is a note payable to the entrepreneur's father-in-law for $20,000.

The final step is to compile all of these items into a projected balance sheet, as shown in Figure 8.5.

4. Understand the basic financial statements through ratio analysis.

Ratio Analysis

Once an entrepreneur has the business "up and running" with the help of a solid financial plan, the next step is to keep the company moving in the right direction with the help of proper financial controls. Establishing these controls—and using them consistently—are keys to keeping a business vibrant and healthy. "If you don't keep a finger on the pulse of your company's finances, you risk making bad decisions," explains one business writer. "You could be in serious financial trouble and not even realize it."[5]

A smoothly functioning system of financial controls is essential to achieving business success. Such a system can serve as an early warning device for underlying problems that could destroy a young business. According to one writer:

A company's financial accounting and reporting systems will provide signals, through comparative analysis, of impending trouble, such as:

Figure 8.5
Projected Balance Sheet For a Small Bookstore

Assets		Liabilities	
Current Assets		**Current Liabilities**	
Cash	$23,126	Accounts Payable	$24,998
Inventory	49,997	Notes Payable	3,750
Miscellaneous	1,800		
Total Current Assets	$74,923	Total Current Liabilities	$28,748
Fixed Assets		**Long-Term Liabilities**	
Fixtures	$7,500	Notes Payable	$20,000
Office Equipment	1,100		
Cash Register	1,200		
Signs	300	Owner's Equity	$36,275
Total Fixed Assets	$10,100		
Total Assets	$85,023	Total Liabilities and Owner's Equity	$85,023

☆ Decreasing sales and falling profit margins.

☆ Increasing corporate overheads.

☆ Growing inventories and accounts receivable.

These are all signals of declining cash flows from operations, the lifeblood of every business. As cash flows decrease, the squeeze begins:

☆ Payments to vendors become slower.

☆ Maintenance on production equipment lags.

☆ Raw material shortages appear.

☆ Equipment breakdowns occur.

All of these begin to have a negative impact on productivity. Now the downward spiral has begun in earnest. The key is hearing and focusing on the signals.[6]

What are these signals, and how does an entrepreneur go about hearing and focusing on them? One extremely helpful tool is ratio analysis. **Ratio analysis** is a method of expressing the relationships between any two accounting elements and provides a convenient technique for performing financial analysis. When analyzed properly, ratios serve as barometers of a company's financial health. "You owe it to yourself to understand each ratio and what it means to your business," says one accountant. "Ratios point out potential trouble areas so you can correct them before they multiply."[7] Ratio analysis allows a small business manager to determine if her firm is carrying excessive inventory, experiencing heavy operating expenses, overextending credit, taking on too much debt, managing to pay its bills on time, and to answer other questions relating to the efficient operation of the firm. Unfortunately, few business owners actually use ratio analysis; one study discovered that just 2 percent of all entrepreneurs compute financial ratios and use them in managing their businesses![8]

Clever business owners use financial ratio analysis to identify problems in their businesses while they are still problems, not business-threatening crises. Tracking these ratios over time permits an owner to spot a variety of "red flags" that are indications of these problem areas. This is critical to business success because business owners cannot solve problems they do not know exist!

At Atkinson-Baker & Associates, a Los Angeles court-reporting service, every one of the firm's 50 employees is responsible every day for tracking a key financial statistic relating

ratio analysis—*a method of expressing the relationships between any two accounting elements that allows business owners to analyze their companies' financial performances.*

to his or her job. CEO Alan Atkinson-Baker believes that waiting until the month's end to compile financial ratios takes away a company's ability to respond to events as they happen. "Employees have statistics for their jobs, and it helps them see how well they are producing," he says. Because the statistics are linked directly to their jobs, employees quickly learn which numbers to track and how to compile or to calculate them. "Each day everybody reports their statistics," explains Atkinson-Baker. "It all goes into a computer . . . , and we keep track of it all." A spreadsheet summarizes the calculations and generates 27 graphs so managers can analyze trends in a meeting the following morning. One rule the company developed from its financial analysis is "Don't spend more today than you brought in yesterday." Atkinson-Baker explains, "You can never run into trouble as long as you stick to that rule." He also notes that effective financial planning would be impossible without timely data. "When we have had problem areas, the statistics have helped us catch them before they become a bigger problem," he says.[9]

Business owners also can use ratio analysis to increase the likelihood of obtaining a bank loan. By analyzing financial statements with ratios, an owner can anticipate potential problems and identify important strengths in advance. And loan officers *do* use ratios to analyze the financial statements of companies applying for loans. One bank loan officer explains, "We look closely at debt to net worth, debt to net income, and the quick ratio . . . We are primarily interested in trends."[10]

But how many ratios should the small business manager monitor to maintain adequate financial control over the firm? The number of ratios that an owner could calculate is limited only by the number of accounts recorded on a firm's financial statements. However, tracking too many ratios only creates confusion and saps the meaning from an entrepreneur's financial analysis. The secret to successful ratio analysis is *simplicity*, focusing on just enough ratios to provide a clear picture of a company's financial standing.

12 Key Ratios

In keeping with the idea of simplicity, we will describe 12 key ratios that will enable most business owners to monitor their companies' financial positions without becoming bogged down in financial details. This chapter presents explanations of these ratios and examples based on the balance sheet and the income statement for Sam's Appliance Shop shown in Figures 8.1 and 8.2. We will group them into four categories: liquidity ratios, leverage ratios, operating ratios, and profitability ratios.

liquidity ratios—*tell whether a small business will be able to meet its short-term obligations as they come due.*

LIQUIDITY RATIOS. **Liquidity ratios** tell whether or not the small business will be able to meet its short-term financial obligations as they come due. These ratios can forewarn a business owner of impending cash flow problems. A small company with solid liquidity not only is able to pay its bills on time, but it also has enough cash to take advantage of attractive business opportunities as they arise. The primary measures of liquidity are the current ratio and the quick ratio.

current ratio—*measures a small firm's solvency by indicating its ability to pay current debts out of current assets.*

1. Current Ratio. The **current ratio** measures the small firm's solvency by indicating its ability to pay current liabilities (debts) from current assets. It is calculated in the following manner:

$$\text{Current ratio} = \frac{\text{current assets}}{\text{current liabilities}}$$

$$= \frac{\$686,985}{\$367,850}$$

$$= 1.87:1$$

Sam's Appliance Shop has $1.87 in current assets for every $1 it has in current liabilities.

Current assets are those which the manager expects to convert into cash in the ordinary business cycle and normally include cash, notes/accounts receivable, inventory, and any other short-term marketable securities. Current liabilities are those short-term obligations that come due within one year and include notes/accounts payable, taxes payable, and accruals.

The current ratio is sometimes called the *working capital ratio* and is the most commonly used measure of short-term solvency. Typically, financial analysts suggest that a small business maintain a current ratio of at least 2:1 (i.e., two dollars of current assets for every one dollar of current liabilities) to maintain a comfortable cushion of working capital. Generally, the higher the firm's current ratio, the stronger its financial position, but a high current ratio does not guarantee that the firm's assets are being used in the most profitable manner. For example, the business may be maintaining excessive balances of idle cash or may be overinvesting in inventory.

With its current ratio of 1.87, Sam's Appliance Shop could liquidate its current assets at 53.5 percent (1 ÷ 1.87 = .535) of its book value and still manage to pay its current creditors in full.

2. Quick Ratio. The current ratio sometimes can be misleading because it does not show the quality of a company's current assets. For instance, a company with a large number of past-due receivables and stale inventory could boast an impressive current ratio and still be on the verge of financial collapse. The **quick ratio** (or the **acid test ratio**) is a more conservative measure of a firm's liquidity since it shows the extent to which its most liquid assets cover its current liabilities. This ratio includes only a company's "quick assets," excluding the most illiquid asset of all—inventory. It is calculated as follows:

$$\text{Quick ratio} = \frac{\text{quick assets}}{\text{current liabilities}}$$

$$= \frac{\$686,985 - \$455,455}{\$367,850}$$

$$= 0.63:1$$

Quick assets include cash, readily marketable securities, and notes/accounts receivables, assets that can be converted into cash immediately if needed. Most small firms determine quick assets by subtracting inventory from current assets because they cannot convert inventory into cash quickly. Also, inventories are the assets on which losses are most likely to occur in case of liquidation.

The quick ratio is a more specific measure of a firm's ability to meet its short-term obligations and is a more rigorous test of its liquidity. It expresses capacity to pay current debts if all sales income ceased immediately. Generally, a quick ratio of 1:1 is considered satisfactory. A ratio of less than 1:1 indicates that the small firm is overly dependent on inventory and on future sales to satisfy short-term debt. A quick ratio of more than 1:1 indicates a greater degree of financial security.

LEVERAGE RATIOS. **Leverage ratios** measure the financing supplied by the firm's owners against that supplied by its creditors; they are a gauge of the depth of a company's debt. These ratios show the extent to which an entrepreneur relies on debt capital (rather than equity capital) to finance operating expenses, capital expenditures, and expansion costs. As such, it is a measure of the degree of financial risk in a company. Generally, small businesses with low leverage ratios are less affected by economic downturns, but the returns for these firms are lower during economic booms. Conversely, small firms with high leverage ratios are more vulnerable to economic slides because their debt loads demolish cash flow; however, they have greater potential for large profits.

debt ratio—*measures the percentage of total assets financed by a company's creditors compared to its owners.*

3. Debt Ratio. The small firm's **debt ratio** measures the percentage of total assets financed by its creditors compared to its owners. The debt ratio is calculated as follows:

$$\text{Debt ratio} = \frac{\text{total debt (or liabilities)}}{\text{total assets}}$$

$$= \frac{\$367,850 + \$212,150}{\$847,655}$$

$$= 0.68:1$$

Total debt includes all current liabilities and any outstanding long-term notes and bonds. Total assets represent the sum of the firm's current assets, fixed assets, and intangible assets. Clearly, a high debt ratio means that creditors provide a large percentage of the firm's total financing and, therefore, bear most of the company's financial risk. Owners generally prefer higher leverage ratios; otherwise, business funds must come either from the owners' personal assets or from taking on new owners, which means giving up more control over the business. Also, with a greater portion of the firm's assets financed by creditors, the owner is able to generate profits with a smaller personal investment. However, creditors typically prefer moderate debt ratios since a lower debt ratio indicates a smaller chance of creditor losses in case of liquidation. To lenders and creditors, high debt ratios mean a great risk of default.

According to a senior analyst at Dun & Bradstreet's Analytical Services, "If managed properly, debt can be beneficial because it's a great way to have money working for you. You're leveraging your assets, so you're making more money than you're paying out in interest." However, excessive debt can be the downfall of a business. "As we pile up debt on our personal credit cards our lifestyles are squeezed," he says. "The same thing happens to a business. Overpowering debt sinks thousands of businesses each year."[11]

debt to net worth ratio—*expresses the relationship between the capital contributions from creditors and those from owners.*

4. Debt to Net Worth Ratio. The small firm's debt to net worth ratio also expresses the relationship between the capital contributions from creditors and those from owners. This ratio shows a company's capital structure by comparing what the business "owes" to "what it owns." It is a measure of the small firm's ability to meet both its creditor and owner obligations in case of liquidation. The debt to net worth ratio is calculated as follows:

$$\text{Debt to net worth ratio} = \frac{\text{total debt (or liabilities)}}{\text{tangible net worth}}$$

$$= \frac{\$367,850 + \$212,150}{\$267,655 - \$3,500}$$

$$= 2.20:1$$

Total debt is the sum of current liabilities and long-term liabilities, and tangible net worth represents the owners' investment in the business (capital + capital stock + earned surplus + retained earnings) less any intangible assets (e.g., goodwill) the firm owns.

The higher this ratio, the more leverage a business is using, and the lower the degree of protection afforded creditors if the business should fail. Also, a higher debt to net worth ratio means that the firm has less capacity to borrow; lenders and creditors see the firm as being "borrowed up." Conversely, a low ratio typically is associated with a higher level of financial security, giving the business greater borrowing potential.

As the firm's debt to net worth ratio approaches 1:1, the creditors' interest in the business approaches that of the owners'. If the ratio is greater than 1:1, creditors' claims exceed those of the owners', and the business may be undercapitalized. In other words, the owner has not supplied an adequate amount of capital, forcing the business to be overextended in terms of debt.

5. Times Interest Earned. The **times interest earned** ratio is a measure of the small firm's ability to make the interest payments on its debt. It tells how many times the company's earnings cover the interest payments on the debt it is carrying. This ratio measures the size of the cushion a company has in covering the interest cost of its debt load. The times interest earned ratio is calculated as follows:

$$\text{Times interest earned} = \frac{\text{earnings before interest and taxes (or EBIT)}}{\text{total interest expense}}$$

$$= \frac{\$60,629 + \$39,850}{\$39,850}$$

$$= 2.52:1$$

times interest earned ratio—*measures the small firm's ability to make the interest payments on its debt.*

EBIT is the firm's profit *before* deducting interest expense and taxes; the denominator measures the amount the business paid in interest over the accounting period.

A high ratio suggests that the company would have little difficulty meeting the interest payments on its loans; creditors would see this as a sign of safety for future loans. Conversely, a low ratio is an indication that the company is overextended in its debts; earnings will not be able to cover its debt service if this ratio is less than 1. "I look for a [times interest earned] ratio of higher than three-to-one," says one financial analyst, "which indicates that management has considerable breathing room to make its debt payments. When the ratio drops below one-to-one, it clearly indicates management is under tremendous pressure to raise cash. The risk of default or bankruptcy is very high."[12] Many creditors look for a times interest earned ratio of at least 4:1 to 6:1 before pronouncing a company to be a good credit risk.

Trouble looms on the horizon for companies whose debt loads are so heavy that they must starve critical operations, research and development, customer service, and others just to pay interest on the debt. Because their interest payments are so large, highly leveraged companies find that they are restricted when it comes to spending cash, whether on an acquisition, normal operations, or capital spending.

Debt is a powerful financial tool, but companies must handle it carefully—just as a demolitionist handles dynamite. And, like dynamite, too much debt can be dangerous. Unfortunately, some companies that have pushed their debt loads beyond the safety barrier (see Figure 8.6 on page 260) and are struggling to survive. Managed carefully, however, debt can boost a company's performance and improve its productivity. Its treatment in the tax code also makes debt a much cheaper means of financing growth than equity. When companies with AA financial ratings borrow at 9.2 percent, the after-tax cost is just 6.6 percent (because interest payments to lenders are tax deductible); equity financing costs more than twice that.

Table 8.1 on page 261 describes how lenders view liquidity and leverage.

OPERATING RATIOS. **Operating ratios** help the owner evaluate the small firm's performance and indicate how effectively the business employs its resources. The more effectively its resources are used, the less capital a small business will require. These five operating ratios are designed to help entrepreneurs spot those areas where they must improve if their businesses are to remain competitive.

operating ratios—*help owners evaluate a small firm's performance and indicate how effectively the business employs its resources.*

Figure 8.6
The Right Amount of Debt Is a Balancing Act

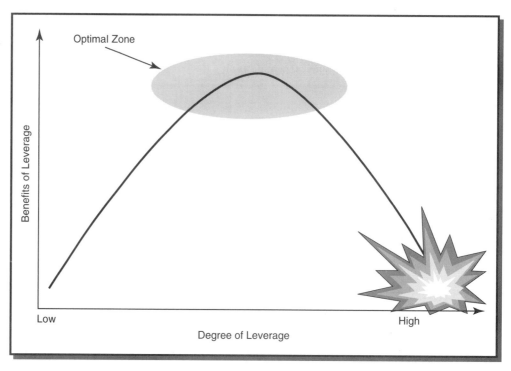

6. Average Inventory Turnover. A small firm's **average inventory turnover ratio** measures the number of times its average inventory is sold out, or turned over, during the accounting period. This ratio tells the owner whether or not the firm's inventory is being managed properly. It apprises the owner of whether the business inventory is understocked, overstocked, or obsolete. The average inventory turnover ratio is calculated as follows:

average inventory turnover ratio—

measures the number of times a company's inventory is sold out, or turned over, during the accounting period.

$$\text{Average inventory turnover ratio} = \frac{\text{cost of goods sold}}{\text{average inventory}}$$

$$= \frac{\$1,290,117}{(\$805,745 + \$455,455) \div 2}$$

$$= 2.05 \text{ times/year}$$

Average inventory is the sum of the value of the firm's inventory at the beginning of the accounting period and its value at the end of the accounting period, divided by 2.

This ratio tells the owner how fast the merchandise is moving through the business and helps to balance the company's inventory on the fine line between oversupply and undersupply. To determine the average number of days units remain in inventory, the owner can divide the average inventory turnover ratio into the number of days in the accounting period (e.g., 365 ÷ average inventory turnover ratio). The result is called *days' inventory* (or *average age of inventory*). An above-average inventory turnover indicates that the small business has a healthy, salable, and liquid inventory and a supply of quality merchandise supported by sound pricing policies. A below-average inventory turnover suggests an illiquid inventory characterized by obsolescence, overstocking, stale merchandise, and poor purchasing procedures.

Table 8.1
How Lenders View Liquidity and Leverage

Source: Adapted from David H. Bangs, Jr., *Financial Troubleshooting* (Dover, NH: Upstart Publishing Company, 1992), p. 124.

	Liquidity	Leverage
Low	If chronic, this is often evidence of mismanagement. It is a sign that the owner has not planned for the company's working capital needs. In most businesses characterized by low liquidity, there is usually no financial plan. This situation is often associated with last minute or "Friday night" financing.	This is a very conservative position. With this kind of leverage, lenders are likely to lend money to satisfy a company's capital needs. Owners in this position should have no trouble borrowing money.
Average	This is an indication of good management. The company is using its current assets wisely and productively. Although they may not be impressed, lenders feel comfortable making loans to companies with adequate liquidity.	If a company's leverage is comparable to that of other businesses of similar size in the same industry, lenders are comfortable making loans. The company is not overburdened with debt and is demonstrating its ability to use its resources to grow.
High	Some lenders look for this because it indicates a most conservative company. However, companies that constantly operate this way usually are forgoing growth opportunities because they are not making the most of their assets.	Businesses that carry excessive levels of debt scare most lenders off. Companies in this position normally will have a difficult time borrowing money unless they can show lenders good reasons for making loans. Owners of these companies must be prepared to sell lenders on their ability to repay.

Businesses that turn their inventories more rapidly require a smaller inventory investment to produce a particular sales volume. That means that these companies tie up less cash in inventory that idly sits on shelves. For instance, if Sam's could turn its inventory *four* times each year instead of just *two*, the company would require an average inventory of just $322,529 instead of the current level of $630,600 to generate sales of $1,870,841. Increasing the number of inventory turns would free up more than $308,000 currently tied up in excess inventory! Sam's would benefit from improved cash flow and higher profits.

The inventory turnover ratio can be misleading, however. For example, an excessively high ratio could mean the firm has a shortage of inventory and is experiencing stockouts. Similarly, a low ratio could be the result of planned inventory stockpiling to meet seasonal peak demand. Another problem is that the ratio is based on an inventory balance calculated from two days out of the entire accounting period. Thus, inventory fluctuations due to seasonal demand patterns are ignored, which may bias the resulting ratio. There is no universal, ideal inventory turnover ratio. Financial analysts suggest that a favorable turnover ratio depends on the type of business, its size, its profitability, its method of inventory valuation, and other relevant factors.

7. Average Collection Period. The small firm's **average collection period ratio** (or **days sales outstanding, DSO**) tells the average number of days it takes to collect accounts receivable. To compute the average collection period ratio, you must first calculate the firm's receivables turnover. If Sam's *credit* sales for the year were $1,309,589, then the company's receivables turnover ratio would be as follows:

average collection period ratio—*measures the number of days it takes a company to collect its accounts receivable.*

$$\text{Receivables turnover ratio} = \frac{\text{credit sales}}{\text{accounts receivable}}$$

$$= \frac{\$1,309,589}{\$179,225}$$

$$= 7.31 \text{ times/year}$$

This ratio measures the number of times the firm's accounts receivable turn over during the accounting period. Sam's Appliance Shop turns over its receivables 7.31 times per year. The higher the firm's receivables turnover ratio, the shorter the time lag between the sale and the cash collection.

Use the following to calculate the firm's average collection period ratio:

$$\text{Average collection period ratio} = \frac{\text{days in accounting period}}{\text{receivables turnover ratio}}$$

$$= \frac{365 \text{ days}}{7.31 \text{ times/year}}$$

$$= 50.0 \text{ days}$$

So, Sam's Appliance Shop's accounts and notes receivable are outstanding for an average of 50 days. Typically, the higher the firm's average collection period ratio, the greater the chance of bad debt losses.

One of the most useful applications of the collection period ratio is to compare it to the industry average and to the firm's credit terms. Such a comparison will indicate the degree of the small company's control over its credit sales and collection techniques. One rule of thumb suggests that the firm's collection period ratio should be no more than one-third greater than its credit terms. For example, if a small company's credit terms are net 45, its average collection period ratio should be no more than 60 days. A ratio greater than 60 days would indicate poor collection procedures.

Slow payers represent a great risk to many small businesses. Many entrepreneurs proudly point to rapidly rising sales only to find that they must borrow money to keep their companies going because credit customers are paying their bills in 45, 60, or even 90 days instead of 30. Slow receivables are a real danger because they usually lead to a cash crisis that threatens a company's survival. Table 8.2 on page 264 shows how to calculate the savings associated with lowering a company's average collection period ratio.

average payable period ratio—*measures the number of days it takes a company to pay its accounts payable.*

8. Average Payable Period. The converse of the average collection period ratio, the **average payable period ratio**, tells the average number of days it takes a company to pay its accounts payable. Like the average collection period, it is measured in days. To compute this ratio, first calculate the payables turnover ratio. Sam's payables turnover ratio is as follows:

$$\text{Payables turnover ratio} = \frac{\text{purchases}}{\text{accounts payable}}$$

$$= \frac{\$939,827}{\$152,580}$$

$$= 6.16 \text{ times/year}$$

Now You See It.
Now You Don't.

It was so easy to do . . . and so easy to justify. Then things began to get out of control.

After years at the helm of the high-flying Comptronix Corporation, an Alabama electronics company, William Hebding admitted that he and two other top officers had improperly inflated the company's profits by engaging in fraudulent accounting practices. The managers disclosed that they had recorded as capital assets some expenses such as salaries and startup costs and had overstated Comptronix's inventory holdings to decrease its cost of goods sold. The reason was to shore up a weakening balance sheet and to give the illusion that profits were holding at the levels to which investors had grown accustomed. After the scandal broke, Mr. Hebding and his two accomplices were quickly fired.

Comptronix's story has become all too common as tough economic times and fierce competitive conditions exert pressure on companies' profits. "When companies are desperate to stay afloat, inventory fraud is the easiest way to produce profits and dress up the balance sheet," says one accounting expert. The tactic is so simple, yet so effective, primarily because detecting fraudulent adjustments to inventory is so difficult, even for auditors at top accounting firms. In a typical audit, accountants take a small sample of the goods and raw materials in stock and compare an actual count with the company's inventory records. One auditor claims that it is extremely difficult, if not impossible, for an outside auditor to spot inventory fraud "if top management is directing it." One accounting expert reports that inventory fraud has increased fourfold within the past five years.

In another case, an auditor spotted a barrel whose contents management had valued at several thousands of dollars. In reality, it was filled with floor sweepings! When the auditor checked the barrel, he forced the company to subtract its value from inventory. Managers meekly apologized to the auditor, who let the incident go unreported. "It never occurred to the auditor that this was an example of intentional and pervasive fraud," observes a colleague.

Companies under pressure to perform, such as those who have gone public recently, are often the perpetrators of such scams, which usually are surprisingly simple. For instance, Kendall Square Research Corporation, a maker of supercomputers, recently acknowledged that it counted as sales numerous computers that it knew customers could not pay for. The company had predicted sales of $60 million, but an investigation showed that sales were only $18.1 million. "There is tremendous pressure on companies such as ours to continue their revenue-growth trend," says the company's new chief financial officer.

At Media Vision Technology, Inc., which makes audio and animation components for personal computers, managers created a phantom warehouse to hide inventory for returned products. Rather than charge the returns against company sales (and lower its profits), they decided to pretend the returns never happened.

One of the most blatant cases of fraud occurred in a New York copper-wire maker, Laribee Wire Manufacturing. The company, plagued by huge debt—almost *seven* times its equity—was trying to buoy a sinking ship by creating fictitious inventories. Both sales and cash flow were spiraling downward rapidly and the company needed cash desperately to stay afloat. Using large amounts of inventory as collateral, Laribee borrowed $130 million from six banks.

The problem was that the inventory didn't really exist.

Some was carried on the books at extremely bloated values. Large amounts of wire were reported at $2.20 per pound when it was selling at only $1.70 to $1.75 per pound. In addition, shipments of wire between plants were recorded in inventory at both plants. Some shipments, supposedly "in transit," never even left the first plant. And 4.5 million pounds of copper rod, supposedly worth more than $5 million, that Laribee said it was storing in two upstate New York warehouses would have required three times the capacity of the buildings!

Within six months of receiving the bank loans, Laribee filed for bankruptcy protection. The court-appointed trustee, John Turbidy, estimates that inventory fraud contributed $5.5 million (before taxes) to Laribee's year-end results. Without the inventory fraud and other accounting sleights-of-hand, Laribee would have reported a loss of $6.5 million for the year, he estimates. "It was one of the biggest inventory overstatements I've ever seen," says Turbidy.

1. Refer to the balance sheet and income statement for Sam's Appliance Shop (Figures 8.1 and 8.2) and do some "creative accounting" of your own. Inflate the inventory values by a significant amount and see what happens to net worth and profits.

2. Recalculate the 12 key ratios for Sam's Appliance Shop. Compare the results. Which version would look better to a banker? Why?

3. Who loses when the managers of a company commit inventory fraud? What are the ethical implications of such practices?

Sources: Adapted from Lee Berton, "Tech Concerns Fudge Figures to Buoy Stocks," *Wall Street Journal*, May 19, 1994, pp. B1, B2; Lee Berton, "Convenient Fiction," *Wall Street Journal*, December 14, 1992, pp. A1, A4.

To find the average payable period, use the following computation:

$$\text{Average payable period} = \frac{\text{days in accounting period}}{\text{payables turnover ratio}}$$

$$= \frac{365 \text{ days}}{6.16}$$

$$= 59.3 \text{ days}$$

Sam's Appliance Shop takes an average of 59 days to pay its accounts with suppliers.

An excessively high average payables period ratio indicates the presence of a significant amount of past-due accounts payable. Although sound cash management calls for a business owner to keep cash as long as possible, slowing payables too drastically can severely damage the company's credit rating. Ideally, the average payable period would match (or exceed) the time it takes to convert inventory into sales and ultimately into cash. In this case, the company's vendors would be financing its inventory and its credit sales.

One of the most meaningful comparisons for this ratio is against the credit terms suppliers offer (or an average of the credit terms offered). If the average payable ratio slips beyond vendors' credit terms, it is an indication that the company is suffering from cash shortages or a sloppy accounts payable procedure and its credit rating is in danger. If this

---

Table 8.2
How Lowering Your Average Collection Period Can Save You Money

Source: "Days Saved, Thousands Earned," *Inc.*, November 1995, p. 98.

Too often, entrepreneurs fail to recognize the importance of collecting their accounts receivable on time. After all, collecting accounts is not as glamorous or as much fun as generating sales. Lowering a company's average collection period ratio, however, *can* produce tangible—and often significant—savings. The following formula shows how to convert an improvement in a company's average collection period ratio into dollar savings:

$$\frac{\text{Annual}}{\text{savings}} = \frac{(\text{Credit sales} \times \text{annual interest rate} \times \text{number of days average collection period is lowered})}{365}$$

where,

   credit sales = company's annual credit sales in $

   annual interest rate = the interest rate at which the company borrows money

   number of days average collection period is lowered = the difference between the previous year's average collection period ratio and the current one

Example:

Sam's Appliance Shop's average collection period ratio is 50 days. Suppose that the previous year's average collection period ratio was 56 days, a six-day improvement. The company's credit sales for the most recent year were $1,309,589. If Sam borrows money at 10.25 percent, this six-day improvement has generated savings for Sam's Appliance Shop of:

$$\text{Savings} = \frac{\$1,309,589 \times 10.25\% \times 6 \text{ days}}{365 \text{ days}} = \$2,207$$

By collecting his accounts receivable just six days faster on the average, Sam has saved his business more than $2,200! Of course, if a company's average collection period ratio rises, the same calculation will tell the owner how much that costs.

---

ratio is significantly lower than vendors' credit terms, it may be a sign that the firm is not using its cash most effectively.

9. Net Sales to Total Assets. The small company's **net sales to total assets ratio** (also called the **total assets turnover ratio**) is a general measure of its ability to generate sales in relation to its assets. It describes how productively the firm employs its assets to produce sales revenue. The total assets turnover ratio is calculated as follows:

$$\text{Total assets turnover ratio} = \frac{\text{net sales}}{\text{net total assets}}$$

$$= \frac{\$1,870,841}{\$847,655}$$

$$= 2.21{:}1$$

The denominator of this ratio, net total assets, is the sum of all of the firm's assets (cash, inventory, land, buildings, equipment, tools, everything owned) less depreciation. This ratio is meaningful only when compared to that of similar firms in the same industry category. A total assets turnover ratio below the industry average may indicate that the small firm is not generating an adequate sales volume for its asset size.

10. Net Sales to Working Capital. The **net sales to working capital ratio** measures how many dollars in sales the business makes for every dollar of working capital (working capital current assets—current liabilities). Also called the **turnover of working capital ratio**, this proportion tells the owner how efficiently working capital is being used to generate sales. It is calculated as follows:

$$\text{Net sales to working capital ratio} = \frac{\text{net sales}}{\text{current assets} - \text{current liabilities}}$$

$$= \frac{\$1,870,841}{\$686,985 - \$367,850}$$

$$= 5.86{:}1$$

An excessively low net sales to working capital ratio indicates that the small firm is not employing its working capital efficiently or profitably. On the other hand, an extremely high ratio points to an inadequate level of working capital to maintain a suitable level of sales, which puts creditors in a more vulnerable position. This ratio is very helpful in maintaining sufficient working capital as the small business grows. It is critical for the small firm to keep a satisfactory level of working capital to nourish its expansion, and the net sales to working capital ratio helps define the level of working capital required to support higher sales volumes.

PROFITABILITY RATIOS. **Profitability ratios** indicate how efficiently the small firm is being managed. They provide the owner with information about the company's bottom line; in other words, they describe how successfully the firm is conducting business.

11. Net Profit on Sales. The **net profit on sales ratio** (also called the **profit margin on sales** or **net profit margin**) measures the firm's profit per dollar of sales. The computed percentage shows the number of cents of each sales dollar remaining after deducting all expenses and income taxes. The profit margin on sales is calculated as follows:

net sales to total assets ratio—*measures a company's ability to generate sales in relation to its assets.*

net sales to working capital ratio—*measures how many dollars in sales a business makes for every dollar of working capital.*

Profitability ratios—*indicate how efficiently a small firm is being managed.*

net profit on sales ratio—*measures a company's profit per dollar of sales.*

$$\text{Net profit on sales ratio} \quad = \quad \frac{\text{net profit}}{\text{net sales}}$$

$$= \frac{\$60,629}{\$1,870,841}$$

$$= 3.24\%$$

Most small business owners believe that a high profit margin on sales is necessary for a successful business operation, but this is a myth. To evaluate this ratio properly, the owner must consider the firm's asset value, its inventory and receivables turnover ratios, and its total capitalization. For example, the typical small supermarket earns an average net profit of only one cent on each dollar of sales, but its inventory may turn over as many as 25 times a year. If the firm's profit margin on sales is below the industry average, it may be a sign that its prices are relatively low, or that its costs are excessively high, or both.

If a company's net profit on sales ratio is excessively low, the owner should check the gross profit margin (net sales minus cost of goods sold expressed as a percentage of net sales). Of course, a reasonable gross profit margin varies from industry to industry. For instance, a service company may have a gross profit margin of 75 percent, while a manufacturer's may be 35 percent. The key is to know what a reasonable gross profit margin is for your particular business. If this margin slips too low, it puts a company's future in immediate jeopardy.

Figure 8.7 shows the net profit margin for corporations across the past five decades.

"I vote we hang the darn thing upside down and go home!"

Source: Copyright 1989 by Patrick Hardin.

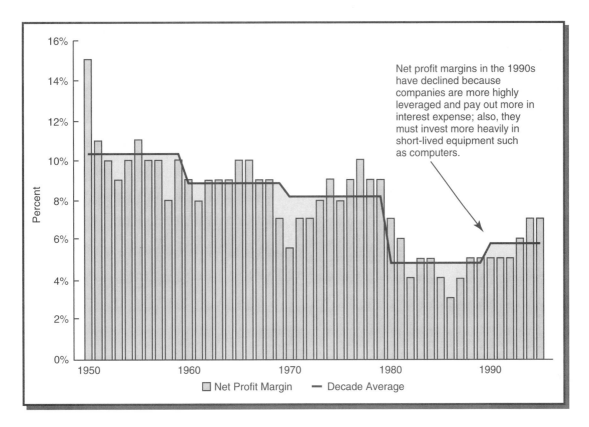

Net profit margins in the 1990s have declined because companies are more highly leveraged and pay out more in interest expense; also, they must invest more heavily in short-lived equipment such as computers.

☐ Net Profit Margin   — Decade Average

Figure 8.7
After-Tax Corporate Net Profit Margin, 1950–1995
Source: Joe Spiers, "The Myth of Corporate Greed," *Fortune*, April 15, 1996, p.67.
© 1996 *Time, Inc.* All rights reserved.

12. Net Profit to Equity. The **net profit to equity ratio** (or **return on net worth ratio**) measures the owners' rate of return on investment. Because it reports the percentage of the owners' investment in the business that is being returned through profits annually, it is one of the most important indicators of a firm's profitability or a management's efficiency. The net profit to equity ratio is computed as follows:

$$\text{Net profit to equity ratio} = \frac{\text{net profit}}{\text{owners' equity (or net worth)}}$$

$$= \frac{\$60,629}{\$267,655}$$

$$= 22.65\%$$

This ratio compares profits earned during the accounting period with the amount the owners have invested in the business during that time. If this interest rate on the owners' investment is excessively low, some of this capital might be better employed elsewhere.

All Is Not Paradise in Eden's Garden: Part 1

Joe and Kaitlin Eden, co-owners of Eden's Garden, a small nursery, lawn, and garden supply business, have just received their year-end financial statements from their accountant. At their last meeting three months ago with their accountant, Shelley Edison, the Edens had mentioned that they seemed to be having trouble paying their bills on time. "Some of our suppliers have threatened to put us on 'credit-hold,'" said Joe.

"I think you need to sit down with me very soon and let me show you how to analyze your financial statements so you can see what's happening in your business," Shelley told them at that meeting. Unfortunately, that was the beginning of Eden's Garden's busy season, and the Edens were so busy running the company that they never got around to setting a time to meet with Shelley.

"Now that business has slowed down a little, perhaps we should call Shelley and see what she can do to help us understand what our financial statements are trying to tell us," said Kaitlin.

"Right. Before it's too late to do anything about it . . ." said Joe, pulling out the following financial statements.

Income Statement, Eden's Garden

Net Sales Revenue*		$689,247
Cost of Goods Sold		
Beginning Inventory, 1/1/xx	$ 78,271	
+ Purchases	403,569	
Goods Available for Sale	$481,840	
− Ending Inventory, 12/31/ss	86,157	
Cost of Goods Sold		$395,683
Gross Profit		$293,564
Operating Expenses		
Advertising	$ 22,150	
Insurance	9,187	
Depreciation		
Building	26,705	
Autos	7,895	
Equipment	11,200	
Salaries	116,541	
Uniforms	4,018	
Repairs and Maintenance	9,097	
Travel	2,658	
Entertainment	2,798	
Total Operating Expenses		$212,249
General Expenses		
Utilities	$ 7,987	
Telephone	2,753	
Professional Fees	3,000	
Postage	1,892	
Payroll Taxes	11,589	
Total General Expenses		$27,221
Other Expenses		
Interest Expense	$21,978	
Bad Check Expense	679	
Miscellaneous Expense	1,248	
Total Other Expenses		$23,905
Total Expenses		$263,375
Net Income		$ 30,189

*Credit sales represented $289,484 of this total.

Balance Sheet, Eden's Garden

Assets

Current Assets

Cash		$ 6,457
Accounts Receivable	$ 29,152	
Less Allowance for Doubtful Accounts	3,200	25,952
Inventory		88,157
Supplies		7,514
Prepaid Expenses		1,856
Total Current Assets		$129,936

Fixed Assets

Land		$ 59,150
Buildings	$51,027	
Less Accumulated Depreciation	2,061	48,966
Autos	$24,671	
Less Accumulated Depreciation	12,300	12,371
Equipment	$22,375	
Less Accumulated Depreciation	1,250	21,125
Furniture and Fixtures	$10,295	
Less Accumulated Depreciation	1,000	9,295
Total Fixed Assets		$150,907

Intangibles (Goodwill)	0
Total Assets	$280,843

Liabilities

Current Liabilities

Accounts Payable	$ 54,258
Notes Payable	20,150
Credit Line Payable	8,118
Accrued Wages/Salaries Payable	1,344
Accrued Interest Payable	1,785
Accrued Taxes Payable	1,967
Total Current Liabilities	$ 87,622

Long-term Liabilities

Mortgage	$72,846
Notes Payable	47,000
Total Long-term Liabilities	$119,846

Owner's Equity

Joe and Kaitlin Eden, Capital	$ 73,375
Total Liabilities and Owner's Equity	$280,843

1. Assume the role of Shelley Edison. Using the financial statements for Eden's Garden, calculate the 12 ratios covered in this chapter.

2. Do you see any ratios that, on the surface, look suspicious? Explain.

Interpreting Business Ratios

Ratios are useful yardsticks in measuring the small firm's performance and can point out potential problems before they develop into serious crises. But calculating these ratios is not enough to ensure proper financial control. In addition to knowing how to calculate these ratios, the owner must understand how to interpret them and apply them to managing the business more effectively and efficiently.

Not every business measures its success with the same ratios. In fact, key performance ratios vary dramatically across industries and even within different segments of the same industry. Every manager must know and understand which ratios are most crucial to his company's success and focus on monitoring and controlling those. Sometimes, business owners develop ratios that are unique to their own operations to help them achieve success. One entrepreneur calls them "critical numbers."[13]

AutoLend Group, Inc.

For instance, Steve Simon, CEO of AutoLend Group, Inc., a used-car financing company, focuses on just a few critical numbers to determine his company's exact financial position every day. He uses several ratios that describe the relationships among his company's cash balance, its total loans outstanding, and its loans in delinquency. Simon and his top financial staffers developed a spreadsheet to monitor the "key numbers we really needed to keep closest track of," he says. The result is AutoLend's "Daily Flash Report," which is available to everyone by 7 a.m. each day! "The relationship between numbers is just as important as the results themselves," says Simon. "We've got very clear goals about how these numbers need to relate for us to achieve profitable growth."[14]

Another valuable way to utilize ratios is to compare them with those of similar businesses in the same industry. By comparing the company's financial statistics to industry averages, the owner is able to locate problem areas and maintain adequate financial controls. "By themselves, these numbers are not that meaningful," says one financial expert on ratios, "but when you compare them to [those of] other businesses in your industry, they suddenly come alive because they put your operation in perspective."[15]

The principle behind calculating these ratios and comparing them to industry norms is the same as that of most medical tests in the health care profession. Just as a healthy person's blood pressure and cholesterol levels should fall within a range of normal values, so should a financially healthy company's ratios. A company cannot deviate too far from these normal values and remain successful for long. When deviations from "normal" do occur (and they will), a business owner should focus on determining the cause of the deviations. In some cases, such deviations are the result of sound business decisions, such as taking on inventory in preparation for the busy season, investing heavily in new technology, and others. In other instances, however, ratios that are out of the normal range for a particular type of business are indicators of what could become serious problems for a company. Properly used, ratio analysis can help owners identify potential problem areas in their businesses early on—*before* they become crises that threaten their very survival.

Several organizations regularly compile and publish operating statistics, including key ratios, summarizing the financial performance of many businesses across a wide range of industries. The local library should subscribe to most of these publications:

Robert Morris Associates. Established in 1914, Robert Morris Associates publishes its *Annual Statement Studies*, showing ratios and other financial data for over 350 different industrial, wholesale, retail, and service categories.

Dun & Bradstreet, Inc. Since 1932, Dun & Bradstreet has published *Key Business Ratios,* which covers 22 retail, 32 wholesale, and 71 industrial business categories. Dun & Bradstreet also publishes *Cost of Doing Business,* a series of operating ratios compiled from the IRS's Statistics of Income.

Vest Pocket Guide to Financial Ratios. This handy guide, published by Prentice Hall, gives key ratios and financial data for a wide variety of industries.

Bank of America. Periodically, the Bank of America publishes many documents relating to small business management, including the *Small Business Reporter*, which details costs of doing business ratios.

Trade Associations. Virtually every type of business is represented by a national trade association, which publishes detailed financial data compiled from its membership. For example, the owner of a small supermarket could contact the National Association of Retail Grocers or the *Progressive Grocer*, its trade publication, for financial statistics relevant to his operation.

Government Agencies. Several government agencies (the Federal Trade Commission, Interstate Commerce Commission, Department of Commerce, Department of Agriculture, and Securities and Exchange Commission) offer a great deal of financial operating data on a variety of industries, although the categories are more general. In addition, the IRS annually publishes *Statistics of Income*, which includes income statement and balance sheet statistics compiled from income tax returns. The IRS also publishes the *Census of Business,* which gives a limited amount of ratio information.

What Do All of These Numbers Mean?

Learning to interpret financial ratios just takes a little practice! This section will show you how it's done by comparing the ratios from the operating data already computed for Sam's to those taken from *Robert Morris Associate's Annual Statement Studies* . (The industry median is the ratio falling exactly in the middle when sample elements are arranged in ascending or descending order.)

	Sam's Appliance Shop	**Industry Median**

Liquidity Ratios—tell whether or not the small business will be able to meet its maturing obligations as they come due.

1. Current Ratio =   1.87:1   1.50:1

   Sam's Appliance Shop falls short of the rule of thumb of 2:1, but its current ratio is above the industry median by a significant amount. Sam's should have no problem meeting its short-term debts as they come due. By this measure, the company's liquidity is solid.

2. Quick Ratio =   0.63:1   0.50:1

   Again, Sam's is below the rule of thumb of 1:1, but the company passes this test of liquidity when measured against industry standards. Sam's relies on selling inventory to satisfy short-term debt (as do most appliance shops). If sales slump, the result could be liquidity problems for Sam's.

Leverage Ratios—measure the financing supplied by the firm's owners against that supplied by its creditors and serve as a gauge of the depth of a company's debt.

3. Debt Ratio =   0.68:1   0.64:1

   Creditors provide 68 percent of Sam's total assets, very close to the industry median of 64 percent. Although Sam's does not appear to be overburdened with debt, the company might have difficulty borrowing additional money, especially from conservative lenders.

	Sam's Appliance Shop	Industry Median

4. Debt to Net Worth Ratio = 2.20:1   1.90:1

Sam's Appliance Shop owes $2.20 to creditors for every $1.00 the owners have invested in the business (compared to $1.90 in debt to every $1.00 in equity for the typical business). Although this is not an exorbitant amount of debt, many lenders and creditors will see Sam's as "borrowed up." Borrowing capacity is somewhat limited since creditors' claims against the business are more than twice those of the owners.

5. Times Interest Earned Ratio = 2.52:1   2.0:1

Sam's earnings are high enough to cover the interest payments on its debt by a factor of 2.52, slightly better than the typical firm in the industry, whose earnings cover its interest payments just two times. Sam's Appliance Shop has a cushion (although a small one) in meeting its interest payments.

Operating Ratios—evaluate the firm's overall performance and show how effectively it is putting its resources to work.

6. Average Inventory Turnover Ratio = 2.05 times/year   4.0 times/year

Inventory is moving through Sam's at a very slow pace, *half* that of the industry median. The company has a problem with slow-moving items in its inventory and, perhaps, too much inventory. Which items are they, and why are they slow moving? Does Sam's need to drop some product lines?

7. Average Collection Period Ratio = 50.0 days   19.3 days

Sam's Appliance Shop collects the average accounts receivable after 50 days (compared with the industry median of 19 days)—more than 2.5 times longer. A more meaningful comparison is against Sam's credit terms; if credit terms are net 30 (or anywhere close to that), Sam's has a dangerous collection problem, one that drains cash and profits and demands *immediate* attention!

8. Average Payable Period Ratio = 59.3 days   43 days

Sam's payables are nearly 40 percent slower than those of the typical firm in the industry. Stretching payables too far could seriously damage the company's credit rating, causing suppliers to cut off future trade credit. This could be a sign of cash flow problems or a sloppy accounts payable procedure. This problem also demands *immediate* attention.

9. Net Sales to Total Assets Ratio = 2.21:1   2.7:1

Sam's Appliance Shop is not generating enough sales, given the size of its asset base. This could be the result of a number of factors—improper inventory, inappropriate pricing, poor location, poorly trained sales personnel, and many others. The key is to find the cause . . . *fast*!

10. Net Sales to Working Capital Ratio = 5.86:1   10.8:1

Sam's generates just $5.86 in sales for every $1 in working capital, just over half of what the typical firm in the industry does. Given the previous ratio, the message is clear: Sam's simply is not producing an adequate level of sales. Improving the number of inventory turns will boost this ratio; otherwise, Sam's is likely to experience a working capital shortage soon.

Profitability Ratios—measure how efficiently the firm is operating and offer information about its bottom line.

	Sam's Appliance Shop	Industry Median
11. Net Profit on Sales Ratio =	3.24%	7.6%

After deducting all expenses, 3.24 cents of each sales dollar remains as profit for Sam's—less than half the industry median. Sam should check his company's gross profit margin and investigate its operating expenses, checking them against industry standards and looking for those that are out of balance.

	Sam's Appliance Shop	Industry Median
12. Net Profit to Equity Ratio =	22.65%	12.6%

Sam's Appliance Shop's owners are earning 22.65 percent on the money they have invested in the business. This yield is nearly twice that of the industry median, and, given the previous ratio, is more a result of the owners' relatively low investment in the business than an indication of its superior profitability. The owners are using O.P.M. (other people's money) to generate a profit.

When comparing ratios for their individual businesses to published statistics, small business owners must remember that the comparison is made against averages. Owners must strive to achieve ratios that are at least as good as these average figures. The goal should be to manage the business so that its financial performance is above average. As owners compare financial performance to those covered in the published statistics, they inevitably will discern differences between them. They should note those items that are substantially out of line from the industry average. However, a ratio that varies from the average does not *necessarily* mean that the small business is in financial jeopardy. Instead of making drastic changes in financial policy, owners must explore *why* the figures are out of line.

Steve Cowan, co-owner of Professional Salon Concepts, a wholesale beauty products distributor, routinely performs such an analysis on his company's financial statements. "I need to know whether the variances for expenses and revenues for a certain period are similar," he says. "If they're not, are the differences explainable? Is an expense category up just because of a decision to spend more, or were we just sloppy?"[16]

Professional Salon
Concepts

In addition to comparing ratios to industry averages, owners should analyze their firms' financial ratios over time. By themselves, these ratios are "snapshots" of the firm's finances at a single instant; but by examining these trends over time, the owner can detect gradual shifts that otherwise might go unnoticed until a financial crisis is looming (see Figure 8.8).

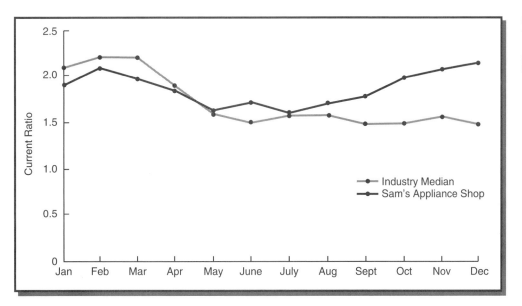

Figure 8.8
Trend Analysis of Ratios

All Is Not Paradise in Eden's Garden: Part 2

Remember Joe and Kaitlin Eden, co-owners of Eden's Garden? Assume the role of Shelley Edison, their accountant. Tomorrow, you have scheduled a meeting with them to review their company's financial statements and to make recommendations about how they can improve their company's financial position. Use the following worksheet to summarize the ratios you calculated earlier in this chapter. Then compare them against the industry averages from *Robert Morris Associates Annual Statement Studies*.

Ratio Comparison			
Ratio	**Eden's Garden**	**Garden Supply Industry Median***	
Liquidity Ratios			
Current ratio		1.4	
Quick ratio		0.5	
Leverage Ratios			
Debt ratio		0.6	
Debt to net worth ratio		1.8	
Times interest earned ratio		2.6	
Operating Ratios			
Average inventory turnover ratio		5.6	
Average collection period ratio		9	days
Average payable period ratios		17	days
Net sales to total assets ratio		3.0	
Net sales to working capital ratio		16.6	
Profitability Ratios			
Net profit on sales ratio		7.5	%
Net profit to equity ratio		15.0	%
*Robert Morris Associates Annual Statement Studies			

1. Analyze the comparisons you have made of Eden's Garden's ratios with those from Robert Morris Associates. What "red flags" do you see?

2. What might be causing the deviations you have observed?

3. What recommendations can you make to the Edens to improve their company's financial performance in the future?

Breakeven Analysis

6. Conduct a breakeven analysis for a small company.

Another key component of every sound financial plan is the breakeven analysis. The small firm's **breakeven point** is the level of operation (sales dollars or production quantity) at which it neither earns a profit nor incurs a loss. At this level of activity, sales revenue equals expenses, that is, the firm "breaks even." By analyzing costs and expenses, the owner can calculate the minimum level of activity required to keep the firm in operation. These techniques can then be refined to project the sales needed to generate the desired profit. Most potential lenders and investors will require the potential owner to prepare a breakeven analysis to assist them in evaluating the earning potential of the new business. In addition to its being a simple, useful screening device for financial institutions, breakeven analysis can also serve as a planning device for the small business owner. It occasionally will show a poorly prepared entrepreneur just how unprofitable a proposed business venture is likely to be.

breakeven point— the level of operation (sales dollars or production quantity) at which a company neither earns a profit nor incurs a loss.

CALCULATING THE BREAKEVEN POINT. A small business owner can calculate a firm's breakeven point by using a simple mathematical formula. To begin the analysis, the owner must determine fixed costs and variable costs. **Fixed expenses** are those that do not vary with changes in the volume of sales or production (e.g., rent, depreciation expense, interest payments). **Variable expenses**, on the other hand, vary directly with changes in the volume of sales or production (e.g., raw material costs, sales commissions).

fixed expenses— expenses that do not vary with change in the volume of sales or production.

variable expenses— expenses that vary directly with changes in the volume of sales or production.

Some expenses cannot be neatly categorized as fixed or variable because they contain elements of both. These semivariable expenses change, although not proportionately, with changes in the level of sales or production (electricity would be one example). These costs remain constant up to a particular production or sales volume, and then climb as that volume is exceeded. To calculate the breakeven point, the owner must separate these expenses into their fixed and variable components. A number of techniques can be used (which are beyond the scope of this text), but a good cost accounting system can provide the desired results.

Here are the steps an entrepreneur must take to compute the breakeven point using an example of a typical small business, the Magic Shop:

Step 1. Determine the expenses the business can expect to incur. With the help of a budget an entrepreneur can develop estimates of sales revenue, cost of goods sold, and expenses for the upcoming accounting period. The Magic Shop expects net sales of $950,000 in the upcoming year, with a cost of goods sold of $646,000 and total expenses of $236,500.

Step 2. Categorize the expenses estimated in step 1 into fixed expenses and variable expenses. Separate semivariable expenses into their component parts. From the budget, the owner anticipates variable expenses (including the cost of goods sold) of $705,125 and fixed expenses of $177,375.

Step 3. Calculate the ratio of variable expenses to net sales. For the Magic Shop, this percentage is $705,125 ÷ $950,000 = 74 percent. So the Magic Shop uses $0.74 out of every sales dollar to cover variable expenses, leaving $0.26 as a contribution margin to cover fixed costs and make a profit.

Step 4. Compute the breakeven point by inserting this information into the following formula:

$$\text{Breakeven sales (\$)} = \frac{\text{total fixed cost}}{\text{contribution margin expressed as a percentage of sales}}$$

For the Magic Shop,

$$\text{Breakeven sales} = \frac{\$177,375}{0.26}$$

$$= \$682,212$$

The same breakeven point will result from solving the following equation algebraically:

Breakeven sales = fixed expense + variable expenses expressed as a percentage of sales

$$S = \$177,375 + 0.74S$$
$$100S = 17,737,500 + 74S$$
$$26S = 17,737,500$$
$$S = \$682,212$$

Thus, the Magic Shop will break even with sales of $682,212. At this point, sales revenue generated will just cover total fixed and variable expense. The Magic Shop will earn no profit and will incur no loss. To verify this, make the following calculations:

Sales at breakeven point	$682,212
− Variable expenses (74% of sales)	− 504,837
Contribution margin	177,375
− Fixed expenses	− 177,375
Net profit (or net loss)	$ 0

ADDING IN A PROFIT. But what if the Magic Shop's owner wants to do better than just break even? His analysis can be adjusted to consider such a possibility. Suppose the owner expects a reasonable profit (before taxes) of $80,000. What level of sales must the Magic Shop achieve to generate this? He can calculate this by treating the desired profit as if it were a fixed cost. In other words, the owner modifies the formula to include the desired net income:

$$\text{Sales (\$)} = \frac{\text{total fixed expenses} + \text{desired net income}}{\text{contribution margin expressed as a percentage of sales}}$$

$$= \frac{\$177,375 + \$80\,000}{0.26}$$

$$= \$989,904$$

To achieve a net profit of $80,000 (before taxes), the Magic Shop must generate net sales of $989,904.

BREAKEVEN POINT IN UNITS. Some small businesses may prefer to express the breakeven point in units produced or sold instead of in dollars. Manufacturers often find this approach particularly useful. The following formula computes the breakeven point in units:

$$\text{Breakeven volume} = \frac{\text{total fixed costs}}{\text{sales price per unit} - \text{variable cost per unit}}$$

For example, suppose that Trilex Manufacturing Company estimates its fixed costs for producing its line of small appliances at $390,000. The variable costs (including materials, direct labor, and factory overhead) amount to $12.10 per unit, and the selling price per unit is $17.50. So, Trilex computes its contribution margin this way:

$$\text{Contribution margin} = \text{price per unit} - \text{variable cost per unit}$$
$$= \$17.50 \text{ per unit} - \$12.10 \text{ per unit}$$
$$= \$5.40 \text{ per unit}$$

Trilex's breakeven volume is as follows:

$$\text{Breakeven volume (units)} = \frac{\text{total fixed costs}}{\text{per unit contribution margin}}$$

$$= \frac{\$390,000}{\$5.40}$$

$$= 72,222 \text{ units}$$

To convert this number of units to breakeven sales dollars, Trilex simply multiplies it by the selling price per unit:

Breakeven sales = 72,222 units $\times$ \$17.50 = \$1,263,889

Trilex could compute the sales required to produce a desired profit by treating the profit as if it were a fixed cost:

$$\text{Sales (units)} = \frac{\text{total fixed costs} + \text{desired net income}}{\text{per unit contribution margin}}$$

For example, if Trilex wanted to earn a \$60,000 profit, its required sales would be:

$$\text{Sales (units)} = \frac{390,000 + 60,000}{5.40} = 83,333 \text{ units}$$

CONSTRUCTING A BREAKEVEN CHART. The following outlines the procedure for constructing a graph that visually portrays the firm's breakeven point (that point where revenues equal expenses).

Step 1. On the horizontal axis, mark a scale measuring sales volume in dollars (or in units sold or some other measure of volume). The breakeven chart for the Magic Shop shown in Figure 8.9 on page 278 uses sales volume in dollars because it applies to all types of businesses, departments, and products.

Step 2. On the vertical axis, mark a scale measuring income and expenses in dollars.

Step 3. Draw a fixed expense line intersecting the vertical axis at the proper dollar level parallel to the horizontal axis. The area between this line and the horizontal axis represents the firm's fixed expenses. On the breakeven chart for the Magic Shop shown in Figure 8.9, the fixed expense line is drawn horizontally beginning at \$177,375 (point *A*). Because this line is parallel to the horizontal axis, it indicates that fixed expenses remain constant at all levels of activity.

Step 4. Draw a total expense line that slopes upward beginning at the point where the fixed cost line intersects the vertical axis. The precise location of the total expense line is determined by plotting the total cost incurred at a particular sales volume. The total cost for a given sales level is found by the following formula:

Total = fixed expenses + variable expenses expressed as a percentage of sales $\times$ sales level expenses

Arbitrarily choosing a sales level of \$950,000, the Magic Shop's total costs would be as follows:

Figure 8.9
**Breakeven Chart,
The Magic Shop**

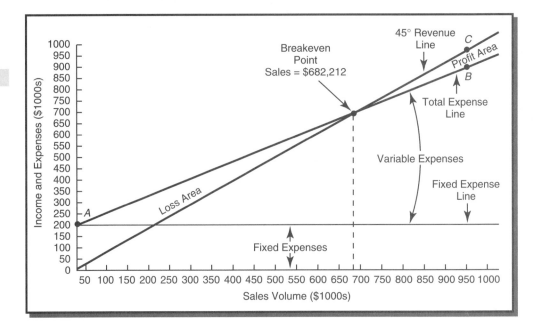

Figure 8.9 Breakeven Chart, The Magic Shop

$$\text{Total expenses} = \$177,375 + (0.74 \times \$950,000)$$
$$= \$880,375$$

Thus, the Magic Shop's total cost is $880,375 at a net sales level of $950,000 (point B). The variable cost line is drawn by connecting points A and B. The area between the total cost line and the horizontal axis measures the total costs the Magic Shop incurs at various levels of sales. For example, if the Magic Shop's sales are $850,000, its total costs will be $806,375.

Step 5. Beginning at the graph's origin, draw a 45-degree revenue line showing where total sales volume equals total income.

For the Magic Shop, point C shows that sales = income = $950,000.

Step 6. Locate the breakeven point by finding the intersection of the total expense line and the revenue line. If the Magic Shop operates at a sales volume to the left of the breakeven point, it will incur a loss because the expense line is higher than the revenue line over this range. This is shown by the triangular section labeled "Loss Area." On the other hand, if the firm operates at a sales volume to the right of the breakeven point, it will earn a profit because the revenue line lies above the expense line over this range. This is shown by the triangular section labeled "Profit Area."

USING BREAKEVEN ANALYSIS. Breakeven analysis is a useful planning tool for the potential small business owner, especially when approaching potential lenders and investors for funds. It provides an opportunity for integrated analysis of sales volume, expenses, income, and other relevant factors. Breakeven analysis is a simple, preliminary screening device for the entrepreneur faced with the business startup decision. It is easy to understand and use. With just a few calculations, the small business owner can determine the effects of various financial strategies on the business operation. It is a helpful tool for evaluating the impact of changes in investments and expenditures. For instance, before Donald Trump opened the billion-dollar Trump Taj Mahal, an opulent casino-hotel complex in Atlantic City, a cost-revenue analysis showed that the complex needed revenues of $400 million a year—*$1.1 million a day*—just to break even![17]

Where Do We Break Even?

Anita Dawson is doing some financial planning for her music store. Based on her budget for the upcoming year, Anita is expecting net sales of $495,000. She estimates that cost of goods sold will be $337,000 and that other variable expenses will total $42,750. Using the past year as a guide, Anita anticipates fixed expenses of $78,100.

Anita recalls an earlier meeting with her accountant, who mentioned that her store had already passed the breakeven point eight-and-one-half months into the year. She was pleased, but really didn't know how the accountant had come up with that calculation.

Now Anita is considering expanding her store into the vacant building next to her existing location and taking on three new product lines. The company's cost structure would change, adding another $66,000 to fixed costs and $22,400 to variable expenses. Anita believes the expansion could generate additional sales of $102,000.

She wonders what she should do.

1. Calculate Anita's breakeven point without the expansion plans. Draw a breakeven chart.

2. Compute the breakeven point assuming that Anita decides to expand.

3. Would you recommend that Anita expand her business? Explain.

Breakeven analysis does have certain limitations. It is too simple to use as a final screening device because it ignores the importance of cash flows. Also, the accuracy of the analysis depends on the accuracy of the revenue and expense estimates. Finally, the assumptions pertaining to breakeven analysis may not be realistic for some businesses. Breakeven calculations assume the following: Fixed expenses remain constant for all levels of sales volume; variable expenses change in direct proportion to changes in sales volume; and changes in sales volume have no effect on unit sales price. Relaxing these assumptions does not render this tool useless, however. For example, the owner could employ nonlinear breakeven analysis using a graphical approach.

CHAPTER SUMMARY

1. Understand the importance of preparing a financial plan.
- Launching a successful business requires an entrepreneur to create a solid financial plan. Not only is such a plan an important tool in raising the capital needed to get a company off the ground, but it also is an essential ingredient in managing a growing business.
- Earning a profit does not occur by accident; it takes planning.

2. Describe how to prepare the basic financial statements and use them to manage the small business.
- Entrepreneurs rely on three basic financial statements to understand the financial conditions of their companies:
  1. *The balance sheet.* Built on the accounting equation: Assets = Liabilities + Owner's Equity (Capital), it provides an estimate of the company's value on a particular date.
  2. *The income statement.* This statement compares the firm's revenues against its expenses to determine its net profit (or loss). It provides information about the company's bottom line.

  3. *The statement of cash flows.* This statement shows the change in the company's working capital over the accounting period by listing the sources and the uses of funds.

3. Create pro forma financial statements.
- Projected financial statements are a basic component of a sound financial plan. They help the manager plot the company's financial future by setting operating objectives and by analyzing the reasons for variations from targeted results. Also, the small business in search of startup funds will need these pro forma statements to present to prospective lenders and investors. They also assist in determining the amount of cash, inventory, fixtures, and other assets the business will need to begin operation.

4. Understand the basic financial statements through ratio analysis.
- The 12 key ratios described in this chapter are divided into four major categories: *liquidity ratios*, which show the small firm's ability to meet its current obligations; *leverage ratios*, which tell how much of the company's

financing is provided by owners and how much by creditors; *operating ratios*, which show how effectively the firm uses its resources; and *profitability ratios*, which disclose the company's profitability.

• Many agencies and organizations regularly publish such statistics. If there is a discrepancy between the small firm's ratios and those of the typical business, the owner should investigate the reason for the difference. A below-average ratio does not necessarily mean that the business is in trouble.

5. Explain how to interpret financial ratios.
   • To benefit from ratio analysis, the small company should compare its ratios to those of other companies in the same line of business and look for trends over time.

• When business owners detect deviations in their companies' ratios from industry standards, they should determine the cause of the deviations. In some cases, such deviations are the result of sound business decisions; in other instances, however, ratios that are out of the normal range for a particular type of business are indicators of what could become serious problems for a company.

6. Conduct a breakeven analysis for a small company.
   • Business owners should know their firm's breakeven point, the level of operations at which total revenues equal total costs; it is the point at which companies neither earn a profit nor incur a loss. Although just a simple screening device, breakeven analysis is a useful planning and decision-making tool.

DISCUSSION QUESTIONS

1. Why is developing a financial plan so important to an entrepreneur about to launch a business?
2. How should a small business manager use the ratios discussed in this chapter?
3. Outline the key points of the 12 ratios discussed in this chapter. What signals do each give the manager?
4. Describe the method for building a projected income statement and a projected balance sheet for a beginning business.
5. Why are pro forma financial statements important to the financial planning process?
6. How can breakeven analysis help an entrepreneur planning to launch a business?

Beyond the Classroom...

Ask the owner of a small business to provide your class with copies of the firm's financial statements (current or past).

1. Using these statements, compute the 12 key ratios described in this chapter.
2. Compare the firm's ratios with those of the typical firm in this line of business.
3. Interpret the ratios and make suggestions for operating improvements.
4. Prepare a breakeven analysis for the owner.

SURFING THE NET

1. Using one of the search engines on the World Wide Web (WWW) such as Lycos, Magellan, Yahoo!, or others, conduct a search on the words *ratio analysis*, and *financial statements*. Select one topic from each of these two searches and prepare a one-page report on what you learn.

2. Find a publicly held company of interest to you that provides its financial statements on the Web. You can conduct a Web search using the company's name or you can find lists of companies at the following Web sites:
   • Hoover's Online at

http://www.hoovers.com/

(Try using Company Capsules and Company Profiles.)

• Securities and Exchange Commission at:

http://www.sec.gov/edgarhp.htm

Analyze the company's financial statements by calculating the 12 ratios covered in this chapter and compare these ratios to industry averages found in *Robert Morris Associates Annual Statement Studies* or Dun & Bradstreet's *The Cost of Doing Business* reports.

CHAPTER

NINE

Crafting a Winning Business Plan

*The more concrete and complete the plan, the more likely it is to earn
the respect of outsiders and their support in necessary financial matters.*
- Jesse Werner

Planning is a process by which you continuously create your own future.
- Roger Fritz

An objective without a plan is a dream.
- W.J. Reddin

LEARNING OBJECTIVES

Upon completion of this chapter, you will be able to:

1. ***Explain*** why every entrepreneur should create a business plan.
2. ***Describe*** the elements of a solid business plan.
3. ***Explain*** the benefits of preparing a business plan
4. ***Understand*** the keys to making an effective business plan presentation.
5. ***Explain*** the "five Cs of credit" and why they are important to potential lenders and investors reading business plans.

Why Develop a Business Plan?

business plan—*a written summary of an entrepreneur's proposed business venture, its operational and financial details, its marketing opportunities and strategy, and its managers' skills and abilities.*

A **business plan** is a written summary of an entrepreneur's proposed business venture, its operational and financial details, its marketing opportunities and strategy, and its managers' skills and abilities. There is no substitute for a well-prepared business plan, and there are no shortcuts to creating one. The plan serves as an entrepreneur's road map on the journey toward building a successful business. It describes the direction the company is taking, what its goals are, where it wants to be, and how it's going to get there. The plan is written proof that the entrepreneur has performed the necessary research and has studied the business opportunity adequately. In short, the business plan is the entrepreneur's best insurance against launching a business destined to fail or mismanaging a potentially successful company.

The business plan serves two essential functions. First and most important, it guides the company's operations by charting its future course and devising a strategy for following it. The plan provides a battery of tools—a mission statement, goals, objectives, budgets, financial forecasts, target markets, strategies—to help managers lead the company successfully. It gives managers and employees a sense of direction, but only if everyone is involved in creating, updating, or altering it. As more team members become committed to making the plan work, it takes on special meaning. It gives everyone targets to shoot for, and it provides a yardstick for measuring actual performance against those targets, especially in the crucial and chaotic startup phase.

The second function of the business plan is to attract lenders and investors. Too often small business owners approach potential lenders and investors without having come prepared to sell themselves and their business concept. Simply scribbling a few rough figures on a note pad to support a loan application is not enough. Applying for loans or attempting to attract investors without a solid business plan rarely attracts needed capital. Rather, the best way to secure the necessary capital is to prepare a sound business plan. The entrepreneur must pay attention to detail because it is germane to her sales presentation to potential lenders and investors. In most cases, the quality of the firm's business plan weighs heavily in the decision to lend or invest funds. It is also potential lenders' and investors' first impression of the company and its managers. Therefore, the finished product should be highly polished and professional in both form and content.

A plan is a reflection of its creator. It should demonstrate that the entrepreneur has thought seriously about the venture and what will make it succeed. Preparing a solid plan demonstrates that the entrepreneur has taken the time to commit the idea to paper. Building a plan also forces the entrepreneur to consider both the positive and the negative aspects of the business. A detailed and thoughtfully developed business plan makes a positive first impression on those who read it. In most cases, potential lenders and investors read a business plan before they ever meet with the entrepreneur behind it. Sophisticated investors will not take the time to meet with an entrepreneur whose business plan fails to reflect a serious investment of time and energy. They know that an entrepreneur who lacks the discipline to develop a good business plan likely lacks the discipline to run a business.

An entrepreneur cannot allow others to prepare the business plan for him because outsiders cannot understand the business nor envision the proposed company as well as the entrepreneur can. The entrepreneur is the driving force behind the business idea and is the one who can best convey the vision and the enthusiasm he has for transforming that idea into a successful business. Also, because the entrepreneur will make the presentation to potential lenders and investors, he must understand every detail of the business plan. Otherwise, an entrepreneur cannot present it convincingly, and in most cases the financial institution or investor will reject it. Alice Medrich, cofounder of Cocolat, a manufacturer of specialty candies and desserts, recalls her first attempt at presenting her business plan:

First of all, I went to the bank, and I was so ill-prepared and so insecure about what I was asking about . . . I was extremely insecure with a banker. I didn't know how to describe what I was doing with any confidence. I did *not* know how to present a business plan. And, he was condescending to me. Looking back on it, I can understand why: I wasn't prepared . . . We didn't get the loan.[1]

Investors want to feel confident that an entrepreneur has realistically evaluated the risk involved in the new venture and has a strategy for addressing it. They also want to see proof that a business will become profitable and produce a reasonable return on their investment.[2]

Perhaps the best way to understand the need for a business plan is to recognize the validity of the "two-thirds rule," which says that only two-thirds of the entrepreneurs with a sound and viable new business venture will find financial backing. Those that do find financial backing will only get two-thirds of what they initially requested, and it will take them two-thirds longer to get the financing than they anticipated.[3] The most effective strategy for avoiding the two-thirds rule is to build a business plan!

The Elements of a Business Plan

2. *Describe* the elements of a solid business plan.

Smart entrepreneurs recognize that every business plan is unique and must be tailor-made. They avoid the off-the-shelf, "cookie-cutter" approach that produces look-alike plans. The elements of a business plan may be standard, but how the entrepreneur tells her story should be unique and reflect her personal excitement about the new venture. If this is a first attempt at writing a business plan, it may be very helpful to seek the advice of individuals with experience in this process. Consultants with Small Business Development Centers, accountants, business professors, and attorneys can be excellent sources of advice in refining your plan.

Initially, the prospect of writing a business plan may appear to be overwhelming. Many entrepreneurs would rather launch their companies and "see what happens" than invest the necessary time and energy defining and researching their target markets, defining their strategies, and mapping out their finances. After all, building a plan is hard work! However, it is hard work that pays many dividends—not all of them immediately apparent. Entrepreneurs who invest their time and energy building plans are better prepared to face the hostile environment in which their companies will compete than those who do not. Earlier, we said that a business plan is like a road map that guides an entrepreneur on the journey to building a successful business. If you were making a journey to a particular destination through unfamiliar, harsh, and dangerous territory, would you rather ride with someone equipped with a road map and a trip itinerary or with someone who didn't believe in road maps or in planning trips, destinations, and layovers? Although building a business plan does *not* guarantee success, it *does* raise an entrepreneur's chances of succeeding in business.

A business plan typically ranges from 25 to 55 pages in length. Shorter plans usually are too sketchy to be of any value, and those much longer than this run the risk of never getting used or read! This section explains the most common elements of a business plan. However, entrepreneurs must recognize that, like every business venture, every business plan is unique. An entrepreneur should view the following elements as a starting point for building a plan and should modify them as needed to better tell the story of his new venture.

The Executive Summary

To summarize the presentation to each potential financial institution or investor, the entrepreneur should write an executive summary. It should be concise—a maximum of two pages—and should summarize all of the relevant points of the proposed deal. The executive summary presents the essence of the plan in a capsulized form. It should explain the purpose of the financial request, the dollar amount requested, how the funds will be used, and how (and when) any loans will be repaid. It is designed to capture the reader's attention. If it misses, the chances of the remainder of the plan being read are minimal. A well-developed, coherent summary introducing the financial proposal establishes a favorable first impression of the entrepreneur and the business and can go a long way toward obtaining financing. Although the executive summary is the first part of the business plan, it should be the last section written.

Mission Statement

As you learned in Chapter 2, a mission statement expresses in words the entrepreneur's vision for what her company is and what it is to become. It is the broadest expression of a company's purpose and defines the direction in which it will move. It serves as the thesis statement for the entire business plan.

Company History

The manager of an existing small business should prepare a brief history of the operation, highlighting the significant financial and operational events in the company's life. This section should describe when and why the company was formed, how it has evolved over time, and what the owner envisions for the future. It should highlight the successful accomplishment of past objectives and should convey the firm's image in the marketplace.

Business and Industry Profile

To acquaint lenders and investors with the nature of the business, the owner should describe it in the business plan. This section should begin with a statement of the company's general business goals and a narrower definition of its immediate objectives. Together they should spell out what the business plans to accomplish, how, when, and who will do it. **Goals** are broad, long-range statements of what a company plans to do in the distant future that guide its overall direction and express its *raison d'être*. In other words, they answer the question. "Why am I in business?" Answering such a basic question appears to be obvious, but, in fact, many entrepreneurs cannot define the basis of their businesses.

Objectives, on the other hand, are short-term, specific performance targets that are attainable, measurable, and controllable. Every objective should reflect some general business goal and include a technique for measuring progress toward its accomplishment. To be meaningful, an objective must have a time frame for achievement. Both goals and objectives should relate to the company's basic mission (see Figure 9.1).

When summarizing the small company's background, an owner should describe the present state of the art in the industry and what she will need to succeed in the market segment in which her business will compete. The owner should then identify the current applications of the product or service in the market and include projections for future applications.

This section should provide the reader with an overview of the industry or market segment in which the new venture will operate. Industry data such as market size, growth trends, and the relative economic and competitive strengths of the major firms in the industry all set the stage for a better understanding of the viability of the new product or service. Strategic issues such as ease of market entry and exit, the ability to achieve economies of scale or scope, and the existence of cyclical or seasonal economic trends further help the reader evaluate the new venture. This part of the plan also should describe significant industry trends and an overall outlook for its future. The *U.S. Industrial Outlook Handbook* is an excellent reference that profiles a variety of industries and offers projections for future trends in them. Information about the evolution of the industry helps the reader comprehend its competitive dynamics.

goals—*broad, long range statements of what a company plans to do in the distant future that guide its overall direction and express its* raison d'être.

objectives—*short-term, specific performance targets that are attainable, measurable, and controllable.*

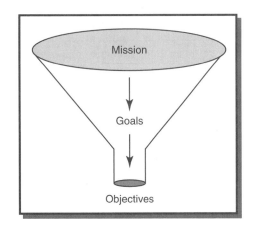

Figure 9.1
*The Relationship
Between Mission, Goals,
and Objectives*

The industry analysis should also focus on the existing and anticipated profitability of the firms in the targeted market segment. Any significant entry or exit of firms or consolidations and mergers should be discussed in terms of their impact on the competitive behavior of the market. The entrepreneur also should mention any events that have significantly altered the industry in the past ten years.

Business Strategy

An even more important part of the business plan is the owner's view of the strategy needed to meet—and beat—the competition. In the previous section, the entrepreneur defined *where* he wants to take his business by establishing goals and objectives. This section addresses the question of *how* to get there—business strategy. It should explain how the entrepreneur plans to gain a competitive edge in the market. He should comment on how he plans to achieve business goals and objectives in the face of competition and government regulation and should identify the image that the business will try to project. An important theme in this section is what makes the company unique in the eyes of its customers. One of the quickest routes to business failure is trying to sell "me-too" products or services that offer customers nothing new, better, bigger, faster, or different. The foundation for this part of the business plan comes from the material in Chapter 2, "Strategic Management and the Entrepreneur."

This segment of the business plan should outline the methods the company can use to meet the key success factors cited earlier. If, for example, a strong, well-trained sales force is considered critical to success, the owner must devise a plan of action for assembling one.

Description of Firm's Product or Service

The business owner should describe the company's overall product line, giving an overview of how customers use its goods or services. Drawings, diagrams, and illustrations may be required if the product is highly technical. It is best to write product and service descriptions so that laypeople can understand them. A statement of a product's position in the product life cycle might also be helpful. The entrepreneur should include a summary of any patents, trademarks, or copyrights protecting the product or service from infringement by competitors. Finally, the owner should honestly compare the company's product or service with those of competitors, citing specific advantages or improvements that make his goods or services unique and indicating plans for creating the next generation of goods and services that will evolve from the present product line.

The emphasis of this section should be on defining the *benefits* customers get by purchasing the company's products or services, rather than on just a "nuts and bolts" description of the features of those products or services. A **feature** is a descriptive fact about a product or service ("an ergonomically designed, more comfortable handle"). A **benefit** is what the customer gains from the product or service feature ("fewer problems with carpal tunnel syndrome and increased productivity"). Advertising legend Leo Burnett once said, "Don't tell the people how good you make the goods; tell them how good your goods make them."[4] This part of the plan must describe how a business will transform tangible product or service *features* into important, but often intangible, customer *benefits*, for example, lower energy bills, faster access to the Internet, less time writing checks to pay monthly bills, greater flexibility in building floating structures, shorter time required to learn a foreign language, or others. *Remember*: Customers buy benefits, *not* product or service features.

Manufacturers should describe their production process, strategic raw materials required, sources of supply they will use, and their costs. They should also summarize the production method and illustrate the plant layout. If the product is based on a patented or proprietary process, a description (including diagrams, if necessary) of its unique market advantages is helpful. It is also helpful to explain the company's environmental impact and how the entrepreneur plans to mitigate any negative environmental consequences the process may produce.

Marketing Strategy

One crucial concern of entrepreneurs and the potential lenders and investors who finance their companies is whether or not there is a real market for the proposed good or service. Every entrepreneur must, therefore, describe the company's target market and its characteristics. Defining the target market and its potential is one of the most important—and most difficult—parts of building a business plan. Building a successful business depends on an entrepreneur's ability to attract real customers who are willing and able to spend real money to buy its products or services. Perhaps the worst marketing error an entrepreneur can commit is failing to define his target market and trying to make his business "everything to everybody." Small companies usually are much more successful focusing on a specific market niche where they can excel at meeting customers' special needs or wants.

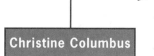

Christine Columbus

Annette Zientek knows that one key to her company's success is focusing on the unique needs of her target market, upscale women who travel frequently. Zientek's company, Christine Columbus, is a mail-order company that sells women-oriented travel products. After two years of extensive market research, much of it with real customers, Zientek was able to determine what to sell and how to sell it to her target customers. With her target audience's profile in place, Zientek was able to purchase mailing lists to reach them. "It is so important to know who your market is," Zientek says. "A good idea is not enough. You need to know what your demographics are and how to find those people." Wanting to expand her catalog and to eventually create her own product line, Zientek has revised her original business plan into a constantly updated five-year plan for success.[5]

Defining a company's target market involves using the techniques described in Chapter 5, "Creating a Powerful Marketing Plan." Questions that this part of the business plan should address include:

- ☆ Who are my target customers (age, sex, income level, and other demographic characteristics)?
- ☆ Where do they live, work, and shop?
- ☆ How many potential customers are in my company's trading area?
- ☆ Why do they buy? What needs and wants drive their purchase decisions?
- ☆ What can my business do to meet those needs and wants better than my competitors?
- ☆ Knowing my customers' needs, wants, and habits, what should be the basis for differentiating my business in their minds?

Successful entrepreneurs know that a solid understanding of their target markets is the first step in building an effective marketing strategy. Indeed, every other aspect of marketing depends on having a clear picture of the customers and their unique needs and wants. Proving that a profitable market exists involves two steps: showing customer interest and documenting market claims.

SHOWING CUSTOMER INTEREST. The entrepreneur must be able to prove that her target customers need or want the company's good or service and are willing to pay for it. This phase is relatively straightforward for a company with an existing product or service but can be quite difficult for one with only an idea or a prototype. In this case the entrepreneur might offer the prototype to several potential customers in order to get written testimonials and evaluations to show to investors. Or the owner could sell the product to several customers at a discount. This would prove that there are potential customers for the product and would allow demonstrations of the product in operation. Getting a product into customers' hands is also an excellent way to get valuable feedback that can lead to significant design improvements and increased sales down the road.

DOCUMENTING MARKET CLAIMS. Too many business plans rely on vague generalizations such as, "This market is so huge that if we get just 1 percent of it, we will break even in eight months." Such statements are not backed by facts and usually reflect an entrepreneur's unbridled optimism. In most cases, they are also unrealistic!

Entrepreneurs must support claims of market size and growth rates with *facts,* and that requires market research. Results of market surveys, customer questionnaires, and demographic studies lend credibility to an entrepreneur's frequently optimistic sales projections. (Refer to the market research techniques and resources in Chapter 5.) Quantitative market data are important because they form the basis for all of the company's financial projections in the business plan.

To get such data before incurring the expense of launching a full-blown barbecue restaurant, entrepreneur Ronald Byrd decided to test the local taste for barbecue by selling his product from a street cart. "This is a marketing research project," he says, pointing to his cart. "I didn't want to invest a lot of money into moving into a restaurant [and have no market]. So, I started with a cart." Sales that outpaced his expectations proved to him (and to bankers) that the demand for his creative barbecue dishes was sufficient to support a restaurant. This aspiring restaurateur also used feedback and suggestions from customers to fine-tune his menu offerings—all before ever opening the doors to his "official" restaurant, Baby Byrd's Q.[6]

| **Baby Byrd's Q** |

One of the essential goals of this section of the plan is to identify the basics for financial forecasts that follow. Sales, profit, and cash forecasts must be founded on more than wishful thinking. An effective market analysis should identify the following:

- *Target market:* Who are the most promising customers or prospects? What are their characteristics? What do they buy? Why do they buy? When do they buy? What expectations do they have about the product or service? Will the business focus on a niche? How does the company seek to position itself in its market(s)?

- *Advertising:* Once an entrepreneur defines her company's target market, she can design a promotion and advertising campaign to reach those customers most effectively and efficiently. Which media are most effective in reaching the target market? How will they be used? How much will the promotional campaign cost? How can the company benefit from publicity?

- *Market size and trends:* How large is the potential market? Is it growing or shrinking? Why? Are the customers' needs changing? Are sales seasonal? Is demand tied to another product or service?

★ *Location*: For many businesses, choosing the right location is a key success factor. For retailers, wholesalers, and service companies, the best location usually is one that is most convenient to their target customers. Using census data and other market research, entrepreneurs can determine the sites with the greatest concentrations of their customers and locate there. Which specific sites put the company in the path of its target customers? Do zoning regulations restrict the use of the site? For manufacturers, the location issue often centers on finding a site near its key raw materials or near its major customers. Using demographic reports and market research to screen potential sites takes the guesswork out of choosing the "right" location for a business.

★ *Pricing:* What does the product or service cost to produce or deliver? What is the company's overall pricing strategy? What image is the company trying to create in the market? Will the planned price support the company's strategy and desired image? (See Figure 9.2.) Can it produce a profit? How does the planned price compare to those of similar products or services? Are customers willing to pay it? What price tiers exist in the market? How sensitive are customers to price changes? Will the business sell to customers on credit? Will it accept credit cards?

★ *Distribution:* How will the product or service be distributed? What is the average sale? How many sales calls does it take to close a sale? What are the incentives for salespeople? What can the company do to make it as easy as possible for customers to buy?

This portion of the plan also should describe the channels of distribution that the business will use (mail, in-house sales force, sales agents, retailers). The owner should summarize the firm's overall pricing and promotion strategies, including the advertising budget, media used, and publicity efforts. The company's warranties and guarantees for its products and services should be addressed as well.

Competitor Analysis

An entrepreneur should discuss the new venture's competition. Failing to assess competitors realistically makes entrepreneurs appear to be poorly prepared, naive, or dishonest. Gathering information on competitors' market shares, products, and strategies is usually

Figure 9.2
The Link Between Pricing, Perceived Quality, and Company Image

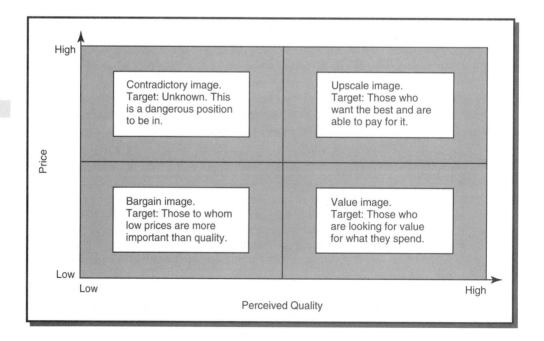

not difficult. Trade associations, customers, industry journals, marketing representatives, and sales literature are valuable sources of data. This section of the plan should focus on demonstrating that the entrepreneur's company has an advantage over its competitors. Who are the company's key competitors? What are their strengths and weaknesses? What are their strategies? What images do they have in the marketplace? How successful are they? What distinguishes the entrepreneur's product or service from others already on the market, and how will these differences produce a competitive edge? This section of the plan should demonstrate that the firm's strategies are clearly customer focused.

Officer's/Owners' Résumés

The most important factor in the success of a business venture is its management, so financial officers and investors weigh heavily the ability and experience of the firm's managers in financing decisions. Thus, the plan should include the résumés of business officers, key directors, and any person with at least 20 percent ownership in the company. *Remember:* Lenders and investors prefer experienced managers.

A résumé should summarize the individual's education, work history (emphasizing managerial responsibilities and duties), and relevant business experience. When compiling a personal profile, an entrepreneur should review the primary reasons for small business failure (refer to Chapter 1) and show how her management team will use its skills and experience to avoid them. Lenders and investors look for the experience, talent, and integrity of the people who will breathe life into the plan. This portion of the plan should show that the company has the right people organized in the right fashion for success. One experienced private investor advises entrepreneurs to remember the following:

- ☆ Ideas and products don't succeed; people do. Show the strength of your management team. A top-notch management team with a variety of proven skills is crucial.
- ☆ Show the strength of key employees and how you will retain them. A Board of Directors or advisers consisting of industry experts lends credibility and can enhance the value of the management team.[7]

Plan of Operation

To complete the description of the business, the owner should construct an organizational chart identifying the business's key positions and the personnel occupying them. Assembling a management team with the right stuff is difficult, but keeping it together until the company is established may be harder. Thus, the entrepreneur should describe briefly the steps taken to encourage important officers to remain with the company. Employment contracts, shares of ownership, and perks are commonly used to keep and motivate such employees.

Finally, a description of the form of ownership (partnership, joint venture, S corporation, LLC) and of any leases, contracts, and other relevant agreements pertaining to the operation is helpful.

Financial Data

One of the most important sections of the business plan is a detailed outline of the loan or investment package—the "dollars and cents" of the proposed deal. Lenders and investors use past financial statements to judge the health of an existing small company and its ability to repay loans or generate adequate returns. The owner should supply copies of the firm's major financial statements from the past three years. Ideally, these statements should be audited by a certified public accountant because most financial institutions prefer that extra reliability, although a financial review of the statements by an accountant sometimes may be acceptable.

Whether assembling a plan for an existing business or a startup, an entrepreneur should carefully prepare monthly projected (or pro forma) financial statements for the operation for the next two to three years (and possibly for two more years by quarters) using past operating data, published statistics, and judgment to derive three sets of forecasts of the income statement, balance sheet, cash budget, and schedule of planned capital expenditures. There should be forecasts under pessimistic, most likely, and optimistic conditions to reflect the uncertainty of the future.

It is essential that all three sets of forecasts be realistic. Entrepreneurs must avoid the tendency to "fudge the numbers" in order to look good. Financial officers compare these projections against published industry standards and can detect unreasonable forecasts. In fact, some venture capitalists automatically discount an entrepreneur's financial projections by as much as 50 percent. Upon completing the forecasts, the owner can perform a breakeven analysis and a ratio analysis on the projected figures.

It is also important to include a statement of the *assumptions* on which these financial projections are based. Potential lenders and investors want to know how the entrepreneur derived forecasts for sales, cost of goods sold, operating expenses, accounts receivable, collections, inventory, and other such items. Spelling out such assumptions gives a plan more credibility. In addition to providing valuable information to potential lenders and investors, these projected financial statements help the entrepreneur run her business more effectively and more efficiently. They establish important targets for financial performance and make it easier for an entrepreneur to maintain control over routine expenses and capital expenditures.

The Loan Proposal

The loan proposal section of the business plan should state the purpose of the loan, the amount requested, and the plans for repayment. When describing the purpose of the loan, the owner must specify the planned use of the funds. General requests for funds using reasons such as "for modernization," "working capital," or "expansion" are unlikely to win approval. Instead, descriptions such as "to modernize production facilities by purchasing five new, more efficient looms that will boost productivity by 12 percent" or "to rebuild merchandise inventory for fall sales peak, beginning in early summer" should be used. The entrepreneur should state the precise amount requested and include relevant backup data, such as vendor estimates of costs or past production levels. Owners should not hesitate to request the amount of money needed but should not inflate the amount anticipating the financial officer to "talk them down." *Remember:* Lenders and investors are familiar with industry cost structures.

Another important element of the loan or investment proposal is the repayment schedule and exit strategy. A lender's main consideration in granting a loan is the reassurance that the applicant will repay, whereas an investor's major concern is earning a satisfactory rate of return. Financial projections must reflect the firm's ability to repay loans and produce adequate yields. Without this proof, a request for additional funds stands little chance of being accepted. It is necessary for the entrepreneur to produce tangible evidence showing the ability to repay loans or to generate attractive returns. "Plan an exit for the investor," says the owner of a financial consulting company. "Generally, the equity investor's objective with early-stage funding is to earn a 30% to 50% annual return over the life of the investment. To enhance the investor's interest in your enterprise, show how they can 'cash out' perhaps through a public offering or acquisition."[8]

Finally, the owner should have a timetable for implementing the proposed plan. He should present a schedule showing the estimated startup date for the project and note any significant milestones along the way. Entrepreneurs tend to be optimistic, so the owner must be sure that his timetable of events is realistic.

It is beneficial to include an evaluation of the risks of a new venture. Evaluating risk in a business plan requires an entrepreneur to walk a fine line. Dwelling too much on everything that can go wrong will discourage potential lenders and investors from financing the venture. Ignoring the project's risks makes those who evaluate the plan tend to believe the entrepreneur to be either naive, dishonest, or unprepared. The best strategy is to identify the most significant risks the venture faces and then to describe what plans the entrepreneur has developed to avoid them altogether or to overcome the negative outcome if the event does occur.

There is a difference between a working business plan—the one the entrepreneur is using to guide her business—and the presentation business plan—the one she is using to attract capital. Although coffee rings and penciled-in changes in a working plan don't matter (in fact, they're a good sign that the entrepreneur is actually *using* the plan), they have no place on a plan going to someone outside the company. A plan is usually the tool that an entrepreneur uses to make a first impression on potential lenders and investors. To make sure that impression is a favorable one, an entrepreneur should follow these tips:

- ☆ Make sure the plan is free of spelling and grammatical errors and "typos." It is a professional document and should look like one.
- ☆ Make it visually appealing. Use color charts, figures, and diagrams to illustrate key points. Don't get carried away, however, and end up with a "comic book" plan.
- ☆ Include a table of contents to allow readers to navigate the plan easily.
- ☆ Make it interesting. Boring plans seldom get read.
- ☆ Use computer spreadsheets to generate financial forecasts. They allow entrepreneurs to perform valuable what-if (sensitivity) analysis in just seconds.
- ☆ *Always* include cash flow projections. Entrepreneurs sometimes focus excessively on their proposed venture's profit forecasts and ignore cash flow projections. Although profitability is important, lenders and investors are much more interested in cash flow because they know that's where the money to pay them back or to cash them out comes from.
- ☆ The ideal plan is "crisp"—long enough to say what it should but not so long that it is a chore to read.
- ☆ Tell the truth. Absolute honesty is always critical in preparing a business plan.

The Benefits of Preparing a Plan

3. Explain the benefits of preparing a business plan.

Preparing a sound business plan clearly requires time and effort, but the benefits greatly exceed the costs. Building the plan forces a potential entrepreneur to look at her business idea in the harsh light of reality. It also requires the owner to assess the venture's chances of success more objectively. A well-assembled plan helps prove to outsiders that a business idea can be successful. To get external financing, an entrepreneur's plan must pass three tests with potential lenders and investors: (1) the reality test, (2) the competitive test, and (3) the value test.[9] The first two tests have both an external and an internal component.

REALITY TEST. The external component of the reality test revolves around proving that a market for the product or service *really* does exist. It focuses on industry attractiveness, market niches, potential customers, market size, degree of competition, and similar factors. Entrepreneurs who pass this part of the reality test prove in the marketing portion of their business plans that there is strong demand for their business idea.

The internal component of the reality test focuses on the product or service itself. Can the company *really* build it for the cost estimates in the business plan? Is it truly different from what competitors are already selling? Does it offer customers something of value?

The Need for a Plan

"I don't know what I was thinking a year ago: a fifth-year senior in college, I got kicked off the staff of the school paper . . . and in a fit of revenge decided to put out my own magazine. Who would have thought that this is how it would turn out?" That's how 23-year-old Shirley Halperin introduced the anniversary issue of *Smug*, an alternative-music magazine that is free to subscribers. The ten-issues-a-year publication is targeted at music fans in the 16-to-30-year-old age group with well-written stories "about musicians that matter, plus bands you haven't even heard of yet," says Halperin. It covers the alternative-music scene between the musical meccas of New York City and Philadelphia. Early issues featured stories on bands with names such as Bent Backed Tulips, Swinging Udders, and Super Chunky Monkey. Halperin, the creative force behind *Smug's* hip look and unique content, has a nose for music, and she invests incredible time and energy checking out the music scene in the Northeast corridor. Her enthusiasm for her subject has spilled over to the writers, editors, designers, and photographers who contribute their work to *Smug*. And they do *contribute*. *Smug's* staff of 30 works, so far, for no pay! They donate their talents for such incentives as by-lines, photo credits, college internships, job experience, free tickets to concerts, free CDs, and others.

To keep startup costs low, Halperin runs *Smug* from her Gramercy Park apartment, which she shares with two roommates. Ads in more established, competing publications such as the *Village Voice*, the *Aquarian Weekly*, and *Spin* range from $7,000 to $29,700; *Smug* charges just $1,000 for the same size ad. Halperin says that her budget ad rates are designed for smaller bands who have a regional following but haven't hit the big time yet. "It doesn't make sense for baby bands to advertise in the bigger publications until awareness of them rises," she says. Halperin's cost-consciousness carries over from the earliest days of *Smug's* startup. Her frugality enabled Halperin to launch *Smug* with just $1,700 in personal savings and $7,000 in "donations" from friends, relatives, and music colleagues. Halperin cuts costs wherever possible. Her father, Eli Halperin, handles all of the company's accounting and recordkeeping duties while his daughter focuses on producing the magazine. He recently cosigned a $10,000 note so Halperin could get a bank line of credit.

Halperin is happy to have someone she can trust to manage *Smug's* financial affairs. She admits that finance is not her strong point, but she is quick to point out that the company is built on her strengths. "I'm very good at knowing what music people are listening to and what people want to read about," she says. *Smug's* results tend to back up what she says. In less than 18 months, *Smug's* circulation has gone from 5,000 to more than 20,000, its readership has expanded to 60,000, and advertising revenues have climbed from zero to $15,000 per month. After publishing its fourth issue, *Smug* beat out its larger and more established competitors to win a prestigious local music award. Reviewers rave about the quality of the magazine's writing, its design, and its photography.

Despite its early success, *Smug's* continued success is not guaranteed. Half of all magazine startups fail within the first year, and those that don't take four to five years to break even. Those that make it, however, can produce attractive profit margins of as much as 15 to 30 percent.

Smug's distribution is limited to 169 music outlets in New York City, New Jersey, and Philadelphia, but none of the major music retailers such as Tower Records has agreed to distribute it yet. Cash flow is also a concern; at the end of its first year, $7,500 of *Smug's* $70,000 in revenues were still in accounts receivable! Although Halperin started *Smug* without a business plan, she realizes now she needs one to raise the $500,000 necessary to take the magazine "to the next level." She needs the capital infusion to upgrade from newsprint to semiglossy paper stock, and, more importantly, to begin paying her staff. She wants the plan to reflect her basic business philosophy: "Every year circulation should go up, your pages should go up, and your ad revenues should go up."

1. Write a memo to Shirley Halperin explaining what topics she should include in her business plan.

2. What advice would you offer Halperin when she begins to use her business plan to locate the capital she needs?

3. If Halperin approached you as a potential investor, what questions would you ask her? Explain. Would your answer change the content of the memo you wrote in question 1? If so, how?

Source: Adapted from Alessandra Bianchi, "What's Love Got to Do With It?" *Inc.*, May 1996, pp. 77-85.

COMPETITIVE TEST. The external part of the competitive test evaluates the company's relative position to its key competitors. How do the company's strengths and weaknesses match up with those of the competition? How are existing competitors likely to react when the new business enters the market? Do these reactions threaten the new company's success and survival?

The internal competitive test focuses on management's ability to create a company that will gain an edge over existing rivals. To pass this part of the competitive test, a plan must prove the quality of the venture's management team. What other resources does the company have that can give it a competitive edge in the market?

VALUE TEST. To convince lenders and investors to put their money into the venture, a business plan must prove to them that it offers a high probability of repayment or an attractive rate of return. Entrepreneurs usually see their businesses as good investments because they consider the intangibles of owning a business such as gaining control over their own destinies, freedom to do what they enjoy, and others; lenders and investors, however, look at a venture in colder terms: dollar-for-dollar returns. A plan must convince lenders and investors that they will earn an attractive return on their money.

Sometimes the greatest service a business plan provides an entrepreneur is the realization that "it just won't work." The time to find out a potential business idea won't succeed is in the planning stages *before* the entrepreneur commits significant resources to the venture. In other cases it reveals important problems to overcome before launching a company. According to one business consultant, "If you do a really good job of writing your business plan, it's more than just putting words on paper. You do a lot of research, and you expose a lot of flaws. Each one that you expose and treat, you enhance the chances of your success."[10]

The real value in preparing a business plan is not so much in the plan itself as it is in the process the entrepreneur goes through to create the plan. Although the finished product is useful, the process of building a plan requires an entrepreneur to subject his idea to an objective, critical evaluation. What the entrepreneur learns about his company, its target market, its financial requirements, and other factors can be essential to making the venture a success. This process allows the entrepreneur to replace "I thinks" with more "I knows" and to make mistakes on paper, which is much cheaper than making them in reality. Simply put, building a business plan reduces the risk and uncertainty in launching a company by teaching the entrepreneur to do it the right way!

The Appendix at the end of this book contains a sample business plan for an actual company, Septic Sense, Inc.

Making the Business Plan Presentation

4. Understand the keys to making an effective business plan presentation.

Lenders and investors are favorably impressed by entrepreneurs who are informed and prepared when requesting a loan or investment. When attempting to secure funds from professional venture capitalists or private investors, the written business plan almost always precedes the opportunity to meet "face-to-face." For the most part an entrepreneur's time for presenting her business opportunity will be quite limited. (When presenting a plan to a venture capital forum, the allotted time is usually 15 to 20 minutes, 30 minutes at the maximum). When the opportunity arises, an entrepreneur must be well prepared. It is important to rehearse, rehearse, and then rehearse more. It is a mistake to begin by leading the audience into a long-winded explanation about the technology on which the product or service is based. Within minutes most of the audience will be lost; and so is any chance the entrepreneur has of obtaining the necessary financing for her new venture.

Some helpful tips for making a business plan presentation to potential lenders and investors include:

☆ Demonstrate enthusiasm about the venture, but don't be overemotional.

☆ "Hook" investors quickly with an up-front explanation of the new venture, its opportunities, and the anticipated benefits to them.

☆ Use visual aids. They make it easier for people to follow your presentation.

☆ Hit the highlights; specific questions will bring out the details later. Don't get caught up in too much detail in early meetings with lenders and investors.

☆ Avoid the use of technological terms that will likely be above most of the audience. Do at least one rehearsal before someone who has no special technical training. Tell him to stop you anytime he does not understand what you are talking about. When this occurs (and it likely will), rewrite that portion of your presentation.

☆ Close by reinforcing the nature of the opportunity. Be sure you have sold the benefits the investors will realize when the business is a success.

☆ Be prepared for questions. In many cases, there is seldom time for a long "Q&A" session, but interested investors may want to get you aside to discuss the details of the plan.

☆ Follow up with every investor to whom you make a presentation. Don't sit back and wait; be proactive. They have what you need—investment capital. Demonstrate that you have confidence in your plan and have the initiative necessary to run a business successfully.

YOU BE THE CONSULTANT...

Dick's Dilemma

Dick Bardow sat quietly in his car, pondering why he had failed to convince Linda Jolly, managing partner of Next Century Venture Capital, to provide the startup capital he needed to launch the business that would launch his new high-tech medical invention. Bardow had spent the past three-and-a-half years researching and developing the concept, and now that he had a product in hand, he was ready to take it to the market. The idea for Bardow's new venture had been simmering for many years during his stints as a researcher for a major medical lab and as a sales representative for a medical products company. Bardow had learned a great deal about selling medical products in his sales job, which he took after earning a master's degree. But it was during his tenure at the medical lab that Bardow saw the importance of staying on the cutting edge of technology in the field of medicine. He also saw the tremendous profit potential of successful medical products.

Driving home, Bardow replayed his meeting with Jolly in his mind. "How could those venture capitalists have missed the tremendous opportunity right in front of them?" he mused. During his 45-minute meeting with Jolly and her staff, Bardow had spent 30 minutes explaining how the technology had evolved over time, how he had developed the product, and why it was technologically superior to anything currently on the market. "I've got them where I want them, now," he remembers thinking. "They can't help but see the incredible power of this technology." Throughout his corporate career, Bardow had earned a reputation for his ability to explain abstract ideas and highly technical concepts to his fellow scientists. Over the years, he had made dozens of presentations at scientific professional meetings, all of which were well received.

Bardow had to admit, however, that he was really puzzled by all of the questions Jolly had asked him toward the end of their meeting. They weren't at all what he was expecting! "She never asked a single question about my product, its design, the technology behind it, or the patent I have pending," he muttered. He remembered her questioning him about a "market analysis" and how and to whom he planned to market his product. "How foolish!" he thought. "You can't forecast exact sales for a new product. Once this product is on the market and the medical industry sees what it can do, we'll have all the sales we'll need—and more." Bardow was convinced that Jolly didn't understand that new, innovative products create their own markets. "I've seen it dozens of times," he said. Dick was beginning to believe that venture capital firms were too focused on revenues, profits, and return on investment. "Don't they know that those things are outcomes?" he thought. "They come . . . in time."

1. Identify the possible problems with Dick Bardow's presentation of his business plan to Linda Jolly.

2. Should potential lenders and investors evaluate new ventures that are based on cutting-edge technology differently from other business ventures? Explain.

3. List at least five suggestions you would make to Dick Bardow to improve his business plan and his presentation of it.

"I can't sleep. I just got this incredible craving for capital."

Source: Drawing by Mankoff; © 1995 The New Yorker Magazine, Inc.

What Bankers Look for in a Loan Application

Banks will rarely be a new venture's sole source of capital because a bank's return is limited by the interest rate it negotiates, but its risk could be the entire amount of the loan if the new business fails. Once the business is operational and has established a financial track record, the bank becomes the traditional source of financing. For this reason the small business owner needs to be aware of the criteria bankers use in evaluating the credit-worthiness of loan applicants. Most bankers refer to these criteria as the **five Cs of credit**: capital, capacity, collateral, character, and conditions.

CAPITAL. A small business must have a stable capital base before a bank will grant a loan. Otherwise the bank would be making, in effect, a capital investment in the business. Most banks refuse to make loans that are capital investments because the potential for return on the investment is limited strictly to the interest on the loan, and the potential loss would probably exceed the reward. In fact, the most common reasons that banks give for rejecting small business loan applications are undercapitalization or too much debt. The bank expects the small business to have an equity base of investment by the owner(s) that will help support the venture during times of financial strain.

CAPACITY. A synonym for capacity is cash flow. The bank must be convinced of the firm's ability to meet its regular financial obligations and to repay the bank loan, and that takes cash. In Chapter 7 we saw that more small businesses fail from lack of cash than from lack of profit. It is possible for a company to be showing a profit and still have no cash—that is, to be technically bankrupt. Bankers expect the small business loan applicant to pass the test of liquidity, especially for short-term loans. The bank studies closely the small company's cash flow position to decide whether or not it meets the capacity required.

5. Explain the "five Cs of credit" and why they are important to potential lenders and investors reading business plans.

five Cs of credit—*criteria bankers use to evaluate the credit-worthiness of loan applicants: capital, capacity, collateral, character, and conditions.*

COLLATERAL. Collateral includes any assets the owner pledges to the bank as security for repayment of the loan. If the company defaults on the loan, the bank has the right to sell the collateral and use the proceeds to satisfy the loan. Typically, banks make very few unsecured loans (those not backed by collateral) to business startups. Bankers view the owner's willingness to pledge collateral (personal or business assets) as an indication of dedication to making the venture a success. A sound business plan can improve a banker's attitude toward a venture.

CHARACTER. Before approving a loan to a small business, the banker must be satisfied with the owner's character. The evaluation of character frequently is based on intangible factors such as honesty, competence, polish, determination, intelligence, and ability. Although the qualities so judged are abstract, this evaluation plays a critical role in the banker's decision.

Loan officers know that most small businesses fail because of incompetent management, and so they try to avoid extending loans to high-risk managers. The business plan described earlier in this chapter and a polished presentation by the entrepreneur can go far in convincing the banker of the owner's capability.

CONDITIONS. The conditions surrounding a loan request also affect the owner's chance of receiving funds. Banks consider factors relating to the business operation such as potential growth in the market, competition, location, form of ownership, and loan purpose. Again, the owner should provide this relevant information in an organized format in the business plan. Another important condition influencing the banker's decision is the shape of the overall economy, including interest rate levels, inflation rate, and demand for money. Although these factors are beyond an entrepreneur's control, they still are an important component in a banker's decision.

The higher a small business scores on these five Cs, the greater its chance will be of receiving a loan. The wise entrepreneur keeps this in mind when preparing a business plan and presentation.

Business Plan Format

Although every company's business plan will be unique, reflecting its individual circumstances, certain elements are universal. The following outline summarizes these components.

I. Executive Summary (not to exceed two typewritten pages)
   A. Company name, address, and phone number
   B. Name(s), address(es), and phone number(s) of all key people
   C. Brief description of the business
   D. Brief overview of the market for your product
   E. Brief overview of the strategic actions you plan to take to make your firm a success
   F. Brief description of the managerial and technical experience of your key people
   G. Brief statement of what the financial needs are and what the money would be used for; also, income statements and balance sheets for the last three years of operation

II. Detailed Business Plan
   A. Industry analysis
      1. Industry background and overview
      2. Trends
      3. Growth rate
      4. Outlook for the future

B. Background of your business
   1. Brief history of the business
   2. Current situation
C. Your business
   1. Complete and detailed description of your business
      a. Your company's mission statement
      b. What makes your business unique—sources of competitive advantage
      c. How does your company create value for others?
      d. Describe the key factors that will dictate the success of your business (i.e., price competitiveness, quality, durability, dependability, technical features, etc.)
D. Market analysis
   1. Who are the potential buyers for your products? (Please be specific)
   2. What is their motivation to buy?
   3. How many customers does the market contain? (How large is the market?)
   4. What are their potential annual purchases?
   5. What is the nature of the buying cycle?
      a. Is this product a durable good that lasts for years or a product that is repurchased on a regular basis?
      b. Is the product likely to be purchased at only seasonal periods during the year?
   6. Specific target market—what do you know about the potential customer you are likely to sell to in your geographic area?
      a. What are the product features that influence the customer's buying decision?
      b. What, if any, research supports your conclusions?
      c. Do the customers have a preference in where they purchase comparable products? How strong is this preference?
   7. Pricing strategies
      a. Cost structure—fixed and variable
      b. Desired image in market
      c. Your prices versus competitors' prices
   8. Advertising and promotion strategies
      a. What media are most effective in reaching your target audience?
      b. Media costs
      c. Frequency of usage
      d. How will you generate publicity for your business?
   9. Distribution strategy
      a. Channels of distribution
      b. How will you get the product or service into the customers' hands?
      c. Sales techniques and incentives
   10. External market influence. How might each of the following external forces affect the sale or profitability of your product?
      a. Economic factors
         (1) Inflation
         (2) Recession
         (3) High or low unemployment
         (4) Interest rates
      b. Social factors
         (1) Age of customers
         (2) Locational demographics
         (3) Income levels
         (4) Size of household
         (5) Social attitudes

  c. Technological factors influencing your business

 E. Competitor analysis

  1. Describe each of the following factors and discuss how these factors will influence your success

   a. Existing competitors

    (1) Who are they? Please list major known competitors

    (2) Why do you believe the potential customers in your target market buy from them now?

   b. Potential firms who might enter the market

    (1) Who are they and when and why might they enter the market?

    (2) What would be the impact in your target market segment if they enter?

   c. What are the strengths and weaknesses of each key competitor's business?

 F. Strategic plan for your business

  1. Core competencies

  2. Market position and image

  3. SWOT analysis

   a. Strengths

   b. Weaknesses

   c. Opportunities

   d. Threats

  4. Business strategy

   a. Cost leadership

   b. Differentiation

   c. Focus

 G. Specifics of your organization and management

  1. How is your business organized?

   a. Legally (corporation, S corporation, partnership, sole proprietorship)

   b. Functionally

  2. Who are the key people in your organization?

   a. What are their backgrounds, and what do they bring to the business that will enhance the chance of success?

   b. Résumés of key managers and employees

  3. Organization chart

 H. Financial plans

  1. How much money do you need to make this product and your business a long-term success?

   a. Tie the response to this question to your production and marketing plan.

   b. Be realistic and specific

  2. Create a budget. Show the banker or investor how much money you need, why you need it, when you need it, and how and when you plan to generate revenues from operations and sales

  3. Have a realistic projection of costs of operations

   a. Materials

   b. Labor

   c. Equipment

   d. Marketing

   e. Overhead

   f. Other (i.e., unique startup costs)

  4. Present actual and projected balance sheets and income statements

  5. Prepare a breakeven analysis

  6. Prepare a ratio analysis

7. Create cash flow projections

I. Strategic action plan
  1. Clear mission statement for your business
  2. Specific performance goals and objectives
  3. Restatement of your production and marketing strategies
  4. How these strategies will be converted into operation action plans
  5. What control procedures you plan to establish to keep the business on track

J. Loan proposal
  1. Loan purpose
  2. Amount requested
  3. Repayment or "cash out" schedule
  4. Timetable for implementation

CHAPTER SUMMARY

1. Explain why every entrepreneur should create a business plan.
- The business plan serves two essential functions. First and most important, it guides the company's operations by charting its future course and devising a strategy for following it. The second function of the business plan is to attract lenders and investors. Applying for loans or attempting to attract investors without a solid business plan rarely attracts needed capital. Rather, the best way to secure the necessary capital is to prepare a sound business plan.

2. Describe the elements of a solid business plan.
- Although a business plan should be unique and tailor-made to suit the particular needs of a small company, it should cover these basic elements: an executive summary, a mission statement, a company history, a business and industry profile, a description of the company's business strategy, a profile of its products or services, a statement explaining its marketing strategy, a competitor analysis, owners' and officers' résumés, a plan of operation, financial data, and the loan or investment proposal.

3. Explain the benefits of preparing a plan.
- Preparing a sound business plan clearly requires time and effort, but the benefits greatly exceed the costs. Building the plan forces a potential entrepreneur to look at his or her business idea in the harsh light of reality. It also requires the owner to assess the venture's chances of success more objectively. A well-assembled plan helps prove to outsiders that a business idea can be successful.
- The *real* value in preparing a business plan is not so much in the plan itself as it is in the process the entrepreneur goes through to create the plan. Although the finished product is useful, the process of building a plan requires an entrepreneur to subject his or her idea to an objective, critical evaluation. What the entrepreneur learns about his or her company, its target market, its financial requirements, and other factors can be essential to making the venture a success.

4. Understand the keys to making an effective business plan presentation.
- Lenders and investors are favorably impressed by entrepreneurs who are informed and prepared when requesting a loan or investment.
- Tips include: Demonstrate enthusiasm about the venture, but don't be overemotional; "hook" investors quickly with an up-front explanation of the new venture, its opportunities, and the anticipated benefits to them; use visual aids; hit the highlights of your venture; don't get caught up in too much detail in early meetings with lenders and investors; avoid the use of technological terms that will likely be above most of the audience; rehearse your presentation before giving it; close by reinforcing the nature of the opportunity; and be prepared for questions.

5. Explain the "five Cs of credit" and why they are important to potential lenders and investors reading business plans.
- Small business owners need to be aware of the criteria bankers use in evaluating the credit-worthiness of loan applicants—the five Cs of credit: capital, capacity, collateral, character, and conditions.
- *Capital.* Lenders expect small businesses to have an equity base of investment by the owner(s) that will help support the venture during times of financial strain.
- *Capacity.* A synonym for capacity is cash flow. The bank must be convinced of the firm's ability to meet its regular financial obligations and to repay the bank loan, and that takes cash.
- *Collateral.* Collateral includes any assets the owner pledges to the bank as security for repayment of the loan.
- *Character.* Before approving a loan to a small business, the banker must be satisfied with the owner's character.
- *Condition*s. The conditions such as interest rates, the health of the nation's economy, industry growth rates, and others surrounding a loan request also affect the owner's chance of receiving funds.

1. Why should an entrepreneur develop a business plan?
2. Describe the major components of a business plan.
3. How can an entrepreneur seeking funds to launch a business convince potential lenders and investors that a market for the product or service really does exist?
4. How would you prepare to make a formal presentation of your business plan to a venture capital forum?
5. What are the five Cs of credit? How does a banker use them when evaluating a loan request?

Beyond the Classroom...

1. Interview a local banker who has experience in making loans to small businesses. Ask him or her the following questions.

   a. How important is a well-prepared business plan?

   b. How important is a smooth presentation?

   c. How does the banker evaluate the owner's character?

   d. How heavily does the bank weigh the five Cs of credit?

   e. What percentage of small business owners are well prepared to request a bank loan?

   f. What are the major reasons for the bank's rejection of small business loan applications?

2. Interview a small business owner who has requested a bank loan or an equity investment from external sources. Ask him or her these questions:

   a. Did you prepare a written business plan before approaching the financial officer?

   b. If the answer is "yes" to part a, did you have outside or professional help in preparing it?

   c. How many times have your requests for additional funds been rejected? What reasons were given for the rejection?

SURFING THE NET

1. Using one of the search engines on the World Wide Web, (WWW), such as Lycos, Magellan, Yahoo!, or others, conduct a search on the phrase *business plan.*

2. From your Web search in exercise 1, locate a sample (or actual) business plan on the Web. Critique the plan and its format. What suggestions can you make for improving the plan?

3. Go to the Web addresses for:

Palo Alto Software at:

http://pasware.com/

and

MoneyHunter at:

http://www.moneyhunter.com/businessplan/

and

Enterprise Support Systems at:

http://www.ess-advisors.com/

and

Strategic Business Planning Company at:

http://www.bizplan.com/

and

Business Resource Software Inc. at:

http://www.brs-inc.com/strategy.html

and

California Small Business Assistance Network at:

http://csban.org:80/bgt/business_plan/

Prepare a brief report on the resources available to entrepreneurs building business plans.

CHAPTER

TEN

Sources of Funds: Equity and Debt

The key to [economic] growth is quite simple: creative people with money.
- George Gilder

*Business is never so healthy as when, like a chicken,
it must do a certain amount of scratching for what it gets.*
- Henry Ford

There's many a pessimist who got that way by financing an optimist.
- Anonymous

LEARNING OBJECTIVES

Upon completion of this chapter, you will be able to:

1. ***Explain*** the differences among the three types of capital small businesses require: fixed, working, and growth.

2. ***Describe*** the differences between equity capital and debt capital and the advantages and disadvantages of each.

3. ***Describe*** the various sources of equity capital available to entrepreneurs, including personal savings, friends and relatives, angels, partners, corporations, venture capital, and public stock offerings, and describe the advantages and disadvantages of each.

4. ***Describe*** the process of "going public," as well as its advantages and disadvantages and the various simplified registrations and exemptions from registration available to small businesses wanting to sell securities to investors.

5. ***Describe*** the various sources of debt capital and the advantages and disadvantages of each.

6. ***Identify*** the sources of government financial assistance and the loan programs offered.

7. ***Discuss*** valuable methods of financing growth and expansion internally.

Raising the money to launch a new business venture has always been a challenge for entrepreneurs. Today, however, entrepreneurs are finding it increasingly difficult to locate the seed capital they need to bring their businesses to life. The blows the financial industry has taken over the past decade have made the entrepreneur's job of fund raising extremely challenging. Banks have tightened their lending criteria, venture capitalists have become more conservative, private investors have grown more cautious, and making a public stock offering remains a viable option for only a handful of fast-growing companies with good track records. The result has been a credit crunch for many entrepreneurs. To many potential lenders and investors, small business has become "(too) risky business."

In the face of this capital crunch, business's need for capital is greater than ever before. One financing expert says that the entrepreneurial segment of our nation's economy needs $60 billion per year in seed capital to fuel its growth.[1] When searching for the capital to launch their companies, entrepreneurs must remember three "secrets" to successful financing in the 1990s:

☆ Choosing the right sources of capital for a business can be just as important as choosing the right form of ownership or the right location. It is a decision that will influence a company for a lifetime, so entrepreneurs must weigh their options carefully before committing to a particular funding source. "It is important that companies in need of capital align themselves with sources that best fit their needs," says one financial consultant. "The success of a company often depends on the success of that relationship."[2]

☆ The money is out there; the key is knowing where to look. "The problem is not a lack of funding sources but a lack of knowledge of how to find them," says Bruce Blechman, coauthor of *Guerrilla Financing*.[3]

☆ Creativity counts. Although many popular sources of funds in the 1980s from venture capital funds to federal loan programs will play a smaller role in financing business startups, entrepreneurs have discovered new sources from large corporations and customers to international venture capitalists and state or local programs to take up the slack. "With so many doors to borrowing closed," says one financing expert, " . . . entrepreneurs are being forced to use as much ingenuity in financing as they did in product and service ideas."[4]

Rather than relying primarily on a single source of funds as they have in the past, entrepreneurs are now having to piece together their capital from multiple sources.

Frederick Sport and Ice Arena

Entrepreneurs Byron and Wendy Dyke demonstrate the "patchwork" of startup financing that has become so common. Over the course of three-and-a-half years, 16 commercial lenders, eight leasing companies, and four venture capitalists turned down the Dykes' business plan for launching Frederick Sport and Ice Arena, a combination ice rink and fitness club. Ultimately, the Dykes won approval for a $1 million Small Business Administration loan, convinced two banks to put up $1.2 million in loans, and persuaded family members to put up $700,000 in equity financing to finance their company. To fill the remaining capital gap, the couple turned to the state of Maryland, which put up the final $250,000 through a loan program that encourages job growth, increasing tax revenues, and improving the quality of life. After just one year in business, Frederick Sport and Ice Arena was so successful that the couple added a second rink.[5]

This chapter will guide you through the myriad financing options available to entrepreneurs, focusing on both sources of equity (ownership) and debt (borrowed) financing.

Planning for Capital Needs

1. Explain the differences among the three types of capital small businesses require: fixed, working, and growth.

Becoming a successful entrepreneur requires one to become a skilled fund raiser, a job that usually requires more time and energy than most business founders realize. In startup companies, raising capital can easily consume as much as one-half of the entrepreneur's time. Most entrepreneurs are seeking less than $1 million (indeed, most need less than $100,000, see Figure 10.1), which may be the toughest money to secure. Where to find this seed money depends, in part, on the nature of the proposed business and on the amount of money required. For example, the originator of a computer software firm would have different capital requirements than the founder of a coal mining operation.

Capital is any form of wealth employed to produce more wealth for the firm. It exists in many forms in a typical business, including cash, inventory, plant, and equipment. Financial managers must plan for the following three different types of capital.

capital—*any form of wealth employed to produce more wealth; it exists in many forms in a business, including cash, inventory, plant, and equipment.*

FIXED CAPITAL. **Fixed capital** is needed to purchase the business's permanent or fixed assets, such as buildings, land, computers, and equipment. Money invested in these fixed assets tends to be frozen since it cannot be used for any other purpose. Typically, large sums of money are involved in purchasing fixed assets, and credit terms are frequently lengthy. Lenders of fixed capital expect the assets purchased to improve the efficiency and, thus, the profitability of the business, and to create improved cash flows to ensure repayment over the years.

fixed capital—*capital needed to purchase the business's permanent or fixed assets such as buildings, land, computers, or equipment.*

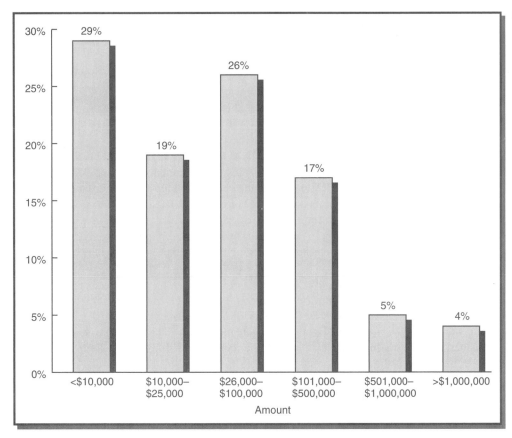

Figure 10.1
Startup Requirements: How Much Capital Did You Need to Start Your Business?
Source: Adapted from BBDO Seidman, New York.

WORKING CAPITAL. **Working capital** represents the business's temporary funds; it is the capital used to support the business's normal short-term operations. Accountants define working capital as current assets minus current liabilities. The need for working capital arises because of the uneven flow of cash into and out of the business due to normal seasonal fluctuations. Credit sales, seasonal sales swings, or unforeseeable changes in demand will create fluctuations in any small company's cash flow. Working capital normally is used to buy inventory, pay bills, finance credit sales, pay wages and salaries, and take care of any unexpected emergencies. Lenders of working capital expect it to produce higher cash flows to ensure repayment at the end of the production/sales cycle.

GROWTH CAPITAL. **Growth capital**, unlike working capital, is not related to the seasonal fluctuations of a small business. Instead, growth capital requirements surface when an existing business is expanding or changing its primary direction. For example, a small manufacturer of silicon microchips for computers saw his business skyrocket in a short time period. With orders for chips rushing in, the growing business needed a sizable cash infusion to increase plant size, expand its sales and production work force, and buy more equipment. During times of such rapid expansion, a growing company's capital requirements are similar to those of a business startup. Like lenders of fixed capital, growth capital lenders expect the funds to improve a company's profitability and cash flow position, thus ensuring repayment.

Although these three types of capital are interdependent, each has certain sources, characteristics, and effects on the business and its long-term growth that entrepreneurs must recognize. Table 10.1 lists the various sources of capital for companies in the various stages of the business life cycle and their likelihood of use.

Equity Capital versus Debt Capital

Equity capital represents the personal investment of the owner (or owners) in a business, and it is sometimes called *risk capital* because these investors assume the primary risk of losing their funds if the business fails. However, if the venture succeeds, they also share in the benefits, which can be quite substantial. The founders of Federal Express, Intel, and Compaq Computers became multimillionaires when their equity investments finally paid off. The primary advantage of equity capital is that it does not have to be repaid like a loan does. Equity investors are entitled to share in the company's earnings (if there are any) and usually to have a voice in the company's future direction.

The primary disadvantage of equity capital is that the entrepreneur must give up some—perhaps *most*—of the ownership in the business to outsiders. Although 50 percent of something is better than 100 percent of nothing, giving up control of your company can be disconcerting and dangerous.

For instance, when Gary Hoover launched Bookstop, Inc., a book superstore, he relied on equity financing so much that he was left with just 6 percent of his company's stock. Seven years after startup, the venture capitalists who owned most of the stock fired Hoover from the company he founded![6] Entrepreneurs are most likely to give up more equity in their businesses in the startup phase than in any other (see Figure 10.2 on page 306).

Bookstop, Inc.

Debt capital is the financing that a small business owner has borrowed and must repay with interest. Very few entrepreneurs have adequate personal savings to finance the complete startup costs of a small business; many of them must rely on some form of debt capital to launch their companies. Lenders of capital are more numerous than investors, although small business loans can be just as difficult (if not more difficult) to obtain. Although borrowed capital allows entrepreneurs to maintain complete ownership of their businesses, it must be carried as a liability on the balance sheet as well as be repaid with

Sources	Startup	Operation	Growth	Initial Maturity
Business Life Cycle*				
Equity:				
Individual Investors	M	M	P	U
Corporations	U	U	P	M
Employee Stock Option Plan	U	U	P	M
Venture Capital	M	M	P	U
Small Business Investment Corp.	P	P/M	P/M	M
Public Offering	U	U/P	M	M
Personal and Business Assoc.	P	M	P	U
Debt Finance:				
Commercial Banks	P	M	M	M
Savings and Loan Assn.	U	P	U	U
Life Insurance Co.	U	U	P	M
Commercial Credit Co.	P	P	M	P
Factors	U	P	M	P
Government Programs				
—Small Business Administration	P	M	M	U
—Community Development Corporation	U	U	M	M
—Economic Development Commission	U	U	M	M
—Small Business Investment Corporation	P	M	U	U
Private Limited Parntership	M	P	P	U
Other:				
Research/Development Grants	P/M	M	P	U
Tax Shelters	P/M	P	P	P
Private Foundations	P	M	P	U
Corporate Annuities	U	U	P	M
Joint Ventures	P	M	P	U
Licensing Ventures	U	U	P	M
Vendor Financing	U	U	P	M
Mezzanine Financing	U	P	M	M
Pension Funds	U	P	P	P

*M, Most likely source; P, Possible source; U, Unlikely source.

Table 10.1
The Source of Capital Matrix

Sources: EMCO Financial Ltd., Los Angeles; Thomas Owens, "Getting Financing in 1990," *Small Business Reports*, June 1990, p. 71.

interest at some point in the future. In addition, because lenders consider small businesses to be greater risks than bigger corporate customers, they require higher interest rates on loans to small companies because of the risk-return tradeoff—the higher the risk, the greater the return demanded. Most small firms pay the prime rate—the interest rate banks charge their most creditworthy customers—*plus* a few percentage points. Still, the cost of debt financing often is lower than that of equity financing. Because of the higher risks associated with providing equity capital to small companies, investors demand greater returns

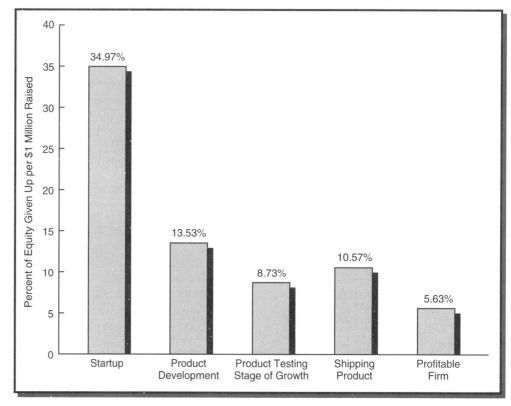

than lenders. Also, unlike equity financing, debt financing does not require an entrepreneur to dilute her ownership interest in the company.

We now turn our attention to nine common sources of equity capital.

3. Describe the various sources of equity capital and the advantages and disadvantages of each.

Sources of Equity Capital

Personal Savings

The first place entrepreneurs should look for startup money is in their own pockets. It's the least expensive source of funds available! "The sooner you take outside money, the more ownership in your company you'll have to surrender," warns one small business expert.[7] Entrepreneurs apparently see the benefits of self-sufficiency; the most common source of equity funds used to start a small business is the entrepreneur's pool of personal savings. In fact, Commerce Department statistics show that 67 percent of all business owners launched or acquired their companies without borrowing capital.[8]

As a general rule, entrepreneurs should expect to provide at least half of the startup funds in the form of equity capital. If the entrepreneur is not willing to risk his own money, potential investors are not likely to risk their money in the business either. Furthermore, if an owner contributes any less than half of the initial capital requirement, he must borrow an excessive amount of capital to fund the business properly, and the high repayment schedule puts intense pressure on cash flow. In some cases, however, a creative entrepreneur is able to invest as little as 10 percent of the initial capital requirement. The important point is that an entrepreneur should not surrender all hope of going into business just because he is unable to provide half of the starting funds.

Friends and Relatives

After emptying their own pockets, entrepreneurs should turn to friends and relatives who might be willing to invest in the business venture. Because of their relationships with the founder, these people are most likely to invest. According to the Census Bureau, nearly 10 percent of small business owners say they rely on relatives and friends for capital.[9] Often, they are more patient than other outside investors. "Most of our relatives just told us to pay them back when we could," says an entrepreneur who used $30,000 from family members to launch a gourmet coffee business."[10]

Inherent dangers lurk in family business investments, however. Unrealistic expectations or misunderstood risks have destroyed many friendships and have ruined many family reunions. To avoid such problems, an entrepreneur must honestly present the investment opportunity and the nature of the risks involved to avoid alienating friends and family members if the business fails. Table 10.2 offers suggestions for structuring family or friendship financing deals.

Angels

After dipping into their own pockets and convincing friends and relatives to invest in their business ventures, many entrepreneurs still find themselves short of the seed capital they need. Frequently, the next stop on the road to business financing is private investors. These

---

Tapping family members and friends for startup capital, whether in the form of equity or debt financing, is a popular method of financing business ideas. Unfortunately, these deals don't always work to the satisfaction of both parties. For instance, when actor Don Johnson needed seed capital to launch DJ Racing, a company that designs and races speedboats, he approached a wealthy Miami friend who made a $300,000 interest-free loan on nothing but a handshake. Within a year, a dispute arose over when Johnson was to pay back the loan. A lawsuit followed, which the two now former friends settled out of court. The following suggestions can help entrepreneurs avoid needlessly destroying family relationships and friendships.

★ *Consider the impact of the investment on everyone involved.* Will it work a hardship on anyone? Is the investor putting up the money because he wants to or because he feels obligated to? Can both parties afford the loan if the business folds?

★ *Keep the arrangement strictly business.* The parties should treat all loans and investments in a business-like manner, no matter how close the friendship or family relationship, to avoid problems down the line. If the transaction is a loan exceeding $10,000, it must carry a rate of interest at least as high as the market rate; otherwise the IRS may consider the loan a gift and penalize the lender.

★ *Settle the details up front.* Before any money changes hands, both parties must agree on the details of the deal. How much money is involved? Is it a loan or an investment? How will the investor cash out? How will the loan be paid off? What happens if the business fails?

★ *Create a written contract.* Don't make the mistake of closing a financial deal with just a handshake. The probability of misunderstandings skyrockets! Putting an agreement in writing demonstrates both parties' commitment to the deal and minimizes the chances of disputes from faulty memories and misunderstandings.

★ *Treat the money as "bridge financing."* Although family and friends can help you launch your business, it is unlikely that they can provide enough capital to sustain it over the long term. Sooner or later, you will need to establish a relationship with other sources of credit if your company is to survive and thrive. Consider money from family and friends as a bridge to take your company to the next level of financing.

★ *Develop a payment schedule that suits both the entrepreneur and the lender or investor.* Although lenders and investors may want to get their money back as quickly as possible, a rapid repayment or cash-out schedule can jeopardize a fledgling company's survival. Establish a realistic repayment plan that works for both parties without putting excessive strain on the young company's cash flow.

Table 10.2
Suggestions for Structuring Family and Friendship Financing Deals

Source: Adapted from Alex Markels, "A Little Help from Their Friends," *Wall Street Journal*, May 22, 1995, p. R10.

angels—*wealthy individuals, often entrepreneurs themselves, who invest in business startups in exchange for equity stakes in the companies.*

Thunder Sports

private investors (or **angels**) are wealthy individuals, often entrepreneurs themselves, who invest in business startups in exchange for equity stakes in the companies.

Angels are a primary source of startup capital for companies in the embryonic stage through the growth stage, and their role in financing small businesses is significant. Some experts conservatively estimate that angels invest between $10 and $20 billion a year in 30,000 to 40,000 small companies. Because the angel market is so fragmented and disorganized, we may never get a completely accurate estimate of its investment in business startups. Although they may disagree on the exact amount of angel investments, experts concur on one fact: Angels are the largest single source of external equity capital for small businesses.[11] Their investments in young companies dwarf those of professional venture capitalists, providing at least three to five times more capital to 20 to 30 times as many companies.[12]

Angels fill a significant gap in the seed capital market. They are most likely to finance startups with capital requirements in the $250,000 to $500,000 range, well below the $1 million minimum investments most professional venture capitalists prefer. Because a $500,000 deal requires about as much of a venture capitalist's time to research and screen as a $5 million deal does, venture capitalists tend to focus on the big deals, where their returns are bigger. Due to the inherent risks in startup companies, many venture capitalists have shifted their investment portfolios away from startups toward more established firms. "Venture capital has become the oxymoron of the 1990s," says one industry expert. "There's no venture and there's no capital—at least for startups."[13] That's why angel financing is so important. Angels will often finance the deals that no venture capitalists will consider.

For example, when Andrew and Glen Ferguson, ages 19 and 23, respectively, wanted to launch an indoor soccer arena, they could find no one, including banks and the Small Business Administration, to bankroll the $100,000 they needed. They watched as potential customers drove 100 miles roundtrip to play indoor soccer in another city. Then, using a connection their father's accountant had, the brothers found a private investor who put up the $100,000 in exchange for 25 percent of the company. After three years, their company, Thunder Sports, was growing so fast that they needed more capital to build their own indoor multisports complex. A business associate introduced the brothers to another angel, who, after reviewing their business plan, agreed to finance the entire $4.5 million project.[14]

The challenge, of course, is *finding* these angels. The typical angel is a 47-year-old white male with a college education earning $100,000 per year and a net worth (excluding a home) of $1 million. Most have substantial business and financial experience and prefer to invest in companies at the startup or infant growth stage. The typical angel accepts 30 percent of the investment opportunities presented; makes an average of two investments every three years; and has invested an average of $131,000 of equity in 3.5 firms (although investments may range from as little as $5,000 to as much as $1 million or more). Ninety percent say they're satisfied with their investment decisions.[15] As the Ferguson brothers' experience demonstrates, locating angels boils down to making the right contacts. Asking friends, attorneys, bankers, stockbrokers, accountants, other business owners, and consultants for suggestions and introductions is a good way to start. "It's all a networking issue," says one active angel.[16]

Angels almost always invest their money locally, so entrepreneurs should look close to home for them—typically within a 50- to 100-mile radius. Angels also look for businesses they know something about and most expect to invest their knowledge, experience, and energy as well as their money in a company. Angels tend to invest in clusters as well. With the right approach, an entrepreneur can attract an angel who might share the deal with some of his cronies.

For instance, the Investors' Circle is an informal organization of angels that specializes in financing socially responsible businesses. Every month, the Investor's Circle sends its 130 members two-page summaries on anywhere from four to twenty business ventures. Interested members, who often team up with one another, contact company founders directly. Cyclean Inc., a company that recycles asphalt, recently raised part of its startup capital from 23 Circle member investors.[17]

Angels are an excellent source of "patient money," often willing to wait seven years or longer to cash out their investments. They earn their returns through the increased value of the business, not through dividends and interest. For example, more than 1,000 early investors in Microsoft Inc. (now a giant in the computer software industry) are now millionaires. The original investors in Genentech Inc. (a genetic engineering company) have seen their investments increase more than 500 times![18] Angels return on investment targets tend to be lower than those of professional venture capitalists. While venture capitalists shoot for 60 percent to 75 percent returns annually, private investors usually settle for 35 percent to 50 percent (depending on the level of risk involved in the venture). Private investors typically take less than 50 percent ownership, leaving the majority ownership to the company founder(s). Sixty percent of angel investments is in seed capital (financing businesses in the startup phase), and 82 percent is for less than $500,000.[19] The lesson: If an entrepreneur needs relatively small amounts of money to launch a company, angels are a primary source.

Partners

As we saw in Chapter 3, an entrepreneur can choose to take on a partner to expand the capital foundation of the proposed business.

When Lou Bucelli and Tim Crouse were searching for the money to launch CME Conference Video, a company that produces and distributes videotapes of educational conferences for physicians, they found an angel willing to put up $250,000 for 40 percent of the business. Unfortunately, their investor backed out when some of his real estate investments went bad, leaving the partners with commitments for several conferences but no cash to produce and distribute the videos. With little time to spare, Bucelli and Crouse decided to form a series of limited partnerships with people they knew, one for each video tape they would produce. Six limited partnerships produced $400,000 in financing, and the tapes generated $9.1 million in sales for the year. As the general partners, Bucelli and Crouse retained 80 percent of each partnership. The limited partners earned returns of up to 80 percent in just six months. Within two years, their company was so successful that venture capitalists started calling. To finance their next round of growth, Bucelli and Crouse sold 35 percent of their company to a venture capital firm for $1.3 million.[20]

Before entering into any partnership arrangement, however, the owner must consider the impact of giving up some personal control over operations and of sharing profits with one or more partners. Whenever an entrepreneur gives up equity in her business (through whatever mechanism), she runs the risk of losing control over it. As the founder's ownership in a company becomes increasingly diluted, the probability of losing control of its future direction and the entire decision-making process increases.

At age 19, Scott Olson started a company that manufactured in-line skates—a company that he had big dreams for. Rollerblades Inc. grew quickly and soon ran into the problem that plagues so many fast-growing companies—insufficient cash flow. Through a series of unfortunate incidents, Olson ended up trading equity in the company for the money he desperately needed to bring his innovative skate designs to market. Ultimately, his investors ended up with 95 percent of the company, leaving Olson with the remaining scant 5 percent. Frustrated at not being able to determine the company's direction, Olson soon left to

start another company. "It's tough to keep control," he says. "For every penny you get in the door, you have to give something up."[21]

Corporations

Large corporations recently have gotten into the business of financing small companies. Today, more than 100 large corporations across the globe from Johnson & Johnson to Genentech maintain their own venture capital funds to finance projects with small businesses. For example, two fast-growing small companies in multimedia technology, Kaleida Labs and General Magic, were financed almost entirely by large U.S. and Japanese electronics companies.[22] Often, the large companies providing the financing are the customers of those receiving it. Recognizing how interwoven their success is with that of their suppliers, corporate giants such as AT&T, J. C. Penney, and Ford now offer financial support to many of the small businesses they buy from.

> **Conner Peripherals Inc.**
>
> *When Finis Conner was launching Conner Peripherals Inc., a small maker of hard disk drives for personal computers, he set out with a prototype disk drive in search of customers and investors. He found both in Compaq Computers. Managers at Compaq were so impressed with Conner's product that they not only decided to buy it, but they also bankrolled the company. Compaq put up $12 million for 40 percent of Conner Peripherals' stock and bought its entire first year's production of disk drives. Conner Peripherals went on to become a Fortune 500 company in just three years.[23]*

YOU BE THE CONSULTANT...

The Hunt for Capital

Micro-Link Technologies, Inc. is a small company that manufactures computer mother boards and equipment for computer makers. It is profitable on annual sales of about $2.2 million. For the past few years, founder Don Duke and chief financial officer Larry Morton have invested heavily in research and development on technologies that could transform the little company into a major player in the computer industry. One of the products Micro-Link developed is a PC mother board that can withstand intense vibrations and temperatures with no loss of performance. Such a product could open the doors to entirely new industries, where using computers was not practical because of the harsh physical environment. Working in a joint venture with a university, Micro-Link also developed StoreMaster, a software package that manages data storage and retrieval on local area networks. "The amount of data on computer networks is growing at an exponential rate, and companies need a turnkey storage solution with intelligent software," says Duke. According to Morton's projections, these two products alone could push Micro-Link's sales to $98 million and profits to $16 million in just five years.

The only barrier is money—or a lack of it.

Micro-Link's bank was recently bought out by a much larger one, and now loan officers have decided to eliminate the company's line of credit. The bank has asked Micro-Link to pay off the $475,000 outstanding balance on its line of credit. When the bank suggested that Duke sell two commercial properties he owned personally below market value to pay off the debt, Duke and Morton decided to find another bank. Within a few months, Micro-Link had established a relationship with a new bank, which extended a new, larger line of credit to the company. Unfortunately, Micro-Link needed more to achieve the goals that Duke and Morton have set for the company. The company's new line of extra-durable computer mother boards and its StoreMaster software are ready to launch, but Micro-Link needs about $6 million for its sales and marketing efforts. Without the money, Micro-Link will most likely continue to be a successful business, but it will be confined to being a niche player in the industry. If Duke and Morton can get the financing they need, they believe they can establish Micro-Link as a major company in the computer business with a very bright future.

1. Identify the possible sources Micro-Link could approach for the financing it needs.

2. Which source(s) would you recommend the company pursue most aggressively? Explain.

3. Which sources would you recommend Micro-Link avoid? Explain.

4. What should Duke and Morton do to prepare for their search for capital?

Source: Adapted from David R. Evanson, "Dollars and Sense," *Entrepreneur*, July 1996, pp. 62-65; David R. Evanson, "Making a Statement," *Entrepreneur*, July 1995, pp. 34-37.

Foreign corporations are also interested in investing in small U.S. businesses. Often, these corporations are seeking strategic partnerships to gain access to new technology, new products, or access to lucrative U.S. markets.

For instance, Ron Posner's CD-ROM publishing company, StarPress, Inc. had grown into a $6 million a year business, but Posner knew that the real growth opportunities for his business lay in Europe. While searching for a company to help finance his European expansion plans, Posner discovered Olivetti Group, one of Europe's largest computer makers. The fit was perfect; Posner needed money and distribution channels, and Olivetti needed CD-ROM titles. Not only did the two companies form a joint venture to sell CD-ROM titles in Europe, but Posner convinced Olivetti's venture capital division to put up $1.5 million for 10 percent of StarPress, Inc.[24]

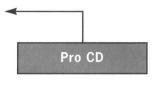

StarPress, Inc.

Venture Capital Companies

Venture capital companies are private, for-profit organizations that purchase equity positions in young businesses they believe have high-growth and -profit potential, producing annual returns of 300 to 500 percent over five to seven years. More than 3,000 venture capital firms operate across the United States today, investing in promising small companies in a wide variety of industries. Venture capitalists have invested billions of dollars in high-potential small companies over the years, including such notable businesses as Apple Computer, Microsoft Inc., Intel, and Data General. Although companies in high-tech industries such as computer software, medical care, biotechnology, and communications are popular targets of venture capital, a company with extraordinary growth prospects has the potential to attract venture capital, whatever its industry. Table 10.3 on page 312 offers a humorous look at deciphering the language of venture capitalists.

Jim Bryant's company, Pro CD, a publisher of telephone directories on CD-ROM, grew so rapidly, reaching $10 million in sales in just three years, that its financing requirements began to outstrip its available cash. Bryant used his network of contacts to initiate meetings with several venture capitalists. "Our first meeting with venture capitalists was a complete disaster," says Bryant, recalling his lack of preparation. The next time he sat down with venture capitalists, however, Bryant made sure he was ready for all of the questions they would ask. Two venture capital firms decided to invest a total of $4.5 million in Pro CD, with each getting 10 percent ownership in the company. "Now we're positioned to maintain our fast growth, and soon, with the help of our venture investors, we'll be ready to go public," says Posner.[25]

Pro CD

"I gave up the honest-man bit, and now I'm looking for someone with a little venture capital."

Source: Copyright © 1997 Sidney Harris.

Table 10.3

Deciphering the Language of the Venture Capital Industry

Sources: Adapted from John F. Budd, Jr., "Cracking the CEO's Code," *Wall Street Journal*, March 27, 1995, p. A20; "Venture-Speak Defined," *Teleconnect*, October 1990, p. 42.

By nature, entrepreneurs tend to be optimistic. When screening business plans, venture capitalists must make an allowance for entrepreneurial enthusiasm. Here's a dictionary of phrases commonly found in business plans and their accompanying venture capital translations.

Acquisition strategy—The current products have no market.

Basically on plan—We're expecting a revenue shortfall of 25 percent.

Biotech business model—Potential bigger fools have been identified.

A challenging year—Competitors are eating our lunch.

Considerably ahead of plan—Hit our plan in one of the last three months.

Company's underlying strength and resilience—We still lost money, but look how we cut our losses.

Core business—Our product line is obsolete.

Currently revising budget—The financial plan is in total chaos.

Cyclical industry—We posted a huge loss last year.

Entrepreneurial CEO—He is totally uncontrollable, bordering on maniacal.

Facing unprecedented economic, political, and structural shifts—It's a tough world out there, but we're coping the best we can.

Highly leverageable network—No longer works but has friends who do.

Ingredients are there—Given two years, we might find a workable strategy.

Investing heavily in R&D—We're trying desperately to catch the competition.

Limited downside—Things can't get much worse.

Long sales cycle—Yet to find a customer who likes the product enough to buy it.

Major opportunity—It's our last chance.

Niche strategy—A small-time player.

On a manufacturing learning curve—We can't make the product with positive margins.

Passive investor—She phones once a year to see if we're still in business.

Positive results—Our losses were less than last year.

Repositioning the business—We've recently written off a a multimillion dollar investment.

Selective investment strategy—The board is spending more time on yachts than on planes.

Solid operating performance in a difficult year—Yes, we lost money and market share, but look how hard we tried.

Somewhat below plan—We expect a revenue shortfall of 75 percent.

Strategic investor—One who will pay a preposterous price for an equity share in the business.

Strongest fourth quarter ever—Don't quibble over the losses in the first three quarters.

Sufficient opportunity to market this product no longer exists—Nobody will buy the thing.

Too early to tell—Results to date have been grim.

A team of skilled, motivated, and dedicated people—We've laid off most of our staff, and those who are left should be glad they still have jobs.

Turnaround opportunity—It's a lost cause.

Unique—We have no more than six strong competitors.

Volume-sensitive—Our company has massive fixed costs.

Window of opportunity—Without more money fast, this company is dead.

Work closely with the management—We talk to them on the phone once a month.

A year in which we confronted challenges—At least we know the questions even if we haven't got the answers.

Venture capital firms usually establish stringent policies to implement their overall investment strategies.

Investment Size and Screening. Depending on the size of the venture capital corporation and its cost structure, minimum investments range from $50,000 to $1,000,000. Investment ceilings, in effect, do not exist. Most firms seek investments in the $250,000 to $1,500,000 range to justify the cost of investigating the large number of proposals they receive.

The venture capital screening process is *extremely* rigorous. The typical venture capital company invests in less than 1 percent of the applications it receives! For example, the average venture capital firm screens about 1,200 proposals a year, but over 90 percent are rejected immediately because they do not match the firm's investment criteria. The remaining 10 percent are investigated more thoroughly at a cost ranging from $2,000 to $3,000 per proposal. At this time, approximately 10 to 15 proposals will have passed the screening process, and these are subjected to comprehensive review. The venture capital firm will invest in three to six of these remaining proposals.

Ownership. Most venture capitalists prefer to purchase ownership in a small business through common stock or convertible preferred stock. The share of ownership a venture capital company purchases may be as low as 1 percent for a profitable company to possibly 100 percent for a financially unstable firm. Although there is no limit on the amount of stock it can buy, a typical venture capital company seeks to purchase 30 to 40 percent of the business. Anything more incurs the risk of draining the entrepreneur's dedication and enthusiasm for managing the firm. Still, the entrepreneur must weigh the positive aspects of receiving needed financing against the negative features of owning a smaller share of the business.

Control. Although the entrepreneur must sacrifice a portion of the business to the venture capitalist, he usually can retain a majority interest and control of its operations. Most venture capitalists prefer to let the founding team of managers employ its skills to operate the business. However, many venture capitalists join the boards of directors of the companies they invest in or send in new managers or a new management team to protect their investments. Sometimes venture capitalists serve as financial and managerial advisors, while others take an active role in the managing of the company by recruiting employees, providing sales leads, choosing attorneys and advertising agencies, and making daily decisions. One recent survey found that 90 percent of venture capitalists eventually either become directly involved in managing or selecting outside managers for the companies they invest in. Seventy-five percent of these active venture capitalists say they are forced to step in because the existing management team lacked the talent to achieve growth targets.[26] One cautionary note for *every* entrepreneur seeking venture capital is to find out *before* the deal is done exactly how much control and hands-on management investors plan to assume.

Investment Preferences. The venture capital industry has undergone important changes over the past decade. Venture capital funds are larger, more numerous, and more specialized. As the industry grows, more venture capitalists are focusing their investments in niches—everything from low-calorie custards to electronics. Some will invest in almost any industry but prefer companies in particular stages. Some 170 funds now specialize in start-up companies alone.[27]

Small business owners must realize that it is *very* difficult for any small business, especially fledgling or struggling firms, to pass the intense screening process of a venture capital company and qualify for an investment. Venture capital firms finance less than 1,000 deals each year.[28] Two factors make a deal attractive to venture capitalists: high returns and a convenient (and profitable) exit strategy. When evaluating potential investments, venture capitalists look for the following features:

☆ *Competent Management.* The most important ingredient in the success of any business is the ability of the manager or the management team, and venture capitalists recognize this. One financing expert explains, "Venture capitalists are really buying into the management of your company. If the light isn't on at the top, it's dim all the way down."[29]

☆ *Competitive Edge.* Investors are searching for some factor that will enable a small business to set itself apart from its competitors. This distinctive competence may range from an innovative product or service to a unique marketing or R&D approach. It must be something with the potential to make the business a leader in its field.

☆ *Growth Industry.* Hot industries attract profits and venture capital. Most venture capitalists focus their searches for prospects in rapidly expanding fields because they believe the profit potential is greater in these areas. Venture capital firms are most interested in young companies that have enough growth potential to become $50 million (or more) businesses in five to seven years.

☆ Intangible Factors. Some other important factors considered in the screening process are not easily measured; they are the intuitive, intangible factors the venture capitalist detects by gut feeling. This feeling might be the result of the small firm's solid sense of direction, its strategic planning process, the chemistry of its management team, or a number of other factors.

Public Stock Sale ("Going Public")

4. Describe the process of "going public," as well as its advantages and disadvantages and the various simplified registrations and exemptions from registration available to small businesses.

In some cases, entrepreneurs can "go public" by selling shares of stock in their corporation to outside investors. This is an effective method of raising large amounts of capital, but it can be an expensive and time-consuming process filled with regulatory nightmares. "Taking your company public will be one of the most difficult transitions it will ever make," says one investment banker.[30] Once a company makes an initial public offering (IPO), *nothing* will ever be the same again. Managers must consider the impact of their decisions not only on the company and its employees but also on its shareholders and the value of their stock.

Going public isn't for every business. In fact, most small companies do not meet the criteria for making a successful public stock offering. Only 20,000 companies in the United States, that is, less than 1 percent of the total, are publicly held. Few companies with less than $5 million in annual sales manage to go public successfully. It is almost impossible for a startup company with no track record of success to raise money with a public offering. Instead, the investment bankers who underwrite public stock offerings typically look for established companies with the following characteristics:

☆ consistently high growth rates

☆ strong record of earnings

☆ three to five years of audited financial statements

☆ a solid position in rapidly-growing markets

☆ a sound management team and a strong board of directors

Figure 10.3 shows the number of IPOs from 1981 to 1995, along with the amount of capital raised during that time.

Entrepreneurs who are considering taking their companies public should first consider carefully the advantages and the disadvantages of an IPO. The *advantages* include the following:

Ability to Raise Large Amounts of Capital. The biggest benefit of a public offering is the capital infusion the company receives. After going public, the corporation has the cash to fund R&D projects, expand plant and facilities, repay debt, or boost working capital bal-

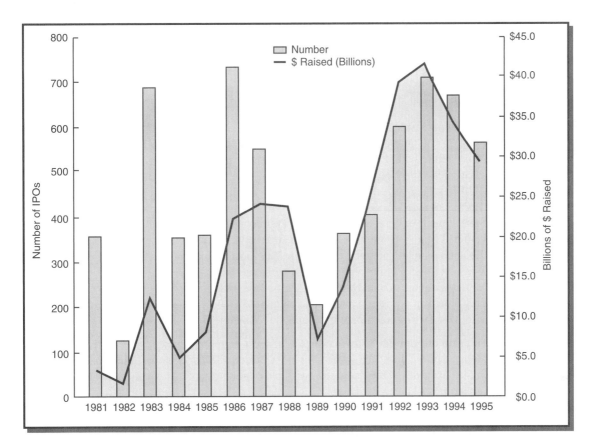

Figure 10.3
Initial Public Offerings
Source: Adapted from Securities Data Company, New York.

ances without incurring the interest expense and the obligation to repay associated with debt financing.

For instance, when Planet Hollywood, the restaurant chain owned by Arnold Schwarzenegger, Bruce Willis, Whoopi Goldberg, and other Hollywood stars, went public, it raised $180 million for the company.[31]

Improved Access for Future Financing. Going public boosts a company's net worth and broadens its equity base. Its improved financial strength makes it easier for the firm to attract more capital—both debt and equity—and to grow.

Improved Corporate Image. All of the media attention a company receives during the registration process makes it more visible. Plus, becoming a public company in some industries improves its prestige and enhances its competitive position, one of the most widely recognized, intangible benefits of going public.

Attracting and Retaining Key Employees. Public companies often use stock-based compensation plans to attract and retain quality employees. Stock options and bonuses are excellent methods for winning employees' loyalty and for instilling a healthy ownership attitude among them. Employee stock ownership plans (ESOPs) and stock purchase plans are popular recruiting and motivational tools in many small corporations, enabling them to hire top-flight talent they otherwise would not be able to afford.

Using Stock for Acquisitions. A company whose stock is publicly traded can acquire other businesses by offering its own shares (rather than cash). Acquiring other companies with shares of stock eliminates the need to incur additional debt.

Listing on a Stock Exchange. Being listed on an organized stock exchange, even a small regional one, improves the marketability of a company's shares and enhances its image. Most publicly held companies' stocks do not qualify for listing on the nation's largest exchanges—the New York Stock Exchange (NYSE) and the American Stock Exchange (AMEX). However, the AMEX recently created a new market for small-company stocks, The Emerging Company Marketplace. Most small companies' stocks are traded on either the National Association of Securities Dealers Automated Quotation (NASDAQ) system's National Market System (NMS) and its emerging small-capitalization exchange or one of the nation's regional stock exchanges. The most popular regional exchanges include the Midwest (MSE), Philadelphia (PHLX), Boston (BSE), and Pacific (PSE).

Despite these advantages, many factors can spoil a company's attempted IPO. In fact, only 5 percent of the companies that attempt to go public ever complete the process.[32] The *disadvantages* of going public include the following:

Dilution of Founder's Ownership. Whenever entrepreneurs sell stock to the public, they automatically dilute their ownership in the business. Most owners retain a majority interest in the business, but they may still run the risk of unfriendly takeovers years later after selling more stock.

Loss of Control. If enough shares are sold in the public offering, the founder risks losing control of the company. If a large block of shares falls into the hands of dissident stockholders, they could vote the existing management team (including the founder) out.

Loss of Privacy. Taking a company public can be a big ego boost for owners, but they must realize that it is no longer solely their company. Information that was once private must be available for public scrutiny. The initial prospectus and the continuous reports filed with the Securities and Exchange Commission (SEC) disclose a variety of information about the company and its operations from financial data and raw material sources to legal matters and patents to *anyone,* including competitors. A recent study found that loss of privacy and loss of control were the most commonly cited reasons why CEOs choose not to attempt IPOs.[33]

Reporting to the SEC. Publicly held companies must file periodic reports with the SEC, which often requires a more powerful accounting system, a larger accounting staff, and greater use of attorneys and other professionals.

Filing Expenses. A public stock offering usually is an expensive way to generate funds for startup or expansion. For the typical small company, the cost of a public offering is around 12 percent of the capital raised. On small offerings, costs can eat up as much as 40 percent of the capital raised, while on offerings above $20 million, just 5 percent will go to cover expenses.[34] Research suggests that once an offering exceeds $10 million, its relative issuing costs drop.[35] The largest cost is the underwriter's commission, which is typically 7 to 10 percent of the offering's proceeds.

Accountability to Shareholders. The capital that the entrepreneur manages and risks is no longer just his own. Managers of a publicly held firm must be accountable to the shareholders. Indeed, the law requires that managers recognize and abide by a relationship built on trust. Profit and return on investment become the primary concerns for investors. If the stock price of a newly public company falls, shareholder lawsuits are inevitable. Investors whose shares decline in value may sue the company's managers for fraud and the failure to disclose the potential risks to which their investment exposes them.

Timing. As impatient as they can be, entrepreneurs often find the time demands of an initial public offering frustrating and distracting. Jeffrey Hollander, CEO of Seventh Generation, a mail-order company selling environmentally friendly products, says, "Doing this public offering was the most intense, complicated process I've ever been involved with. From start to finish, after completion of the business plan, the process took 11 months. During this period it took 50 to 75 percent of my time, including some very long hours."[36]

During this time, the company runs the risk that the market for IPOs or for a particular issue may go sour. Declines in the stock market and potential investors' jitters can quickly slam shut a company's "window of opportunity" for an IPO.

For example, the IPO from A Pea in the Pod, an upscale maternity-wear retailer, suffered from poor timing caused by something completely beyond its control: The stock price of a similar new stock took a nose dive. Investors watching the decline became nervous about buying A Pea in the Pod's new stock issue, dampening the prospects for A Pea in the Pod's premium IPO.[37]

| A Pea in the Pod |

THE REGISTRATION PROCESS. Taking a company public is a complicated, bureaucratic process that usually takes several months to complete. The typical entrepreneur *cannot* take his company public alone. It requires a coordinated effort from a team of professionals, including company executives, an accountant, a securities attorney, a financial printer, and at least one underwriter. The key steps in taking a company public follow.

Choose the Underwriter. Probably the single most important ingredient in making a successful IPO is selecting a capable **underwriter** (or **investment banker**). The underwriter's primary role is to sell the company's stock through an underwriting syndicate of other investment bankers it develops. The underwriter also serves as a consultant and advisor in preparing the registration statement, promoting the issue, pricing the stock, and providing after-market support.

Negotiate a Letter of Intent. To begin an offering, the entrepreneur and the underwriter must negotiate a **letter of intent**, which outlines the details of the deal. The letter of intent covers a variety of important issues, including the type of underwriting, its size and price range, the underwriter's commission, and any warrants and options included. It almost always states that the underwriter is not bound to the offering until it is executed—usually the day before or the day of the offering. However, the letter usually creates a binding obligation for the company to pay any direct expenses the underwriter incurs relating to the offer.

Prepare the Registration Statement. After the company signs the letter of intent, the next task is to prepare the **registration statement** to be filed with the Securities and Exchange Commission (SEC). This document describes both the company and the stock offering and discloses information about the risks of investing. It includes information on the use of the proceeds, the company's history, its financial position, its capital structure, any risks it faces, its managers, and many other details. The statement is extremely comprehensive and may take months to develop. To prepare the statement, the owner must rely on her team of professionals.

File with the SEC. When the statement is finished (with the exception of pricing the shares, proceeds, and commissions, which cannot be determined until just before the issue goes to market), the company officially files the statement with the SEC and awaits the review of the Division of Corporate Finance. The Division sends notice of any deficiencies in the registration statement to the company's attorney in a comment letter. The company and its

underwriter (or investment banker)— *a financial company that sells a company's stock through an underwriting syndicate of other investment bankers and guides the company through the process of going public.*

letter of intent—*an agreement between the underwriter and the company about to go public that outlines the details of the deal.*

registration statement— *a document a company must file with the SEC that describes both the company and its stock offering and discloses information about the risk of investing.*

team of professionals must cure all of the deficiencies in the statement noted by the comment letter. Finally, the company files the revised registration statement, along with a pricing amendment (giving the price of the shares, the proceeds, and the commissions).

Wait to Go Effective. While waiting for the SEC's approval, the managers and the underwriters are busy. The underwriters are building a syndicate of other underwriters who will market the company's stock. (No sales can be made prior to the effective date of the offering, however.) The SEC also limits the publicity and information a company may release during this quiet period (which officially starts when the company reaches a preliminary agreement with the managing underwriter and ends 90 days after the effective date).

Securities laws do permit a **road show**, a gathering of potential syndicate members sponsored by the managing underwriter. Its purpose is to promote interest among potential underwriters in the IPO by featuring the company, its management, and the proposed deal. The managing underwriter and key company officials barnstorm major financial centers at a grueling pace.

On the last day before the registration statement becomes effective, the company signs the formal underwriting agreement. The final settlement, or closing, takes place a few days after the effective date for the issue. At this meeting the underwriters receive their shares to sell and the company receives the proceeds of the offering.

Typically, the entire process of going public takes from 60 to 180 days, but it can take much longer if the issuing company fails to "do its homework."

Meet State Requirements. In addition to satisfying the SEC's requirements, the company also must meet the securities laws in all states in which the issue is sold. These state laws (or "blue-sky" laws) vary drastically from one state to another, and the company must comply with them.

Simplified Registrations and Exemptions

The IPO process just described requires maximum disclosure in the initial filing and discourages most small businesses from using it. Fortunately, the SEC allows several exemptions from this full-disclosure process for small businesses. Many small businesses that go public choose one of these simplified options the SEC has designed for small companies. The SEC has established the following simplified registration statements and exemptions from the registration process:

REGULATION S-B. In August 1992, the SEC approved Regulation S-B, which created a simplified registration process for small companies seeking to make initial or subsequent public offerings. Not only does this regulation simplify the initial filing requirements with the SEC, but it also reduces the ongoing disclosure and filings required of companies. Its primary goals are to open the doors to capital markets to smaller companies by cutting the paperwork and the costs of raising capital. Companies using the simplified registration process have two options: Form SB-1, a "transitional" registration statement for companies issuing less than $10 million worth of securities over a 12-month period, and Form SB-2, which is reserved for small companies seeking more than $10 million in a 12-month period.

To be eligible for the simplified registration process under Regulation S-B, a company:

- ☆ must be based in the United States or Canada
- ☆ must have revenues of less than $25 million
- ☆ must have outstanding securities of less than $25 million
- ☆ must not be an investment company

The goal of Regulation S-B's simplified registration requirements is to enable smaller companies to go public without incurring the expense of a full-blown registration.

road show—a gathering of potential syndicate members by the managing underwriter for the purpose of promoting a company's initial public offering.

Pierre de Champfleury used Form SB-2 to sell 1.75 million shares of stock in his fragrance firm Erox Corporation at $4 per share. de Champfleury had launched Erox through private investors and venture capitalists, but he had used that money for product development. Now he needed to finance the launch of the company's newest fragrance, Realm. Before Regulation S-B, de Champfleury would have had to spend tens of thousands of dollars and many months wading through reams of paperwork to go public. Under the new rules, however, Erox spent just $2,275 and filed only 126 pages of documents with the SEC. de Champfleury says that the registration process was quite easy, and, best of all, Erox got the money it needed for a successful product launch. Its stock is now traded on the NASDAQ small capital exchange.[38]

Erox Corporation

SMALL COMPANY OFFERING REGISTRATION (SCOR). Created in the late 1980s, the Small Company Offering Registration (also known as the Uniform Limited Offering Registration, ULOR) now is available in 46 states. A little known tool, SCOR is designed to make it easier and less expensive for small companies to sell their stock to the public. The whole process typically costs less than half of what a traditional public offering costs. Entrepreneurs using SCOR will need an attorney and an accountant to help them with the issue, but many can get by without a securities lawyer, which can save tens of thousands of dollars. Some entrepreneurs even choose to market their companies' securities themselves (for example, to customers), saving the expense of hiring a broker. However, selling an issue is both time and energy consuming, and most SCOR experts recommend hiring a professional securities or brokerage firm to sell the company's shares. The SEC's objective in creating SCOR was to give small companies the same access to equity financing that large companies have via the stock market while bypassing many of the same costs and filing requirements.

The capital ceiling on a SCOR issue is $1 million, and the price of each share must be at least $5. That means that a company can sell no more than 200,000 shares (making the stock less attractive to stock manipulators). A SCOR offering requires only minimal notification to the SEC. The company must file a standardized disclosure statement, the U-7, which consists of 50 fill-in-the-blank questions. The form, which asks for information such as how much money the company needs, what the money will be used for, what investors receive, how investors can sell their investments, and other pertinent questions, also serves as a business plan, a state securities offering registration, a disclosure document, and a prospectus. Entrepreneurs using SCOR may advertise their companies' offerings and can sell them directly to any investor with no restrictions and no minimums. An entrepreneur can sell practically any kind of security through a SCOR, including common stock, preferred stock, convertible preferred stock, stock options, stock warrants, and others.

For example, Michael Kaufman and Willie Jones raised $193,000 from their own pockets and those of friends and family members to launch WillieMichael's Southern Cafe in New York City's Harlem district. Business boomed, and the entrepreneurs are using a SCOR offering to raise $1 million to expand their concept into a national soul-food franchise.[39]

WillieMichael's Southern Cafe

A SCOR offering offers entrepreneurs needing equity financing several *advantages*:

☆ Access to a huge pool of equity funds without the expense of full registration with the SEC.

☆ Few restrictions on the securities to be sold and on the investors to whom they can be sold.

☆ The ability to market the offering through advertisements.

☆ New or startup companies can qualify.

☆ No requirement of audited financial statements for offerings less than $500,000.

☆ Faster approval of the issue from regulatory agencies.

☆ The ability to make the offering in several states at once.

There are, of course, some *disadvantages* to using SCOR to raise needed funds:

☆ Not every state yet recognizes SCOR offerings.

☆ Partnerships cannot make SCOR offerings.

☆ A company can raise no more than $1 million in a 12-month period.

☆ Every state in which the offering is to be made must approve it.

☆ The process can be time consuming, distracting the entrepreneur from the daily routine of running the company.

☆ A limited secondary market for the securities may limit investors' interest. Currently, SCOR shares must be traded through brokerage firms that make small markets in specific stocks. However, the Pacific Stock Exchange and the NASDAQ's electronic bulletin board recently began listing SCOR stocks, which broadens the secondary market for them.

Every securities offering must be registered unless the law allows a specific exemption from registration. Small businesses can choose from four exemptions from the tedious and expensive registration process: Regulation A; Regulation D (Rules 504, 505, and 506); private placements (Section 4(6)); and intrastate offerings (Rule 147).

REGULATION A. Regulation A, although currently not used often, allows an exemption for offerings up to $5 million over a 12-month period. Regulation A imposes few restrictions, but it is more costly than the other types of exempted offerings, usually running between $80,000 and $120,000. The primary difference between a SCOR offering and a Regulation A offering is that a company must register its SCOR offering only in the states where it will sell its stock; in a Regulation A offering, the company also must file those documents with the SEC. Like a SCOR offering, a Regulation A offering allows a company to sell its shares directly to investors

For instance, Blue Fish Clothing Inc., a natural clothing company, made a direct public offering under Regulation A, selling 800,000 shares at $5 each. It publicized the $4 million offering through fish-shaped hanging tags on its garments and word of mouth from loyal customers and supporters. Blue Fish, whose shares are traded on the Chicago Stock Exchange, used the offering's proceeds to build new retail stores, to install a computerized information system, and to fund the company's growth.[40]

Blue Fish Cothing Inc.

REGULATION D. The SEC adopted Regulation D in 1982 to give small businesses another avenue to equity capital markets. This exemption gives emerging companies the opportunity to sell stock (usually convertible preferred stock) themselves through private placements without actually going public. In a private placement, the company sells its shares directly to private investors without having to register them with the SEC. Private deals typically are in the $8 million to $25 million range, with investors usually buying between 10 percent and 30 percent of a company's stock.

When John Cook's company, The Profit Recovery Group, a financial services firm, needed outside capital to fuel its rapid growth, Cook raised the money through a private placement. Cook, who sees the private placement as "bridge financing" until the company makes a public stock offering, says," I raised $12.5 million and had to give up only 15 percent of my company and one board seat to do it."[41]

The Profit Recovery Group

For small businesses, Regulation D has become the most common method of raising capital from private investors. *Rule 504* has the least restrictive provisions (no information requirements and no restrictions on the number or the type of investors), but it is limited to $1 million in any 12-month period. It is best suited for small corporations needing a relatively small amount of capital. Rule 504 offerings are relatively simple to prepare and are the most commonly used of the three private placement options. Rule 504 allows a company to advertise its private placement and to solicit potential investors.

A *Rule 505* offering has a higher capital ceiling of $5 million, but imposes more restrictions (no more than 35 "nonaccredited" investors, limits on advertising, and others). Its disclosure requirements also are more stringent, requiring a company to publish information on the company, its operating history, its financial performance, its managers and directors, and the nature of the offering itself.

Rule 506 imposes no ceiling on the amount that can be raised, but it does limit the issue to 35 "nonaccredited" investors. There is no limit on the number of accredited investors, however. Rule 506 also requires detailed disclosure of relative information, but the extent depends on the dollar size of the offering.

These Regulation D rules minimize the expense and the time required to raise equity capital for small businesses. They do impose limitations and demand some disclosure, but they only require a company to file a simple form (Form D) with the SEC within 15 days of the first sale of stock.

SECTION 4(6). Section 4(6) covers private placements and is similar to Regulation D, Rule 505. It does not require registration on offers up to $5 million if they are made only to accredited investors.

RULE 147. Rule 147 governs intrastate offerings, which are those sold only to investors in a single state by a company doing business in that state. To qualify, a company must be incorporated in the state, maintain its executive offices there, have 80 percent of its assets there, derive 80 percent of its revenues from the state, and use 80 percent of the offering proceeds for business in the state. There is no ceiling on the amount of the offering.

Gary Hoover put up just $5,000 of his own money and convinced several private investors to purchase $850,000 worth of preferred stock to launch TravelFest, a retail store that caters to travelers. As the company grew, Hoover decided to make an intrastate offering under Rule 147 to raise the money he needed for expansion. He registered the offering in TravelFest's home state of Texas, where resident investors purchased $5.6 million in convertible preferred stock.[42]

TravelFest

DIRECT STOCK OFFERINGS ON THE WORLD WIDE WEB (WWW). The World Wide Web (WWW) is one the fastest-growing sources of capital for small businesses. Much of the Web's appeal as a fund-raising tool stems from its ability to reach large numbers of prospective investors very quickly and at a low cost. "This is the only form of instantaneous international contact with an enormous population," says one Web expert. "You can put your prospectus out to the world."[43]

Spring Street Brewery, a New York City-based microbrewer, was one of the first companies to use the Web to make a Regulation A public stock offering, which raised $1.6 million. Company founder Andrew Klein spent just $200 to develop Spring Street's home page and another $150 per month to maintain it—a fraction of what it would have cost to do a traditional IPO! "Dollar for dollar, it was the most effective method for getting information to potential investors," says Klein.[44]

Spring Street Brewery

Even though Klein made the offering electronically, he had to file the necessary legal documents with the SEC and the state of New York. Experts caution Web-based fund seekers to make sure their electronic prospectuses meet SEC and state requirements.

Table 10.4 on page 322 provides a summary of the major types of exemptions and simplified offerings. Of these, the limited offerings and private placements are most commonly used.

Foreign Stock Markets

Sometimes foreign stock markets offer entrepreneurs access to equity funds more readily than U.S. markets. The United Kingdom's Unlisted Securities Market and the Vancouver Stock Exchange are especially attractive to small companies. Both encourage equity listings of small companies, and the costs of offerings are usually lower than in the United States.

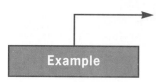

Example

Kim Jones raised $2.5 million for his software development company with an initial public offering made through the Vancouver Stock Exchange. Jones, who had explored the possibility of a U.S. IPO, found that he could get a better price for his company's stock on the Vancouver market.[45]

Table 10.4
Simplified Registration and Exemptions: Comparative Table
Source: Deciding to Go Public, New York: Ernst & Young, 1993, pp. 70–71.

Private and Limited Offerings Regulation D		
Rule 504	**Rule 505**	**Rule 506**

	Rule 504	Rule 505	Rule 506
Dollar Limit	$1 million in any 12-month period	$5 million in any 12-month period	None
Limit on Number of Purchasers	No	35 nonaccredited, unlimited accredited	35 nonaccredited, unlimited accredited
Qualification for Purchasers	No	No	Nonaccredited must be sophisticated
Qualifications of Issuers	Not available for investment companies, blank check companies, or reporting companies	Not available for investment companies or those disqualified by "bad boy" provisions	No
Disclosure Requirements	Not specified	Only if one or more nonaccredited purchasers	Only if one or more nonaccredited purchasers
Financial Statement Requirements	Not specified	Period varies for audited statements	Period varies for audited statements
General Solicitation and Advertising Prohibited	No	Yes	Yes
Resale Restrictions	No	Yes	Yes

Private Placements Section 4(6)	**Intrastate Offerings Rule 147**	**Unregistered Public Offerings Regulation A**	**Small Business Issuers Registration Form SB-1**	**Small Business Issuers Registration Form SB-2**
$5 million	None	$5 million in any 12-month period	$10 million in any 12-month period	None
No	No	No	No	No
All must be accredited	All must be registrants of a single state	No	No	No
No	Must be resident and do business in same state as purchasers	Available for U.S. and Canadian companies only; not available for reporting companies, blank check companies, investment companies, sale of oil and gas or mineral rights, or those disqualified by "bad boy" provisions	Available for U.S. and Canadian companies with revenue and public float of less than $25 million; not available for investment companies or subsidiaries whose parent is not qualified to use the form	Available for U.S. and Canadian companies with revenue and public float of less than $25 million; not available for investment companies or subsidiaries whose parent is not qualified to use the form
Not specified	Not specified	Yes	Yes	Yes
Not specified	Not specified	2 years of unaudited statements	2 years of audited statements	2 years of audited statements
Yes	No	No	No	No
Yes	Yes	Yes	No	No

Going. . . Going. . . Gone. . . Public?

Too Small? Joe Falsetti, founder of ROM Tech, a publisher of multimedia CD-ROM software, knows his company is riding the crest of a wave that is pushing the popularity of CD-ROMs to record levels. From his experience in strategic planning at a large technology company, Falsetti also knows that successfully cracking a market driven by new technology requires large amounts of capital. In his conversations about financing with venture capitalists and private investors, Falsetti has noticed a common theme: They all wanted to know about an exit strategy—"How do we cash out and win?" The answer they were looking for was for ROM Tech to go public so they could sell their equity positions in the company at a handsome profit.

Falsetti set up a meeting with a New York City investment banker to explore the possibility of a public offering. ROM Tech is profitable on annual sales of $1.2 million, but the investment banker was afraid that ROM Tech is too small to make a successful IPO. To raise $5 million, the minimum deal size for most underwriters, the broker estimated that Falsetti would have to sell nearly 100 percent of the company rather than the usual 25 to 33 percent. At $1.2 million in sales, "the company didn't have enough meat on its bones to get them excited," says Falsetti.

Growth Spiral. Kwik Goal, a sports-equipment manufacturer, is constantly experiencing cash shortages because of its tremendous appetite for capital that resulted from the growing popularity of soccer in the United States. "We are in a growth spiral," says company founder Vincent Caruso. "Our debt is getting bigger each year by the difference between what we are making (total revenue) and what we need to keep growing." Like many fast-growing companies, Kwik Goal's cash demands are simply outstripping its ability to generate cash. With the company approaching the $4 million sales mark, Caruso figures he needs $6 million in capital to take Kwik Goal to the next level of growth. Caruso has met with several investment bankers, but because he lacks a strong background in financial management, he does not feel comfortable selling the benefits of his company to strangers who happen to be financial experts.

Go or No Go? Best Programs Inc., a company that develops accounting and human resources software, is flush with cash but is in an industry full of competitors. To establish a stronger position in the industry, managers at Best Programs see the need to buy out some existing companies whose product lines complement their own. To make those acquisitions, however, requires big money. Best Programs is considering filing for a $23 million IPO. The company has more than $20 million in annual revenues, attractive pre-tax profit margins of 14 percent, and an annual growth rate of 30 percent. Because of its impressive record of success, Best was able to interest two regional underwriters in making its public offering. In their letter of intent, the underwriters recommend selling 2.1 million shares at $9 to $11 per share.

1. What advice would you offer these entrepreneurs who are considering taking their companies public? (Consider the advantages and the disadvantages of going public.)

2. Would you advise any of these companies *not* to make a public offering? Explain. What other financing options would you suggest they explore?

3. Which of these companies do you believe has the greatest chance at making a successful public offering? Why?

Source: Adapted from David R. Evanson, "Tales of Caution in Going Public," *Nation's Business*, June 1996, pp. 57-59.

The Nature of Debt Financing

5. Describe the various sources of debt capital and the advantages and disadvantages of each.

Debt financing involves the funds that the small business owner borrows and must repay with interest. Lenders of capital are more numerous than investors, although small business loans can be just as difficult (if not more difficult) to obtain. Although borrowed capital allows entrepreneurs to maintain complete ownership of their businesses, it must be carried as a liability on the balance sheet as well as be repaid with interest at some point in the future. In addition, because small businesses are considered to be greater risks than bigger corporate customers, they must pay higher interest rates because of the risk-return trade-off—the higher the risk, the greater the return demanded. Most small firms pay the prime rate, the interest rate banks charge their most creditworthy customers, plus a few percentage points. Still, the cost of debt financing often is lower than that of equity financing.

Because of the higher risks associated with providing equity capital to small companies, investors demand greater returns than lenders. Also, unlike equity financing, debt financing does not require an entrepreneur to dilute her ownership interest in the company.

Entrepreneurs seeking debt capital are quickly confronted with an astounding range of credit options varying greatly in complexity, availability, and flexibility. Not all of these sources of debt capital are equally favorable, however. By understanding the various sources of capital—commercial and government lenders—and their characteristics, entrepreneurs can greatly increase the chances of obtaining a loan.

We now turn to the various sources of debt capital.

Sources of Debt Capital

Commercial Banks

Commercial banks are the very heart of the financial market, providing the greatest number and variety of loans to small businesses. A recent study by the Federal Reserve concluded that commercial banks provide almost half the financing available to small businesses![46] Business owners consider banks to be lenders of *first* resort. The same study found that 80 percent of all loans to existing small businesses come from banks, and bank loans are second only to entrepreneurs' personal capital as a source of capital for launching businesses.[47]

Banks tend to be conservative in their lending practices and prefer to make loans to established small businesses rather than to high-risk startups. Bankers want to see evidence of a company's successful track record before committing to a loan. They are concerned with a firm's operating past and will scrutinize its records to project its position in the immediate future. They also want proof of the stability of the firm's sales and about the ability of the product or service to generate adequate cash flows to ensure repayment of the loan. If they do make loans to a startup venture, banks like to see sufficient cash flows to repay the loan, ample collateral to secure it, or an SBA guarantee to insure it. Studies suggest that the small banks (those with less than $300 million in assets) are most likely to lend money to small businesses.[48]

Banks also focus on a company's capacity to create positive cash flow because they know that's where the money to repay their loans will come from. The first question in most bankers' minds when reviewing an entrepreneur's business plan is "Can this business generate sufficient cash to repay the loan?" Even though they rely on collateral to secure their loans, the last thing banks want is for a borrower to default, forcing them to sell the collateral (often at "fire sale" prices) and use the proceeds to pay off the loan. *That's* why bankers stress cash flow when analyzing a loan request, especially for a business startup. "Cash is more important than your mother," jokes one experienced borrower.[49]

Short-Term Loans

Short-term loans, extended for less than one year, are the most common type of commercial loan granted to small firms. These funds typically are used to replenish the working capital account to finance the purchase of more inventory, boost output, finance credit sales to customers, or take advantage of cash discounts. As a result, the owner repays the loan after converting inventory and receivables into cash. There are several types of short-term loans.

COMMERCIAL LOANS (OR TRADITIONAL BANK LOANS). The basic short-term loan is the commercial bank's specialty. It is usually repaid as a lump sum within three to six months and is unsecured because secured loans are much more expensive to administer and maintain. In other words, the bank grants a loan to the small business owner without requiring him to pledge any specific collateral to support the loan in case of default. The owner is expected to repay the total amount of the loan at maturity. Sometimes the interest due on the loan is prepaid, that is deducted from the total amount borrowed. Until a small business is able to prove its financial strength to the bank's satisfaction, it will probably not qualify for this kind of commercial loan.

LINES OF CREDIT. One of the most common requests entrepreneurs make of banks is to establish a **line of credit**, a short-term loan with a preset limit which provides much-needed cash flow for day-to-day operations. With an approved line of credit, business owners can borrow up to the predetermined ceiling at any time during the year quickly and conveniently by writing themselves a loan.

> **line of credit**—*a short-term bank loan with a preset limit which provides working capital for day-to-day operations.*

Todd Heim, owner of Future Cure Inc., a manufacturer of paint-spray booths for auto body shops, relies on a line of credit to meet his company's seasonal cash needs, covering payroll and other expenses and financing inventory and accounts receivable. "There's a big neon sign in every business owner's office that says 'Game Over' when the checking account gets to zero," he says. "You need a line of credit for those cash flow shortfalls."[50]

Future Cure Inc.

Banks usually limit the open line of credit to 40 to 50 percent of the firm's present working capital, although they will lend more for highly seasonal businesses. It is usually extended for one year (or more) and is secured by collateral, although some banks offer unsecured lines of credit to small companies with solid financial track records. A business typically pays a small handling fee (1 to 2 percent of the maximum amount of credit) plus interest on the amount borrowed, usually prime plus three points or more. A recent study of small businesses with lines of credit found that 76 percent used them; the remaining 24 percent have established their lines as a safety net but have not activated them.[51]

Two types of lines of credit are available: seasonal and sustained growth. *Seasonal lines of credit* are more common and are used to finance a company's seasonal cash needs, such as financing inventory or accounts receivable. Banks allow borrowers to draw on seasonal lines as needed; however, once a year, they require business owners to pay them down to zero for a short time (usually 30 to 60 days). This annual cleanup is scheduled when a firm's cash balance is at its highest level, usually at the end of the busy season when inventories and receivables have been converted into cash. This standard repayment protects the bank against default by forcing the firm to prove its credit-worthiness before continuing the line of credit for another year. "Think of your credit line as a yo-yo," advises one bank president. "Your borrowing will go up and down—bankers expect that—but your borrowing should match your business cycles." That means paying off ("resting") the company's line of credit when its cash flow peaks. "If you can rest your credit line for 30 consecutive days, you banker won't worry about your misusing the line to hide losses," she says.[52]

Sustained-growth lines of credit are designed to finance rapidly growing companies' cash flow needs over a longer time period. Because they cover a longer time horizon and are designed to finance growth, sustained growth lines usually do not call for a 30-day annual cleanup.

Table 10.5 on page 326 describes the five most common reasons bankers reject small business loan applications and how to avoid them.

FLOOR PLANNING. Floor planning is a form of financing frequently employed by retailers of big-ticket items that are easily distinguishable from one another (usually by serial number), such as automobiles, boats, and major appliances. For example, a commercial bank finances Auto City's purchase of its inventory of automobiles and maintains a security interest in each car in the order by holding its title as collateral. Auto City pays interest on the loan monthly and repays the principal as the cars are sold. The longer a floor-planned item sits in inventory, the more it costs the business owner in interest expense. Banks and other

Table 10.5

The Five Most Common Reasons Bankers Reject Small Business Loan Applications (and How You Can Avoid Them)

Source: Adapted from J. Tol Broome, Jr., "How to get a 'Yes' From Your Banker," *Nation's Business*, April 1996, p. 37.

Reason 1. "I don't know enough about you or your business." Cure: Develop a detailed business plan that explains what your company does (or will do) and describes how you will gain a competitive edge over your rivals. Also, be prepared to supply business credit references and a personal credit history.

Reason 2. "You haven't told me why you need the money." Cure: A solid business plan will explain how much money you need and how you plan to use it. Make sure your request is specific; avoid requests for loans "for working capital." Don't make the mistake of answering the question, "How much money do you need?" with "How much will you lend me?"

Reason 3. "Your numbers don't support your loan request." Cure: Include a cash flow forecast in your business plan. Bankers analyze a company's balance sheet and income statement to judge the quality of its assets and its profitability, but bankers lend primarily on the basis of cash flow. They know that's how you'll repay the loan. If adequate cash flow isn't available, don't expect a loan. Prove to the banker that you know what your company's cash flow is and how to manage it.

Reason 4. "You don't have enough collateral." Cure: Be prepared to pledge your company's assets—and perhaps your personal assets—as collateral for the loan. Bankers like to have the security of collateral before they make a loan. They also expect more than $1 in collateral for every $1 of money they lend. Banks typically lend 80 to 90 percent of the value of real estate, 70 to 80 percent of the value of accounts receivable, and just 10 to 50 percent of the value of inventory pledged as collateral.

Reason 5. "Your business does not support the loan on its own." Cure: Be prepared to provide a personal guarantee on the loan. By doing so, you're telling the banker that if your business cannot repay the loan, you will. Many bankers see their small business clients and their companies as one and the same. Even if you choose a form of ownership that provides you with limited personal liability, most bankers will ask you to override that protection by personally guaranteeing the loan.

There's no magic to getting a bank to approve your loan request. The secret is proper preparation and building a solid business plan that enhances your credibility as a business owner with your banker. Use your plan to prove that you have what it takes to survive and thrive.

floor planners often discourage retailers from using their money without authorization by performing spot checks to verify prompt repayment of the principal as items are sold.

Intermediate and Long-Term Loans

Banks primarily are lenders of short-term capital to small businesses, although they will make certain intermediate and long-term loans. Intermediate and long-term loans are extended for one year or longer and are normally used to increase fixed- and growth-capital balances. Commercial banks grant these loans for starting a business, constructing a plant, purchasing real estate and equipment, and other long-term investments. Loan repayments are normally made monthly or quarterly. One of the most common types of intermediate-term loans are installment loans, which banks make to small firms for purchasing equipment, facilities, real estate, and other fixed assets. In financing equipment, a bank usually lends the small business from 60 to 80 percent of the equipment's value in return for a security interest in the equipment. The loan's amortization schedule typically coincides with the length of the equipment's usable life. In financing real estate (commercial mortgages), banks typically will lend up to 75 to 80 percent of the property's value and will allow a lengthier repayment schedule of 10 to 30 years.

Nonbank Sources of Debt Capital

Although they are usually the first stop for entrepreneurs in search of debt capital, banks are not the only lending game in town. We now turn our attention to other sources of debt capital that entrepreneurs can tap to feed their cash-hungry companies.

Asset-Based Lenders

Asset-based lenders, which are usually smaller commercial banks, commercial finance companies, or specialty lenders, allow small businesses to borrow money by pledging otherwise idle assets such as accounts receivable, inventory, or purchase orders as collateral. Even unprofitable companies whose financial statements could not convince loan officers to make traditional loans can get asset-based loans. These cash-poor but asset-rich companies can use normally unproductive assets such as accounts receivable, inventory, fixtures, and purchase orders to finance rapid growth and the cash crises that often accompany it.

For example, JSG (NY) Inc., a small, rapidly growing apparel maker, desperately needed money to pay for manufacturing several large orders the company had received. Using the purchase orders from the customers as collateral, JSG applied for a $500,000 loan from New York's MTB Bank, which specializes in such loans. JSG, which could not meet conventional lender's standards, got the money it needed to fill its customers' orders by using those same orders as security for the loan.[53]

JSG (NY) Inc.

The amount a small business can borrow through asset-based lending depends on the **advance rate**, the percentage of an asset's value that a lender will lend. For example, a company pledging $100,000 of accounts receivable might negotiate a 70 percent advance rate and qualify for a $70,000 asset-based loan. Advance rates can vary dramatically depending upon the quality of the assets pledged and the lender. Because inventory is an illiquid asset (i.e., hard to sell), the advance rate on inventory-based loans is quite low, usually 10 percent to 50 percent. A business pledging high-quality accounts receivable as collateral, however, may be able to negotiate up to an 85 percent advance rate. The most common types of asset-based financing are discounting accounts receivable and inventory financing.

advance rate—*the percentage of an asset's value that a lender will lend.*

DISCOUNTING ACCOUNTS RECEIVABLE. The most common form of secured credit is accounts receivable financing. Under this arrangement, the small business pledges its accounts receivable as collateral; in return, the commercial bank advances the owner a loan against the value of approved accounts receivable. The amount of the loan tendered is not equal to the face value of the accounts receivable, however. Even though the bank screens the firm's accounts and accepts only qualified receivables, it makes an allowance for the risk involved because some will be written off as uncollectible. A small business usually can borrow an amount equal to 55 to 80 percent of its receivables, depending on their quality. Generally, banks hesitate to finance receivables that are past due, and no bank will accept accounts that are as much as 90 days past due. Many commercial finance companies also engage in accounts receivable financing.

INVENTORY FINANCING. Here the small business loan is secured by the firm's inventory of raw materials, work in process, and finished goods. If the owner defaults on the loan, the bank can claim the firm's inventory, sell it, and use the proceeds to satisfy the loan (assuming the bank's claim is superior to the claims of other creditors). Because inventory usually is not a highly liquid asset and its value can be difficult to determine, banks are willing to lend only a portion of its worth, usually no more than 50 percent of the inventory's value. Most asset-based lenders avoid inventory-only deals; they prefer to make loans backed by inventory *and* more secure accounts receivable.

Asset-based financing is a powerful tool. A small business that could obtain a $1 million line of credit with a bank would be able to borrow as much as $3 million by using accounts receivable as collateral.[54] It is also an efficient method of borrowing because small business owners have the money they need when they need it. In other words, the business pays only for the capital it actually needs and uses.

Asset-based loans are more expensive than traditional bank loans because of the cost of originating and maintaining them and the higher risk involved. Rates usually run from two to seven percentage points above the prime rate. Because of this rate differential, small business owners should not use asset-based loans over the long term; their goal should be to establish their credit through asset-based financing and then to move up to a line of credit.

Trade Credit

Because of its ready availability, trade credit is an extremely important source of financing to most entrepreneurs. When banks refuse to lend money to a startup business because they see it as a bad credit risk, the owner usually is able to turn to trade credit as a viable source of capital. Getting vendors to extend credit in the form of delayed payments (e.g., "net 30" credit terms) usually is much easier for small businesses than obtaining bank financing.

It is no surprise that businesses receive three dollars of credit from suppliers for every two dollars they receive from banks as loans.[55] Vendors and suppliers usually are willing to finance a small business owner's purchase of goods from 30 to 90 or more days, interest free.

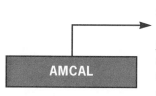

For instance, Gus Walboldt, owner of AMCAL, a fine-art publishing company, uses supplier financing as an integral part of his company's 20-year growth plan. Because calendars represent a large portion of AMCAL's sales, its business is highly seasonal, which creates significant cash flow problems. "We would spend half the year flush with cash [and the other half] cash poor," says Walboldt. Walboldt worked out a financing arrangement with the companies that print the calendars. AMCAL pays the printers' labor and material costs when the calendars are printed during the summer months and then covers their profit margins when its cash flow swells in the fall. "We have since approached all our major production vendors to work out similar terms," Walboldt says.[56]

Equipment Suppliers

Most equipment vendors encourage business owners to purchase their equipment by offering to finance the purchase. This method of financing is similar to trade credit but with slightly different terms. Usually, equipment vendors offer reasonable credit terms with only a modest down payment with the balance financed over the life of the equipment (usually several years). In some cases, the vendor will repurchase equipment for salvage value at the end of its useful life and offer the business owner another credit agreement on new equipment. Startup companies often use trade credit from equipment suppliers to purchase equipment and fixtures such as counters, display cases, refrigeration units, machinery, and the like. It pays to scrutinize vendors' credit terms, however; they may be less attractive than those of other lenders.

Commercial Finance Companies

When denied a bank loan, a small business owner often looks to a commercial finance company for the same type of loan. Unlike their conservative counterparts, commercial finance companies are usually willing to tolerate more risk in their loan portfolios. Of course, their primary consideration is collecting their loans, but they tend to rely more on obtaining a security interest in some type of collateral, given the higher-risk loans that make up their portfolios. Because commercial finance companies depend on collateral to recover most of their losses, they do not require the complete financial projections of future operations that most banks do. However, this does *not* mean that they do not carefully evaluate a company's financial position before making a loan.

Their most common methods of providing credit to small businesses are accounts receivable financing and inventory loans, and they operate exactly as commercial banks do. In fact, commercial finance companies usually offer many of the same credit options as commercial banks do. However, because their loans are subject to more risks, finance companies charge a higher interest rate than commercial banks. In addition to short-term financing for small businesses, commercial finance companies also extend intermediate and long-term loans for real estate and fixed assets.

Savings and Loan Associations

Savings and loan (S&L) associations specialize in loans for real property. In addition to their traditional role of providing mortgages for personal residences, savings and loan associations offer financing on commercial and industrial property. In the typical commercial or industrial loan, the S&L will lend up to 80 percent of the property's value with a repayment schedule of up to 30 years.

Minimum loan amounts are typically $50,000, but most S&Ls hesitate to lend money for buildings specially designed for a particular customer's needs. S&Ls expect the mortgage to be repaid from the firm's future profits.

Stock Brokerage Houses

Stockbrokers are getting into the lending business, too, and many of them offer loans to their customers at lower interest rates than banks. These **margin loans** carry lower rates because the collateral supporting them—the stocks and bonds in the customer's portfolio—is of high quality and is highly liquid. "There isn't a bank in the country that can lend more cheaply than you can borrow on margin," claims one stockbroker.[57] Moreover, brokerage firms make it easy to borrow. Usually, brokers set up a line of credit for their customers when they open a brokerage account. To tap that line of credit, the customer simply writes a check or uses a debit card. Typically, there is no fixed repayment schedule for a margin loan; the debt can remain outstanding indefinitely, as long as the market value of the borrower's portfolio of collateral meets minimum requirements.

Aspiring entrepreneurs can borrow up to 85 percent of the value of their portfolios. For example, one woman borrowed $60,000 to buy equipment for her New York health club, and a St. Louis doctor borrowed $1 million against his brokerage account to help finance a medical clinic.[58] Brokers typically lend a maximum of 50 percent of the value of stocks and bonds in a portfolio, 70 percent for corporate bonds, and 85 to 90 percent for government securities.[59]

There is risk involved in using stocks and bonds as collateral on a loan. Brokers typically require a 30 percent cushion on margin loans. If the value of the borrower's portfolio drops, the broker can make a **margin call**; that is, the broker can call the loan in and require the borrower to provide more cash and securities as collateral. Such a margin call could require an entrepreneur to repay a significant portion of the loan within a matter of days—or hours. If the account lacks adequate collateral, the broker can sell off the customer's portfolio to pay off the loan.

Insurance Companies

For many small businesses, life insurance companies can be an important source of business capital. Insurance companies offer two basic types of loans: policy loans and mortgage loans.

Policy loans are extended on the basis of the amount of money paid through premiums into the insurance policy. It usually takes about two years for an insurance policy to accumulate enough cash surrender value to justify a loan against it. Once cash value is accumulated in a policy, an entrepreneur may borrow up to 95 percent of that value for any length of time. Interest is levied annually, but repayment may be deferred indefinitely. However, the amount of insurance coverage is reduced by the amount of the loan. Policy loans typically offer very favorable interest rates—often around 8 percent or less. Only insurance policies that build a cash value, that is, combine a savings plan with insurance

margin loans—*loans from stockbrokers that use the stocks and bonds in the borrower's portfolio as collateral.*

margin call—*occurs when the value of a borrower's portfolio drops and the broker calls the loan in and requires the borrower to put up more cash and securities as collateral.*

policy loan— *a loan insurance companies make on the basis of the amount of money a customer has paid into a policy in the form of premiums.*

coverage offer the option of borrowing. These include whole life (permanent insurance), variable life, universal life, and many corporate-owned life insurance policies. Term life insurance, which offers only pure insurance coverage, has no borrowing capacity.

Insurance companies make **mortgage loans** on a long-term basis on real property worth a minimum of $500,000. They are based primarily on the value of the real property being purchased. The insurance company will extend a loan of up to 75 or 80 percent of the real estate's value, and will allow a lengthy repayment schedule over 25 or 30 years so that payments do not strain the firm's cash flows excessively.

Insurance companies also make intermediate-term loans in addition to the long-term loans in which they specialize.

For example, when the C. E. Niehoff Company, a manufacturer of heavy-duty alternators, needed to refinance a five-year loan on one of its plants, the bank agreed, but only for $750,000, $200,000 less than the original amount. Ralph Hermann, vice president of finance, began the frustrating search for other lenders. He eventually found the corporate lending division of Metropolitan Life Insurance Company, where he negotiated a new loan for $1.2 million (which allowed Niehoff to pay down its variable-rate line of credit at the bank) at a fixed rate of 10.25 percent. Total fees came to just 2 percent of the loan. "We were very pleased," says Hermann.[60]

mortgage loan—*a loan insurance companies make on a long-term basis for real property worth at least $500,000.*

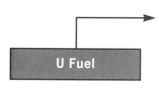

C.E. Niehoff Company

Credit Unions

Credit unions, nonprofit financial cooperatives that promote savings and provide credit to their members, are best known for making consumer and car loans. However, many are now willing to lend money to their members to launch businesses, especially since many banks have restricted loans to higher-risk startups. Of the 12,000 state and federally chartered credit unions operating in the United States, more than 1,000 are actively making member business loans, those of more than $25,000 granted without personal collateral for the purpose of starting a business. Most credit union officials believe that business lending makes up a significant part of their loan portfolios, but the majority of loans are personal loans to entrepreneurs who use the proceeds to launch companies.

Credit unions don't make loans to just anyone; to qualify for a loan, an entrepreneur must be a member. Lending practices at credit unions are very much like those at banks, but they usually are willing to make smaller loans.

For instance, when Michael Webb, president of U Fuel, needed $50,000 for his young automated-fueling-systems business, he turned to a local credit union of which he was a member. The credit union approved his application and established a $50,000 line of credit for U Fuel, allowing the company to grow.[61]

credit union—*a nonprofit financial cooperative that promotes savings and provides credit to its members.*

U Fuel

Bonds

Bonds, which are corporate IOUs, have always been a popular source of debt financing for large companies. Few small business owners realize that they can also tap this valuable source of capital. Although the smallest businesses are not viable candidates for issuing bonds, a growing number of small companies are finding the funding they need through bonds when banks and other lenders say no. Because of the costs involved, issuing bonds usually is not practical for companies with capital requirements below $10 or $12 million.

Although they can help small companies raise much-needed capital, bonds have certain disadvantages. The issuing company must follow the same regulations that govern businesses selling stock to public investors. Even if the bond issue is private, the company must register the offering and file periodic reports with the SEC.

Small manufacturers have access to an attractive, relatively inexpensive source of funds in industrial revenue bonds (IRBs). A company wanting to issue IRBs must get authorization from the appropriate municipality and the state before proceeding. Typically, the amount of money small companies issuing IRBs seek to raise is at least $1 million, but some small manufacturers have raised as little as $500,000 using IRBs. Even though the paperwork and legal costs associated with making an IRB issue can run up to 2 to 3 percent of the financing amount, that is a relative bargain for borrowing long-term money at a fixed interest rate.

To open IRBs up to even smaller companies, some states pool the industrial bonds of several small companies too small to make an issue. By joining together to issue composite industrial bonds, companies can reduce their issuing fees and attract a greater number of investors. The issuing companies typically pay lower interest rates than they would on conventional bank loans, often below the prime interest rate.

Private Placements

Earlier in this chapter, we saw how companies can raise money by making private placements of their stock (equity) without going public. Private placements are also available for debt instruments. A **private placement** involves selling debt to one or a small number of investors, usually insurance companies or pension funds. Private placement debt is a hybrid between a conventional loan and a bond. At its heart, it is a bond, but its terms are tailored to the borrower's individual needs, as a loan would be.

Privately placed securities offer several advantages over standard bank loans. First, they usually carry fixed interest rates, rather than the variable rates banks often charge. Second, the maturity of private placements is longer than most bank loans—fifteen years rather than five years. Private placements do not require complex filings with the SEC or hiring expensive investment bankers. Finally, because private investors can afford to take greater risks than banks, they are willing to finance deals for small companies.

private placement— *involves selling debt instruments that are a hybrid between a conventional loan and a bond to one or a small number of investors.*

Small Business Investment Companies (SBICs)

Small Business Investment Companies (SBICs), created in 1958 when Congress passed the Small Business Investment Act, are privately owned financial institutions that are licensed and regulated by the SBA. Their function is to use a combination of private capital and federally guaranteed debt to provide long-term capital to small businesses. There are two types of SBICs: regular SBICs and specialized SBICs (SSBICs). Approximately 103 SSBICs provide credit and capital to small businesses that are at least 51 percent owned by minorities and socially or economically disadvantaged people. Since its inception in 1969, SSBICs have helped finance more than 19,000 minority-owned companies.[62] Most SBICs prefer later-round financing (mezzanine financing) and leveraged buyouts (LBOs) over funding raw startups. Still, SBICs invest twice as much in startup companies as do private venture capitalists. Funding from SBICs helped launch companies such as Apple Computer and Federal Express.

Over the past 30 years, SBICs have provided more than $12.0 billion in financing to some 77,000 small businesses, adding many thousands of jobs to the American economy. Both SBICs and SSBICs must be capitalized privately with a minimum of $500,000, at which point they qualify for up to four dollars in long-term SBA loans for every dollar of private capital invested in small businesses. As a general rule, both SBICs and SSBICs may provide financial assistance only to small businesses with a net worth of less than $18 million and average after-tax earnings of $6 million during its past two years. However, employment and total annual sales standards vary from industry to industry. SBICs are limited to a maximum investment or loan amount of 20 percent of their private capital to a single client, while SSBICs may lend or invest up to 30 percent of their private capital in a single small business.

SBICs can provide both debt and equity financing to small businesses. But, because of SBA regulations affecting the financing arrangements an SBIC can offer, most SBICs

Small Business Investment Companies (SBICs)— *privately owned financial institutions that are licensed and regulated by the SBA; they use a combination of private and public funds to provide long-term capital to small businesses.*

extend their investments as loans with an option to convert the debt instrument into an equity interest later. In addition, SBICs are prohibited from obtaining a controlling interest in the companies in which they invest. The most common forms of SBIC financing (in order of their frequency) are a loan with an option to buy stock, a convertible debenture, a straight loan, and preferred stock.

Small Business Lending Companies (SBLCs)

Small Business Lending Companies (SBLCs) make only intermediate and long-term SBA-guaranteed loans. They specialize in loans that many banks would not consider and operate on a nationwide basis. For instance, most SBLC loans have terms extending for at least ten years. The maximum interest rate for loans of seven years or longer is 2.75 percent above the prime rate; for shorter-term loans, the ceiling is 2.25 percent above prime. Another feature of SBLC loans is the expertise the SBLC offers borrowing companies in critical areas.

SBLCs also screen potential investors carefully, and most of them specialize in particular industries. The result is a low loan default rate of roughly 4 percent. Corporations own most of the nation's SBLCs, giving them a solid capital base. States one executive, "This is the only program I know of that attracts Wall Street money for small businesses."[63]

<table>
<tr><td>**6. Identify** the sources of government financial assistance and the loan programs offered.</td></tr>
</table>

Federally Sponsored Programs

Federally sponsored lending programs have suffered from budget reductions in the past several years. Current trends suggest that the federal government is reducing its involvement in the lending business, but many programs are still quite active, and some are actually growing.

Economic Development Administration (EDA)

The Economic Development Administration, a branch of the Commerce Department, offers loan guarantees to create new business and to expand existing businesses in areas with below-average income and high unemployment. Loan requirements are strict and only a small number of loan guarantees are granted each year. In addition, the loan application process is lengthy and confusing. For example, guarantees for up to 85 percent of the loan value are permitted to purchase fixed assets only if the applicant supplies at least 14 percent of their cost in the form of equity capital. To qualify for a guaranteed loan for working capital, the borrower must supply 15 percent of the amount. Funds for direct loans from the EDA have dried up, and loan guarantee activity has dwindled significantly over the past five years.

EDA business loans are designed to help replenish economically distressed areas by creating or expanding small businesses that provide employment opportunities in local communities. To qualify for a loan the business must be located in the disadvantaged area, and its presence must directly benefit local residents. Because the application process is lengthy and detailed, entrepreneurs should seek assistance from EDA personnel before filing an application.

Farmers Home Administration (FmHA)

The U.S. Department of Agriculture provides financial assistance to certain small businesses through the Farmer's Home Administration (FmHA). The FmHA loan program is open to all types of businesses and is designed to create nonfarm employment opportunities in rural areas—those with populations below 50,000 and not adjacent to a city where densities exceed 100 persons per square mile. Entrepreneurs in many small towns, especially those with populations below 25,000, are eligible to apply for loans through the FmHA program, which makes about $100 million in loan guarantees each year.

The FmHA does not make direct loans to small businesses, but it will guarantee as much as 90 percent of a bank's loan up to $10 million (although actual guarantee amounts are almost always far less) for qualified applicants. Entrepreneurs apply for loans through private lenders, who view applicants with loan guarantees much more favorably than those without such guarantees. An FmHA guarantee reduces the lender's risk dramatically because the guarantee means that the government agency would pay off the loan balance (up to the ceiling) if the entrepreneur defaults on the loan.

To make a loan guarantee, the FmHA requires much of the same documentation as most banks and most other loan guarantee programs. Because of its emphasis on developing employment in rural areas, the FmHA requires an environmental-impact statement describing the jobs created and the effect the business has on the area.

When Dorene Miller launched Black Tie Affair, Inc. in Wooster, Ohio in 1980 as a catering service, she had a dream of expanding her company to include a full-service conference and party center. The opportunity to realize her dream occurred in 1993, when a partially finished conference center in Wooster came up for sale. Miller convinced an adventurous banker to assemble a consortium of five banks to lend Miller $2 million to buy and to finish the building. However, she still needed $450,000 for furnishings and equipment before the banks would approve the $2 million loan. After some searching, Miller discovered the FmHA's loan guarantee program, and the agency approved her $450,000 loan.[64]

Black Tie Affair, Inc.

Department of Housing and Urban Development (HUD)

HUD sponsors several loan programs to assist qualified entrepreneurs in raising needed capital. The Urban Development Action Grants (UDAG) are extended to cities and towns that, in turn, lend or grant money to entrepreneurs to start small businesses that will strengthen the local economy. Grants are aimed at cities and towns that HUD considers economically distressed. Funds are normally used to construct buildings and plants to be leased to entrepreneurs, sometimes with an option to buy. No ceilings or geographic limitations are placed on UDAG loans and grants.

UDAG loan and grant terms are negotiated individually between the town and the entrepreneur. One entrepreneur might negotiate a low-interest, long-term loan, while another might arrange for a grant in return for a promise to share a portion of the company's profits for several years with the town.

Local Development Companies (LDCs)

The federal government encourages local residents to organize and fund **local development companies (LDCs)** on either a profit or nonprofit basis. After raising initial capital by selling stock to at least 25 residents, the company seeks loans from banks and from the SBA. Each LDC can qualify for up to $1 million per year in loans and guarantees from the SBA to assist in starting small businesses in the community. Most LDCs are certified to operate locally or regionally, but each state may have one LDC that can operate *anywhere* within its boundaries. LDCs enable towns to maintain a solid foundation of small businesses even when other attractive benefits such as trade zones and tax breaks are not available.

Three parties are involved in providing the typical LDC loan—the LDC, the SBA, and a participating bank. An LDC normally requires the small business owner to assist by supplying about 10 percent of a project's cost, and then arranges for the remaining capital through SBA guarantees and bank loans. LDCs finance only the fixed assets of a small business—acquiring land or buildings and modernizing, renovating or restoring existing facil-

local development companies—*profit-seeking or nonprofit organizations that combine private funds and public funds to lend money to small businesses.*

ities and sites. They cannot provide funds for working capital to supply inventory, supplies, or equipment, but they can help arrange loans from banks for working capital. LDCs usually purchase real estate, refurbish or construct buildings and plants, equip them, and then lease the entire facility to the small business. The lessee's payments extend for 20 to 25 years to allow repayment of SBA, bank, and LDC loans. When the lease expires, the LDC normally gives the small business owners an option to purchase the facility, sometimes at prices well below market value.

Small Business Administration (SBA)

The Small Business Administration (SBA) has several programs designed to help finance both startup and existing small companies that cannot qualify for traditional loans because of their thin asset base and their high risk of failure. In its 45-plus years of operation, the SBA has helped some 14 million companies get the financing they need for startup or for growth.[65] To be eligible for SBA funds, a business must be within the SBA's criteria for defining a small business. Also, some types of businesses, such as those engaged in gambling or those in "mind-molding" businesses (e.g., newspaper publishers, broadcasters, etc.) are ineligible for SBA loans.

The loan application process can take from between three days to many months, depending on how well prepared the entrepreneur is and which bank is involved. To speed up processing times, the SBA has established a Certified Lender Program (CLP) and a Preferred Lender Program (PLP). Both are designed to encourage banks to become frequent SBA lenders. When a bank makes enough good loans to qualify as a certified lender, the SBA promises a fast turnaround time for the loan decision—typically three to ten business days. When a bank becomes a preferred lender, it makes the final lending decision itself, subject to SBA review. In essence, the SBA delegates the application process, the lending decision, and other details to the preferred lender. The SBA guarantees up to 75 percent of PLP loans in case the borrower fails and defaults on the loan. The minimum PLP loan guarantee is $100,000, while the maximum is $500,000. Using certified or preferred lenders can reduce the processing time for an SBA loan considerably.

To further reduce the paperwork requirements involved in its loans, the SBA recently instituted the **Low Doc Loan Program**, which allows small businesses to use a simple one-page application for loans up to $50,000; loans between $50,000 and $100,000 require the one-page application plus personal tax returns for three years and a personal financial statement from the entrepreneur. Before the Low Doc Program, a typical SBA loan application required an entrepreneur to complete at least ten forms, and the SBA often took 45 to 90 days to decide on an application. Under the Low Doc Program, response time is just a few days. To qualify for a Low Doc loan, a company must have average sales below $5 million during the previous three years and employ less than 100 people. Businesses can use Low Doc loans for working capital, machinery, equipment, and real estate.[66]

Emilio Mendoza, CEO of a defense contracting firm, is a believer in the new, streamlined SBA loan application process. When Mendoza's company, Galactic Technologies, ran into a cash crunch because of delayed payments on several defense contracts, he approached his banker Terri Saenz for a loan. On Wednesday, he told Saenz that he needed a $95,000 loan to cover payroll and other operating expenses due that Friday. Saenz, who knew of the SBA's push to speed loan applications, decided to put the agency to the test. She explained the need for speed on Mendoza's request to the SBA district office and faxed his Low Doc application to the office on Thursday morning. That afternoon, Saenz got a call from the SBA authorizing the loan guarantee. On Friday morning, Mendoza went to the bank, signed the necessary paperwork, and picked up the check.[67]

Low Doc Loan Program—*a program initiated by the SBA in an attempt to simplify its loan application process.*

Galactic
Technologies

Limited Choices

Jackie DiBella planned to launch a computer software company that would enable other entrepreneurs to start their own travel agencies at just a fraction of what it normally costs. The company, Global Alliance of Travel Entrepreneurs, would operate a software system that would link travel agents across the nation into a centralized office to make travel bookings. Rather than having to spend up to the usual $200,000 to start up their agencies, Global Alliance affiliates could be in the travel business for $10,000 or less. "We're putting together a travel agency for individuals who can't afford to operate independently," says Ms. DiBella.

DiBella's plan was to invest $75,000 of her own money to develop and test the software system. Then she would use $300,000 from investors to implement an aggressive marketing campaign to sign up travel agents as Global Alliance affiliates. Within ten months, she forecasted that the company would have 110 customers generating more than $500,000 in revenues. She figured that the $375,000 seed capital would carry the company until it could generate enough cash to support its own operations.

Unfortunately, it didn't work that way.

DiBella's original investors convinced her that $150,000 would be enough to launch the company successfully because customers would see the benefits of her system and would join quickly. But travel agents didn't sign up as quickly as DiBella had hoped, and many balked at paying $8,000 to sign up for the system. DiBella estimated that customers would come on board within 45 to 60 days of their first meeting with Global Alliance, but most took 95 to 120 days before they committed. That meant that the company's revenue projections were falling farther and farther behind schedule. To sign up affiliates faster, DiBella decided to cut the sign-up fee by as much as 25 percent, putting more pressure on the company's revenues. The fledgling company took another hit when DiBella and her partner (her son) decided to expand into the national market, which required a much larger capital investment than originally planned.

In an effort to conserve the company's cash, DiBella and her son decided not to cash their paychecks from the company, but that, too, proved to be a mistake. The IRS informed Global Alliance that it had neglected to pay the necessary payroll taxes and placed a lien on the company's accounts, seizing $21,000, which left less than $2,000 in cash on hand. As her company's actual financial picture spiraled farther away from the projections DiBella had made, she realized that the company needed an injection of capital to survive. She has managed to pay off the debt to the IRS, and is now looking for a cash infusion of $500,000 to get the Global Alliance back on track.

1. Looking back at Global Alliance's journey, what mistakes can you identify in DiBella's financial plan and decisions?

2. How have these past mistakes affected the company's ability to attract capital today?

3. Which sources of funds would you suggest Ms. DiBella approach? Which ones would you rule out? Explain.

Source: Adapted from Udayan Gupta, "How Much?" *Wall Street Journal*, May 22, 1995, p. R7.

Another program designed to streamline the application process for SBA loan guarantees is the **FA$TRAK Program**, in which participating banks use their own loan procedures and applications to make loans of up to $100,000 to small businesses. Because the SBA guarantees up to 50 percent of the loan, banks are often more willing to make smaller loans to entrepreneurs who might otherwise have difficulty meeting lender's standards.

SBA Loan Programs

The SBA offers three basic types of loans in administering its 19 different programs: direct, immediate participation, and guaranteed.

Direct loans are made by the SBA directly to the small business with public funds and no bank participation. Generally, a direct loan cannot exceed $150,000. (A lower ceiling, $100,000, applies to a direct Economic Opportunity loan.) The interest rate charged on direct loans depends on the cost of money to the government, and it changes as general interest rates fluctuate. Activity in direct loans is very limited; they account for less than one-half of 1 percent of the SBA's total loan activity.

Immediate participation loans are made from a pool of public funds and private loans. The SBA provides a portion of the total loan and a private lender supplies the remaining

FA$TRAK Program—*an SBA program that allows participating banks to use their own loan procedures to make SBA -guaranteed loans.*

direct loans—*loans made by the SBA directly to small businesses with public funds.*

immediate participation loans—*loans the SBA makes to small businesses that combine public and private funds.*

portion. The SBA's general policy is to fund no more than 75 percent of a participation loan, but there are exceptions. The SBA's portion of an immediate participation loan may not exceed $150,000 (except that Economic Opportunity loans are limited to $100,000). The interest rate the SBA charges on its share of the loan is usually the same as that charged on direct loans.

By far, the most popular type of SBA loan is the **guaranteed loan** (or **7(A) loan**) (see Figure 10.4). Private lenders (usually commercial banks) extend these loans to small businesses, but the SBA guarantees them (80 percent of loans up to $100,000; 75 percent of loans above $100,000 up to the loan guarantee ceiling of $750,000). In other words, the SBA does not actually lend any money; it merely guarantees the bank this much repayment in case the borrower defaults on the loan. Because the SBA assumes most of the credit risk, banks are more willing to consider riskier deals that they normally would refuse.

For instance, when their sports-equipment-bag company, Buck's Bags, began to experience explosive growth that outstripped cash flow, Larry Lee and Dara Lee Howerton applied for an SBA guaranteed loan at their banker's suggestion. The Howertons have received four SBA-guaranteed loans totaling more than $600,000, using the loans to move into a larger plant, buy new equipment, and hire new workers. With the SBA loan guarantees, Buck's Bags sales have soared. "The SBA was very helpful in getting us through our rapid-growth years," says Larry Lee. "I don't know what we would have done without them."[68]

guaranteed loans—*loans made by commercial banks to small companies and guaranteed by the SBA.*

Buck's Bags

Figure 10.4
SBA Guaranteed Loans
Source: Adapted from the U.S. Small Business Administration.

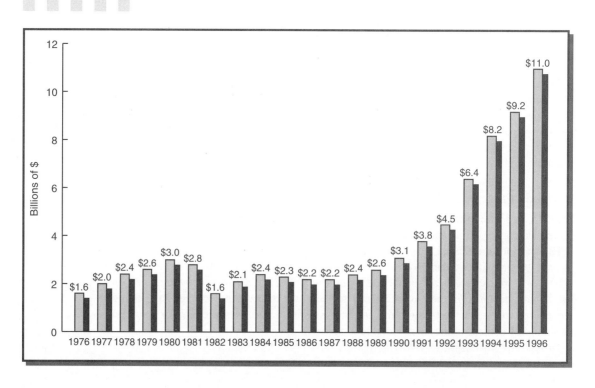

Qualifying for an SBA loan guarantee requires cooperation among the entrepreneur, the participating bank, and the SBA. The participating bank determines the loan's terms and sets the interest rate within SBA limits. Contrary to popular belief, SBA guaranteed loans do *not* carry special deals on interest rates. Typically, rates are negotiated with the participating bank, with a ceiling of prime plus 2.25 percent on loans of less than seven years and prime plus 2.75 percent on loans of seven to 25 years. Interest rates on loans of less than $25,000 can run up to prime plus 4.75 percent. The average interest rate on SBA-guaranteed loans is prime plus 2 percent (compared to prime plus 1 percent on conventional bank loans). The SBA also assesses a one-time guaranty fee of up to 3.875 percent for all loan guarantees.

The median loan through the guarantee program is $175,000 and the average duration of an SBA loan is 12 years—longer than the average commercial small business loan. In fact, longer loan terms are a distinct advantage of SBA loans. At least half of all bank business loans are for less than one year.[69] By contrast, SBA real estate loans can extend for up to 25 years (compared to just 10 to 15 years for a conventional loan), and working capital loans have maturities of seven years (compared with two to five years at most banks). These longer terms translate into lower payments, which are better suited for young, fast-growing, cash-strapped companies.

In addition to its basic 7(a) loan guarantee program (through which the SBA makes about 75 percent of its loans), the SBA provides guarantees to small businesses for startup, real estate, machinery and equipment, fixtures, working capital, exporting, and restructuring debt through several other methods. About two-thirds of all SBA's loan guarantees are for machinery and equipment or working capital. The **Seasonal Line of Credit Program** offers short-term capital to growing companies needing to finance seasonal buildups of inventory or accounts receivable. The maximum loan is $500,000 and its maturity cannot exceed 12 months, and the company must repay it from cash flow. Accounts receivable and inventory are collateral for the loan. The **Contract Loan Program** is another short-term loan guarantee, but it is designed to finance the cost of labor and materials needed to perform a contract. Maturity times are up to 18 months.

For small businesses going global, the SBA has the **Export Working Capital Program**. Under this program, the SBA will guarantee 90 percent of a bank credit line up to $750,000. Loan proceeds must be used to finance small business exports.

SECTION 504 CERTIFIED DEVELOPMENT COMPANY PROGRAM. The SBA's Section 504 program is designed to encourage small businesses to expand their facilities and to create jobs. Section 504 deals provide long-term, fixed-asset financing to small companies to purchase land, buildings, or equipment. Three lenders play a role in every 504 loan: a bank, the SBA, and a **certified development company (CDC)**. A CDC is a nonprofit organization designed to promote economic growth in a community. Some 290 CDCs operate across the United States The entrepreneur generally is required to make a down payment of 10 percent of the total project cost. The CDC puts up 40 percent at a long-term fixed rate, supported by an SBA loan guarantee in case the entrepreneur defaults. The bank provides long-term financing for the remaining 50 percent, also supported by an SBA guarantee.

When Jerry and Loretta Schutten's manufacturing company, Commercial Lighting, outgrew the location it was renting, the Schuttens worked with their bank, the Evergreen Community Development Association (a CDC), and the SBA to finance the purchase of a new location. The Evergreen CDC provided a $148,400 loan, which the SBA guaranteed, and their bank made a $192,000 loan. The Schuttens put up the remaining 10 percent of the cost of the new building.[70]

As attractive as they are, 504 loans are not for every business owner. The SBA imposes several restrictions on 504 loans:

Seasonal Line of Credit Program—*an SBA program offering short-term capital to finance growing companies' seasonal needs for working capital.*

Contract Loan Program—*an SBA program providing short-term loan guarantees to finance the cost of labor and materials needed to perform a contract.*

certified development company—*a nonprofit organization designed to promote economic growth in a community by working with commercial banks and the SBA to make loans to small companies.*

Commercial Lighting

☆ For every $35,000 the CDC lends, the project must create at least one new job.

☆ Machinery and equipment financed must have a useful life of at least ten years.

☆ The borrower must occupy at least two-thirds of a building constructed with the loan.

☆ The borrower must occupy at least half of a building purchased or remodeled with the loan.

☆ The borrower must qualify as a small business under the SBA's definition and must not have a tangible net worth in excess of $6 million and does not have an average net income in excess of $2 million after taxes for the preceding two years.

Because of strict equity requirements, existing small businesses usually find it easier to qualify for 504 loans than do startups.

MICROLOAN PROGRAM. Recall from Figure 10.1 that about three-fourths of all entrepreneurs need less than $100,000 to launch their businesses. Indeed, research suggests that most entrepreneurs require less than $50,000 to start their companies. Unfortunately, loans of that amount can be the most difficult to get. Lending these relatively small amounts to entrepreneurs starting businesses is the purpose of the SBA's Microloan Program. Called microloans because they range from just a hundred dollars to as much as $25,000, these loans have helped thousands of people take their first steps toward entrepreneurship. Banks typically have shunned loans in such small amounts because they considered them to be unprofitable. So, in 1992, the SBA began funding microloan programs at 96 private non-profit lenders in 44 states in an attempt to "fill the void" in small loans to startup companies. The average microloan is for $9,916 over three years (the maximum term is six years), and lenders' standards are less demanding than those on conventional loans.[71]

Although microloans are available to anyone, the SBA hopes to target those entrepreneurs who have the greatest difficulty getting startup capital—women, minorities, and those with low incomes. More than 37 percent of microloans go to minority entrepreneurs, and nearly 45 percent go to women.[72]

SBA'S 8(a) PROGRAM. The SBA's 8(a) program is designed to help minority-owned businesses get a fair share of federal government contracts. Through this program, the SBA directs about $4 million each year to small businesses with "socially and economically disadvantaged" owners. Once a small business convinces the SBA that it meets the program's criteria, it finds a government agency needing work done. The SBA then approaches the federal agency that needs the work done and arranges for a contract to go to the SBA. The agency then subcontracts the work to the small business. Government agencies cooperate with the SBA in its 8(a) program because the law requires them to set aside a portion of their work for minority-owned firms.

DISASTER LOANS. As their name implies, disaster loans are made to small businesses devastated by some kind of financial or physical losses. The maximum disaster loan usually is $500,000, but Congress often raises that ceiling when circumstances warrant. For instance, in response to the tremendous flooding in the Midwest during the summer of 1993 and again in the wake of the Los Angeles earthquake in early 1994, the SBA tripled the ceiling on disaster loans for physical damage to $1.5 million. Disaster loans carry below-market interest rates, for example, 4 percent on the loans to small companies after the L.A. earthquakes. Loans for physical damage above $10,000 and financial damage of more than $5,000 require the entrepreneur to pledge some kind of collateral, usually a lien on the business property. The SBA's coffers have been stretched thin by a string of disasters in recent years, ranging from hurricanes Hugo, Andrew, and Fran on the southeastern coast and earthquakes on the western coast to the Los Angeles riots and floods in the Midwest.

GREENLINE REVOLVING LINE OF CREDIT PROGRAM. Started in early 1994, the SBA's GreenLine program is designed to increase small companies' access to working capital by providing them with revolving lines of credit. Rather than use traditional SBA term loans, which require fixed monthly payments, the GreenLine program employs highly flexible revolving loans, in which cash-hungry small businesses draw on a credit line only when they need the money. Banks extend lines of credit to small companies for up to five years at 2.75 percent over the prime interest rate, and the SBA guarantees 75 percent of the loan (up to $750,000). The average GreenLine loan is $100,000. SBA lenders monitor these revolving credit lines more carefully than their usual term loans because they are secured by accounts receivable and inventory, which are less reliable than the real estate, buildings, and machinery that secure term loans. That means that revolving credit loans are riskier than term loans.

Loans built around lines of credit are just what small businesses need most because they are so flexible, efficient, and, unfortunately, so hard to get. This loan program is designed to provide short-term credit to allow small businesses to finance the sale of their products and services until they can collect payment for them.

SMALL BUSINESS INNOVATION RESEARCH (SBIR) PROGRAM. Started as a pilot program by the National Science Foundation in the 1970s, the SBIR program has expanded to 11 federal agencies and has an annual budget in excess of $900 million. These agencies award cash grants or long-term contracts to small companies wanting to initiate or to expand their research and development (R&D) efforts. The SBIR process includes three phases. Phase I grants, which determine the feasibility of a technology or product, last for up to six months and have a ceiling of $100,000. Phase II grants, designed to develop the concept into a specific technology or product, run for up to 24 months with a ceiling of $750,000. Approximately 40 percent of all Phase II applicants receive funding. Phase III is the commercialization phase, in which the company pursues commercial applications of the research and development conducted in phases I and II and must use private or non-SBIR federal funding to bring a product to market.

More than 29,000 SBIR awards totaling in excess of $4 billion have gone to small companies, which traditionally have had difficulty competing with big corporations for federal R&D dollars.[73] The government's dollars have been well invested. About one out of four small businesses receiving SBIR awards has achieved commercial success for its products. Indeed, federal contract officers consistently report that their SBIR projects are superior in quality to those with large corporations and universities and are more likely to lead to technological innovation and commercialization of ideas.

For example, Ross-Hime, a small business with just 35 employees, recently received an SBIR grant to develop a sophisticated computer-controlled robotic wrist module that allows humans to avoid exposure to toxic fumes in closed-environment, spray-painting operations. Ross-Hime's innovative product is used extensively in the automotive industry as well as in others.[74]

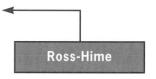

Ross-Hime

THE SMALL BUSINESS TECHNOLOGY TRANSFER PROGRAM. The Small Business Technology Transfer Program (STTR) program complements the Small Business Innovation Research (SBIR) program. While SBIR focuses on developing commercially promising ideas which originate in small businesses, STTR allows small companies to exploit a vast new reservoir of commercially promising ideas which originate in universities, federally funded R&D centers, and nonprofit research institutions. Researchers at these institutions can join forces with small businesses and can spin off commercially promising ideas while remaining employed at their research institutions. Five federal agencies award grants of up to $500,000 in two phases to these research partnerships.

State and Local Loan Development Programs

Just when many federally funded programs are facing cutbacks, state-sponsored loan and development programs are becoming more active in providing funds for business startups and expansions. Many states have decided that their funds are better spent encouraging small business growth rather than "chasing smokestacks" - trying to entice large businesses to locate in their boundaries. These programs come in a wide variety of forms, but they all tend to focus on developing small businesses that create the greatest number of jobs and economic benefits. For example, South Carolina's Jobs Economic Development Authority (JEDA) is a direct lending arm of the state, offering low-interest loans to manufacturing, industrial, and service businesses. JEDA also provides financial and technical assistance to small companies seeking to develop export markets.

Although each state's approach to economic development is somewhat special, one common element is some kind of small business financing program—loans, loan guarantees, development grants, venture capital pools, and others.

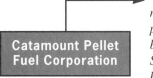

Catamount Pellet Fuel Corporation

Averill Cook got the idea for the Catamount Pellet Fuel Corporation, a company that manufactures clean-burning, cheap fuel pellets from sawdust, after he started his first company, a firewood business. After spending four years researching the project and building a business plan, he concluded that it would take about $1 million to launch the company. Several family members agreed to guarantee $500,000 of the loans Cook negotiated with a bank. Then he pitched his idea to industrial development organizations in Massachusetts, who offered him a package of low-cost grants and loans. In the end, Catamount's startup capital totaled $1.3 million.[75]

Even cities and small towns have joined in the effort to develop small businesses and help them grow.

Weaver Street Market

For example, when a group of entrepreneurs wanted to open a specialty-food store in tiny Carrboro, North Carolina, they convinced a nonprofit funding organization, the Center for Community Self-Help, in nearby Durham to put up $100,000. But there was a catch: The entrepreneurs had to find $100,000 in matching funds. Carrboro quickly came up with $100,000 from its own revolving loan fund, and the town's 8,000 residents pitched in another $100,000 in loans to help launch Weaver Street Market. Today, the company has annual sales of more than $4 million and employs more than 50 workers.[76]

Internal Methods of Financing

bootstrap financing— *internal methods of financing a company's need for capital.*

factor—*a financial institution that buys businesses' accounts receivable at a discount.*

Small business owners do not have to rely solely on financial institutions and government agencies for capital. Instead, the business itself has the capacity to generate capital. This type of financing, called **bootstrap financing**, is available to virtually every small business and encompasses factoring, leasing rather than purchasing equipment, using credit cards, and managing the business frugally.

FACTORING ACCOUNTS RECEIVABLE. Instead of carrying credit sales on its own books (some of which may never be collected), a small business can sell outright its accounts receivable to a **factor**. Under deals arranged "with recourse," the small business owner retains the responsibility for customers who fail to pay their accounts. The business owner must take back these uncollectible invoices. Under deals arranged "without recourse," however, the owner is relieved of the responsibility for collecting them. If some accounts are not collected, the factor bears the loss. Because the factoring company assumes the risk of collecting the accounts, it normally screens the firm's credit customers, accepts those judged to be credit-worthy, and advances the small business owner a portion of the value of the accounts receivable. Factors will pay anywhere from 60 to 95 percent of the face value of a company's accounts receivable, depending on four conditions:[77]

⭐ the small company's customers' financial strength and credit ratings.
⭐ the small company's industry and its customers' industries since some industries have a reputation for slow payments.
⭐ the small company's financial strength, especially in deals arranged with recourse.
⭐ the small company's credit policies.

Once the factor collects the accounts, it releases the balance of the funds less its factoring fees and interest. Because factors assume certain risks when buying a small company's accounts receivable, factoring is more expensive than bank loans. Factors normally charge interest (at 1 to 3 points over prime) on the cash they advance on a batch of receivables plus a "discount" (factoring fee) ranging from 0.75 percent to 7 percent of the full amount of the receivables.

Factoring is ideally suited for fast-growing companies—especially startups that cannot qualify for bank loans.

For example, when sales at his gourmet ice-cream company, Belmont Gourmet Ice Cream, were growing so fast that they were exhausting its cash flow, Larry Baras turned to a factor for some fast cash. The factor advanced Belmont $50,000 for its receivables, enough to purchase supplies and raw materials in bulk (at a discount) and win a contract with a chain of superstores it had been trying to sell to for years.[78]

Belmont Gourmet Ice Cream

LEASING. Leasing is another common bootstrap financing technique. Today, small businesses can lease virtually any kind of asset from office space and telephones to computers and heavy equipment. By leasing expensive assets, the small business owner is able to use them without locking in valuable capital for an extended period of time. In other words, the manager can reduce the long-term capital requirements of the business by leasing equipment and facilities, and she is not investing her capital in depreciating assets. Also, because no down payment is required and because the cost of the asset is spread over a longer time (lowering monthly payments), the firm's cash flow improves.

CREDIT CARDS. Unable to find financing elsewhere, some entrepreneurs have launched their companies using the most convenient source of debt capital available: credit cards! A recent study by Robin Leonard found that 60 percent of entrepreneurs could not get the startup capital they needed through traditional sources, and 40 percent of those entrepreneurs used credit cards to launch their companies.[79] Putting business startup costs on credit cards charging 21 percent or more in annual interest is expensive and risky, but some entrepreneurs have no other choices.

When Beverly and John Zeiss launched Critical Care Associates Inc., a company that finds and places nurses in critical care hospital units, they got $87,000 from family and friends and even took out a $100,000 second mortgage. As sales took off, the copreneurs discovered they needed $300,000 to keep the company growing. But when the Zeisses went to their local bank to request a loan, they were turned down, despite a long-term relationship with the bank and a good credit record. Because the couple's company was a service business, it lacked the assets the bank wanted for collateral. So Beverly and John turned to their credit cards, which carried annual interest rates from 13.9 percent to 20.4 percent. Using 19 different cards, the Zeisses charged $92,483 of business expenses, incurring interest charges of more than $15,000 for the year! The risk paid off; Critical Care Associates Inc.'s sales continued to climb, and the Zeisses were able to pay off their credit card balances, although it took several years to do so.[80]

Critical Care Associates Inc.

1. Explain the differences among the three types of capital small businesses require: fixed, working, and growth.

- Capital is any form of wealth employed to produce more wealth. Three forms of capital are commonly identified: fixed capital, working capital, and growth capital.
- Fixed capital is used to purchase a company's permanent or fixed assets; working capital represents the business's temporary funds and is used to support the business's normal short-term operations; growth capital requirements surface when an existing business is expanding or changing its primary direction.

2. Describe the differences between equity capital and debt capital and the advantages and disadvantages of each.

- Equity financing represents the personal investment of the owner (or owners), and it offers the advantage of not having to be repaid with interest.
- Debt capital is the financing that a small business owner has borrowed and must repay with interest. It does not require entrepreneurs to give up ownership in their companies.

3. Describe the various sources of equity capital available to entrepreneurs, including personal savings, friends and relatives, angels, partners, corporations, venture capital, and public stock offerings.

- The most common source of financing a business is the owner's personal savings. After emptying their own pockets, the next place entrepreneurs turn for capital is family members and friends. Angels are private investors who not only invest their money in small companies, but they also offer valuable advice and counsel to them. Some business owners have success financing their companies by taking on limited partners as investors or by forming an alliance with a corporation, often a customer or a supplier. Venture capital companies are for-profit, professional investors looking for fast-growing companies in "hot" industries. When screening prospects, venture capital firms look for competent management, a competitive edge, a growth industry, and important intangibles that will make a business successful. Some owners choose to attract capital by taking their companies public, which requires registering the public offering with the SEC.

4. Describe the process of "going public," as well as its advantages and disadvantages and the various simplified registrations and exemptions from registration available to small businesses wanting to sell securities to investors.

- Going public involves: (1) choosing the underwriter, (2) negotiating a letter of intent, (3) preparing the registration statement, (4) filing with the SEC, and (5) meeting state requirements.
- Going public offers the advantages of raising large amounts of capital, improved access to future financing, improved corporate image, and gaining listing on a stock exchange. The disadvantages include dilution of the founder's ownership, loss of privacy, reporting to the SEC, filing expenses, and accountability to shareholders.
- Rather than go through the complete registration process, some companies use one of the simplified registration options and exemptions available to small companies: Regulation S-B, Small Company Offering Registration (SCOR), Regulation D (Rule 504, Rule 505, and Rule 506), Section 4(6), Rule 147, and Regulation A.

5. Describe the various sources of debt capital and the advantages and disadvantages of each: banks, asset-based lenders, vendors (trade credit), equipment suppliers, savings and loan associations, stockbrokers, insurance companies, credit unions, bonds, Small Business Investment Companies (SBICs), and Small Business Lending Companies (SBLCs).

- Commercial banks offer the greatest variety of loans, although they are conservative lenders. Typical short-term bank loans include commercial loans, lines of credit, discounting accounts receivable, inventory financing, and floor planning.
- Trade credit is used extensively by small businesses as a source of financing. Vendors and suppliers commonly finance sales to businesses for 30, 60, or even 90 days.
- Equipment suppliers offer small businesses financing similar to trade credit, but with slightly different terms.
- Commercial finance companies offer many of the same types of loans that banks do, but they are more risk oriented in their lending practices. They emphasize accounts receivable financing and inventory loans.
- Savings and loan associations specialize in loans to purchase real property—commercial and industrial mortgages—for up to 30 years.
- Stock brokerage houses offer loans to prospective entrepreneurs at lower interest rates than banks because they have high-quality, liquid collateral—stocks and bonds in the borrower's portfolio.
- Insurance companies provide financing through policy loans and mortgage loans. Policy loans are extended to the owner against the cash surrender value of insurance policies. Mortgage loans are made for large amounts and are based on the value of the land being purchased.
- Small business investment companies are privately owned companies licensed and regulated by the SBA that qualify for SBA loans to be invested in or loaned to small firms.
- Small business lending companies make only intermediate and long-term loans that are guaranteed by the SBA.

6. Identify the sources of government financial assistance and the loan programs offered.

- The Economic Development Administration, a branch of the Commerce Department, makes loan guarantees to create and expand small businesses in economically depressed areas.

- The Farmers Home Administration's loan program is designed to create nonfarm employment opportunities in rural areas through loans and loan guarantees.
- The Department of Housing and Urban Development extends loans to cities that, in turn, lend and grant money to small businesses in an attempt to strengthen the local economy.
- The Small Business Administration has three types of loans: direct, immediate participation, and guaranteed. Almost all SBA loan activity now is in the form of loan guarantees. Popular SBA programs include the Seasonal Line of Credit, the Contract Loan program, Export Working Capital program, the Section 504 Certified Development Company program, the Microloan program, the 8(a) program, the Disaster Loan program, the Greenline Revolving Line of Credit, the Small Business Innovation Research program, and the Small Business Technology Transfer program.
- State loan and development programs have taken up much of the slack left by dwindling federal programs.

7. Discuss valuable methods of financing growth and expansion internally.
- Small business owners may also look inside their firms for capital. By factoring accounts receivable, leasing equipment instead of buying it, and by minimizing costs, owners can stretch their supplies of capital.

DISCUSSION QUESTIONS

1. Why is it so difficult for most small business owners to raise the capital needed to start, operate, or expand their ventures?
2. What is capital? List and describe the three types of capital a small business needs for its operations.
3. Define equity financing. What advantage does it offer over debt financing?
4. What is the most common source of equity funds in a typical small business? If an owner lacks sufficient equity capital to invest in the firm, what options are available for raising it?
5. What guidelines should an entrepreneur follow if friends and relatives choose to invest in her business?
6. What is an "angel?" Put together a brief profile of the typical private investor. How can entrepreneurs locate potential angels to invest in their businesses?
7. What advice would you offer an entrepreneur about to strike a deal with a private investor to avoid problems?
8. What types of businesses are most likely to attract venture capital? What investment criteria do venture capitalists use when screening potential businesses? How do these compare to the typical angel's criteria?
9. How do venture capital firms operate? Describe their procedure for screening investment proposals.
10. What role do commercial banks play in providing debt financing to small businesses? Outline and briefly describe the major types of short-term, intermediate, and long-term loans commercial banks offer.
11. What is trade credit? How important is it as a source of debt financing to small firms?
12. What function do SBICs serve? How does an SBIC operate? What methods of financing do SBICs rely on most heavily?
13. Briefly describe the loan programs offered by the following:
    a. Economic Development Administration
    b. Farmers Home Administration
    c. Department of Housing and Urban Development
    d. local development companies
14. How can a firm employ bootstrap financing to stretch its current capital supply?
15. How does a factor operate?

Beyond the Classroom...

1. Interview several local business owners about how they financed their businesses. Where did their initial capital come from? Ask the following questions:
   a. How did you raise your starting capital? What percent did you supply on your own? What percent was debt capital and what percent was equity capital?
   b. Which of the sources of funds described in this chapter do you use? Are they used to finance fixed, working, or growth capital needs?
   c. How much money did you need to launch your businesses? Where did subsequent capital come from? What advice do you offer others seeking capital?

Continued

2. Contact a local private investor and ask him or her to address your class. (You may have to search to locate one!). What kinds of businesses does this angel prefer to invest in? What screening criteria does he or she use? How are the deals typically structured?

3. Contact a local venture capitalist and ask him or her to address your class. What kinds of businesses does his or her company invest in? What screening criteria does the company use? How are deals typically structured?

4. Invite an investment banker or a financing expert from a local accounting firm to address your class about the process of taking a company public. What do they look for in a potential IPO candidate? What is the process, and how long does it usually take?

5. After a personal visit, prepare a short report on a nearby factor's operation. How is the value of the accounts receivable purchased determined? Who bears the loss on uncollected accounts?

6. Interview the administrator of a financial institution program offering a method of financing with which you are unfamiliar, and prepare a short report on its method of operation.

7. Contact your state's business development board and prepare a report on the financial assistance programs it offers small businesses.

SURFING THE NET

1. Visit Khera Communications Inc.'s Business Resource Center at the following address:

http://www.kcilink.com/brc/

Explore the "Financing Guide" section. Choose a method of financing that interests you and prepare a one-page report on it.

2. Visit the Web site for the Price Waterhouse LLP National Venture Capital Survey at:

http://www/pw.com/vc/

How much did venture capital companies invest in small businesses in the latest quarter reported? What were the "hot" industry sectors? What regions of the country attracted the most venture capital? In what stage of development were the majority of the companies that received venture capital investments?

3. Go to the Small Business Administration's home page at:

http://www.sba.gov

Enter the "Financing Your Business" section or the "Financing Your Business Workshop" section. Choose two of the SBA's loan programs and prepare a short report explaining their purposes, methods of operation, and target audiences. How do SBA loan programs benefit entrepreneurs?

4. Access the home page for Capital Quest, a showcase for entrepreneurs looking for private investors, at:

http://www.usbusiness.com/capquest/home.html

Explore the "Venture Index" to find an executive summary of a business plan for a company that interests you. Prepare a brief report highlighting the company, its target market, and its competitive advantage. How much capital is the entrepreneur seeking? If you were an angel, would you invest in this company? Explain.

ELEVEN

Choosing a Location and Layout

The error of one moment becomes the sorrow of a whole life.
- Chinese proverb

How little do they see what is, who frame their hasty judgments upon that which seems.
- Robert Southey

Nothing looks as good close up as it does from far away.
- Anonymous

LEARNING OBJECTIVES

Upon completion of this chapter, you will be able to:

1. **Explain** the stages in the location decision—choosing the region, the state, the city, and the final site.

2. **Describe** the location criteria for retail and service businesses.

3. **Outline** the basic location options for retail and service businesses: central business districts (CBDs), neighborhoods, shopping centers and malls, near competitors, outlying areas, and at home.

4. **Explain** the site selection process for manufacturers.

5. **Discuss** the benefits of locating a startup company in a business incubator.

6. **Describe** the criteria used to analyze the layout and design considerations of a building, including the Americans with Disabilities Act.

7. **Evaluate** the advantages and disadvantages of building, buying, and leasing a building.

8. **Explain** the principles of effective layouts for retailers, service businesses, and manufacturers.

The Basics of the Location Decision: From Region to State to City to Site

Almost everyone has heard the old adage that business success, especially retail businesses, depends on three factors; location, location, location! This may be an overstatement, but most authorities on small business would quickly agree that failing to do your homework in searching for the best location is a serious mistake. Too many small business owners never look for a location beyond their own home cities or towns. When entrepreneurs stay in this "comfort zone," they often fail to discover locations that would be far superior and contribute significantly to the success of their new ventures.

The location selection process is like an interactive computer game where each decision opens the way to make another decision on the way to solving the puzzle. The answer to the puzzle, of course, is the best location for the new business. At each step in the decision process the entrepreneur studies a set of specific facts, reaches a conclusion, and goes to the next level in the location selection process. Location selection decisions are not difficult to make; like the interactive computer game there are lots of clues, or in this case facts, that guide the entrepreneur to the best solution. The "secret" to selecting the ideal location goes back to knowing who the company's target customers are (see Chapter 5) and then finding a site that makes it most convenient for those customers to do business with the company!

For instance, David Chang, owner of Coastal Cotton, a small retail chain specializing in casual cotton clothing, has seen his company grow from a single store in Hialeah, Florida to 12 locations in outlet centers across the Southeast and in California. Because Coastal Cotton's primary target is value-hunting tourists, Chang chooses locations with high concentrations of potential customers. "You have to know your customer base and be strategic about choosing sites," Chang explains.[1]

Coastal Cotton

The Region

The first step in selecting the best location is to focus at the regional level. Which region of the country has the characteristics necessary for a new business to succeed? Common requirements include rapid growth in the population of a certain age group, rising disposable incomes, or the existence of specific infrastructure. Choosing an appropriate location is essentially a matter of selecting the site that best serves the needs of the business's target market most efficiently. The first phase is to determine which regions of the country are experiencing substantial growth. Every year many popular business publications prepare reports on the various regions of the nation—which ones are growing, which are stagnant, and which are declining. Studying shifts in population and industrial growth will give an entrepreneur an idea of where the action is—and isn't. For example, how large is the population? How fast is it growing? What is the makeup of the overall population? Which segments are growing fastest? Slowest? What is the population's income? Is it increasing or decreasing? Are other businesses moving into the region? If so, what kind of businesses? Generally, owners want to avoid dying regions; these regions simply cannot support a broad base of potential customers. A firm's customers will be people, businesses, and industry, and if it is to be successful, the business must locate in a place that is convenient to them.

One of the first stops entrepreneurs should make when conducting a regional evaluation is the U.S. Census Bureau. The Census Bureau produces many publications to aid entrepreneurs in their search for the best location (far too many to list here!), but two that are based on the most recent nationwide census are quite helpful: *Census '90: Introduction to Product and Services* and *1990 Census Basics*. The Census Bureau also publishes a monthly newsletter, *Census and You*, which is especially helpful to business owners.

In addition, the Census Bureau makes most of the information contained in its valuable data banks available to entrepreneurs researching potential sites through its easy-to-use World Wide Web (WWW) site at: http://www.census.gov/. There entrepreneurs can access for specific locations vital demographic information such as age, income, educational level, employment level, occupation, ancestry, commuting times, housing data (house value, number of rooms, mortgage or rent status, number of vehicles owned, etc.), and many other characteristics. Sorting through each report's 92 fields, entrepreneurs can prepare customized reports on the potential sites they are considering. Oregon State University has compiled much of the data from the Census Bureau, the Bureau of Economic Analysis, the National Center for Education Statistics, and the Mesa Group into the World Wide Web's Government Information Sharing Project (http:/govinfo.kerr.orst.edu/). This Web site gives users an easy and powerful system for mining information from the vast and valuable resources the U.S. government has collected and compiled. These WWW resources give entrepreneurs instant access to important site-location information that only a few years ago would have taken *many* hours of intense research to compile!

The Small Business Administration also has a number of valuable aids to help you throughout your location search. Some of these include *Practical Use of Government Statistics*, *Using Census Data to Select a Store Site*, and *Using Census Data in Small Plant Marketing*. *American Demographics* magazine has two valuable booklets also: *The 1990 Census: The Counting of America* and *A Researcher's Guide to the 1990 Census*.

Four other helpful publications merit mentioning as well: *Sales and Marketing Management's Survey of Buying Power*, *Editor and Publisher Market Guide*, *Rand McNally's Commercial Atlas and Marketing Guide,* and *Zip Code Atlas and Market Planner*. The *Survey of Buying Power*, published annually, provides a detailed breakdown of population, retail sales, spendable income, and other characteristics for census regions, states, metropolitan areas, counties, and cities. The survey includes highlights and summary sections, analyses of changes in metro markets, projections for metro markets, descriptions of newspaper and TV markets, and summaries of sales of certain merchandise.

The *Editor and Publisher Market Guide* is similar to the *Survey of Buying Power*, but provides additional information on markets. The guide includes detailed information on key cities.

The *Commercial Atlas and Marketing Guide* reports on more than 128,000 places in the United States, many of which are not available through census reports. It includes 11 economic indicators for every major geographic market; tables showing population trends, income, buying power, trade, and manufacturing activity; and large, cross-reference maps. Its format makes it easy to collect large amounts of valuable data on any region in the country (and specific areas within that region).

The *Zip Code Atlas and Market Planner* is an extremely useful location and market-planning tool. It combines a breakdown of zip codes (often the basis of psychographic customer profiles) with maps featuring physical features such as mountains, rivers, and major highways. The planner contains loose-leaf, full-color maps, each with a reusable acetate overlay showing five-digit zip code boundaries. There are detailed maps of all 50 states, plus 85 specific inset maps and 11 vicinity maps.

The task of analyzing various potential locations—gathering and synthesizing data on a wide variety of demographic and geographic variables—is one ideally suited for a computer. In fact, a growing number of entrepreneurs are relying on geographic information systems (GIS), powerful software programs that combine map drawing with database management capability, to pinpoint the ideal location for their businesses. GIS packages allow users to search through virtually *any* database containing a wealth of information and plot the results on a map of the country, an individual state, a specific city, or even a single city block. The visual display highlights what otherwise would be indiscernible business trends.

For instance, using a GIS program, an entrepreneur could plot her existing customer base on a map, with various colors representing the different population densities. Then she could zoom in on those areas with the greatest concentration of customers, mapping a detailed view of zip code borders or even city streets. GIS street files originate in the U.S. Census Department's TIGER (Topological Integrated Geographic Encoding Referencing) file, which contains map information broken down for every square foot of metropolitan statistical areas. TIGER contains the name and location of every street in the country and detailed block statistics for the 345 largest urban areas. In essence, TIGER is a computerized map of the entire United States, and, when linked with a database, gives small business owners incredible power to pinpoint existing and potential customers.

The Small Business Administration's Small Business Development Center (SBDC) program also offers location analysis assistance to entrepreneurs. These centers, numbering some 600 nationwide, provide training, counseling, research and other specialized assistance to entrepreneurs and existing business owners on a wide variety of subjects—all at no charge! They are an important resource, especially for those entrepreneurs who may not have access to a computer. (To locate the SBA nearest you, contact the SBA office in your state or go to the SBA's home page at http://www.sbaonline.sba.gov/).

Once an entrepreneur has identified the best region of the country, the next step is to evaluate the individual states in that region.

The State

Every state has a business development office to recruit new businesses to that state. Even though the publications produced by these offices will be biased in favor of locating in that state, they still are an excellent source of facts and can help you assess the business climate in each state. Some of the key issues to explore include the laws, regulations, and taxes that govern businesses and any incentives or investment credits the state may offer to businesses locating there. Other factors to consider include proximity to markets, proximity to raw materials, quantity and quality of the labor supply, general business climate, and wage rates.

PROXIMITY TO MARKETS. Locating close to markets that manufacturing firms plan to serve is extremely critical when the cost of transportation of finished goods is high relative to their value. Locating near customers is necessary to remain competitive. Service firms often find that proximity to their clients is essential. If a business is involved in repairing equipment used in a specific industry, it should be located where that industry is concentrated. The more specialized the business, or the greater the relative cost of transporting the product to the customer, the more likely it is that proximity to the market will be of critical importance in the location decision.

PROXIMITY TO NEEDED RAW MATERIALS. If a business requires raw materials that are difficult or expensive to transport, it may need a location near the source of those materials.

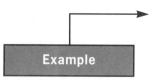

For instance, one producer of kitty litter chose a location on a major vein of kaolin, the highly absorbent clay from which kitty litter is made. Transporting the heavy, low-value material over long distances would be impractical—and unprofitable.

In other situations in which bulk or weight is not a factor, locating in close proximity to suppliers can facilitate quick deliveries and reduce holding costs for inventories. The value of products and materials, their cost of transportation, and their unique function all interact in determining how close a business needs to be to its source of supplies.

LABOR SUPPLY NEEDS. There are two distinct factors when analyzing labor supply needs: the number of workers available in the area, and their level of education, training, and experience. The potential business owner wants to know how many qualified people available in the area to do the work required in the business. However, unemployment and labor cost statistics can be misleading if a company needs people with specific qualifications. Some states have attempted to attract industry with the promise of cheap labor. Unfortunately, businesses locating there found exactly what the term implied—unskilled, low-wage labor. Unskilled laborers can be difficult to train, and many have poor work habits.

Knowing the exact nature of the labor needed and preparing job descriptions and job specifications in advance will help a business owner determine whether or not there is a good match with the available labor pool. Checking with the high schools, colleges, and universities in the state to determine the number of graduates in relevant fields of study will provide an idea of the local supply of qualified workers. Such planning will result in choosing a location with a steady source of quality labor.

BUSINESS CLIMATE. What is the state's overall attitude toward your kind of business? Has it passed laws that impose restrictions on the way a company can operate? Does the state impose a corporate income tax? Is there an inventory tax? Are there "blue laws" that prohibit certain business activity on Sundays? Does the state offer small business support programs or financial assistance to entrepreneurs? These are just some of the issues an owner must compare on a state-by-state basis to determine the most suitable location.

Some states are more "small business friendly" than others.

For instance, Entrepreneur *magazine recently named Minnesota's Minneapolis/St. Paul as one of the best areas for small businesses, citing its positive attitude toward growing and developing small companies as major assets. Many factors make the Twin Cities a desirable location, including its diversified industrial base, a strong base of private investors anxious to invest in promising small companies, one of the nation's highest SBA loan rates, and several state and local government support systems offering entrepreneurial assistance and advice. The area also boasts the Mall of America, the country's largest retail mall, and an innovative plan for revitalizing the city's downtown riverfront areas will create new opportunities for small businesses in the future.*[2]

Example

Gateway 2000

WAGE RATES. The existing wage rates will provide another measure for comparison among states. Entrepreneurs must be sure to measure the wage rates for jobs that relate to their particular industries or companies. In addition to government surveys, local newspapers will give you some idea of wages paid by competitors. Study the trend in wage rates. How does the rate of increase in wage rates compare among states? Another factor influencing wage rates is the level of union activity in a state. How much union organizing activity has the state seen within the past two years? Is it increasing or decreasing? Which industries have unions targeted in the recent past?

Gateway 2000, a mail-order personal computer maker offering high-performance hardware at bargain-basement prices, uses its location to gain a competitive edge in a hotly competitive industry. With constant downward pressure on computer prices, Gateway must keep its costs low. The company's location, North Sioux City, South Dakota—not exactly the heart of Silicon Valley—is one variable in its low-cost formula. South Dakota has no state corporate or personal income taxes, and the low cost of living appeals to employees. Gateway's starting wage for assembly workers—a bargain by national standards—is quite attractive in the local market. Most of the company's workers come from Iowa, known for the quality of its schools. The company's mid-continent location also keeps shipping costs low for a company selling computers nationwide, and managers are pleased with their employees' midwestern work ethic.[3]

Most entrepreneurs are amazed at the amount of specific information that exists if they search in the right places and ask the right questions. Obtaining and analyzing the information about a region and the states in it provide the entrepreneur with a clear picture of the most favorable location. The next phase of the location selection process concentrates on selecting the best city.

The City

POPULATION TRENDS. An entrepreneur should know more about a city and its various neighborhoods than do the people who live there. By analyzing population and other demographic data, an entrepreneur can examine a city in detail, and the location decision becomes more than a shot in the dark. Studying the characteristics of a city's residents, including population size and density, growth trends, family size, age breakdowns, education, income levels, job categories, sex, religion, race, and nationality gives an entrepreneur the facts she needs to make an informed location decision. In fact, using only basic census data, entrepreneurs can determine the value of the homes in an area, how many rooms they contain, how many bedrooms they contain, what percentage of the population own their homes, and how much residents' monthly rental or mortgage payments are. Imagine how useful such information would be to someone about to launch a bed and bath shop!

A company's location should match the market for its products or services, and assembling a demographic profile will tell an entrepreneur how well a particular site measures up to her target market's profile. For instance, an entrepreneur planning to open a fine china shop would likely want specific information on family income, size, age, and education. Such a shop would need to be in an area where people appreciate the product and have the discretionary income to purchase it.

Trends or shifts in population components may have more meaning than total population trends. For example, if a city's population is aging, its disposable income may be decreasing and the city may be gradually dying. On the other hand, a city may be experiencing rapid growth in the population of high-income, professional young people. For example, Atlanta, where the average age of inhabitants is 29, has seen an explosion of businesses aimed at young people with rising incomes and hearty appetites for consumption.

THE INDEX OF RETAIL SATURATION. For retailers, the number of customers in the trading area is an essential factor in predicting success. One traditional way to analyze potential sites is to compare them on the basis of the index of retail saturation (IRS).[4] The **index of retail saturation** is a measure of the potential sales per square foot of store space for a given product within a specific trading area. The index is the ratio of a trading area's sales potential for a particular product or service to its sales capacity:

$$IRS = \frac{C \times RE}{RF}$$

where

C = number of customers in the trading area

RE = retail expenditures—the average expenditure per person (\$) for the product in the trading area

RF = retail facilities—the total square feet of selling space allocated to the product in the trading area

This computation is an important one for any retailer to make. Locating in an area already saturated with competitors results in dismal sales volume and often leads to failure.

To illustrate the index of retail saturation, suppose that an entrepreneur looking at two sites for a shoe store finds that he needs sales of \$175 per square foot to be profitable. Site 1 has a trading area with 25,875 potential customers who spend an average of \$42 on shoes annually; the only competitor in the trading area has 6,000 square feet of selling space. Site 2 has 27,750 potential customers spending an average of \$43.50 on shoes annually; two competitors occupy 8,400 square feet of space.

index of retail saturation—*a measure of the potential sales per square foot of store space for a given product within a specific trading area; it is the ratio of a trading area's sales potential for a product or service to its sales capacity.*

Site 1

$$IRS = \frac{25,875 \times 42}{6,000}$$

$$= \$181.12 \text{ sales potential per square foot}$$

Site 2

$$IRS = \frac{27,750 \times 43.50}{8,400}$$

$$= \$143.71 \text{ sales potential per square foot}$$

Although site 2 appears to be more favorable on the surface, site 1 is superior on the index: site 2 fails to meet the minimum standard of $175 per square foot.

The amount of available data on the population of any city or town is staggering. These statistics allow a potential business owner to compare a wide variety of cities or towns and to narrow the choices to those few that warrant further investigation. The mass of data may make it possible to screen out undesirable locations, but it does not make a decision for an entrepreneur. The owner needs to see the locations firsthand. Only by personal investigation will the owner be able to add that intangible factor of intuition into the decision-making process.

LOCAL LAWS AND REGULATIONS. Before selecting a particular site within a city, the small business owner must explore the local zoning laws to determine if there are any ordinances that would place restrictions on business activity or that would prohibit establishing a business altogether. **Zoning** is a system that divides a city or county into small cells or districts to control the use of land, buildings, and sites. Its purpose is to contain similar activities in suitable locations. For instance, one section of a city may be zoned residential, while the primary retail district is zoned commercial and another is zoned industrial to house manufacturing operations. Before choosing a site, an entrepreneur must explore the zoning regulations governing it to make sure it is not "out of bounds." In some cases, an entrepreneur may appeal to the local zoning commission to rezone a site or to grant a **variance** (a special exception to a zoning ordinance), but this is risky and could be devastating if the board disallows the variance.

zoning—*a system that divides a city or county into small cells or districts to control the use of land, buildings, and sites.*

variance—*a special exemption to a zoning ordinance.*

COMPETITION. For some retailers, it makes sense to locate near competitors because similar businesses located near one another may serve to increase traffic flow. This location strategy works well for products for which customers are most likely to comparison shop. For instance, in many cities, auto dealers locate next to one another in a "motor mile," trying to create a shopping magnet for customers. The convenience of being able to shop for dozens of brands of cars all within a few hundred yards of one another draws customers from a sizable trading area. Of course, this strategy has limits. Overcrowding of businesses of the same type in an area can create an undesirable impact on the profitability of all competing firms. Consider the specific nature of the businesses in the area. Do they offer the same quality merchandise or comparable services? The products or services of a business may be superior to those which competitors presently offer.

Studying the size of the market for a product or service and the number of existing competitors will help an entrepreneur determine whether she can capture a sufficiently large market share to earn a profit. Again, Census Bureau reports can be a valuable source of information. The *County Business Patterns Economic Profile* shows the breakdown of businesses in manufacturing, wholesale, retail, and service categories and estimates companies' annual payrolls and number of employees. The *Economic Census*, which covers 15 million businesses and is produced in years that end in "2" and "7," gives an overview of the businesses in an area—their sales (or other measure of output), employment, payroll, and form of organization. It covers eight industry categories including retail, wholesale, service, manufacturing, construction, and others, giving statistics at not only the national level, but also by state, MSA, county, places with 2,500+ inhabitants, and zip code. The *Economic Census* is a useful tool for helping an entrepreneur determine whether or not an area he is considering as a location is already saturated with competitors.

COMPATIBILITY WITH THE COMMUNITY. One of the intangibles that can be determined only by a visit is the degree of compatibility a business has with the surrounding community. In other words, a company's image must fit in with the character of a town and the needs and wants of its residents. Consider the costs associated with opening a business in a high-income community. The business would need to match the flavor of the surrounding businesses. Rents, along with fixtures and other decor items, would likely be expensive. Is there an adequate markup in your merchandise to justify such costs?

TRANSPORTATION. Manufacturers and wholesalers must investigate the quality of local transportation systems. If you need to locate on a railroad spur, is such a location available in the city you are considering? How regular is truck service? Are the transportation rates reasonable? In some situations, double or triple handling of merchandise and inventory

---

YOU BE THE CONSULTANT...

From Theory to Practice

After serving six years in the United States Air Force, Mark Dickerson knew what he did not want to do: work for someone else. Instead, his goal was to use the skills and knowledge he had gained in his two years of technical school and his years in the Air Force and start a business of his own. From his teenage years, Mark had loved to work with metals. His inspiration was his father, who had been a machinist at a local factory for his entire career and had a workshop in the family garage, where Mark grew up learning important skills at his father's side. After graduating from high school, Mark enrolled in the metallurgical science program at a nearby technical school, where he excelled in his classes. His associate's degree in metallurgy helped Mark land a highly desirable work assignment in specialty metals in the Air Force, where he further honed his metallurgy skills. "It was almost like a continuation of school," says Mark. "For five years, I had the chance to work with people who were experts in the field of metallurgy." Those years not only increased his knowledge and experience base in metals, but they also deepened his commitment to a career in metallurgy.

During his years in the Air Force, Mark noticed that industries such as automaking and jet building were using more exotic metals and metal composites—the same ones he had experience with in the Air Force—in their manufacturing processes. He also saw that heavy manufacturers were installing increasingly complex tools made from these new

metals to meet rising productivity and quality targets. "They're going to need someone to work with those metals and to repair those tools," Mark thought. "Why not me?!"

Mark had saved some money while in the Air Force. He had $20,000 of his own money and a firm commitment from his father to lend him another $25,000 to get his business off the ground. For the past four months, he has been working with a local Small Business Development Center and a small bank on a business plan and an application for a Small Business Administration guaranteed loan. According to the banker, the odds of Mark getting the loan are very high.

Everything about Mark's plan seems to be on track except one thing: Mark has yet to pick the exact location of his business.

1. Assume the role of consultant. What questions would you ask Mark about his business and his target customers before helping him choose a location?

2. What potential environmental problems might be associated with this type of business? What impact might they have on Mark's final location decision?

3. Modify Table 11.1 (see page 360) to include the factors you think would most likely affect Mark's decision on the ideal location for his business.

4. Using library resources and the World Wide Web, analyze two potential sites for Mark's business and be prepared to defend your recommendation.

causes transportation costs to skyrocket. For retailers, the availability of loading and unloading zones is an important feature of a suitable location. Some downtown locations suffer from a lack of sufficient space for carriers to unload deliveries of merchandise.

POLICE AND FIRE PROTECTION. Does the community in which you plan to locate offer adequate police and fire protection? If these services are not adequate, it will be reflected in the cost of the company's business insurance.

PUBLIC SERVICES. The location should be served by some governmental unit that provides water and sewer services, trash and garbage collection, and other necessary utilities. The streets should be in good repair with adequate drainage. If the location is not within the jurisdiction of a municipality that provides these services, they will become a continuing cost to the business.

THE LOCATION'S REPUTATION. Like people, a city or parts of a city can have a bad reputation. In some cases the reputation of the previous business will lower the value of the location. Sites where businesses have failed again and again create negative impressions in customers' minds; they view the business as just another that will soon be gone.

One restaurateur struggled early on to overcome the negative image his new location had acquired over the years as one restaurant after another had failed there. He eventually established a base of loyal customers and succeeded, but it was a slow and trying process.

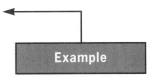

Example

The Site

The final step in the location selection process is choosing the actual site for the business. Again, *facts* will guide the entrepreneur to the best location decision. Each type of business has different evaluation criteria for what makes an ideal location. A manufacturer's prime consideration may be access to raw materials, suppliers, labor, transportation, and customers. Service firms need access to customers but can generally survive in lower-rent properties. A retailer's prime consideration is customer traffic. The one element common to all three is the need to locate where customers want to do business.

Site location draws on the most precise information available on the makeup of the area. Through the use of the published statistics mentioned earlier in this chapter, an owner can develop valuable insights regarding the characteristics of people and businesses in the immediate community.

Would you like to know how many people or families are living in your trading area, what type of jobs they have, how much money they make, their ages, the value of their homes, and their education level, as well as a variety of other useful information? Sometimes businesses pay large fees to firms and consultants for this market research information. However, this information is available *free* from your public library and the various publications of the Census Bureau. (There are fees for some Census Bureau publications and reports, however.) Every decade, the U.S. government undertakes the most ambitious market research project in the world, collecting incredibly detailed statistics on the nation's 267 million residents! The Census Bureau has divided the United States into 255 metropolitan statistical areas (MSAs). These MSAs are then subdivided into census tracts. The average census tract contains 4,000 to 5,000 people. These census tracts are subdivided into block statistics and are available only for urban areas.

This mother lode of market research is available to entrepreneurs through some 1,300 state data centers across the country. As always, the data come in a multitude of printed reports. Two reports entrepreneurs find especially useful when choosing locations are *Summary Population and Housing Characteristics*, which provides a broad demographic

"This looks like a good spot."

Source: Drawing by Chas. Addams. © 1987 The New Yorker Magazine, Inc.

look at an area, and *Population and Housing Characteristics for Census Tracts and Block Numbering Areas*, which offers a detailed breakdown of areas as small as city blocks. The data are available on CD-ROM and on the World Wide Web at the Census Bureau's home page. Any small business owner with a properly equipped personal computer can access this incredible wealth of data with a few clicks of a mouse.

Location Criteria for Retail and Service Businesses

2. Describe the location criteria for retail and service businesses.

RETAIL BUSINESSES. Few decisions are as important for retailers than the choice of a location. Because their success depends upon a steady flow of customers, retailers must locate their businesses with their target customers' convenience and preferences in mind. The following are important considerations.

trade area—*the region from which a business can expect to draw customers over a reasonable time span.*

TRADE AREA SIZE. Every retail business should determine the extent of its **trade area**—the region from which a business can expect to draw customers over a reasonable time span. The primary variables that influence the scope of a trading area are the type and size of the operation. If a retailer is a specialist with a wide assortment of products, he may draw customers from a great distance. In contrast, a convenience store with a general line of merchandise may have a small trading area because it is unlikely that customers would drive across town to purchase what is available within blocks of their homes or businesses. As a rule, the larger the store and the greater the selection, the broader its trading area.

The following environmental factors influence the retail trading area size.

retail compatibility— *the benefits a company receives by locating near other businesses selling complementary products and services.*

Retail Compatibility. Shoppers tend to be drawn to clusters of related businesses. That's one reason shopping malls and outlet shopping centers are popular destinations for shoppers and are attractive locations for retailers. The concentration of businesses pulls customers from a larger trading area than a single free-standing business does. **Retail compatibility** describes the benefits a company receives by locating near other businesses selling complementary products and services. Clever business owners choose their locations with an eye on the surrounding mix of businesses.

When Vic and Suzette Brounsuzian started Meg-A-Nut Inc., a retail shop selling fine chocolates and nuts, they wanted to find just the right location for it. Vic invested considerable time investigating potential sites and studying their demographic profiles using census data and information from a local Small Business Development Center. He also analyzed each site's existing businesses to judge their retail compatibility with Meg-A-Nut. "I learned all about the kinds of people who live in the area," he says, "their salary ranges, purchasing habits, and all that—and I made sure to choose a location where other businesses were coming in to provide a solid merchant mix." Relying on the concept of retail compatibility, the Brounsuzians decided to locate their shop in a growing shopping plaza near a movie theater. "Since we're so close to the theater, we expected that people on the way to see a movie would stop in, pick up a little snack, . . . and munch on it . . . It's working out that way," explains Vic.[5]

Meg-A-Nut Inc.

Degree of Competition. The size, location, and activity of competing businesses also influence the size of the trading area. If a business will be the first of its kind in a location, its trading area might be quite extensive. However, if the area already has eight or ten nearby stores that directly compete with a business, its trading area might be very small. How does the size of your planned operation compare with those that presently exist? Your business may be significantly larger and have more drawing power, giving it a competitive advantage.

Transportation Network. The transportation networks are the highways, roads, and public service routes that presently exist or are planned. If it is inconvenient to get to an area, its trading area is reduced. Entrepreneurs should check to see if the transportation system works smoothly and is free of barriers that might prevent customers from reaching their stores. Is it easy to cross traffic if the customer is traveling in the opposite direction? Are there turn signals or well-planned traffic patterns?

Physical, Racial, or Political Barriers. Trading area shape and size also are influenced by physical, racial, or political barriers that may exist. Physical barriers may be parks, rivers, lakes, or any other obstruction that hinders customers' access to the area. Locating on one side of a large park may reduce the number of customers that will drive around it to get to the store. If high-crime areas exist in any direction from the site, most of a company's potential customers will not travel through those neighborhoods to reach the business.

In urban areas, new immigrants tend to cluster together, sharing a common culture and language. Some areas are defined by cultural barriers, where inhabitants patronize only the businesses in their neighborhoods. The Little Havana section of Miami or the Chinatown sections of San Francisco, New York, and Los Angeles are examples.

Political barriers are creations of law. County, city, or state boundaries—and the laws within those boundaries—are examples. For instance, in South Carolina, some counties have outlawed video poker machines while others allow them. In the counties where betting on video poker is legal, hundreds of small video parlors have sprung up, especially near the borders of the counties that no longer permit the practice. State tax laws also create conditions where customers cross over to the next state to save money. For instance, North Carolina imposes a very low cigarette tax, and shops located on its borders do a brisk business in the product.

Other factors retailers should consider when evaluating potential sites follow.

CUSTOMER TRAFFIC. Perhaps the most important screening criteria for a potential retail (and often for a service) location is the number of potential customers passing by the site during business hours. To be successful, a business must be able to generate sufficient sales to surpass its breakeven point, and that requires an ample volume of customer traffic going past its doors. One of the key success factors for a convenience store, for instance, is a high-volume location with easy accessibility. Entrepreneurs should know the traffic counts (pedestrian and/or auto) at the sites they are considering as potential locations.

Express Shipping Centers, a network of UPS shipping centers, knows that locating in convenient, high-traffic destinations is central to its success. In just five years, the company has set up more than 4,000 locations across the United States, almost all within supermarkets. "Our whole business is making UPS convenient for consumers, and supermarkets are the best place to do that," says CEO Ken Ross. With no self-standing storefronts of its own, Express Shipping Center's "store within a store" concept generates $11 million in annual sales.[6]

ADEQUATE PARKING. If customers cannot find convenient and safe parking, they are not likely to stop in the area. Many downtown areas have lost customers because of inadequate parking. Although shopping malls typically average five parking spaces per 1,000 square feet of shopping space, many central business districts get by with 3.5 spaces per 1,000 square feet. Customers generally will not pay to park if parking is free at shopping centers or in front of competing stores. Even when free parking is provided, some potential customers may not feel safe on the streets, especially after dark. Many large city downtown business districts become virtual ghost towns at the end of the business day. A location where traffic vanishes after 6 p.m. may not be as valuable as mall and shopping center locations that mark the beginning of the prime sales time at 6 p.m.

ROOM FOR EXPANSION. A location should be flexible enough to provide for expansion if success warrants it. Failure to consider this factor can result in a successful business being forced to open a second store when it would have been better to expand in its original location.

VISIBILITY. No matter what a small business sells and how well it serves customers' needs, it cannot survive without visibility. Highly visible locations simply make it easy for customers to make purchases. A site lacking visibility puts a company at a major disadvantage before it ever opens its doors for business.

Coffee, Etc.

Consider the story of Coffee, Etc., a small gourmet coffee store/restaurant in San Francisco. Located on the outside of a suburban mall, the store attracted shoppers and mall employees. Then mall owners remodeled the center, building a large department store over the old parking lot. Coffee, Etc. found itself literally hidden in the shadow of the new store, completely invisible to automobile traffic. Sales dropped off, and within a year the store went out of business. Several other restaurants tried the location, but all of them failed. The site remains vacant.[7]

3. Outline the basic location options for retail and service businesses.

Basic Location Options for Retail and Service Businesses

There are six basic areas where the retailer and the service business owner can locate: the central business district (CBD); neighborhoods; shopping centers and malls; near competitors; outlying areas; and at home. According to the International Council of Shopping Centers, the average cost to lease space in a shopping center is about $15 per square foot. At a regional mall, rental rates run from $20 to $40 per square foot, and in central business locations, the average cost is $43 per square foot (although rental rates can vary significantly in either direction of that average, depending upon the city.)[8] Of course, cost is just one factor a business owner must consider when choosing a location.

central business district—the traditional center of town where businesses located in the early development of towns and cities.

CENTRAL BUSINESS DISTRICT. The **central business district (CBD)** is the traditional center of town—the downtown concentration of businesses established early in the development of most towns and cities. The small business owner derives several advantages from a downtown location. Because the firm is centrally located, it attracts customers from the entire trading area of the city. Also, the small business usually benefits from the customer traffic generated by the other stores in the district. However, locating in a CBD does have certain disadvantages. Many CBDs are characterized by intense competition, high rental rates, traffic congestion, and inadequate parking facilities. In addition, many cities are experiencing difficulty in preventing the decay of their older downtown business districts as a result of "mall withdrawal." Many shoppers simply prefer the convenience of modern shopping malls to the unique atmosphere of the traditional downtown.

NEIGHBORHOOD LOCATIONS. Small businesses that locate near residential areas rely heavily on the local trading areas for business. For example, many convenience stores located just outside residential subdivisions count on local clientele for successful operation. The primary advantages of a neighborhood location include relatively low operating costs and rents, and close contact with customers.

SHOPPING CENTERS AND MALLS. Shopping centers and malls have experienced explosive growth over the last three decades. Since 1960 the number of shopping centers and malls in the United States has increased 1500 percent! More than 41,000 of them now dot our nation's landscape, occupying 4.97 billion square feet of retail space.[9] Because many different types of stores exist under a single roof, shopping malls give meaning to the term *one-stop shopping*. Following are four types of shopping centers.

★ *Neighborhood Shopping Centers*. The typical neighborhood shopping center is relatively small, containing from three to twelve stores and serving a population of up to 40,000 people who live within a 10-minute drive.

★ *Community Shopping Centers*. The community shopping center contains from 12 to 50 stores and serves a population ranging from 40,000 to 150,000 people.

★ *Regional Shopping Malls*. The regional shopping mall serves a much larger trading area, usually from 10 to 15 miles or more in all directions. It contains from 50 to 100 stores and serves a population in excess of 150,000 people living within a 20- to 40-minute drive.

★ *Power Centers*. A power center combines the drawing strength of a large regional mall with the convenience of a neighborhood shopping center. Anchored by large specialty retailers, these centers target older, wealthier baby boomers, who want selection and convenience.

When evaluating a mall or shopping center location, an entrepreneur should consider these questions: [10]

★ Is there a good fit with other products and brands sold in the mall or center?

★ Who are the other tenants? Which stores are the anchors that will bring people into the mall or center?

★ Demographically, is the center a good fit for your products or services? What are its customer demographics?

★ How much foot traffic does the mall or center generate? How much traffic passes the specific site you are considering?

★ How much vehicle traffic does the mall or center generate? Check its proximity to major population centers, the volume of tourists it draws, and the volume of drive-by freeway traffic. A mall or center that scores well on all three is probably a winner.

★ What is the vacancy rate? The turnover rate?

★ Is the mall or center successful? How many dollars in sales does it generate per square foot? Compare its record against industry averages. (The International Council of Shopping Centers in New York [telephone (212) 421-8181] is a good source of industry information. Its Web address is: http://www.icsc.org/).

NEAR COMPETITORS. One of the most important factors in choosing a retail or service location is the compatibility of nearby stores with the retail or service customer. For example, stores selling high-priced goods find it advantageous to locate near competitors to facilitate comparison shopping. Locating near competitors might be a key factor for success in those businesses selling goods that customers shop for and compare on the basis of price, quality, color, and other factors.

OUTLYING AREAS. Generally, it is not advisable for a small business to locate in a remote area because accessibility and traffic flow are vital to retail and service success, but there are exceptions. Some small firms have turned their remote locations into trademarks. One small gun shop was able to use its extremely remote location to its advantage by incorporating this into its advertising to distinguish itself from its competitors.

HOME-BASED BUSINESSES. For 27.1 million people (14 million full-time and 13.1 million part-time), home is where the business is, and their numbers are swelling. Home-based businesses represent 25 percent of all newly created small companies.[11] Although a home-based retail business is usually not feasible, locating a service business at home is quite popular. Many service companies do not have customers come to their places of business, so an expensive office location is not necessary. For instance, customers typically contact plumbers or exterminators by telephone, and the work is performed in the customers' homes.

Entrepreneurs locating their businesses at home reap several benefits. Perhaps the biggest benefit is the low cost of setting up the business. Most often, home-based entrepreneurs set up shop in a spare bedroom or basement, avoiding the cost of renting, leasing, or buying a building. With a few basic pieces of office equipment such as a computer, fax machine, copier, telephone answering system, and scanner, a lone entrepreneur can perform just like a major corporation.

> **Truth and Fun Inc.**

For instance, David Gans runs Truth and Fun Inc., a state-of-the-art production studio, from a spare bedroom in his Oakland, California home. From his high-tech, in-home studio, Gans produces a weekly radio show, the Grateful Dead Hour, that he beams by satellite to 90 radio stations across the country. "The equipment has gotten so powerful and inexpensive that one human being working from home can produce the exact same-quality program as National Public Radio," says Gans.[12]

Choosing a home location has certain disadvantages, however. Interruptions are more frequent, the refrigerator is all too handy, work is always just a few steps away, and isolation can be a problem. Another problem for some entrepreneurs running businesses from their homes involves zoning laws. As their businesses grow and become more successful, entrepreneurs' neighbors often begin to complain about the increased traffic, noise, and disruptions from deliveries, employees, and customers who drive through their residential neighborhoods to conduct business. Many states now face the challenge of passing updated zoning laws that reflect the reality of today's home-based businesses while protecting the interests of residential homeowners.

4. Explain the site selection process for manufacturers.

The Location Decision for Manufacturers

The criteria for the location decision for manufacturers is very different from those of retailers and service businesses; however, the decision can have just as much impact on the company's success. In some cases, a manufacturer has special needs that influence the choice of a location. For instance, when one manufacturer of photographic plates and film was searching for a location for a new plant, it had to limit its search only to those sites with a large supply of available fresh water, a necessary part of its process.

Local zoning ordinances will limit a manufacturer's choice of location. If the manufacturing process creates offensive odors or noise, the business may be even further restricted

Too Spicy, or Just Right?

Scott Shaw is in the restaurant business, and he and his partner had been very successful since opening their first eatery, Austin Grill, in Washington, DC in 1987. Their southwestern-style restaurant was not a carbon copy of the typical Mexican chain. In fact, its unique—and spicy—menu was one of the keys to their success. Their formula was a hit from the start, and within a few years, the partners opened a second Austin Grill in Alexandria, VA. That restaurant's success led Shaw and his partner to open Jaleo, an authentic Spanish tapas restaurant.

Then, as they decided to expand, they faced a series of tough location decisions that would determine the future of their company. Shaw had moved to Miami, and he approached his partner with the idea of expanding their unique brand of "Tex-Mex" restaurants to Florida. His partner eagerly agreed. Shaw recalls, "A funny thing happened on the way to the real estate office. We began to look around at the growing success of other Tex-Mex chains around the country and saw an opportunity to join the stampede. Our location strategy was a big problem, however. To raise big dollars, we needed to prove that our concept would work outside the urban markets we had been successful in. So we went off to look for the same kind of suburban locations in South Florida that the big chains were looking for."

Shaw and his partner chose upscale Boca Raton for their restaurant's location. It's an affluent city-suburb whose demographic profile shows a strong concentration of high-income young people. Even though other Tex-Mex restaurants had failed there, Shaw and his partner took the plunge and opened Austin Grill. After all, they reasoned, there were no other Tex-Mex restaurants in town. Plus, Boca Raton is home to some of the highest-volume restaurants of several major chains. How could they miss?

They leased an expensive site just a few doors down from one of the city's most successful restaurants that catered to young families and singles. The layout they created had seating space for 250 customers, 50% larger than anything they had done before. But, with more seats available, they figured they could break even at sales of $8,000 per seat, versus the $19,000 per seat their top restaurant in Washington, DC was generating.

Still, Shaw couldn't help but wonder. Would customers like the spicy salsas, the tartness of the fresh lime margaritas, and the lack of "traditional" Mexican dishes—all the things that made their Washington restaurant a success? Shaw knew the importance of making the correct location decision. "In our business you get only one chance to make a good impression and get word of mouth going," he says.

1. What information would you recommend Shaw and his partner collect before they make the decision about the Boca Raton market?

2. How should they collect this information?

3. Do you see any indications of red flags that might warn Shaw and his partner that Boca Raton might not be the best site for their new location?

4. Use the library or the World Wide Web to collect demographic information on the city of Boca Raton, Florida. What would you recommend to Shaw? Explain.

Source: Adapted from Scott Shaw, "The Wrong Move," *Inc.*, August 1995, pp. 21–22.

---

in its choices. City and county planners will be able to show potential manufacturers the areas of the city or county set aside for industrial development. Some cities have developed industrial parks in cooperation with private industry. These industrial parks typically are equipped with sewage and electrical power sufficient for manufacturing. Many locations are not so equipped, and it can be extremely expensive for a small manufacturer to have such utilities brought to an existing site.

Location of the plant can, in some cases, be dictated by the type of transportation facilities needed. Some manufacturers may need to locate on a railroad siding, while others may only need reliable trucking service. If raw materials are purchased by the carload for economies of scale, the location must be convenient to a railroad siding. Bulk materials are sometimes shipped by barge and, consequently, require a facility convenient to a navigable river or lake. The added cost of using multiple shipping (i.e., rail-to-truck or barge-to-truck) can significantly increase shipping costs and make a location unfeasible for a manufacturer.

In some cases the perishability of the product dictates location. Vegetables and fruits must be canned in close proximity to the fields in which they are harvested. Fish must be processed and canned at the water's edge. Location is determined by quick and easy access to the perishable products.

Table 11.1
Rating the Suitability of
Sites for a Business

Common Factors	Factor Importance (10 high—1 low)	
Located to serve the customer (demographic trends)		
Cost of the location (rent or purchase price)		
Quantity and quality of the labor supply		
Zoning restrictions		
General business climate		
Transporation —For customers (highways, public transportation)		
—For raw material or inventories (rail, barge, air freight)		
Proximity to raw material or inventory		
Quality of public services (fire and police protection)		
Taxes (if owning)		
Adequacy for future expansion		
Value of the site in future years		
Labor cost and anticipated productivity		

Needed utilities, zoning, transportation, and special requirements all work together to limit the number of locations that are suitable for a manufacturer. Table 11.1 provides a rating system to determine the suitability of various locations.

5. Discuss the benefits of locating a startup company in a business incubator.

Business Incubators: A Low-Cost Alternative for Business Startups

For many startup companies, a business incubator may make the ideal initial location. A **business incubator** is an organization that combines low-cost, flexible rental space with a multitude of support services for its small business residents. The overwhelming reason for establishing an incubator is to enhance economic development in an area and to diversify the local economy. Common sponsors of incubators include government agencies (49 percent), colleges or universities (13 percent), partnerships among government, nonprofit agencies, and/or private developers (18 percent), and private investment groups (12 percent). Business and technical incubators vary to some degree as to the types of clients they

	Actual Scores for Alternative Sites (10 high—1 low)				Total Scores for Alternative Sites (Factor Importance × Actual Score)			
	Site A	Site B	Site C	Site D	Site A	Site B	Site C	Site D

TOTAL _____ _____ _____ _____

_____ _____ _____ _____

Highest-scoring site is:_____

attempt to attract, but most incubator residents are engaged in light manufacturing, service businesses, and technology- or research-related fields. [13]

The shared resources incubators typically provide their tenants include secretarial services, a telephone system, a computer and software, fax machines, and meeting facilities; and, sometimes, management consulting services. An incubator will normally have entry requirements that are tied to its purpose and that detail the nature and scope of the business activities to be conducted. Incubators also have criteria that establish the conditions a business must meet to remain in the facility as well as the expectations for "graduation" into the business community.

More than 550 active incubators operate across the United States, and a new incubator opens, on average, every week. Most receive some type of financial assistance from their sponsors to continue operations. The investment that supports the incubator is generally a wise one because firms that graduate from incubators have only an 11 percent failure rate. The average incubator houses 17 ongoing businesses employing 55 people.

business incubator—*an organization that combines low-cost, flexible rental space with a multitude of support services for its small business residents.*

Layout and Design Considerations

Once an entrepreneur chooses the best location for her business, she must begin thinking about designing the proper layout for the building to maximize sales (retail) or productivity (manufacturing or service). **Layout** is the logical arrangement of the physical facilities in a business that contributes to efficient operations, increased productivity, and higher sales. To begin this process, an entrepreneur must set forth the criteria for her building.

layout—*the logical arrangement of the physical facilities in a business that contributes to efficient operations, increased productivity, and higher sales.*

Criteria Analysis for the Building

Planning for the most effective and efficient use of space in a business environment can produce dramatic improvements in a company's operating effectiveness and efficiency. Wise small business owners understand that attention to detail is crucial when designing a proper layout for a business. The following factors have a significant impact on a building's layout and design.

SIZE. A building must be large enough to accommodate a business's daily operations comfortably. If it is too small at the outset of operations, efficiency will suffer. There must be room enough for customers' movement, inventory, displays, storage, work areas, offices, and restrooms. Haphazard layouts undermine employee productivity and create organizational chaos. Too many small business owners start their operations in locations that are already overcrowded and lack room for expansion. The result is that the owner is forced to make a costly move to a new location within the first few years of operation.

If an owner plans to expand in any way, will the building accommodate it? Will hiring new employees, purchasing new equipment, expanding production areas, increasing service areas, and other growth require a new location? How fast is the company expected to grow over the next three to five years? Lack of adequate room in the building may become a limitation on the growth of the business. Most small businesses wait too long before moving into larger quarters, and they fail to plan the new space arrangements properly. To avoid such problems, some experts recommend that new businesses plan their space requirements one to two years ahead and update the estimates every six months. When preparing the plan, managers should include the expected growth in the number of employees, manufacturing, selling, or storage space requirements, and the number and location of branches to be opened.

CONSTRUCTION AND EXTERNAL APPEARANCE. Is the construction of the building sound? It pays to have an expert look it over before buying or leasing the property. Beyond the soundness of construction, does the building have an attractive external and internal appearance? The physical appearance of the building provides customers with their first impression of a business. This is especially true in retail businesses. Many retailers provide the customer with a consistent building appearance as they expand (e.g., fast-food restaurants and motels). Is the building's appearance consistent with the entrepreneur's desired image for the business?

Small retailers must recognize the importance of creating the proper image for their stores and how their shops' layouts and physical facilities influence this image. The store's external appearance contributes significantly to establishing its identity in the customer's mind. In many ways the building's appearance sets the tone for what the customer can expect in the way of quality and service. The appearance should, therefore, reflect the business's "personality." Should the building project an exclusive image or an economical one? Is the atmosphere informal and relaxed or formal and businesslike? Physical facilities send important messages to customers.

Externally, the storefront, its architectural style and color, signs, entrances, and general appearance give important clues to customers about a business's image. Internally, store layout, fixtures, colors, and displays perform the same function. An owner must strive to create the appropriate image in the customer's mind. Communicating the right signal through layout and physical facilities is an important step in creating a competitive edge over rivals.

ENTRANCES. All entrances to a business should invite customers in. Wide entryways and attractive merchandise displays that are set back from the doorway can draw customers into a business. Retailers with heavy traffic flows such as supermarkets or drugstores often install automatic doors to ensure a smooth traffic flow into and out of their stores. Retailers should remove any barriers that interfere with customers' easy access to the storefront. Broken sidewalks, sagging steps, mud puddles, and sticking or heavy doors not only create obstacles that might discourage potential customers but they also create legal hazards for a business if they cause customers to be injured.

THE AMERICANS WITH DISABILITIES ACT. **The Americans with Disabilities Act (ADA)**, passed in July 1990, requires practically all businesses to make their facilities available to physically challenged customers and employees. In addition, the law requires businesses with 15 or more employees to accommodate physically challenged candidates in their hiring practices. The rules of the ADA's Title III are designed to ensure that mentally and physically challenged customers have equal access to a firm's goods or services. For instance, the act requires business owners to remove architectural and communication barriers when "readily achievable." The ADA allows flexibility in how a business achieves this equal access, however. For example, a restaurant could either provide menus in Braille or could offer to have a staff member read the menu to blind customers. Or, a small dry cleaner might not be able to add a wheelchair ramp to its storefront without incurring significant expense, but the owner could comply with the ADA by offering curbside pickup and delivery services for disabled customers at no extra charge.

Although the law allows a good deal of flexibility in retrofitting existing structures, buildings that were occupied after January 25, 1993 must be designed to comply with all aspects of the law. For example, buildings with three stories or more must have elevators; anywhere the floor level changes by more than one-half inch, an access ramp must be in place. In retail stores, checkout aisles must be wide enough—at least 36 inches—to accommodate wheelchairs. Restaurants must have 5 percent of their tables accessible to wheelchair-bound patrons.

Complying with the ADA does not necessarily require businesses to spend large amounts of money. The Justice Department estimates that more than 20 percent of the cases customers have filed under Title III involved changes the business owners could have made at no cost![14] In addition, companies with $1 million or less in annual sales or with 30 or fewer full-time employees that invest in making their locations more accessible to all qualify for a tax credit. The credit is 50 percent of their expenses exceeding $250 but not more than $10,250.

The ADA also prohibits any kind of employment discrimination against anyone with a physical or mental disability. A physically challenged person is considered to be "qualified" if he can perform the essential functions of the job. The employer must make "reasonable accommodation" for a physically challenged candidate or employee without causing "undue hardship" to the business.

The following are some of the specific provisions of Title III of the act, which requires businesses to make public accommodations and services available to everyone.

☆ Restaurants, hotels, theaters, shopping centers and malls, retail stores, museums, libraries, parks, private schools, daycare centers, and other similar places of public accommodation may not discriminate on the basis of disability.

Americans with Disabilities Act (ADA)— *a law that requires businesses with 15 or more employees to make their facilities available to physically challenged customers and employees.*

★ Physical barriers in existing places of public accommodation must be removed if readily achievable (i.e., easily accomplished and able to be carried out without much difficulty or expense). If not, alternative methods of providing services must be offered, if those methods are readily achievable.

★ New construction of places of public accommodation and commercial facilities (nonresidential facilities affecting commerce) must be accessible.

★ Alterations to existing places of public accommodation and commercial facilities must be done in an accessible manner. When alterations affect the utility of or access to "primary function" areas of a facility, an accessible path of travel must be provided to the altered areas, and the restrooms, telephones, and drinking fountains serving the altered areas must also be accessible, to the extent that the cost of making these features accessible does not exceed 20 percent of the cost of the planned alterations. The additional accessibility requirements for alterations to "primary function" areas do not apply to measures taken solely to comply with readily achievable barrier removal.

★ Elevators are not required in newly constructed or altered buildings under three stories or with less than 3,000 square feet per floor, unless the building is a shopping center, shopping mall, professional office of a health care provider, terminal, depot, or other station used for specific public transportation, or an airport passenger terminal.

The Americans with Disabilities Act has affected, in a positive way, how businesses deal with this segment of their customers and employees.

SIGNS. One of the most low-cost and effective methods of communicating with customers is a business sign. Signs tell potential customers what a business does, where it is, and what it is selling. America is a very mobile society, and a well-designed, well-placed sign can be a powerful tool for reaching potential customers.

A sign should be large enough for passersby to read it from a distance, taking into consideration the location and speed of surrounding traffic arteries. To be most effective, the message should be short, simple, and clear. A sign should be legible in both daylight and at night; proper illumination is a must. Contrasting colors and simple typefaces are best. The most common problems with business signs are that they are illegible, poorly designed, improperly located, poorly maintained, and have color schemes that are unattractive or are hard to read.

Before investing in a sign, an entrepreneur should investigate the local community's sign ordinance. In some cities and towns, local regulations impose restrictions on the size, location, height, and construction materials used in business signs.

BUILDING INTERIORS. Like exterior considerations, the functional aspects of building interiors are very important and require careful evaluation. Designing a functional, efficient interior is not easy. Technology has changed drastically the way employees, customers, and the environment interact with one another.

ergonomics—the science of adapting work and the work environment to complement employees' strengths and to suit customers' needs.

Piecing together an effective layout is not a haphazard process. **Ergonomics,** the science of adapting work and the work environment to complement employees' strengths and to suit customers' needs, is an integral part of a successful design. For example, chairs, desks, and table heights that allow people to work comfortably can help employees perform their jobs faster and more easily. Design experts claim that improved lighting, better acoustics, and proper climate control benefit the company as well as employees. Proper layout is an important ingredient in projecting the appropriate business image for both employees and customers. It reflects the way a company projects itself to those inside and outside the business.

When planning store, office, or plant layouts, business owners too often focus on minimizing costs. Although staying within a budget is important, enhancing employees' productivity or maximizing sales with an effective layout should be the overriding issue. One extensive six-year study concluded that changes in office design have a direct impact on workers' performance, job satisfaction, and ease of communication. The report also concluded that the savings generated by effective layouts are substantial, and conversely, that poorly planned designs involve significant costs.[15] Plus, retailers know that an effective store layout can increase traffic in their shops and boost sales and profits.

When evaluating an existing building's interior, an entrepreneur must be sure to determine the integrity of its structural components. Are the building's floors sufficiently strong to hold the business's equipment, inventories, and personnel? Strength is an especially critical factor for manufacturing firms that use heavy equipment. When multiple floors exist, are the upper floors anchored as solidly as the primary floor? Can inventory be moved safely and easily from one area of the plant to another? Is the floor space adequate for safe and efficient movement of goods and people? Consider the cost of maintaining the floors. Hardwood floors may be extremely attractive but require expensive and time-consuming maintenance. Carpeted floors may be extremely attractive in a retail business but may be totally impractical for a quality manufacturing firm. The small business manager must consider both the utility and durability of flooring materials as well as their maintenance requirements, attractiveness, and, if important, effectiveness in reducing noise.

Like floors, walls and ceilings must be both functional and attractive. On the functional side, walls and ceilings should be fireproof and soundproof. Are the colors of walls and ceilings compatible, and do they create an attractive atmosphere here? Retail stores should have a light and bright appearance. Ceilings should therefore be done in light colors to reflect the store's lighting.

Walls may range from purely functional, unpainted cement block in a factory to wallpapered showpieces in expensive restaurants and exclusive shops. Wall coverings are traditionally expensive and should be considered only when the additional cost will enhance the sale of goods or services.

For many businesses, a drive-through window adds another dimension to the concept of customer convenience and is a relatively inexpensive way to increase sales. Although drive-through windows are standard at fast-food restaurants and banks, they can add value for customers in a surprising number of businesses.

For instance, when Marshall Hoffman relocated his business, Steel Supply Company, to a building that had been used as a bank, the idea of using the drive-through window intrigued him. Looking for a way to improve customer service, Hoffman transformed the former bank lobby into his showroom floor and began advertising the convenience of buying steel at the drive-through window. Customers place their steel orders by telephone, pull up to the window and pay, and receive a ticket. The order goes by computer to a warehouse Hoffman built on the site. By the time the customer pulls up to the warehouse, the order is waiting! The window has been a hit with customers. Since moving into its new location, Steel Supply's sales have grown from $3.5 million to more than $6 million.[16]

> Steel Supply Company

LIGHTS AND FIXTURES. Good lighting allows employees to work at maximum efficiency. Proper lighting is measured by what is ideal for the job being done. Proper lighting in a factory may be quite different from that required in an office or retail shop. Retailers often use creative lighting to attract customers to a specific display. Jewelry stores provide excellent examples of how lighting can be used to display merchandise.

Lighting is often an inexpensive investment when considering its impact on the overall appearance of the business. Few people seek out businesses that are dimly lit because they convey an image of untrustworthiness. The use of natural and artificial light in combination can give a business an open and cheerful look. Many restaurant chains have added greenhouse glass additions to accomplish this.

The Big Decision: Build, Buy, or Lease

Now that the entrepreneur has a good idea of the specific criteria to be met for a building to serve the needs of her business, the issue turns to what she can afford to spend. The ability to obtain the best possible physical facilities in relation to available cash may depend largely on whether the entrepreneur decides to build, buy, or lease a building.

The Decision to Build

If a business had unlimited funds, the owner could design and build a perfect facility. However, few new business owners have this luxury. Constructing a new facility can project a positive image to potential customers. The business looks new and consequently creates an image of being modern, efficient, and top quality. A new building can incorporate the most modern features during construction, and these might significantly lower operating costs. When such costs are critical to remaining competitive, it may be reasonable to build.

In some rapidly growing areas, there are few or no existing buildings to buy or lease that match the entrepreneur's requirements. In these situations, a business owner must consider the cost of constructing a building as a significant factor in her initial estimates of capital needs and breakeven point. Constructing a building has high initial fixed expenses that an owner must weigh against the facility's ability to attract additional sales revenue and to reduce operating costs.

The Decision to Buy

In many cases, there may be an ideal building in the area where an entrepreneur wants to locate. Buying the facility allows her to remodel it without seeking permission from anyone else. As with building, buying can put a drain on the business's financial resources, but the owner knows exactly what her monthly payments will be. Under a lease, rental rates can (and usually do) increase over time. If an owner believes that the property will actually appreciate in value, a decision to purchase may prove to be a wise investment. In addition, the owner can depreciate the building each year, and both depreciation and interest are tax-deductible expenses.

When considering the purchase of a building, the owner should use the same outline of facilities requirements developed for the building option to ensure that this property will not be excessively expensive to modify for his use. Remodeling can add a significant initial expense. The layout of the building may be suitable in many ways, but it may not be ideal for a particular business. Even if a building housed the same kind of business, its existing layout may be completely unsuitable for the way the new owner plans to operate.

Building or buying a building greatly limits an entrepreneur's mobility, however. Some business owners prefer to stay out of the real estate business to retain maximum flexibility and mobility. Plus not all real estate appreciates in value. Surrounding property can become run-down and consequently lower a property's value despite the owner's efforts to keep it in excellent condition. Many downtown locations have suffered from this problem.

The Decision to Lease

The major advantage of leasing is that it requires no large initial cash outlay, so the business's funds are available for purchasing inventory or for current operations. Firms that are short on cash will inevitably be forced to lease facilities. All lease expenses are tax deductible.

One major disadvantage of leasing is that the property owner might choose not to renew the lease. A successful business might be forced to move to a new location, and such relocation can be extremely costly and could result in a significant loss of established customers. In many cases it is almost like starting the business again. Also, if a business is successful, the property owner may ask for a significant increase in rent when the lease renewal is negotiated. The owner of the building is well aware of the costs associated with moving and has the upper hand in the negotiations. In some lease arrangements the owner is compensated, in addition to a monthly rental fee, by a percentage of the tenant's gross sales. This is common in shopping centers.

Still another disadvantage to leasing is the limitation on remodeling. If the building owner believes that modifications will reduce the future rental value of the property, he will likely require a long-term lease at increased rent. In addition, all permanent modifications of the structure become the property of the building owner.

Whatever choice an entrepreneur makes, it is important that the selection matches the plan she has for her business. Throughout this chapter, you will be presented with questions to guide you in evaluating the options.

Layout: Maximizing Revenues, Increasing Efficiency, or Reducing Cost

8. Explain the principles of effective layouts for retailers, service businesses, and manufacturers.

The ideal layout for a building depends on the type of business it houses and on the entrepreneur's strategy for gaining a competitive edge. Retailers design their layouts with the goal of maximizing sales revenue while manufacturers see layout as an opportunity to increase efficiency and productivity and to lower costs.

Layout for Retailing

Retail layout is the arrangement of merchandise in a store and its method of display. A retailer's success depends, in part, on a well-designed floor display. It should pull customers into the store and make it easy for them to locate merchandise, compare price, quality, and features, and ultimately to make a purchase. In addition, the floor plan should take customers past displays of other items that they may buy on impulse. Retailers have always recognized that some locations within a store are superior to others. Customer traffic patterns give the owner a clue to the best location for the highest gross margin items. Merchandise purchased on impulse and convenience goods should be located near the front of the store. Items people shop around for before buying and specialty goods will attract their own customers and should not be placed in prime space. Prime selling space should be restricted to products that carry the highest markups. Table 11.2 on page 368 offers suggestions for locating merchandise in a small retail store.

retail layout—*the arrangement of merchandise in a store and its method of display.*

Layouts in a retail store evolve from a clear understanding of customers' buying habits. If customers come into the store for specific products and have a tendency to walk directly to those items, it will benefit retailers to place complementary products in their path. Observing customer behavior can help the owner identify the "hot spots" where merchandise sells briskly and "cold spots" where it may sit indefinitely. By experimenting with factors such as traffic flow, lighting, aisle size, noise levels, signs, and colors, an owner can discover the most productive store layout.

Retailers have three basic layout patterns to choose from: the grid, the free-form layout, and the boutique. The **grid layout** arranges displays in rectangular fashion so that aisles are parallel. It is a formal layout that controls the traffic flow through the store. Most supermarkets and many discount stores use the grid layout because it is well suited to self-service stores. This layout uses the available selling space most efficiently, creates a neat, organized environment, and facilitates shopping by standardizing the location of items. Figure 11.1 on page 368 shows a typical grid layout.

grid layout—*a formal arrangement of displays in rectangular fashion so that aisles are parallel.*

Table 11.2

Classification and Arrangement of Merchandise in Small Retail Stores

Source: U.S. Small Business Administration, "Small Business Location and Layout," *Administrative Management Course Program,* Topic 13, Washington, 1980, p. 6.

Merchandise Type	How or Why Bought	Placement in Store
Impulse Goods	As a result of attractive visual merchandising displays	Small store—near entrance Larger store—on main aisle
Convenience Goods	With frequency in small quantities	Easily accessible feature locations along main aisle
Necessities or Staple Goods	Because of need	Rear of one-level stores, upper floor(s) of multilevel stores (not a hard-and-fast rule)
Utility Goods	For home use—brooms, dust-pans, similar items	As impulse items, up front or along main aisle
Luxury and Major Expense Items	After careful planning and considerable "shopping around"	Some distance from entrance

free-form layout—*an informal arrangement of displays of various shapes and sizes.*

Unlike the grid layout, the **free-form layout** is informal, using displays of various shapes and sizes. Its primary advantage is the relaxed, friendly shopping atmosphere it creates, which encourages customers to shop longer and increases the number of impulse purchases they make. Still, the free-form layout is not as efficient as the grid layout in using selling space, and it can create security problems if not properly planned. Figure 11.2 illustrates a free-form layout.

boutique layout—*an arrangement that divides a store into a series of individual shopping areas, each with its own theme.*

The **boutique layout** divides the store into a series of individual shopping areas, each with its own theme. It is like building a series of specialty shops into a single store. The boutique layout is more informal and can create a unique shopping environment for the customer. Small department stores sometimes use this layout (see Figure 11.3 on page 370).

Every business owner should display merchandise as attractively as her budget will allow. Customers' eyes focus on displays, which tell them the type of merchandise the busi-

Figure 11.1
The Grid Layout

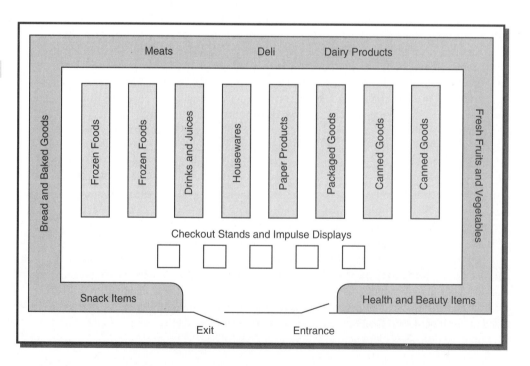

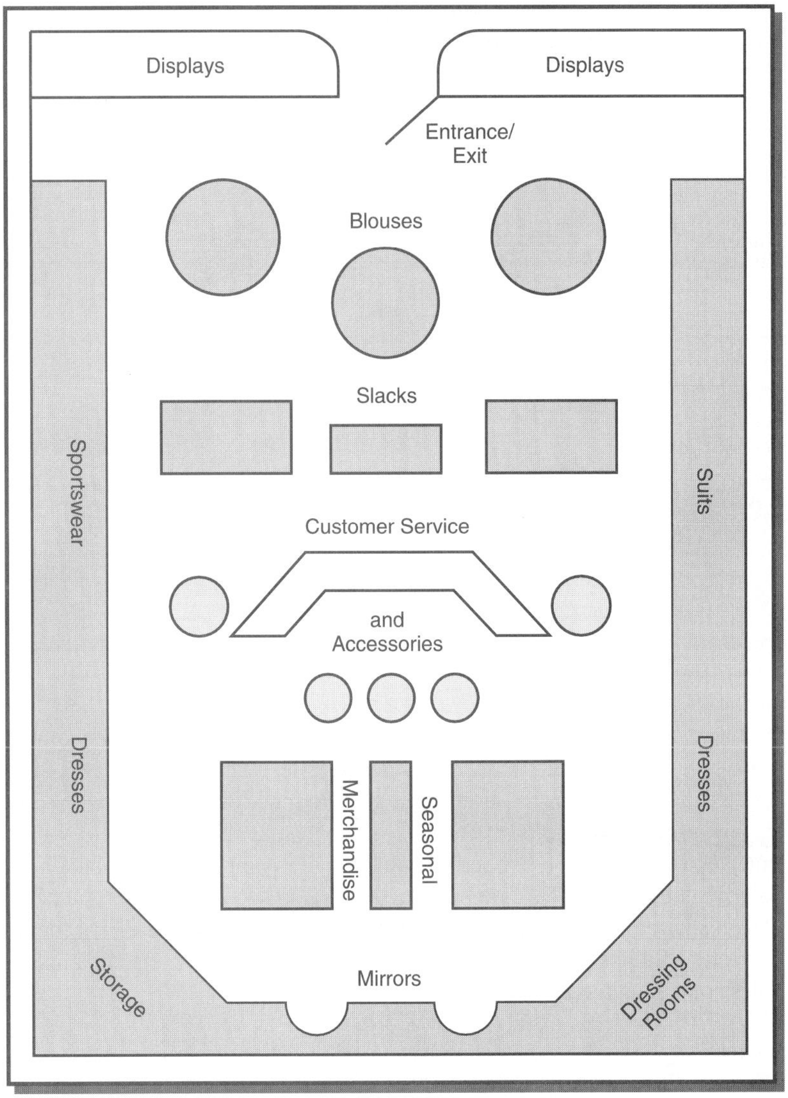

Figure 11.2
The Free-form Layout

ness sells. It is easier for customers to relate to one display than to a rack or shelf of merchandise. Open displays of merchandise can surround the focus display, creating an attractive selling area.

Retailers can boost sales by displaying together items that complement each other. For example, displaying ties near dress shirts or handbags next to shoes often leads to multiple sales.

Spacious displays provide shoppers an open view of merchandise and reduce the likelihood of shoplifting. An open, spacious image is preferable to a cluttered appearance.

Retailers must remember to separate the selling and nonselling areas of a store. Never waste prime selling space with nonselling functions (storage, office, dressing area, etc.). Although nonselling activities are necessary for a successful retail operation, they should not take precedence and occupy valuable selling space. Many retailers place their non-selling departments in the rear of the building, recognizing the value of each foot of space in a retail store and locating their most profitable items in the best selling areas.

Figure 11.3
The Boutique Layout

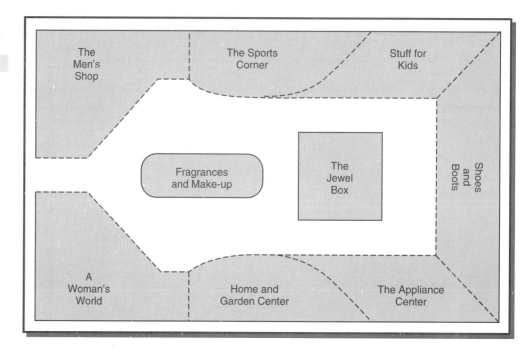

Clearly, not every portion of a small store's interior space is of equal value in generating sales revenue. Certain areas contribute more to revenue than others. The value of store space depends on floor location in a multistory building, location with respect to aisles and walkways, and proximity to entrances. Space values decrease as distance from the main entry-level floor increases. Selling areas on the main level contribute a greater portion to sales than those on other floors in the building because they offer greater exposure to customers than either basement or higher-level locations. Therefore, main-level locations carry a greater share of rent than other levels. Figure 11.4 offers one example of how rent and sales could be allocated by floors.

Figure 11.4
**Rent Allocation
By Floors**
Source: From Dale M. Lewison, *Retailing*, 6th ed. ©1997. Reprinted by permission of Prentice-Hall, Inc., Upper Saddle River, NJ.

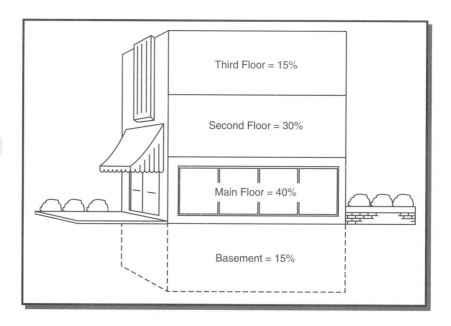

The layout of aisles in the store has a major impact on the customer exposure that merchandise receives. Items located on primary walkways should be assigned a higher share of rental costs and should contribute a greater portion to sales revenue than those displayed along secondary aisles. Figure 11.5 shows that high-value areas are exposed to two primary aisles.

Space values also depend on their relative position to the store entrance. Typically, the farther away an area is from the entrance, the lower its value. Another consideration is that most shoppers turn to the right entering a store and move around it counterclockwise. Finally, only about one-fourth of a store's customers will go more than halfway into the store. Using these characteristics, Figure 11.6 on page 372 illustrates space values for a typical small store layout.

Understanding the value of store space ensures proper placement of merchandise. The items placed in the high-rent areas of the store should generate adequate sales and contribute enough profit to justify their high-value locations.

The decline in value of store space from front to back of the shop is expressed in the 40-30-20-10 rule. This rule assigns 40 percent of a store's rental cost to the front quarter of the shop, 30 percent to the second quarter, 20 percent to the third quarter, and 10 percent to the final quarter. Similarly, each quarter of the store should contribute the same percentage of sales revenue.

For example, suppose that a small department store anticipates $120,000 in sales this year. Each quarter of the store should generate the following sales volume:

Front quarter	$120,000 × 0.40 =	$ 48,000
Second quarter	$120,000 × 0.30 =	$ 36,000
Third quarter	$120,000 × 0.20 =	$ 24,000
Fourth quarter	$120,000 × 0.10 =	$ 12,000
Total		$120,000

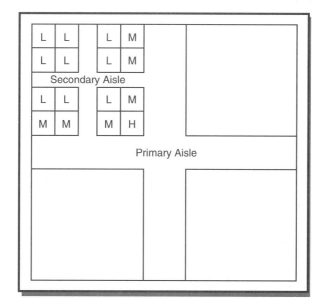

Figure 11.5
Rent Allocation
Based on Traffic Aisles
Source: From Dale M. Lewison, *Retailing*, 6th ed. ©1997. Reprinted by permission of Prentice-Hall, Inc., Upper Saddle River, NJ.

Figure 11.6
**Space Values For
a Small Store**
Source: From Dale M. Lewison,
Retailing, 6th ed.
©1997. Reprinted by
permission of Prentice-Hall, Inc.,
Upper Saddle River, NJ.

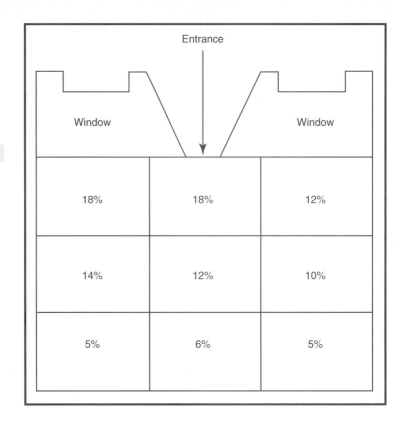

Layout for Manufacturing

Manufacturing layout decisions take into consideration the arrangement of departments, workstations, machines, and stock-holding points within a production facility. The general objective is to arrange these elements to ensure a smooth work flow (in a production facility) or a particular traffic pattern (in a service facility or organization).

Manufacturing facilities have come under increasing scrutiny as firms attempt to improve quality, decrease inventories, and increase productivity through facilities that are integrated, flexible, and controlled. Facility layout has a dramatic effect on product mix, product processing, and material handling, storage, and control, as well as production volume and quality.

FACTORS IN MANUFACTURING LAYOUT. The ideal layout for a manufacturing operation depends on a number of factors, including the following:

- ☆ *Type of product*—product design and quality standards; whether the product is produced for inventory or for order; and the physical properties such as the size of materials and products, special handling requirements, susceptibility to damage, and perishability.

- ☆ *Type of production process*—technology used; types of materials handled; means of providing a service; and processing requirements in terms of number of operations involved and amount of interaction between departments and work centers.

- ☆ *Economic considerations*—volume of production; costs of materials, machines, workstations, and labor; pattern and variability of demand; and length of permissible delays.

- ☆ *Space availability* within the facility itself.

TYPES OF MANUFACTURING LAYOUTS. Manufacturing layouts are categorized by either the work flow in a plant or by the production system's function. There are three basic types of layouts that manufacturers can use separately or in combination—product, process, and fixed position—and they are differentiated by their applicability to different conditions of manufacturing volume.

PRODUCT LAYOUTS. In a **product (or line) layout**, a manufacturer arranges workers and equipment according to the sequence of operations performed on the product (see Figure 11.7). Conceptually, the flow is an unbroken line from raw material input or customer arrival to finished goods or customer's departure. This type of layout is applicable to rigid-flow, high-volume, continuous or mass-production operations, or when the service or product is highly standardized. Automobile assembly plants, paper mills, and oil refineries are examples of product layouts.

Product layouts offer the advantages of lower material handling costs; simplified tasks that can be done with low-cost, lower-skilled labor; reduced amounts of work-in-process inventory and relatively simplified production control activities. All units are routed along the same fixed path, and scheduling consists primarily of setting a production rate.

Disadvantages of product layouts are their inflexibility, monotony of job tasks, high fixed investment in specialized equipment, and heavy interdependence of all operations. A breakdown in one machine or at one workstation can idle the entire line. Such a layout also requires the owner to duplicate many pieces of equipment in the manufacturing facility, which for a small firm can be cost prohibitive.

PROCESS LAYOUTS. In a **process layout**, a manufacturer groups workers and equipment according to the general function they perform, without regard to any particular product or customer (see Figure 11.8 on page 374). Process layouts are appropriate when production runs are short, when demand shows considerable variation and the costs of holding finished goods inventory are high, or when the service or product is customized.

Process layouts have the advantages of being flexible for doing custom work and promoting job satisfaction by offering employees diverse and challenging tasks. Its disadvantages are the higher costs of materials handling, more skilled labor, lower productivity, and more complex production control. Because the work flow is intermittent, each job must be individually routed through the system, scheduled at the various work centers, and have its status monitored.

FIXED POSITION LAYOUTS. In **fixed position layouts**, materials do not move down a line as in a production layout but rather, due to the bulk or weight of the final product, are assembled in one spot. In other words, workers and equipment go to the material rather than having the material flow down a line to them. Aircraft assembly shops and shipyards typify this kind of layout.

product layout—*an arrangement of workers and equipment according to the sequence of operations performed on the product.*

process layout—*an arrangement of workers and equipment according to the general function they perform, without regard to any particular product or customer.*

fixed position layout—*an arrangement in which materials do not move down a production line but rather, because of their weight or bulk, are assembled on the spot.*

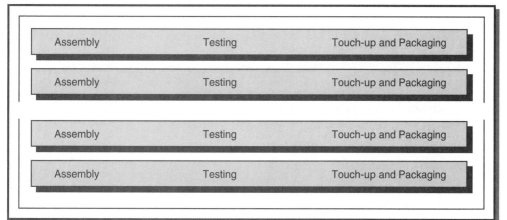

Figure 11.7
Product Layout

Assembly	Testing	Touch-up and Packaging
Assembly	Testing	Touch-up and Packaging
Assembly	Testing	Touch-up and Packaging
Assembly	Testing	Touch-up and Packaging

Figure 11.8
Process Layout

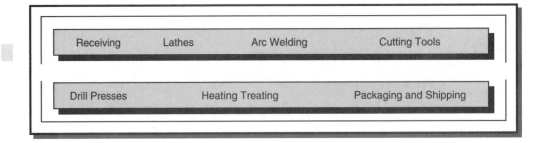

| Receiving | Lathes | Arc Welding | Cutting Tools |

| Drill Presses | Heating Treating | Packaging and Shipping |

FUNCTIONAL LAYOUTS. Many layouts are designed with more than one objective or function in mind and, therefore, combinations of the various layouts are common. For example, a supermarket, though primarily arranged on the basis of marketing, is partly a storage layout; a cafeteria represents not only a layout by marketing function but also by work flow (a food assembly line); and a factory may arrange its machinery in a process layout but perform assembly operations in a fixed sequence, as in a product layout.

DESIGNING LAYOUTS. The starting point in layout design is determining how and in what sequence product parts or service tasks flow together. One of the most effective techniques is to create an overall picture of the manufacturing process using assembly charts and process flow charts. Given the tasks and their sequence, plus knowledge of the volume of products to be produced or of customers to be served, an owner can analyze space and equipment needs to get an idea of the facility's demands. When using a product or line layout, these demands have precedence, and manufacturers must arrange equipment and workstations to fit the production tasks and their sequence. With a process or functional layout, different products or customers with different needs place demands on the facility. Rather than having a single best flow, there may be one flow for each product or customer, and compromises are necessary. As a result, any one product or customer may not get the ideal layout.

ANALYZED PRODUCTION LAYOUTS. Although there is no general procedure for analyzing the numerous interdependent factors that enter into layout design, specific layout problems lend themselves to detailed analysis. Two important criteria for selecting and designing a layout are worker effectiveness and materials-handling costs.

The layout should be designed to improve job satisfaction and to use workers at the highest skill level for which they are being paid. This applies just as much to an office layout, where an engineer may spend half of a working day delivering blueprints, as it does to a plant layout, where a machinist must travel a long distance for tools.

Manufacturers can lower materials-handling costs by using layouts designed so that product flow is automated whenever possible and flow distances and times are minimized. The extent of automation depends on the level of technology and amount of capital available, as well as behavioral considerations of employees. Flow distances and times are usually minimized by locating sequential processing activities or interrelated departments in adjacent areas. The following features are important to a good manufacturing layout:

1. planned materials flow pattern
2. straight-line layout where possible
3. straight, clearly marked aisles
4. backtracking kept to a minimum
5. related operations close together
6. minimum of in-process inventory
7. easy adjustment to changing conditions
8. minimum materials-handling distances

9. minimum of manual handling

10. no unnecessary rehandling of material

11. minimum handling between operations

12. materials delivered to production employees

13. materials efficiently removed from the work area

14. materials handling being done by indirect labor

15. orderly materials handling and storage

16. good housekeeping

CHAPTER SUMMARY

1. Explain the stages in the location decision—choosing the region, the state, the city, and the final site.

- The location decision is one of the most important decisions an entrepreneur will make, given its long-term effects on the company. An entrepreneur should look at the choice as a series of increasingly narrow decisions: Which region of the country? Which state? Which city? Which site? Choosing the right location requires an entrepreneur to evaluate potential sites with her target customers in mind. Demographic statistics are available from a wide variety of sources, but government agencies such as the Census Bureau have a wealth of detailed data that can guide an entrepreneur in her location decision.

2. Describe the location criteria for retail and service businesses.

- For retailers, the location decision is especially crucial. Retailers must consider the size of the trade area, the volume of customer traffic, number of parking spots, availability of room for expansion, and the visibility of a site.

3. Outline the basic location options for retail and service businesses.

- Retail and service businesses have six basic location options: central business districts (CBDs), neighborhoods, shopping centers and malls, near competitors, outlying areas, and at home.

4. Explain the site selection process for manufacturers.

- A manufacturer's location decision is strongly influenced by local zoning ordinances. Some areas offer industrial parks designed specifically to attract manufacturers. Two crucial factors for most manufacturers are the accessibility to (and the cost of transporting) raw materials and the quality and quantity of available labor.

5. Discuss the benefits of locating a startup company in a business incubator.

- Business incubators are locations that offer flexible, low-cost rental space to their tenants as well as business and consulting services. Their goal is to nurture small companies until they are ready to "graduate" into the business community. Many government agencies and universities offer incubator locations.

6. Describe the criteria used to analyze the layout and design considerations of a building, including the Americans with Disabilities Act.

- When evaluating the suitability of a particular building, an entrepreneur should consider several factors: size (is it large enough to accommodate the business with some room for growth?); construction and external appearance (is the building structurally sound and does it create the right impression for the business?); entrances (are they inviting?); legal issues (does the building comply with the Americans with Disabilities Act? If not, how much will it cost to bring it up to standard?); signs (are they legible, well located, and easy to see?); interior (does the interior design contribute to our ability to make sales? Is it ergonomically designed?); lights and fixtures (is the lighting adequate for the tasks workers will be performing and what is the estimated cost of lighting?).

7. Evaluate the advantages and disadvantages of building, buying, and leasing a building.

- Building a new building gives an entrepreneur the opportunity to design exactly what he wants in a brand-new facility; however, not every small business owner can afford to tie up significant amounts of cash in fixed assets. Buying an existing building gives a business owner the freedom to renovate as needed, but this can be an expensive alternative. Leasing a location is a common choice because it is economical, but the business owner faces the uncertainty of lease renewals, rising rents, and renovation problems.

8. Explain the principles of effective layouts for retailers, service businesses, and manufacturers.

- Layout for retail stores and service businesses depends on the owner's understanding of her customers' buying habits. Retailers have three basic layout options from which to choose: grid, free-form pattern, and boutique. Some areas of a retail store generate more sales per square foot and are, therefore, more valuable.

- The goal of a manufacturer's layout is to create a smooth, efficient work flow. Three basic options exist: product layout, process layout, and fixed position layout. Two key considerations are worker productivity and materials-handling costs.

1. How do most small business owners choose a location? Is this wise?
2. What factors should a manager consider when evaluating a region in which to locate a business? Where are such data available?
3. Outline the factors important when selecting a state in which to locate a business.
4. What factors should a seafood processing plant, a beauty shop, and an exclusive jewelry store consider in choosing a location? List factors for each type of business.
5. What intangible factors might enter into the entrepreneur's location decision?
6. What are zoning laws? How do they affect the location decision?
7. What is the trade area? What determines a small retailer's trade area?
8. Why is it important to discover more than just the number of passersby in a traffic count?
9. What types of information can the entrepreneur collect from census data?
10. Why may a cheap location not be the best location?
11. Summarize the advantages and disadvantages of building, buying, and leasing a building.
12. Why is it costly for a small firm to choose a location that is too small?
13. What function does a small firm's sign serve? What are the characteristics of an effective business sign?
14. Explain the statement: "Not every portion of a small store's interior space is of equal value in generating sales revenue." What areas are most valuable?
15. What are some of the major features that are important to a good manufacturing layout?

Beyond the Classroom...

1. Select a specific type of business you would like to go into one day and use census data and Commerce Department reports from the local library to choose a specific site for the business in the local region. What location factors are critical to the success of this business? Would it be likely to succeed in your hometown?

2. Interview a sample of local small business owners. How did they decide on their particular locations? What are the positive and negative features of their existing locations?

3. Locate the most recent issue of either *Entrepreneur* or *Fortune* describing the "best cities for (small) business." (For *Entrepreneur*, it is usually the October issue, and for *Fortune*, it is normally an issue in November.) Which cities are in the top 10? What factors did the magazine use to select these cities? Pick a city and explain what makes it an attractive destination for locating a business there.

4. Select a manufacturing operation, a wholesale business, and a retail store, and evaluate their layouts using the guidelines presented in this chapter. What changes would you recommend? Why? Does the layout contribute to a more effective operation?

5. Choose one of the businesses studied in exercise 4 and design an improved layout for the operation. How expensive would these alterations be?

1. Access the home page of York, Nebraska at:

http://www.ci.york.ne.us/

How has this city presented itself as a possible location for a new business venture? What other details would you want to know about York, Nebraska before locating there? Use the Web site of the Government Information Sharing Project at:

http://govinfo.kerr.orst.edu/index.html

to collect demographic information about York, Nebraska. Looking at this profile, what kind of businesses would be best suited for this town?

2. Access the Small Business Administration gopher listing at:

gopher://www.sbaonline.sba.gov/

Search for specific information on two of topics of interest to you from this chapter and write a one-page report on what you find.

3. Access the Web site for the Census Bureau at:

http://www.census.gov/

Go to the Census data for your town and use it to recommend a location for the following types of businesses:

a new motel with 25 units
a bookstore
an exclusive women's clothing shop

a Mexican restaurant
a residential plumber
a day care center
a high-quality stereo shop
a family hair care center

4. Go to the Web site of the Government Information Sharing Project at:

http://govinfo.kerr.orst.edu/index.html

a. Prepare a demographic profile of your hometown or city or of the town or city in which you attend college. Using the demographic profile as an analytical tool, what kinds of businesses do you think would be successful there? Unsuccessful? Explain.

b. Using this same Web site, prepare an analysis of the competition in the area using the economic census data.

5. Access the Web site for the International Council of Shopping Centers in New York at:

http://www.icsc.org/

and the National Business Incubation Association in Athens Ohio at:

http://www.nbia.org/

Prepare a one-page report describing the current status and recent trends in shopping centers and malls and in business incubators.

TWELVE

Purchasing, Quality, and Inventory Control

Buying correctly is more important than selling correctly.
- Lewis Paul

Quality is a common standard; it makes sense to everybody, everywhere.
It can bind and build a core of corporate values worldwide.
- Francis Lorentz

We've got it if we can find it.
- sign in hardware store

LEARNING OBJECTIVES

Upon completion of this chapter, you will be able to:

1. ***Understand*** the components of a purchasing plan: quality, quantity, price, timing, and vendor.

2. ***Explain*** the elements of total quality management (TQM) and its impact on a small company's quality.

3. ***Conduct*** economic order quantity (EOQ) analysis to determine the proper levels of inventory.

4. ***Differentiate*** among the three types of purchase discounts vendors offer: trade, quantity, and cash.

5. ***Calculate*** a company's reorder point.

6. ***Develop*** a vendor or supplier analysis model.

7. ***Explain*** the various inventory control systems available and the advantages and disadvantages of each.

8. ***Describe*** how just-in-time (JIT) inventory control techniques work.

Purchasing is an important function in every business because it determines a firm's ability to sell a quality product or service at a reasonable price. How effectively a business owner purchases goods and services, manages quality, works with vendors and suppliers, and controls inventory are the operational elements of strategy that determine a company's ability to satisfy customers, control costs, and earn a profit. The effects of these decisions ripple throughout the entire company, affecting everything it does and producing a dramatic impact on its bottom line. The average manufacturer, for example, spends 55 cents of each dollar in sales on purchases of goods and services. By finding savings in its purchasing bill of 5 percent, the typical manufacturer can add 3 percent to its net profit![1]

The Purchasing Plan

Purchasing involves the acquisition of needed materials, supplies, services, and equipment of the right quality, in the proper quantities, for reasonable prices, at the appropriate time, from the right vendor or supplier. A major objective of purchasing is to acquire enough (but not too much!) stock to ensure smooth, uninterrupted production or sales and to see that the merchandise is delivered on time. Companies large and small are purchasing goods and supplies from all across the globe, and coordinating the pieces of that global puzzle requires a comprehensive purchasing plan. The plan must identify a company's quality requirements, its cost targets, and the criteria for determining the best supplier, considering such factors as reliability, service, delivery, and cooperation. A small company's purchasing plan should focus on five critical elements: quality, quantity, price, timing, and vendor (see Figure 12.1).

Quality

The last few decades have taught every businessperson that quality goods and services are absolutely essential to staying competitive. The benefits earned by pursuing quality products, services, and processes come not only in the form of fewer defects but also as lower costs, higher productivity, reduced cycle time, greater market share, increased customer satisfaction, and higher customer retention rates. W. Edwards Deming, one of the founding fathers of the modern quality movement, always claimed that "higher quality is less expensive to produce than lower quality."[2] Internally, companies with a quality focus report significant improvements in work-related factors such as enhanced quality of work life, increased employee moral, and lower employee turnover. Benefits such as these can result in earning a significant competitive advantage in the marketplace.

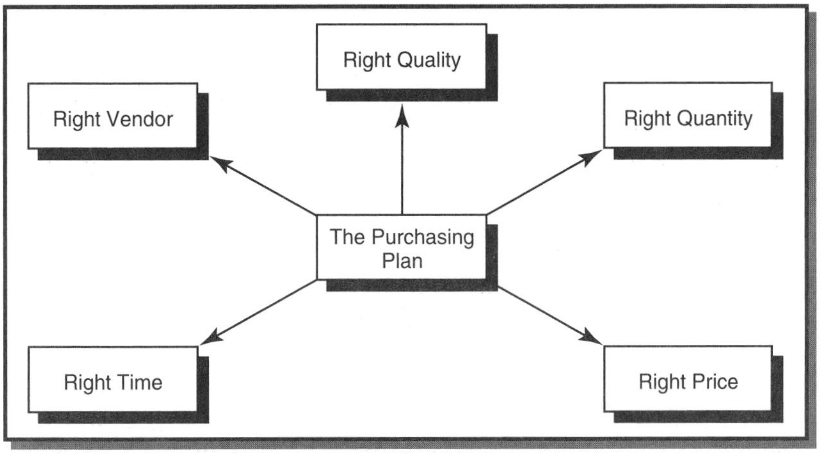

1. Understand the components of a purchasing plan: quality, quantity, price, timing, and vendor.

purchasing—*the acquisition of needed materials, supplies, services, and equipment of the right quality, in the proper quantities, for reasonable prices, at the appropriate time, from the right vendor or supplier.*

2. Explain the elements of total quality management (TQM) and its impact on a small company's quality.

Figure 12.1
Components of a Purchasing Plan

Alexander Doll Company

Total quality companies believe in and manage with the attitude of continuous improvement, a concept the Japanese call **kaizen**. The *kaizen* philosophy holds that small improvements made continuously over time accumulate into a radically reshaped and improved process.

The Alexander Doll Company of New York knows the value of improving quality through continuous improvement. The company fell into such bad financial shape that it declared bankruptcy before managers decided to try to turn it around with kaizen. *Managers began by setting up a cross-functional team (a team of workers from different functional areas of the business) to identify problems with the production process and to make suggestions for solving them. The first problem the team tackled was the manufacturing process itself, which was spread out over three floors, causing a high breakage rate. The team recommended moving the production process onto one floor and rearranging it to minimize handling. Alexander created more teams, which went to work on 65 projects covering all phases of its operation. The results: The distance dolls traveled during manufacturing fell from 630 feet to just 40 feet. The inventory of unfinished doll pieces dropped from 29,000 to 34, and productivity went from eight dolls per person per day to 25! In addition, the lead time to produce a doll went from 90 days to just 90 minutes. Managers cannot credit any single change with producing such dramatic results; rather, they are the outcome of many small changes teams of creative workers came up with over time.*[3]

Despite the benefits their companies can reap from quality improvements, many managers have yet to get on the quality bandwagon. According to one recent study, 83 percent of managers at mid-sized companies said that quality was a top priority, However, only 31 percent had actually calculated the cost of quality—the costs associated with scrap, rework, inspections, training, technology, and other factors.[4] Other studies show that executives estimate the cost of bad quality to be just 5 percent (or less) of sales when, in reality, the actual percentage is between 20 and 30 percent of sales![5] For a quality improvement system to be successful, *everyone* in the company must understand the real cost of bad quality and make a commitment to lowering it.

Source: Reprinted by permission of Harley Schwardron.

Under the total quality management (TQM) philosophy, companies define a quality product as one that conforms to predetermined standards that satisfy customers' demands. The goal is to get *everything*—from delivery and invoicing to installation and follow-up—right the first time. Although they know that they may never reach their targets of zero defects, they never stop striving for perfection in their relationships with their customers. The businesses, both large and small, that have effectively implemented these programs understand that the process involves a total commitment from strategy to practice from the top of the organization to the bottom.

TQM is *not* a "quick-fix," short-term program that can magically push a company to world-class status overnight. Because it requires such fundamental, often drastic, changes in the way a company does business, TQM takes time both to implement and to produce results. Patience is a must. Although some small businesses that use TQM begin to see some improvements within just a matter of weeks, the *real* benefits take longer to realize. Studies show that it takes at least three to four years before TQM principles gain acceptance among employees, and that eight to ten years are necessary to fully implement TQM in a company.[6]

To implement TQM successfully, a small business owner must rely on ten fundamental principles:

☆ *Shift from a management-driven culture to a participative, team-based one.* Two basic tenets of TQM are employee involvement and teamwork. Business owners must be willing to push decision-making authority down the organization to where the real experts are. Teams of employees working together to identify and solve problems can be a powerful force in an organization of any size. "Brain power is the sum of all the intelligence of the people in a company, not just one person," says one TQM consultant. "If [managers] can tap into that brain power, their company will be far ahead of the competition."[7]

☆ *Modify the reward system to encourage teamwork and innovation.* Because the team, not the individual, is the building block of TQM, companies often have to modify their compensation systems to reflect team performance. Traditional compensation methods pit one employee against another, undermining any sense of cooperation. Often, they are based on seniority rather than on how much an employee contributes to the company. Compensation systems under TQM usually rely on incentives, linking pay to performance. However, rather than tying pay to individual performance, these systems focus on *team-based* incentives. Each person's pay depends on whether or not the entire team (or, sometimes, the entire company) meets a clearly defined, measurable set of performance objectives.

   For instance, when Laitram Corporation, a small manufacturing company, implemented TQM, it determined employees' base pay on their "market value" using regional and local surveys. Managers also set up a profit-sharing incentive system based on overall company and team performances. Workers have input into the system because they evaluate their coworkers' performances as well as those of their managers. "Employees were skeptical of the whole system," says human resource manager James Evans, "until they started getting checks."[8]

☆ *Train workers constantly to give them the tools they need to produce quality and to upgrade the company's knowledge base.* One of the most important factors in making long-term, constant improvements in a company's processes is teaching workers the philosophy and the tools of TQM. Admonishing employees to "produce quality" or offering them rewards for high quality is futile unless a company gives them the tools and the know-how to achieve that end. Managers must be dedicated to making their companies "learning organizations" that encourage people to upgrade their skills and to giving them the opportunities and incentives to do so. The most successful companies spend anywhere from 1 to 5 percent of their employees' time on training, most of it invested in workers, not managers. To give employees a sense of how the quality of their jobs fits

cross-training—*teaching workers to do other jobs in the company.*

Pareto's law (the 80/20 rule)—*a law stating that 80 percent of a company's quality problems arise from just 20 percent of all causes.*

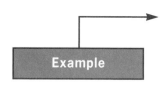

into the "big picture," many TQM companies engage in **cross-training**, teaching workers to do other jobs in the company.

⭐ *Train employees to measure quality with the tools of statistical process control (SPC).* The only way to ensure gains in quality is to measure results objectively and to track the company's progress toward its quality objectives. That requires teaching employees how to use statistical process control techniques such as fishbone charts, Pareto charts, control charts, and measures of process capability. Without knowledgeable workers using these quantitative tools, TQM cannot produce the intended results.

⭐ *Use Pareto's law to focus TQM efforts.* One of the toughest decisions managers face in companies embarking on TQM for the first time is "Where do we start?" The best way to answer that fundamental question is to use **Pareto's law** (also called the **80/20 rule**), which states that 80 percent of a company's quality problems arise from just 20 percent of all causes. By identifying this small percentage of causes and focusing quality improvement efforts on them, a company gets maximum returns for minimum efforts. This simple, yet powerful rule forces workers to concentrate resources on the most significant problems first, where payoffs are likely to be biggest and help build momentum for a successful TQM effort.

For instance, when one company's customers began complaining about product losses during shipment, a team of salespeople used Pareto analysis to identify the small percentage of shippers who were responsible for the bulk of the losses. They collected the data they needed, analyzed it, and solved the problem with a just a few telephone calls and visits.[9]

⭐ *Share information with everyone in the organization.* Asking employees to make decisions and to assume responsibility for creating quality necessitates that the owner share information with them. Employees cannot make sound decisions consistent with the company's quality initiative if managers are unwilling to give them the information they need to make those decisions.

For instance, at City Concrete Products, a small building supply company that embraces the TQM philosophy, owner Mel Chambers has created work teams and an employee council that meet regularly for the purpose of sharing key information about the company's processes and results. Chambers also makes sure that information flows both ways at employee council meetings; workers routinely offer ideas and suggestions for improvement (most of which the company implements) because they know that managers will listen and act on them.[10]

⭐ *Focus quality improvements on astonishing the customer.* The heart of TQM is customer satisfaction—better yet, customer astonishment. Unfortunately, some companies focus their quality improvement efforts on areas that never benefit the customer. Quality improvements with no customer focus (either internal or external customers) are wasted.

⭐ *Don't rely on inspection to produce quality products and services.* The traditional approach to achieving quality was to create a product or service and then to rely on an army of inspectors to "weed out" all of the defects. Not only is such a system a terrible waste of resources (consider the cost of scrap, rework, and no-value-added inspections), but it gives managers no opportunity for continuous improvement. The only way to improve a process is to discover the cause of poor quality, fix it (the sooner, the better), and learn from it so that workers can *avoid* the problem in the future. Using the statistical tools of the TQM approach allows a company to learn from its mistakes with a consistent approach to constantly improving quality.

⭐ *Avoid using TQM to place blame on those who make mistakes.* In many firms, the only reason managers seek out mistakes is to find someone to blame for them. The result is a culture based on fear and an unwillingness on the part of workers to take chances to innovate. The goal of TQM is to improve the processes in which people work, *not* to lay blame on workers. Searching out "the guilty party" is fruitless! The TQM philosophy sees each problem that arises as an opportunity for improving the company's system.

☆ *Strive for continuous improvement in processes as well as in products and services.* There is no finish line in the race for quality. A company's goal must be to improve the quality of its processes, products, and services constantly, no matter how high it currently stands!

Many of these principles are evident in Deming's 14 points, a capsulized version of how to build a successful TQM approach (see Table 12.1). Figure 12.2 on page 384 shows the four absolutes of quality.

Table 12.1
Deming's 14 Points

Total quality management cannot succeed as a piecemeal program or without true commitment to its philosophy. W. Edwards Deming, the man most visibly connected to TQM, drove home these concepts with his 14 points, the essential elements for integrating TQM successfully into a company.

1. *Constantly strive to improve products and services.* This requires total dedication to improving quality, productivity, and service—*continuously.*

2. *Adopt a total quality philosophy.* There are no shortcuts to quality improvement; it requires a completely new way of thinking and managing.

3. *Correct defects* as they happen, rather than relying on mass inspection of end products. Real quality comes from improving the process, not from inspecting finished products and services. At that point, it's too late. Statistical process control charts can help workers detect when a process is producing poor-quality goods and services. Then, they can stop it, make corrections, and get the process back on target.

4. *Don't award business on price alone.* Rather than choosing the lowest-cost vendor, businesses should work toward establishing close relationships with suppliers offering the highest quality.

5. *Constantly improve the system of production and service.* Management must lead the way toward continuous improvement. Managers must focus the entire company on customer satisfaction and must measure results. There is no finish line in the race for quality.

6. *Institute training.* Workers cannot improve quality and lower costs without proper training to erase "old ways" of doing things.

7. *Institute leadership.* The supervisor's job is not to "boss" workers around; it is to lead. The nature of the work is more like coaching than controlling.

8. *Drive out fear.* People often are afraid to point out problems because they fear the repercussions. Managers must encourage and reward employee suggestions.

9. *Break down barriers among staff areas.* Departments within organizations often erect needless barriers in the interest of "protecting their own turf." Total quality requires a spirit of teamwork and cooperation across the entire organization.

10. *Eliminate superficial slogans and goals.* These only offend employees since they imply that workers could do a better job if they would only try.

11. *Eliminate standard quotas.* They emphasize quantity over quality. Not everyone can move at the same rate and still produce quality.

12. *Remove barriers to pride of workmanship.* Most workers want to do quality work. Eliminating "demotivators" frees them to achieve quality results.

13. *Institute vigorous education and retraining.* Managers must teach employees the new methods of continuous improvement, including statistical process control techniques.

14. *Management must take demonstrated action to achieve the transformation.* Although success requires involvement of all levels of the organization, the impetus for change must come from the top.

These 14 interrelated elements contribute to a chain reaction effect. As a company improves its quality, costs decline, productivity increases, the company gains additional market share due to its ability to provide high-quality products at competitive prices, and the company and its employees prosper.

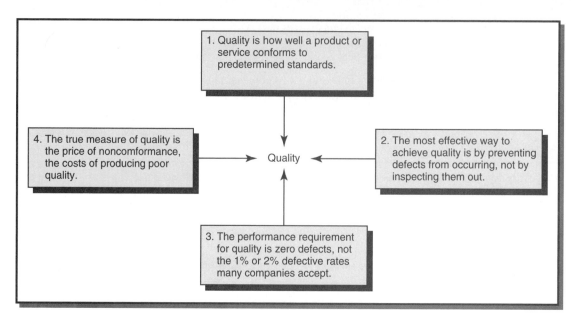

1. Quality is how well a product or service conforms to predetermined standards.

4. The true measure of quality is the price of noncomformance, the costs of producing poor quality.

Quality

2. The most effective way to achieve quality is by preventing defects from occurring, not by inspecting them out.

3. The performance requirement for quality is zero defects, not the 1% or 2% defective rates many companies accept.

Figure 12.2
The Four Absolutes of Quality

3. Conduct economic order quantity (EOQ) analysis to determine the proper levels of inventory.

Quantity

The typical small business has its largest investment in inventory. But an investment inventory is not profitable because dollars return nothing until the inventory is sold. In a sense, the small firm's inventory is its largest non-interest-bearing "account." The owner must focus on controlling this investment and on maintaining proper inventory levels.

A primary objective of this portion of the purchasing plan is to generate an adequate turnover of merchandise by purchasing proper quantities. Maintaining extra inventory means that an excessive amount of the company's capital is tied up in inventory, which limits the firm's working capital and exerts pressure on its cash flows. Also, the firm risks the danger of being stuck with spoiled or obsolete merchandise, an extremely serious problem for many small businesses. Excess inventory also takes up valuable store or selling space that could be used for items with higher turnover rates and more profit potential. On the other hand, maintaining too little inventory can be extremely costly. An owner will be forced to reorder merchandise frequently, escalating total inventory costs. Also, inventory stockouts will occur when customer demand exceeds the firm's supply of merchandise, causing customer ill will. Persistent stockouts are inconvenient for customers, and many will eventually choose to shop elsewhere.

THE ECONOMIC ORDER QUANTITY (EOQ). Clearly the small business must maintain enough inventory to meet customer orders, but not so much that storage costs and inventory investment are excessive. The analytical techniques used to determine economic order quantities (EOQ) will help the manager compute the amount of stock to purchase with an order or to produce with each production run to minimize total inventory costs. To compute the proper amount of stock to order or to produce, the small business owner must first determine the three principal elements of total inventory costs: the cost of the units, the holding (or carrying) cost, and the setup (or ordering) cost.

COST OF UNITS. The cost of the units is simply the number of units demanded for a particular time period multiplied by the cost per unit. Suppose that a small manufacturer of lawn movers forecasts demand for the upcoming year to be 100,000 mowers. He needs to order enough wheels at $1.55 each to supply the production department. So, he computes:

$$\text{Cost of units} = D \times C$$

where

$$D = \text{annual demand}$$
$$C = \text{cost of a single unit}$$

In this example,

$$D = 100,000 \text{ mowers} \times 4 \text{ wheels per mower}$$
$$= 400,000 \text{ wheels}$$
$$C = \$1.55/\text{wheel}$$

$$\text{Cost of units} = D \times C$$
$$= 400,000 \text{ wheels} \times \$1.55$$
$$= \$620,000$$

HOLDING (CARRYING) COSTS. The typical costs of holding inventory include the costs of storage, insurance, taxes, interest, depreciation, spoilage, obsolescence, and pilferage. The expense involved in physically storing the items in inventory is usually substantial, especially if the inventories are large. The owner may have to rent or build additional warehousing facilities, pushing the cost of storing the inventory even higher. The firm may also incur expenses in transferring items into and out of inventory. The cost of storage also includes the expense of operating the facility (e.g., heating, lighting, refrigeration), as well as the depreciation, taxes, and interest on the building. Most small business owners purchase insurance on their inventories to shift the risk of fire, theft, flood, and other natural disasters to the insurer. The premiums paid for this coverage are also included in the cost of holding inventory. Generally, the larger the firm's average inventory, the greater its storage cost.

Many small business owners fail to recognize the interest expense associated with carrying large inventories. In many cases the interest expense is evident when the firm borrows money to purchase inventory. But a less obvious interest expense is the opportunity cost associated with investing in inventory. In other words, the owner could have used the money invested in inventory (a non-interest-bearing investment) for some other purpose, such as plant expansion, research and development, or reducing debt. Thus, the cost of independent financing of inventory is the cost of forgoing the opportunity to use these funds elsewhere. A substantial inventory investment means that a large amount of money is tied up unproductively.

Depreciation costs represent the reduced value of inventory over time. Some businesses are strongly influenced by the depreciation of inventory. For example, a small auto dealer's inventory is subject to depreciation because he must sell models left over from one year at reduced prices.

Spoilage, obsolescence, and pilferage also add to the costs of holding inventory. Some small firms, especially those that deal in fad merchandise, assume an extremely high risk of obsolescence. For example, a fashion merchandiser with a large inventory of the latest styles may be left with worthless merchandise when styles suddenly change. Small companies selling perishables must always be aware of the danger of spoilage. For example, the owner of a small fish market must plan purchases carefully to ensure a fresh inventory. And unless the owner establishes sound inventory control procedures, the business will suffer losses from employee theft and shoplifting.

Let us use the lawn mower manufacturer example to illustrate the cost of holding inventory:

$$\text{Holding cost} = \frac{Q}{2} \times H$$

where

Q = quantity of inventory ordered (EOQ)

H = holding cost per unit per year

$\dfrac{Q}{2}$ = average inventory

The greater the quantity ordered, the greater the inventory carrying cost. This relationship is shown in Table 12.2, assuming that the cost of carrying a single unit of inventory for one year is $1.25.

SETUP (ORDERING) COSTS. The various expenses incurred in actually ordering materials and inventory or in setting up the production line to manufacture them determine the level of setup or ordering costs of a product. The costs of obtaining materials and inventory typically include preparing purchase orders; analyzing and choosing vendors; processing, handling, and expediting orders; receiving and inspecting items; and performing all the required accounting and clerical functions. Even if the small company produces its own supply goods, it encounters most of these same expenses. Ordering costs are usually relatively fixed, regardless of the quantity ordered.

Setup or ordering cost is found by multiplying the number of orders made per year (or the number of production runs per year) by the cost of placing a single order (or the cost of setting up a single production run). If we use the earlier lawn mower manufacturing example, where the annual requirement is 400,000 wheels per year and the cost to place an order is $9.00, the ordering costs are as follows:

$$\text{Setup (ordering) costs} = \frac{D}{Q} \times S$$

where

Table 12.2
Economic Order Quantity and Carrying Cost

If Q Is . . .	$\dfrac{Q}{2}$ Average Inventory Is . . .	$\dfrac{Q}{2} \times H$ Carrying Cost Is . . .
500	250	$312.50
1,000	500	625.00
2,000	1,000	1,250.00
3,000	1,500	1,875.00
4,000	2,000	2,500.00
5,000	2,500	3,125.00
6,000	3,000	3,750.00
7,000	3,500	4,375.00
8,000	4,000	5,000.00
9,000	4,500	5,625.00
10,000	5,000	6,250.00

$$D = \text{annual demand}$$

$$Q = \text{quantity of inventory ordered (EOQ)}$$

$$S = \text{setup (ordering) costs for a single run (or order)}$$

The greater the quantity ordered, the smaller the number of orders placed. This relationship is shown in Table 12.3, assuming an ordering cost of $9 per order.

SOLVING FOR EOQ. Clearly, if carrying costs were the only expense involved in obtaining inventory, the small business manager would purchase the smallest number of units possible in each order to minimize the cost of holding the inventory. For example, if the lawn mower manufacturer purchased one wheel per order, carrying cost would be minimized:

$$\text{Carrying Cost} = \frac{Q}{2} \times H$$

$$= \frac{1}{2} \times \$1.25$$

$$= \$.625$$

but his ordering cost would be outrageous:

$$\text{Ordering costs} = \frac{D}{Q} \times S$$

$$= \frac{400,000}{1} \times \$9$$

$$= \$3,600,000$$

Obviously, this is not the small manufacturer's ideal inventory solution!

Similarly, if ordering costs were the only expense involved in procuring inventory, the small business manager would purchase the largest number of units possible in order to minimize the ordering cost. In our example, if the lawn mower manufacturer purchased 400,000 wheels per order, ordering cost would be minimized:

Table 12.3
Economic Order Quantity and Setup Cost

If Q Is . . .	$\frac{D}{Q}$ Number of Orders per Year Is . . .	$\frac{D}{Q} \times S$ Ordering (Setup) Cost is . . .
500	800	$7,200
1,000	400	3,600
2,000	200	1,800
3,000	134	1,206
4,000	100	900
5,000	80	720
6,000	67	603
7,000	58	522
8,000	50	450
9,000	45	405
10,000	40	360

$$\text{Ordering costs} = \frac{D}{Q} \times S$$

$$= \frac{400,000}{400,000} \times \$9$$

$$= \$9$$

but his carrying cost would be tremendously high:

$$\text{Carrying Cost} = \frac{Q}{2} \times H$$

$$= \frac{400,000}{2} \times \$1.25$$

$$= \$250,000$$

A quick inspection shows that neither of these solutions minimizes the total cost of the manufacturer's inventory. As indicated in the last section, total cost is composed of the cost of the unit, carrying cost, and ordering costs:

$$\text{Total cost} = (D \times C) + \left(\frac{Q}{2} \times H\right) + \left(\frac{D}{Q} \times S\right)$$

These cost are graphed in Figure 12.3. Notice that as the quantity ordered increases, the ordering costs decrease and the carrying costs increase.

The EOQ formula simply balances the ordering cost and the carrying cost of the small business owner's inventory so that total costs are minimized. Table 12.4 summarizes the total costs for various values of Q for our lawn mower manufacturer.

Figure 12.3
Inventory Costs

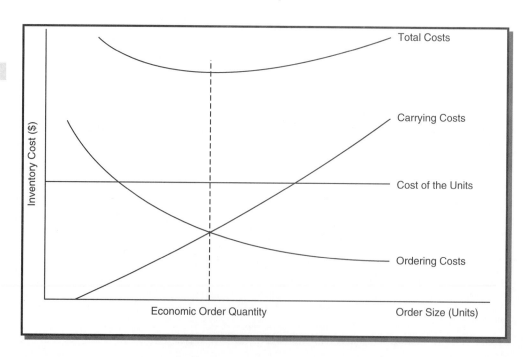

If Q Is . . .	D × C Cost of Units Is . . .	$\frac{Q}{2} \times H$ Carrying Cost Is . . .	$\frac{D}{Q} \times S$ Ordering Cost Is . . .	Total Cost Is . . .
500	$620,000	$312.50	$7,200.00	$627,512.50
1,000	$620,000	$625.00	$3,600.00	$624,225.00
2,000	$620,000	$1,250.00	$1,800.00	$623,050.00
2,400	**$620,000**	**$1,500.00**	**$1,500.00**	**$623,000.00**
3,000	$620,000	$1,875.00	$1,206.00	$623,081.00
4,000	$620,000	$2,500.00	$900.00	$623,400.00
5,000	$620,000	$3,125.00	$720.00	$623,845.00
6,000	$620,000	$3,750.00	$603.00	$624,353.00
7,000	$620,000	$4,375.00	$522.00	$624,897.00
8,000	$620,000	$5,000.00	$450.00	$625,450.00
9,000	$620,000	$5,625.00	$405.00	$626,030.00
10,000	$620,000	$6,250.00	$360.00	$626,610.00

Table 12.4
**Economic Order Quantity
and Total Cost**

As Table 12.4 and Figure 12.3 illustrate, the EOQ formula locates the minimum point on the total cost curve, which occurs where the cost of carrying inventory ($\frac{Q}{2} \times H$) equals the cost of ordering inventory ($\frac{D}{Q} \times S$). If the small business places the smallest number of orders possible per year, its ordering cost is minimized but its carrying cost is maximized. Conversely, if the firm orders the smallest number of units possible per order, its carrying cost is minimized, but its ordering cost is maximized. Total inventory cost is minimized when carrying costs and ordering costs are balanced.

Let us return to our lawn mower manufacturer and compute his economic order quantity, EOQ, using the following formula:

$$S = \$9.00 \text{ per order}$$
$$C = \$1.55 \text{ per wheel}$$

$$EOQ = \sqrt{\frac{2 \times D \times S}{H}}$$

$$= \sqrt{\frac{2 \times 400,000 \times 9.00}{1.25}}$$

$$= 2,400 \text{ wheels}$$

To minimize total inventory cost, the lawn mower manufacturer should order 2,400 wheels at a time. Furthermore,

$$\text{Number of orders per year} = \frac{D}{Q}$$

$$= \frac{400,000}{2,400}$$

$$= 166.67 \text{ orders}$$

This manufacturer will place approximately 167 orders this year at a total cost of $623,000, computed as follows:

$$\text{Total Cost} = (D \times C) + \left(\frac{Q}{2} \times H \right) + \left(\frac{D}{Q} \times S \right)$$

$$= (400,000 \times 1.55) + \left(\frac{2,400}{2} \times 1.25 \right) + \left(\frac{400,000}{2,400} + 9.00 \right)$$

$$= \$620,000 + \$1,500 + \$1,500$$

$$= \$623,000$$

ECONOMIC ORDER QUANTITY (EOQ) WITH USAGE. The preceding EOQ model assumes that orders are filled instantaneously, that is, fresh inventory arrives all at once. Because this does not hold true for many small manufacturers, it is necessary to consider a variation of the basic EOQ model, which allows inventory to be added over a period of time rather than instantaneously. In addition, the manufacturer is likely to be taking items from inventory for use in the assembly process over the same time period. For example, the lawn mower manufacture may be producing blades to replenish his supply, but, at the same time, assembly workers are reducing the supply of blades to make finished mowers. The key feature of this version of the EOQ model is that inventories are used while inventories are being added.

Using the lawn mower manufacturer as an example, we can compute the EOQ for the blades. To make the calculation, we need two additional pieces of information: the usage rate for the blades, U, and the plant's capacity to manufacture the blades, P. Suppose that the maximum number of lawn mower blades the company can manufacture is 480 per day. We know from the previous illustration that annual demand for mowers is 100,000 units (therefore, 100,000 blades). If the plant operates five days per week for 50 weeks, its usage rate is

$$U = \frac{100,000}{50 \times 5} \approx 400 \text{ units per day}$$

It costs $325 to set up the blade manufacturing line and $8.71 to store one blade for one year. The cost of producing a blade is $4.85. To compute EOQ, we modify the basic formula:

$$\text{EOQ} = \frac{2 \times D \times S}{H \times \left(1 - \dfrac{U}{P} \right)}$$

For the lawn mower manufacturer,

$$D = 100,000 \text{ blades}$$
$$S = \$325 \text{ per production run}$$
$$H = \$8.71 \text{ per blade per year}$$
$$U = 400 \text{ blades per day}$$
$$P = 480 \text{ blades per day}$$

$$\text{EOQ} = \sqrt{\frac{2 \times 100{,}000 \times 325}{8.71 \times \left(1 - \frac{400}{480}\right)}}$$

$$= 6{,}691.50 \text{ blades}$$

$$= 6{,}692 \text{ blades}$$

Therefore, to minimize total inventory cost, the lawn mower manufacturer should produce 6,692 blades per production run. Also,

$$\text{Number of production runs per year} = \frac{D}{Q}$$

$$= \frac{100{,}000}{6{,}692}$$

$$= 14.9$$

$$= 15 \text{ runs}$$

The manufacturer will make fifteen production runs during the year at a total cost of:

$$\text{Total cost} = (D \times C) + \left(\frac{1 - \dfrac{U}{P} \times Q}{2} \times H\right) + \left(\frac{D}{Q} \times S\right)$$

$$= (100{,}000 \times \$4.85) + \left(\frac{1 - \dfrac{400}{480} \times 6{,}692}{2} \times 8.71\right) + \left(\frac{100{,}000}{6{,}692} \times \$325\right)$$

$$= \$485{,}000 + \$4{,}857 + \$4{,}857$$

$$= \$494{,}714$$

The small business manager must remember that the EOQ analysis is based on estimations of cost and demand. The final result is only as accurate as the input used. Thus, this analytical tool serves only as a guideline for decision making. The answer may not be the ideal solution due to intervening factors, such as opportunity costs or seasonal fluctuations. The knowledgeable entrepreneur will employ EOQ analysis as a starting point in making a decision and then will use managerial judgment to produce a final ruling.

Price

4. Differentiate among the three types of purchase discount vendors offer: trade, quantity, and cash.

For the typical small business owner, price is always a substantial factor in purchasing inventory and supplies. In many cases, an entrepreneur can negotiate price with potential suppliers on large orders of frequently purchased items. In other instances, perhaps when small quantities of items are purchased infrequently, the small business owner must pay list price.

The typical small business owner shops around at several different vendors and then orders from the supplier offering the best price. Still, this does not mean the small business manager should always purchase inventory and supplies at the lowest price available. The best purchase price is the lowest price at which the owner can obtain goods and services *of acceptable quality*. This guideline usually yields the best value more often than simply purchasing the lowest-priced goods.

Recall that one of Deming's 14 points is "End the practice of awarding business solely on the basis of price tag." Without proof of quality, an item with the lowest initial price may

OK Tire Store

Rick Newbury had worked for 14 years at the OK Tire Store. He was an ideal employee, always willing to work hard and put in the hours necessary to get a job done to the customer's satisfaction. Wes Cassell, the founder of OK Tire, saw Rick as the son he never had. Rick and all of the employees at OK Tire were shocked when they received a phone call on Monday morning from Cassell's neighbor, telling them that they had discovered Wes dead in his recliner. He had apparently died in his sleep on Sunday.

Rick was even more surprised when Cassell's attorney told him that Wes had left the entire business to him. Rick had always managed the tire store's floor operations, but Wes and his secretary, Flora, had always handled all of the office work.

One of the first tasks facing Rick is placing an order for the company's best-selling tire to replenish OK's inventory. With Flora's help, Rick found records for the previous year. They showed that OK typically sold about 9,850 of these tires per year. The cost to place an order is approximately $74, and it costs OK $17 to carry one tire in inventory for one year. The tires cost OK $48.75 at wholesale.

1. Assume the role of consultant. What is OK's economic order quantity for this type of tire?
2. How many orders will OK place if it purchases in the EOQ amount?
3. What is OK's annual total inventory cost for these tires if Rick purchases in the EOQ amount?

---

produce the highest total cost. Deming condemned the practice of constantly switching suppliers in search of the lowest initial price because it increases the variability of a process and lowers its quality. Instead he recommends that businesses establish long-term relationships built on mutual trust and cooperation with a single supplier.

For instance, when New Pig Inc., a small manufacturer of contained absorbents (sock-like bundles of absorbent materials used to soak up industrial leaks and spills), set out to improve quality, reduce the time required to introduce new products, and innovate new product development, it turned to its suppliers for help. New Pig depends on its suppliers for some element of every one of the 3,000 items it sells, so establishing closer supplier relationships was one of management's top priorities. The company began forming strategic alliances with its 30 largest-volume suppliers, improving communication with them and involving them in product development and quality improvement efforts. One joint project resulted in changing a shipping method that produced savings of hundreds of thousands of dollars. "We've developed a synergy and are moving forward together [with our suppliers] to cut costs, be more efficient, and increase profits," says Doug Evans, New Pig's director of strategic purchasing.[11]

New Pig Inc.

PURCHASE DISCOUNTS. When evaluating a supplier's price, small business owners must consider not only the actual price of the goods and services but also the selling terms accompanying them. In some cases the selling terms can be more important than the price itself. Sometimes a vendor's terms might include some type of purchase discount. Vendors typically offer three types of discounts: trade discounts, quantity discounts, and cash discounts.

Trade Discounts. Trade discounts are established on a graduated scale and depend on a small firm's position in the channel of distribution. In other words, trade discounts recognize the fact that manufacturers, wholesalers, and retailers perform a variety of vital functions at various stages in the channel of distribution and compensate them for providing these needed activities. Figure 12.4 illustrates a typical trade discount structure.

Quantity Discounts. Quantity discounts are designed to encourage businesses to order large quantities of merchandise and supplies. Vendors are able to offer lower prices on bulk purchases because of the lower cost per unit of handling large orders. Quantity discounts normally exist in two forms: noncumulative and cumulative. Noncumulative quantity discounts are granted only if a large enough volume of merchandise is purchased in a single

trade discounts—
discounts established on a graduated scale that depend on a small firm's position in the channel of distribution.

quantity discounts—
discounts designed to encourage businesses to order large quantities of merchandise and supplies.

Figure 12.4
Trade Discount Structure

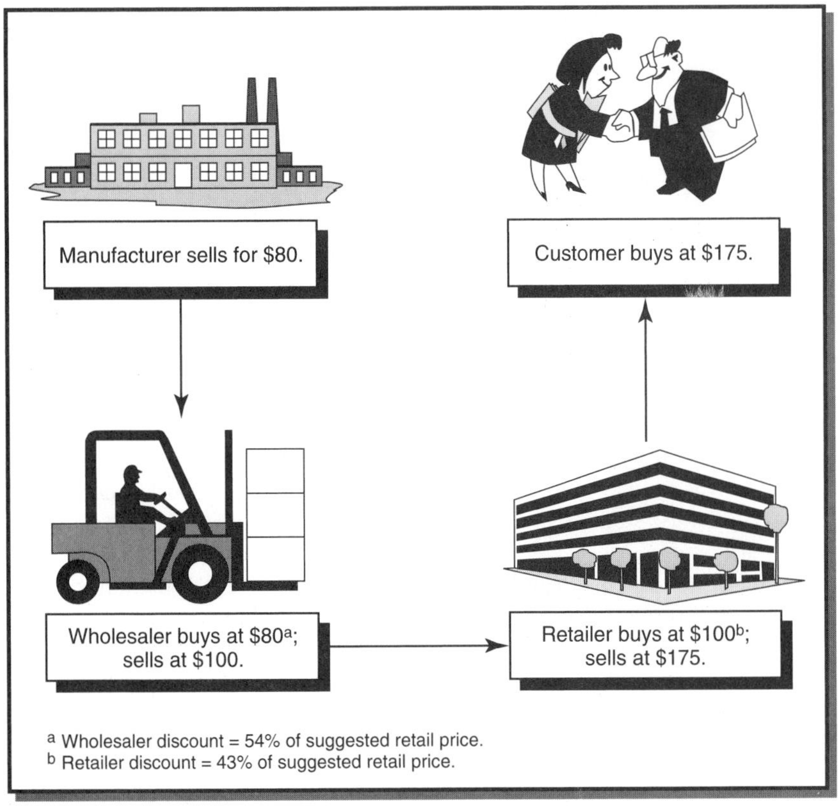

Manufacturer sells for $80.

Customer buys at $175.

Wholesaler buys at $80ᵃ;
sells at $100.

Retailer buys at $100ᵇ;
sells at $175.

a Wholesaler discount = 54% of suggested retail price.
b Retailer discount = 43% of suggested retail price.

order. For example, a wholesaler may offer a small retailer a 3 percent discount only if she purchases 10 gross of Halloween masks in a single order. Table 12.5 shows a typical noncumulative quantity discount structure.

Cumulative quantity discounts are offered if a firm's purchases from a particular vendor exceed a specified quantity or dollar value over a predetermined time period. The time frame varies, but a yearly basis is most common. For example, a manufacturer of appliances may offer a small firm a 3 percent discount on subsequent orders if its purchases exceed $10,000 per year.

Some small business owners who normally buy in small quantities and are unable to qualify for quantity discounts can earn such discounts by joining buying groups, purchasing pools, or buying cooperatives.

For instance, Edward Reagan, owner of Performance Audio, joined a purchasing pool in an attempt to cut his company's health insurance costs. By joining with more than 4,300 other small business owners in California's state-sponsored Health Insurance Plan of California, Reagan was able to cut health insurance costs for himself and his eight employees by 42 percent![12]

Performance Audio

Order Size	Price
1—1,000 units	List price
1,001—5,000 units	List price—2%
5,001—10,000 units	List price—4%
10,001 units and above	List price—6%

Table 12.5
Noncumulative Quantity Discount Structure

cash discounts—
discounts offered to customers as an incentive to pay for merchandise promptly.

Cash Discounts. Cash discounts are offered to customers as an incentive to pay for merchandise promptly. Many vendors grant cash discounts to avoid being used as an interest-free bank by customers who purchase merchandise and then neglect to pay by the invoice due date. To encourage prompt payment of invoices, many vendors allow customers to deduct a percentage of the purchase amount if payment is remitted within a specified time. Cash discount terms "2/10, net 30" are common in many industries. This notation means that the total amount of the invoice is due 30 days after its date, but if the bill is paid within 10 days, the buyer may deduct 2 percent from the total. A discount offering "2/10, EOM" (EOM means "end of month") indicates that the buyer may deduct 2 percent if the bill is paid by the tenth of the month after purchase.

Generally, it is sound business practice to take advantage of cash discounts The money saved by paying invoices promptly is freed up for use elsewhere. Conversely, there is an implicit (opportunity) cost of forgoing a cash discount. By forgoing a cash discount, the small business owner is, in effect, paying an annual interest rate to retain the use of the discounted amount for the remainder of the credit period. For example, suppose that the Print Shop receives an invoice for $1,000 from a vendor offering a cash discount of 2/10, net 30. Figure 12.5 illustrates this situation and shows how to compute the cost of forgoing the cash discount.

Actually, it costs the Print Shop $20 to retain the use of its $980 for an extra 20 days. Translating this into an annual interest rate:

$$I = P \times R \times T$$

where

I = interest in $ \qquad R = rate of interest in %

P = principle in $ \qquad T = time factor (number of days/360)

So, to compute R, the annual interest rate,

$$R = \frac{I}{P \times T}$$

In our example,

$$R = \frac{\$20}{980 \times \dfrac{20}{360}}$$

$$= 36.735\%$$

Figure 12.5
A Cash Discount

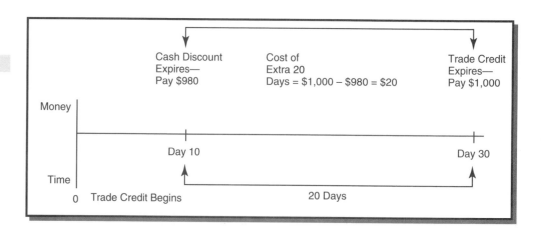

Cash Discount Expires— Pay $980

Cost of Extra 20 Days = $1,000 – $980 = $20

Trade Credit Expires— Pay $1,000

Money

Day 10   Day 30

Time

0   Trade Credit Begins   20 Days

Cash Discount Terms	Cost of Forgoing (Annually)
2/10, net 30	36.735%
2/30, net 60	34.490%
2/10, net 60	14.693%
3/10, net 30	55.670%
3/10, net 60	22.268%

Table 12.6
The Cost of Forgoing Cash Discounts

The cost to the Print Shop of forgoing the cash discount is 36.735 percent per year! If there is $980 available on day 10 of the trade credit period, the owner should pay the invoice unless he is able to earn a return greater than 36.735 percent on it. If the owner does not have $980 on day 10 but can borrow it at less than 36.735 percent, he should do so to take advantage of the cash discount. Table 12.6 summarizes the cost of forgoing cash discounts offering various terms.

Timing

Timing the purchase of merchandise and supplies is also a critical element of any purchasing plan. The owner must schedule delivery dates so that the firm does not lose customer goodwill from stockouts. Also, the owner must concentrate on maintaining proper control over the firm's inventory investment without tying up an excessive amount of working capital. There is a trade-off between the cost of running out of stock and the cost of carrying additional inventory.

When planning delivery schedules for inventory and supplies, the owner must consider the **lead time** for an order, that is, the time gap between placing an order and receiving it. Generally, business owners cannot expect instantaneous delivery of merchandise. As a result the manager must plan reorder points for inventory items with lead time in mind.

To determine when to order merchandise for inventory, a small business manager must calculate the reorder point for key inventory items. Developing a reorder point model involves determining the lead time for an order, the usage rate for the item, the minimum level of stock allowable, and the economic order quantity (EOQ). The lead time for an order is the time gap between placing an order with a vendor and actually receiving the goods. It may take as little as a few hours or as long as several weeks to process purchase requisitions and orders, contact the supplier, receive the goods, and sort them into the inventory. Obviously, owners who purchase from local vendors encounter shorter lead times than those who rely on distant suppliers.

The usage rate for a particular product can be determined from past inventory and accounting records. The small business owner must estimate the speed at which the supply of merchandise will be depleted over a given time. The anticipated usage rate for a product determines how long the supply will last. For example, if an owner projects that she will use 900 units in the next 6 months, the usage rate is five units per day (900 units/180 days). The simplest reorder point model assumes that the firm experiences a linear usage rate; that is, depletion of the firm's stock continues at a constant rate over time.

The small business owner must determine the minimum level of stock allowable. If the firm runs out of a particular item (i.e., incurs stockouts), customers may lose faith in the business, and customer ill will may develop. To avoid stockouts many firms establish a minimum level of inventory greater than zero. In other words, they build a cushion, called **safety stock**, into their inventories in case demand runs ahead of the anticipated usage rate.

5. Calculate a company's reorder point.

lead time—*the time gap between placing an order and receiving it.*

safety stock—*a cushion of extra inventory in case demand runs ahead of the anticipated usage rate.*

In such cases the owner can dip into the safety stock to fill customer orders until the stock is replenished.

To compute the reorder point for an item, the owner must combine this inventory information with the product's EOQ. The following example will illustrate the reorder point technique:

$$L = \text{lead time for an order} = 5 \text{ days}$$
$$U = \text{usage rate} = 18 \text{ units/day}$$
$$S = \text{safety stock (minimum level)} = 75 \text{ units}$$
$$\text{EOQ} = \text{economic order quantity} = 540 \text{ units}$$

The formula for computing the reorder point is:

$$\text{Reorder point} = (L \times U) + S$$

In this example,

$$\text{Reorder point} = (5 \text{ days} \times 18 \text{ units/day}) + 75 \text{ units}$$
$$= 165 \text{ units}$$

Thus, this owner should order 540 more units when inventory drops to 165 units. Figure 12.6 illustrates the reorder point situation for this small business.

The simple reorder technique makes certain assumptions that may not be valid in particular situations. First, the model assumes that the firm's usage rate is constant, when in fact for most small businesses demand varies daily. Second, the model assumes that lead time for an order is constant, when, in fact, few vendors deliver precisely within lead time estimates. Third, in this sample model, the owner never taps safety stock; however, late deliveries or accelerated demand may force the owner to dip into this inventory reserve. Although more advanced models relax some of these assumptions, the simple model can be a useful inventory guideline for making inventory decisions in a small company. For many small businesses these assumptions are not realistic. More often, demand is not known and constant. Using the previous model under these conditions would lead to stock-outs, lost sales, and customer ill will.

Another popular reorder point model assumes that the demand for a product during its lead time is normally distributed (see Figure 12.7). The area under the normal curve at any

Figure 12.6
Reorder Point Model

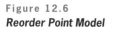

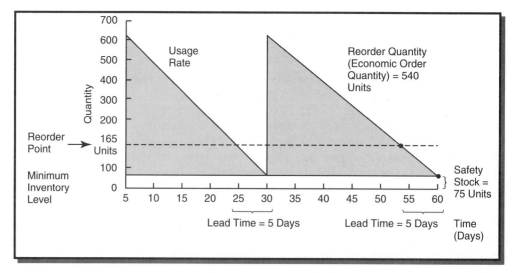

Figure 12.7
Demand During Lead Time

given point represents the probability of that particular demand level occurring. Figure 12.8 illustrates the application of this normal distribution to the reorder point model *without* safety stock. The model recognizes that three different demand patterns can occur during a product's lead time. Demand pattern 1 is an example of below-average demand during lead time; demand pattern 2 is an example of average demand during lead time; and demand pattern 3 is an example of an above-average demand during lead time.

If the reorder point for this item is $\bar{D}_L$, the average demand for the product during lead time, 50 percent of the time demand will be below average (note that 50 percent of the area under the normal curve lies below average). Similarly, 50 percent of the time demand during lead time will exceed the average, and the firm will experience stockouts (note that 50 percent of the area under the normal curve lies above average).

To reduce the probability of inventory shortage, the small business owner can increase the reorder point above $\bar{D}_L$ (average demand during lead time). But how much should the owner increase the reorder point? Rather than attempt to define the actual costs of carrying extra inventory versus the costs of stockouts (remember the trade-off described earlier), this

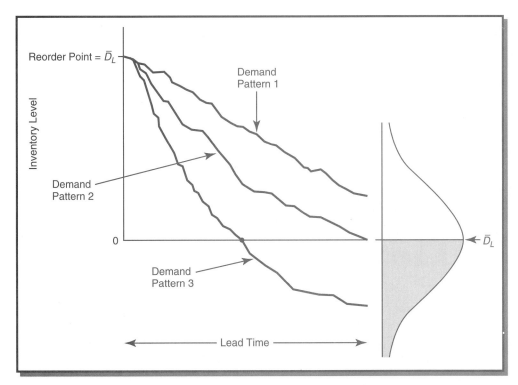

Figure 12.8
Reorder Point Without Safety Stock

model allows the small business owner to determine the appropriate reorder point by setting a desired customer service level. For example, the owner may wish to satisfy 95 percent of customer demand for a product during lead time. This service level determines the amount of increase in the reorder point. In effect, these additional items serve as a safety stock:

$$\text{Safety Stock} = \text{SLF} \times \text{SD}_L$$

where

SLF = service level factor (the appropriate Z score)

SD_L = standard deviation of demand during lead time

Table 12.7 shows the appropriate service level factor *(Z* score) for some of the most popular target customer service levels.

Figure 12.9 shows how this normally distributed reorder point model *with* safety stock works. In this case the manager has set a 95 percent customer service level—that is, to meet 95 percent of the demand during lead time. The normal curve in the model without safety stock (from Figure 12.8) is shifted up so that 95 percent of the area under the curve lies above the zero inventory level. The result is a reorder point that is higher than the original reorder point by the amount of the safety stock:

$$\text{Reorder point} = \overline{D}_L + (\text{SLF} \times \text{SD}_L)$$

where

$\overline{D}_L$ = average demand during lead time (original reorder point)

SLF = service level factor (the appropriate Z score)

SD_L = standard deviation of demand during lead time

To illustrate, suppose that the demand for a product during its lead time (one week) is normally distributed with an average of 325 units and a standard deviation of 110 units. If the service level is 95 percent, the service level factor (from Table 12.7) would be 1.645. The reorder point would be:

$$R = 325 + (1.645 \times 110) = 325 + 181$$
$$= 506 \text{ units}$$

Figure 12.10 on page 400 illustrates the shift from a system without safety stock to one with safety stock for this example. With a reorder point of 325 units ($\overline{D}_L$), this small business owner will experience inventory shortages during lead time 50 percent of the time. With a reorder point of 506 units (i.e., a safety stock of 181 units), the business owner will experience inventory stockouts during lead time only 5 percent of the time (i.e., a customer service level of 95 percent).

Table 12.7
Service Level Factors and Z Scores*

Target Customer Service Level	Z Score
99.0%	2.33
97.5%	1.96
95.0%	1.645
90.0%	1.275
80.0%	0.845
75.0%	0.675

*Any basic statistics book will provide a table of areas under the normal curve, which will give the appropriate *Z* score for *any* service level factor.

Figure 12.9
***Reorder Point
With Safety Stock***

Reorder Point

Demand
Pattern 1

Inventory Level

Demand
Pattern 2

Demand
Pattern 3

Safety
Stock

0

Lead Time

$\bar{D}_L$

0.05

YOU BE THE CONSULTANT...

OK Tire Store, Part 2

Since Wes Cassell's death, Rick and Flora have been managing the OK Tire Store without any major problems. Of course, there were many times when they wished they could have been able to ask Wes how to handle a particular matter, but with every passing day, they were learning and gaining more confidence. Managing inventory was still their greatest challenge, however. On one of the store's busiest days, an employee ran up to Rick and said, "Boss, we're out of our best-selling tire . . . Thought you'd want to know."

Rick couldn't believe it, but in the mad rush over the previous few days, he had totally forgotten about placing an order with their wholesale supplier. Flora had not been around to catch the error since Rick had given her a few days off to rest since they had both been keeping long hours for months. "I want to make sure this never happens again," Rick muttered to

himself. "I'm going to start carrying 100 of these tires as safety stock just to make sure we don't run out. But, if it takes four days for our supplier to fill an order, and we operate 310 days per year, when should I reorder?"

1. Assume the role of consultant. Using the EOQ calculation you helped Rick make earlier in this chapter, compute his reorder point using the simple reorder point model.

2. What are the disadvantages of this reorder point model?

3. Suppose that Rick has determined that the demand for these tires is normally distributed during the lead time with a standard deviation of 18.4 tires. If Rick wants to establish a service level of 90 percent, what should OK's reorder point be? Suppose that Rick decides to boost OK's desired service level to 99 percent. What would the company's reorder point be? Which reorder point would you recommend to Rick? Explain.

Figure 12.10
**Shift From a No-Safety
Stock System to a
Safety Stock System**

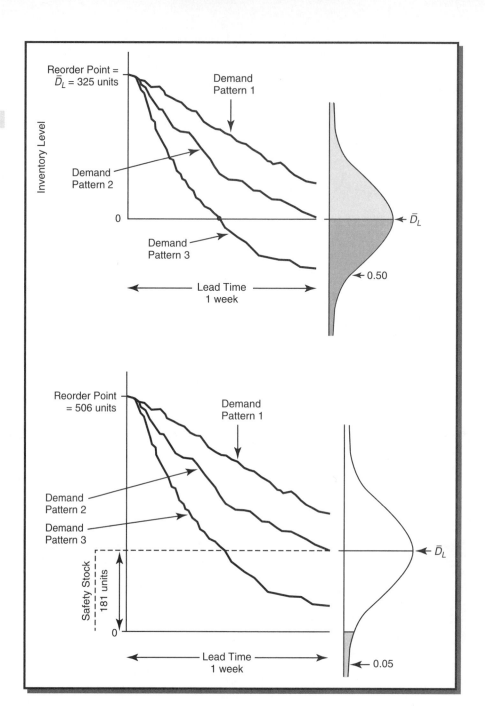

Vendor/Supplier Analysis

6. Develop a
vendor or supplier
analysis model.

Selecting the right vendors or suppliers for a business can have an impact well beyond simply obtaining the lowest cost. Although searching for the best price will always be an important factor, successful small business owners must always consider other factors in vendor selection such as reliability, reputation, quality, support services, and proximity. To add some objectivity to the selection process, many firms develop a vendor rating system. Obviously, each company's system differs based on its relevant purchasing criteria.

The first step in developing a scale is to determine which criteria are most important in selecting a vendor (e.g., price, quality, prompt delivery). The next step is to assign weights to each criterion to reflect its relative importance. The third step involves developing a grading scale for comparing vendors on the criteria. Developing a usable scale requires that the owner maintain proper records of past vendor performances. Finally, the owner must compute a weighted total score for each vendor and select the vendor scoring the highest on the set of criteria.

Consider the following example.

Bravo Bass Boats, Inc. is faced with choosing from among several suppliers of a critical raw material. The company's owner has decided to employ a vendor rating scale to select the best vendor using the following procedure.

Step 1. Determine important criteria. The owner of Bravo has selected the following criteria:

Quality
Price
Prompt delivery
Service
Assistance

Step 2. Assign weights to each criterion to reflect its relative importance.

Criteria	*Weight*
Quality	35
Price	30
Prompt delivery	20
Service	10
Assistance	5
Total	100

Step 3. Develop a grading scale for each criterion.

Criteria	*Grading Scale*
Quality	$\dfrac{\text{Number of acceptable lots from vendor X}}{\text{Total number of lots from vendor X}}$
Price	$\dfrac{\text{Lowest quoted price of all vendors}}{\text{Price offered by vendor X}}$
Prompt delivery	$\dfrac{\text{Number of on-time deliveries from vendor X}}{\text{Total number of deliveries from vendor X}}$
Service	A subjective evaluation of the variety of service offered by each vendor
Assistance	A subjective evaluation of the advice and assistance provided by each vendor

Step 4. *Compute a weighted score for each vendor.*

Criteria	Weight	Grade	Weighted Score (Weight x Grade)
Vendor 1			
Quality	35	9/10	31.5
Price	30	12.5/12.5	30.0
Prompt delivery	20	10/10	20.0
Service	10	8/10	8.0
Assistance	5	5/5	5.0
Total weighted score			**94.5**
Vendor 2			
Quality	35	8/10	28.0
Price	30	12.5/13.5	27.8
Prompt delivery	20	8/10	16.0
Service	10	8/10	8.0
Assistance	5	4/5	4.0
Total weighted score			**83.8**
Vendor 3			
Quality	35	7/10	24.5
Price	30	12.5/12.5	30.0
Prompt delivery	20	6/10	12.0
Service	10	7/10	7.0
Assistance	5	1/5	1.0
Total weighted score			**74.5**

Based on this analysis of the three suppliers, Bravo should purchase the majority of this raw material from Vendor 1.

This vendor analysis procedure assumes that the business owner has a detailed working knowledge of the supplier's network. In the case of new startup business, this will seldom be the case. The entrepreneur will need to focus on finding suppliers and then gathering data to conduct the vendor analysis.

Finding Supply Sources

Many new entrepreneurs have difficulty locating supplies of inventory and materials to start their businesses. One obvious way to find vendors for your products is to approach established businesses selling similar lines and interview the managers. Clearly, local competitors are not likely to be very cooperative with new competition, but a beginning entrepreneur may get the necessary information from businesses outside the immediate trading area.

Another source for establishing vendor relationships is the industry trade association. These associations often have available to members lists of vendors and suppliers as well as other useful information. They also sponsor trade shows, where large numbers of vendors and suppliers promote their versions of the latest styles, product innovations, and technological advancements. The local chamber of commerce may be able to provide vendor and supplier connections, especially if a company is located in a large city.

A number of publications offer the entrepreneur a great deal of assistance in locating vendors. A ready source of cheap information for any new owner is the telephone directory's Yellow Pages. Scouring the appropriate product category should yield a good list of prospective vendors. Vendor advertisements in trade publications also offer a great deal of information about needed merchandise and materials. Library reference books that list national distributors and their product lines are another information source. Publications such as *American Wholesalers and Distributors Directory; MacRae's Blue Book; Standard and Poor's Register of Corporations, Executives, and Industries; Ward's Service Industries, USA*; and the *Thomas Register of American Manufacturers* provide lists of products and services along with names, addresses, telephone numbers, and ratings of manufacturers and suppliers. The *U.S. Industrial Directory* is similar to the *Thomas Register*, although its coverage is not as broad. The owner also should consult the U.S. Chamber of Commerce publication, *Sources of State Information and State Industrial Directories*, which lists state directories of manufacturers. Entrepreneurs whose product lines have an international flair may look to *Kelly's Manufacturers and Merchants Directory, Marconi's International Register*, or *Trade Directories of the World* for information on companies throughout the world dealing in practically every type of product or service. The well-prepared entrepreneur who utilizes these resources should have little difficulty in locating vendors and suppliers and in establishing sound relationships with them.

Selecting a Vendor

Once the small business owner identifies potential vendors and suppliers, she must decide which one (or ones) to do business with. A critical task in this process is specifying key factors in selecting a vendor and then employing them in analyzing the options. The following discusses some of the factors relevant to choosing the right supplier.

NUMBER OF SUPPLIERS. One important question the small business owner faces is, "Should I buy from a single supplier or from several different sources?" Concentrating purchases at a single supplier gives the owner several advantages. First, the small business receives a good deal of individual attention from the sole supplier, especially if orders are substantial. Second, the firm may receive quantity discounts if its orders are large enough.

For example, Duds 'n Suds, the combination bar and laundromat chain, purchases all of the equipment for its franchised outlets from a single supplier so that it can negotiate the best package of price, quality, warranties, and service.[13]

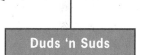

Duds 'n Suds

Finally, the firm is able to cultivate a closer, more cooperative relationship with the supplier. Suppliers are more willing to assist companies they consider to be their loyal customers. The results of such a partnership can be better-quality goods and services. "Companies win by treating suppliers not as adversaries but as partners," says one purchasing specialist.[14]

However, using a single vendor also has disadvantages. The small firm may experience shortages of critical materials if its only supplier suffers a catastrophe, such as a fire, strike, or bankruptcy. In such cases business owners might have trouble establishing an alternate supply source and be forced to shut down for a time.

The advantages of developing close, cooperative relationships with a single supplier outweigh the risks of sole sourcing in most cases. A business owner must exercise great caution in choosing a supplier to make sure she picks the right one, however. Otherwise the outcome could be disastrous.

RELIABILITY. The business owner must evaluate the potential vendor's ability to deliver adequate quantities of quality merchandise as needed. The most common complaint purchasing managers have against suppliers is late delivery.[15] Late deliveries or shortages cause lost sales and create customer ill will unnecessarily.

PROXIMITY. The small firm's physical proximity to the vendor is an important factor in choosing a supplier. Costs for transporting merchandise can substantially increase the cost of merchandise to the buyer. Also, some vendors offer better service to local small businesses because they know the owners. In addition, a small business owner is better able to solve coordination problems with nearby vendors than with distant vendors.

SERVICES. The small business owner must evaluate the range of services vendors offer. Do salespeople make regular calls on the firm, and are they knowledgeable about their product line? Will the sales representatives assist in planning store layout and in creating attractive displays? Will the vendor make convenient deliveries on time? Is the supplier reasonable in making repairs on equipment after installation and in handling returned merchandise? Are sales representatives able to offer useful advice on purchasing and other managerial functions? Before choosing a vendor, the small business owner should answer these and other relevant questions about potential suppliers.

7. Explain the various inventory control systems available and the advantages and disadvantages of each.

Inventory Control

So far in this chapter we have focused on the decisions related to buying the goods and services the company needs to conduct business. Now it is time to explore procedures designed to maximize the value of the firm's inventory while reducing both the costs and the risks of owning that inventory. For most small businesses, next to payroll cost, inventory is the biggest expense as well as an essential component of the firm's assets. Carrying too much of it "lowers a company's profitability—and not just because of the money spent to produce all those goods . . . sitting unsold on . . . the shelves, but also because it eats up additional and unnecessary warehouse space; boosts personnel needs . . .; necessitates the purchase of extra inventory insurance; and increases borrowing needs," according to one banker.[16] For these reasons, once an owner has established proper purchasing procedures and has selected the best vendors or suppliers, her focus shifts to establishing techniques for monitoring and controlling inventory. The payoff can be huge. "Companies can increase their profitability 20 to 50 percent through prudent inventory management," says one expert.[17]

Managing inventory involves the following interrelated steps:

1. *Develop an accurate sales forecast.* The proper inventory levels for each item are directly related to the demand for that item. A business can't sell what it does not have, and conversely, an owner does not want what will not sell.

2. *Develop a plan to make inventory available when and where customers want it.* Inventory will not sell if customers have a difficult time finding it.

3. *Build relationships with your most critical suppliers to ensure that you can get the merchandise you need when you need it.* Business owners must keep suppliers and vendors aware of how their merchandise is selling and communicate their needs to them. Vendors and suppliers can be an entrepreneur's greatest allies in managing inventory.

4. *Set realistic inventory turnover objectives.* Keeping in touch with their customers' likes and dislikes and monitoring their inventory allows owners to better estimate the most likely buying patterns for different types of merchandise. One of the factors having the greatest impact on a company's sales, cash flow, and ultimate success is its inventory turnover ratio.

5. *Compute the actual cost of carrying inventory.* Carrying costs would include such items as interest on borrowed money, insurance expenses associated with the inventory, and all other related operating costs. Without an accurate cost of carrying inventory, it is impossible to determine an optimum inventory level.

6. *Use the most timely and accurate information system the business can afford to provide the facts and figures necessary to make critical inventory decisions.* Computers and modern point-of-sale terminals that are linked to a company's inventory records allow business owners to know exactly which items are selling and which ones are not.

7. *Teach employees how inventory control systems work so that they can contribute to managing the firm's inventory on a daily basis.* All too often, the employees on the floor have no idea of how the various information systems and inventory control techniques operate or interact with one another. Consequently, the people closest to the inventory and the sale of merchandise contribute little to controlling the firm's inventory.

The owner's goal is to find the balance between the cost of holding inventory and the requirement to have the needed merchandise when the customer demands it. Walking this inventory tightrope is never easy. If a firm focuses solely on minimizing costs, it is likely to lose sales and generate ill will due to a failure to meet customer needs. If, on the other hand, the firm strives to meet every peak customer demand, inventory costs will climb out of control.

Inventory Control Systems

Regardless of the type of inventory control system an owner chooses, he must recognize the importance of Pareto's law (or the 80/20 rule, described earlier in this chapter)**,** which holds that about 80 percent of the value of the firm's inventory comes from about 20 percent of the items kept in stock. Some of the firm's items are high dollar volume goods, while others account for only a small portion of sales volume. Because most sales are generated by a small percentage of items, the owner should focus the majority of his inventory control efforts on this 20 percent. Observing this simple principle ensures that an entrepreneur will spend time controlling only the most productive—and, therefore, most valuable—inventory items. With this technique in mind, we now examine three basic types of inventory control systems: perpetual, visual, and partial.

PERPETUAL INVENTORY SYSTEMS. **Perpetual inventory systems** are designed to maintain a running count of the items in inventory. Though a number of different perpetual inventory systems exist, they all have a common element: They all keep a continuous tally of each item added to or subtracted from the firm's stock of merchandise. The basic perpetual inventory system uses a perpetual inventory sheet that includes fundamental product information such as the item's name, stock number, description, economic order quantity (EOQ), and reorder point.

These perpetual inventory sheets are usually placed next to the merchandise in the warehouse or storage facility. Whenever a shipment is received from a vendor, the quantity is entered in the receipts column and added to the total. When an item is sold and taken from inventory, it is simply deducted from the total. As long as this procedure is followed consistently, the owner can quickly determine the number of each item on hand.

Although consistent use of the system yields accurate inventory counts at any moment, sporadic use creates problems. If managers or employees take items out of stock or place them in inventory without recording them, the perpetual inventory sheet will yield incorrect totals and can foul up the entire inventory control system. Another disadvantage of this system is the cost of maintaining it. Keeping such records for a large number of items and ensuring the accuracy of the system can be excessively expensive. Therefore, these systems are used most frequently and most successfully in controlling high dollar volume items that require strict monitoring. Management must watch these items closely and ensure that inventory records are accurate.

Technical advances in computerized cash registers have overcome many of the disadvantages of using the basic perpetual inventory system. Small businesses now are able to

perpetual inventory systems—*inventory control systems designed to maintain a running count of the items in inventory.*

**point-of-sale (POS)
systems**—*computerized
systems that double as
both cash registers and
inventory control systems.*

afford computerized **point-of-sale (POS) systems** that perform all of the functions of a traditional cash register and maintain an up-to-the-minute inventory count. While POS systems are not new (major retailers have been using them for more than 25 years), their affordable prices are. Not so long ago most systems required mini- or mainframe computers and cost $20,000 or more. Today small business owners can set up POS systems on personal computers for less than $1,000! These systems rely on an inventory database, and as items are rung up on the register, product information is recorded and inventory balances are adjusted. Using the system, a business owner can get up-to-the-minute information on which items are selling fastest, which ones are not selling at all, and how many are in stock at any time. Plus, his inventory records are more accurate and are always up-to-date. He also can generate instantly a variety of reports to aid in making purchasing decisions! The system can be programmed to alert the owner when the supply of a particular item drops below a predetermined reorder point, or even to print automatically a purchase order for the EOQ indicated. Computerized systems such as these make it possible for the owner to employ a basic perpetual inventory system on a large number of items—a task that, if performed manually, would be virtually impossible. A well-designed POS system gives an owner the information he needs to make sound inventory and purchasing decisions on a timely basis without spending a small fortune to do it.

SPECIFIC PERPETUAL INVENTORY SYSTEMS. Perpetual inventory systems operate in a number of ways, but three basic variations are particularly common: the sales ticket method, the sales stub method, and the floor sample method.

The Sales Ticket Method. Most small businesses use sales tickets to summarize individual customer's transactions. These tickets serve two major purposes: They provide the customer with a sales receipt for the merchandise purchased, and they provide the owner with a daily record of the number of specific inventory items sold. The **sales ticket method** operates by gathering all the sales tickets at the end of each day and transcribing the data onto the appropriate perpetual inventory sheet. By posting inventory deductions to the perpetual inventory system from sales tickets, the small business manager can monitor sales patterns and keep close control on inventory. The primary disadvantages of using such a system is the time required to make it function properly. Most mangers find it difficult to squeeze in the time needed to post sales tickets to the perpetual inventory system.

sales ticket method—*an
inventory control system
that operates by gathering
the sales tickets at the
end of each day and
transcribing the data onto
the appropriate perpetual
inventory sheet.*

sales stub method—*an
inventory control system
that uses a pull-apart
ticket to post sales from
inventory at the end of
each day.*

The Sales Stub Method. The principle behind the **sales stub method** of inventory control is the same as that underlying the sales ticket method, but its mechanics are slightly different. Retail stores often attach a ticket with two or more parts containing relevant product information to each inventory item in stock. When an employee sells an item, he removes a portion of the stub and places it in a container. At the end of the day the owner posts the inventory deductions recorded by the stubs to the proper perpetual inventory sheet.

floor sample method—
*an inventory control
system for big-ticket items
that uses a small pad with
numbered sheets
indicating how many units
are left in stock.*

The Floor Sample Method. The **floor sample method** of controlling inventory is commonly used by businesses selling big-ticket items with high unit cost. In many cases these items are somewhat bulky and are difficult to display in large numbers. For example, the owner of a small furniture store might receive a shipment of 15 roll-top desks in a particular style. A simple technique for maintaining control of these items is to attach a small pad to the display desk with sheets numbered in descending order from 15 to 1. Whenever an employee sells a roll-top desk, he removes a sheet from the pad. As long as the system is followed consistently, the owner is able to determine accurate inventory levels with a quick pass around the sales floor. When the supply of a particular item dwindles, the owner simply calls the vendor to replenish the inventory. The procedure is simple and serves its purpose.

ee sells a roll-top desk, he removes a sheet from the pad. As long as the system is followed consistently, the owner is able to determine accurate inventory levels with a quick pass around the sales floor. When the supply of a particular item dwindles, the owner simply calls the vendor to replenish the inventory. The procedure is simple and serves its purpose.

VISUAL INVENTORY CONTROL SYSTEMS. One common method of controlling inventory in a small business is the **visual control system**, in which the manager simply conducts a periodic visual inspection to determine the quantity of various items she should order. As mentioned earlier, manual perpetual inventory systems can be excessively costly and time consuming. Such systems are impractical when the business stocks a large number of low-value items with low dollar volume. Therefore, many owners rely on the simplest, quickest inventory control method: the visual system. Unfortunately, this method is also the least effective for ensuring accuracy and reliability. Oversights of key items often lead to stock-outs and resulting lost sales. The biggest disadvantage of the visual control system is its inability to detect and to foresee shortages of inventory items.

Generally, a visual inventory control system works best in firms where daily sales are relatively consistent, the owner is closely involved with the inventory, the variety of merchandise is small, and items can be obtained quickly from vendors. For example, small firms dealing in perishable goods use visual control systems very successfully, and rarely, if ever, rely on analytical inventory control tools. For these firms, shortages are less likely to occur under a visual system; when they do occur, they are less likely to create major problems. Still, the manager who uses a visual inventory control system should leave reminders to make regular inspections and be alert to shifts in customer buying patterns that alter required inventory levels.

PARTIAL INVENTORY CONTROL SYSTEMS. For the small business owner with limited time and money, the most viable option for inventory management is a partial inventory control system. Such a system relies on the validity of the 80/20 rule. For example, if a small business carries 5,000 different items in stock, roughly 1,000 of them account for about 80 percent of the firm's sales volume. Experienced business owners focus their control efforts on those 1,000 items. Still, many managers seek to maintain tight control over the remaining 4,000 items, a frustrating and wasteful practice. The wise small business owner will design an inventory control system with this principle in mind. One of the most popular partial inventory control systems is the ABC system.

The ABC Method of Inventory Control. Too many managers apply perpetual inventory control systems universally across every item maintained in stock when a partial control system would be much more practical. Partial inventory systems minimize the expense involved in analyzing, processing, and maintaining records, a substantial cost of any inventory control system. The ABC method is one such approach, focusing control efforts on that small percentage of items that account for the majority of the firm's sales. The typical **ABC system** divides a firm's inventory into three major categories:

A items: those items that account for a high dollar usage volume

B items: those items that account for a moderate dollar usage volume

C items: those items that account for a low dollar usage volume

The dollar usage volume that an item accounts for measures the relative importance of that item in the firm's inventory. Note that value is not necessarily synonymous with high unit cost. In some instances a high-cost item that generates only a small dollar volume can be classified as an A item. But, more frequently, A items are those that are low to moderate in cost and high volume by nature.

visual control system—*a simple inventory control system in which a manager conducts a periodic visual inspection to determine the quantity of items she should order.*

ABC system—*an inventory control system that divides a firm's inventory into three categories: A (high dollar usage volume), B (moderate dollar usage volume), and C (low dollar usage volume) so that an owner can exercise the proper degree of control over each category.*

annual dollar usage volume— *the cost per unit of an item multiplied by the annual quantity used.*

$$190 \times \$75 = \$14,250$$

The next step is to arrange the products in descending order based on the computed annual dollar usage volume. Once so arranged, they can be divided into appropriate classes by applying the following rule:

A items: roughly the top 15 percent of the items listed

B items: roughly the next 35 percent

C items: roughly the remaining 50 percent

For example, Florentina's small retail shop is interested in establishing an ABC inventory control system to lower losses from stockouts, theft, or other hazards. The manager has computed the annual dollar usage volume for the store's merchandise inventory, as shown in Table 12.8. (For simplicity, we show only 12 inventory items.)

The ABC inventory control method divides the firm's inventory items into three classes depending on the items' value. Figure 12.11 graphically portrays the segmentation of the items listed in Table 12.8.

The purpose of classifying items according to their value is to establish the proper degree of control over each item held in inventory. Clearly, it is wasteful and inefficient to exercise the same level of control over C items as A items. Items in the A classification should be controlled under a perpetual inventory system with as much detail as necessary. Analytical tools and frequent counts may be required to ensure accuracy, but the extra cost of tight control for these valuable items is usually justified. The manager should not retain a large supply of reserve or safety stock because this ties up excessive amounts of money in inventory, but she must monitor the stock closely to avoid stockouts and lost sales.

Control of B items should rely more on periodic control systems and basic analytical tools such as EOQ and reorder point analysis. The manager can maintain moderate levels

Table 12.8
Calculating Annual Dollar Usage Volume and an ABC Inventory for Florentina's

Item	Annual Dollar Usage Volume	Percent of Annual Dollar Usage
Paragon	$374,100	42.0
Excelsior	294,805	33.1
Avery	68,580	7.7
Bardeen	54,330	6.1
Berkeley	27,610	3.1
Tara	24,940	2.8
Cattell	11,578	1.3
Faraday	9,797	1.1
Humboldt	8,016	0.9
Mandel	7,125	0.08
Sabot	5,344	0.06
Wister	4,453	0.05
Total	$890,678	100.00

Classification	Items	Annual Dollar Usage	Percent of Total
A	Paragon, Excelsior	$668,905	75.1%
B	Avery, Bardeen, Berkeley, Tara	175,460	19.7%
C	Cattell, Faraday, Humboldt, Mandel, Sabot, Wister	46,313	5.2%
Total		$890,678	100.0%

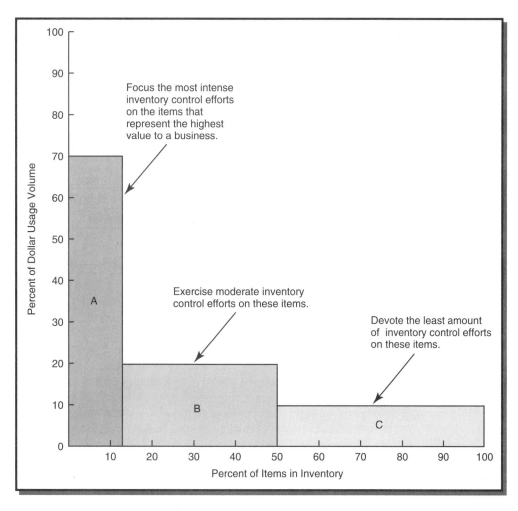

Figure 12.11
ABC Inventory Control

of safety stock for these items to guard against shortages, and can afford monthly or even bimonthly merchandise inspections. Because B items are not as valuable to the business as A items, less rigorous control systems are required.

C items typically comprise a minor proportion of the small firm's inventory value and, as a result, require the least effort and expense to control. These items are usually large in number and small in total value. The most practical way to control them is to use uncomplicated records and procedures. Large levels of safety stock for these items are acceptable because the cost of carrying them is usually minimal. Substantial order sizes often enable the business to take advantage of quantity discounts without having to place frequent orders. The cost involved in using detailed recordkeeping and inventory control procedures greatly outweighs the advantages gleaned from strict control of C items.

One practical technique for maintaining control simply is the two-bin system, which keeps two separate bins full of material. The first bin is used to fill customer orders, while the second bin is filled with enough safety stock to meet customer demand during the lead time. When the first bin is empty, the owner places an order with the vendor large enough to refill both bins. During the lead time for the order, the manager uses the safety stock in the second bin to fill customer demand. A variation of this technique is the level control system. Here the manager fills the bin with the usual amount of safety stock and marks the level with a brightly colored line. When the supply of material reaches the colored line, she orders enough stock to refill the bin.

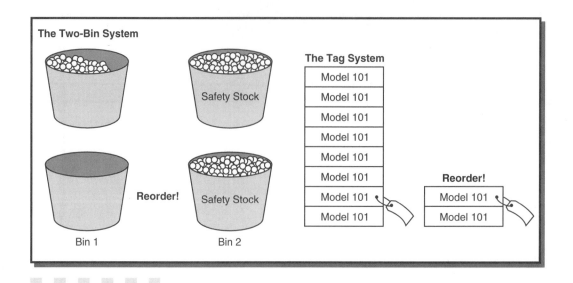

Figure 12.12
The Two-Bin and Tag Systems of Inventory Control

When storage space or the type of item does not suit the two-bin system, the owner can use a tag system. Based on the same principle as the two-bin system, which is suitable for many manufacturers, the tag system applies to most retail, wholesale, and service firms. Instead of placing enough inventory to meet customer demand during lead time into a separate bin, the owner marks this inventory level with a brightly colored tag. When the supply is drawn down to the tagged level, the owner reorders the merchandise. Figure 12.12 illustrates the two-bin and tag system of controlling C items.

In summary, a business owner minimizes total inventory costs when she spends time and effort controlling items that represent the greatest inventory value. Some inventory items require strict, detailed control techniques, while others cannot justify the cost of such systems. Because of its practicality, the ABC inventory system is commonly used in industry. In addition, the technique is easily computerized, speeding up the analysis and lowering its cost. Table 12.9 summarizes the use of the ABC control system.

Table 12.9
ABC Control Features

Feature	A Items	B Items	C Items
Level of control	Monitor closely and maintain tight control	Maintain moderate control	Maintain loose control
Reorder	Based on forecasted requirements	Based on EOQ calculations and past experience	When level gets low, reorder
Recordkeeping	Keep detailed records of receipts and disbursements	Use periodic inspections and control procedures	No records required
Safety stock	Low levels of safety stock	Moderate levels of safety stock	High levels of safety stock
Inspection frequency	Frequent monitoring of schedule changes	Periodic checks on changes in requirements	Few checks on requirements

The Shirt Store

Carol Konop learned the business of making and selling men's shirts by starting at the bottom. In the 1970s, she took a part-time job as a bookkeeper for a shirt manufacturer and retailer on New York's Lower East Side. When Konop worked her way up to vice president of operations, she met Yale Shanfield, a supplier with a reputation for reliability and quality. Then, in 1986, Konop decided to launch her own retail shirt company, and she knew she wanted Shanfield to be her supplier. Using $100,000 of her own money and $30,000 from two friends, she leased a prime location in the path of thousands of New York City commuters, just across from Grand Central Station. Today her company, The Shirt Store, stocks a uniquely large and select inventory of men's shirts in a wide variety of patterns, colors, and sizes. The store keeps an average of 1,200 dozen shirts in stock at any time and is always looking for new styles and designs. For instance, in Konop's first year of business, a customer asked for a shirt with horizontal stripes that he had seen a character in a hit movie wearing. The shirt remains a popular seller.

A key ingredient in Konop's strategy for success is her decision to have a labor contractor such as Shanfield manufacture her shirts rather than farm out production to cut-and-sew shops overseas. Shanfield's factory, the Barnesboro Shirt Company, lies just 300 miles west of New York City, which means that Konop's orders are filled quickly, giving her the ability to stock the latest styles and patterns. Konop pays about 48 percent of her gross revenues to Shanfield for manufacturing shirts; but because the two have such a close, cooperative relationship, she can offer top-quality shirts at prices 25 percent below those of her competitors. Her prices range from $37.50 to $85.00 for off-the-shelf shirts and from $75.00 to $260.00 for custom-made shirts, which are made at a nearby plant on Long Island.

The Shirt Store orders fabric, buttons, labels, and linings for collars and cuffs and has them delivered to Shanfield's warehouse. When Konop gives her design specifications to Shanfield, his factory launches into production. "Yale can just look at a sketch for a collar and say, 'This is what I have to do to sew it, and this is what it will cost,'" says Konop. Not only does Shanfield have to keep close control of costs, but he also must be able to make rapid deliveries. "Clients want faster turnaround for smaller lot sizes," he says. "To survive, I must practically run a custom-shirt business."

Konop purchases all of The Shirt Store's ready-to-wear shirts from Shanfield, and her orders account for 10 percent of Bamesboro's sales volume. Their customer/supplier relationship is built on trust, respect, and honesty. "He won't lie to me," says Konop. "If I say, 'Can you have the shirts here in time for my January sale?' and he can't do it, he'll say, 'Forget it; I can't make it.'" Konop and Shanfield stay in close contact with one another. In addition to the two or three visits each makes to the other's business every year, Konop calls the shirt factory anywhere from one to five times a day. When Konop places a shirt order, the "ticket" goes to the ordering-processing room, where Shanfield's son David calculates the cost for every operation required on the shirt. Shanfield's son-in-law Jeffrey Boyer figures out how to use each bolt of fabric most efficiently to minimize waste. Shanfield manages the factory, where the typical shirt goes through 52 different sewing operations. A collar alone may require 13 or 14 different steps. After four inspections, each shirt is pressed and packed and then shipped to the customer.

Konop's success with The Shirt Store has led her to look for a second location. She is currently looking for space in New York City's financial district, and has dreams of expanding beyond that. "If the United States can import all those shirts from abroad," she says with a grin, "Why can't we export mine?"

1. What dangers does Konop face by using Barnesboro as her sole supplier of off-the-shelf shirts? What benefits does Konop receive from such a close relationship with Barnesboro?

2. Would you recommend such close relationships with suppliers for most small businesses? Explain.

3. What suggestions would you make for further strengthening the supplier/customer relationship between The Shirt Store and Barnesboro?

4. What methods would you suggest to Konop for controlling her inventory of shirts?

Source: Adapted from Corinne K. Hoexter, "A Shirt Tale," *Your Company,* Spring 1993, pp. 22-25.

PHYSICAL INVENTORY COUNT. Regardless of the type of inventory control system used, the small business owner must always conduct a periodic physical inventory count. Even when the firm employs a perpetual inventory system, the owner must still count the actual number of items on hand because of the possibility of human error. A physical inventory count allows the manager to reconcile the actual amount of inventory in stock with the amount reported through the inventory control system. These counts give the manager a fresh start in determining the actual number of items on hand, and enable her to evaluate the effectiveness and the accuracy of her inventory control system.

The typical method of taking inventory involves two employees, one who calls out the relevant information for each inventory item and the other who records the count on a tally sheet. There are two basic methods of conducting a physical inventory count. One alternative is to take inventory at a regular interval. Many businesses take inventory at the end of the year. In an attempt to minimize counting, many managers run special year-end inventory reduction sales. This periodic physical count generates the most accurate measurement of inventory. The other method of taking inventory, called **cycle counting**, involves counting a number of items on a continuous basis. Instead of waiting until year-end to tally the entire inventory of items, the manager counts a few types of items each week and checks the numbers against the inventory control system. Such a system allows for continuous correction of mistakes in inventory control systems and detects inventory problems sooner.

Once again, technology can make the job of taking inventory much easier for the small business owner. **Electronic Data Interchange (EDI)** systems allow business owners to track their inventories and to place orders with vendors much faster and with fewer errors by linking them electronically. These systems often rely on hand-held computer terminals equipped with a scanning wand. The employee runs the wand across a bar-code label on the shelf that identifies the inventory item; then he counts the items on the shelf and enters that number using the number pad on the terminal. Then, by linking the hand-held terminal to a personal computer, he can download the physical inventory count into the company's inventory control software in seconds!

In some EDI systems, the vendor is tied into a company's POS system, monitoring it constantly; when its supply of a particular item drops to a preset level, the vendor automatically sends a shipment to replenish its stock.

For example, Cedar Works, a small manufacturer of cedar birdfeeders and mailboxes, went on-line with EDI to keep one of its biggest customers, Wal-Mart, happy. Cedar Works has formed such a close alliance with the retail giant that it no longer waits for Wal-Mart to send purchase orders. Using its EDI connection, the company replenishes the retailer's supplies based on anticipated demand at individual stores. Today, Cedar Works is linked via EDI with ten other retailers, including Home Depot and Nature Company.[18]

Just-in-Time (JIT) Techniques

Many U.S. manufacturers have turned to a popular inventory control method called the **just-in-time (JIT)** technique to reduce costly inventories and turn around their fortunes. Until recently these firms had accepted and practiced without question the following long-standing principles of manufacturing: Long production runs of standard items are ideal; machines should be up and running as much as possible; machines must produce a large number of items to justify long setup times and high costs; similar processes should be consolidated into single departments; tasks should be highly specialized; and inventories (raw material, work-in-process, and finished goods) should be large enough to avoid emergencies such as supply interruptions, strikes, and breakdowns.

The just-in-time philosophy, however, views excess inventory as a blanket that masks problems and as a source of unnecessary costs that inhibit a firm's competitive position. Under a JIT system, materials and inventory should flow smoothly through the production process without stopping. They arrive at the appropriate location just in time instead of becoming part of a costly inventory stockpile. JIT is a manufacturing philosophy that seeks to improve a company's efficiency. The key measure of manufacturing efficiency is the level of inventory maintained; the lower the level of inventory, the more efficient the production system. In the past, only large companies could reap the benefits of computerized

cycle counting—
counting the number of items in stock on a continuous basis.

Electronic Data Interchange (EDI)—a
system that allows business owners to track their inventories and to place orders with vendors much faster and with fewer errors by linking them electronically.

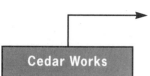
Cedar Works

8. Describe how just-in-time (JIT) inventory control techniques work.

just-in-time (JIT)—an
inventory control technique that views excess inventory as a blanket that masks problems; its goal is to minimize a company's inventory investment and to get items where they are needed "just in time."

JIT and inventory control software, but now a proliferation of inexpensive programs designed for personal computers gives small companies that ability.

At Mothers Work Inc., a chain of 450-plus maternity shops, Rebecca and Dan Mathias rely on a computerized inventory management system to tell them exactly what is selling, what isn't, and how long it will take to make or order more. Mothers Work uses the system to test market fashion ideas in its stores before committing to long production runs of goods that might not sell. With the system, if the Mathiases discover a hot-selling item, they can fill their store shelves with it in less than two weeks, compared to about six months at their competitors. The company also can replenish its inventory at its stores on a daily basis. The result: a leaner stock of inventory that turns over much more quickly and is much less likely to require markdowns to move off the shelf.[19]

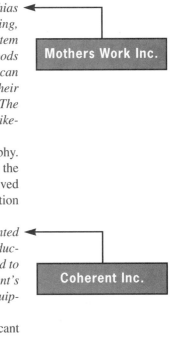

Almost any change that has this aim can be counted as part of the JIT philosophy. Companies adopting the JIT system look for ways to cut machine setup times, reduce the number of adjustments made during production, redesign plants so that machines involved in the same processes are closer together, and move parts to each manufacturing station only when they are needed.

When Coherent Inc., a California-based maker of printed circuit boards, implemented JIT in its factory, the results were astounding. Overhead costs fell by 58 percent, productivity climbed by more than 60 percent, and the company's cycle time (the time required to fill a customer's order) dropped by 90 percent! Also, teams of workers have used Coherent's computerized JIT system to help them reduce the setup time for the manufacturing equipment to practically zero.[20]

JIT is most effective in repetitive manufacturing operations where there are significant inventory levels, where production requirements can be forecast accurately, and where suppliers are an integral part of the system. Today, many suppliers recognize that extremely high quality and absolutely on-time delivery are essential elements of remaining competitive. JIT systems work because suppliers recognize that if they are unable to meet demands set forth by their customers, somebody else surely will.

At Bose Corporation's electronics manufacturing plant in Framingham, Massachusetts, vendors and suppliers have set up "in-plants," locations inside the company's factory, so that they can provide a seamless flow of materials into the production process. Part of the company's JIT II program, the concept is designed to reduce both the costs and the time involved in day-to-day transactions with suppliers. Other benefits Bose has reaped include improved product engineering and design, increased efficiency, and fewer vendor problems. "These people have total authority to create an order," says JIT II's creator Lance Dixon. "All they have to do is keep my materials going. It's a fresh, nontraditional relationship based on trust."[21]

Turning Slow-Moving Inventory into Cash

Managing inventory effectively requires that the business owner monitor her firm's inventory turnover ratio and compare it with other firms of similar size in the same industry. As you recall, the inventory turnover ratio is computed by dividing the firm's cost of goods sold by its average inventory. This ratio expresses the number of times per year the business turns over its inventory. In most cases, the higher the inventory turnover ratio, the better the small firm's financial position will be. A very low inventory turnover ratio indicates that much of its inventory may be stale and obsolete or that its inventory is too large.

Slow-moving items carry a greater chance of loss resulting from spoilage or obsolescence. Firms dealing in trendy fashion merchandise or highly seasonal items often experience losses as a result of being stuck with unsold inventory for long time periods (retail clothing stores that sell high-fashion styles are an example). Some small business owners are reluctant to sell these slow-moving items by cutting prices, but it is much more profitable to dispose of this merchandise as quickly as possible than to hold it in stock at regular prices. The owner who postpones marking down stale merchandise, fearing it would reduce profit and hoping that the goods will sell eventually at regular price, is making a huge mistake. The longer the merchandise sits, the dimmer the prospects of ever selling it, much less selling it at a profit. Pricing these items below regular price or even below cost is difficult, but it is much better than having valuable working capital tied up in unproductive assets.

The most common technique for liquidating slow-moving merchandise is the markdown. Not only is the markdown effective in eliminating slow-moving goods, but it also is a successful promotional tool. Advertising special prices on such merchandise helps the small business garner a larger clientele and contributes to establishing a favorable business image. Using special sales to promote slow-moving items helps create a functional program for turning over inventory more quickly. To get rid of a large supply of out-of-style neckties, one small business offered a "one cent sale" to customers purchasing neckwear at the regular price. One retailer of stereos and sound equipment chooses an unusual holiday—George Washington's birthday—to sponsor an all-out blitz, including special sales, prices, and promotions, to reduce its inventory. Other techniques that help eliminate slow-moving merchandise include the following:

- ☆ middle-of-the-aisle display islands that attract customer attention
- ☆ one-day-only sales
- ☆ quantity discounts for volume purchases
- ☆ bargain tables with a variety of merchandise for customers to explore
- ☆ eye-catching lights and tickets marking sale merchandise

CHAPTER SUMMARY

1. Understand the components of a purchasing plan: quality, quantity, price, timing, and vendor.

- The purchasing function is vital to every small business's success because it influences a company's ability to sell quality goods and services at reasonable prices. Purchasing is the acquisition of needed materials, supplies, services, and equipment of the right quality, in the proper quantities, for reasonable prices, at the appropriate time, and from the right suppliers.

2. Explain the elements of total quality management (TQM) and its impact on a small company's quality.

- Under the total quality management (TQM) philosophy, companies define a quality product as one that conforms to predetermined standards that satisfy customers' demands. The goal is to get *everything*—from delivery and invoicing to installation and follow-up—right the first time.
- To implement TQM successfully, a small business owner must rely on ten fundamental principles: Shift from a management-driven culture to a participative, team-based one; modify the reward system to encourage teamwork and innovation; train workers constantly to give them the tools they need to produce quality and to upgrade the company's knowledge base; train employees to measure

quality with the tools of statistical process control (SPC); use Pareto's law to focus TQM efforts; share information with everyone in the organization; focus quality improvements on astonishing the customer; don't rely on inspection to produce quality products and services; avoid using TQM to place blame on those who make mistakes; and strive for continuous improvement in processes as well as in products and services.

3. Conduct economic order quantity (EOQ) analysis to determine the proper levels of inventory.

- Many small businesses encounter difficulty controlling their inventory investments. A major goal is to generate adequate inventory turnover by purchasing proper quantities of merchandise. A useful device for computing the proper quantity is economic order quantity (EOQ) analysis. EOQ analysis yields the ideal order quantity, the amount that minimizes total inventory costs. Total inventory costs consist of three components: the cost of the units, holding (carrying) costs, and ordering (setup) costs. The EOQ balances the costs of ordering merchandise and the costs of carrying merchandise to yield minimum total inventory cost.

4. Differentiate among the three types of purchase discounts vendors offer: trade, quantity, and cash.

- Purchase discounts can lower the price of goods and services substantially, and the small business owner should take advantage of them. Discounts come in three versions: trade discounts, quantity discounts, and cash discounts.
- Trade discounts are established on a graduated scale and depend on a small firm's position in the channel of distribution. Quantity discounts are designed to encourage businesses to order large quantities of merchandise and supplies. Cash discounts are offered to customers as an incentive to pay for merchandise promptly.

5. Calculate a company's reorder point.
   - Timing of purchases is also a crucial element in administering a purchasing plan. A small business owner must recognize that there is a time gap between the placing of an order and actual receipt of the goods. The reorder point model tells the owner when to place an order to replenish the company's inventory.

6. Develop a vendor or supplier analysis model.
   - Creating a vendor or supplier analysis model involves four steps. Step 1: Determine the important criteria (i.e., price, quality, prompt delivery, service, etc.). Step 2: Assign weights to each criterion to reflect its relative importance. Step 3: Develop a grading scale for each criterion. Step 4: Compute a weighted score for each vendor.

7. Explain the various inventory control systems available and the advantages and disadvantages of each.
   - Three basic types of inventory control systems are available to the small business owner: perpetual, visual, and

periodic. Perpetual inventory control systems include the sales ticket method, which uses daily sales tickets to post inventory deductions to the perpetual inventory sheet; the sales stub method, which uses a sales stub of two or more parts to accomplish the same purpose as the sales ticket method; and the floor sample method, which involves attaching pads with numbered sheets to display items to keep track of the items in inventory.

- The visual inventory system is the most common method of controlling merchandise in the small business. Although it is simple and easy to use, it cannot detect shortages.
- The ABC system divides a firm's inventory into three categories depending on each item's dollar usage volume (cost per unit multiplied by quantity used per time period). The purpose of classifying items according to their value is to establish the proper degree of control over them.

8. Describe how just-in-time (JIT) inventory control techniques work.
   - The just-in-time system of inventory control sees excess inventory as a blanket that masks production problems and adds unnecessary costs to the production operation. Under a JIT philosophy, the level of inventory maintained is the measure of efficiency. Materials and parts should not build up as costly inventory. They should flow through the production process without stopping, arriving at the appropriate location "just in time."

DISCUSSION QUESTIONS

1. What is purchasing? Why is it important for the small business owner to develop a purchasing plan?
2. What is TQM? How can it help small business owners achieve the quality goods and services they require? Outline some of the basic principles of the TQM philosophy.
3. What is the economic order quantity? How does it minimize total inventory costs?
4. Should a small business owner always purchase the products with the lowest prices? Why or why not?
5. Briefly outline the three types of purchase discounts. Should the owner take advantage of them?
6. What is lead time? Outline the procedure for determining a product's reorder point.
7. Explain how a small business entrepreneur could locate suppliers and vendors for a new business.
8. Explain the procedure for developing a vendor rating scale. What factors are commonly used to evaluate suppliers?
9. Describe some of the incidental costs of carrying and maintaining inventory for the small business owner.

10. What is a perpetual inventory system? How does it operate? What are the advantages and disadvantages of using such a system.?
11. List and describe briefly the four versions of a perpetual inventory system.
12. What advantages and disadvantages does a visual inventory control system have over other methods?
13. What is the 80/20 rule, and why is it important in controlling inventory?
14. Outline the ABC inventory control procedure. What is the purpose of classifying inventory items using this procedure? Briefly describe the types of control techniques that should be used for A, B, and C items.
15. What is the basis for the JIT philosophy? Under what conditions does a JIT system work best?
16. Outline the two methods of taking a physical inventory count. Why is it necessary for every small business manager to take inventory?
17. Why are slow-moving items dangerous to the small business? What can an owner do to convert them into cash?

1. Interview the owner of a local small business about his or her purchasing plan. How does the owner locate and evaluate suppliers? How does the owner compute order quantities? Does he or she take advantage of purchase discounts? What factors are most important to him or her in selecting vendors?

2. Assume that you are about to open a small business. Describe how you would locate reliable suppliers for your product. Use some of the sources described in this chapter to prepare a list of vendors for your product line.

3. Contact a local small business owner and request the following information: What type of inventory control system is used? How does it work? Does the 80/20 rule apply to the inventory? Does the owner's inventory control system reflect the 80/20 rule? How does the owner liquidate slow-moving merchandise?

4. Visit a small manufacturer and ask if it is using a just-in-time system to integrate inventory and production. If so, ask what the results have been. What problems were initially encountered? Were these problems solved? What improvements, if any, has the manufacturer experienced?

SURFING THE NET

1. Visit the home page of the National Association of Purchasing Management at:

http://www.napm.org/napm.html

and the National Association of Purchasing Management-Silicon Valley, Inc. at:

http://catalog.com/napmsv/welcome.html

Write a short paper on the activities of these associations and the assistance they offer business owners.

2. Visit the Web site of the American Productivity and Inventory Control Society (APICS) at:

http://lionhrtpub.com/APICS.html

Go into the "Article Index" and research one of the topics covered in this chapter. Prepare a one-page paper on what you learn.

3. Using one of the search engines on the World Wide Web (WWW) such as Lycos, Magellan, Yahoo!, or others, conduct a search on the phrase *Electronic Data Interchange (EDI)*. What are some of the advantages and disadvantages of EDI? Prepare a brief report on your findings.

4. A. Working with a team of your classmates, go to the case study, "Electronic Commerce on the World Wide Web" at:

http://www/cox.smu.edu/mis/cases/webcase/home.html

Analyze the facts of this case and answer the discussion questions listed at this site.

B. Go to the Web site on EDI at the following address:

http://www.ecrc.gmu.edu/edistone/ediqztop.html

Test your knowledge of EDI by taking the 12-question quiz at this site. How did you score?

5. Access MIT's W. Edwards Deming home site at:

http://www-caes.mit.edu/products/deming/home.html

or the Web site of the W. Edwards Deming Institute at:

http://www.deming.org/

Explore the features of one of these sites and prepare a one-page report on W. Edwards Deming and the quality principles he taught.

Leading the Growing Company and Planning for Management Succession

A leader is someone I'll follow somewhere I'd never go by myself.
- George Grant

Next to doing a good job yourself, the greatest joy is in having someone else do a first-class job under your direction.
- William Feather

Enthusiasm finds the opportunities, and energy makes the most of them.
- Henry S. Haskins

LEARNING OBJECTIVES

Upon completion of this chapter, you will be able to:

1. **Explain** the challenges involved in the entrepreneur's role as leader and what it takes to be a successful leader.

2. **Describe** the importance of hiring the right employees and how to avoid making hiring mistakes.

3. **Explain** how to build the kind of company culture and structure which supports the entrepreneur's mission and goals and motivates employees to achieve them.

4. **Discuss** the ways in which entrepreneurs can motivate their workers to higher levels of performance.

5. **Describe** the steps in developing a management succession plan for a growing business that will allow a smooth transition of leadership to the next generation.

leadership—*the process of influencing and inspiring others to work to achieve a common goal and then giving them the power and the freedom to achieve it.*

The Entrepreneur's Role as Leader

To be successful, a small business manager must assume a wide range of roles, tasks, and responsibilities, but none is more important than the role of *leader*. Some entrepreneurs are uncomfortable in this role, but they must learn to be effective leaders if their companies are to grow and reach their potential. **Leadership** is the process of influencing and inspiring others to work to achieve a common goal and then giving them the power and the freedom to achieve it. Without leadership ability, entrepreneurs—and their companies—never rise above mediocrity. Yet, leadership is not an easy task to learn; the skills needed to do it well are constantly changing. In the past, many small business managers relied on fear and intimidation as their primary leadership tools. Today, however, the work force is more knowledgeable, more skilled, and demands a more sophisticated style of leadership.

Until recently, experts compared the leader's job to that of a symphony orchestra conductor. Like the symphony leader, a small business manager made sure that everyone in the company was playing the same score, coordinated individual efforts to produce a harmonious sound, and directed the orchestra members as they played. The conductor (manager) retained virtually all of the power and made all of the decisions about how the orchestra would play the music without any input from the musicians themselves. Today's successful small business leader, however, is more like the leader of a jazz band, which is known for its improvisation, innovation, and creativity. Max DePree, former head of Herman Miller, Inc., a highly successful office furniture manufacturer, explains the connection this way:[1]

> Jazz band leaders must choose the music, find the right musicians, and perform—in public. But the effect of the performance depends on so many things—the environment, the volunteers playing in the band, the need for everybody to perform as individuals and as a group, the absolute dependence of the leader on the members of the band, the need for the followers to play well . . . The leader of the jazz band has the beautiful opportunity to draw the best out of the other musicians. We have much to learn from jazz-band leaders, for jazz, like leadership, combines the unpredictability of the future with the gifts of individuals.

In short, management and leadership are not the same, yet both are essential to a small company's success. Leadership without management is unbridled; management without leadership is uninspired. Leadership gets a small business going; management keeps it going. Stephen Covey, author of *Principle-Centered Leadership*, explains the difference between management and leadership this way:[2]

> Leadership deals with people; management deals with things. You manage things; you lead people. Leadership deals with vision; management deals with logistics toward that vision. Leadership deals with doing the right things; management focuses on doing things right. Leadership deals with examining the paradigms on which you are operating; management operates within those paradigms. Leadership comes first, then management, but both are necessary.

Leadership and management are intertwined; one without the other means that a small business is going nowhere.

Effective leaders should exhibit the following behaviors:

☆ *Create a set of values and beliefs for employees and passionately pursue them.* Employees look to their leaders for guidance in making decisions. Leaders should be like beacons in the night, constantly shining light on the principles, values, and beliefs on which they founded their companies.

☆ *Respect and support employees.* To gain the respect of their employees, leaders must first respect those who work for them.

☆ *Set the example for employees.* A leader's words ring hollow if he fails to "practice what he preaches." Few signals are transmitted to workers more quickly than a leader who sells employees on one set of values and principles and then acts according to a different set. One manager explains, "You've got to walk the talk. If there is ambiguity about your message or values, people will opt out."[3]

☆ *Focus employees' efforts on challenging goals and keep them driving toward those goals.* Effective leaders have a clear vision of where they want their companies to go, and they are able to communicate their vision to those around them. Leaders must repeatedly reinforce the goals they set for their companies.

☆ *Provide the resources employees need to achieve their goals.* Effective leaders know that workers cannot do their jobs well unless they have the tools they need. They not only provide workers with the physical resources they need to excel but also the necessary intangible resources such as training, coaching, and mentoring.

☆ *Communicate with employees.* Leaders recognize that helping workers see the company's overarching goal is just one part of effective communication; encouraging employee feedback and then listening is just as vital. In other words, they know that communication is a two-way street.

☆ *Value the diversity of workers.* Smart business leaders recognize the value of their workers' varied skills, abilities, backgrounds, and interests. When channeled in the right direction, such diversity can be a powerful weapon in achieving innovation and maintaining a competitive edge.

☆ *Celebrate workers' successes.* Effective leaders recognize that workers want to be winners and do everything they can to encourage top performance among their people. The rewards they give are not always financial; in many cases, it may be as simple as a handwritten congratulatory note.

☆ *Encourage creativity among workers.* Rather than punish workers who take risks and fail, effective leaders are willing to accept failure as a natural part of innovation and creativity. They know that innovative behavior is the key to future success and do everything they can to encourage it among workers.

☆ *Maintain a sense of humor.* One of the most important tools a leader can have is a sense of humor. Without it, work can become dull and unexciting for everyone.

☆ *Keep an eye on the horizon.* Effective leaders are never satisfied with what they and their employees accomplished yesterday. They know that yesterday's successes are not enough to sustain their companies indefinitely. They see the importance of building and maintaining sufficient momentum to carry their companies to the next level.

Leading an organization—whatever its size—is one of the biggest challenges any manager faces. Yet, for an entrepreneur, leadership success is one of the key determinants of the company's success. In addition to the uncertainties of dealing with people, the job of the organizational leader is constantly changing. One business writer explains, "The new leader is...the one who sees clearly the goal, shares repeatedly and forcefully the vision, provides the tools, trains and enables co-workers to manage and improve their processes, remains persistent in the face of adversity, and inspires others to take an ownership position in the completion of the mission—by example." Table 13.1 on pages 420–421 offers a short quiz to test your leadership skills.

To be effective, a small business leader must perform four vital tasks:

☆ Hire the right employees and constantly improve their skills.

☆ Build an organizational culture and structure that allow both workers and the company to reach their potential.

☆ Motivate workers to higher levels of performance.

☆ Plan for "passing the torch" to the next generation of leadership.

Table 13.1

Take this quiz to test your leadership skills

Source: *Your Company,* June/July 1996, p. 61.

As commanders from Attila the Hun to GE's Jack Welch have shown, you can't get your troops to advance your cause unless you know how to lead them. To help assess your leadership capabilities, answer the following nine questions and then score yourself. The test was developed by Development Dimensions International (DDI), a respected leadership training firm in Pittsburgh.

Questions

1. Sharing with employees my personal feelings and rationale about decisions (such as why we have to cut budgets) is a sign of a weak leader. **TRUE   FALSE**

2. As the owner, I should step in and take charge if an employee's project runs into major problems. **TRUE   FALSE**

3. Delegating makes employees resentful because their responsibilities or workload will increase; it also takes less time to do the work myself. **TRUE   FALSE**

4. When two of my employees are having a conflict, it's best for me to step in and resolve the problem. **TRUE   FALSE**

5. It's critical for me to keep an open, honest dialogue with my employees, including sharing aspects of the company's financial health or future plans. **TRUE   FALSE**

6. Leaders should give employees continual feedback on what they are doing wrong, to increase productivity and ensure that important goals are met. **TRUE   FALSE**

7. Because I own the business, I'm really the best person to inspire and motivate employees as they work on projects. **TRUE   FALSE**

8. The best way to build employee confidence is to supervise projects closely. **TRUE   FALSE**

9. The most important characteristic of a leader is remaining consistent. **TRUE   FALSE**

Answers

1. **FALSE**. Disclosing your own feelings, thoughts and rationale about a situation in a balanced way will instill loyalty, motivation and enthusiasm in employees. When disclosing information, however, consider what's appropriate for you, the other person, and the company.

2. **FALSE**. Although tempting, taking over when projects falter sends the wrong message to everyone. Instead, assess the situation before you jump in. A leader's role is to provide support without removing responsibility and to coach staffers to find their own solutions. Work with your employees to fix the problem.

3. **FALSE.** Delegation is an important leadership tool. New assignments will help staffers improve their skills and learn more about the business. The challenge is to match the right person or work group to the assignment and then provide the necessary resources. Don't forget, however, to carefully establish the boundaries of these new responsibilities and levels of authority.

4. **FALSE** Taking charge, or even ignoring conflict, is not the best approach because you remove responsibility for solving problems from the employee. As a leader, your best choices are to listen and mediate or provide support as the parties work through the source of conflict.

5. **TRUE**. Fear is the most common reaction to change. The best way to allay fears is to keep your employees informed about your plans and how these changes will impact their jobs.

6. **FALSE**. Feedback should be balanced and specific and should include advice that will help staffers improve their performance. Remember, a constant stream of negative feedback is demotivating.

7. **FALSE**. Today's most effective leaders maximize and stimulate the talents and skills of others. These leaders who place an emphasis on sharing responsibility, coaching, providing resources, helping people through change and forming partnerships can be found at all levels of an organization.

8. **FALSE**. When you're running a small business, you can't look over everyone's shoulder. Instead, teach your employees how to think through problems, ideas, and opportunities.

9. **TRUE.** Being consistent was considered the most desirable quality of a leader in a recent leadership study by DDI that surveyed nearly 1,500 people representing a cross section of positions. That way, employees aren't wondering whether "good boss" or "bad boss" will show up today.

Hiring the Right Employees

*2. **Describe** the importance of hiring the right employees and how to avoid making hiring mistakes.*

The decision to hire a new employee is an important one for every business, but its impact is magnified many times in a small company. Every new hire a business owner makes determines the heights to which the company can climb—or the depths to which it will plunge. "Bad hires" are incredibly expensive, and no organization, especially small ones, can afford too many of them. One study concluded that an employee hired into a typical entry-level position who quits after six months costs a company about $17,000 in salary, benefits, and training. In addition, the intangible costs—time invested in the new employee, lost opportunities, reduced morale among coworkers, and business setbacks—are seven times the direct costs of a bad hire. In other words, the total price tag for this bad hire is about $136,000![5]

In 1992, after four years in business, Erler Industries, an industrial painting and finishing service, earned a large contract with Dell Computer Corporation. After working with just six employees since its founding, the company was in the awkward position of having to hire 175 people into entry-level positions almost overnight! Desperate for employees, Linda and Mark Erler ran a coupon in the North Vernon, Indiana paper offering a $50 bonus to anyone they hired. The coupon enticed enough applicants so that the Erlers met their staffing goals. Unfortunately, they had to hire workers so rapidly that they could not check references, and problems quickly surfaced. "It was very risky," says Linda, recalling the night that one group of new hires came to work with "whiskey in their soda cans." Employee turnover skyrocketed. "Everyone had to be replaced five or six times before we found a person who really wanted to work," she says.[6]

Erler Industries

Avoiding Hiring Mistakes

As crucial as finding good employees is to a small company's future, it is no easy task. One expert estimates that of every three employees a business hires, one makes a solid contribution, one is a marginal worker, and one is a hiring mistake.[7] For instance, the owner of four franchised fast-food restaurants who deals with an annual turnover rate of 150 to 175 percent says, "Sometimes we have to hire people, knowing full well that they aren't going to work out for the long term."[8] Even though the importance of hiring decisions is magnified in small companies, small businesses are most likely to make hiring mistakes because they lack the human resources experts and the disciplined hiring procedures large companies have. In the early days of a company, an entrepreneur rarely takes the time to create job descriptions and specifications; instead, he usually hires people because he knows or trusts them rather than for their job skills. Then, as the company grows, the business owner hires people to fit in around these existing employees, often creating a very unusual, inefficient organization structure built around jobs that are poorly planned and designed.

The following guidelines can help small business managers avoid making costly hiring mistakes.

CREATE PRACTICAL JOB DESCRIPTIONS AND JOB SPECIFICATIONS. Small business owners must recognize that what they do *before* they ever start interviewing candidates for a position determines to a great extent how successful they will be at hiring winners. The first step is to perform a **job analysis**, the process by which a firm determines the duties and nature of the jobs to be filled and the skills and experience required of the people who are to fill them. The first objective of a job analysis is to develop a **job description**, a written statement of the duties, responsibilities, reporting relationships, working conditions, and materials and equipment used in a job. A results-oriented job description explains what a job entails and the duties the person filling it is expected to perform. One small business owner uses the following "recipe" for writing job descriptions in his company: job title, job summary, duties to be performed, nature of supervision, job's relationship to other jobs in the company, working conditions, definitions of job-specific terms, and general comments needed to clarify any of the preceding categories.[9]

Preparing job descriptions is a task most small business owners overlook; however, this may be one of the most important parts of the hiring process because it creates a "blueprint" for the job. One hiring consultant explains, "It's important for a small company to spend a good amount of time defining the tasks that need to be accomplished." If they do, he says, "they've gone a long way toward finding the right person."[10] Without this blueprint, a manager tends to hire the person with experience whom they like the best. Useful sources of information for writing job descriptions include the manager's knowledge of the job, the worker(s) currently holding the job, and the *Dictionary of Occupational Titles (D.O.T)*, available at most libraries. The *Dictionary of Occupational Titles*, published by the Department of Labor, lists more than 20,000 job titles and descriptions and serves as a useful tool for getting a small business owner started when writing job descriptions. Table 13.2 provides an example of the description drawn from the D.O.T. for an unusual job.

The second objective of a job analysis is to create a **job specification**, a written statement of the qualifications and characteristics needed for a job stated in such terms as education, skills, and experience. A job specification shows the small business manager the kind of person to recruit and establishes the standards an applicant must meet to be hired. When writing job specifications, some managers define the traits a candidate needs to do a job well. Does the person have to be a good listener, empathetic, well organized, decisive, or a "self-starter?" Table 13.3 provides an example that links the tasks for a sales representative's job (drawn from a job description) to the traits or characteristics a small business owner identified as necessary to succeed in that job.

PLAN AN EFFECTIVE INTERVIEW. Once the manager knows what she must look for in a job candidate, then she can develop a plan for conducting an informative job interview. Too often, small business owners go into an interview unprepared, and as a result, they fail to get the information they need to judge the candidate's qualifications, qualities, and suitability for the job. Conducting an effective interview requires a small business owner to know what she wants to get out of the interview in the first place and to develop a series of questions to extract that information. The following guidelines will help an owner develop interview questions that will give her meaningful insight into an applicant's qualifications, personality, and character.

job analysis—*the process by which a firm determines the duties and the nature of the jobs to be filled and the skills and experience of the people who are to fill them.*

job description—*a written statement of the duties, responsibilities, reporting relationships, working conditions, and materials and equipment used in a job.*

job specification—*a written statement of the qualifications and characteristics needed for a job stated in such terms as education, skills, and experience.*

Table 13.2

A Sample Job Description from the Dictionary of Occupational Titles

Worm Picker—gathers worms to be used as fish bait; walks about grassy areas, such as gardens, parks, and golf courses and picks up earthworms (commonly called dew worms and nightcrawlers). Sprinkles chlorinated water on lawn to cause worms to come to the surface, and locates worms by use of lantern or flashlight. Counts worms, sorts them, and packs them into containers for shipment. (# 413.687 - 014 *D.O.T.*)

Job task	Trait or Characteristic
Generate and close new sales.	"outgoing"; persuasive; friendly
Make 15 "cold calls" per week.	a "self-starter"; determined; optimistic; independent; confident
Analyze customers' needs and recommend proper equipment.	good listener; patient; empathetic
Counsel customers about options and features needed.	organized; polished speaker; "other-oriented"
Prepare and explain financing methods; negotiate finance contracts.	honest; "numbers-oriented"; comfortable with computers
Retain existing customers	customer-oriented; relationship builder

Table 13.3

Linking Tasks from a Job Description to the Traits Necessary to Perform a Job Successfully

★ *Develop a series of core questions and ask them of every candidate.* To give the screening process more consistency, smart business owners rely on a set of relevant questions they ask in every interview. Of course, they also customize each interview using impromptu questions based on an individual's responses.

★ *Ask open-ended questions (including on-the-job scenarios) rather than questions calling for "yes" or "no" answers.* These types of questions are most effective because they encourage candidates to talk about their work experience in a way that will disclose the presence or the absence of the traits and characteristics the business owner is seeking.

★ *Create hypothetical situations candidates would be likely to encounter on the job and ask how they would handle them.* Building the interview around such questions gives the owner a preview of the candidate's work habits and attitudes.

★ *Probe for specific examples in the candidate's past work experience that demonstrate the necessary traits and characteristics.* A common mistake interviewers make is failing to get candidates to provide the details they need to make an informed decision.

★ *Ask candidates to describe a recent success and a recent failure and how they dealt with them.* Smart entrepreneurs look for candidates who describe them both with equal enthusiasm because they know that peak performers put as much into their failures as they do their successes and usually learn something valuable from their failures.

Table 13.4 on page 424 shows an example of some interview questions one manager uses to uncover the traits and characteristics he seeks in a top-performing sales representative.

CONDUCT THE INTERVIEW. An effective interview contains three phases: breaking the ice, asking questions, and selling the candidate on the company.

★ *Breaking the ice.* In the opening phase of the interview the manager's primary job is to diffuse the tension that exists because of the nervousness of both parties. Many skilled interviewers use the job description to explain the nature of the job and the company's culture to the applicant. Then they use "ice-breakers"—questions about a hobby or special interest—to get the candidate to relax.

> *For instance, to loosen up one very tense but promising candidate, one entrepreneur asked about his hobby, military history. "He launched into a description of the Battle of Midway that was so enthralling, I told him, 'Since you can come across like that, I'm going to give you a shot,'" recalls the business owner. "He went on to be a star salesman."*[11]

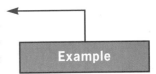

Example

★ *Asking questions.* During the second phase of the interview, the employer asks the questions from her question bank to determine the applicant's suitability for the job. Her primary job at this point is to *listen.* Effective interviewers spend about 25 percent of the

Trait or Characteristic	Question
"outgoing"; persuasive; friendly; "a self-starter"; determined; optimistic; independent; confident.	How do you persuade reluctant prospects to buy?
good listener; patient; empathetic; organized; polished speaker; "other-oriented."	What would you say to a fellow salesperson who was getting more than his share of rejections and was having difficulty getting appointments?
honest; customer-oriented; relationship builder.	How do you feel when someone questions the truth of what you say? What do you do in such situations?

Other questions: If you owned a company, why would you hire yourself?

If you were head of your department, what would you do differently? Why?

How do you recognize the contributions of others in your department?

interview talking and about 75 percent listening. They also take notes during the interview to help them ask follow-up questions based on a candidate's comments and to evaluate a candidate after the interview is over. Experienced interviewers also pay close attention to a candidate's nonverbal clues, or body language, during the interview. They know that candidates may be able to say exactly what they want with their words, but that their body language does not lie! One interviewer refers to an applicant's body language as "music," saying, "An interviewer who listened only to the words without taking the music . . . into account would miss [much] make-or-break data about the candidate."[12]

"Human Resources."

Source: Drawing by P. Steiner; © 1995 The New Yorker Magazine, Inc.

Small business owners must be careful to make sure they avoid asking candidates illegal questions. At one time, interviewers could ask wide-ranging questions covering just about every area of an applicant's background. Today, interviewing is a veritable minefield of legal liabilities, waiting to explode in the unsuspecting interviewer's face. Companies are more vulnerable to job discrimination lawsuits now than ever before. Although the Equal Employment Opportunity Commission (EEOC), the government agency responsible for enforcing employment laws, does not outlaw specific interview questions, it does recognize that some questions can result in employment discrimination. If a candidate files charges of discrimination against a company, the burden of proof shifts to the employer to prove that all preemployment questions are job related and are nondiscriminatory. In addition, many states have passed laws that forbid the use of certain questions or screening tools in interviews. To avoid trouble, a business owner should keep in mind why he is asking a particular question. The goal is to find someone who is qualified to do the job well. By steering clear of questions about subjects that are peripheral to the job itself, employers are less likely to ask questions that will land them in court. Wise business owners ask their attorneys to review their bank of questions before using them in an interview. Table 13.5 offers a quiz entitled "Is It Legal?" to help you understand which kinds of questions are most likely to create charges of discrimination.

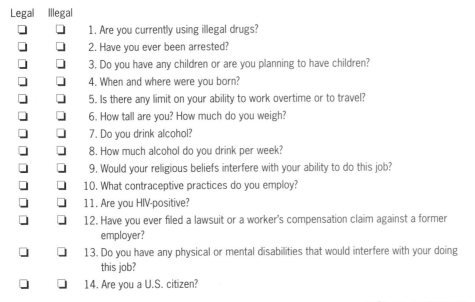

Table 13.5
Is It Legal?

Some interview questions can land an employer in legal hot water. Review the following interview questions and then decide whether you think each one is "legal" or "illegal."

Legal	Illegal	
❏	❏	1. Are you currently using illegal drugs?
❏	❏	2. Have you ever been arrested?
❏	❏	3. Do you have any children or are you planning to have children?
❏	❏	4. When and where were you born?
❏	❏	5. Is there any limit on your ability to work overtime or to travel?
❏	❏	6. How tall are you? How much do you weigh?
❏	❏	7. Do you drink alcohol?
❏	❏	8. How much alcohol do you drink per week?
❏	❏	9. Would your religious beliefs interfere with your ability to do this job?
❏	❏	10. What contraceptive practices do you employ?
❏	❏	11. Are you HIV-positive?
❏	❏	12. Have you ever filed a lawsuit or a worker's compensation claim against a former employer?
❏	❏	13. Do you have any physical or mental disabilities that would interfere with your doing this job?
❏	❏	14. Are you a U.S. citizen?

Answers: 1. Legal. 2. Illegal. Employers cannot ask about an applicant's arrest record, but they can ask if a candidate has ever been convicted of a crime. 3. Illegal. Employers cannot ask questions that would lead to discrimination against a particular group, e.g., women. 4. Illegal. The Civil Rights Act of 1964 bans discrimination on the basis of race, color, sex, religion, or national origin. 5. Legal. 6. Illegal. Unless a person's physical characteristics are important for high job performance (e.g., lifting 100-pound sacks of flour), employers cannot ask candidates such questions. 7. Legal. 8. Illegal. Notice the fine line between question number 7 and question number 8; this is what makes interviewing a challenge! 9. Illegal. This question would violate the Civil Rights Act of 1964. 10. Illegal. What relevance would this have to an employee's job performance? 11. Illegal. Under the Americans with Disabilities Act, which prohibits discrimination against people with disabilities, people with HIV or AIDS are considered disabled. 12. Illegal. Workers who file such suits are protected from retribution by a variety of federal and state laws. 13. Illegal. This question also would violate the Americans with Disabilities Act. 14. Illegal. This question violates the Civil Rights Act of 1964.

Continued

Table 13.5
Is It Legal? Continued

Small business owners can use the **"OUCH"** test as a guide for determining whether or not an interview question might be considered discriminatory:

☆ Does the question **O**mit references to race, religion, color, sex, or national origin?

☆ Does the question **U**nfairly screen out a particular class of people?

☆ Can you **C**onsistently apply the question to every applicant?

☆ Does the question **H**ave job-relatedness and business necessity?

☆ *Selling the candidate on the company.* In the final phase of the interview, the employer tries to sell her company to desirable candidates. This phase begins by allowing the candidate to ask questions about the company, the job, or other issues. Again, experienced interviewers note the nature of these questions and the insights they give into the candidate's personality. This part of the interview offers the employer a prime opportunity to explain to the candidate why her company is an attractive place to work. Remember: The best candidates will have other offers, and it's up to you to make sure they leave the interview wanting to work for your company. Finally, before closing the interview, the employer should thank the candidate and tell him what happens next (e.g., "We'll be contacting you about our decision within two weeks.")

Table 13.6 describes ten interviewing mistakes small business owners must avoid.

CHECK REFERENCES. Small business owners should take the time to check *every* applicant's references. Although many business owners see checking references as a formality and pay little attention to it, others realize the need to protect themselves (and their customers) from hiring unscrupulous workers. Is it really necessary? Yes! According to the American Association for Personnel Administration, approximately 25 percent of all résumés and applications contain at least one *major* fabrication.[13] Checking references thoroughly can help an employer uncover such false or exaggerated information. Rather than contacting only the references listed, experienced employers call an applicant's previous employers and talk to their immediate supervisors to get a clear picture of the applicant's job performance, character, and work habits.

Experienced small business owners know that the hiring process provides them with one of the most valuable raw materials their companies count on for success—capable, hardworking people. They know that hiring an employee is not a single event but the beginning of a long-term relationship.

Table 13.6
Ten Interviewing Mistakes

1. Succumbing to pressure to hire fast, which often arises as a result of failing to begin the search process far enough in advance. Plan ahead!

2. Falling victim to the halo effect, the tendency to attribute a host of positive attributes (e.g., intelligence, sense of humor, honesty, etc.) to a candidate based on one positive attribute (e.g. well spoken). This tendency is called the horn effect when it works in a negative fashion.

3. Asking leading or "canned" questions, those in which it is obvious to everyone involved, including the job applicant, what the "right" answer should be.

4. Talking too much. A common mistake inexperienced interviewers make is doing most of the talking while the candidate has to work hard just to become part of the conversation. Remember the 25/75 rule!

5. Failing to take notes during the interview. Jotting down key points, questions, and impressions as they occur will be of tremendous value when it's time to make a final decision about a particular candidate.

6. Accepting generalizations from a candidate. Effective interviewers probe for specific results and examples from candidates so they can verify applicants' qualifications and characteristics more objectively.

7. Asking questions that could lead to charges of discrimination and land the company in a nasty lawsuit. Keep questions job focused and consistent.

8. Failing to check a candidate's references. This routine procedure may uncover inconsistencies and false-hoods in the candidate's background. It can help small business owners avoid making a bad hire and law-suits charging them with negligent hiring. Ask former employers, "Would you hire him or her again?"

9. Making snap judgments. A common tendency among novice interviewers is to make a decision about a candidate in the first few minutes of an interview and then to spend the rest of the interview justifying that decision.

10. Committing candidate-order error. Experienced interviewers know that the order in which they interview candidates can affect their evaluation of them. Most recent candidates tend to have the advantage. Be aware of this tendency.

Table 13.6
Ten Interviewing Mistakes, Continued

Building the Right Culture and Structure

Culture

Company culture is the distinctive, unwritten code of conduct that governs the behavior, attitudes, relationships, and style of an organization. It is the essence of "the way we do things around here." In many small companies, culture plays as important a part in gaining a competitive edge as strategy does. It has a powerful impact on the way people work together in a business, how they do their jobs, and how they treat their customers. Company culture manifests itself in many ways—from how workers dress and act to the language they use. For instance, at some companies, the unspoken dress code requires workers to wear suits and ties, but at companies such as Apple Computer, employees routinely come to work in jeans and T-shirts. Bing Gordon, cofounder of Electronic Arts, a fast-growing video game company, owns only two suits, but he never wears them—certainly not to work. Electronic Arts' culture is *very* informal. "If somebody wears a suit to work around here, it's a sure sign that he is interviewing," says Gordon.[14]

In many companies, the culture creates its own language. At Disney, for instance, work-ers are not "employees"; they are "cast members." They don't merely go to work; their jobs are "parts in a performance." Disney's customers are "guests." When a cast member treats someone to lunch, it's "on the mouse." Anything negative, such as a cigarette butt on a walkway, is "a bad Mickey," and anything positive is "a good Mickey."

Creating a culture that supports a company's strategy is no easy task, but the entrepre-neurs who have been most successful at it "have a set of overarching beliefs that serve as powerful guides for everyday action—and that are reinforced in a hundred different ways, both symbolic and substantive," explains one business writer.[15] Culture arises from an entrepreneur's consistent and relentless pursuit of a set of core values that everyone in the company can believe in.

For instance, Amy Miller, founder of Amy's Ice Creams, a seven-store chain of gourmet ice-cream shops, knows that her company's competitive edge comes not only from selling quality products and friendly service but also from selling entertainment. Miller hires employees who enjoy performing for customers. They juggle their serving spades, toss scoops of ice cream to one another behind the counter, and dance on top of the freezer. They offer free ice cream to customers who will sing, dance, or recite poetry. Walking into an Amy's Ice Creams shop, customers might see employees wearing pajamas (on Sleep-over Night) or masks (on Star Wars Night); candles decorating the store (on Romance Night) or strobe lights (on Disco Night). Because of the culture Miller has created, employees know that part of their jobs is to create fun and entertainment for their customers; that's what keeps them coming back! Amy Miller has created a culture that values creativity in her com-pany. It allows her employees to have fun, entertains the customers, and keeps the compa-ny growing at 30 percent a year![16]

3. Explain how to build the kind of company culture and structure which supports the entrepreneur's mission and goals and motivates employees to achieve them.

company culture—*the distinctive, unwritten code of conduct that governs the behavior, attitudes, relationships, and style of an organization.*

Amy's Ice Creams

As companies grow from seedling businesses into leggy saplings and beyond (perhaps into giants in the business forest), they often experience dramatic changes in their cultures. Procedures become more formal, operations grow more widespread, jobs take on more structure, communication becomes more difficult, and the company's personality begins to change. As more workers come on board, employees find it more difficult to know everyone in the company and what their jobs are. Unless an entrepreneur works hard to maintain her company's unique culture, she may wake up one day to find that she has sacrificed that culture—and the competitive edge that goes with it—in the name of growth.

Ironically, growth can sometimes be a small company's biggest enemy, causing a once successful business to spiral out of control into oblivion. The problem stems from the fact that the organizational structure (or lack of it!) and the style of management that makes an entrepreneurial startup so successful often cannot support the business as it grows into adolescence and maturity. As a company grows, not only does its culture tend to change but so does its need for a management infrastructure capable of supporting that growth. Compounding the problem is the entrepreneur's tendency to see all growth as good. After all, who wouldn't want to be the founder of a small company whose rapid growth makes it destined to become the next rising star in the industry? Yet, *achieving* rapid growth and *managing* it are two distinct challenges. Entrepreneurs must be aware of the challenges rapid growth brings with it; otherwise they may find their companies crumbling around them as they reach warp speed.

Looking back, one entrepreneur whose specialty-food business "crashed into the wall" sees fast, uncontrolled growth as the primary cause of his company's troubles. In just five years, James Bildner took his business from startup to a publicly held company with 20 retail stores, 1,250 employees, and $48 million in sales. Uncontrolled growth, which magnified J. Bildner and Sons' other problems, sent the company careening into "the wall." Bildner says, "Rapid growth itself—too many locations, new products, new people; too much or too little capital; and always too little investment up front in financial systems and controls—makes everything worse." Like many entrepreneurs, Bildner never saw (or chose to ignore) the signs of trouble—diminishing cash flow, rapid turnover of good people, expanding general and administrative expenses, and increasing distance from the core of the business—until it was too late. The company survived, but, according to Bildner, is "a shadow of its former self."[17]

In many cases, small companies achieve impressive growth because they bypass the traditional organizational structures, forgo rigid policies and procedures, and maintain maximum flexibility. One recent study of business growth found that small companies have the edge over their larger rivals:[18]

- ☆ Large companies' inability to react quickly is a major barrier to their growth. Small companies are naturally quick to respond.
- ☆ Rigid internal structures keep big companies from growing rapidly. Small companies typically bypass traditional structures.
- ☆ Large companies focus on expanding existing product and service lines, while small businesses concentrate more on creating new ones.
- ☆ Large companies are concerned with minimizing risks and defending their market share. Small companies are more willing to take the risks necessary to conquer new markets.
- ☆ Large companies are reluctant to eradicate market research and technology that have worked in the past. Entrepreneurial companies have more of a "clean-slate" approach to research and technology.

J. Bildner and Sons

But growth brings with it change: changes in management style, organizational strategy, and methods of operations. Growth produces organizational complexity. In this period of transition, the entrepreneur's challenge is to walk a fine line between retaining the small-company traits that are the seeds of the business's success and incorporating the elements of the infrastructure essential to supporting and sustaining the company's growth.

Structure

Entrepreneurs rely on six different management styles to guide their companies as they grow. The first three (craftsman, classic, and coordinator) involve running a company without any management assistance and are best suited for small companies in the early stages of growth; the last three (entrepreneur-plus-employee team, small partnership, big-team venture) rely on a team approach to run the company as its growth rate heats up.[19]

THE CRAFTSMAN. One of the earliest management styles to emerge was the craftsman. These entrepreneurs literally run a one-man (or one-woman) show; they do everything themselves because their primary concern is with the quality of the products or services they produce. Woodworkers, cabinet makers, glassblowers, and other craftsmen rely on this style of management. The benefits of this style include minimal operating expenses (no

---

YOU BE THE CONSULTANT...

A Change Is in the Air

Roxanne Coady, owner of R. J. Julia Books, is happy that her bookstore has grown 400 percent in just five years.

After spending 20 years as a CPA, Coady decided to blend her love for books with her business acumen and opened a friendly little store with lots of ambiance and a skilled staff. She invested in a unique, diverse, and large selection of books and offered superb customer service. Customers loved her approach to business, and soon the company was growing at 30 percent to 75 percent a year. In its fourth year, R. J. Julia Books earned the coveted Bookseller of the Year award from *Publishers Weekly*.

Despite the company's popularity with customers and its rapid growth rate, R. J. Julia Books was losing money, forcing Coady to invest more of her own money to make up the shortfall. Before she knew it, she had put $250,000 into the business, but its financial position was no better than before the cash injections. Coady says, "My inventory turnover was too low and my costs were too high . . . Whenever I became concerned about monitoring costs, I assured myself that the way we were spending money—on a first-class newsletter, author events, and extra staff—was right and that the numbers would turn around. Unfortunately, they didn't. The irony was that after I'd spent 20 years as an accountant, it seemed that my strength was in marketing and my weakness in accounting." Coady assumed that because her company was small, the "big business" management principles she had learned in her career as an accountant didn't apply. She had never established a procedure for setting goals or productivity standards, nor had she ever involved her staff in setting and meeting financial objectives.

One day, Coady realized that for R.J. Julia Books to be successful, she would have to change her management style drastically. She would have to get serious about running the bookstore as a *business*. "I believe that my business has incredible opportunity," she says, "but it also needs to be bigger to be competitive. In retail, economy of scale matters."

Coady estimates that she will need $1 million to take the company to the next level of growth. In the meantime, however, she knows that she must get her company under control and start earning a profit. Otherwise, she'll never be able to attract that amount of money. After all, who wants to lend money to or invest in a small, money-losing bookstore?

Coady called her employees together and announced that the company would be making several dramatic changes . . .

1. What changes would you recommend that Coady make in the way she manages R. J. Julia Books? Explain.

2. What should she tell her employees at the meeting she has called?

3. What advice would you offer Coady about her company's growth? Explain.

Source: Adapted from Roxanne Coady, "The Cobbler's Shoes," *Inc.*, January 1996, pp. 21-22.

---

employees to pay), very simple operations (no workers' compensation, incentive plans, or organizational charts), no supervision problems, and the entrepreneur's total control over both the business and its quality.

Of course, one disadvantage of the craftsman management style is that the entrepreneur must do *everything* in the business, including those tasks that she does not enjoy. The biggest disadvantage of this style, however, is the limitations it puts on a company's ability to grow. A business can grow only so big without the craftsman taking on other workers and delegating authority to them. Before choosing this management style, a craftsman must decide: "How large do I want my business to become?"

THE CLASSIC. As business opportunities arise, a craftsman quickly realizes that she could magnify the company's capacity to grow by hiring other people to work. The classic entrepreneur brings in other people but does not delegate any significant authority to them, choosing instead to "watch over everything" herself. She insists on tight supervision, constantly monitors employees' work, and performs all of the critical tasks herself. Classic entrepreneurs do not feel comfortable delegating the power and the authority for making decisions to anyone else; they prefer to keep a tight rein on the business and on everyone who works there.

Even though this management style gives a business more growth potential than the craftsman style, there is a limit to how much an entrepreneur can accomplish. Therefore, entrepreneurs who choose to operate this way must limit the complexity of their businesses if they are to grow at all. An inherent danger of this style is the entrepreneur's tendency to "micromanage" every aspect of the business rather than spend her time focusing on those tasks that are most important and most productive for the company.

THE COORDINATOR. The coordinator style of management gives an entrepreneur the ability to create a fairly large company with very few employees. In this type of business (often called a virtual corporation because the company is actually quite "hollow"), the entrepreneur farms out a large portion of the work to other companies and then coordinates all of the activities from "headquarters." By hiring out at least some of the work (in some cases, most of the work), the entrepreneur is free to focus on pumping up sales and pushing the business to higher levels. Some coordinators hire someone to manufacture their products, pay brokers to sell them, and arrange for someone to collect their accounts receivable! With the help of just a few workers, a coordinator can build a multi million-dollar business!

Although the coordinator style sounds like an easy way to build a business, it can be very challenging to implement. The business's success is highly dependent on its suppliers and their ability to produce quality products and services in a timely fashion. Getting suppliers to perform on time is one of the hardest tasks. Plus, if the entrepreneur hires someone else to manufacture the product, she loses control over its quality.

THE ENTREPRENEUR-PLUS-EMPLOYEE TEAM. As their companies grow, many entrepreneurs see the need to shift to a team-based management style. The entrepreneur-plus-employee team gives an entrepreneur the power to grow the business beyond the scope of the manager-only styles. In this style, the entrepreneur delegates authority to key employees, but she retains the final decision-making authority in the company. Of course, the transition from a management style where the entrepreneur retains almost total authority to one based on delegation requires some adjustments for employees and especially for the entrepreneur! Employees have to learn to make decisions on their own, and the manager must learn to give workers the authority, the responsibility, and the information to make them. Delegating requires a manager to realize that there are several ways to accomplish a task and that sometimes employees will make mistakes. Still, delegation allows a manager to get the maximum benefit from each employee while freeing herself up to focus on the most important tasks in the business.

THE SMALL PARTNERSHIP. As the business world grows more complex and interrelated, many entrepreneurs find that there is strength in numbers. Rather than manage a company alone, they choose to share the managerial responsibilities with one or more partners (or shareholders). As we saw in Chapter 3 concerning forms of ownership, the benefits are many. Perhaps the biggest advantage is the ability to share responsibility for the company with others who have a real stake in the company and are willing to work hard to make it a success. Some of the most effective partnerships are those where the owners' skills complement one another, creating natural "fault lines" for dividing responsibilities. Of course, the downside to this management style includes the necessity of giving up total control over the business and the potential for personality conflicts and disputes over the company's direction.

THE BIG-TEAM VENTURE. The broadest-based management style is the big-team venture, which typically emerges over time as a company grows larger. The workload demands on a small number of partners can quickly outstrip the time and energy they can devote to them, even if they are effective delegators. Once a company reaches this point, managers must expand the breadth of the management team's experience to handle the increasing level of responsibility that results from the sheer size of the company. If the company's operations have become global in scope as it has grown, the need for such a management team is even more pronounced. For entrepreneurial ventures that have grown to this size, the big-team venture is almost a necessity.

Any of these management styles can be successful for an entrepreneur if it matches her personality and the company's goals. The key is to plan for the company's growth and to lay out a strategy for managing the changes the company will experience as it grows. "Ask yourself whether your management style is really effective for a business of this particular size, shape, and complexity," advise the authors of *The New Venture Handbook*. "If the answer is no, modify your plan."[20]

TEAM-BASED MANAGEMENT. Large companies have been using self-directed work teams for years to improve quality, increase productivity, raise morale, lower costs, and boost motivation; yet, team-based management is just now beginning to catch on in small firms. In fact, a team approach may be best suited for small companies. Even though converting a traditional company to teams requires a major change in management style, it is usually easier to implement with a small number of workers. A **self-directed work team** is a group of workers from different functional areas of a company that work together as a unit largely without supervision, making decisions and performing tasks that once belonged only to managers. Some teams may be temporary, attacking and solving a specific problem, but many are permanent components of an organization's structure. As their name implies, these teams manage themselves, performing such functions as setting work schedules, ordering raw materials, evaluating and purchasing equipment, developing budgets, hiring and firing team members, solving problems, and a host of other activities. The goal is to get people working together to serve customers better.

Managers in companies using teams don't just sit around drinking coffee, however. In fact, they work just as hard as before, but the nature of their work changes dramatically. Before teams, managers were "bosses" who made most of the decisions affecting their subordinates alone and hoarded information and power for themselves. In a team environment, managers take on the role of "coaches" who empower those around them to make decisions affecting their work and share information with workers. As facilitators, their job is to sup-

self-directed work team—*a group of workers from different functional areas of a company that work together as a unit largely without supervision, making decisions and performing tasks that once belonged only to managers.*

port and to serve the teams functioning in the organization and to make sure they produce results. "It's not easy for an entrepreneur to take this role, but it is the way to get a productive team," says one management consultant.[21]

Companies have strong competitive reasons for using team-based management. Companies that use teams effectively report significant gains in quality, reductions in cycle time, lower costs, increased customer satisfaction, and improved employee motivation and morale. "Your competitiveness is your ability to use the skills and knowledge of people most effectively, and teams are the best way to do that," says one manager.[22] A team-based approach is not for every organization, however. Teams are *not* easy to start, and switching from a traditional organizational structure to a team-based one is filled with potential pitfalls. Teams work best in environments where the work is interdependent and people must interact with one another to accomplish their goals. Although a team approach might succeed in a small plant making gas grills, it would most likely fail miserably in a real estate office, where salespeople work independently of one another with little interaction required to make a sale.

In some cases, teams have been a company's salvation from failure and extinction; in others, the team approach has flopped. What's the difference? What causes teams to fail? The following errors are common: [23]

⭐ *Assigning teams inappropriate tasks.* One of the biggest mistakes managers make with teams is assigning them to tasks that individuals ought to be performing.

⭐ *Creating "make-nice" teams.* For a team to perform effectively, it must have a clear purpose and every team member must understand it. Unfortunately, managers sometimes create a team but fail to give it any meaningful work assignments other than to "make nice with one another."

⭐ *Inadequate training for team members and team leaders.* Some organizations form teams and then expect employees, long accustomed to individual responsibilities, to magically become team players and contributors. Teams are very complex social systems influenced by pressures from within and buffeted by forces from without, and workers need training to become effective team players.

⭐ *Sabotaging teams with underperformers.* Rather than fire poor performers (always an unpleasant task), some managers put them on teams, hoping that the members will either discipline them or get rid of them. It never works. Underperfomers undermine team performance.

⭐ *Switching to team responsibilities but keeping pay individually oriented.* One of the quickest ways to destroy a team system is to pay team members based on their individual performances.

Building a successful team-based structure requires some effort on the manager's part. One writer explains:[24]

. . . Teams run counter to conventional individualism and internal competition that work against cooperation and trust. Teams can be thwarted by the organization's systems for performance appraisal, promotion, compensation, and financial incentives. They simply don't fit the usual hierarchical layers or functional divisions. Top management must initiate and nurture team activity so teams won't be crushed out by the organization in its day-to-day practices.

To ensure teams' success, managers must:

⭐ *Make sure that teams are appropriate for the company and the nature of its work.* A good starting point is to create a "map" of the company's work flow that shows how workers build a product or deliver a service. Is the work interdependent, complex, and interactive? Would teamwork improve the company's performance?

- ☆ *Form teams around the natural work flow and give them specific tasks to accomplish.* Teams can be effective only if managers challenge them to accomplish specific, measurable objectives.
- ☆ *Provide adequate support and training for team members and leaders.* Team success requires a new set of skills. Workers must learn how to communicate, resolve conflict, support one another, and solve problems as a team. Smart managers see that workers get the training they need.
- ☆ *Involve team members in determining how their performances will be measured, what will be measured, and when it will be measured.* Doing so gives team members a sense of ownership and pride about what they are accomplishing.
- ☆ *Make at least part of team members' pay dependent on team performance.* Companies that have used teams successfully still pay members individually, but they make successful team work a major part of an individual's performance review. "Teams will not work unless compensation is at least partly team-based," says one expert.[25]

Table 13.7 shows the four stages that teams go through on their way to performing effectively and accomplishing goals.

Entrepreneur Eric Greshman, founder of Published Image, a publisher of mutual fund literature, turned to self-managed teams to help turn his struggling company around. Published Image had grown rapidly but had sacrificed quality, customer service, and employee morale in the process. The company's documents were laden with errors, employee turnover was running at 50 percent per year, and turnover among customers was about 30 percent per year. Greshman knew he had to do a complete overhaul of his company. Given the complexity and interdependence of the company's work, Greshman decided to switch to a team-based structure. "We blew up the old company and totally changed people's thinking about what their jobs are," he says. The company's 26 employees serve on

Published Image

Stage	Description	Leader Focus
1. Startup	High expectations. Unclear goals and roles.	Task focus. Provide goals and structure. Supervise startup and define accountability.
2. Reality strikes	Recognition of time and effort required. Roadblocks. Frustration.	Task and process emphasis. Clarify expectations and roles. Encourage open discussions and address concerns. Ensure proper skills and resources.
3. Realigning expectations	Goals and roles reset. Cooperation and trust begin to produce progress.	Process focus. Promote participation and team decision making. Encourage peer support. Provide feedback.
4. Performance	Involvement, openness, and teamwork. Commitment to process and task achievement.	Monitoring and feedback focus. Let team take responsibility for solving problems and making decisions. Monitor progress and supply feedback.

Table 13.7
The Stages of Team Development
Source: Mark A. Frohman, "Do Teams. . . But Do Them Right," *Industry Week*, April 3, 1995, p. 22.

teams (Gershman calls them "little Published Images") that set their own schedules, prepare budgets, and earn bonuses based on their teams' performances. Each team acts like a self-contained business, courting clients, negotiating prices, producing their customers' newsletters start to finish, and even collecting their accounts receivable. Managers, now called coaches, serve as advisors and facilitators. Since the change, Published Image's revenues have doubled and its profit margin has increased from 3 percent to 20 percent. In addition, employee turnover has dropped to zero, and the customer defection rate has fallen to less than 5 percent a year. The teams at Published Image have been so successful that Greshman's goal is to ultimately eliminate his own job! "I hope this business can run without me," he says.[26]

4. Discuss the ways in which entrepreneurs can motivate their workers to higher levels of performance.

The Challenge of Motivating Workers

Motivation is the degree of effort an employee exerts to accomplish a task; it shows up as excitement about work. Motivating workers to higher levels of performance is one of the most difficult and challenging tasks facing a small business manager. Few things are more frustrating to a business owner than an employee with a tremendous amount of talent who lacks the desire to use it. This section discusses four aspects of motivation: empowerment, job design, rewards and compensation, and feedback.

motivation—*the degree of effort an employee exerts to accomplish a task; it shows up as excitement about work.*

empowerment—*the process of giving workers at every level of the organization the power, the freedom, and the responsibility to control their own work, to make decisions, and to take action to meet the company's objectives.*

Empowerment

One of the principles underlying the team-based management style discussed in the previous section is empowerment. **Empowerment** involves giving workers at every level of the organization the power, the freedom, and the responsibility to control their own work, to make decisions, and to take action to meet the company's objectives. Competitive forces and a more demanding work force challenge business owners and managers to share power with everyone in the organization, whether they use a team-based approach or not.

Empowering employees requires a different style of management and leadership from that of the traditional manager. Many old-style managers are unwilling to share power with anyone because they fear doing so weakens their authority and reduces their influence. In fact, exactly the *opposite* is true! Business owners who share information, responsibility, authority, and power soon discover that their success (and their companies' success, too) is magnified many times over. Empowered workers become more successful on the job, which means the entrepreneur also becomes more successful.

Empowerment builds on what real business leaders already know: that the people in their organizations bring with them to work an amazing array of talents, skills, knowledge, and abilities. Workers are willing—even anxious—to put these to use; unfortunately, in too many small businesses, suffocating management styles and poorly designed jobs quash workers' enthusiasm and motivation. Enlightened business owners recognize their workers' abilities, develop them, and then give workers the freedom and the power to use those abilities. "Employees work best when you give them the opportunity to use their own creativity and imagination," explains one manager.[27]

When implemented properly, empowerment can produce impressive results, not only for the small business but also for newly empowered employees. For the business, benefits typically include significant productivity gains, quality improvements, more satisfied customers, improved morale, and increased employee motivation.

Rheacom

When Rheacom, a supplier of parts to the aerospace industry, switched to empowered work teams, workers unleashed a torrent of new ideas aimed at improving the company's

"Henderson has his own unique way of empowering his staff."

Source: Drawing by Mike Shapiro. Reprinted by permission of Cartoon Features Syndicate.

performance. One suggestion led to a reduction in the machine time required for a brake shoe the company had been making for 25 years from more than three and a half hours to less than one hour. [28]

For workers, empowerment offers the chance to do a greater variety of work that is more interesting and challenging. Empowerment challenges workers to make the most of their creativity, imagination, knowledge, and skills. This method of management encourages them to take the initiative to identify and solve problems on their own and as part of a team. As empowered workers see how the various parts of a company's manufacturing or service systems fit together, they realize their need to acquire more skills and knowledge to do their jobs well. Entrepreneurs must realize that empowerment and training go hand-in-hand.

Not every worker *wants* to be empowered, however. Some will resist, wanting only to "put in their eight hours and go home." One expert estimates that companies moving to empowerment can expect to lose about 5 percent of their work force. "Out of every 100 employees, five are diehards who will be impossible to change," he says. Another 75 percent will accept empowerment and thrive under it, if it is done properly. The remaining 20 percent will pounce eagerly on empowerment because it is something they "have been waiting to do. . . their whole [work] lives," he says. [29] Empowerment works best when a business owner: [30]

⭐ *is confident enough to give workers all of the authority and responsibility they can handle.* Early on, this may mean giving workers the power to tackle relatively simple assignments. But, as their confidence and ability grow, most workers are eager to take on more responsibility.

⭐ *plays the role of coach and facilitator, not the role of meddlesome boss.* One sure-fired way to make empowerment fail is to give associates the power to attack a problem and then to hover over them, criticizing every move they make. Smart owners empower their workers and then get out of the way so they can do their jobs!

★ *recognizes that empowered employees will make mistakes.* The worst thing an owner can do when empowered employees make mistakes is to hunt them down and punish them. That teaches everyone in the company to avoid taking risks and to always play it safe—something no innovative small business can afford.

★ *hires people who can blossom in an empowered environment.* Empowerment is not for everyone. Owners quickly learn that as costly as hiring mistakes are, such errors are even more costly in an empowered environment. Ideal candidates are high-energy self-starters who enjoy the opportunity to grow and to enhance their skills.

★ *trains workers continuously to upgrade their skills.* Empowerment demands more of workers than traditional work methods. Managers are asking workers to solve problems and make decisions they have never made before. To handle these problems well, workers need training, especially in effective problem-solving techniques, communication, teamwork, and technical skills.

★ *trusts workers to do their jobs.* Once workers are trained to do their jobs, owners must learn to trust them to assume responsibility for their jobs. After all, they are the *real* experts; they face the problems and challenges every day. One Japanese study found that workers "in the trenches" knew 100 percent of the problems in a company; supervisors knew 74 percent; and top managers knew just 4 percent![31]

★ *listens to workers when they have ideas, solutions, or suggestions.* Because they are the experts on the job, employees often come up with incredibly insightful, innovative ideas for improving jobs—*if* business owners give them the chance. Failing to acknowledge or to act on employees' ideas sends them a clear message: Your ideas really don't count. "The greatest source of motivation is giving people some input into what they do everyday," explains one expert.[32]

★ *shares information with workers.* For empowerment to succeed, business owners must make sure workers get adequate information, the raw material for good decision making. Some companies have gone beyond sharing information to embrace **open-book management**, in which employees have access to *all* of a company's records, including its financial statements. The goal of open-book management is to enable employees to understand why they need to raise productivity, improve quality, cut costs, and improve customer service. Under open-book management, employees: (1) see and learn to understand the company's financial statements and other critical numbers in measuring its performance; (2) learn that a significant part of their jobs is making sure those critical numbers move in the right direction; and (3) have a direct stake in the company's success through profit sharing, ESOPs, or performance-based bonuses. In short, open-book management establishes the link between employees' knowledge and their performance. One expert writes, "Instead of telling employees how to cut defects, [open-book management] asks them to boosts profits—and lets them figure out how. Instead of giving them a reengineered job, it turns them into businesspeople. They experience the challenge—and the sheer fun and excitement—of matching wits with the marketplace, toting up the score, and sharing in the proceeds. . . . There's no better motivation." [33]

★ *recognizes workers' contributions.* One of the most important tasks a business owner has is to recognize jobs well done. Some businesses reward workers with monetary awards; others rely on recognition and praise; still others use a combination of money and praise. Whatever system an owner chooses, the key to keeping a steady flow of ideas, improvements, suggestions, and solutions is to recognize the people who supply them.

open-book management—*the process of giving employees access to all of a company's records, including its financial statements, so they can understand why they need to raise productivity, improve quality, cut costs, and improve customer service.*

Job Design

Over the years, managers have learned that the job itself and the way it is designed can be a source of motivation (or demotivation!) for workers. In some companies, work is organized on the principle of **job simplification**, breaking the work down into its simplest form and standardizing each task, as in some assembly-line operations. The scope of jobs organized in such a way is extremely narrow, resulting in impersonal, monotonous, and boring work that creates little challenge or motivation for workers. Job simplification invites workers to "check their brains at the door" and offers them little opportunity for excitement, enthusiasm, or pride in their work. The result can be apathetic, unmotivated workers who don't care about quality, customers, or costs.

To break this destructive cycle, some companies have redesigned jobs so that they offer workers intrinsic rewards and motivation. Three strategies are common: job enlargement, job rotation, and job enrichment.

Job enlargement (or **horizontal job loading**) adds more tasks to a job to broaden its scope. For instance, rather than an employee simply mounting four screws in computers coming down an assembly line, a worker might assemble, install, and test the entire motherboard (perhaps as part of a team). The idea is to make the job more varied and to allow employees to perform a more complete unit of work.

Job rotation involves cross-training employees so they can move from one job in the company to others, giving them a greater number and variety of tasks to perform. As employees learn other jobs within an organization, both their skills and their understanding of the company's purpose and processes rise. Cross-trained workers are more valuable because they give a company the flexibility to shift workers from low-demand jobs to those where they are most needed. As an incentive for workers to learn to perform other jobs within an operation, some companies offer **skill-based pay**, a system under which the more skills workers acquire, the more they earn.

Job enrichment (or **vertical job loading**) involves building motivators into a job by increasing the planning, decision-making, organizing, and controlling functions, that is, traditional managerial tasks, which workers perform. The idea is to make every employee a manager—at least a manager of his own job. Notice that empowerment, the management technique discussed in the previous section, is based on the principle of job enrichment.

To enrich employees' jobs, a business owner must build five core characteristics into them:

★ *skill variety*—the degree to which a job requires a variety of different skills, talents, and activities from the worker. Does the job require the worker to perform a variety of tasks that demand a variety of skills and abilities or does it force him to perform the same task repeatedly?

★ *task identity*—the degree to which a job allows the worker to complete a whole or identifiable piece of work. Does the employee build an entire piece of furniture (perhaps as part of a team) or does he merely attach four screws?

★ *task significance*—the degree to which a job substantially influences the lives or work of others—employees or final customers. Does the employee get to deal with customers, either internal or external? One effective way to establish task significance is to put employees in touch with customers so they can see how customers use the product or service they make.

★ *autonomy*—the degree to which a job gives a worker the freedom, independence, and discretion in planning and performing tasks. Does the employee make decisions affecting his work or must he rely on someone else (e.g., the owner, a manager, or a supervisor) to "call the shots"?

★ *feedback*—the degree to which a job gives the worker direct, timely information about the quality of his performance. Does the job give employees feedback about the quality of their work or does the product (and all information about it) simply disappear after it leaves the worker's station?

job simplification—*the type of job design that breaks work down into its simplest form and standardizes each task.*

job enlargement—*the type of job design that adds more tasks to a job to broaden its scope.*

job rotation—*the type of job design that cross-trains employees so they can move from one job in the company to others, giving them a greater number and variety of tasks to perform.*

skill-based pay—*a system under which the more skills workers acquire, the more they earn.*

job enrichment—*the type of job design that builds motivators into a job by increasing the planning, decision-making, organizing, and controlling functions.*

Tom Warner, a fourth generation plumber who took over his father's heating, ventilation, and air conditioning (HVAC) company in 1989, has used innovative job designs to transform his employees' motivation and attitudes toward their jobs, and, in the process, to revitalize the company's sales and profits. Until 1992, Warner Corporation was a traditional HVAC business with a crew of workers waiting for "the boss" to tell them where to go, what to do, and when to do it. Warner Corporation was also a company headed for financial trouble. That's when Warner decided to redesign the jobs in his company. The HVAC technicians, plumbers, and electricians would become area technical directors (ATDs), who would, in essence, manage their own businesses within Warner Corporation. ATDs got their own territories (based on zip codes) in which they developed customer relationships, handled their own equipment, did their own sales work, and collected their own accounts. By transforming his technicians into businesspeople who make decisions and are responsible for generating profits and keeping customers happy, Warner has instilled in them a sense of pride and ownership in their work that was missing before. "This program is a real ego booster," he says. "Running their own businesses, these guys really feel good about themselves."

Feeling good about themselves plays a part in making them want to take better care of their customers, who couldn't be happier because they now have "personal ATDs." Describing Ron Inscoe, "her" ATD, one satisfied customer says, "Ron told me to call him if I have any problems because this is his territory. I think it's a great idea. I have somebody to relate to—not just some corporation." That satisfaction is showing up in rising profits, sales, and market share. The ATDs share in Warner's success; the more money the company makes, the more money they make. Warner credits the job redesign with his company's turnaround. "Two or three years ago, I had to think of everything, and people just waited for me," he says. "Now our people come up with their own ideas, and I'm cheering more than leading."[34]

As the nation's work force and the companies employing them continue to change, business is changing the way people work, moving away from a legion of full-time employees in traditional 8-to-5, on-site jobs. Organizational structures, even in small companies, are flatter than ever before, as the lines between traditional managers and workers get blurrier. Rather than resembling the current pyramid, the organization of tomorrow will more closely resemble a spider's web, with a network of interconnected employee specialists working in teams and using lightning-fast communication to make decisions without having to go through three of four layers of management. One expert in organizational change says, "There is going to be a tremendous shift during the next 25 years toward independence, autonomy, and self-directedness with people and teams accountable for their own performances. Companies [won't] be able to compete without redefining the way that work is done and how organizations are managed."[35] Many of these shifts are already taking place in the form of flextime, job sharing, flexplace, and telecommuting.

Flextime is an arrangement under which employees build their work schedules around a set of "core hours," such as 11 a.m. to 2 p.m., but have flexibility about when they start and stop work. For instance, one worker might choose to come in at 7 a.m. and leave at 3 p.m. to attend her son's soccer game, while another may work from 11 a.m. to 7 p.m. Flextime not only raises worker morale, but it also makes it easier for companies to attract high-quality young workers who want rewarding careers without sacrificing their lifestyles. In addition, companies using flextime schedules often experience lower levels of tardiness and absenteeism.

Job sharing is a work arrangement in which two or more people share a single full-time job. For instance, two college students might share the same 40-hour-a-week job, one working mornings and the other working afternoons. Although job sharing affects a relatively

flextime—
an arrangement under which employees build their work schedules around a set of "core hours" but have flexibility about when they start and stop work.

job sharing—*a work arrangement in which two or more people share a single full-time job.*

small portion of the nation's work force, it is an important job design strategy for some companies that find it difficult to recruit capable, qualified full-time workers.

Flexplace is a work arrangement in which employees work at a place other than the traditional office, such as a satellite branch closer to their homes or, in some cases, at home. Flexplace is an easy job design strategy for companies to use because of **telecommuting**. Using modern communication technology such as e-mail, fax machines, and laptop computers, employees have more flexibility in choosing where they work. Today, it is quite simple for workers to hook up electronically to their workplaces (and to all of the people and the information there) from practically anywhere on the planet! According to Link Resources, approximately 12 million workers are telecommuters, and the number is growing rapidly; by 2002, the Department of Transportation estimates that 15 percent of the U.S. work force will be telecommuting.[36]

Richard Grove, owner of PrimeTime Publicity and Media Consulting, reaps the many benefits of telecommuting, including increased productivity, fewer sick days, the need for less office space, and, perhaps most important, the ability to recruit top-quality workers. Eight of the 15 employees at Grove's public relations firm telecommute from their homes. He sees them face-to-face just twice a year, but that doesn't interfere with their ability to perform their jobs well.[37]

Before shifting to telecommuting, Grove had to address some important issues:

☆ Does the nature of the work fit telecommuting? Obviously, some jobs are better suited to telecommuting than others.

☆ Can you monitor compliance with federal wage and hour laws for telecommuters? Generally, employers must keep the same employment records for telecommuters that they do for traditional office workers.

☆ Are you adequately insured? Employers should be sure that the telecommuting equipment employees use in their homes is covered under their insurance policies.

☆ Can you keep in touch? Telecommuting works well as long as long-distance employees stay in touch with headquarters.

Rewards and Compensation

The rewards an employee gets from the job itself are intrinsic rewards, but managers have at their disposal a wide variety of extrinsic rewards (those outside the job itself) to motivate workers. The key to using rewards to motivate involves tailoring them to the needs and characteristics of the workers. "The core of successful motivation is tapping into the things that are really important to people—taking the time to find out what those are, and structuring your recognition around those in the context of the job," says one motivation expert.[38] For instance, to a technician making $25,000 a year, a chance to earn a $3,000 performance bonus would most likely be a powerful motivator. To an executive earning $125,000 a year, it would not be.

One of the most popular rewards is money. Cash is an effective motivator—up to a point. Over the last 20 years, many companies have moved to **pay-for-performance compensation systems**, in which employees' pay depends upon how well they perform their jobs. In other words, extra productivity equals extra pay. By linking employees' compensation directly to the company's financial performance, a business owner increases the likelihood that workers will achieve performance targets that are in their best interest and in the company's best interest. Such systems work only when employees see a clear connection between their performances and their pay.

flexplace—an arrangement under which employees work at a place other than the traditional office, such as a satellite branch closer to their homes, or at home.

PrimeTime Publicity and Media Consulting

telecommuting—an arrangement under which employees working from their homes use modern communications equipment to hook up electronically to their workplaces.

pay-for-performance compensation system—a compensation system in which employees' pay depends upon how well they perform their jobs.

For example, Mark Swepston, owner of Atlas Butler Heating and Cooling, was looking for a way to increase sales and to improve his company's cash flow, so he decided to enlist the help of his sales force. Swepston switched to a pay-for-performance system under which his six full-time sales representatives receive sales commissions rather than salaries. A salesperson gets 50 percent of a job's net income, but only after the company receives the customer's payment. Since the switch, Atlas receives customer payments four times faster than before, and its bad debt losses have dropped from 2.7 percent to just 0.3 percent. In addition to improving the company's financial performance, the new compensation system is also producing better customer service. "It's made [the sales representatives] pay more attention to the customers' needs . . . This practice brings them one step closer to customers because their pocketbooks are affected," says Swepston.[39]

Money isn't the only motivator business owners have at their disposal, of course. In fact, nonfinancial incentives can be more important sources of employee motivation than money! "Money is only a short-term motivator," claims one manager.[40] After its initial motivational impact, money loses its impact; it does not have a lasting motivational effect (which for small businesses, with their limited resources, is a plus). Often, the most meaningful motivating factors are the simplest ones—praise, recognition, feedback, job security, promotions, and others—things that any small business, no matter how limited its budget, can do. "To get the right kind of people, you have to put together a compensation package for them," says one entrepreneur, "but what people really work for is appreciation and the feeling that success brings to them."[41] For instance, one innovative home builder rewards his employees for exceptional work by naming streets after them in his subdivisions. [42]

Ariat International

At Ariat International, an equestrian footwear maker, president Beth Cross shut the company down for an afternoon and took her 12 employees horseback riding to show her appreciation for their hard work. A few months earlier, after an especially busy period, she let everyone take an afternoon off to go to a big sale at a local department store.[43]

Small companies find that younger workers, especially "Generation Xers," respond best to intangible rewards and not to monetary rewards. Wanting more balance in their work and personal lives than their baby-boomer parents, Generation X workers are looking for workplaces that offer challenging assignments coupled with a sense of fun. They respond best to constant feedback that is specific and accurate and to managers who take the time to celebrate their successes.

Trinity Communications

When Trinity Communications, a small marketing-communications company surveyed its 11 Generation X employees to find out what attracts and motivates them, managers were a bit surprised to find that employees ranked a good 401(k) retirement plan, not salary, at the top of their financial concerns. Other motivating factors the employees ranked high were opportunities to learn, access to up-to-date technology, work force diversity, and flexibility in job design and schedules. Based on the results of its survey, Trinity changed its benefits package to one more consistent with its employees' desires, including a more aggressive 401(k) plan, a more generous and flexible vacation policy, and home computers with Internet access for all workers.[44]

Praise is another simple, yet powerful motivational tool. People enjoy getting praise, especially from a manager or business owner; it's just human nature. As Mark Twain once said, "I can live for two months on a good compliment." Praise is an easy and inexpensive reward for employees producing extraordinary work.

Mary Kay Cosmetics

For instance, at Mary Kay Cosmetics' annual meeting, praise is the watchword; indeed, it is one of the main reasons more than 36,000 beauty consultants from around the world gather in Dallas every year. At the meeting, superstar saleswomen receive praise and recognition from their peers and from company founder Mary Kay Ash in sessions that resemble a cross between an awards banquet and a tent revival. Women come away with crowns, sashes, pins, bracelets, and, of course, those coveted pink Cadillacs—and a zealous fervor to go out and sell lots of makeup![45]

One of the surest ways to kill high performance is simply to fail to recognize it and the employees responsible for it. Failing to praise good work eventually conveys the message that the owner either doesn't care about exceptional performance or cannot distinguish between good work and poor work. In either case, through inaction, the manager destroys employees' motivation to excel.

Because they lack the financial resources of bigger companies, small business owners must be more creative when it comes to giving rewards that motivate workers. In many cases, however, using rewards other than money gives small businesses an advantage because they usually have more impact on employee performance over time. One expert on employee motivation says, "To consistently enjoy [high] levels of performance, you've got to give them more than a paycheck. What gets people to excel on a daily basis, to stay late, to work weekends in a pinch is when you regularly communicate to them that you value what they do."[46] In short, rewards do *not* have to be expensive to be effective. At one company, high-performing employees get a free car wash from the boss in the employee parking lot at lunchtime. Employees gather around to hear about how the worker earned such an honor—a real source of motivation![47] In the future, managers will rely more on nonmonetary rewards—praise, recognition, car washes, pins, letters of commendation, and others—to create a work environment where employees take pride in their work, enjoy it, are challenged by it, and get excited about it—in short, act like owners of the business themselves. The goal is to let employees know that "every person is important."

Table 13.8 on page 442–443 offers "the 20 Top Ways to Motivate Employees," which is based on the results of a survey of some of the nation's leading motivational experts.

Feedback

Business owners not only must motivate employees to excel in their jobs, but they must also focus their efforts on the right targets. Providing feedback on progress toward those targets can be a powerful motivating force in a company. To ensure that the link between her vision for the company and its operations is strong, an entrepreneur must build a series of specific performance measures that serve as periodic monitoring points. For each critical element of the organization's performance (e.g., product or service quality, financial performance, market position, productivity, employee development, etc.), the owner should develop specific measures that connect daily operational responsibilities with the company's overall strategic direction. These measures become the benchmarks for measuring employees' performances and the company's progress. The adage "what gets measured and monitored gets done" is true for most organizations. By connecting the company's long-term strategy to its daily operations and measuring performance, an entrepreneur makes it clear to everyone in the company what is most important. Jack Stack, CEO of Springfield Remanufacturing Corporation, explains the importance of focusing every employee's attention on key performance targets:

> To be successful in business, you have to be going somewhere, and everyone involved in getting you there has to know where it is. That's a basic rule, a higher law, but most companies miss. . . the fact that you have a much better chance of winning if everyone knows what it takes to win.[48]

In other words, getting or giving feedback implies that a business owner has established meaningful targets that serve as standards of performance for her, her employees, and the company as a whole. One characteristic successful people have in common is that they set goals and objectives—usually challenging ones—for themselves. Business owners are no different. Successful entrepreneurs usually set targets for performance that make them stretch to achieve, and then they encourage their employees to do the same. The result is that they keep their companies constantly moving forward.

J.J. Stupp, founder of TableTalk, a company that produces decks of cards imprinted with fascinating facts and questions designed to stimulate meaningful conversations, makes goal setting a regular part of her business routine. "Goals are vital to the work plan of any small business," she says. "Writing down short-term and long-term goals for my business helps me stay focused."[49]

For feedback to have impact as a motivating force in a business requires business owners to follow the procedure illustrated in Figure 13.1.

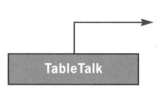

TableTalk

Table 13.8
The Top 20 Ways to Motivate Employees

Source: Shari Caudron, "The Top 20 Ways to Motivate Employees," *Industry Week,* April 3, 1995, pp. 12-18.

1. *Give employees the information they need to do a good job.* Employees need timely information to do their jobs, starting with the company's mission and goals and moving down to information on their specific job responsibilities.
2. *Provide regular feedback.* Communication should be an ongoing event, giving employees the opportunity to measure and improve their performances.
3. *Ask employees for their input and involve them in the decisions that affect their jobs.* The people who are performing a job are the real experts, so why not involve them in the decision-making process? At one manufacturing plant, workers, not managers, made all of the decisions relating to the purchase of a $3 million piece of equipment. After all, they were the ones who would be using it.
4. *Establish easy-to-use channels of communication.* Managers should give employees the opportunity to express their ideas and suggestions on workplace issues. Effective managers learn to become good listeners.
5. *Learn from employees themselves what motivates them.* Because what motivates each employee is different, managers must customize the rewards they offer. The best way to find out what employees want? (1) Get to know them, and (2) ask them.
6. *Learn what on-the-job activities employees choose to do when they have free time and then create opportunities for them to perform those activities on a more regular basis.* Employees do well at those tasks they enjoy most.
7. *Personally congratulate employees for jobs well done.* A survey of 1,500 employees from a variety of work settings found that the most powerful motivator was recognition. Not only is it powerful, but it also doesn't cost anything.
8. *Recognize the power of a manager's presence.* Employees like frequent contact with their managers, however brief, because it indicates that the manager recognizes the importance of their work.
9. *Write personal notes to employees about their performances.* Such tangible recognition is a powerful motivator. These notes often make it to the home hall of fame—the refrigerator door.
10. *Publicly recognize employees for good work.* Given that one-on-one recognition is such an important motivator, consider the power of public recognition to accelerate an employee's performance.

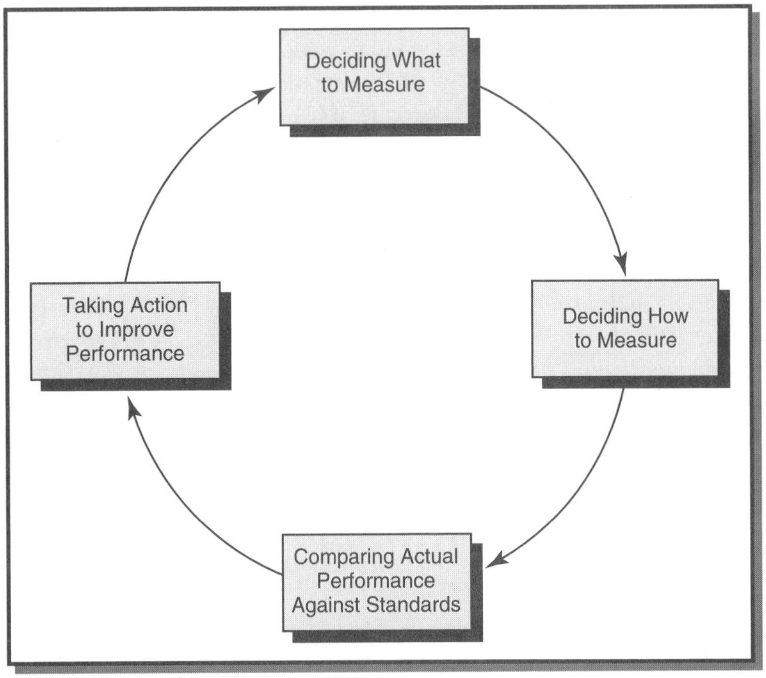

Figure 13.1
The Feedback Loop

Deciding What to Measure

Deciding How to Measure

Comparing Actual Performance Against Standards

Taking Action to Improve Performance

11. *Include morale-building meetings that celebrate team success.* Although they don't have to be elaborate, team success celebrations help employees build camaraderie and a sense of togetherness.

12. *Give employees good jobs to do.* Boring, routine, unchallenging work saps employee motivation faster than anything. Proper job design is an important part of effective motivation.

13. *Make sure employees have the tools available to do their best work.* Like good mechanics, smart managers know that doing a job well requires the right tools. Plus, when managers provide good equipment, employees see it as an investment in their abilities.

14. *Recognize employees' personal needs.* With so many dual-career families in our society, workers appreciate companies that acknowledge and care for their personal needs by offering flextime, on-site day care, personal time allowances, and other conveniences.

15. *Use performance as the basis for promotions.* Although it makes sense to promote those employees who are the best and most productive, too many companies continue to use seniority or politics to determine who gets promoted.

16. *Establish a comprehensive promote-from-within policy.* One of the best ways to spur employees to higher levels of performance is to show them that doing so leads to promotions within the company.

17. *Emphasize the company's commitment to long-term employment.* Although no company can offer a blanket "no-layoff" guarantee in this age, managers can communicate a "lifetime employment without guarantees" attitude. Job security for top performers is an important source of motivation.

18. *Foster a sense of community.* Forming a company around teams is a great way to start, but encouraging employees to recognize fellow workers for top performances can do wonders.

19. *Pay people competitively based on what they are worth.* If employees believe they are compensated fairly, they won't be preoccupied with their paychecks, and a company can get the most from its nonfinancial awards.

20. *Give employees a financial reason to excel by offering them a share of the profits or a share of the company.* Employees begin to act like owners when they *are* owners. Sharing ownership—or at least profits—gives them a major incentive to do everything they can to see that the company prospers.

Chapter 13: Leading the Growing Company and Planning for Management Succession **443**

Deciding What to Measure. The first step in the feedback loop is deciding what to measure. Every business is characterized by a set of numbers that are critical to its success, and these critical numbers are what the entrepreneur should focus on. Obvious critical numbers include sales, profits, profit margins, cash flow, and other standard financial measures. However, running beneath these standard and somewhat universal measures of performance is an undercurrent of critical numbers that are unique to a company's operations. In most cases, these are the numbers that actually drive profits, cash flow, and other financial measures and are the company's *real* critical numbers.

Example

For instance, in a conversation with another business owner, a hotel franchisee said that his company's critical number was profit and that the way to earn a profit was to control costs. His managerial efforts focused on making sure that his employees knew exactly what to do, how to do it, and how much they could spend doing it. The only problem was that the hotel was losing money.

"Tell me," said his friend, "how do you make money in this business?"

"We fill rooms," said the hotelier.

"How many rooms do you have to fill to break even?"

"Seventy-one percent," came the reply, "but we're only running at 67 percent."

"How many people know that?" asked his friend.

"Two," he said.

"Maybe that's your problem," observed his friend.

The hotel owner quickly realized that one of his company's most critical numbers was occupancy rate; that's what drove profits! His managerial focus had been misguided, and he had failed to get his employees involved in solving the problem. The hotel owner put together an incentive plan for employees based on occupancy rate. Once the rate surpassed 71 percent, employees qualified for bonuses; the higher the occupancy rate, the bigger the bonuses. He also involved employees in identifying other critical numbers, such as customer retention rates and customer satisfaction levels, and began tracking results and posting them for everyone to see. Before long, every employee in the hotel was involved in and excited about exceeding their targets. The occupancy rate, customer retention rate, and customer satisfaction scores all shot up. The hotel owner had learned not only what his company's critical number was but how to use it to motivate employees![50]

Deciding How to Measure. Once a business owner identifies his company's critical numbers, the issue of how to best measure them arises. In some cases, identifying the critical numbers defines the measurements the owner must make, for example, the occupancy rate at the hotel just mentioned, and measuring them simply becomes a matter of collecting and analyzing data. In other cases, the method of measurement is not as obvious or as tangible. For instance, in some businesses, social responsibility is a key factor, but how should a manager measure his company's performance on such an intangible concept? One of the best ways to develop methods for measuring such factors is to use brainstorming sessions involving employees, customers, and even outsiders. For example, one company used this technique to develop a "fun index," which used the results of an employee survey to measure how much fun employees had at work (and, by extension, how satisfied they were with their work, the company, and their managers).

Whatever method a business owner designs to measure a company's critical numbers, it must meet two criteria: validity and reliability. **Validity** is the extent to which a measuring device or technique actually measures what it is intended to measure and how well it measures that factor. **Reliability** is the extent to which a measurement device or technique produces consistent measurements of a factor over time. To be reliable, a measurement technique must be stable. Without measurements that are both valid and reliable, a company could be chasing after solutions to performance gaps that do not really exist! The performance gap appears only because the measurements are faulty or misleading. To avoid this

validity—*the extent to which a measuring device or technique actually measures what it is intended to measure and how well it measures that factor.*

reliability—*the extent to which a measuring device or technique produces consistent measurements of a factor over time.*

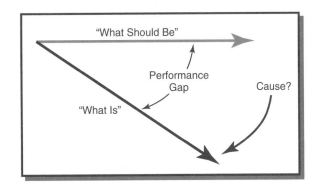

Figure 13.2
Comparing Actual Results with Performance Standards

"What Should Be"

Performance Gap

"What Is"

Cause?

problem, managers and employees should carefully define the measurements they will use to track performance and determine the procedure used to collect and to analyze the data.

Comparing Actual Results with Standards. In this stage of the feedback loop, the idea is to look for deviations *in either direction* from the performance standards the company has set for itself. In other words, opportunities to improve performance arise when there is a gap between "what should be" and "what is" (see Figure 13.2). The most serious deviations usually are those where actual performance falls far below the standard. Managers and employees must focus their efforts on figuring out *why* actual performance is substandard. The goal is *not* to hunt down the guilty party (or parties) for punishment, but to discover the cause of the subpar performance and fix it! Managers should not ignore deviations in the other direction, however. When actual performance consistently exceeds the company's standards, it is an indication that the standards are set too low. The company should look closely at "raising the bar another notch" to spur motivation.

Taking Action to Improve Performance. When managers or employees detect a performance gap, their next challenge is to decide on which course of action will eliminate it most effectively. Typically, several suitable alternatives to solving a performance problem exist; the key is finding an acceptable solution that solves the problem quickly, efficiently, and effectively.

PERFORMANCE APPRAISAL. One of the most common methods of providing feedback on employee performance is through **performance appraisal**, the process of evaluating an employee's actual performance against desired performance standards. Most performance appraisal programs strive to accomplish three goals: (1) to give employees feedback about how they are doing their jobs, which can be an important source of motivation; (2) to provide a business owner and an employee the opportunity to devise a plan for developing the employee's skills and abilities and for improving his performance; and (3) to establish a basis for determining promotions and salary increases. Although the primary purpose of performance appraisals is to encourage and to help employees improve their performances, too often they turn into uncomfortable confrontations that do nothing more than upset the employee, aggravate the business owner, and destroy trust and morale. Why? Because most business owners don't understand how to conduct an effective performance appraisal. Although American businesses have been conducting performance appraisals for about 75 years, most companies, their managers, and their employees are dissatisfied with the entire process. Common complaints include unclear standards and objectives; managers who lack information about employees' performances; managers who are unprepared or who lack honesty and sincerity; and managers who use general, ambiguous terms to describe employees' performances. Perhaps the biggest complaint concerning appraisals is that they happen only periodically—most often just once a year. Employees do not have the oppor-

performance appraisal—*the process of evaluating an employee's performance against desired performance standards.*

tunity to receive any ongoing feedback on a regular basis. All too often, a manager saves up all of the negative feedback to give an employee and then dumps it on him in the annual performance review. Not only does it destroy the employee's motivation, but it does *nothing* to improve the employee's performance. What good does it do to tell an employee that six months before, he botched an assignment that caused the company to lose a customer? One writer compares the lack of ongoing feedback to asking employees to bowl in the dark. They can hear some pins falling, but they have no idea which ones are left standing for the next frame. "Two pins left," comments the manager. "Which ones?" asks the employee. "Don't bother me. Just keep bowling," says the manager. "I'll be back tomorrow to tell you how you did." At the end of the next day, the manager tells the worker, "You bowled poorly yesterday." "What was my score?" asks the employee. "I don't know, but it is terrible," the manager replies.[51] How motivated would you be to keep bowling? Managers should address problems when they occur rather than wait until the performance appraisal session. Continuous feedback, both positive and negative, is a much more effective way to improve employees' performances and to increase their motivation.

Making Performance Appraisals Work. If done properly, performance appraisals can be effective ways to provide employee feedback and to improve workers' performances. However, it takes some planning and preparation on the business owner's part. The following guidelines can help a business owner create a performance appraisal system that actually works:

- ☆ *Link the employee's performance criteria to the job description discussed earlier in this chapter.* To evaluate an employee's performance effectively, a manger must understand the job that employee is in very well.

- ☆ *Establish meaningful, job-related, observable, measurable, and fair performance criteria.* The criteria should describe behaviors and actions, not traits and characteristics. What kind of behavior constitutes a solid performance in this job?

- ☆ *Prepare for the appraisal session by outlining the key points you want to cover with the employee.* Important points to include are the employee's strengths and weaknesses and developing a plan for improving his performance.

- ☆ *Invite the employee to provide an evaluation of his own job performance based on the performance criteria.* In one small company, workers rate themselves on a one-to-five scale in categories of job-related behavior and skills as part of the performance appraisal system. Then they meet with their supervisors to compare their evaluations with those of their supervisors and discuss them. Workers there also evaluate their bosses as part of the review process. [52]

- ☆ *Be specific.* One of the most common complaints employees have about the appraisal process is that managers' comments are too general to be of any value. Offer the employee specific examples of his desirable or undesirable behavior.

- ☆ *Keep a record of employees' critical incidents—both positive and negative.* The most productive evaluations are those based on a manager's direct observation of his employees' on-the-job performances. Such records also can be vital in case legal problems arise.

- ☆ *Discuss an employee's strengths and weaknesses.* An appraisal session is not the time to "unload" about everything an employee has done wrong over the past year. Use it as an opportunity to design a plan for improvement and to recognize employees' strengths, efforts, and achievements.

- ☆ *Incorporate employees' goals into the appraisal.* Ideally, the standard against which to measure an employee's performance is the goals he has played a role in setting. Workers are more likely to be motivated to achieve goals that they have helped establish.

- ☆ *Keep the evaluation constructive.* Avoid the tendency to belittle employees. Do not dwell on past failures. Instead, point out specific things they should do better and help them develop meaningful goals for the future and a strategy for getting there.

⭐ *Focus on behaviors, actions, and results.* Problems arise when managers move away from tangible results and actions and begin to critique employees' abilities and attitudes. Such criticism creates a negative tone for the appraisal session and undercuts its primary purpose.

⭐ *No surprises.* If a business owner is doing her job well, performance appraisals should contain no surprises for employees or the business owner. The ideal time to correct improper behavior or slumping performance is when it happens, not months later. Managers should provide employees with continuous feedback on their performances and use the appraisal session to keep employees on the right track.

⭐ *Plan for the future.* Smart business owners use appraisal sessions as gateways to workers' future success. They spend only about 20 percent of the time discussing past performance; they use the remaining 80 percent of the time to develop goals, objectives, and a plan for the future.

Many companies are encouraging employees to evaluate each other in **peer reviews** or to evaluate their bosses in **upward feedback**, both part of a technique called *360-degree feedback.* Studies suggest that 30 percent of U.S. companies use 360-degree evaluations as part of their performance appraisal systems.[53] Peer appraisals can be especially useful because an employee's coworkers see his on-the-job performance every day. As a result, peer evaluations tend to be more accurate and more valid than those of some managers. Plus, they may capture behavior that managers might miss. Disadvantages of peer appraisals include potential retaliation against coworkers who criticize, the possibility that appraisals will be reduced to "popularity contests," and workers who refuse to offer any criticism because they feel uncomfortable evaluating others. Some bosses using upward feedback report similar problems, including personal attacks and extreme evaluations by vengeful subordinates.

peer reviews—*an appraisal technique in which an employee's coworkers evaluate his job performance.*

upward feedback—*an appraisal technique in which employees evaluate their manager's job performance.*

Management Succession and the Growing Business

5. Describe the steps in developing a management succession plan for a growing business that will allow a smooth transition of leadership to the next generation.

There never seems to be an end to the new and different opportunities facing a business during the growth stage. A fast-growing business is much like a fast break in basketball. A business has a step or two lead on its competitors, but the ballhandler (the entrepreneur) must keep the lead while controlling the wild and fast pace of the action. Any stumble or inability to implement the necessary strategic actions can result in the opponent (competitor) catching up and even stealing the ball. Control of the market segment is always up for grabs, and an entrepreneur must retain an aggressive strategic posture while mastering the new roles and responsibilities that growth brings with it.

For most entrepreneurs, growth is one way of measuring the success of their business ventures. Yet, growth brings with it a multitude of problems and challenges. The entrepreneur must change as the company changes, learning to adjust her management style to suit a larger, more visible organization. Many entrepreneurs have trouble making the transition from the role of freewheeling founder to that of disciplined manager. Because the skills these roles require are so vastly different, some entrepreneurs cannot make the transition as their companies grow. They must either limit their companies' growth or bring in "professional" managers to guide the company through its growing pains.

Success in business brings with it the seeds of change, however. Organizations with the ability to retain their entrepreneurial initiative and focus on ever-changing market demands are those which must eventually come to grips with possibly the biggest decision a company founder will ever have—the exit decision. Three options are available: (1) sell the business to an outsider (often a competitor); (2) sell the business to an insider or a group of insiders; or (3) sell or transfer the business to a family member.

Selling to Outsiders

Selling a business to an outsider is no simple task. Done properly, it takes time, patience, and preparation to locate a suitable buyer, strike a deal, and make the transition. Advance preparation and maintaining accurate financial records are keys to a successful sale. Too often, however, business owners postpone selling their businesses until the last minute—when they reach retirement age or when they face a business crisis. Such a "fire sale" approach rarely yields the maximum price for a business.

A straight sale may be best for those entrepreneurs who want to step down and turn the reins of the company over to someone else. Selling a business outright is not an attractive exit strategy for those who want to stay on with the company or for those who want to surrender control of the company gradually rather than all at once.

Potential buyers of the business can belong to one of the following categories and can have one or more of the following motivations for acquiring the business:

Direct Competitors and Their Possible Motivations

☆ They can gain market share through acquisitions, which is often less expensive.

☆ Acquiring a firm already in the market segment can eliminate potential competitors.

☆ Acquisition is the fastest and often the least expensive method of obtaining additional production capacity, market outlets, or distribution channels.

☆ Through acquisitions, they can create production or distribution economies of scale and on-line operational efficiencies not previously possible.

☆ They can acquire tangible or intangible assets that otherwise cannot be duplicated (patent, trademarks, brand names).

Indirect Competitors in Related Market Segments and Their Possible Motivations

☆ They can enter a market immediately through acquisition.

☆ They can extend their product lines through acquisition.

☆ They can acquire new technical knowledge and economies of scale that serve as an entry barrier to competitors.

Noncompetitors and Their Possible Motivations

☆ A business's profitability makes it an attractive acquisition target.

☆ Potential buyers believe that they can apply their management skills to increase the profitability of the business.

☆ Potential buyers are cash-rich firms in search of an opportunity-rich acquisition.

Before taking any steps to sell their businesses, entrepreneurs need to address some fundamental questions. First, what is a reasonable price for the business? Chapter 4 discussed the various techniques for valuing a business. The range of values determined using those methods will be affected by conditions such as the current economic climate or the time constraints placed on the sale. When economic conditions influencing the firms' profitability are positive, entrepreneurs who are willing to be patient can obtain a premium selling price.

The financial terms of a sale also influence the selling price of the business and the number of potential bidders. Does the owner want "clean, cash-only, 100 percent at closing" offers, or is he willing to finance a portion of the sale? The 100 percent, cash-only requirement dramatically reduces the number of potential buyers. On the other hand, the owner can exit the business "free and clear" and does not incur the risk that the buyer may fail to operate the business in a profitable fashion and to complete the financial transition. Thus,

Table 13.9
*Sale Options:
Advantages and Risks*

100% Cash at Closing Sale
☆ A lower selling price due to a smaller pool of potential buyers and more demanding terms for the buyer.
☆ No financial risk to the seller.
☆ Seller walks away from the deal with cash in hand and no future obligations.

Cash Down Payment Plus Notes
☆ A higher selling price due to more favorable terms for the buyer.
☆ Notes the seller accepts usually bear interest rates that are 2 to 3 percent above the prime interest rate and can be an excellent source of income.
☆ The less cash the seller receives at closing, the greater the risk to her.
☆ No guarantee that the buyer will be able to manage the business profitably and generate the cash to pay off the seller's notes.
☆ If the buyer cannot pay off the notes, the seller may have no choice but to return to the company to try to salvage it. In some cases, the buyer may have damaged the business beyond repair.

the owner may be required to return to the business only to discover that the buyer's incompetent management has destroyed its value. In some cases, the buyer may have been unethical or even illegal in his management practices. Entrepreneurs who don't look beyond the financial issues to the character and competence of the buyer unknowingly accept more risk than expected (see Table 13.9).

Selling to Insiders

When entrepreneurs have no family members to whom they want to transfer ownership or who want to assume the responsibilities of running a company, selling the business to employees is often the preferred option. In most situations, the options available to owners are: (1) sale for cash plus a note, (2) a leveraged buyout, and (3) an employee stock ownership plan.

CASH SALE PLUS NOTE. The first option involves the sale of the business for a specific dollar amount to one or more employees. The seller holds a promissory note for a major portion of the selling price. With its many creative financial methods, this option is similar to the sale of the business to outsiders. However, in this case, the seller has considerable knowledge of the buyers' competencies. In many cases, the owner's risk is lower, and he may even retain a seat on the board of directors to ensure that the new owners are keeping the business on track.

LEVERAGED BUYOUTS (LBOs). The second option—the **leveraged buyout (LBO)**—was one of the most popular exit strategies employed in the 1980s. In an LBO, managers and/or employees borrow money from a financial institution and pay the owner the total agreed-upon price at closing; then they use the cash generated from the company's operations to pay off the debt. During the economic boom of the 1980s, financial institutions were willing to accept the risks associated with highly leveraged businesses. Because of the high levels of debt they had taken on, the new managements had very little room for error. Unfortunately, as the booming economy slowed, many highly leveraged businesses ended up in bankruptcy.

leveraged buyout (LBO)—*an exit strategy in which the managers and/or employees of a company borrow money from a financial institution to buy out the owner and then use the cash from the company's operations to pay off the debt.*

Just as with any cashout sale at closing, the seller can take the cash from the LBO and move on, sometimes using the proceeds to finance another venture. Many entrepreneurs thrill at the opportunity to build their businesses to a size that proves the success of their ideas. Once they have attained that level of success in one business, they are ready to move on to a new challenge. They are very willing to cash out, knowing that they leave the business in good hands. Many entrepreneurs create and build dozens of businesses in their lifetimes. Their need to continually form new ventures that put their skills to the test is almost addictive.

EMPLOYEE STOCK OWNERSHIP PLANS (ESOPs). The third option—the **employee stock ownership plan (ESOP)**—allows employees and/or managers (that is, the future owners) to purchase the business gradually, thus enabling the entrepreneur to finance the venture's growth. With an ESOP, employees contribute a portion of their earnings over time toward purchasing shares of the company's stock. Through their ESOP contributions, participants gradually achieve total ownership of the business. It is a long-term exit strategy that benefits everyone involved. The owner sells the business to the people he can trust the most—his managers and employees. The managers and employees buy a business they already know how to run successfully. Plus, because they own the company, the managers and employees have a huge incentive to see that it operates effectively and efficiently.

Planning for Management Succession

An overwhelming number of founders hope to keep the businesses "all in the family." In fact, approximately 80 percent of all U.S. businesses are family owned, and they employ about half of the nation's work force and produce 40 percent of the nation's GDP.[54] Not all of them are small; about one-third of *Fortune* 500 companies are family-owned![55] Unfortunately, 70 percent of first-generation businesses fail to survive into the second generation. Of those that do survive, only half make it to the third generation.[56] A common cause of this high mortality rate from one generation to the next is the failure to prepare a management succession plan. Although 85 percent of all small business owners with teenage children plan for their children to join them in the business and 78 percent of all family business founders intend to pass their business to their children, only 25 percent actually create a formal succession plan.[57] Without a succession plan, family businesses face an increased risk of not succeeding in the next generation. Those businesses with the greatest probability of surviving are the ones whose owners prepare a succession plan well before it is time to "pass the torch of leadership" to the next generation.

Management succession planning requires, first, an attitude of trusting others. It recognizes that other family members have a stake in the future of the business and want to participate in planning its future. Planning is an attitude that demonstrates that decisions made with open discussion are more constructive than those made without family input. Another attitude hindering succession planning is that, in planning the future of the business, the owner is forced to accept the painful reality of her own mortality.

Second, management succession as an evolutionary process must reconcile the entrepreneur's inevitable anguish and even pain with her successors' desire for autonomy. Perhaps the owner is afraid to release the business into the hands of another person, even a family member. Often, the business has been such a focal point in the owner's life that it has become her "personal identity." One succession planning expert says, "[Planning] is very difficult because for years the family and the business have been intertwined. [The

Early Involvement With the Business in Routine Tasks (While Very Young and in High School) Little	Rotation Among Various Assignments Summer/Holiday Vacation Time (While in College)	Entry-Level Position With Planned Job Rotations, Regular Performance Evaluations and Mentoring by Both Insiders and Outsiders	Greater Responsibility Department or Functional Manager—Service on Advisory Board	General Manager Transition Phase Membership on the Board Great
Stage I	Stage II	Stage III	Stage IV	Stage V Ascension to CEO Position

Figure 13.3
Stages in the Management Succession Process

business] is clearly the most valuable family asset and yet the most vulnerable because people don't view it separately from their lives."[58] The owner's emotional ties to the business may be as strong as—or stronger than—the financial ties. On the other side are the successors, who may desire or even crave autonomy. Their attitude is "It's my turn to make decisions and run this business." As a result, each side sees the other as greedy or selfish.

Succession planning reduces the tension and stress created by these conflicts by gradually "changing the guard." A well-developed succession plan can be compared to the smooth, graceful exchange of a baton between runners in a relay race. The new runner still has maximum energy; the concluding runner has already spent his or her energy by running at maximum speed. The athletes never come to a stop to exchange the baton, which takes place on the move. The race is a skillful blend of the talents of all team members. Such an exchange of leadership is so smooth and powerful that the business never falters, but accelerates, fueled by a new source of energy at each leg of the race.

Management succession planning involves a lengthy series of interconnected stages that begin very early in the life of the owner's children and extend to the point of final ownership transition (see Figure 13.3). If management succession is to be effective, it is necessary for the process to begin early in the successor's life. In most cases, this means involving the child in the business while he is still in junior high or high school. In this period the tasks are routine, but the child is learning the basics of how the business operates. Young adults begin to appreciate the role the business plays in the life of the family. They learn firsthand about the values and responsibilities of running the company. While in college the successor moves to stage II of the continuum. During this stage, the individual rotates among a variety of job functions to both broaden his base of understanding of the business and to permit the parents to evaluate his skills. Upon graduation from college, the successor enters stage III. At this point, the successor becomes a full-time worker and ideally has already earned the respect of coworkers through his behavior in the first two stages of the process. Stage III focuses on the successor's continuous development. A formal program for mentoring the successor involves both internal and external people. As the successor develops his skills and performance, he moves to stage IV, in which real decision-making authority grows rapidly. Stage IV of the succession continuum is the period when the founder makes a final assessment of the individual's abilities to take full and complete control over the firm. The skills the successor will need include financial abilities, technical knowledge, negotiating ability, communication skills, leadership qualities, and a commitment to the business.[59] The final stage involves the ultimate transition of organizational leadership. The successor becomes the organizational CEO, while the former CEO retains the title of chairman of the board.

Superior Metal Products

Henry Hawk, founder of Superior Metal Products, a maker of metal parts for appliances, started the business in 1951 and immediately began grooming his son, Leo, to take over the business upon his retirement. After college and at his father's suggestion, Leo worked for three years outside the family business before joining Superior in 1958. Over the next several years, he held a variety of jobs in the company and helped it grow from just $5,000 in annual sales to more than $240 million in sales. Learning from his father, Leo began grooming his four sons for possible leadership positions in the company. Only one, Jeffrey, had any desire to manage the family business. Now 63 and approaching his own retirement, Leo is shifting more responsibility to Jeffrey. All indications are that Superior will be one of the few family businesses that makes the successful transition to a third generation.[60]

How to Develop a Management Succession Plan

Developing a plan takes time and dedication, yet the benefits are well worth the cost.

Step 1: *Select the successor.* Entrepreneurs should never assume that their children want to take control of the business. Above all, they should not be afraid to ask the question: "Will you take over the family business?" Too often, children in this situation tell Mom and Dad what they want to hear out of loyalty, pressure, or guilty feelings. It is critical to remember at this juncture in the life of a business that entrepreneurial skills and desires are not necessarily inherited. By leveling with the children about the business and their options regarding a family succession, the owner will know which heirs, if any, are willing to assume leadership of the business. When naming a successor, merit is a better standard to use than birth order.

Once the founder identifies potential candidates, he can choose his successor. The selection should not remain a secret. Rather, the owner should announce who the new leader will be and then should put that decision in writing. The successor will need a list of key advisors, people who have provided good advice and who have demonstrated their trustworthiness over the years. This list should include the names of individuals who can give counsel and advice as needed by the successor, for example, attorney, accountant, banker, insurance agent, and board members.

Step 2: *Create a survival kit for the successor.* The entrepreneur should brief the selected successor concerning all critical documents (will, trust, insurance policies, financial statements, bank accounts, key contracts, corporate bylaws, and so forth) and should be sure that the successor reads and understands all relevant documents. Other important steps the owner should take preparing a successor survival kit include the following:

☆ On a regular basis, share his vision of the business's future direction, describing key factors that have led to its success and those that will bring future success.

Who Gets the Business? Family or "Uncle Sam"?

Barbara Balter (known as "Bobbie") suddenly found herself at the helm of her family's engineering firm, Robert B. Balter Company, when her husband Bob died suddenly. The company is in the geotechnical business, designing subsurface structures to support buildings and other construction. It employs 65 workers and generates more than $1 million in sales annually.

Bobbie, now 66, wonders about her impending retirement and whether the company can survive another transition. As they were growing up, Bobbie's three daughters and two sons worked at a variety of jobs in the business. Two of them, Edward, 35, and Lori, 40, decided to stay with the family business after graduating from college. At that point, Bobbie decided that Balter needed a management succession plan and that it would not include selling the business to the employees through an ESOP or selling it to outsiders.

After her husband died, Bobbie owned 70 percent of Balter's common stock, which is an S corporation. Each of her five children owned 6 percent, which their father had given to them through a lifetime gifting program. "Control has to be in the hands of the people working in the business," says Bobbie. They need the majority vote." That means that Lori and Edward would get controlling interest in the company, but Bobbie believes the children should earn the stock they get.

Bobbie's goals for Balter's management succession plan include keeping the business alive and in the family, generating adequate income for herself after she retires, producing adequate income for Lori and Edward as they run the business, and minimizing the estate tax burden when she dies. She also wants the arrangement to be fair to all five of her children. "Our family is a close family," she says. "I want both the business and the family to function."

1. What advice would you offer Bobbie Balter about developing a management succession plan for the family business? What issues should the plan address?

2. How should Bobbie achieve the goals she has set for the succession plan?

3. What steps do you recommend she take to minimize the effects of estate taxes on the transition to the next generation? Why is this such an important issue for business owners?

4. Do you agree with Bobbie's assessment that Lori and Edward should get the controlling interest in the company? Explain.

5. Why is it important for entrepreneurs to begin planning to "pass the torch of leadership" on to the next generation well in advance?

Source: Ronaleen R. Roha, "Estate Planning Solutions for Small Business Owners," *Kiplinger's Personal Finance Magazine*, August 1994, pp. 77-80.

☆ Be open and listen to the successor's views.

☆ Teach and learn at the same time.

☆ Relate specifically how the firm's key success factors have produced tangible results.

☆ Tie the key success factors to performance and profitability.

☆ Explain the strategies of the business and the operational key success factors.

☆ Discuss the values and philosophy of the business and how they have inspired and influenced past actions.

☆ Discuss the people in the business and their strengths and weaknesses.

☆ Discuss the philosophy underlying the firm's compensation policy and explain why employees are paid what they are.

☆ Make a list of the firm's most important customers and its key suppliers or vendors and review the history of all dealings with the parties on both lists.

☆ Discuss how these key players should be treated to ensure the company's continued success and its smooth and error-free transition.

Step 3: *Groom the successor.* These discussions that set the stage for the transition of leadership are time-consuming and require openness on the part of both parties. Grooming the successor is the founder's greatest teaching and development responsibility. In implementing the succession plan, the founder must be:

⭐ Patient, realizing that the transfer of power is gradual and evolutionary and that the successor should earn responsibility and authority one step at a time until the final transfer of power takes place.

⭐ Willing to accept that the successor will make mistakes.

⭐ Skillful at using the successor's mistakes as a teaching tool.

⭐ An effective communicator and an especially tolerant listener.

⭐ Capable of establishing reasonable expectations for the successor's performance.

⭐ Able to articulate the keys to success for the business.

Teaching is in reality the art of assisting discovery. Teaching also requires letting go rather than controlling. When a problem arises in the business, the founder should consider whether or not he should delegate it to the successor in training. If so, he must resist the tendency to wade in and fix the problem unless it is beyond the scope of the successor's ability. Realize that most great teachers and leaders are remembered more for the success of their students and followers than for their own.

Step 4: *Promote an environment of trust and respect.* Another priceless gift a founder can leave a successor is an environment of trust and respect. Trust and respect on the part of the founder and others fuel the successor's desire to learn and excel and build the successor's confidence in making decisions. Developing a competent successor over a five-to-ten-year period is realistic. Empowering the successor by gradually delegating responsibilities creates an environment in which all parties can objectively view the growth and development of the successor. Clients, creditors, suppliers, and staff members can gradually develop confidence in the successor. The final transfer of power is not a dramatic, wrenching change but a smooth, coordinated passage.

Step 5: *Cope with the financial realities of estate taxes.* Experts estimate that by 2005, a staggering $10 trillion in assets will pass from one generation to the next.[61] One of the primary concerns of entrepreneurs transferring their businesses to the next generation is minimizing the tax bite of the transfer. Although the law allows individuals to pass up to $600,000 to their heirs without incurring any estate taxes, the tax rate on transfers above that floor *starts* at 37 percent! The tax rate climbs to 55 percent on estates valued at more than $3 million and to 60 percent for estates worth between $10 and $21 million.[62] Without proper estate planning, the heirs to a successful business may be forced to sell it just to pay the estate tax bill. A variety of tools exists to help the founder who wants to make a smooth transfer of the business ownership and to pay the lowest possible estate taxes:

OPTION 1. *Lifetime gifting.* The owners of a successful business may transfer money to their children (or other recipients) from their estate throughout the parents' lives. Current federal tax regulations allow individuals to make gifts of $10,000 per year, per parent, per recipient, that are exempt from federal gift taxes. Each child would be required to pay income taxes on the $10,000 gift they receive, but the children are usually in lower tax brackets than those of the giver. For instance, husband and wife business owners could give $1.2 million worth of stock to their three children and their spouses over a period of ten years without incurring any estate taxes.

OPTION 2. *Setting up a trust.* A **trust** is a contract between a grantor (the founder) and a trustee (generally a bank officer or an attorney). The grantor gives the trustee legal title to assets (for example, stock in the company), which the trustee agrees to hold for the beneficiaries (children). The beneficiaries can receive income from the trust, or they can receive the property in the trust, or both, at some specified time. Under present tax codes, the only trust that provides a tax benefit is an **irrevocable trust**, in which the grantor cannot require the trustee to return the assets held in trust. The value of the grantor's estate is lowered because the assets in an irrevocable trust are excluded from the value of the estate. However, an irrevocable trust places severe restrictions on the grantor's control of the property placed in the trust.

OPTION 3. *Grantor-retained annuity trust.* A **grantor-retained annuity trust (GRAT)** is a special type of irrevocable trust and has become one of the most popular tools for entrepreneurs to transfer ownership of a business while maintaining control over it and minimizing estate taxes. Under a GRAT, an owner can put property in an irrevocable trust for a maximum of ten years. While the trust is in effect, the grantor retains the voting power and receives the interest income from the property in the trust. At the end of the trust (not to exceed ten years), the property passes to the beneficiaries (heirs). The beneficiaries are required to pay a gift tax on the value of the assets placed in the GRAT. However, the IRS taxes GRAT gifts only according to their discounted present value because the heirs did not receive use of the property while it was in trust. There are presently some disadvantages of using a GRAT in estate planning. If the grantor dies during the life of the GRAT, its assets pass back into the grantor's estate. These assets then become subject to the full estate tax.

OPTION 4. *Estate freeze.* An **estate freeze** attempts to minimize estate taxes by having family members create two classes of stock for the business: (1) preferred voting stock for the parents and (2) nonvoting common stock for the children. The value of the preferred stock is frozen while the common stock reflects the anticipated increased market value of the business. Any appreciation in the value of the business after the transfer is not subject to estate taxes. However, the parent must pay gift taxes on the value of the common stock given to the children. The value of the common stock is the total value of the business less the value of the voting preferred stock retained by the parent. The parents also must accept taxable dividends at the market rate on the preferred stock they own.

trust—*a contract between a grantor (the founder) and a trustee in which the grantor gives the trustee title to assets (e.g., company stock), which the trustee holds for the trust's beneficiaries (e.g., the grantor's heirs).*

irrevocable trust—*a trust in which the grantor cannot require the trustee to return the assets held in trust.*

grantor-retained annuity trust (GRAT)—*an irrevocable trust which allows a business owner to transfer ownership of a business to the next generation while maintaining control over it and minimizing estate taxes.*

estate freeze—*a strategy that attempts to minimize estate taxes by creating two classes of stock for a business: preferred voting stock for the parents and nonvoting common stock for the children.*

CHAPTER SUMMARY

1. Explain the challenges involved in the entrepreneur's role as leader and what it takes to be a successful leader.
- Leadership is the process of influencing and inspiring others to work to achieve a common goal and then giving them the power and the freedom to achieve it.

- Management and leadership are not the same, yet both are essential to a small company's success. Leadership without management is unbridled; management without leadership is uninspired. Leadership gets a small business going; management keeps it going.

2. Describe the importance of hiring the right employees and how to avoid making hiring mistakes.

- The decision to hire a new employee is an important one for every business, but its impact is magnified many times in a small company. Every new hire a business owner makes determines the heights to which the company can climb—or the depths to which it will plunge.
- To avoid making hiring mistakes, entrepreneurs should develop meaningful job descriptions and job specifications, plan and conduct an effective interview, and check references before hiring any employee.

3. Explain how to build the kind of company culture and structure to support the entrepreneur's mission and goals and to motivate employees to achieve them.

- Company culture is the distinctive, unwritten code of conduct that governs the behavior, attitudes, relationships, and style of an organization. Culture arises from an entrepreneur's consistent and relentless pursuit of a set of core values that everyone in the company can believe in. Small companies' flexible structures can be a major competitive weapon.
- Entrepreneurs rely on six different management styles to guide their companies as they grow. The first three (craftsman, classic, and coordinator) involve running a company without any management assistance and are best suited for small companies in the early stages of growth; the last three (entrepreneur-plus-employee team, small partnership, big-team venture) rely on a team approach to run the company as its growth rate heats up.
- Team-based management is growing in popularity among small firms. Companies that use teams effectively report significant gains in quality, reductions in cycle time, lower costs, increased customer satisfaction, and improved employee motivation and morale.

4. Discuss the ways in which entrepreneurs can motivate their workers to higher levels of performance.

- Motivation is the degree of effort an employee exerts to accomplish a task; it shows up as excitement about work. Four important tools of motivation include empowerment, job design, rewards and compensation, and feedback.
- Empowerment involves giving workers at every level of the organization the power, the freedom, and the responsibility to control their own work, to make decisions, and to take action to meet the company's objectives.
- Job design techniques for enhancing employee motivation include job enlargement, job rotation, job enrichment, flextime, job sharing, and flexplace (which includes telecommuting).
- Money is an important motivator for many workers, but not the only one. The key to using rewards such as recognition and praise and to motivate involves tailoring them to the needs and characteristics of the workers.
- Giving employees timely, relevant feedback about their job performances through a performance appraisal system can also be a powerful motivator.

5. Describe the steps in developing a management succession plan for a growing business that will allow a smooth transition of leadership to the next generation.

- As their companies grow, entrepreneurs must begin to plan for passing the leadership baton to the next generation well in advance. Three options are available: (1) sell the business to an outsider (often a competitor); (2) sell the business to an insider or a group of insiders; or (3) sell or transfer the business to a family member.
- A succession plan is a crucial element in transferring a company to the next generation. Preparing a succession plan involves five steps: (1) Select the successor. (2) Create a survival kit for the successor. (3) Groom the successor. (4) Promote an environment of trust and respect. (5) Cope with the financial realities of estate taxes.

1. What is leadership? What is the difference between leadership and management?
2. What behaviors do effective leaders exhibit?
3. Why is it so important for small companies to hire the right employees? What can small business owners do to avoid making hiring mistakes?
4. What is a job description? A job specification? What functions do they serve in the hiring process?
5. Outline the procedure for conducting an effective interview.
6. What is company culture? What role does it play in a small company's success? What threats does rapid growth pose for a company's culture?
7. Explain the six different management styles entrepreneurs rely on to guide their companies as they grow (craftsman, classic, coordinator, entrepreneur-plus-employee team, small partnership, and big-team venture).
8. What mistakes do companies make when switching to team-based management? What can they do to avoid these mistakes? Explain the four phases teams typically go through.

9. What is empowerment? What benefits does it offer workers? The company? What must a small business manager do to make empowerment work in a company?

10. Explain the differences among job simplification, job enlargement, job rotation, and job enrichment. What impact do these different job designs have on workers?

11. Is money the "best" motivator? How do pay-for-performance compensation systems work? What other rewards are available to small business managers to use as motivators? How effective are they?

12. Suppose that a mail-order catalog company selling environmentally friendly products identifies its performance as a socially responsible company as a critical number in its success. Suggest some ways for the owner to measure this company's social responsibility index.

13. What is performance appraisal? What are the most common mistakes managers make in performance appraisals? What should small business managers do to avoid making these mistakes?

14. Why is it so important for a small business owner to develop a management succession plan? Why is it so difficult for most business owners to develop such a plan? What are the steps that are involved in creating a succession plan?

15. Briefly describe the options a small business owner wanting to pass the family business on to the next generation can take to minimize the impact of estate taxes.

Beyond the Classroom...

1. Visit a local business that has experienced rapid growth in the past three years and ask the owner about the specific problems he or she had to face due to the organization's growth. How did the owner handle these problems? Looking back, what would he or she do differently?

2. Contact a local small business with at least 20 employees. Does the company have job descriptions and job specifications? What process does the owner use to hire a new employee? What questions does the owner typically ask candidates in an interview?

3. Ask the owner of a small manufacturing operation to give you a tour of his or her operation. During your tour, observe the way jobs are organized. Explain how the company uses the following job design concepts: job simplification, job enlargement, job rotation, job enrichment, flextime, and job sharing. Based on your observations, what recommendations would you make to the owner about the company's job design?

4. Contact five small business owners about their plans for passing their businesses on to the next generation. Do they intend to pass the business along to a family member? Do they have a management succession plan? Have they developed a plan for minimizing the effects of estate taxes? How many more years do they plan to work before retiring?

SURFING THE NET

1. Visit the Web site on leadership at Princeton University's Outdoor Action Guide to Group Dynamics & Leadership at:

http://www.princeton.edu/~oa/sect9.html

a. Scroll down the page to the section on leadership. What roles does a leader play? Summarize the situational leadership theory and give an example of its application. What is the basic premise of the situational leadership theory?

b. Scroll down the page to the section on group development. Summarize the stages of group development.

2. Visit the Web site for Ernst and Young's *Vision Newsletter* at:

http://www.idirect.com/hroffice/vision/index.html

or the HR Homepage: The Internet Center for Human Resource Professionals at:

http://www.hrhome.com/Articles/articles.htm

Continued

Select one of the articles on a topic relating to human resources management and prepare a one-page summary of it.

3. Visit American Express's Small Business Exchange home page at:

http://www.americanexpress.com/smallbusiness/ resources/managing/index.html

Explore the "Managing Your Business" section. Select a topic discussed in this chapter and prepare a one-page report on it.

4. There are many sources of information on management succession and the construction of a management succession plan. Visit the following Web sites and write a short paper on the advice provided:

http://nmq.com/fambiznc/cntprovs/orgs/baylor/ legacy/buscont.htm

or

http://www.aednet.org/ced/jun96/perryx.htm

or

http://199.103.128.199/fambiznc/cntprovs/orgs/ Cornell/articles/real/erven.htm

5. Conduct a Web search and prepare a report on finding employees on the World Wide Web. Two sites you might find helpful as a starting point is the Society of Human Resources Management at:

http://www.shrm.org/

and HR Professional's Gateway to the Internet at:

http://www.teleport.com/~erwilson/

From here, you can access a variety of human resources information.

6. Go to the HR Cyberspace's Top 20: A Highly Subjective Guide to Essential HR home page at:

http://www.shrm.org/cyberspace/top20.html

Use the links at this site to explore one of the topics in this chapter in more depth. Prepare a brief report on what you learn.

CHAPTER

FOURTEEN

Global Aspects of Entrepreneurship

A small business owner experienced in conducting international business was talking to another business owner about the benefits of going global. Unconvinced, the novice asked his well-traveled friend what he regarded as the most important language for world trade. Expecting the answer to be English, he was quite surprised when his colleague said, "My customer's language."

- Bits & Pieces

On a political map, the borders between countries are as clear as ever. But on a competitive map, a map showing the real flows of financial and industrial activity, those boundaries have largely disappeared.

- Kenichi Ohmae

LEARNING OBJECTIVES

Upon completion of this chapter, you will be able to:

1. **Explain** why "going global" has become an integral part of many small companies' strategies.

2. **Describe** the seven principal strategies small businesses have for going global: relying on trade intermediaries, joint ventures, foreign licensing, international franchising, countertrading and bartering, exporting, and establishing international locations.

3. **Explain** how to build a thriving export program.

4. **Discuss** the major barriers to international trade and their impact on the global economy.

5. **Describe** the trade agreements that will have the greatest influence on foreign trade into the twenty-first century—GATT and NAFTA.

Until recently, the world of international business was much like the world of astronomy before Copernicus, who revolutionized the study of the planets and the stars with his theory of planetary motion. In the sixteenth century, his Copernican system replaced the Ptolemaic system, which held that the earth was the center of the universe with the sun and all the other planets revolving around it. The Copernican system, however, placed the sun at the center of the solar system with all of the planets, including the earth, revolving around it. Astronomy would never be the same.

In the same sense, business owners across the globe have been guilty of having Ptolemaic tunnel vision when it came to viewing international business opportunities. Like their pre-Copernican counterparts, owners saw an economy that revolved around the nations that served as their home bases. Market opportunities stopped at their homeland's borders. Global trade was only for giant corporations who had the money and the management to tap foreign markets and enough resources to survive if the venture flopped.

But no more.

Today, the global marketplace is as much the territory of small, upstart companies as it is that of giant multinational corporations.

For example, when Bicknell Manufacturing Company, a manufacturer of drill bits for construction equipment, saw its sales falter due to a severe recession in the construction industry, manager John Purcell began scrambling for new business. The 102-year-old company saw little hope of a fast recovery in its traditional domestic market, so managers began exploring market opportunities abroad. Through their research, they discovered building booms in several foreign countries, including Brazil, Mexico, and Colombia. Despite the fact that none of the company's 65 employees had any experience in international trade, Bicknell soon was selling its drill bits through distributors in Latin America. Within a few years, the company had signed a deal to sell its products in China and Vietnam. Today, international sales account for 20 percent of Bicknell's total revenue.[1]

Political, social, cultural, and economic changes are sweeping the world, creating a new world order—and a legion of both problems and opportunities for businesses of all sizes. These changes are enough to make businesses of *any* size hesitant to go global, but they also are creating tremendous opportunities for small companies ready to capitalize on them.

For instance, Michael Giles recently left his $160,000-a-year job at IBM to move to Soweto, a black township outside Johannesburg, South Africa. "People back home thought I was crazy," he says, referring to the squatter camps without running water or sewage systems that surrounded the area. But where others saw squalor, Giles saw opportunity. He noticed that only four laundromats served the township's 4.5 million residents. After arranging a $9.3 million loan from the U.S. government's Overseas Private Investment Corporation, Giles began building a chain of 108 coin-operated laundromats called QuickWash-Dry Clean USA to serve South Africa's black townships. "There's something intangible and immensely satisfying in helping bring about change," he says.[2]

Expanding a business beyond its domestic borders may actually enhance a company's overall performance. A recent study by The Conference Board concluded that American manufacturers with global operations earn more and grow faster than those who remain purely domestic. In addition, multinational firms were 50 percent more likely to survive the decade than those who limited their businesses to American borders.[3] Another study from the Commerce Department found that companies that export create better, higher-paying jobs for their workers than their purely domestic counterparts.

Bicknell Manufacturing Company

QuickWash-Dry Clean USA

Why Go Global?

1. Explain why "going global" has become an integral part of many small companies' strategies.

Businesses can no longer consider themselves to be domestic companies in this hotly competitive, global environment. "In the global economy, the competitor six time zones away is potentially as serious a threat as the competitor six blocks away," says one expert. [5] For companies across the world, going global is a matter of survival, not preference. No matter where a company's home base is, competitors are forcing it to think globally. For example, the executives of a small Oregon company manufacturing robotic-vision systems to cut french fries discovered that a Belgian company had developed a similar, competing device. [6] "There are an awful lot of people in the rest of the world who think they are pretty good at doing your business," warns Lester Thurow. [7] For instance, in the 1950s just 5 percent of the goods made in America faced foreign competition; today, 80 percent will go up against foreign goods. [8] "Like it or not, virtually all businesses are facing global competition," says the owner of a small ginseng business that operates globally. "Companies that fail to see the world as a global marketplace risk being blindsided at home and abroad." [9]

Failure to cultivate global markets can be a lethal mistake for modern businesses—whatever their size. To thrive in the twenty-first century, small businesses must take their place in the world market! Globalization is no longer on the horizon; it is already here. Increasingly, small businesses will be under pressure to expand into international markets. To be successful, companies must consider themselves businesses without borders. "If a company really is a global competitor, it is going to be shipping all over the place from all over the place," says one executive. [10]

Entrepreneurs who take the plunge into global business can reap the following benefits:

★ *Offset sales declines in the domestic market.* As Bicknell Manufacturing Company discovered, markets in foreign countries may be booming as those in the United States are sagging.

★ *Increase sales and profits.* "Companies are realizing that [by] relying only on the domestic market, they have been ignoring four billion other [potential] customers," says one export consultant. [11]

★ *Extend their products' life cycles.* Some companies have been able to take products that had reached the maturity stage of the product life cycle in the United States and sell them very successfully in foreign markets.

★ *Lower manufacturing costs.* In industries characterized by high levels of fixed costs, businesses that expand into global markets can lower their manufacturing costs by spreading these fixed costs over a larger number of units.

★ *Improve competitive position.* Going up against some of the toughest competition in the world forces a company to hone its competitive skills.

★ *Raise quality levels.* Customers in many global markets are much tougher to satisfy than those in the United States. One reason Japanese products have done so well worldwide is that Japanese companies must build products to satisfy their customers at home, who demand extremely high quality and are sticklers for detail. Businesses who compete in global markets learn very quickly how to boost their quality levels to world-class standards.

★ *Become more customer oriented.* Delving into global markets teaches business owners about the unique tastes, customs, preferences, and habits of customers in many different cultures. Responding to these differences imbues these businesses with a degree of sensitivity toward their customers, both domestic and foreign.

Unfortunately, not enough entrepreneurs have learned to see their companies from a global perspective. A recent report from the Competitiveness Policy Council warns that "an absence of global thinking is one of the elements that permeates our society and most directly hurt(s) its competitive position." [12] Indeed, learning to *think globally* may be the first—and most threatening—obstacle an entrepreneur must overcome on the way to creating a truly global business. **Global thinking** is the ability to appreciate, understand, and respect the different beliefs, values, behaviors, and business practices of companies and people in different cultures and countries. A British manager explains:

> If you are operating in South America, you'd better know how to operate in conditions of hyperinflation. If you're operating in Africa, you'd better know a lot about government relations and the use of local partners. If you're operating in Germany, you'd better understand the mechanics of codetermination and some of the special tax systems that one finds in that country. If you're operating in China, it's quite useful in trademark matters to know how the People's Court of Shanghai works. . . . If you're operating in Japan, you'd better understand the different trade structures.[13]

Gaining a foothold in newly opened foreign markets or maintaining a position in an existing one is no easy task, however. "The key to the problem of how to truly become global can be summarized in one word: *attitude*," says one U.S. manager. "Until you have the attitude that you are truly an international company, not just a U.S. company also doing business abroad, you cannot achieve your goals."[14] Success in the global economy also requires constant innovation; staying nimble enough to use speed as a competitive weapon; maintaining a high level of quality and constantly improving it; being sensitive to foreign customers' unique requirements; adopting a more respectful attitude toward foreign habits and customs; hiring motivated, multilingual employees; and retaining a desire to learn constantly about global markets. In short, the path to success requires businesses to become "insiders" rather than just "exporters."

Before venturing into the global marketplace, a small business owner should consider five questions:[15]

1. Are we willing to commit adequate resources of time, people, and capital to our international campaign?
2. Can we make money there?
3. If so, can we get it out? (That is, is the currency convertible?)
4. Will we feel comfortable doing business there? (That is are we sensitive to the cultural differences of conducting international business?)
5. Can we afford *not* to go global?

Going Global: Strategies for Small Businesses

A growing number of small businesses are recognizing that "going global" is not a strategy reserved solely for industry giants such as General Motors, IBM, and Boeing. In fact, John Naisbitt, trend-spotting author of *The Global Paradox,* says that the increasing globalization of business actually *favors* smaller companies. Naisbitt states:

> In the huge global economy, there will be smaller and smaller market niches." In this global economy, . . . the competitive edge is swiftness to market and innovation. Small units are much better at speed to market and innovation ... As a result, they can innovate faster, not just in products but in internal operations, to take advantage of the new technologies."[16]

Their agility and adaptability give small firms the edge in today's highly interactive, fast-paced global economy. "The bigger the world economy, the more powerful its smallest players," concludes Naisbitt.[17]

Small companies go global for a variety of reasons. Some move into foreign markets because their domestic sales have sagged.

For example, after Artais Weather Check Inc. captured 80 percent of the U.S. market in airport weather-observation systems, sales reached a plateau. That's when Artais turned its *attention to building sales in foreign markets. The payoff was immediate—and large. Foreign sales jumped to $3.7 million, two-thirds of the company's total sales. To date, Artais has sold its computerized airport weather information systems in Taiwan, Ecuador, China, Saudi Arabia, and Egypt. Charles Shanklin, president of the family-owned company, expects foreign sales to grow as many developing nations increase expenditures on upgrading their airports' technology.*[18]

Other small businesses have discovered soaring demand for their products and services among foreign customers.

For instance, when Rostilav Ordovsky-Tanaevsky traveled for the first time to the former Soviet Union, he stumbled upon his father's relatives, many of whom had been missing since the 1917 Bolshevik Revolution. When he went to buy film for his camera to record the event, "I couldn't find a single roll," he recalls. On another trip, Ordovsky-Tanaevsky tried to have lunch but couldn't find an open restaurant! Sensing the business opportunities before him, Ordovsky-Tanaevsky spent the next five years building his business, Rostik International. Today, he owns more than 200 Fokus photo retail stores and is Moscow's leading restaurateur. His restaurants include a string of hamburger stands, pizzerias, New-York style delicatessens, and theme restaurants. "Growth is here for the next 20 years," Ordovsky-Tanaevsky says.[19]

Still other entrepreneurs realize that their future success depends on their ability to go global.

Copreneurs Edward Wierzbowski and Pamela Roberts saw global markets as the key to success for their small TV production company, Global American Television. Although small in size (annual revenues of less than $500,000), Global American Television has big aspirations—to help create a successful commercial TV industry in Russia. Because it has been working with Russian television companies since the early 1980s, the company has a head start on its much larger competitors and does plenty of high-profile business in Russia. Global American has coproduced several projects with Russian companies and was the first to persuade Russian television companies to sell commercial air time to Western companies. "We compete as a small company by being willing to take risks and always looking for a new niche," says Wierzbowski, who is interested in developing other foreign markets as well.[20]

Becoming a global business depends on instilling a global culture throughout the organization so that it permeates *everything* the company does. Entrepreneurs who routinely conduct international business have developed a global mind-set for themselves and their companies. As one business writer explains:

> The global (business] . . . looks at the whole world as *one market*. It manufactures, conducts research, raises capital, and buys supplies wherever it can do the job best. It keeps in touch with technology and market trends around the world. National boundaries and regulations tend to be irrelevant, or a mere hindrance. [Company] headquarters might be anywhere.[21]

As cultures from around the globe become increasingly interwoven, the ability to "go global" will determine the relative degree of success (or lack of it!) for more and more small businesses.

Small companies pursuing a global presence have seven principal strategies available: relying on trade intermediaries, joint ventures, foreign licensing, franchising, countertrading and bartering, exporting, and establishing international locations (see Figure 14.1 on page 464).

Relying on Trade Intermediaries

Perhaps the least complex way of getting into international markets is by using a trade intermediary. Trade intermediaries serve as distributors in foreign countries for domestic companies of all sizes. They rely on their networks of contacts, their extensive knowledge of

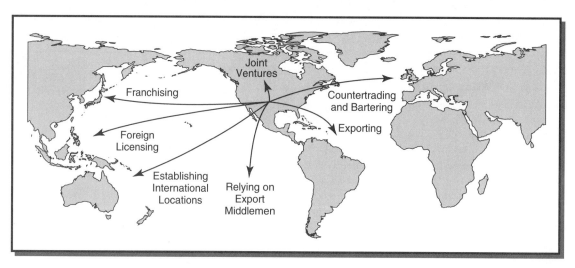

Figure 14.1
Seven Principal Strategies for Pursuing Global Markets

local customs and markets, and their experience in international trade to market products effectively and efficiently all across the globe.

Trade intermediaries currently account for about 10 percent of all U.S. exports. Although a broad array of trade intermediaries is available, the following are ideally suited for small businesses.

export management companies (EMCs)—
merchant intermediaries that provide small businesses with a low-cost, efficient, independent international marketing department.

EXPORT MANAGEMENT COMPANIES (EMCs). **Export management companies (EMCs)** are an important channel of foreign distribution for small companies just getting started in international trade or for those lacking the resources to assign their own people to foreign markets. Most EMCs are merchant intermediaries, working on a buy-and-sell arrangement with domestic small companies. They provide small businesses with a low-cost, efficient, independent international marketing department, offering services ranging from market research and advice on patent protection to arranging financing and handling shipping. More than 1,000 EMCs operate across the United States, and many of them specialize in particular products or product lines.

Hamilton Manufacturing Corporation, a small maker of machines that exchange coins for paper currency, used an export management company to break into foreign markets. James Nesmith, president of the small concern, turned to International Projects Inc., a Toledo-based EMC, for help in selling Hamilton's newly developed machines designed to exchange foreign currency. Going global alone "was a lot more than I could handle," says Nesmith. So Hamilton signed a five-year agreement with International Projects to sell the machines abroad, and its foreign sales are climbing rapidly.[22]

Hamilton Manufacturing Corporation

export trading companies (ETCs)—
businesses that buy and sell products in a number of countries and offer a wide variety of services to their clients.

EXPORT TRADING COMPANIES (ETCs). Another tactic for getting into international markets with a minimum of cost and effort is through an export trading company (ETC). ETCs have been an important vehicle in international trade throughout history. The Hudson's Bay Company and the East India Company were dominant powers in world trade in the sixteenth, seventeenth, and eighteenth centuries.

Export trading companies (ETCs) are businesses that buy and sell products in a number of countries, and they typically offer a wide range of services such as exporting, importing, shipping, storing, distributing, and others to their clients. Unlike EMCs, which tend to focus on exporting, ETCs usually perform both import and export trades across many countries' borders. However, like EMCs, ETCs lower the risk of exporting for small businesses. Some of the largest trading companies in the world are based in the United States and Japan. In fact, many businesses that have navigated successfully Japan's complex system of distribution have done so with the help of ETCs.

In 1982, Congress passed the Export Trading Company Act to allow producers of similar products to form ETC cooperatives without the fear of violating antitrust laws. The goal was to encourage U.S. companies to export more goods by allowing businesses in the same industry to band together to form export trading companies.

MANUFACTURER'S EXPORT AGENTS (MEAs). **Manufacturer's export agents (MEAs)** act as international sales representatives in a limited number of markets for various noncompeting domestic companies. Unlike the close, long-term partnering relationship formed with most EMCs, the relationship between an MEA and a small company is a short-term one, where the MEA typically operates on a commission basis.

EXPORT MERCHANTS. **Export merchants** are domestic wholesalers who do business in foreign markets. They buy goods from many domestic manufacturers and then market them in foreign markets. Unlike MEAs, export merchants often carry competing lines, which means they have little loyalty to suppliers. Most export merchants specialize in particular industries such as office equipment, computers, industrial supplies, and others.

RESIDENT BUYING OFFICES. Another approach to exporting is to sell to a **resident buying office**, a government-owned or privately owned operation established in a country for the purpose of buying goods made there. Many foreign governments and businesses have set up buying offices in the United States. Selling to them is just like selling to domestic customers because the buying office handles all the details of exporting.

FOREIGN DISTRIBUTORS. Many small businesses work through foreign distributors to reach international markets. Domestic small companies export their products to these distributors who handle all of the marketing, distribution, and service functions in the foreign country. Distributors often request contracts giving them exclusive distribution rights for a company's product in their markets. They offer exporting small businesses the benefits of knowledge of their local markets, the ability to cover a given territory thoroughly, and prompt sales and service support.

For example, when managers at Mardel Laboratories, a manufacturer of water conditioners and other supplies for tropical-fish aquariums, decided to sell its products in the Far East, it hired a Hong Kong distributor to handle the transactions. Mardel found the foreign distributor with the help of Penn Plax Plastics, a company that sells complementary (but not competing) aquarium supplies. [23]

Trade intermediaries such as these are becoming increasingly popular among businesses attempting to branch out into world markets because they make that transition so much faster and easier. Most small businesses simply do not have the knowledge, resources, confidence, or the connections to go global alone. Intermediaries' global networks of buyers and sellers allow their small business customers to build their international sales efforts much more quickly and with fewer hassles and mistakes.

The key to establishing a successful relationship with a trade intermediary is conducting a thorough screening to determine what type of intermediary—and which one in particular—will best serve a small company's needs. A company looking for an intermediary should compile a list of potential candidates using some of the sources listed in Table 14.1 on page 466. The 50 World Trade Centers (most of which are affiliated with the U.S. government) and the 15 Export Assistance Centers located across the United States offer valuable advice and assistance to small businesses wanting to get started in conducting global business.

manufacturer's export agents—*businesses that act as international sales representatives in a limited number of markets for various noncompeting domestic companies.*

export merchants—*domestic wholesalers who do business in foreign markets.*

resident buying office—*a government-owned or privately owned operation established in a country for the purpose of buying goods from businesses there.*

Mardel Laboratories

████ ████ ████ ████ ████ ████

Trade intermediaries make doing business around the world much easier for small companies, but finding the right one can be a challenge. Fortunately, several government agencies offer a wealth of information to businesses interested in reaching into global markets with the help of trade intermediaries. Entrepreneurs looking for help in breaking into global markets should contact the International Trade Administration and the U.S. Commerce Department first to take advantage of the following services:

★ *Agent/Distributor Service (ADS)*—provides customized searches to locate interested and qualified foreign distributors for a product or service (search cost = $250 per country).

★ *Commercial Service International Contacts (CSIC) List*—provides contact and product information for more than 82,000 foreign agents, distributors, and importers interested in doing business with U.S. companies.

★ *Country Directories of International Contacts (CDIC) List*—provides the same kind of information as the CSIC list but is organized by country.

★ *Industry Sector Analysis (ISA)*—offers in-depth reports on industries in foreign countries, including information on distribution practices, end users, and top sales prospects.

★ *International Market Insights (IMIs)*—include reports on specific foreign market conditions, upcoming opportunities for U.S. companies, trade contacts, trade show schedules, and other information.

★ *Trade Opportunity Program (TOP)*—provides up-to-the-minute, prescreened sales leads around the world for U.S. businesses, including joint venture and licensing partners, direct sales leads, and representation offers.

★ *International Company Profiles (ICPs)*—Commercial specialists will investigate potential partners, agents, distributors, or customers for U.S. companies and will issue profiles on them.

★ *Commercial News USA*—a government-published magazine (ten issues per year) that promotes U.S. companies' products and services to 259,000 business readers in 152 countries at a fraction of the cost of commercial advertising. Small companies can use *Commercial News USA* to reach new customers around the world for as little as $395!

★ *Gold Key Service*—For a small fee, business owners wanting to target a specific country can use the Department of Commerce's Gold Key Service, in which experienced trade professionals arrange meetings with prescreened contacts whose interests match their own.

★ *Matchmaker Trade Delegations Program*—helps small U.S. companies establish business relationships in major markets abroad by introducing them to the right contacts.

★ *Multi-State/Catalog Exhibition Program*—Working with state economic development offices, the Department of Commerce presents companies' product and sales literature to hundreds of interested business prospects in foreign countries.

★ *International Fair Certification Program*—promotes U.S. companies' participation in foreign trade shows that represent the best marketing opportunities for them.

★ *National Trade Data Bank (NTDB)*—Most of the information listed here is available on the NTDB, the U.S. government's most comprehensive database of world trade data. With the NTDB, small companies have access to information that only *Fortune* 500 companies could afford.

★ *Economic Bulletin Board (EBB)*—provides on-line trade leads and valuable market research on foreign countries compiled from a variety of federal agencies.

domestic joint venture—*an alliance of two or more U.S. small businesses for the purpose of exporting their goods and services abroad.*

Joint Ventures

Joint ventures, both domestic and foreign, lower the risk of emerging global markets for small businesses. They also give small companies more clout in foreign lands. In a **domestic joint venture**, two or more U.S. small businesses form an alliance for the purpose of exporting their goods and services abroad. For export ventures, participating companies get antitrust immunity, allowing them to cooperate freely. The businesses share the responsibility and the costs of getting export licenses and permits, and they split the venture's prof-

Where Do We Start?

Specialty Building Supplies is a small company with $6.4 million in annual sales that manufactures and sells a line of building supply products such as foundation vents, innovative insulation materials, and fireplace blowers to building supply stores in the northeastern United States. The eight-year-old company, founded by Tad Meyers, has won several awards for its unique and innovative products and has earned a solid reputation among its supply store customers and the builders and homeowners who ultimately buy its products. Before launching the company, Meyers had been a home builder. As he watched the price of home heating fuels climb dramatically over time, Meyers began to incorporate into the houses he built simple, inexpensive ways to help homeowners save energy. He began tinkering with existing products, looking for ways to improve them. The first product he designed (and the product that ultimately led him to launch Specialty Building Supplies) was an automatic foundation vent that was thermostatically controlled (no electricity needed). The vent would automatically open and close based on the outside temperature, keeping cold drafts from blowing under a house. Simple and inexpensive in its design, the Autovent was a big hit in newly constructed homes in the Northeast because it not only saved energy but it also avoided a major headache for homeowners in cold climates: water pipes that would freeze and burst. Before long, Meyers stopped building houses and focused on selling the Autovent. Its success prompted him to add other products to the company's line.

Specialty's sales have been lackluster for more than a year now, primarily due to a slump in new home construction in its primary market. Tad Meyers recently met with the company's top marketing managers and salespeople to talk about their options for getting Specialty's sales and profit growth back on track. "What about selling our products in international markets?" asked Dee Rada, the company's marketing manager. "I read an article just last week about small companies doing good business in other countries, and many of them were smaller than we are."

"Interesting idea," Meyers said, pondering the concept. "I've never really thought about selling anything overseas. In fact, other than my years in the military, I've never traveled overseas and don't know anything about doing business there."

"It's a big world out there. Where should we sell our products?" said Hal Milam, Specialty's sales manager. "How do we find out what the building codes are in foreign countries? Would we have to modify our designs to meet foreign standards?"

"I don't know," shrugged Meyers. "Those are some good questions . . ."

"How would we distribute our products?" asked Rada. "We have an established network of distributors here in the United States, but how do we find *foreign* distributors?"

"I wonder if exporting is our only option," said Meyers. "There must be other ways to get into the global market besides exporting. What do you think? Where do we start?"

1. What advice would you offer Meyers and the other managers at Specialty Building Supplies about their prospects of "going global"?

2. How would you suggest these managers go about finding the answers to the questions they have posed? What other questions would you advise them to answer?

3. Outline the steps these managers should take to assemble an international marketing plan.

---

its. Establishing a joint venture with the right partner has become an essential part of maintaining a competitive position in global markets for a growing number of industries.

Yamas Controls Inc., a small California maker of environmental control systems, formed a joint venture with Bechtel Group Inc., the giant construction and engineering company, to provide its systems to the Chinese government. Without the joint venture, Yamas most likely would not have been able to break into the Chinese market. With it, the company's annual sales have grown from $4 million to $40 million in just eight years. Not only did the joint venture lower Yamas's risk of selling in foreign markets, but it also opened the door for similar projects with several American, European, and Chinese firms.[24]

In a **foreign joint venture,** a domestic small business forms an alliance with a company in the target nation. The host partner brings to the joint venture valuable knowledge of the local market and its method of operation as well as of the customs and the tastes of local customers. Sometimes foreign countries place certain limitations on joint ventures. Some nations, for example, require host companies to own at least 51 percent of the venture. "The only way to be German in Germany, Canadian in Canada, and Japanese in Japan is through alliances," says one international manager.[25]

> **Yamas Controls Inc., Bechtel Group Inc.**

foreign joint venture—
an alliance between a U.S. small business and a company in the target nation.

For example, Conveyant Systems, Inc., a small distributor of PC-based telecommunications equipment, has captured 3 percent of the gigantic market in China for private branch exchange (PBX) products. The tiny company beat out larger rivals by entering into a foreign joint venture with Tianchi Telecommunications Corporation, the municipal government in Tainjin, China, and a local economic development group. The venture's 90 Chinese employees turn out about $10 million worth of equipment a year, most of which is snapped up immediately by Chinese companies starved for communications equipment.[26]

The most important ingredient in the recipe for a successful joint venture is choosing the right partner. A productive joint venture is much like a marriage, requiring commitment and understanding. In addition to picking the right partner(s), a second key to creating a successful alliance is to establish common objectives. Defining exactly what each party in the joint venture hopes to accomplish at the outset will minimize the possibility of misunderstandings and disagreements later on. One important objective should always be to use the joint venture as a learning experience.

Unfortunately, most joint ventures fail. According to a recent study, the average success rate is just 43 percent; the average life of a joint venture is only 3.5 years. That makes it essential for the companies in an alliance to establish a contingency plan for getting out in case the joint venture doesn't work. Common problems leading to failure include improper selection of partners, incompatible management styles, failure to establish common goals, inability to be flexible, and failure to trust one another. "The usual problem," says one recent study of joint ventures, "is growing discontent between the partners as they discover how differently they view the world, how hard it is to keep their relationships in balance, and how easy it is... to forget what [they have] learned about making alliances work."[27]

Foreign Licensing

Rather than sell their products or services directly to customers overseas, some small companies enter foreign markets by licensing businesses in other nations to use their patents, trademarks, copyrights, technology, processes, or products. In return for licensing such assets, the small company collects royalties from the sales of its foreign licenses. Licensing is a relatively simple way for even the most inexperienced business owner to extend his reach into global markets. Eugene M. Lang, a foreign licensing expert, says, "Many small companies can't afford to invest capital in foreign facilities, and they don't have the personnel to send over there. Often, small company owners don't even have the time to acquaint themselves with foreign markets. The alternative is to license—to find someone who can capture the market for you who is already at home in that market."[28]

Joe Boxer Corporation, the highly successful maker of underwear, activewear, lingerie, sleepware, bedding, towels, tablecloths, and placemats, licenses its uniquely designed collections (picture boxer shorts adorned with pink pigs or glow-in-the-dark lips) to companies across the globe. Because of Joe Boxer's licensing arrangements, even the most conservative dressers in Canada, Australia, New Zealand, the United Kingdom, Mexico, Belgium, and the Netherlands can add a splash of excitement to their wardrobes—even if it is underneath![29]

Although many business owners consider licensing only their products to foreign companies, the licensing potential for intangibles such as processes, technology, copyrights, and trademarks often is greater. "You often make more money from licensing your know-how for production or product control than you could from actually selling your finished product in a highly competitive market," explains Lang.[30] Disney often licenses its famous cartoon characters, including Mickey and Minnie Mouse, Goofy, Roger Rabbit, and others, to manufacturers in countries across the world.

Catesby Jones, president of Peace Frogs, a small retailer, explains why his company used a foreign licensing arrangement for its copyrighted designs in Spain. "We export our Peace Frogs T-shirts directly to Japan, but in Spain per capita income is lower, competition from domestic producers is stronger, and tariffs are high, so we licensed a Barcelona-based company the rights to manufacture our product," he says.[31]

Foreign licensing enables a small business to enter foreign markets quickly, easily, and with virtually no capital investment. Risks to the company include the potential of losing control over its manufacturing and marketing and creating a competitor if the licensee gains too much knowledge and control. Securing proper patent, trademark, and copyright protection beforehand can minimize these risks, however.

International Franchising

Franchising has become a major export industry for the United States. The International Franchise Association estimates that more than 20 percent of the nation's 4,000-plus franchisers have outlets in foreign countries.[32] Over the past decade, a growing number of franchises have been attracted to international markets to boost sales and profits as the domestic market has become increasingly saturated with outlets and much tougher to wring growth from. International franchisers sell virtually every kind of product or service imaginable—from fast food to child day care—in international markets. In some cases, the products and services sold in international markets are identical to those sold in the United States. However, most franchisers have learned that they must modify their products and services to suit local tastes and customs.

For instance, Domino's Pizza operates 1,160 restaurants in 46 countries, where local managers have developed new pizza flavors such as mayonnaise and potato (Japan), pickled ginger (India), and reindeer sausage (Iceland) to cater to customers' palates.[33] *Although McDonald's builds its foreign menus around the same items and standardized assembly-line approach that have made it such a success in the United States, it makes changes to accommodate local tastes. In Germany, McDonald's restaurants sell beer, and in Great Britain they offer British Cadbury chocolate sticks.*[34]

Although franchise outlets span the globe, Canada is the primary market for U.S. franchisers, with Japan and Europe following. These markets are most attractive to franchisers because they are similar to the U.S. market—rising personal incomes, strong demand for consumer goods, growing service economies, and spreading urbanization. Europe holds special interest for many American franchises as trade barriers there continue to topple, opening up the largest—and one of the most affluent—markets in the world. Although large franchisers are already well established in many European nations, a new wave of smaller franchisers is seeking to establish a foothold there. Growth potential is the primary attraction.

Eastern European countries that recently have thrown off the chains of communism are turning to franchising to help them move toward a market economy. "Nothing better suits the startup of a free-market economy than franchising," says a franchising attorney.[35] Some countries of Eastern Europe, including Hungary and Poland, are attracting franchises. Southeast Asian countries such as Indonesia, Malaysia, and Vietnam hold promise for franchising in the future, as do India and Russia with their large populations and blooming economies. For franchisers entering these emerging nations, many of which are still in the volatile stages of formation, patience is the key. Profits may be years in coming, but franchisers see the long-term benefits of establishing a presence in these markets early on. Future growth is likely to occur in other countries as well. Because of its growing middle class and recent free-trade agreement with the United States, Mexico is becoming a popular target for franchises.

Countertrading and Bartering

As business becomes increasingly global, companies are discovering that attracting customers is just one part of the battle. Another problem global businesses face when selling to some countries is that their currencies are virtually worthless outside their borders, so getting paid in a valuable currency is a real challenge! In fact, 70 percent of all countries do not have either convertible currencies or sufficient cash flow to pay for imported goods.[36] Companies wanting to reach these markets must countertrade or barter. A **countertrade** is a transaction in which a company selling goods and services in a foreign country agrees to help promote investment and trade in that country. The goal of the transaction is to help offset the capital drain from the foreign country's purchases. Experts estimate that countertrading accounts for 20 to 30 percent of all global trade, and its use will continue to escalate.[37]

countertrade—*a transaction in which a company selling goods in a foreign country agrees to help promote investment and trade in that country.*

Big businesses are accustomed to countertrading to reach certain markets, but small- and medium-sized companies usually lack the skills and the resources needed to conduct countertrades on their own. However, they can tie into deals made by large corporations.

For instance, when export giant McDonnell Douglas sold $1.5 billion worth of jets to Spain recently, it agreed to a countertrade. As part of the deal, Cornnuts, Inc., a small maker of snack foods, agreed to open an office in Spain and to introduce hybrid corn technology there. Cornnuts had been eyeing Spain as an export market but didn't know how to get started. McDonnell Douglas arranged key meetings with Spanish officials and even helped the small company write its presentation and translate it into Spanish. The countertrade has proved to be a winner for Spain, McDonnell Douglas, and Cornnuts.[38]

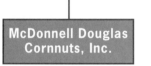

McDonnell Douglas
Cornnuts, Inc.

Countertrading does suffer from numerous drawbacks. Countertrade transactions can be complicated, cumbersome, and time consuming. They also increase the chances that a company will get stuck with useless merchandise that it cannot move. They can lead to unpleasant surprises concerning the quantity and quality of products required in the countertrade. Still, countertrading offers one major advantage: Sometimes it's the only way to make a sale!

Entrepreneurs must weigh the advantages against the disadvantages for their companies before committing to a countertrade deal. Because of its complexity and the risks involved, countertrading is not the best choice for a novice entrepreneur looking to break into the global marketplace.

Bartering, the exchange of goods and services for other goods and services, is another way of trading with countries lacking convertible currency. In a barter exchange, a company that manufactures electronics components might trade its products for the coffee that a business in a foreign country processes, which it then sells to a third company for cash. Barter transactions require finding a business with complementary needs, but they are much simpler than countertrade transactions.

bartering—*the exchange of goods and services for other goods and services.*

Exporting

3. Explain how to build a thriving export program.

For years, small businesses in the United States could afford the luxury of conducting business at home in the world's largest market, never having to venture outside its borders. With increased global competition putting pressure on domestic markets and trade agreements opening up foreign markets as never before, small companies increasingly are looking toward exporting as a global business strategy. Large companies still dominate exporting. Although small companies account for 97 percent of the companies involved in exporting, they generate only 30 percent of the dollar value of the nation's exports.[39] However, small companies, realizing the incredible profit potential it offers, are making exporting an ever-expanding part of their marketing plans (see Figure 14.2). Nearly half of U.S. companies with annual revenues under $100 million export goods, up from only 36 percent in 1990.[40] In short, there is plenty of opportunity for small businesses looking to grow, and much of that opportunity lies outside the borders of the United States.

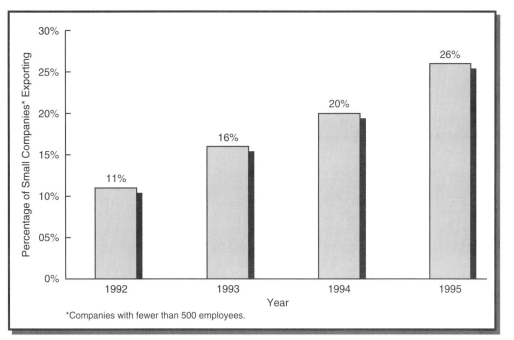

Figure 14.2
Small Business Go Global! (Percentage of Small Companies* Exporting)
Source: Adapted from Arthur Anderson and National Small Business United, Washington, D.C.

Katherine Allen, who with her mother runs Allen Filters, a maker of oil-cleanup products and services, is one business owner who discovered that exporting is not meant only for giants such as Bechtel and Ford. Allen, who spends up to a third of her time cultivating relationships abroad, says that half of her company's $4 million in sales comes from exports. One key to success, she says, is understanding local markets and customers. "If they have a good foundation, I think the world is open to most small businesses," says Allen.[41]

Allen Filters

Approximately 100,000 U.S. companies currently export; however, experts estimate that at least twice as many are capable of exporting but are not doing so.[42] The biggest barrier facing companies that have never exported is not knowing where or how to start. Paul Hsu, whose company sells ginseng across the globe, explains, "Exporting . . . starts with a global mind-set, which unfortunately, is not all that common among owners of small- and medium-sized businesses in the United States. . . . Most entrepreneurs in the United States envision markets only within domestic and sometimes even state borders, while Japanese and other foreign entrepreneurs look at export markets first."[43] Breaking the psychological barrier to exporting is the first and most difficult step in setting up a successful program. What other steps must an entrepreneur take to get an export program underway?

1. *Recognize that even the tiniest companies and least-experienced entrepreneurs have the potential to export.*

   Richie Harral, owner of Windchimes by Russco III, started making windchimes with his brother at age 10 in 1978 in the cellar of his home. Their company started really small—two kids selling windchimes to neighbors door-to-door. Their big break came seven years later when Wal-Mart ordered 30,000 chimes. In 1992, Windchimes experienced another stroke of luck when a British distributor, whose parents had bought a chime in a Missouri Wal-Mart, placed a $2,500 order. Today, the United Kingdom accounts for 6 percent of the company's $2 million in sales, and Harral predicts that by 2000, exports will rise to 30 percent of sales.[44]

   Windchimes by Russco III

   Exporting not only can boost a small company's sales, but it also can accelerate its growth rate. A recent study found that small companies that export grow markedly faster than those that do not. The study also concluded that the growth gap is widening as business becomes increasingly global in scope.[45]

2. *Analyze your product or service.* Is it special? New? Unique? High quality? Priced favorably due to lower costs or exchange rates? In which countries would there be sufficient demand for it?

Ron Schutte, president of Creative Bakers of Brooklyn, a company that makes presliced cheesecakes for restaurants, saw an opportunity to sell in Japan. The only modification Schutte made to his high-quality cheesecakes was reducing the portion size from 4.5 ounces to 2.25 ounces. "The Japanese aren't as gluttonous as we are," he explains.[46]

3. *Analyze your commitment.* Selling products or services in foreign markets usually takes more time, energy, and money than selling them in the domestic market. Are you willing to devote the time and the energy to develop export markets? Does your company have the necessary resources? Few business owners realize "the amount of management resources it will suck up at the top levels of the company," says one export consultant.[47] Export startups can take from six to eight months (or longer), but entering foreign markets isn't as tough as most entrepreneurs think, and the payoffs can be huge. Table 14.2 summarizes key issues managers must address in the export decision.

4. *Research markets and pick your target.* Before investing in a costly sales trip abroad, entrepreneurs should make a trip to the local library or the nearest branch of the Department of Commerce. Exporters can choose from a multitude of guides, manuals, books, newsletters, videos, and other resources to help them research potential markets. Armed with research, small businesses can avoid wasting valuable resources on markets with limited potential for their products or services and can concentrate on those with the greatest promise. The World Bank projects that by 2020, the world's largest economies will be China, the United States, Japan, India, Indonesia, Germany, and Korea. It predicts that other "hot" export markets will include France, Taiwan, Brazil, Italy, Russia, Great Britain, and Mexico.[48]

Managers at Ekkwill Tropical Fish Farm, a wholesale fish supplier, discovered through research that collecting fish is an even more popular hobby in Japan than in the United States,. Ekkwill now flies one-third of its production—some 4 million fish—to Japan as well as to Latin America, Asia, Canada, and the West Indies. Its best-selling fish in international markets are Florida gars, red swordtails, and new world cichlids, all common breeds in North America but considered exotic in other lands.[49]

Research shows export entrepreneurs whether or not they need to modify their existing products and services to suit the tastes and preferences of their foreign target customers.

For instance, when Rodney Robbins, CEO of Robbins Industries, a measuring cup and spoon maker, was negotiating with a distributor prior to entering the Swedish and British markets, he learned that he would have to modify his products slightly. The British use measuring utensils labeled in milliliters while the Swedes prefer deciliters.[50]

Such modifications can sometimes spell the difference between success and failure in the global market.

In other cases, products destined for export need little or no modification.

For example, for more than 40 years Richland Beverage Corporation has been exporting its Texas brand of nonalcoholic beer and soft drinks to Asia, Canada, and Mexico in exactly the same form used in the United States.

Experts estimate that one-half of exported products require little modification; one-third require moderate modification; only a few require major changes. Entrepreneurs should let market research be their guide when deciding how to modify their products for global markets.

Table 14.3 on page 474 offers questions to guide entrepreneurs conducting export research.

5. *Develop a distribution strategy.* Should you use an export intermediary or sell directly to foreign customers? Small companies just entering international markets may prefer to rely on export intermediaries to break new ground.

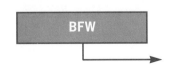

Lynn Cooper, president of BFW, a 25-year-old medical lighting supplier, uses wholesale distributors to sell her company's products in 25 countries. Exports account for 30

Table 14.2

Management Issues in the Export Decision

Source: Adapted from *A Basic Guide to Exporting* (Washington, DC: U.S. Department of Commerce, 1986), p. 3.

I. Experience

1. With what countries has your company already conducted business (or from what countries have you received inquiries about your product or service)?

2. What product lines do foreign customers ask about most often?

3. Prepare a list of sales inquiries for each buyer by product and by country.

4. Is the trend of inquiries or sales increasing or decreasing?

5. Who are your primary domestic and foreign competitors?

6. What lessons has your company learned from past export experiences?

II. Management and Personnel

1. Who will be responsible for the export organization's organization and staff? (Do you have an export "champion"?)

2. How much top management time

   a. should you allocate to exporting?

   b. can you afford to allocate to exporting?

3. What does management expect from its exporting efforts? What are your company's export goals and objectives?

4. What organizational structure will your company require to ensure that it can service export sales properly? (Note the political implications, if any.)

5. Who will implement the plan?

III. Production Capacity

1. To what extent is your company using its existing production capacity? Is there any excess? If so, how much?

2. Will filling export orders hurt your company's ability to make and service domestic sales?

3. What will additional production for export markets cost your company?

4. Are there seasonal or cyclical fluctuations in your company's workload? When? Why?

5. Is there a minimum quantity foreign customers must order for a sale to be profitable?

6. How much would your company need to modify its products, packaging, and design specifically for its export targets? Is your product quality adequate for foreign customers?

7. What pricing structure will your company use? Will prices be competitive?

8. How will your company collect payment on its export sales?

IV. Financial Capacity

1. How much capital will your company need to begin exporting? Where will it come from?

2. How will you allocate the initial costs of your company's export effort?

3. Does your company have other expansion plans that would compete with an exporting effort?

4. By what date do you expect your company's export program to pay for itself?

5. How important is establishing a global presence to your company's future success?

> percent of BFW's sales, and Cooper is happy with her method of distribution. "With distributors, the risk to us is minimal, but we still know just where the products are going," she says.[51]

6. *Find your customer.* Small businesses can rely on a host of export specialists to help them track down foreign customers. (Refer to Table 14.1 for a list of some of the resources available from the government.) The U.S. Department of Commerce and the International Trade Administration should be the first stops on an entrepreneur's agenda for going global. These agencies have the market research available for locating the best target markets for a particular company and specific customers in those markets.

★ Is there an overseas market for your company's products or services?

★ Are there specific target markets that look most promising?

★ Which new markets abroad are most likely to open up or expand?

★ How big are the markets your company is targeting and how fast are they growing?

★ What are the major economic, political, legal, social, technological, and other environmental factors affecting the target market?

★ What are the demographic and cultural factors affecting the target market, for example, disposable income, occupation, age, sex, opinions, activities, interests, tastes, and values?

★ Who are your company's present and potential customers abroad?

★ What are their needs and desires? What factors influence their buying decisions—price, credit terms, delivery terms, quality, brand name, and so on?

★ How would they use your company's product or service? What modifications, if any, would be necessary to sell to your target customers?

★ Who are your primary competitors in the foreign market?

★ How do competitors distribute, sell, and promote their products? What are their prices?

★ What are the best channels of distribution for your product?

★ What is the best way for your company to gain exposure in this market?

★ Are there any barriers such as tariffs, quotas, duties, or regulations to selling your products in this market? Are there any incentives?

★ Are there any potential licensing or joint venture partners already in this market?

Industry Sector Analysis (ISA), International Market Insights (IMIs), and Customized Market Analysis (CMA) are just some of the reports and services global entrepreneurs find most useful.

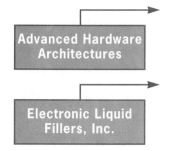

Advanced Hardware Architectures

When he identified France as an export target for his company's semiconductor devices, John Overby, owner of Advanced Hardware Architectures, used Commerce Department research and trade shows to locate both distributors and customers.[52]

Other entrepreneurs search out customers on their own.

Electronic Liquid Fillers, Inc.

For instance, Jeff Ake, co-owner of Electronic Liquid Fillers, Inc., a small packaging equipment company, spent seven weeks calling on potential customers in the Pacific Rim. He identified his target customers with the help of foreign-based English-language industry trade magazines. During his travels, Ake used the local English-language equivalent of the Yellow Pages to find others.[53]

7. *Find financing.* One of the biggest barriers to small business exports is lack of financing. Access to adequate financing is a crucial ingredient in a successful export program since the cost of generating foreign sales often is higher and collection cycles are longer. The trouble is that bankers and other sources of capital don't always understand the intricacies of international sales and view financing them as excessively risky. Also, among major industrialized nations, the U.S. government spends the least per capita to promote exports.

Several federal, state, and private programs are operating to fill this export financing void, however. Programs such as the SBA's Export Working Capital Program (90 percent loan guarantees up to $750,000), the Export-Import Bank, the Overseas Private Investment Corporation, and a variety of state-sponsored programs offer export-minded entrepreneurs both direct loans and loan guarantees. (A list of all state foreign trade assistance offices is available on the Commerce Department's National Export Directory.) The Bankers Association for Foreign Trade (telephone number 1-800 49-AXCAP) is an association of 450 banks that matches exporters needing foreign trade financing with interested banks.

Western Sunflower Company

Western Sunflower Company, a small processor of sunflower seeds, used a $575,000 Export Working Capital loan guarantee to begin selling its seeds in Spain, Taiwan, the Virgin Islands, and Mexico. Almost 90 percent of the company's sales comes from exports![53]

8. *Ship your goods.* Export novices usually rely on freight forwarders and custom-house agents—experienced specialists in overseas shipping—for help in navigating the bureaucratic morass of packaging requirements and paperwork demanded by customs. These specialists are to exporters what travel agents are to passengers and normally charge relatively small fees for a valuable service.

9. *Collect your money.* Collecting foreign accounts can be more complex than collecting domestic ones, but by picking their customers carefully and checking their credit references closely, entrepreneurs can minimize bad-debt losses. Financing foreign sales often involves special credit arrangements such as letters of credit and bank (or documentary) drafts. A **letter of credit** is an agreement between an exporter's bank and the foreign buyer's bank that guarantees payment to the exporter for a specific shipment of goods. In essence, a letter of credit reduces the financial risk for the exporter by substituting a bank's credit-worthiness for that of the purchaser (see Figure 14.3). A **bank draft** is a document the seller draws on the buyer, requiring the buyer to pay the face amount (the purchase price of the goods) either on sight (a sight draft) or on a specified date (a time draft) once the goods are shipped. Rather than use letters of credit or drafts, some exporters simply require cash in advance or cash on delivery (C.O.D.). Insisting on cash payments up front, however, may cause some foreign buyers to reject a deal. The parties to an international deal should always come to an agreement in advance on an acceptable method of payment.

Planned carefully and taken one step at a time, exporting can be a highly profitable route for small businesses. Table 14.4 on pages 476–477 describes the 12 most common mistakes exporters make.

letter of credit—*an agreement between an exporter's bank and the foreign buyer's bank that guarantees payment to the exporter for a specific shipment of goods.*

bank draft—*a document the seller draws on the buyer, requiring the buyer to pay the face amount (the purchase price of the goods) either on sight (a sight draft) or on a specified date (a time draft).*

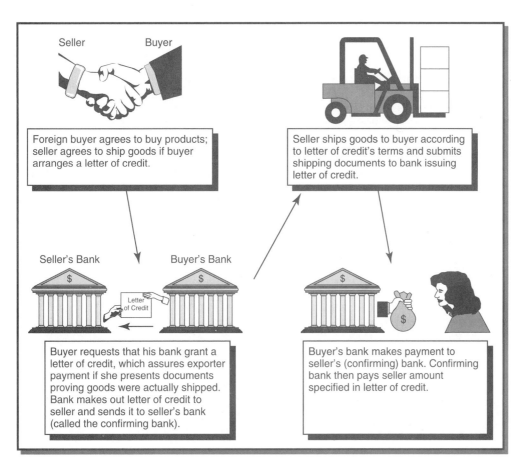

Figure 14.3
How a Letter of Credit Works

Seller **Buyer**

Foreign buyer agrees to buy products; seller agrees to ship goods if buyer arranges a letter of credit.

Seller ships goods to buyer according to letter of credit's terms and submits shipping documents to bank issuing letter of credit.

Seller's Bank **Buyer's Bank**

Buyer requests that his bank grant a letter of credit, which assures exporter payment if she presents documents proving goods were actually shipped. Bank makes out letter of credit to seller and sends it to seller's bank (called the confirming bank).

Buyer's bank makes payment to seller's (confirming) bank. Confirming bank then pays seller amount specified in letter of credit.

Table 14.4

The 12 Most Common Mistakes Exporters Make

Sources: Adapted from Denis Csizmadia, "Exporters Can Avoid 12 Common Mistakes," *Upstate Business*, August 11, 1996, p. 3; Martha Mangelsdorf, "Unfair Trade," *Inc.*, April 1991, pp. 28-36; *A Basic Guide to Exporting* (Washington, DC: U.S. Department of Commerce, 1986), pp. 85-86.

Exporting can be intimidating, especially for an inexperienced small business owner, and overcoming export barriers puts an extra burden on small companies that usually have thin resources. When a small company runs into export trouble, it is usually because it fell victim to one or more of the 12 most common mistakes exporters make:

1. *Not obtaining qualified export counseling and developing a master international marketing plan before starting an export business.* To become a successful exporter, a business must first define its global goals and objectives and identify the problems it is likely to encounter in its global expansion. Then it must develop a workable plan to achieve these objectives and to overcome the problems. Unless a small firm is fortunate enough to have a staff with considerable export expertise, it may not be able to take this crucial first step without qualified outside assistance.

2. *Not obtaining enough commitment from top management to overcome the initial difficulties and financial requirements of exporting.* Although the early delays, costs, and problems may seem difficult to justify when compared to established domestic markets, the long-term benefits of establishing a successful export program will be worth it. Wise exporters take a long-term view and shepherd their international marketing efforts through these early difficulties (which *will* occur). That takes total support from top managers in the company.

3. *Not taking sufficient care in selecting overseas distributors.* The choice of every foreign distributor is crucial. The sheer distance and resulting complications with communication and transportation require a company's distributors to act with greater independence than their domestic counterparts do. Also, because a new exporter's products, trademarks, and reputation are usually unknown in foreign markets, customers may buy on the strength of distributors' reputations. A company must evaluate carefully every distributor handling its products or services, its reputation, and its facilities.

4. *Chasing orders from around the world instead of establishing a basis for profitable international operations and orderly growth.* If exporters expect distributors to sell their products successfully, they must train them, motivate them, and evaluate their performances. Often, this requires putting a marketing executive in a distributor's geographic territory. New exporters should concentrate on one or two markets initially before expanding into multiple markets to avoid stretching their managerial and financial resources too thin.

5. *Neglecting export business when the U.S. market booms.* Many small companies turn to export markets when business falls off in the United States. Then when their domestic business picks up again, some neglect their export customers or relegate them to a secondary place. Such neglect can seriously harm an exporter's reputation in the global market and can jeopardize its long-term global business prospects. Even if its domestic business remains strong, the exporter usually realizes that it has closed off a valuable source of additional sales and profits.

6. *Not treating international distributors on an equal basis with their domestic counterparts.* Often companies have institutional advertising campaigns, special discount offers, sales incentive programs, special credit terms, warranty offers, and the like in the U.S. domestic market but fail to offer similar assistance to their international distributors. This is a mistake that can destroy the vitality of overseas marketing efforts.

7. *Assuming that a given marketing technique and product will be successful in all countries.* What works in one market may not work in another, so an exporter must treat each target market separately. Successful exporters are willing to modify their products, packaging, and promotion techniques to suit local tastes, preferences, and habits.

8. *Not being willing to modify products to meet other countries' regulations or cultural preferences.* Exporters cannot ignore the regulations, customs, tastes, preferences, and import restrictions affecting their products in foreign markets. Although most products exporters sell need only minor modifications to be suitable for their target customers, the key to their success lies in the exporter's willingness to make those modifications. Successful exporters are not so arrogant as to think that the domestic way is the best and only way of using or selling a product.

9. *Not printing service, sales, and warranty messages in the local language.* Although a foreign distributor's top managers may speak English, it is unlikely that all sales and service people have this ability. Without a clear understanding of the sales or service message in their own language, these people will be unable to perform their jobs effectively. Smart exporters use locals to translate these messages so that they retain their accuracy.

10. *Not using an export management company or other trade intermediary.* If a company decides that it cannot afford its own export department (or has tried to organize one unsuccessfully), it should consider using an export management company or other appropriate trade intermediary.

11. *Not considering licensing or joint venture arrangements.* Import restriction in some countries, insufficient personnel or financial resources, or limited product lines cause many companies to dismiss international marketing as unfeasible. Yet, many products that are successful in the United States can be successful in the global marketplace as well. Perhaps the best way to break into the global market may be a licensing arrangement or a joint venture with a foreign partner.

12. *Not providing readily available sales and service support for a product.* A product without proper sales and service support is doomed to failure. When planning their ventures into foreign markets, companies must address not only the sales issue but also the service aspects.

Establishing International Locations

Once established in international markets, some small businesses set up permanent locations there. Establishing an office or a factory in a foreign land can require a substantial investment reaching beyond the budgets of many small companies. Plus, setting up an international office can be an incredibly frustrating experience in some countries. Business infrastructures are in disrepair or are nonexistent. Getting a telephone line installed can take months in some places and finding reliable equipment to move goods to customers is nearly impossible. Securing necessary licenses and permits from bureaucrats often takes more than filing the necessary paperwork; in some nations, bureaucrats expect payments to "grease the wheels of justice." Finding the right person to manage an international office is crucial to success; it also is a major challenge, especially for small businesses. Small companies usually have lean management staffs and cannot afford to send key people abroad without running the risk of losing their focus.

Few small businesses begin their global ventures by establishing international locations, preferring, instead, to build a customer base through some of the other strategies covered in this section.

For example, in 1984, managers at Santec Inc., a U.S.-based manufacturer of electronic connectors, saw the tremendous potential the European market offered. Rather than plunge into the market by establishing a location on the continent, however, they decided to begin by exporting. "We have worked our way up to full-scale manufacturing," says Santec's president John Shine. The sales channels the company established in Europe in 1984 have evolved into a full-fledged manufacturing facility at Cumbernauld, Scotland. The move was a natural extension of Santec's globalization strategy. To ensure its long-term success, "it's just a necessity" to have operations for sales, service, and manufacturing in North America, Europe, and Asia, which is Santec's next stop on its global agenda, according to Shine.[55]

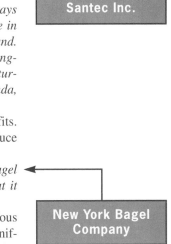

Santec Inc.

New York Bagel
Company

Small companies that establish international locations can reap significant benefits. Startup costs often are lower in many foreign countries, and lower labor costs can produce significant savings as well.

For example, Robert Brooker and Adam Haven-Weiss launched their New York Bagel Company in Budapest, Hungary with just $40,000 in seed money, a fraction of what it would have cost in the United States.[56]

Going global by employing one or more of these seven strategies can put tremendous strain on a small company, but the benefits of cracking international markets can be significant. Not only does going global offer attractive sales and profit possibilities, but it also strengthens the company's competitive skills and enhances its overall reputation. Pleasing tough foreign customers also keeps companies on their competitive toes.

Barriers to International Trade

Governments have always used a variety of barriers to block free trade among nations, in an attempt to protect businesses within their own borders. The benefit of protecting their own companies, however, comes at the expense of foreign businesses, which face limited access to global markets. Numerous trade barriers—both domestic and international—restrict the freedom of businesses in global trading. Even with these barriers, international trade has grown 24-fold to over *$6 trillion* over the past 30 years.[57]

Domestic Barriers

Sometimes the biggest barriers potential exporters face are right here at home. Three major domestic roadblocks are common: attitude, information, and financing. Perhaps the biggest barrier to small businesses exporting is the attitude: "I'm too *small* to export. That's just for big corporations." The first lesson of exporting is "Take nothing for granted about who can export and what you can and cannot export." The first step to building an export program is recognizing that the opportunity to export exists.

Another reason entrepreneurs neglect international markets is a lack of information about how to get started. The key to success in international markets is choosing the correct target market and designing the appropriate strategy to reach it. That requires access to information and research. Although a variety of government and private organizations make volumes of exporting and international marketing information available, many small business owners never use it. A successful global marketing strategy also recognizes that not all markets are the same. Companies must be flexible, willing to make necessary adjustments to their products and services, promotional campaigns, packaging, and sales techniques.

Another significant obstacle is the lack of export financing available. A recent survey of exporters found that 53 percent said they had lost export business because they couldn't get financing.[58] "There is no such thing as export financing for small companies in this country," says one trade consultant, exaggerating only slightly.[59]

For example, N & N Contact Lens International, Inc. recently got an order from a Brazilian customer for $247,000 worth of contact lenses. The buyer had good credit with its Brazilian bank, and a credit check produced a favorable report. But N & N's bank refused to finance the deal. "We just don't finance foreign receivables," explained one bank official. N & N's president laments, "[Yet] I can get an order from Atlanta from a guy who went bankrupt and the bank will finance it, without question."[60]

N & N Contact Lens International, Inc.

International Barriers

Domestic barriers aren't the only ones export-minded entrepreneurs must overcome. Trading nations also erect obstacles to free trade. Two types of international barriers are common: tariff and nontariff.

tariff—*a tax, or duty, that a government imposes on goods and services imported into that country.*

TARIFF BARRIERS. A **tariff** is a tax, or duty, that a government imposes on goods and services imported into that country. Imposing tariffs raises the price of the imported goods—making them less attractive to consumers—and protects the makers of comparable domestic products and services. Established in the United States in 1790 by Alexander Hamilton, the tariff system generated the majority of federal revenues for about 100 years. Today, the U.S. tariff code lists duties on 8,862 items—from brooms and olives to flashlights and teacups.[61]

NONTARIFF BARRIERS. Many nations have lowered the tariffs they impose on products and services brought into their borders, but they rely on other nontariff structures as protectionist trade barriers.

Quotas. Rather than impose a direct tariff on certain imported products, nations often use quotas to protect their industries. A **quota** is a limit on the amount of a product imported into a country. Worried about the Japanese economic juggernaut, the European Community has limited Japanese automakers' share of the European market to just 16 percent. In the U.S. auto market, the Japanese have agreed to "voluntary quotas," limiting the number of autos shipped here.

Japan, often criticized for its protectionist attitude toward imports, traditionally used tariffs and quotas to keep foreign competitors out. However, Japan's tariffs are now among the world's lowest—averaging just 2 percent—but quotas still exist on many products.

The Dexter Shoe Company faces a formidable trade barrier in its attempt to sell its leather shoes in Japanese markets. Because leather working is a traditional craft of a Japanese social underclass called the burakumin, *the shoe industry is protected by a strong quota-tariff system. Every year, Dexter must fight for even a modest expansion in its quota allotment, which now stands at a measly 50,000 pairs.*[62]

Embargoes. An **embargo** is a total ban on imports of certain products. The motivation for embargoes is not always economic. For instance, because of South Africa's history of apartheid policies, many nations have embargoed imports of Krugerrands (gold coins). Traditionally, Taiwan, South Korea, and Israel have banned imports of Japanese autos.

Dumping. In an effort to grab market share quickly, some companies have been guilty of **dumping** products—selling large quantities of them in foreign countries below cost. The United States has been a dumping target for steel, televisions, shoes, and computer chips in the past. Under the U.S. Antidumping Act, a company must prove that the foreign company's prices are lower here than in the home country and that U.S. companies are directly harmed.

quota—a limit on the amount of a product imported into a country.

Dexter Shoe Company

embargo—a total ban on imports of certain products.

dumping—the practice of selling large quantities of products in foreign countries below cost in an attempt to gain market share.

Political Barriers

Entrepreneurs who go global quickly discover a labyrinth of political tangles. Although many American business owners complain of excessive government regulation in the United States, they are often astounded by the complex web of governmental and legal regulations and barriers they encounter in foreign countries.

Companies doing business in politically risky lands face the very real dangers of government takeovers of private property; attempts at coups to overthrow ruling parties; kidnappings, bombings, and other violent acts against businesses and their employees; and other threatening events. Their investments of millions of dollars may evaporate overnight in the wake of a government coup or the passage of a law nationalizing an industry (i.e., giving control of an entire industry to the government).

Some nations welcome foreign business investment while others do everything they can to discourage competition from foreign companies.

For example, the Japanese recently used a web of complex regulations and bizarre rules to prevent International Game Technology, an American manufacturer of slot machines, from competing in their home market. IGT battled one ridiculous rule (most of them unwritten) after another for four years to no avail. Finally, with the help of a former Japanese official (whose job had been to keep competitors such as IGT out of the Japanese market), IGT was able to file its legal documents with regulators. After 19 modifications (none affecting its machines' performance and one because the paper was not the right size), IGT finally won the right to sell its slot machines in Japan.[63]

International Game Technology

On to Japan . . .

"It's hard to believe how far we've come in just 14 months," said Tad Meyers, president of Specialty Building Supplies.

"That's true," chimed in Dee Rada, the company's sales manager. "When we started this whole international business idea, we had no notion of how complicated and time consuming it would be. We were total rookies! Which one of us would have thought we'd be trying to sell our products in Japan?"

"True. But now it looks like the big payoff is just around the corner," said Hal Milam, the company's sales manager.

As the three celebrated their success to date in taking their company into the exciting world of international business, each was proud of what they had accomplished and how much they had learned in just a short time. Yet, their excitement was tinged with anxiety because Meyers and Rada were about to travel abroad to meet with several potential distributors for the company's building supplies. In one week, they would be in Japan, negotiating deals with businesspeople that they had never met before and whose native language neither spoke.

"I do know how to say 'Thank you' in Japanese," said Rada. "It's pronounced *Du-omo ah-ree-gha-toe.*"

"You should probably find out how to say, 'Where's the bathroom' and 'We're lost. Will you take us home?' in Japanese too," joked Milam.

"You know, we probably should find out as much as possible about how the Japanese do business," said Meyers. "I understand their way is very different from what we're used to."

"Such as . . .?" said Milam.

"You know . . . little things," said Rada. "I do know that they make a big deal out of exchanging business cards. They call it *meishi*. In fact, I've had cards printed for Tad and me with English on one side and Japanese on the other. When you take their cards, don't just stick them in your pocket or scribble notes on the backs of them. That's an insult."

"No kidding?" said Meyers. "I didn't know that . . .'"

"I thought we'd take some gifts along to give to our guests," said Rada. "I've had them wrapped in pure white paper with these big red ribbons."

"What are you going to give them?" asked Milam.

"I had some nice golf shirts printed up with our logo, and then I had them add the U.S. and Japanese flags crossing one another."

"Cool! They ought to love that."

"We're taking along some brochures detailing our product line, emphasizing its unique nature and superb quality," said Rada. "I had them printed in Japanese just for this trip. Full color, lots of pictures. They cost a few bucks, but I thought it would be a wise investment."

"We will be on a tight schedule while we're there," said Meyers. "We'll have to get right down to business, close the deal, and then get on to the next appointment. There won't be a lot of time for sightseeing or small talk. I hope we can have these deals done by the time we get back on the plane for home."

"I just hope they don't try to impress us with authentic Japanese meals while we're there," said Meyers. "I'm pretty much a 'meat-and-potatoes' kind of guy. I *don't* do sushi. But I hear that McDonald's has restaurants in Japan. I just hope there's one nearby!"

"Where's your sense of adventure?" teased Rada. "Remember: We can't afford to offend our guests. We need to be sensitive to their culture, habits, and tastes. I just hope we don't do something unintentional that upsets somebody . . . ."

1. Evaluate the preparations that Meyers and Rada have made for their upcoming trip to Japan.

2. Using the library and the World Wide Web as resources, read about Japanese culture and Japanese business practices.* Based on what you learn, would you advise them to change any of their plans? Explain.

*The Do's and Taboos of International Trade, Gestures: The Do's and Taboos of Body Language Around the World, and Do's and Taboos Around the World: A Guide to International Behavior, all by Roger Axtell, are excellent resources.

Cultural Barriers

culture—*the beliefs, values, views, and mores that the inhabitants of a country share.*

The **culture** of a nation includes the beliefs, values, views, and mores that its inhabitants share. Differences in cultures among nations create another barrier to international trade. The diversity of languages, business philosophies, practices, and traditions make international trade more complex than selling to the business down the street. "It's essential for anyone wanting to do business in an international market to have a clear understanding and appreciation of the culture in which they plan to do business," says one international consultant.[64] Consider the following examples:

☆ An American business woman in London was invited to a party hosted by an advertising agency. Unsure of her ability to navigate the streets and subways of London alone, she approached a British colleague who was driving to the party and asked him, "Could I get a ride with you?" After he turned bright red from embarrassment, he regained his composure and politely said, "Lucky for you I know what you meant." Unknowingly, the young woman had requested a sexual encounter with her colleague, not a lift to the party![65]

☆ An American was in the final stages of contract negotiations with an Indonesian company. Given the size of the contract and his distance from home, the American business executive was nervous. Sitting across from his Indonesian counterpart, the American propped his feet up. Obviously angered, the Indonesian business owner stormed out of the room, refusing to sign the contract and leaving the American executive totally bewildered. Only later did he discover that exposing the soles of one's shoes to an Indonesian is an insult. Profuse apologies and some delicate negotiations salvaged the deal.[66]

☆ In another incident, an American went to Malaysia to close a sizable contract. In an elaborate ceremony, he was introduced to a man he thought was named "Roger." Throughout the negotiations, he called the man "Rog," not realizing that his potential client was a "rajah"—a title of nobility, not a name.[67]

☆ On his first trip to the Middle East, an American executive was touring the city with his Arab business contact. As they strolled along the dusty streets, the host reached over, took the executive's hand in his, and the two continued to walk, the host's hand holding the executive's. Totally stunned, the American didn't even have the presence of mind to jerk his hand away—much to his good fortune. He learned later that in his host's country, taking his hand was a sign of great respect and friendship. Jerking his hand away from his host would have been considered a major insult.[68]

☆ One U.S. supermarket trying to impress Japanese visitors served sushi and tea to its guests. Unfortunately, the fish was cooked not raw, and the tea was Chinese! The company did *not* create the impression it was hoping for.[69]

Entrepreneurs who fail to learn the differences in the habits and customs of the cultures in which they hope to do business are at a distinct disadvantage. "In the business arena . . . a lack of understanding of cultures and business practices can be as great an impediment to structuring and implementing a business transaction as an error in the basic assumptions of the deal," says one international expert.[70]

When American businesspeople enter international markets for the first time, they often are amazed at the differences in foreign cultures' habits and customs. Understanding and heeding these often subtle cultural differences is one of the most important keys to international business success. Conducting a business meeting with a foreign executive in the same manner as one with an American businessperson could doom the deal from the outset. "People can be on their best American behavior and go overseas and offend the locals," says one expert in international etiquette.[71] Business customs and behaviors that are acceptable— even expected—in this country may be taboo in others. For instance, American businesspeople usually conduct business in an informal fashion, using slang and calling one another by their first names (or nicknames). Executives in France, England, and Japan, however, would consider such behavior to be rude and highly improper. In many countries such as Spain, China, and Japan, entrepreneurs will need an ample dose of the "three Ps": patience, patience, patience. Unlike the United States, nothing in these cultures—especially business—happens fast!

International Trade Agreements

In an attempt to boost world trade, nations have created a variety of trade agreements over the years. While hundreds of agreements are paving the way for freer trade across the world, two stand out with particular significance: The General Agreement on Tariffs and Trade (GATT) and the North American Free Trade Agreement (NAFTA).

5. Describe the trade agreements that will have the greatest influence on foreign trade into the twenty-first century— GATT and NAFTA.

GATT

Created in 1947, the General Agreement on Tariffs and Trade (GATT) became the first global tariff agreement. It was designed to reduce tariffs among member nations and to facilitate trade across the globe. Originally signed by the United States and 22 other nations, GATT has grown to include 124 member countries today. Together, they account for nearly 90 percent of world trade. The latest round of GATT negotiations, called the Uruguay Round, was completed in December 1993 and took effect on July 1, 1995. Prior to this round, the trade agreement had been successful in reducing trade barriers around the world by 90 percent since its inception. Average tariffs in industrial countries had fallen to just 4.7 percent, down from an average of 40 percent in 1947.

The Uruguay Round continues this trend. Negotiators reduced the remaining industrial tariffs by 40 percent, established new rules governing dumping goods at unfairly low prices, strengthened the global protection of patents, and cut the level of government subsidies on agricultural products. In addition, negotiators agreed to form a World Trade Organization (WTO) with more power to settle trade disputes among member nations than GATT had. Experts estimate that GATT will expand the U.S. economy by approximately $1 trillion over the next decade and create as many as 2 million jobs.[72]

NAFTA

free trade area—*an association of countries that have agreed to knock down trade barriers—both tariff and nontariff— among partner nations.*

The North American Free Trade Agreement (NAFTA) created a free trade area among Canada, Mexico, and the United States. A **free trade area** is an association of countries that has agreed to knock down trade barriers—both tariff and nontariff—among partner nations. Under the provisions of NAFTA, these barriers were eliminated for trade among the three countries, but each remained free to set its own tariffs on imports from non-member nations.

NAFTA forged a unified U.S.-Canada-Mexico market of 370 million people with a total annual output of $6.5 trillion of goods and services. This important trade agreement binds together the three nations on the North American continent into a single trading unit stretching from the Yukon to the Yucatan. Because Canada and the United States already have a free trade agreement in effect, the businesses that will benefit most from NAFTA are those already doing business—or those wanting to do business—with Mexico. Before NAFTA took effect on January 1, 1994, the average tariff on U.S. goods entering Mexico was 10 percent. Under NAFTA, these tariffs will be reduced to zero on most goods over the next 10 to 15 years.[73]

NAFTA's provisions will encourage trade among the three nations, make that trade more profitable and less cumbersome, and open up new opportunities for a wide assortment of companies.

Treatment Products Limited

For instance, Jeff Victor, manager of Treatment Products Limited, a manufacturer of car cleaners and waxes, says that the trade agreement is the primary force behind his company's boom in exports to Mexico. Treatment Products had tried to enter the Mexican market years earlier but met with limited success, primarily because of stiff Mexican tariffs that ran as high as 20 percent. Within months of NAFTA's passage, the tariffs began dropping, and the company's export sales to Mexico began climbing, ultimately totaling 20 percent of its sales. Today, Treatment Products has landed contracts with every major retail chain in Mexico.[74]

Among NAFTA's provisions are:

☆ *Tariff reductions.* Immediate reductions and then gradual phasing out of most tariffs on goods traded among the three countries.

☆ *Nontariff barriers eliminated.* Elimination of most nontariff barriers to free trade by 2008.

☆ *Simplified border processing.* Mexico, in particular, opens its borders and interior to U.S. truckers and simplifies border processing.

☆ *Tougher health and safety standards.* Industrial standards involving worker health and safety become more stringent and more uniform.

☆ *Increased protection of patents, copyrights, and trademarks.* Under NAFTA, companies have greater protection of their patents, trademarks, and copyrights across national borders.

Conclusion

For a rapidly growing number of small businesses, conducting business on a global basis will be the key to future success. To remain competitive, businesses must assume a global posture. Global effectiveness requires managers to be able to leverage workers' skills, company resources, and customer know-how across borders and throughout cultures across the world. Managers also must concentrate on maintaining competitive costs structures and a focus on the core of every business—the *customer*! Robert G. Shaw, CEO of International Jensen Inc., a global maker of home and automobile stereo speakers, explains the importance of retaining that customer focus as his company pursues its global strategy: "We want [our customers] to have the attitude of [our] being across the street. If we're going to have a global company, we have to behave in that mode—whether [the customer is] across the street—or seven miles, seven minutes, or 7,000 miles away."[75]

Few businesses can afford the luxury of basing the definition of their target market on the boundaries of their home nation's borders. The manager of one global business, who discourages the use of the word *domestic* among his employees, says, "Where's 'domestic' when the world is your market?"[76] Although there are no sure-fire rules for going global, small businesses wanting to become successful international competitors should observe these guidelines:[77]

☆ Make yourself at home in all three of the world's key markets—North America, Europe, and Asia. This triad of regions is forging a new world order in trade that will dominate global markets for years to come.

☆ Develop new products for the world market.

☆ Familiarize yourself with foreign customs and languages; constantly scan, clip, and build a file on other cultures—their lifestyles, values, customs, and business practices.

☆ "Glocalize"—make global decisions about products, markets, and management, but allow local employees to make tactical decisions about packaging, advertising, and service.

☆ Train employees to think globally, send them on international trips, and equip them with state-of-the-art communications technology.

☆ Hire local managers to staff foreign offices and branches.

☆ Do whatever seems best wherever it seems best, even if people at home lose jobs or responsibilities.

☆ Consider using partners and joint ventures to break into foreign markets you cannot penetrate on your own.

By its very nature, going global can be a frightening experience for an entrepreneur considering the jump into international markets. Most of those who have already made the jump, however, have found that the benefits outweigh the risks and that their companies are much stronger because of it.

1. Explain why "going global" has become an integral part of many small companies' strategies.

- Businesses large and small can no longer consider themselves to be domestic companies in this hotly competitive, global environment. But gaining a foothold in foreign markets is no easy task for a small company.
- Companies that move into international business can reap many benefits, including offsetting sales declines in the domestic market; increasing sales and profits; extending their products' life cycles; lowering manufacturing costs; improving competitive position; raising quality levels; and becoming more customer oriented.

2. Describe the seven principal strategies small businesses have for going global: (relying on trade intermediaries, joint ventures, foreign licensing, international franchising, countertrading and bartering, exporting, and establishing international locations).

- Businesses looking to "go global" do not have to chart their courses alone. Trade intermediaries such as export management companies, export trading companies, manufacturer's export agents, export merchants, and resident buying offices can serve as a small company's "export department."
- In a domestic joint venture, two or more U.S. small companies form an alliance for the purpose of exporting their goods and services abroad. In a foreign joint venture, a domestic small business forms an alliance with a company in the target nation.
- Some small businesses enter foreign markets by licensing businesses in other nations to use their patents, trademarks, copyrights, technology, processes, or products.
- Franchising has become a major export industry for the United States. The International Franchise Association estimates that more than 20 percent of the nation's 4,000 franchisers have outlets in foreign countries.
- Some countries lack a hard currency that is convertible into other currencies, so companies doing business there must rely on countertrading or bartering. A countertrade is a transaction in which a business selling its goods in a foreign country agrees to promote investment and trade in that country. Bartering involves trading goods and services for other goods and services.

- Although small companies account for 97 percent of the companies involved in exporting, they generate only 30 percent of the dollar value of the nation's exports. However, small companies, realizing the incredible profit potential it offers, are making exporting an ever-expanding part of their marketing plans. Nearly half of U.S. companies with annual revenues under $100 million export goods.
- Once established in international markets, some small businesses set up permanent locations there. Although they can be very expensive to establish and maintain, international locations give businesses the opportunity to stay in close contact with their international customers.

3. Explain how to build a thriving export program.

- Building a successful export program takes patience and research. Steps include realizing that even the tiniest firms have the potential to export, analyzing your product or service, analyzing your commitment to exporting, researching markets and picking your target, developing a distribution strategy, finding your customer, finding financing, shipping your goods, and collecting your money.

4. Discuss the major barriers to international trade and their impact on the global economy.

- Three domestic barriers to international trade are common: the attitude that "we're too small to export;" lack of information on how to get started in global trade; and a lack of available financing.
- International barriers include tariffs, quotas, embargoes, dumping, political barriers, and cultural barriers.

5. Describe the trade agreements that will have the greatest influence on foreign trade into the twenty-first century— GATT and NAFTA.

- Created in 1947, the General Agreement on Tariffs and Trade (GATT), the first global tariff agreement, was designed to reduce tariffs among member nations and to facilitate trade across the globe.
- The North American Free Trade Agreement (NAFTA) created a free trade area among Canada, Mexico, and the United States. The agreement created an association that knocked down trade barriers—both tariff and nontariff—among these partner nations.

1. What is "global thinking"? Why must small businesses think globally?

2. What forces are driving small businesses into international markets?

3. What advantages does going global offer a small business owner? What are the risks?

4. Outline the seven strategies that small businesses can use to go global.

5. Describe the various types of trade intermediaries small business owners can use. What functions do they perform?

6. What is a domestic joint venture? A foreign joint venture? What advantages does taking on an international partner through a joint venture offer? What are the disadvantages?

7. What mistakes are first-time exporters most likely to make? Outline the steps a small company should follow to establish a successful export program.

8. What are the benefits of establishing international locations? ? What are the disadvantages?

9. Describe the barriers businesses face when trying to conduct business internationally. How can a small business owner overcome these obstacles?

10. What is a tariff? A quota? What impact do they have on international trade?

11. What impact have the GATT and NAFTA trade agreements had on small companies wanting to go global? What provisions are included in these trade agreements?

12. What advice would you offer an entrepreneur interested in launching a global business effort?

Beyond the Classroom....

1. Go to lunch with a student from a foreign country. What products and services are most needed there? How does the business system there differ from ours? How much government regulation affects business? What cultural differences exist? What trade barriers has the government erected?

2. A. Review several current business publications and prepare a brief report on which nations seem to be the most promising for U.S. entrepreneurs. What steps should a small business owner take to break into those markets?

   B. Which nations are the least promising? Why?

3. Select a nation which interests you and prepare a report on its business customs and practices. How are they different from those in the United States.? How are they similar? What advice would you offer an entrepreneur interested in conducting business there?

SURFING THE NET

1. Visit the Web site for the International Trade Administration at:

http://www.ita.doc.gov/

Explore the features of this Web site and prepare a one-page report on what you find. What are the top ten exporting states in the United States? What is the current status of the U.S. balance of payments? Which countries are the United States' top five trading partners? For those top five trading partners, determine the trend in their currencies' exchange rates against the dollar. What impact would these trends have on exports of U.S. goods and services to these countries? What is the impact of these trends on imports from these countries into the United States?

2. Using one of the search engines on the World Wide Web such as Lycos, Magellan, Infoseek, Yahoo!, or others, conduct a search on "GATT" and "NAFTA." Prepare a one-page report on what you learn about each trade agreement.

3. Select a foreign country that interests you (perhaps one to which you have traveled). Using one of the search engines on

the World Wide Web such as Lycos, Magellan, Infoseek, Yahoo! or others, conduct a search on the cultural aspects of that country. (Hint: If you choose Japan, try searching for the phrase *Japanese culture*.) Prepare a brief report on what you find. What advice would you give an entrepreneur wanting to conduct business there? What is the economic outlook for business in that country?

4. Visit the Web site for the Export-Import Bank of the United States at:

http://www.exim.gov/

Prepare a brief report on the programs available to small businesses. What is the Export-Import Bank's purpose?

5. Using one of the search engines on the World Wide Web such as Lycos, Magellan, Infoseek, Yahoo!, or others, conduct a search on *International Trade*. Choose a topic that you find interesting and prepare a one-page report on what you learn about it.

CHAPTER

FIFTEEN

The Ethical, Legal, and Regulatory Environment

Don't mistake personality with character.
- Wilma Askinas

A verbal contract isn't worth the paper it's written on.
- Samuel Goldwyn

I have never accepted a bad check from anyone I did not trust.
- Ron Rasmus

LEARNING OBJECTIVES

Upon completion of this chapter, you will be able to:

1. **Define** business ethics and explain how entrepreneurs can establish and maintain high ethical standards in their businesses.

2. **Define** social responsibility and discuss some of the various stakeholders—the environment, employees, customers, investors, and the community—to whom businesses are responsible.

3. **Explain** some of the government regulations affecting small businesses.

4. **Explain** the basic elements required to create a valid, enforceable contract.

5. **Outline** the major components of the portion of the Uniform Commercial Code governing sales contracts.

6. **Explain** the workings of the law of agency.

7. **Explain** the basics of bankruptcy law.

8. **Describe** the protection that patents, trademarks, and copyrights offer business owners.

The first responsibility of a business is an economic one: earning a profit so that it can stay in business, serve its customers, and create jobs. However, our society demands that businesses meet their social, ethical, and legal responsibilities as well. Our nation's business system operates in an environment where ethical behavior, social responsibility, government regulation, and the law are tightly intertwined.

Business ethics involve the moral values and behavioral standards that businesspeople face as they make decisions and solve problems. However, defining what is ethical is not always easy. In some cases, the ethical dilemma is obvious, the implications of unethical behavior are obvious, and established guidelines for handling the situation exist. In most situations, however, ethical dilemmas are less obvious, cloaked in the garb of mundane business decisions and everyday routine. Because they can easily catch entrepreneurs off guard, these ethical problems are the ones most likely to ensnare the unwary. Ethical "sleepers" often catch unprepared entrepreneurs, usually destroying their reputations and those of their companies. The first step toward managing a company ethically is raising the entrepreneur's level of consciousness concerning ethical issues. Too many business owners and managers get into trouble unintentionally, blundering into ethical traps before they ever realize it.

Entrepreneurs quickly discover that various groups of **stakeholders**—the groups and individuals who affect and are affected by a business—exert influence over the decisions they make and the actions they take. Figure 15.1 highlights some of the internal and external stakeholders that influence how a typical business operates. Every company must consider the roles these and other key stakeholders play in the operation of its business. For example, when the founders of a small company producing frozen foods make business decisions, they must consider how those decisions will influence and be influenced by its team of employees; the farmers and the companies that supply it with raw materials; the union that represents its workers in collective bargaining; the government that regulates a multitude of its activities; the banks that provide it with financing; the investors who own

business ethics—*the moral values and behavioral standards that businesspeople face as they make decisions and solve problems.*

stakeholders—*the groups and individuals who affect and are affected by a business.*

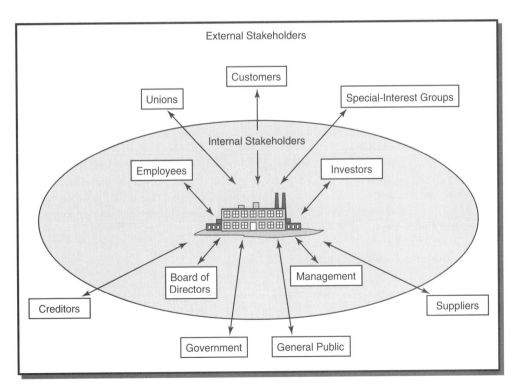

Figure 15.1
Key Stakeholders

its stock; the general public it serves; and, of course, the customers who purchase its products. The power these stakeholders wield determines to a great extent the degree of success a company can achieve. It is this vital link between businesses and the people of society that gives rise to the key concepts of ethics and social responsibility. No business can ignore society's ethical demands and expect to thrive.

Ethical Behavior and Small Business Management

Ethics are the fundamental moral values and behavioral standards that form the foundation for the people of an organization as they make decisions and interact with organizational stakeholders. Employees in companies derive their ethical standards from three sources: the law, company policies and procedures, and their own moral stances. Laws establish the minimum standards of behavior, but simply obeying the law is not a dependable guide to ethical behavior. Few ethical issues are so simple that the law can serve as the acid test for making a decision. Edmund Burke once said, "It is not what a lawyer tells me I may do, but what humanity, reason, and justice tell me I ought to do."[1] Organizations also establish ethical standards through their policies and procedures. Their intent is to set forth clear and specific guidelines for employees as they make daily decisions. The vast majority of businesses make use of this method to communicate a written code of ethics. The third influence on ethical behavior is personal values. Individuals learn these values through interaction with parents, family, religious teachings, and school. In many ways, a positive organizational culture continues to teach and reinforce positive ethical behavior.

Building a reputation for ethical behavior and integrity takes a long time; unfortunately, destroying that reputation takes practically no time at all, and the negative effects linger for years. An entrepreneur's goal is to build a solid ethical reputation for the business and then do everything possible to maintain it. The pressure to take shortcuts or to violate ethical standards is always present. Without a company ethical framework and a supportive ethical work environment, employees may make the wrong decision or display improper behaviors.

Who is responsible for ethical behavior in a company? Although companies establish guidelines for their employees' behavior, the ultimate decision of whether or not to abide by ethical standards rests with the *individual*. In other words, companies are not ethical or unethical; individuals are. Yet, as every business owner knows, managers' and employees' actions determine a company's reputation—good or bad—in its stakeholders' eyes. Managers have tremendous influence over individual behavior in a company, however, because they set the moral tone throughout the entire organization. "In an entrepreneurial organization, the values of the entrepreneur become the values driving the company," says one ethics expert.[2] Employees look to the business owner for clues about what kinds of behavior are acceptable and unacceptable. Plus, the company's culture can either serve to support or to undermine its employees' perceptions of what constitutes ethical behavior. Table 15.1 summarizes three approaches to management ethics: immoral management, amoral management, and moral management.

The Benefits of Moral Management

One of the most common misconceptions about business is the contradiction between ethics and profits. As one business founder says, "It is perfectly possible to make a decent living without compromising the integrity of the company or the individual."[3] Although behaving ethically and acting as a good corporate citizen is reason enough, many companies have discovered that such behavior brings with it many other benefits. First, a company avoids all of the damaging effects associated with a reputation as an unethical busi-

Table 15.1
**Approaches to
Management Ethics**

Source: Archie B. Carroll, "In
Search of the Moral Manager."
Reprinted from *Business Horizons*,
March/April. Copyright 1987 by
the Foundation for the School of
Business at Indiana University.
Used with permission.

		Immoral Management	Amoral Management	Moral Management
Organizational Characteristics	Ethical Norms	Management decisions, actions, and behavior imply a positive and active opposition to what is moral (ethical). Decisions are discordant with accepted ethical principles. An active negation of what is moral is implied.	Management is neither moral nor immoral, but decisions lie outside the sphere to which moral judgments apply. Management activity is outside or beyond the moral order of a particular code. May imply a lack of ethical perception and moral awareness.	Management activity conforms to a standard of ethical, or right, behavior. Conforms to accepted professional standards of conduct. Ethical leadership is commonplace on the part of management.
	Motives	Selfish. Management cares only about its or the company's gains.	Well intentioned but selfish in the sense that impact on others is not considered.	Good. Management wants to succeed but only within the confines of sound ethical precepts (fairness, justice, due process).
	Goals	Profitability and organizational success at any price.	Profitability. Other goals are not considered.	Profitability within the confines of legal obedience and ethical standards.
	Orientation Toward Law	Legal standards are barriers that management must overcome to accomplish what it wants.	Law is the ethical guide, preferably the letter of the law. The central question Is what we can do legally.	Obedience toward letter and spirit of the law. Law is a minimal ethical behavior. Prefer to operate well above what law mandates.
	Strategy	Exploit opportunities for corporate gain. Cut corners when it appears useful.	Give managers free rein. Personal ethics may apply but only if managers choose. Respond to legal mandates if caught and required to do so.	Live by sound ethical standards. Assume leadership position when ethical dilemmas arise. Enlightened self-interest.

ness. Unethical businesses may benefit in the short run, but over time improper behavior takes its toll. It's simply not good business. Second, a solid ethical framework guides managers and employees as they cope with the increasingly complex demands of a network of company stakeholders. Dealing with these diverse demands is much easier if a small business has a solid ethical foundation on which to build. Third, ethical companies earn the respect of two essential groups—their customers and their employees. The ethics factor is intangible and virtually impossible to quantify, yet it is something that customers and employees definitely consider when deciding where to shop and where to work. Finally, many companies discover that ethical behavior can add dollars to their bottom lines. In a recent study, Alfred Marcus at the University of Minnesota found a positive correlation between ethical and socially responsible behavior and higher profits.[4]

Although small in stature, small businesses are anything but small in their impact on their stakeholders. A recent Small Business Administration study found that small businesses contribute more per employee to charitable causes than do large corporations.[5]

Goode and Fresh Pizza Bakery

For instance, Jay Phillips, owner of the Goode and Fresh Pizza Bakery in Glenview, Illinois, set up a summer program with local elementary schools to encourage students to read. For six years, Phillips has donated gift certificates for free pizzas at his restaurant to children who reach a preset reading goal over the summer months. Not only have Phillips and his employees earned the satisfaction of helping children boost their reading skills, but they also have found that the program has added to the company's sales and profits. Phillips estimates that 50 percent of the restaurant's new business each summer comes from the parents of the children enrolled in the reading program![6]

Establishing Ethical Standards

Ethics are not defined by a set of relative guidelines that change from one situation to another. They are an enduring part of an individual's life or a company's culture. Several ethical "tests" for judging behavior exist, including the following:[7]

★ *The utilitarian principle.* Choose the option that offers the greatest good for the greatest number of people.

★ *Kant's categorical imperative.* Act in such a way that the action you take under the circumstances could become a universal law or rule of behavior.

★ *The professional ethic.* Take only those actions that a disinterested panel of professional colleagues would view as proper.

★ *The golden rule.* Treat other people the way you expect them to treat you.

★ *The television test.* Would you or your colleagues feel comfortable explaining your actions to a national television audience?

★ *The family test.* Would you be comfortable explaining to your children, your spouse, and your parents why you took this action?

★ *The emulation test.* How would the person you most admire handle the situation?

★ *The future test.* If you were to look back on your decision or actions in the future, would you be embarrassed or ashamed?

Although these tests do not offer universal solutions to ethical dilemmas, they do help owners and employees identify the moral implications of the decisions they face. People must understand the ethical implications of their actions before they can make responsible decisions.

An Ethical Framework

To cope successfully with the myriad of ethical decisions they face, entrepreneurs must develop a workable ethical framework to guide all employees. While many such frameworks exist, the following four-step process can work quite well.

Step 1. Recognize the ethical dimensions involved in the dilemma or decision. Before an entrepreneur can make an informed ethical decision, he must recognize that an ethical situation exists. Only then is it possible to define the specific ethical issues involved. Too often, business owners fail to take into account the ethical impact of a particular course of action until it is too late. To avoid ethical quagmires, entrepreneurs must consider the ethical forces at work in a situation— honesty, fairness, respect for community, concern for the environment, trust, and others—to have a complete view of the decision.

Step 2. *Identify the key stakeholders involved and determine how the decision will affect them.* As Figure 15.1 demonstrated, every business influences and is influenced by a multitude of stakeholders. Frequently the demands of these stakeholders conflict, and a business has to choose which groups to satisfy and which to forgo. Before making a decision, managers must sort out the stakeholders' conflicting interests by determining which stakeholders have important stakes in the situation. Although this may not resolve the conflict, it will prevent the company from inadvertently causing harm to people it may have failed to consider.

Step 3. *Generate alternative choices and distinguish between ethical and unethical responses.* When generating alternative courses of action and evaluating their positive and negative consequences, small business managers will find the questions in Table 15.2 to be helpful.

Table 15.2

Questions to Help Identify the Ethical Dimensions of a Situation

Source: Sherry Baker, "Ethical Judgment," *Executive Excellence*, March 1992, pp. 7–8.

Principles and Codes of Conduct

★ Does this decision or action meet my standards for how people should interact?

★ Does this decision or action agree with my religious teachings and beliefs (or with my personal principles and sense of responsibility)?

★ How will I feel about myself if I do this?

★ Do we (or I) have a rule or policy for cases like this?

★ Would I want everyone to make the same decision and take the same action if faced with these same circumstances?

★ What are my true motives for considering this action?

Moral Rights

★ Would this action allow others freedom of choice in this matter?

★ Would this action involve deceiving others in any way?

Justice

★ Would I feel that this action was just (ethical or fair) if I were on the other side of the decision?

★ How would I feel if this action were done to me or to someone close to me?

★ Would this action or decision distribute benefits justly?

★ Would it distribute hardships or burdens justly?

Consequences and Outcome

★ What will be the short- and long-term consequences of this action?

★ Who will benefit from this course of action?

★ Who will be hurt?

★ How will this action create good and prevent harm?

Public Justification

★ How would I feel (or how will I feel) if (or when) this action becomes public knowledge?

★ Will I be able to explain adequately to others why I have taken this action?

★ Would others feel that my action or decision is ethical or moral?

Intuition and Insight

★ Have I searched for all alternatives? Are there other ways I could look at this situation? Have I considered all points of view?

★ Even if there is sound rationality for this decision or action, and even if I could defend it publicly, does my inner sense tell me this is right?

★ What does my intuition tell me is the ethical thing to do in this situation? Have I listened to my inner voice?

Step 4. Choose the "best" ethical response and implement it. At this point there will likely be several possible ethical choices. The final choice must be consistent with the company's goals, culture, and value system as well as those of the individual decision maker(s). Making ethical decisions "in the trenches" of corporate combat is no easy task; yet this framework can make entrepreneurs and managers conscious of the impact their decisions are likely to have on those around them. It also will help them to envision the ethical dimensions of their decisions as well as their revenue, cost, or profit impact.

Maintaining Ethical Standards

Establishing ethical standards is the first step; maintaining those standards is a continual challenge facing management. The following are a few techniques used to integrate ethical principles into practice and reinforce the ethical standards of the business.

☆ *Create a company credo.* A company credo defines the company's underlying values and its ethical responsibilities to its stakeholders.

☆ *Develop a code of ethics.* A code of ethics is a written statement of the standard of behavior and ethical principles a company expects from its employees. Codes of ethics do not ensure ethical behavior, but they do establish minimum standards of behavior that are expected from every employee. Much like the Ten Commandments, a code of ethics spells out what kind of behavior is expected (and what kind of behavior will not be tolerated) and offers everyone in the company concrete guidelines for behaving ethically every day on the job.

"Honesty is the best policy, Fernbaugh, but it's not company policy."

Source: Drawing by Leo Cullum; © 1995 The New Yorker Magazine, Inc.

"A Number's Just a Number"

Carla Rigoli, the financial officer for Gifts and More, a small importer of gift items, was sitting at her computer when the founder of the company, Rod Hallman, walked in and asked, "Got a minute?"

"Sure," Carla said, "I've always got a minute for the boss."

As Rod closed the door, Carla noticed that he had an unusual look on his face. "What's up?" she asked.

Gifts and More had been struggling for the past few months, and nobody knew that any better than Carla. She was meticulous in her work, and she understood the company's weakening financial position all too well. Hallman had been trying to sell the company for the past seven months, but no serious buyers had emerged until recently. Hallman confided in Carla, telling her that he "had lost his entrepreneurial drive" and that "running the company just wasn't any fun anymore." He was anxious to make a sale because the company was starting to lose money, and he knew that if the sale stretched out much longer, the price he could get would fall dramatically.

"I've been talking with this prospective buyer, and he's probably our last shot at selling this company," Rod said. "He's been analyzing some of the general financial figures I've given him and he's pretty pleased with what he's seen, but now he wants some more details. That's where you come in."

"I'll be glad to put together some spreadsheets for him," Carla offered.

"Great!" said Rod, handing her a few sheets of figures. "This is what he's seen so far."

Carla studied the numbers for a minute and then looked up at Rod in disbelief. "These numbers aren't right!" she said. "I wish our income statement actually looked this good. Where did these come from?"

As she looked at Rod, he just smiled. Then Carla realized why Rod had come to see her. He wanted her to falsify the company's financial records to make its financial position look better than it actually was! She was furious.

She was about to order Rod out of her office when he said, "Carla, you'd be doing a noble deed by adjusting these numbers. You'd be saving a lot of people's jobs. If this guy doesn't buy the company, I'm afraid we'll have to shut down, and everyone, including you, will be out of a job. Surely you don't want to be responsible for that. We've only got two more days."

As he stood up to leave, Rod said," I've got to go to a meeting with a buyer. Gosh, I hope I can remember which made-up number I gave him last time," he said with a boyish grin. "Oh yes, I remember. After all, a number's just a number," he said as he walked out the door.

Carla sat in a daze, still clutching the numbers that Rod had given her. As she spun her chair around, she looked at the real financial statements she had been preparing on the spreadsheet and pondered her predicament. "What am I going to do now?" she said aloud.

1. What advice would you offer Carla as she deals with this dilemma?

2. Use the four steps in creating an ethical framework to analyze Carla's situation and to make a specific recommendation to her for handling it.

3. What results do you forsee if Carla does what Rod has asked?

Adapted from Doug Wallace, "Cooking the Books," *Business Ethics*, July/August 1995, pp. 50-51.

☆ *Enforce the code fairly and consistently.* Managers and employees must take action when they discover an ethical violation. If employees learn that everyone ignores ethical breaches or lets them go unpunished, the code becomes meaningless.

☆ *Conduct ethical training.* Instilling ethics in an organization's culture requires more than creating a code of ethics and enforcing it. Managers must show employees that the organization truly is committed to practicing ethical behavior. One of the most effective ways to display that commitment is through ethical training designed to raise employees' consciousness of potential ethical dilemmas. Ethics training programs not only raise employees' awareness of ethical issues, but also communicate to them the company's core value system.

☆ *Hire the right people.* Ultimately, the decision in any ethical situation belongs to the individual. Hiring people with strong moral principles and values is the best insurance against ethical violations. To make ethical decisions, people must have (1) *ethical commitment*— the personal resolve to act ethically and do the right thing; (2) *ethical consciousness*— the ability to perceive the ethical implications of a situation; and (3) *ethical competency*—the ability to engage in sound moral reasoning and develop practical problem-solving strategies.

☆ *Perform periodic ethical audits.* One of the best ways to evaluate the effectiveness of an ethics system is to perform periodic audits. These reviews send a signal to employees that ethics is not just a passing fad.

☆ *Establish high standards of behavior, not just rules.* No one can legislate ethics and morality, but managers can let people know the level of performance they expect. It is crucial to emphasize to everyone in the organization the importance of ethics. All employees must understand that ethics are not negotiable.

☆ *Set an impeccable ethical example at all times.* Remember that ethics starts at the top. Far more important than credos and codes are the examples set by the company's leaders. If managers talk about the importance of ethics and then act unethically, they send mixed signals to employees.

☆ *Create a culture that emphasizes two-way communication.* A thriving ethical environment requires two-way communication. Employees must have the opportunity to report any ethical violations they observe. Such a two-way system is integral to a **whistle-blowing program**, in which employees anonymously report breaches of ethical behavior through established channels.

☆ *Involve employees in setting ethical standards.* Encourage employees to offer feedback on how standards should be established. Involving employees improves the quality of a firm's ethical standards and increases the likelihood of employee compliance.

Establishing a workable ethics program is no easy task, but the benefits of doing so are tremendous. It involves creating a culture that supports ethical behavior and an attitude that high moral standards are important throughout the company. Such a program recognizes that a company has a greater responsibility than just earning a profit.

whistle-blowing program—*a two-way communication system in which employees anonymously report breaches of ethical behavior through established channels.*

2. Define social responsibility and discuss some of the various stakeholders—the environment, employees, customers, investors, and the community—to whom businesses are responsible.

social responsibility—*the awareness by a company's managers of the social, environmental, political, human, and financial consequences of their actions.*

Little Earth Productions

Putting Social Responsibility Into Action

Society imposes a higher standard on businesses than it once did: Companies must go beyond just "doing well" by earning a profit, and "do good" by living up to their social responsibility. **Social responsibility** is the awareness by a company's managers of the social, environmental, political, human, and financial consequences of their actions. A socially responsible business considers not only what is best for the firm but also what is best for society. Businesses have responsibilities to several key stakeholders, including the environment, employees, customers, investors, and the community.

The Environment

Most companies are keenly aware of the need to ensure that their products and processes are "environmentally friendly." Sound environmental policies are good business. In addition to lowering operating costs, environmentally safe products attract environmentally conscious customers and can give a company a competitive market advantage.

For instance, Little Earth Productions draws customers with its hip clothing made from recycled materials, including car seat belts, bottle caps, license plates, and tuna cans. "The trouble with most eco-clothing is it's dull," says co-owner Ava De Marco. Little Earth's unusual garments don't suffer from blandness, however. The company sells fashion in a variety of unique forms: shoulder bags made from recycled rubber and hubcaps; purses made with recycled rubber and beer cans; and notebooks made from recycled license plates; but, its best-selling item is a belt made from a car seat belt decorated with bottle caps.[8]

Increasingly, companies are following the 3 Rs—reduce, reuse, and recycle—in the products, packaging, and processes they design. These companies *reduce* the amount of materials they use; *reuse* whatever materials they can; and *recycle* the materials that they must dispose of. "Clean" manufacturing systems further contribute through efforts to avoid waste and pollution in the first place.

Adolph Coors Company, the Golden, Colorado brewery, has been reaping the benefits of a recycling and waste-reduction strategy since the 1950s. By using 100 percent recycled paperboard to ship its products, Coors saves 1,695 acres of virgin forest annually. The company also recycles wood, oil, spent grains, and just about anything else it uses in production. Coors also has discovered ways to avoid creating waste and pollution. Since 1987, Coors has reduced the amount of hazardous wastes it produces by more than 90 percent. Its recycling and waste-reduction efforts are not only good for the environment, but they are also good for business. The company benefits from hundreds of thousands of dollars in savings each year.[9]

> **Adolph Coors Company**

Employees

Few other stakeholders are as important to a business as its employees. It is common for managers to *say* that their employees are their most valuable resource, but the truly excellent ones *treat* them that way. Several important issues face small business owners trying to meet their social responsibility to their employees.

CULTURAL DIVERSITY IN THE WORKPLACE. America has always been recognized as a nation of astonishing cultural diversity, a trait that has imbued it with an incredible richness of ideas and creativity. Indeed, this diversity is one of the driving forces behind the greatest entrepreneurial efforts in all the world, and it continues to grow. Significant demographic shifts will affect virtually every aspect of business, but nowhere will the changes be more visible than in our nation's work force. For instance, in 1995, 57 percent of the country's workers were women or minorities, and that percentage will rise to 62 percent by 2005.[10] This rich mix of cultures within the work force presents both opportunities and challenges to employers. One of the chief benefits of a diverse work force is the rich blend of perspectives and ideas employees have to offer. Managing a culturally diverse work force can present a real challenge for employers, however. Leading employees with highly varied backgrounds, beliefs, and values takes both time and commitment. Stereotypes, biases, and prejudices create barriers that workers and managers must work to overcome. Communication often requires more effort because of language differences.

Managing a culturally diverse work force requires a different way of thinking, and that requires training. Diversity training has as its goal an increased awareness of the negative impacts of bias, prejudice, and discrimination, however subtle or unintentional they may be. Managing a culturally diverse work force requires owners to do the following:

1. *Assess your company's diversity needs.* The starting point of an effective diversity management program is an assessment of the company's needs and problems. Surveys, interviews, and informal conversations with employees can be valuable.

2. *Learn to recognize your own biases and stereotypes.* One of the best ways to identify your own cultural biases is to get exposure to people who are not like you! By spending time with those who are different from you, you will learn quickly that stereotypes simply don't hold up.

3. *Avoid making invalid assumptions.* Decisions based on faulty assumptions are bound to be flawed. Making false assumptions about others based on inaccurate perceptions has kept many qualified women and minorities from getting jobs and promotions.

4. *Push for diversity in your management team.* To get maximum benefit from a culturally diverse work force, a company must promote nontraditional workers into management.

A culturally diverse management team that can serve as mentors and role models provides visible evidence that nontraditional workers can succeed.

5. *Concentrate on communication.* Any organization, especially a culturally diverse one, will stumble if lines of communication break down. Frequent training sessions and regular opportunities for employees to talk with one another in a nonthreatening environment can be extremely helpful.

6. *Make diversity a core value in the organization.* For a cultural diversity program to work, top managers must champion the program and take active steps to integrate diversity throughout the entire organization.

7. *Continue to adjust your company to your workers.* Rather than pressure workers to conform to the company, those entrepreneurs with the most successful cultural diversity programs are constantly looking for ways to adjust their businesses to their workers. Flexibility is the key.

Michele Luna, president of Atlas Headwear, a small maker of military and sports hats, sees the diversity of her work force as a competitive advantage in a fast-changing market. About 94 percent of the company's employees are Asian and Hispanic, and 80 percent are women. Luna follows a promote-from-within policy that has produced a culturally rich top-management team that is sensitive to customers' needs and is capable of responding to a dynamic market. Rather than focus on job candidates' physical characteristics, Atlas looks at their skills and abilities. "We've always considered people on their ability to get the job done," says Luna.[11]

DRUG TESTING. Although some managers would rather ignore the problem, illegal substance abuse has infiltrated the workplace. Drug and alcohol abuse, with its direct impact on employee absenteeism and lost productivity, can cripple a small company's ability to remain competitive. In fact, a recent survey of managers found that substance abuse was the number-one workplace issue across the country.[12]

Small companies bear a disproportionate share of the burden of costs from substance abuse. Most substance abusers—74 percent—are employed, and 23 percent of them use drugs on the job! However, only 3 percent of all small businesses have drug-testing programs, and only 12 percent have formal drug policies.[13] Because they are less likely to screen out substance abusers, small companies are more likely to hire them than larger companies. Small business owners are more likely to be casualties in the war on drugs because they either lack the resources to fight the battle or they do not believe that drug problems exist in their businesses.

Entrepreneurs should develop drug prevention programs that include the following four key elements.

1. *A written substance abuse policy.* The first step in the war against drugs is creating a written policy that spells out the company's position on drugs. The policy should state the purpose of the policy, prohibit the use of drugs on the job (or off the job if it affects job performance), specify the consequences of violating the policy, explain any drug-testing procedures to be used, and describe the resources available to help troubled employees.

2. *Training supervisors to detect drug-using workers.* Supervisors are in the best position to identify employees with drug problems and to encourage them to get help. The supervisor's job, however, is not to play cop or therapist. The supervisor should identify problem employees early and encourage them to seek help. The focal point of the supervisor's role is to track employees' performances against their objectives to identify those with performance problems.

3. *A drug-testing program, when necessary.* Experts recommend that business owners seek the advice of an experienced attorney before establishing a drug-testing program. Preemployment testing of job applicants is generally a safe strategy to follow, as long as it is followed consistently. Testing current employees is a more complex issue. Unless

carefully planned, random drug tests may violate employees' right to privacy and lead to charges of discrimination, slander, and defamation of character.

4. *An employee assistance program (EAP).* No drug-battling program is complete without a way to help addicted employees. An **employee assistance program (EAP)** is a company-provided benefit designed to help reduce workplace problems such as alcoholism, drug addiction, a gambling habit, and other conflicts and to deal with them when they arise. Although some troubled employees may balk at enrolling in an EAP, the company controls the most powerful weapon in motivating them to seek and accept help—their jobs. The greatest fear that substance-abusing employees have is losing their jobs, and the company can use this to help workers recover.

employee assistance program (EAP)—*a company-provided benefit designed to help reduce workplace problems such as alcoholism, drug addiction, a gambling habit, and other conflicts and to deal with them when they arise.*

AIDS. One of the most serious, yet least understood, health problems to strike the world recently is Acquired Immune Deficiency Syndrome (AIDS). The National Center for Health Statistics reports that AIDS is the leading cause of death for Americans aged 25 to 44. It costs businesses an estimated $75 billion annually in medical care and lost productivity.[14] This disease, for which no cure yet exists, poses an array of ethical dilemmas for business, ranging from privacy to discrimination. For most business owners, however, the question is not if one of their employees will contract AIDS but *when*.

Despite AIDS becoming a workplace phenomenon, few businesses are prepared adequately to deal with it. When faced with the disease, business owners and employees usually respond out of fear and misunderstanding. One study found that 75 percent of employers knew little or nothing about their legal obligations to employees with AIDS.[15] In addition, many of the actions employers said they would take with an AIDS-infected employee (including firing and telling coworkers) were illegal.[16] In fact, AIDS is considered a disability and is covered by the Americans with Disabilities Act (ADA), which applies to companies with 15 or more employees. (Small business owners with fewer than 15 employees may be covered by state and local laws.) The ADA prohibits discrimination against any person with a disability, including AIDS, in hiring, promoting, discharging, or compensating. In addition, employers must make "reasonable accommodations" to allow an AIDS-stricken employee to continue working. That could mean job sharing, flexible work schedules, job reassignment, sick leave, and part-time work.

Studies suggest that less than 10 percent of companies have an AIDS program or policy. Yet, coping with AIDS in a socially responsible manner requires a written policy and an educational program, ideally implemented *before* the need arises. Decisions on dealing with AIDS must be based on facts rather than on emotions, so owners must be well informed.

As with drug testing, it is important to ensure that any company policies are legal. Generally, a company's AIDS policy should include the following:

1. *Employment.* Companies must allow employees with AIDS to continue working as long as they can perform the job.

2. *Discrimination.* Because AIDS is a "disability," employers cannot discriminate against qualified people with the disease who can meet job requirements.

3. *Employee benefits.* Employees with AIDS have the right to the same benefits as those with any other life-threatening illness.

4. *Confidentiality.* Employers must keep employees' medical records strictly confidential.

5. *Education.* An AIDS education program should be a part of every company's AIDS policy. The time to create and implement one is before the problem arises. As part of its AIDS program, one small company conducted informational seminars, distributed brochures and booklets, established a print and video library, and even set up individual counseling for employees.

6. *"Reasonable accommodations."* Under the ADA, employers must make "reasonable accommodations" for AIDS-infected employees. This may include extended leaves of

absence, flexible work schedules, restructuring a job to require less strenuous duties, purchasing special equipment to assist affected workers, and other modifications.

SEXUAL HARASSMENT. **Sexual harassment** is any unwelcome sexual advance, request for sexual favors, and other verbal or physical sexual conduct made explicitly or implicitly as a condition of employment. Both the number of sexual harassment lawsuits and the damages awarded in them are on the rise. The average verdict in favor of an employee is $350,000, but awards reaching into the millions are not uncommon.[17]

For instance, a jury awarded a woman who worked as a secretary in a law firm for three months $7.1 million in a sexual harassment lawsuit. The award was more than twice the amount the woman had been seeking in the suit, but the jury punished the law firm because it had tolerated the harassment and had not done enough to prevent it.[18]

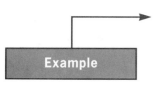

Example

---

sexual harassment—
any unwelcome sexual advance, request for sexual favors, and other verbal or physical sexual conduct made explicitly or implicitly as a condition of employment.

Small businesses are prime targets for sexual harassment lawsuits. "They usually say 'we operate like a family. We're good to our employees and allow them latitude,'" explains one attorney. "But those companies get into the most trouble because they didn't adhere to [a] policy. [Now,] they are learning they have to have a policy [just] as if they were a big company."[19] Three types of behavior most often result in charges of sexual harassment.

1. *Quid pro quo harassment.* The most blatant—and most potentially damaging form of sexual harassment is quid pro quo ("something for something"), in which a superior conditions the granting of a benefit (promotion, raise, etc.) upon the receipt of sexual favors from a subordinate. Only managers and supervisors, not coworkers, can engage in quid pro quo harassment. Unfortunately, this form of harassment is all too common.

2. *Hostile environment.* Behavior that creates an abusive, intimidating, offensive, or hostile work environment also constitutes sexual harassment. A hostile environment usually requires a pattern of offensive sexual behavior rather than a single, isolated remark or display. In judging whether or not a hostile environment exists, courts base their decisions on how a "reasonable woman" would perceive the situation. (The previous standard was that of a "reasonable person.") Although less easily defined than quid pro quo harassment, a hostile work environment is one in which continuing unwelcome sexual conduct in the workplace interferes with an employee's work performance.

3. *Harassment by nonemployees.* An employer can be held liable for third parties (customers, sales representative, and others) who engage in sexual harassment if the employer has the ability to stop the improper behavior.

An effective program for fighting sexual harassment involves three elements: educating workers about sexual harassment, creating a clear policy forbidding it, and establishing a simple procedure to deal effectively with any charges that do arise.

Education. Because there is some uncertainty and disagreement about what constitutes sexual harassment, educational programs are essential. Training programs are designed to raise employees' awareness of what might be offensive to other workers. Table 15.3 offers guidelines for battling sexual harassment in the workplace.

Policy. Another essential ingredient is a meaningful policy against sexual harassment that management can enforce. The policy should (1) state in clear language that harassment will not be tolerated in the workplace; (2) identify the responsibilities of supervisors and employees in preventing harassment; (3) define the sanctions and penalties for engaging in harassment; and (4) spell out the steps to take in reporting an incident of sexual harassment. Employers must also communicate the policy regularly to every employee in the company—from top to bottom.

Procedure. Socially responsible companies provide a channel for all employees to express their complaints. Choosing a person inside the company (perhaps someone in the human resources area) and one outside the company (a close advisor or attorney) is a good strat-

Before You Speak, Ask Yourself . . .	To Keep the Workplace Harassment-free . . .
☆ Would you say it in front of your spouse, parent, or child?	☆ Have a clear, written policy prohibiting sexual harassment.
☆ Would you say it if you were going to be quoted on the front page of the newspaper?	☆ Have mandatory training programs.
☆ Would you say it to a member of your same sex?	☆ Ensure the workplace is free of offensive materials.
☆ Would you behave the same way with a member of your same sex?	☆ Establish a program outlining the steps to take to file a complaint.
☆ Does it need to be said at all?	☆ Keep informed of all complaints and their resolutions

Table 15.3
Guidelines for Battling Sexual Harassment

Sources: Ann Meyer, "Getting to the Heart of Sexual Harasssment," *HR Magazine*, July 1992, p. 82; Jan Bohren, "Six Myths of Sexual Harassment," *Management Review*, May 1993, p. 62.

egy. At least one of these should be a woman. When a complaint arises, managers should (1) listen to the complaint carefully without judging. Taking notes is a good idea. Tell the complainant what the process involves. Never treat the complaint as a joke. (2) Investigate the complaint promptly. Failure to act quickly is irresponsible and illegal. (3) Interview the accused party and any other witnesses privately. (4) Keep findings confidential. (5) Decide what action to take, relying on company policy as a guideline, and (6) document the entire investigation. Acting promptly on a complaint is vital. One of the criteria used to determine a company's liability in sexual harassment cases is how quickly it responds to an employee's complaint. Recently, a jury awarded one woman $2 million in damages because the managers in her company failed to investigate and act on her claim of sexual harassment.[20]

WHISTLE-BLOWING. Whistle-blowers are employees who risk their jobs to alert managers or the public to dangerous or illegal activities in which a company may engage. Despite the fact that they are acting ethically, whistle-blowers are often punished for their behavior by being ostracized by their peers, treated as outcasts, and usually fired (although it is illegal to do so). The high degree of loyalty to the organization expected of employees is part of the problem. When taken to the extreme, such loyalty can lead to socially irresponsible and illegal activities. For example, employees at one oil processing plant failed to speak out about numerous safety violations and other improper practices. The result was a fiery explosion that killed seven workers and severely damaged the plant. Their loyalty to the company and the fear of retaliation kept them from blowing the whistle.

Customers

One of the most important groups of stakeholders that a business must satisfy is its customers. Building and maintaining a base of loyal customers is no easy task, however. It requires more than just selling buyers a product or a service; the key is to build relationships with customers. Socially responsible companies recognize their duty to abide by the Consumer Bill of Rights, first put forth by President John Kennedy. This document gives consumers the following rights:

1. *Right to safety.* This is the most basic consumer right. Companies are responsible for providing their customers with safe, quality products and services. The greatest breach of trust occurs when businesses produce products that, when properly used, injure customers.

2. *Right to know.* Consumers have the right to honest communication about the products and services they buy and the companies from which they buy them. In a free market economy, information is one of the most valuable commodities available. Customers often

depend on companies for this information to make decisions about price, quality, features, and other factors. As a result, companies have a responsibility to customers to be truthful in their advertising.

3. *Right to be heard.* This consumer right suggests that the channels of communication between companies and their customers run in both directions. Socially responsible businesses provide customers with a mechanism for resolving complaints about products and services. Some companies have established consumer ombudsmen to address customer questions and complaints. Others have created customer hotlines, toll-free numbers designed to serve customers more effectively.

4. *Right to education.* Socially responsible companies give customers access to educational programs about their products and services and how to use them properly. The goal is to give customers enough information to make informed purchase decisions.

5. *Right to choice.* Inherent in the free enterprise system is the consumer's right to choose among competing products and services. Socially responsible companies do not restrict competition, and they abide by the U.S. antitrust policy, which promotes free trade and competition in the market. The foundation of this policy is the Sherman Antitrust Act of 1890, which forbids agreements among sellers that restrain trade or commerce and outlaws any attempts to monopolize a market.

Investors

Companies are responsible for providing their investors with an attractive rate of return on their investments. However, as we have seen, earning a profit may be a company's *first* responsibility, but it is certainly not its *only* responsibility. Meeting its ethical and social responsibilities is also an important part of any company's long-term success. Many entrepreneurs believe that managing their businesses in an ethical, socially responsible manner is the only way to generate a profit. For them, maintaining high social and ethical standards translates into profits for investors.

Community

As corporate citizens, businesses have a responsibility to the communities in which they operate. In addition to providing jobs and creating wealth, companies contribute to the local community in many different ways. Socially responsible businesses recognize their duty to put back into the community some of what they take out as they generate profits. These companies are the ones who donate money, time, and personnel to civic clubs and volunteer organizations such as the Red Cross, the United Way, literacy programs, and a host of other groups.

Many entrepreneurs use their businesses as tools to work for solutions to problems in society that are important to them. "A company now is responsible to its *stakeholders* rather than just its *shareholders*," says the head of a company specializing in social responsibility research. "And, increasingly, its competitiveness depends upon its ability to be part of the solution to societal needs."[21] To maximize the impact of their community involvement, many small businesses are linking their philanthropy to their business strategies.

> **The Cheshire Tree**
>
> *When Sue Meany and Kent Thomas opened The Cheshire Tree, a small flower and garden store, they wanted to begin their community involvement immediately. Of course, as a startup business, they had very little cash to spare, but that did not stop them from contributing. "We decided to offer one graduating senior at the local high school a $100 environmental scholarship because environmental studies relate to our business," says Thomas. The Cheshire Tree also supports Students Against Drunk Driving (SADD) by donating the profits from the sale of prom corsages and boutonnieres.*[22]

Woodruff Manufacturing

Woodruff Manufacturing is a small manufacturer of specialty machine parts used in the automotive industry. Lex Woodruff, founder of the company, had run the business for most of its 50 years of operation. Just five years ago, Mike Woodruff, Lex's son, had taken over the company, but Lex remained as chairman of the board and still ran much of the business. Three years ago, the head of a large manufacturing company approached Lex about acquiring Woodruff Manufacturing. Woodruff had been a supplier to this company for almost three decades, and each company's managers knew the product lines and the reputation of the other quite well.

At first, Lex was not terribly interested in talking about selling the company he had worked so hard to build. But Lex was stunned when he heard the terms of the proposed acquisition. The price was almost too good to believe. In addition to the attractive price, the terms called for a substantial cash payment up front and a steady flow of income over the next 20 years. The terms also included a five-year management contract for Mike as CEO at a very competitive salary.

Lex and Mike and their families spent the weekend at their lakeside cabin in the mountains and discussed the offer. By Sunday afternoon, they had decided that the deal was too good to pass up. Within two months, they closed the sale of Woodruff Manufacturing, Lex retired, and Mike formally became the company's second CEO.

The working relationship with the new owners started out well. "For the most part," recalls Mike, "no one saw any major changes in the way the business operated. Other than making some suggestions about making some organizational changes involving cross-training and team-based management, the new owners let us run things the way we saw fit." Mike went to local union officials with the changes, but they wanted no part of any changes in the way their members did their jobs or were paid. Over the next several months, Mike repeatedly tried to involve the union in discussions about new work methods that could improve the company's productivity. Each time, the union representatives refused the changes. Mike was convinced that the changes were necessary because the competitive environment in which Woodruff Manufacturing operated was changing fast and was getting much tougher. Unfortunately, he had no success in convincing the union of the need for change. Like Mike himself, the union leaders had grown up in this small town. For most, Woodruff Manufacturing, which was one of the largest employers in the county, was the only place they had ever worked.

The first shock wave hit Mike when he took a call from the corporate CEO, Alex McKinney, asking him to visit three different sites in Mexico. McKinney said that the company was considering relocating Woodruff Manufacturing to one of these sites and asked Mike to prepare a report on the expected cost savings the company could expect by doing so. Alex made his position clear: "We need to raise productivity or lower costs to remain competitive, but so far, we've gotten little help from your employees. We don't know what else to do."

Mike knew that if the plant closed, 1,275 employees would lose their jobs and the town's economy would be devastated. The company's wage rates ranged from $7.00 per hour to $16.75 per hour. In addition, Lex Woodruff had set up an attractive benefits package years ago that the company had improved upon over time.

At the end of his ten-day Mexican journey, Mike had the details McKinney had sent him to gather. On the plane trip back home, he did some preliminary calculations on his laptop computer. Of course, wage rates in the Mexican locations were much lower than those at Woodruff Manufacturing. However, Mike knew that productivity would be lower and that quality might suffer until the company could train the workers and upgrade their skills. Although productivity at Woodruff Manufacturing was nothing to brag about, Mike estimated that productivity in Mexico would be significantly lower. Factoring in the lower productivity, Mike estimated that moving the operation to Mexico would lower cost over the existing plant by about 28 percent. As he closed his laptop computer, Mike thought about the employees in the plant back home . . .

1. What responsibilities does Woodruff Manufacturing have to:
   a. its present employees?
   b. the local community?
   c. the stockholders of the parent company?
   d. the labor union representing its workers?
   e. its customers?

2. Based on your responses to question 1, what advice would you give Mike Woodruff? What actions should he take over the next few months?

Government Regulation

One of the most influential stakeholders (refer to Figure 15.1) that businesses must deal with is the government. Government regulation had its place in our economy as far back as 1887, when Congress created the Interstate Commerce Commission to regulate railroad rates and to avoid monopolies in the railway industry. Then as today, regulation generally helps some individuals or groups and imposes a cost or duty on others—often consumers. Experts estimate that federal regulations alone make up 9 cents of every $1 of consumer prices.[23] For most of this country's history, government imposed little, if any, regulation on business. From the 1930s forward, laws regulating business practices and government agencies to enforce the regulations have expanded continuously. Not to be outdone by the federal regulators, most states have created their own regulatory agencies to create and enforce a separate set of rules and regulations. In many instances, small business owners are overwhelmed by the paperwork required to respond to all the governmental agencies trying to regulate and protect them. It is not surprising that small business owners laugh at the old line, "Hi, I am from the government, and I am here to help you."

The major issues of small business and regulation revolve around the cost of compliance. For small companies, regulatory compliance cost per employee is significantly higher than those of large businesses with whom they must compete. In a competitive market, small companies cannot simply pass these additional costs forward to their customers and, consequently, small businesses experience a squeeze on their profit margins.

Most business owners agree that some government regulation is necessary. There must be laws governing working safety, environmental protection, package labeling, consumer credit, and other relevant issues because dishonest, unscrupulous managers will abuse the opportunity to serve the public's interest. It is not the regulations that protect workers and consumers and achieve social objectives that businesses object to, but those that produce only marginal benefits relative to their costs. Owners of small firms, especially, seek relief from wasteful and meaningless government regulations, charging that the cost of compliance exceeds the benefits gained.

Trade Practices

Contemporary society places great value on free competition in the marketplace, and antitrust laws reflect this. The notion of *laissez-faire*—that government should not interfere with the operation of the economy—that once dominated U.S. markets no longer prevails. One of the earliest trade laws was the **Sherman Antitrust Act**, which was passed in 1890 to promote competition in the U.S. economy. This act is the foundation on which antitrust policy in the United States is built. Although its language is very general, the Sherman Antitrust Act contains two primary provisions affecting growth and trade among businesses.

Sherman Antitrust Act— *an antitrust law passed in 1890 to promote competition in the U.S. economy.*

Section I forbids "every contract, combination in the form of trust or otherwise, or conspiracy, in restraint of trade or commerce among the several states, or with foreign nations." This section outlaws any agreement among sellers that might create a restraint on free trade in the marketplace. For example, a group of small and medium-size regional supermarkets formed a cooperative association to purchase products to resell under private labels only in restricted geographic regions. The U.S. Supreme Court ruled that this was an attempt to restrict competition by allocating territories. Such concerted activity was an example of "horizontal territorial limitations," which "are naked restraints of trade with no purpose except stifling of competition."

Section II of the Sherman Antitrust Act makes it illegal for any person to "monopolize or attempt to monopolize or combine or conspire with any other person or persons to monopolize any part of the trade or commerce among the several states, or with foreign nations." The primary focus of Section II is on preventing the undesirable effects of monopoly power in the marketplace.

Congress passed the **Clayton Act** in 1914 to strengthen federal antitrust laws by spelling out specific monopolistic activities. The major provisions of the Clayton Act forbid the following activities:

1. *Price discrimination.* A firm cannot charge different customers different prices for the same product, unless the price discrimination is based on an actual cost savings, is made to meet a lower price from competitors, or is justified by a difference in grade, quality, or quantity sold.

2. *Exclusive dealing and tying contracts.* A seller cannot require a buyer to purchase only her product to the exclusion of other competitive sellers' products (an **exclusive dealing agreement**). Also, the act forbids sellers to sell a product on the condition that the buyer agrees to purchase another product the seller offers (a **tying arrangement**). For example, a computer manufacturer could not sell a computer to a business and, as a condition of the sale, require the firm to purchase software as well.

3. *Purchasing stock in competing corporations.* A business cannot purchase the stock or assets of another business when the effect may be to substantially lessen competition. This does not mean that a corporation cannot hold stock in a competing company; it is designed to prevent horizontal mergers that would reduce competition. The Federal Trade Commission and the Antitrust Division of the Justice Department enforce this section (Section 7), evaluating the market shares of the companies involved and the potential effects of a horizontal merger before ruling on its legality.

4. *Interlocking directorates.* The act forbids **interlocking directorates**—a person serving on the board of directors of two or more competing companies. The act establishes specific provisions for the interlocking directorate requirement.

To supplement the Clayton Act, Congress passed the **Federal Trade Commission Act** in 1914, which created its namesake agency and gave it a broad range of powers. Section 5 gives the FTC the power to prevent "unfair methods of competition in commerce and unfair or deceptive acts or practices in commerce." Recent amendments have expanded the FTC's powers. The FTC's primary targets are those businesses that engage in unfair trade practices, often brought to the surface by consumer complaints. In addition, the agency has issued a number of trade regulation rules defining acceptable and unacceptable trade practices in various industries. Its major weapon is a "cease and desist order," commanding the violator to stop its unfair trade practices.

The FTC Act and the Lanham Trademark Act of 1988 (plus state laws) govern the illegal practice of deceptive advertising. In general, the FTC can review any advertisement that might mislead people into buying a product or service they would not buy if they knew the truth. For instance, if a small business advertised a "huge year-end inventory reduction sale" but kept its prices the same as its regular prices, it is violating the law. One video rental store ran afoul of the FTC Act by advertising 99-cent rentals, then charging a 25-cent "tape-protection fee" on each tape rented. Because customers could not rent videos at the advertised price of 99 cents, the company's ads were false and misleading.[24]

Although the Clayton Act addressed price discrimination and the Federal Trade Commission forbade the practice, Congress found the need to strengthen the law because many businesses circumvented original rules. In 1936 Congress passed the **Robinson-Patman Act**, which further restricted price discrimination in the marketplace. The act forbids any seller "to discriminate in price between different purchases of commodities of like grade and quality" unless there are differences in the cost of manufacture, sale, or delivery of the goods. Even if a price-discriminating firm escaped guilt under the Clayton Act, it violated the Robinson-Patman Act. Traditionally, the FTC has had the primary responsibility of enforcing the Robinson-Patman Act.

Clayton Act—*a law passed in 1914 to strengthen federal antitrust laws by spelling out specific monopolistic activities.*

exclusive dealing agreement—*a contract which requires a buyer to purchase only a seller's product to the exclusion of other seller's competitive products.*

tying arrangement—*a contract that requires a buyer to purchase other products the seller offers as a condition of the sale.*

interlocking directorates—*when a person serves on the board of directors of two or more competing companies.*

Federal Trade Commission Act—*an act passed in 1914 that created the Federal Trade Commission and gave it the power to prevent unfair trade practices.*

Robinson—Patman Act—*a law passed in 1934 to restrict price discrimination in the marketplace.*

The **Celler-Kefauver Act** of 1950 gave the FTC the power to review certain proposals for mergers so it could prevent too much concentration of power in any particular industry.

Congress created the Miller-Tydings Act in 1937 to introduce an exception to the Sherman Antitrust Act. This act made it legal for manufacturers to use **fair-trade agreements**—agreements that prohibit sellers of the manufacturer's product from selling it below a predetermined fair trade price. This form of price fixing was outlawed when Congress repealed the Miller-Tydings Act in 1976. Manufacturers can no longer mandate minimum or maximum prices on their products to sellers.

Consumer Protection

Since the early 1960s, legislators have created many laws aimed at protecting consumers from unscrupulous sellers, unreasonable credit terms, and mislabeled or unsafe products. Early laws focused on ensuring that food and drugs sold in the marketplace were safe and of proper quality. The first law, the Pure Food and Drug Act, passed in 1906, regulated the labeling of various food and drug products. Later amendments empowered government agencies to establish safe levels of food additives and to outlaw carcinogenic (cancer-causing) additives. In 1938, Congress passed the **Food, Drug, and Cosmetics Act**, which created the Food and Drug Administration (FDA). The FDA is responsible for establishing standards for safe over-the-counter drugs; inspecting food and drug manufacturing operations; performing research on food, additives, and drugs; regulating drug labeling; and other related tasks. Other acts regulating the food industry include the Agricultural Marketing Act of 1946, the Poultry Products Inspection Act of 1957, the Wholesome Meat Act of 1967, and the Egg Products Inspection Act of 1970.

Congress has also created a number of laws to establish standards pertaining to product labeling for consumer protection. Since 1976, manufacturers have been required to print accurate information about the quantity and content of their products in a conspicuous place on the package. Generally, labels must identify the raw materials used in the product, the manufacturer, the distributor (and its place of business), the net quantity of the contents and the quantity of each serving if the package states the number of servings. The law also requires labels to be truthful. For example, a candy bar labeled "new bigger size" must actually be bigger. These requirements, created by the Fair Packaging and Labeling Act of 1976, were designed to improve the customer's ability to comparison shop. A 1970 amendment to the Fair Packaging and Labeling Act, the Poison Prevention Packaging Act, required manufacturers to install child-proof caps on all products that could be dangerous to children if ingested. Other labeling acts include the Fur Products Labeling Act, the Wool Products Labeling Act, and the Cigarette Labeling and Advertising Act.

In 1953, Congress passed the Flammable Fabrics Act to control the sale of flammable material and clothing. The Consumer Product Safety Commission (CPSC) enforces the act. With the passage of the **Consumer Products Safety Act** in 1972, Congress created the CPSC to control potentially dangerous products sold to consumers, and it has broad powers to rule over manufacturers and sellers of consumer products. For instance, the CPSC can set safety requirements for consumer products, and it has the power to ban the production of any product it considers hazardous to consumers. It can also order vendors to remove unsafe products from their shelves. In addition to enforcing the Consumer Product Safety Act, the CPSC is also charged with enforcing the Refrigerator Safety Act, the Federal Hazardous Substance Act, the Child Protection and Toy Safety Act, the Poison Prevention Packaging Act, and the Flammable Fabrics Act. The Consumer Product Safety Act was created to do the following:

✯ Protect the public against unreasonable risk of injury from consumer products.

✯ Help customers compare products on the basis of safety.

☆ Create safety standards for products and consolidate inconsistent state regulations.

☆ Research the causes and possible prevention of injuries and illness from consumer products.

The Magnuson-Moss Warranty Act, passed in 1975, regulates written warranties that companies offer on the consumer goods they sell. The act does not require companies to offer warranties; it only regulates the warranties companies choose to offer. It also requires businesses to state warranties in easy-to-understand language and defines the conditions warranties must meet before they can be designated as "full warranties."

Consumer Credit

Another area subject to intense government regulation is consumer credit. This section of the law has grown in importance since credit has become a major vehicle for consumer purchases. The primary law regulating consumer credit is the **Consumer Credit Protection Act (CCPA)**, passed in 1968. More commonly known as the Truth-in-Lending Act, this law requires sellers who extend credit and lenders to fully disclose the terms and conditions of credit arrangements. The Federal Trade Commission is responsible for enforcing the Truth-in-Lending Act. The law outlines specific requirements that any firm that offers, arranges, or extends credit to customers must meet. The two most important terms of the credit arrangement that lenders must disclose are the finance charge and the annual percentage rate. The finance charge represents the total cost—direct and indirect—of the credit, and the annual percentage rate (APR) is the relative cost of credit stated in annual percentage terms. Because computing the annual percentage rate can be quite tedious, the Federal Reserve Board publishes a booklet, *Annual Percentage Rate Tables, Volume 1*, to assist business owners in complying with the law.

Consumer Credit Protection Act—*a law passed in 1968 to require sellers who extend credit and lenders to fully disclose the terms and conditions of credit arrangements.*

The Truth-in-Lending Act applies to any installment contract that includes more than four installments. Merchants extending credit to customers must state clearly the following information, using specific terminology:

☆ The price of the product.

☆ The down payment and any trade-in allowance made.

☆ The unpaid balance owed after the down payment.

☆ Total dollar amount of the finance charge.

☆ Any prepaid finance charges or required deposit balances, such as points, service charges, or lenders' fees.

☆ Any other charges not included in the finance charge.

☆ The total amount to be financed.

☆ The unpaid balance.

☆ The deferred payment price, including the total cash price and finance and incidental charges.

☆ The date on which the finance charge begins to accrue.

☆ The annual percentage rate of the finance charge.

☆ The number, amounts, and due dates of payments.

☆ The penalties imposed in case of delinquent payments.

☆ A description of any security interest the creditor holds.

☆ A description of any penalties imposed for early repayment of principal.

Another provision of the Truth-in-Lending Act limits the credit card holder's liability in case the holder's card is lost or stolen. As long as the holder notifies the company of the missing card, she is liable for only $50 of any amount that an unauthorized user might charge on the card (or zero if the holder notifies the company before any unauthorized use of the card).

In 1974 Congress passed the Fair Credit Billing Act, an amendment to the Truth-in-Lending Act. Under this law, a credit card holder may withhold payment on a faulty product, providing she has made a good faith effort to settle the dispute first. A credit card holder can also withhold payment to the issuing company if she believes her bill is in error. The card holder must notify the issuer within 60 days but is not required to pay the bill until the dispute is settled. The creditor cannot collect any finance charges during this period unless there was no error.

Another credit law designed to protect consumers is the Equal Credit Opportunity Act of 1974, which prohibits discrimination in granting credit on the basis of race, religion, national origin, color, sex, marital status, or whether the individual receives public welfare payments.

In 1971, Congress created the Fair Credit Reporting Act to protect consumers against the circulation of inaccurate or obsolete information pertaining to credit applications. Under this act, the consumer can request the nature of any credit investigation, the type of information assembled, and the identity of those persons receiving the report. The law requires that any obsolete or misleading information contained in the file be updated, deleted, or corrected.

Congress enacted the Fair Debt Collection Practices Act in 1977 to protect consumers from abusive debt collection practices. The law does not apply to business owners collecting their own debts, but only to debt collectors working for other businesses. The act prevents debt collectors from doing the following:

⭐ Contacting the debtor at his workplace if the employer objects.

⭐ Using intimidation and harassment to pester the debtor.

⭐ Calling on the debtor at inconvenient times.

⭐ Contacting third parties (except parents, spouses, and financial advisers) about the debt.

⭐ Contacting the consumer after receiving notice of refusal to pay the debt (except to inform the debtor of the involvement of a collection agency).

4. Explain the basic elements required to create a valid, enforceable contract.

Business Law—Contract Basics

The last part of this chapter deals with the basics of business law. The purpose of this section of the chapter is not to make the reader a attorney, but to introduce the most critical legal concepts which most businesses will encounter: contracts, the Uniform Commercial Code, the law of agency, bankruptcy, trademarks, and copyrights.

Contracts

contract—a promise or set of promises for the breach of which the law gives a remedy, or the performance of which the law recognizes as a duty.

Contract law governs the rights and obligations among the parties to an agreement (contract). It is a body of laws that affects virtually every business relationship. A **contract** is simply a legally binding agreement. It is a promise or a set of promises for the breach of which the law gives a remedy, or the performance of which the law in some way recognizes as a duty. A contract arises from an agreement, and it creates an obligation among the parties involved. It is a promise to be fulfilled. Although almost everyone has the capacity to enter into a contractual agreement (freedom of contract), not every contract is valid and enforceable. A valid contract has four separate elements:

⭐ Agreement

⭐ Consideration

★ Contractual capacity

★ Legality

In addition, two supplemental requirements must be met: genuineness of assent and form.

AGREEMENT. **Agreement** requires a meeting of the minds and is established by an offer and an acceptance. One party must make an offer to another party, who must accept that offer. Agreement is governed by the **objective theory of contracts**, which states that a party's intention to create a contract is measured by outward facts—words, conduct, and circumstances—rather than by subjective, personal intentions. In settling contract disputes, courts interpret the objective facts surrounding the contract from the perspective of an imaginary reasonable person.

For instance, Klick-Lewis, a car dealership, offered a new Chevrolet Beretta as a prize to any person who hit a hole-in-one on the ninth hole of a golf tournament. It displayed the car at the tee box of the ninth hole with a sign saying, "HOLE-IN-ONE Wins this 1988 Chevrolet Beretta GI Courtesy of Klick-Lewis Buick-Chevrolet-Pontiac $49.00 OVER FACTORY INVOICE in Palmyra." Amos Carbaugh was playing in the East End Open Golf Tournament and scored a hole-in-one on the ninth hole, but when he attempted to claim the prize, Klick-Lewis refused to sell him the car at $49.00 over invoice. The dealer said that it had offered the car as a prize in another golf tournament, which had taken place two days earlier and that it had simply neglected to remove the car and the sign before the tournament Carbaugh was playing in. Carbaugh filed a lawsuit against Klick-Lewis and won the right to buy the car at $49.00 over invoice. The court said that, based on the objective theory of contracts, an imaginary reasonable person in Carbaugh's position would have believed that the dealership was making an offer, citing the presence of the sign, the car, and no mention of a specific golf tournament. Klick-Lewis's subjective intent was irrelevant.[25]

Agreement requires that one of the parties to a contract make an offer and the other an acceptance.

Offer. An **offer** is a promise or commitment to do or refrain from doing some specified thing in the future. For an offer to stand, there must be an intention to be bound by it, reasonably certain terms, and communication of the offer. The party making the offer must genuinely intend to make an offer, and the offer's terms must be definite, not vague. The following terms must either be expressed or be capable of being implied in an offer: the parties involved; the identity of the subject matter; and the quantity. Other terms offerors should specify include price, delivery terms, payment terms, timing, and shipping terms. Although these elements are not required, the more terms a party specifies, the more likely it is that an offer exists.

Courts often supply missing terms in a contract when there is a reliable basis for doing so. For instance, the court usually supplies a time term that is reasonable for the circumstances. It supplies a price term if a readily ascertainable market price exists; otherwise, a missing price term defeats the contract. On rare occasions, the court supplies a quantity term, but a missing quantity term usually defeats a contract. And courts never specify the identity of a product; lack of identity always defeats a contract. For example, the small retailer who mails an advertising circular to a large number of customers is not making an offer; one major term—quantity—is missing.

An offer must always be communicated to the other party because one cannot agree to a contract unless she knows it exists. The offeror may communicate by verbal expression, written word, or implied action.

Acceptance. Only the offeree can accept an offer and create a contract. The offeree must accept voluntarily, agreeing to the terms exactly as the offeror presents them. When the offeree suggests alternative terms or conditions, he is implicitly rejecting the original offer

agreement—*a meeting of the minds established by an offer and an acceptance.*

objective theory of contracts—*a principle which states that a party's intent to create a contract is measured by outward facts—words, conduct, and circumstances—rather than by subjective, personal intentions.*

Klick-Lewis

offer—*a promise or a commitment to do or refrain from doing something in the future.*

and making a counteroffer. Common law requires that the offeree's acceptance exactly match the offer.

Generally, silence by the offeree cannot constitute acceptance, even if the offer contains statements to the contrary. For instance, when the offeror claims, "If you do not respond to this offer, I conclude your silence to be your acceptance," no acceptance exists even if the offeree does remain silent. The law requires an offeree to act affirmatively to accept an offer in most cases.

An offeree must accept an offer by the means of communication authorized by and within the time limits specified by the offeror. Generally, offers accepted by alternative media or after specified deadlines are ineffective. If the offeror specifies no means of communication, the offeree must use the same medium used to extend the offer (or a faster method). According to the "mailbox rule," if an offeree accepts by mail, the acceptance is effective when the letter is dropped in the mailbox, even if it never reaches the offeror. Also, all offers must be properly dispatched; that is, they must be properly addressed, noted, and stamped.

CONSIDERATION. Contracts are based on promises, and because it is often difficult to distinguish between promises that are serious and those that are not, courts require that consideration be present in virtually every contract. **Consideration** is something of legal value (not necessarily economic value) bargained for and exchanged as the "price" for the promise given. Consideration can be money, but parties most often swap promises for promises. For example, when a buyer promises to buy an item and a seller promises to sell it, valuable consideration exists. To comprise valuable consideration, a promise must impose a liability or create a duty.

Consideration—
something of legal value, bargained for and exchanged as the "price" for the promise given.

For a contract to be binding, the two parties involved must exchange valuable consideration. The absence of consideration makes a promise not binding. A promise to perform something one is already legally obligated to do is not valuable consideration. Also, because consideration is what the promisor requires in exchange for his promise, it must be given *after* the promisor states what is required. In other words, past consideration is not valid. Also, under the common law, new promises require new consideration. For instance, if two businesspeople have an existing contract for performance of a service, any modifications to that contract must be supported by new consideration. Also, promises made in exchange for "love and affection" are not enforceable because this does not constitute valuable consideration.

promissory estoppel—
an exception to the rules of consideration under which a promise that induces another person to act can be enforceable without consideration if the promisee substantially and justifiably relies on that promise.

One important exception to the requirement for valuable consideration is **promissory estoppel.** Under this rule, a promise that induces another party to act can be enforceable *without consideration* if the promisee substantially and justifiably relies on the promise. Suppose, for example, that Singleton promises to sell a franchise to Barlow if Barlow purchases a tract of land in a nearby town. Barlow sells some of her personal assets to purchase the land, but Singleton refuses to grant her the franchise. If Barlow sues Singleton on the basis of promissory estoppel, she would be awarded damages even though she gave Singleton no consideration. Thus, promissory estoppel is a substitute for consideration.

In most cases, courts do not evaluate the adequacy of consideration given for a promise. In other words, there is no legal requirement that the consideration the parties exchange be of approximately equal value. Even if the value of the consideration one party gives is small compared with the value of the bargain to the other party, the bargain stands. Why? The law recognizes that people have the freedom to contract and that they are just as free to enter into "bad bargains" as they to enter into "good" ones. Only in extreme cases (e.g., mistakes, fraud, duress, undue influence) will the court examine the value of the consideration provided in a trade.

CONTRACTUAL CAPACITY. The third element of a valid contract requires that the parties involved in it must have contractual capacity for it to be enforceable. Not every individual who enters into a contract has the capacity to do so. Under the common law, minors, intoxicated people, and insane people lack contractual capacity. As a result, contracts these people enter into are considered to be voidable—that is, the party can annul or disaffirm the contract at his option.

Minors. Minors constitute the largest group of individuals without contractual capacity. In most states, anyone under age 18 is a minor, although a few states establish 21 as the age of majority. With a few exceptions, any contract made by a minor is voidable *at the minor's option*. In addition, a minor can avoid a contract during minority and for "a reasonable time" afterwards. The adult involved in the contract *cannot* avoid it simply because he is dealing with a minor.

If a minor receives the benefit of a completed contract and then disaffirms that contract, she must fulfill her *duty of restoration* by returning the benefit. In other words, the minor must return any consideration she has received under the contract to the adult, and she is entitled to receive any consideration she gave the adult under the contract. The minor must return the benefit of the contract no matter what form or condition it is in. For instance, suppose that Brighton, a 16-year-old minor purchases a mountain bike for $415 from Cycle Time, a small bicycle shop. After riding the bike for a little more than a year, Brighton decides to disaffirm the contract. Under the law, all he must do is return the mountain bike to Cycle Time, whatever condition it is in (pristine, used, wrecked, or rubble), and he is entitled to get *all* of his money back. In most states, he does not have to pay Cycle Time for the use of the bike or the damage done to it. Adults enter into contracts with minors at their own risk.

Parents are usually not liable for any contracts made by their children, although a cosigner is bound equally with the minor. The small business owner can protect himself in dealing with minors by requiring an adult to cosign. If the minor disaffirms the contract, the cosigner remains bound by it.

Intoxicated People. A contract entered into by an intoxicated person can be either voidable or valid, depending on the person's condition when entering into the contract. If reason and judgment are impaired so that the person does not realize a contract is being made, the contract is voidable (even if the intoxication was voluntary) and the benefit must be returned. However, if the intoxicated person understands that a contract is being made, although it may be foolish, the contract is valid and enforceable.

Insane People. A contract entered into by an insane person can be void, voidable, or valid, depending on the mental state of the person. Those who have been judged to be so mentally incompetent that a guardian is appointed for them cannot enter into a valid contract. If such a person does make a contract, it is void (i.e., it does not exist). An insane person who has not been legally declared insane nor appointed a guardian (e.g., someone suffering from Alzheimer's disease) is bound by a contract if he was lucid enough at the time of the contract to comprehend its consequences. On the other hand, if, at the time of entering the contract, that same person was so mentally incompetent that he could not realize what was happening or could not understand the terms, the contract is voidable. Like a minor, he must return any benefit received under the contract.

LEGALITY. The final element required for a valid contract is legality. Because society imposes certain standards of conduct on its members, contracts that are illegal (criminal or tortuous) or against public policy are void. If an illegal contract has not been completed, the injured party cannot obtain performance or damages through the courts. If the illegal contract has been executed, neither party can sue to have it rescinded.

If a contract contains both legal and illegal elements, the courts will enforce the legal parts as long as they can separate the legal portion from the illegal portion. However, in some contracts, certain clauses are so unconscionable that the courts will not enforce them. Usually, the courts do not concern themselves with the fairness and equity of a contract between parties because individuals are supposed to be intelligent. But in the case of unconscionable contracts, the terms are so harsh and oppressive to one party that the courts often rule the clause to be void. These clauses, called exculpatory clauses, frequently attempt to free one party of all responsibility and liability for an injury or damage that might occur.

Genuineness of Assent and the Form of Contracts

A contract that contains the four elements just discussed—agreement, consideration, capacity, and legality—is valid, but a valid contract may still be unenforceable because of two possible defenses against it: genuineness of assent and form. Genuineness of assent serves as a check on the parties' agreement, verifying that it is genuine and not subject to mistakes, misrepresentation, fraud, duress, or undue influence. The existence of a contract can be

---

YOU BE THE CONSULTANT...

"A Peach of a Deal"

As soon as Kyle Pannabecker saw the 1993 Ford Mustang on the lot at Anson's Auto World, he knew it was the car for him. Its sleek profile, flowing lines, and powerful look radiated through the deep, rich, black clearcoat finish. "Man, I have got to have *that* car," he thought to himself. "The only things it needs is a pair of fuzzy dice hanging from the rear view mirror and me sitting behind the wheel." Remembering what his Dad had told him about car shopping, Kyle tried to stifle his enthusiasm. "Dad said to never let them know how much you want the car," he reminded himself. "Otherwise, you lose all of your bargaining power." This was Kyle's first major purchase on his own, and he wanted to do it right. He was just 17, but he asked his dad to let him buy a car all by himself.

As he stood there kicking a tire on the Mustang, Ron Anson, owner of the small car dealership, approached him. "She's a real beauty, isn't she?" asked Anson.

"It's an OK car, I guess," said Kyle, trying his best to keep his true feelings for the car from bubbling to the surface. "I can see a few scratches in the paint."

"'An OK car?!? said Anson. "Man, this is the best buy on the *entire* lot. It's a peach of a deal. You obviously know cars because you came to this one first."

"Well," said Kyle forgetting his disinterested attitude for a moment, "cars are a hobby of mine and I do read about them a lot." Then, slipping back into his serious car-buyer role, Kyle said, "How much would you take for this car, taking into consideration that it is a high-mileage vehicle?"

"Well," said Anson, rubbing his chin, "I'm asking $14,000 for it, but I'll take $13,500. After all, this car has had only one owner, and she bought it from me new. She had all of the maintenance done here, so I know she took good care of it. Do you want a test drive?"

"Sure," said Kyle.

After the test drive, Kyle and Anson sat down in Anson's office to negotiate a deal. Kyle was proud when he finally talked Anson down to $12,700, including tax. They signed a contract, and soon Kyle was driving off in his new Mustang.

Three weeks later, Kyle was in a wreck, and although he sustained only minor injuries, the car wasn't so lucky. It was damaged so severely that it was a complete loss. Kyle filed an insurance claim and collected $12,250 from his insurance company.

Then, he returned to Anson's Auto World, dropped the wrecked car on the lot, and demanded that Anson return the full purchase price of $12,700! Anson couldn't believe what he was hearing. "You think I'm going to give you your money back for that wrecked pile of junk?!" he asked Kyle. "You *are* crazy!"

"No sir," Kyle said. "I'm not crazy, but I am a minor—just 17 years old—and I'm disaffirming this contract."

"Disaffirm *this*!" Anson said, slamming the door in Kyle's face.

Kyle left the lot and went to see his family's attorney. Later that afternoon, Anson phoned his attorney to find out just what Kyle was talking about. "What nerve . . ." he muttered as his attorney picked up the line.

1. What will Anson's attorney tell him?

2. What should Anson have done to avoid this legal entanglement?

3. If they turned out to be false, could any of the claims Anson made in his sales pitch become the basis for a claim of fraud? Explain.

---

affected by mistakes that one or both parties to the contract make. Different types of mistakes exist, but only mistakes of *fact* permit a contract to be voided. Suppose that a small contractor submits a bid on the construction of a bridge, but the bidder mistakenly omits the cost of some materials. The client accepts the contractor's bid because it is $12,000 below all others. If the client knew or should have known of the mistake, the contractor can avoid the contract; otherwise, he must build the bridge at the bid price.

Fraud also voids a contract because no genuineness of assent exists. **Fraud** is the intentional misrepresentation of a material fact, justifiably relied on, that results in injury to the innocent party. The misrepresentation with the intent to deceive can result from words or conduct. Suppose a small retailer purchases a new security system from a dealer who promises it will provide 20 years of reliable service and lower the cost of operation by 40 percent. The dealer knowingly installs a used, unreliable system. In this case, the retailer can either rescind the contract with his original position restored or enforce it and seek damages for injuries.

Duress, forcing an individual into a contract by fear or threat, eliminates genuineness of assent. The innocent party can choose to carry out the contract or to avoid it. For example, if a supplier forces the owner of a small video arcade to enter a contract to lease his machines by threat of personal injury, the supplier is guilty of duress. Blackmail and extortion used to induce another party into a contract also constitute duress.

Generally, the law does not require contracts to follow a prescribed form; a contract is valid whether it is written or oral. Most contracts do *not* have to be in writing to be enforceable, but for convenience and protection, a small business owner should insist that every contract be in writing. If a contract is oral, the party attempting to enforce it must first prove its existence and then establish its actual terms. Although each state has its own set of statutes, the law requires the following contracts to be in writing:

- ☆ Contracts for the sale of land.
- ☆ Contracts involving lesser interests in land (e.g., rights-of-way or leases lasting more than one year).
- ☆ Contracts that cannot by their terms be performed within one year.
- ☆ Collateral contracts such as promises to answer for the debt or duty of another.
- ☆ Promises by the administrator or executor of an estate to pay a debt of the estate personally.
- ☆ Contracts for the sale of *goods* (as opposed to services) priced above $500.

Breach of Contract

The majority of contracts are discharged by full performance of their terms. Occasionally, however, one party fails to perform as agreed. This failure is called breach of contract, and the injured party has certain remedies available. Generally, the nonbreaching party is entitled to sue for compensatory damages, the monetary damages that will place him in the same position he would have been in had the contract been performed.

In addition to compensatory damages, the nonbreaching party may also be awarded consequential damages (also called special damages) that arise as a consequence of the breach. For the nonbreaching party to recover consequential damages, the breaching party must have known the consequences of the breach. Suppose a fireworks manufacturer fails to deliver a shipment of merchandise by June 30 in anticipation of the busy July 4 holiday celebration. The retailer can sue for the profits lost because of the late delivery since the manufacturer could have foreseen the damages late delivery would cause. Of course, the injured party has the duty to mitigate the damages incurred. In other words, the nonbreaching party must make a reasonable effort to minimize the damages incurred by the breach.

fraud—*the intentional misrepresentation of a material fact, justifiably relied on, that results in injury to the innocent party.*

duress—*the act of forcing an individual into a contract by fear or threat.*

In some cases, monetary damages are inadequate to compensate the injured party for the breach of contract. The only remedy that would compensate the nonbreaching party might be specific performance of the act promised in the contract. Specific performance is usually the remedy for breached contracts dealing with unique items (antiques, land, animals). For example, if an antique auto dealer enters a contract to purchase a Dusenberg and the other party breaches the contract, the dealer may sue for specific performance. That is, she may ask the court to order the breaching party to sell the antique car. Courts rarely invoke the remedy of specific performance. Generally, contracts for performance of personal services are not subject to specific performance.

5. *Outline* the major components of the portion of the Uniform Commercial Code governing sales contracts.

Business Law—The Uniform Commercial Code (UCC)

In the 1950s, a group of legal scholars compiled the **Uniform Commercial Code** (or the UCC or the Code) to replace the hodge-podge collection of confusing, often conflicting state laws that governed basic commercial transactions with a document designed to provide uniformity and consistency. The UCC replaced numerous statutes governing trade when each of the states adopted it. The Code does not alter the basic tenets of business law established by the common law; instead, it unites and modernizes them into a single body of law. In some cases, however, the Code changes some of the specific rules under the common law. The Code consists of ten articles:

The Uniform Commercial Code (UCC)—*a unified body of law governing routine business transactions such as sales contracts, bank deposits, letters of credit, documents of title, and investment securities.*

1. General Provisions
2. Sales
3. Negotiable Instruments
4. Bank Deposits and Collections
5. Letters of Credit
6. Bulk Transfers
7. Documents of Title—Warehouse Receipts, Bills of Lading, and Others
8. Investment Securities
9. Secured Transactions
10. Effective Date and Repealer

This section covers some of the general principles relating to sales (UCC Article 2), but the small business owner should also become familiar with the basics of the other parts of the Code. The UCC creates a "caste system" of merchants and nonmerchants and requires merchants to have a higher degree of knowledge and understanding of the Code.

Sales and Sales Contracts

Every sales contract is subject to the basic principles of law that govern all contracts—agreement, consideration, capacity, and legality. But when a contract involves the sale of goods, the UCC imposes rules that may vary slightly or substantially from basic contract law. Article 2 governs *only* the sale of *goods*. To be considered "goods," an item must be tangible and moveable (e.g., not real estate), and a "sale" is "the passing of title from the seller to the buyer for a price" (UCC Sec. 2-106[1]). The UCC does *not* cover the sale of services, although certain "mixed transactions," such as the sale by a garage of car parts (goods) and repairs (a service) will fall under the Code's jurisdiction if the goods are the dominant element of the contract.

In addition to the rules it applies to the sale of goods in general, the Code imposes special standards of conduct in certain instances when merchants sell goods to one another.

Usually, a person is considered a professional **merchant** if he "deals in goods of the kind" involved in the contract and has special knowledge of the business or of the goods; employs a merchant agent to conduct a transaction for him; or holds himself out to be a merchant.

Although the UCC requires that the same elements outlined in common law be present in forming a sales contract, it relaxes many of the specific restrictions. For example, the UCC states that a contract exists even if one or more terms (price, delivery date, place of delivery, quantity) are omitted, as long as the parties intended to make a contract and there is a reasonably certain method for the court to supply the missing terms. For example, suppose a manufacturer orders a shipment of needed raw materials from her usual supplier without asking the price. When the order arrives, the price is substantially higher than she expected, and she attempts to disaffirm the contract. The Code verifies the existence of a contract and assigns to the shipment a price that was reasonable at the time of delivery.

Common law requires the acceptance of an offer to be exactly the same as the offer; and acceptance that adds some slight modification is no acceptance at all, and no contract exists. Any modification constitutes a counteroffer. But the UCC states that as long as an offeree's response indicates a sincere willingness to accept the offer, it is judged as a legitimate acceptance even though varying terms are added. In dealings between buyers and sellers, these added terms become "proposals for addition." Between merchants, however, these additional proposals automatically become part of the contract unless they materially alter the original contract, the offer expressly states that no terms other than those in the offer will be accepted, or the offeror has already objected to the particular terms. Unless the offeror objects to the added terms, they *will* become part of the contract. For example, suppose an appliance wholesaler offers to sell a retailer a shipment of appliances for $5,000 plus freight. The retailer responds with an acceptance but adds "Price is $5,100 including freight." A contract exists, and the addition will become part of the contract unless the wholesaler objects within a reasonable time. If the wholesaler objects, a contract still exists, but it is formed on the wholesaler's original terms of $5,000 plus freight.

The UCC significantly changes the common law requirement that any contract modification requires new consideration. Under the Code, modifications to contract terms are binding *without* new consideration if they are made in good faith. For example, suppose a small paint contractor contracts to paint a house for $500. After the agreement, the price of the paint doubles, and the contractor notifies the client of the need to charge $800. The client agrees to the additional cost but later refuses to pay. According the UCC, the client is bound by the modification because no new consideration is required.

The Code also has its own Statute of Frauds provision relating to the form of contracts for the sale of goods. If the price of the goods is $500 or more, the contract must be written to be enforceable. Of course, the parties can agree orally and then follow it with a written memorandum. The Code does not require both parties to sign the written agreement, but it must be signed by the party against whom enforcement is sought (which is impossible to tell *before* a dispute arises, so it's a good idea for both parties to sign the agreement).

Once the parties create a sales contract, they are bound to perform according to its terms. Both the buyer and the seller have certain duties and obligations under the contract. Generally, the Code assigns the obligations of "good faith" (defined as "honesty in fact in the conduct or transaction concerned") and "commercial reasonableness" (commercial standards of fair dealing) to both parties.

The seller must make delivery of the items involved in the contract, but "delivery" is not necessarily physical delivery. The seller simply must make the goods available to the buyer. The contract normally outlines the specific details of the delivery, but occasionally the parties omit this provision. In this instance, the place of delivery will be the seller's place of business, if one exists; otherwise, it is the seller's residence. If both parties know the usual location of the identified goods, that is the place of delivery (e.g., a warehouse). In addition,

merchant—one who deals in goods of the kind involved in the contract and has special knowledge of the business or of the goods; employs a merchant agent to conduct a transaction for him; or holds himself out to be a merchant.

the seller must make the goods available to the buyer at a reasonable time and in a reasonable manner, and the buyer must give the seller proper notice of the goods' availability. Unless otherwise noted, all goods covered in the contract must be tendered in one delivery.

The buyer must accept the delivery of conforming goods from the buyer. Of course, the buyer has the right to inspect the goods in a reasonable manner and at any reasonable time or place to ensure that they are conforming goods before making payment. However, C.O.D. terms prohibit the right to advance inspection unless the contract specifies otherwise. Under the perfect tender rule in Section 2-601 of the Code, "if goods or tender of delivery fail, in any respect, to conform to the contract," the buyer is not required to accept them.

The buyer can indicate his acceptance of the goods in several ways. Usually the buyer indicates acceptance by an express statement that the goods are suitable. This expression can be by words or by conduct. For example, suppose a small electrical contractor orders a truck to use in the business. When she receives it, she equips it to suit her trade, including a company decal on each door. Later the contractor attempts to reject the truck and return it. Clearly, the buyer has acted inconsistently with continued ownership by the seller, and this constitutes acceptance of the truck. Also, the Code assumes acceptance if the buyer has a reasonable opportunity to inspect the goods and has failed to reject them within a reasonable time.

The buyer has the duty to pay for the goods on the terms stated in the contract when they are received. The seller cannot require payment before the buyer receives the goods. Unless otherwise stated in the contract, payment must be in cash.

Breach of Sales Contract

When a party to the sales contract fails to perform according to its terms, that party is said to have breached the contract. The law provides the innocent (nonbreaching) party numerous remedies, including payment for damages and the right to retain possession of the goods. The object of these remedies is to place the innocent party in the same position as if the contract had been carried out. The parties to the contract may specify their own damages in case of breach. These provisions, called **liquidated damages,** must be reasonable and cannot be in the nature of a penalty. For example, suppose that Alana Mitchell contracts with a local carpenter to build a booth from which she plans to sell crafts. The parties agree that if the booth is not completed by September 1, Mitchell will receive $500. If the liquidated damages had been $50,000, they would be unenforceable because such a large amount of money is clearly a penalty.

An unpaid seller has certain remedies available under the terms of the Code. Under a seller's lien, every seller has the right to maintain possession of the goods until the buyer pays for them. In addition, if the buyer uses a fraudulent payment to obtain the goods, the seller has the right to recover them. If the seller discovers the buyer is insolvent, the seller can withhold delivery of the goods until the buyer pays in cash. If goods are shipped to an insolvent buyer, the seller can require their return within ten days after receipt. In some cases, the buyer breaches a contract while the goods are still unfinished in the production process. When this occurs, the seller must use "reasonable commercial judgment" in deciding whether to sell them for scrap or complete them and resell them elsewhere. In either case, the buyer is liable for any loss the seller incurs. Of course, the seller has the right to withhold performance when the buyer breaches the sales contract.

When the seller breaches a contract, the buyer also has specific remedies available. For instance, if the goods do not conform to the contract's terms, the buyer has the right to reject them. Or, if the seller fails to deliver the goods, the buyer can sue for the difference between the contract price and the market price at the time the breach became known. When the buyer accepts goods and then discovers they are defective or nonconforming, he must notify the seller of the breach. In this instance, damages amount to the difference between

liquidated damages— damages a party to a contract receives from a breaching party to put the innocent party in the same position as if the contract had been carried out.

the value of the goods delivered and their value if they had been delivered as promised. If a buyer pays for goods that the seller retains, he can have the goods if the seller becomes insolvent within ten days after receiving the first payment. If the seller unlawfully withholds the goods from the buyer, the buyer can use the legal action of replevin to recover them. Under certain circumstances, a buyer can obtain specific performance of a sales contract; that is, the court orders the seller to perform according to the contract's terms. As mentioned earlier, specific performance is a remedy only when the goods involved are unique or unavailable on the market. Finally, if the seller breaches the contract, the buyer has the right to rescind the contract; if the buyer has paid any part of the purchase price, it must be refunded.

Whenever a party breaches a sales contract, the innocent party must bring suit within a specified period of time. The Code sets the statute of limitations at four years. In other words, any action for a breach of a sales contract must begin within four years after the breach occurred.

Sales Warranties and Product Liability

The U.S. economy once promulgated the philosophy of caveat emptor—"let the buyer beware"—but today the marketplace enforces a policy of caveat venditor—"let the seller beware." The small business owner must be aware of two general categories involving the quality and reliability of the products sold: sales warranties and product liability.

SALES WARRANTIES. Simply stated, a **sales warranty** is a promise or a statement of fact by the seller that a product will meet certain standards. Because a breach of warranty is a breach of promise, the buyer has the right to recover damages from the seller. Several different types of warranties can arise in a sale. A seller creates an **express warranty** by making statements about the condition, quality, and performance of the good that the buyer substantially relies on. Express warranties can be created by words or actions. For example, a vendor selling a shipment of cloth to a customer with the promise that "it will not shrink" clearly is creating an express warranty. Similarly, the jeweler who displays a watch in a glass of water for promotional purposes creates an express warranty that "this watch is waterproof" even though no such promise is ever spoken. Generally, an express warranty arises if the seller indicates that the goods conform to any promises of fact the seller makes, to any description of them (e.g., printed on the package or statements of fact made by salespersons), or to any display model or sample (e.g., a floor model used as a demonstrator).

Whenever a seller makes a sale of goods, she automatically implies certain warranties unless she specifically excludes them. These implied warranties take several forms. Every seller, simply by offering goods for sale, implies a **warranty of title**, which promises that his title is good (i.e., no liens or claims exist) and that transfer of title is legitimate. A seller can disclaim a warranty of title only by using very specific language in a sales contract.

An implied warranty of merchantability applies to every merchant seller, and the only way to disclaim it is by mentioning the *term warranty of merchantability* in a conspicuous manner. A **warranty of merchantability** assures the buyer that the product will be of average quality—not the best and not the worst. In other words, merchantable goods are "fit for the ordinary purposes for which such goods are used" (UCC Sec. 2-314[1-C]). For example, a refrigeration unit purchased by a small food store should keep food cold.

An implied **warranty of fitness for a particular purpose** arises when a seller knows the particular reason for which a buyer is purchasing a product and knows that the buyer is depending on the seller's judgment to select the proper item. For example, suppose a customer enters a small hardware store requesting a chemical to kill poison ivy. The owner hands over a gallon of chemical, but it fails to kill the weed; the owner has violated the warranty of fitness for a particular purpose.

sales warranty—a promise or a statement of fact by the seller of a product that will meet certain standards.

express warranty—a warranty created when a seller makes statements about the condition, quality, and performance of a good that the buyer substantially relies on.

warranty of title—a warranty offered by a seller that promises the title to an item is good.

warranty of merchantability—a warranty offered by a seller that assures the buyer that the product will be of average quality—not the best and not the worst.

warranty of fitness for a particular purpose—a warranty a seller offers when he knows the particular reason a buyer is buying a product and knows that the buyer is depending on the seller's judgment to select the proper item.

The Code also states that the only way a merchant can disclaim an implied warranty is to include the words "as is" or "with all faults," stating that the buyer purchases the product as it is, without any guarantees. The following statement is usually sufficient to disclaim most warranties, both express and implied: *Seller hereby disclaims all warranties, express and implied, including all warranties of merchantability and all warranties of fitness for a particular purpose.* Such statements must be printed in bold letters and placed in a conspicuous place on the product or its package.

PRODUCT LIABILITY. At one time, only the parties directly involved in the execution of a contract were bound by the law of sales warranties. Today, the UCC and the states have expanded the scope of warranties to include any person (including bystanders) incurring personal or property damages caused by a faulty product. In addition, most states allow an injured party to sue any seller in the chain of distribution for breach of warranty. Courts have awarded billions of dollars to consumers who incur loss of injury from products that break, are improperly designed, are improperly inspected, are incorrectly labeled, contain faulty instructions, or have other dangerous faults. More than 40,000 product lawsuits are filed in federal and state courts in the United States annually.[26] Figure 15.2 shows the trend in the number of product liability suits filed in federal courts. A recent survey by the National Federation of Independent Businesses found that 25 percent of small companies had been involved in or threatened by a product liability lawsuit within the past five years.[27] The costs of these lawsuits and the insurance to protect against them add significantly to the prices of some products and services. For instance, liability costs account for 20 percent of the cost of a stepladder, 50 percent of the cost of a football helmet, 40 percent of the cost of diphtheria vaccine, and one-third of a doctors' fee for a tonsillectomy.[28] In product liability cases, awards exceeding $1 million are commonplace.

Fortunately for businesses, less than 5 percent of product-related injuries result in some type of claim for compensation.[29] A common basis of recovery for those who do file claims

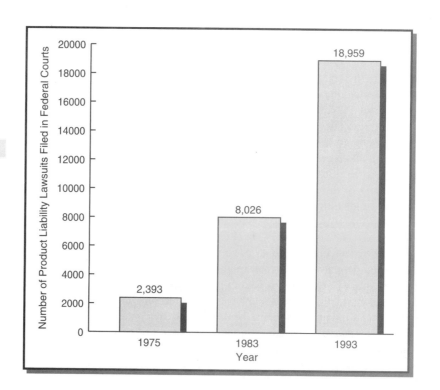

Figure 15.2
Product Liability Lawsuits (Number of Suits Filed in Federal Courts

Source: Paula Mergerhagen, "Product Liability," *American Demographics*, June 1995, pp. 26–34.

is **negligence**, when a manufacturer or distributor fails to do something that a "reasonable" person would do. Typically, negligence claims arise from one or more of the following charges:[30]

☆ *Negligent design.* A buyer claims an injury occurred because the manufacturer designed the product improperly. To avoid liability charges, a company does not have to design products that are 100 percent safe, but it must design products that are free of "unreasonable" risks.

☆ *Negligent manufacture.* A buyer claims that a company's failure to follow proper manufacturing, assembly, or inspection procedures allowed a defective product to get into the customer's hands and cause injury. A company must exercise "due care" (including design, assembly, and inspection) to make its products safe when they are used for their intended purpose.

☆ *Failure to warn.* Although manufacturers do not have to warn customers about obvious dangers of using their products, they must warn them about the dangers of normal use and of foreseeable misuse of the product. (Have you ever read the warning label on a stepladder?) Many businesses hire attorneys to write the warning labels they attach to their products and include in their instructions.

John Hatfield, president of Archbold Ladder, says that his $6.5 million company has faced 63 product liability lawsuits related to ladder accidents involving customers over the past 20 years. The company has lost only one case but has spent more than $2 million defending itself in court. A court found the 96-year-old ladder manufacturer liable for negligence when an elderly woman fell from one of its ladders and was injured, and ordered Archbold to pay damages of $160,000.[31]

Another common basis for product liability claims against businesses is **strict liability**, which states that a manufacturer is liable for its actions no matter what its intentions or the extent of its negligence. Unlike negligence, a claim of strict liability does not require the injured party to prove that the company's actions were unreasonable. The injured person must prove only that the company manufactured or sold a product that was defective and that it caused the injury. For instance, suppose the head of an ax flies off its handle, injuring the user. To sue the manufacturer under strict liability, the customer must prove that the defendant sold the ax in a defective condition, the defendant is normally engaged in the business of selling axes, the ax was unreasonably dangerous to the customer because it was defective, the customer incurred physical harm to a person or to property, and the defective ax was the proximate cause of the injury or damage. If these allegations are true, the ax manufacturer's liability is virtually unlimited.[32]

Business Law—The Law of Agency

An **agent** is one who stands in the place of and represents another in business dealings. Although he has the power to act for the principal, an agent remains subject to the principal's control. Many small business managers do not realize that their employees are agents while performing job-related tasks. But the employer is liable only for those acts that employees perform within the scope of employment. For example, if an employee loses control of a flower shop's delivery truck while making a delivery and crashes into several parked cars, the owner of the flower shop (the principal) and the employee (the agent) are liable for any damages caused by the crash. Even if the accident occurred while the employee was on a small detour of his own (e.g., to stop by his house), the owner is still liable for damages as long as the employee is "within the scope of employment." Normally, an employee is considered to be within the scope of his employment if he is motivated in part by the principal's action and if the place and time for performing the act is not significantly different from what is authorized.

negligence—*a basis for a product liability claim based on a manufacturer's failure to do something that a "reasonable" person would do.*

Archbold Ladder

strict liability—*a basis for a product liability claim that holds a manufacturer liable for its actions no matter what its intentions or the extent of its negligence.*

6. Explain the workings of the law of agency.

agent—*one who stands in the place of and represents another in business dealings.*

Any person, even those lacking contractual capacity, can serve as an agent, but a principal must have the legal capacity to create contracts. Both the principal and the agent are bound by the requirements of a fiduciary relationship—one characterized by trust and good faith. In addition, each party has specific duties to the other. An agent's duties include the following:

- ☆ *Loyalty.* Every agent must be faithful to the principal in all business dealings.
- ☆ *Performance.* An agent must perform his duties according to the principal's instructions.
- ☆ *Notification.* The agent must notify the principal of all facts concerning the subject matter of the agency.
- ☆ *Duty of care.* An agent must act with reasonable care when performing duties for the principal.
- ☆ *Accounting.* An agent is responsible for accounting for all profits and property received or distributed on the principal's behalf.

A principal's duties include the following:

- ☆ *Compensation.* Unless a free agency is created, the principal must pay the agent for her services.
- ☆ *Reimbursement.* The principal must reimburse the agent for all payments made for the principal or any expenses incurred in the administration of the agency.
- ☆ *Cooperation.* Every principal has the duty to cooperate with and assist the agent in carrying out his duties.
- ☆ *Indemnification.* A principal has the duty to indemnify the agent for any authorized payments or any loss or damages incurred by the agency, unless the liability is the result of the agent's mistake.
- ☆ *Safe working conditions.* The law requires a principal to provide a safe working environment for all agents. Workers' compensation laws cover an employer's liability for injuries agents receive on the job.

As agents, employees can bind a company to agreements, even if the owner did not intend for them to do so. An employee can create a binding obligation, for instance, if the business owner represents her as authorized to perform such transactions. As an example, the owner of a flower shop who routinely permits a clerk to place orders with suppliers has given that employee apparent authority for purchasing. Similarly, employees have implied authority to create agreements when performing the normal duties of their jobs. For example, the chief financial officer of a company has the authority to create binding agreements when dealing with the company's bank.

When an agent achieves the specific purpose of the agency, the agency ends, and the principal no longer binds the agent. For example, if the agent's task is to purchase a supply of pork bellies, the agency terminates when the agent completes the transaction. In addition, the two parties can limit the existence of the agency, or they can cancel the agency by mutual agreement. If either the principal or the agent dies or becomes mentally incompetent, the agency terminates immediately. Only when the two parties have terminated the agency themselves must the principal notify any third parties who might know of the agency relationship.

7. Explain the basics of bankruptcy law.

Business Law—Bankruptcy

Bankruptcy occurs when a business is unable to pay its debts as they come due. Early bankruptcy laws were aimed at forcing debtors into court, where they were required to give their property to their creditors. This prevented the debtors from hiding assets from creditors and escaping repayment of debts. But in 1978 Congress passed the Bankruptcy Reform Act, drastically changing the nature of bankruptcy law. The law has removed much of the stigma from being bankrupt; in fact, a bankrupt person is now called a debtor.

Forms of Bankruptcy

Filing for bankruptcy was once akin to contracting a social disease. Today, however, as the number of bankruptcies steadily climbs, it is becoming an accepted business strategy. Many of those filing for bankruptcy are small business owners seeking protection from creditors under one of the eight chapters of the Bankruptcy Reform Act of 1978. Under the act, three chapters (7, 11, and 13) govern the majority of bankruptcies related to small business ownership. Usually, the small business owner in danger of failing can choose from two types of bankruptcies: **liquidation** (once the owner files for bankruptcy, the business ceases to exist) and **reorganization** (after filing for bankruptcy, the owner formulates a reorganization plan under which the business continues to operate).

CHAPTER 7: LIQUIDATIONS. The most common type of bankruptcy is filed under Chapter 7 (called straight bankruptcy), which accounts for 70 percent of all filings. Under Chapter 7, a debtor simply declares all of his firm's debts; he must then turn over all assets to a trustee, who is elected by the creditors or appointed by the court. The trustee sells the assets and distributes all proceeds first to secured creditors and then to unsecured creditors (which include stockholders). Depending on the outcome of the asset sale, creditors can receive anywhere between 0 and 100 percent of their claims against the bankrupt company. Once the bankruptcy proceeding is complete, any remaining debts are discharged. The company disappears.

Straight bankruptcy proceedings can be started by filing either a voluntary or an involuntary petition. A voluntary case starts when the debtor files a petition with a bankruptcy court, stating the names and addresses of all creditors, the debtor's financial position, and all property the debtor owns. On the other hand, creditors start an involuntary case by filing a petition with the bankruptcy court. If there are 12 or more creditors, at least three of them whose unsecured claims total $10,000 or more must file the involuntary petition. If a debtor has fewer than 12 creditors, only one of them having a claim of $10,000 or more is required to file. As soon as a petition (voluntary or involuntary) is filed in a bankruptcy court, all creditors' claims against the debtor are suspended. In other words, no creditor can begin or continue to pursue debt collection once the petition is filed.

Not every piece of property the bankrupt debtor owns is subject to court attachment. According to the Code certain assets are exempt, although each state establishes its own exemptions. Most states make an allowance for equity in a home, interest in an automobile, interest in a large number of personal items and other personal assets. Federal law allows a $4,000 exemption for household items, and clothing, a $3,750 ($7,500 for a married couple) exemption for equity in a house, and a $400 exemption for other property.

The law does not allow a debtor to transfer the ownership of property to others to avoid its seizure in a bankruptcy. If a debtor transfers property within one year of the filing of a bankruptcy petition, the trustee can ignore the transfer and claim the assets. In addition, any transfer of property made for the express purpose of avoiding repayment of debts (called fraudulent conveyance) will be overturned. The new law also enables a judge to dismiss a Chapter 7 bankruptcy petition if it is a "substantial abuse" of the bankruptcy code.

CHAPTER 11: REORGANIZATION. For the small business weakened by a faltering economy or management mistakes, Chapter 11 provides a second chance for success. The philosophy behind this form of bankruptcy is that ailing companies can prosper again if given a fresh start with less debt. Under Chapter 11, a company is protected from creditors' legal actions while it formulates a plan for reorganization and debt repayment or settlement. In

bankruptcy—*occurs when a business is unable to pay its debts as they come due.*

liquidation—*a form of bankruptcy in which the company sells its assets to pay a portion of its debts and then ceases to exist.*

reorganization—*a form of bankruptcy in which a company develops a plan for paying a portion of its debts and then continues to operate.*

most cases, the small firm and its creditors negotiate a settlement in which the company repays its debts at a fraction on the dollar—in other words, the debtor agrees to repay a portion of his debts and is freed of the remainder. The business continues to operate under the court's direction, but creditors cannot foreclose on it, nor can they collect any prebankruptcy debts the company owes.

A Chapter 11 bankruptcy filing can be either voluntary or involuntary. Once the petition is filed, the debtor has 120 days to file a reorganizational plan with the court. Usually, the court does not replace management with an appointed trustee. If the debtor fails to file a plan within the 120-day limit, any party involved in the bankruptcy, including creditors, may propose a plan. The plan must identify the various classes of creditors and their claims, outline how each class will be treated, and establish a method to implement the plan. It also must spell out which debts cannot be paid, which can be paid, and what methods the debtor will use to repay them.

Once the plan is filed, the court must decide whether or not to approve it. A court will approve a plan if a majority of each of the three classes of creditors—secured, priority, and unsecured—votes in favor of it. The court will confirm the plan if it is reasonable and is submitted in good faith—if it is "in the best interest of the creditors."

Filing under Chapter 11 offers the weakened small business a number of advantages, the greatest of which is a chance to survive (although most of the companies that file under Chapter 11 ultimately are liquidated). In addition, employees keep their jobs, and customers get an uninterrupted supply of goods and services. But there are costs involved in bankruptcy proceedings. Customers, suppliers, creditors, and often employees lose confidence in the firm's ability to succeed. Creditors frequently incur substantial losses in Chapter 11 bankruptcies.

CHAPTER 13. Individual debtors (not businesses) with a regular income who owe unsecured debts of less than $250,000 or secured debts under $750,000 may file for bankruptcy under Chapter 13. Many proprietors who have the choice of filing under Chapters 11 or 13 find that Chapter 13 is less complicated and less expensive. Chapter 13 proceedings must begin voluntarily. Once the debtor files the petition, creditors cannot start or continue legal action to collect payment. Under Chapter 13, only the debtor can file a repayment plan, whose terms cannot exceed five years. If the court approves the plan, the debtor may pay off the obligations—either in full or partially—on an installment basis. The plan is designed with the debtor's future income in mind, and when the debtor completes the payments under the plan, all debts are discharged.

8. Describe the protection that patents, trademarks, and copyrights offer business owners.

patent—*a grant from the federal government to the inventor of a product, giving the exclusive right to make, use, or sell the invention in this country for 17 years.*

Business Law—Patents, Trademarks, and Copyrights

Patents

A **patent** is a grant from the federal government's Patent and Trademark Office (PTO) to the inventor of a product, giving the exclusive right to make, use, or sell the invention in this country for 17 years from the date on which the patent is granted. The purpose of giving an inventor a 17-year monopoly over a product is to stimulate creativity and innovation. After 17 years, the patent expires and cannot be renewed. Most patents are granted for new product inventions, but design patents, extending for 3.5, 7, or 14 years as the inventor chooses, are given to inventors who make new, original, and ornamental changes in design to products that enhance their sales. To be patented, a device must be new (but not necessarily better!) and not obvious to a person of ordinary skill or knowledge in the related field. A device *cannot* be patented if it has been publicized in print anywhere in the world or if it has been used or offered for sale in this country prior to the date of the patent application. A U.S. patent is granted only to the true inventor, not a person who discovers another's invention. No one can copy or sell a patented invention without getting a license from its creator. A patent does not give one the right to make, use, or sell an invention, but the right to exclude others from making, using, or selling it.

Although no inventor is assured of getting a patent, she can enhance her chances considerably by following the basic steps suggested by the PTO. Before beginning the often lengthy and involved procedure, the inventor should obtain professional assistance from a patent practitioner—a patent attorney or a patent agent—who is registered with the PTO. Only those attorneys and agents who are officially registered may represent an inventor seeking a patent. Approximately 98 percent of all inventors rely on these patent experts to steer them through the convoluted process.

THE PATENT PROCESS. Since George Washington signed the first patent law in 1790, the U.S. Patent and Trademark Office (PTO) has issued more than 5 million patents, and 150,000 new applications pour in each year. The PTO has issued patents on everything imaginable (and some unimaginable items, too), including mouse traps (of course!), animals (genetically engineered mice), games, and various fishing devices. To receive a patent, an inventor must follow these steps:

- ✮ *Establish the invention's novelty.* An invention is not patentable if it is known or has been used in the United States or has been described in a printed publication in this or a foreign country.

- ✮ *Document the device.* To protect his patent claim, an inventor should be able to verify the date he first conceived the idea for his invention. An inventor can document a device by keeping dated records (including drawings) of his progress on the invention and by having knowledgeable friends witness these records. Inventors also can file a disclosure document with the PTO—a process that includes writing a letter describing the invention and sending a check for $10 to the PTO.

- ✮ *Search existing patents.* To verify that the invention truly is new, nonobvious, and useful, an inventor must conduct a search of existing patents on similar products. The purpose of the search is to determine whether or not the inventor has a chance of getting a patent. Most inventors hire professionals trained in conducting patent searches to perform the research.

- ✮ *Study search results.* Once the patent search is finished, the inventor must study the results to determine his chances of getting a patent. To be patentable, a device must be sufficiently different from what has been used or described before and must not be obvious to a person having ordinary skill in the area of technology related to the invention.

- ✮ *Submit the patent application.* If an inventor decides to seek a patent, he must file an application describing the invention with the PTO. Most inventors hire patent attorneys or agents to help them complete their patent applications. Two useful resources available from the Superintendent of Documents in Washington, DC are the *Official Gazette of the United States Patent and Trademark Office* and the *Directory of Registered Patent Attorneys and Agents.*

- ✮ *Prosecute the patent application.* Before the PTO will issue a patent, one of its examiners studies the application to determine whether or not the invention warrants a patent. If the PTO rejects the application, the inventor can amend his application so that the PTO can accept it.

Trademarks

A **trademark** is any distinctive word, phrase, symbol, design, name, logo, slogan, or trade dress that a company uses to identify the origin of a product or to distinguish it from other goods on the market. (A **service mark** is the same as a trademark except that it identifies and distinguishes the source of a service rather than a product.) A trademark serves as a company's "signature" in the marketplace. There are 1.5 million trademarks registered in the United States, 900,000 of which are in actual use. Federal law permits a manufacturer

trademark—*any distinctive word, phrase, symbol, design, name, logo, slogan, or trade dress that a company uses to identify the origin of a product or to distinguish it from other goods on the market.*

service mark—*the same as a trademark except that it identifies and distinguishes the source of a service rather than a product.*

to register a trademark, which prevents other individuals from employing a similar mark to identify their goods. Before 1989, a business could not reserve a trademark in advance of use. Today, the first party who either uses a trademark in commerce or files an application with the PTO has the ultimate right to register that trademark.

Unlike patents and copyrights, which are issued for limited amounts of time, trademarks last indefinitely. However, a registered trademark cannot keep competitors from producing the same item or from selling it under a different trademark. It merely prevents other from using the same or confusingly similar trademark for the same or similar products. A recent change in trademark law even allows scents and smells to be registered as trademarks.

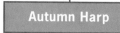

Autumn Harp

Andy Harper, founder of Autumn Harp, a small manufacturer of skin and lip care products, recently battled industry giant Unilever in a trademark dispute. Unilever, with global sales of $55 billion, owns the trademark for Vaseline Petroleum Jelly® and opposed Autumn Harp's attempt to register its Un-Petroleum Jelly® name as a trademark with the Canadian trademark office. Autumn Harp's product line is based on high-quality skin care products that contain no petrochemicals; similar products from Unilever and other manufacturers are petroleum-based derivatives. In the end, Autumn Harp, whose sales are just $10 million a year, won the legal battle and the right to register its trademark, a victory that Harper says will help his company sell its products in international markets. "This case was a threat to the heart and soul of our company," says Harper. "Our Un-Petroleum® name is what sets us apart in our industry. We . . . have been investing heavily in developing and marketing this brand for years."[33]

An owner may lose the exclusive right to a trademark if it loses its unique character and becomes a generic name. Aspirin, escalator, thermos, brassiere, super glue, yo-yo, and cellophane all were once enforceable trademarks that have become common words in the English language. Such generic terms can no longer be licensed as a company's trademark.

Copyrights

copyright—*an exclusive right that protects the creators of original works of authorship, such as literary, dramatic, musical, and artistic works.*

A **copyright** is an exclusive right that protects the creators of original works of authorship such as literary, dramatic, musical, and artistic works (choreography, sculptures, motion pictures, recordings). The internationally recognized symbol © denotes a copyrighted work. A copyright protects only the form in which an idea is expressed, not the idea itself. Copyright applications (Form TX) must be filed with the Copyright Office in the Library of Congress for a fee of $10 per application. A valid copyright on a work lasts for the life of the creator plus 50 years after her death. When a copyright expires, the work becomes public property and can be used by anyone free of charge.

CHAPTER SUMMARY

1. Define business ethics and explain how entrepreneurs can establish and maintain high ethical standards in their businesses.

- Business ethics involve the moral values and behavioral standards that businesspeople face as they make decisions and solve problems.
- Companies can establish high ethical standards by creating a company credo; developing a code of ethics; enforcing the code fairly and consistently; conducting ethical training; hiring the right people; performing periodic ethical audits; establishing high standards of behavior, not just rules; setting an impeccable ethical example at all times; creating a culture that emphasizes two-way

communication; and involving employees in setting ethical standards.

2. Define social responsibility and discuss some of the various stakeholders—the environment, employees, customers, investors, and the community—to whom businesses are responsible.

- Social responsibility is the awareness by a company's managers of the social, environmental, political, human, and financial consequences of their actions.
- Companies have a social responsibility to a variety of stakeholders, including the environment, employees (cultural diversity, drug testing, AIDS, sexual harass-

ment, and whistle-blowing), customers, investors, and the community.

3. Explain some of the government regulations affecting small businesses.

- Businesses operate under a multitude of government regulations governing many areas, including trade practices, where laws forbid restraint of trade, price discrimination, exclusive dealing and tying contracts, purchasing controlling interests in competitors, and interlocking directorates. Other areas subject to government regulations include consumer protection (the Food, Drug, and Cosmetics Act and the Consumer Product Safety Act) and consumer credit (the Consumer Credit Protection Act (CCPA), the Fair Debt Collection Practices Act, and the Fair Credit Reporting Act).

4. Explain the basic elements required to create a valid, enforceable contract.

- A valid contract must contain these elements: agreement (offer and acceptance), consideration, capacity, and legality. A contract can be valid and yet unenforceable because it fails to meet the two other conditions of genuineness of assent and proper form.

- Most contracts are fulfilled by both parties performing their promised actions; occasionally, however, one party fails to perform as agreed, thereby breaching the contract. Usually, the nonbreaching party is allowed to sue for monetary damages that would place her in the same position she would have been in had the contract been performed. In cases where money is an insufficient remedy, the injured party may sue for specific performance of the contract's terms.

5. Outline the major components of the portion of the Uniform Commercial Code governing sales contracts.

- The Uniform Commercial Code (UCC) was an attempt to create a unified body of law governing routine business transactions. Of the ten articles in the UCC, Article 2 on the sale of goods affects many business transactions.

- Contracts for the sale of goods must contain the same four elements of a valid contract, but the UCC relaxes many of the specific restrictions the common law imposes on contracts. Under the UCC, once the parties create a contract, they must perform their duties in good faith.

- The UCC also covers sales warranties. A seller creates an express warranty when he makes a statement about the performance of a product or indicates by example certain characteristics of the product. Sellers automatically create other warranties—warranties of title, implied warranties of merchantability, and, in certain cases, implied warranties of fitness for a particular purpose—when they sell a product.

6. Explain the workings of the law of agency.

- In an agency relationship, one party (the agent) agrees to represent another (the principal). The agent has the power to act for the principal but remains subject to the principal's control. While performing job-related tasks, employees play an agent's role.

- An agent has the following duties to a principal: loyalty, performance, notification, duty of care, and accounting. The principal has certain duties to the agent: compensation, reimbursement, cooperation, indemnification, and safe working conditions.

7. Explain the basics of bankruptcy law.

- Entrepreneurs whose businesses fail often have no other choice but to declare bankruptcy under one of three provisions: Chapter 7 liquidations, where the business sells its assets, pays what debts it can, and disappears; Chapter 11 reorganizations, where the business asks that its debts be forgiven or restructured and then reemerges; and Chapter 13, straight bankruptcy, which is for individuals only.

8. Describe the protection that patents, trademarks, and copyrights offer.

- A patent is a grant from the federal government that gives an inventor exclusive rights to an invention for 17 years. To submit a patent, an inventor must establish novelty, document the device, search existing patents, study the search results, submit a patent application to the U.S. Patent and Trademark Office, and prosecute the application.

- A trademark is any distinctive word, symbol, or trade dress that a company uses to identify its product or to distinguish it from other goods. It serves as the company's "signature" in the marketplace.

- A copyright protects original works of authorship. It covers only the form in which an idea is expressed and not the idea itself and lasts for 50 years beyond the creator's death.

DISCUSSION QUESTIONS

1. What are the business ethics? Summarize the three approaches to management ethics: immoral management, amoral management, and moral management.

2. In any organization, who determines ethical behavior? Is it possible for a business owner to earn a profit and run a business ethically? Explain.

3. What benefits can a business owner reap by running a company ethically?

4. What can business owners do to establish and maintain high ethical standards in their companies?

5. Describe business's social responsibility to each of the following areas: the environment, employees, customers, investors, the community.

6. What can business do to improve the quality of our environment?

7. What can a business owner do to manage a culturally diverse work force more effectively?

8. Should companies be allowed to test employees for drugs? Why or why not? What should be included in a socially responsible drug-testing program?

9. What elements should an effective drug policy contain?

10. What responsibilities does an employer have to an employee who has AIDS?

11. What is sexual harassment? Explain the three types of sexual harassment. What can a business owner do to combat harassment in the workplace?

12. What rights do customers have under the Consumer Bill of Rights? How can businesses ensure those rights?

13. Outline the major pieces of legislation regulating trade practices, consumer behavior, and consumer credit.

14. Explain the statement "For each benefit gained by regulation, there is a cost."

15. What is a contract? List and describe the four elements required for a valid contract. Must a contract be written to be enforceable?

16. What constitutes an agreement?

17. What groups of people lack contractual capacity? Are contracts entered into by minors always void? By intoxicated people? By insane people?

18. What circumstances eliminate genuineness of assent?

19. What is breach of contract? What remedies are available to a party injured by a breach?

20. What is the Uniform Commercial Code? How does it alter the requirements for a sales contract?

21. Under the UCC, what remedies does a seller have when a buyer breaches a sales contract? What remedies does a buyer have when a seller breaches a contract?

22. What is a sales warranty? Explain the types of warranties companies offer.

23. What is product liability? Explain the charges that most often form the basis for product liability claims. What must a customer prove under these charges?

24. What is an agent? What duties does an agent have to a principal? What duties does a principal have to an agent?

25. Explain the differences among the three major forms of bankruptcy: Chapter 7, Chapter 11, and Chapter 13.

26. Explain the differences between a patent, a trademark, and a copyright. What is each one designed to protect?

Beyond the Classroom....

1. Obtain copies of codes of ethics from several different companies or associations and compare them. What are the similarities and differences among them? Do you think these codes would be useful to an employee facing an ethical dilemma?

2. Contact several local business owners. How do they view their responsibility to society? Have they altered their management styles and their companies to reflect society's changing demands for socially responsible companies?

3. "Job safety and performance are more important than the slight invasion of privacy caused by drug testing," says one plant manager. Another, who refuses to test employees, claims, "Drug testing is an outright invasion of employee privacy." Conduct a debate in your class on these two positions.

4. Interview a local small business owner and ask him or her to show you the paperwork and reports he or she must prepare to comply with federal and state regulations of his or her business. How much of the owner's time does complying with these regulations require? Prepare a report on what you learn.

5. Visit a local attorney and ask about his or her experiences regarding the most typical legal problems small business owners must resolve to avoid legal problems.

1. Go to Herman Miller Inc.'s Research Summaries Web page at:

**http://www.hmiller.com/
RESEARCH/RESEARCHIDX.HTML**

a. Find the section entitled "Companies Go Green: Recycling and Waste Management." Using some of the statistics in the article, describe the environmental problems the United States and the world face. What can businesses and individuals do to solve the problems?

b. Find the section entitled "The Changing Work Force." Using some of the statistics in the article, describe the changing nature of our nation's work force. What are the implications of these changes for businesses? What strategies can companies use to manage the new work force more effectively?

2. Visit the home page of the American Psychological Association at:

http://www.apa.org/pubinfo/harass.html

Look under the heading "Information on psychology for the general public" for a page entitled "Sexual Harassment: Myths and Realities." Prepare a one-page report on what you find on this Web page. What steps should a victim of sexual harassment take?

3. Go to the home page for Collier and Associates, a Texas law firm, at:

http://rampages.onramp.net/~collier/index.htm

Can an entrepreneur copyright computer software? If so, how? What can the author of a work do to protect a copyright?

4. Using one of the search engines on the World Wide Web (WWW), find an example of a company that is successfully meeting its responsibility of protecting the environment. Describe the actions the company is taking.

5. Go to the web page for the Legal Information Institute at Cornell Law School at:

http://www.law.cornell.edu/topical.html

Select a legal topic of interest to you and research it. Prepare a one-page report on what you learn.

6. Go to the home page of the U.S. Patent and Trademark Office (PTO) at:

http://www.uspto.gov/

Select one the following topics—patents, trademarks, or copyrights—and prepare a summary of the protection it offers, the requirements for acquiring it, and the process entrepreneurs must follow to get it.

7. Using one of the search engines on the World Wide Web (WWW), conduct a search on *product liability*. Prepare a brief report on what you learn.

SEPTIC SENSE®

A Sample Business Plan

Developed By:

Karen Czuchry
Joseph Kirkpatrick
Michael Reynolds

Executive Summary

A. *Company Name, Address, and Phone Number:*

Septic Sense®
1000 Buckiner Drive
Bristol, Tennessee 37707
423-929-8000

B. *Key Personnel:*

Ms. Karen Czuchry
Mr. Joseph Kirkpatrick
Mr. Michael Reynolds

C. *Brief Description of the Business*

Septic Sense has developed a product that provides homeowners with an easy, simple, quick method for determining whether or not their septic tanks are full and thus require pumping. The Septic Sense device is new, innovative, and provides added value to the homeowner's septic system. Presently there is not a similar device on the market. A patent and trademark have been pursued on the Septic Sense device.

D. Brief Overview of the Market

One in four households in the United States uses septic tanks as a means for waste disposal. Regular maintenance of these residential sewage systems is essential to avoid possible groundwater contamination as well as problems with normal functioning of the septic tank. However, many homeowners neglect their septic systems. Authorities on the subject all conclude that when it comes to maintaining a septic tank, one of the worst mistakes a homeowner can make is to forget it's there. Maintenance of a septic tank involves regular inspection and/or inspecting the tank. Current inspection methods are involved, unpleasant, and in some cases, physically demanding. Consequently, many homeowners forgo inspection and hope that no problem will be encountered. The suggested emptying/pumping schedule is every two years. For some septic systems, pumping a septic tank every two years is too frequent and homeowners can incur unnecessary costs. Septic Sense is a device which determines the level of a septic tank, and indicates whether or not the tank requires pumping. Our initial market is septic tank manufactures and new septic tanks. There are 184 septic tank manufacturers across the United States and 17 septic tank manufacturers in Canada. An estimated 138,000 new septic tanks are installed per year across the United States.

E. Brief Overview of Strategic Actions

The Septic Sense device evolved after three design iterations. After the first two designs were aborted, the final design was pursued and verified to be successful. A prototype using the third design was manufactured and tested for proof of concept. All tests performed have verified the concept and operation of the prototype.

The founders of Septic Sense retained a patent attorney in Knoxville, Tennessee, to pursue a patent.

Septic Sense has manufactured 50 Septic Sense units for Bolton Concrete of Johnson City, Tennessee. Bolton Concrete agreed to purchase each Septic Sense unit for $195. The 50 units were manufactured and delivered in lots of ten. Total sales from this agreement were $9,750. These 50 units were used as a pilot study for the Septic Sense device.

Septic Sense obtained a profit of $100 on each device sold. This amount was based on initial market research, which indicated that septic tank manufacturers are willing to purchase this device for around $200. Exhibit 1 shows sales and net income forecasts for the company's first five years.

Septic Sense adds value to the septic system. Using Septic Sense avoids potential leaching fields and other septic system problems. Repairing a septic system can cost tens of thousands of dollars.[1]

Manufacturing will occur in three production phases. In phase 1, including a pilot study of 50 units, we will be using Bolton Concrete's facilities. For phase 2, Septic Sense will be moving to its own facilities and will be employing a process improvement plan. For phase 3, Septic Sense is going to expand to a larger facility.

F. Brief Description of the Managerial and Technical Experience of Key People

Management of Septic Sense will be handled by the original investors and an additional staff person. Karen Czuchry, who has five years experience in project management, will be president. Mike Reynolds, who has five years experience in aircraft systems and equipment, is a designated engineering representative (DER) for the FAA, and has technical expertise in level-sensing technology, will be the vice president of research and development. Joseph Kirkpatrick, who has expertise in the manufacturing area, will be vice presi-

Exhibit 1
*Septic Sense Sales
and Net Income*

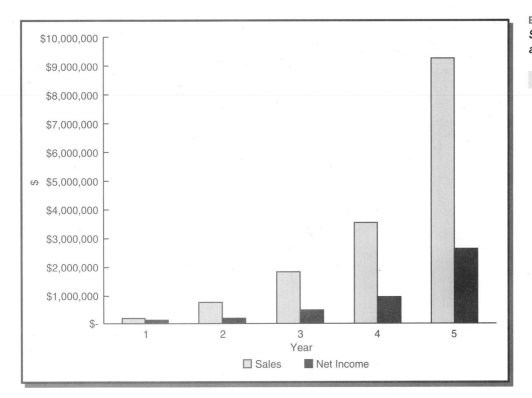

dent of operations and manufacturing. A recent business school graduate will be employed to assist in marketing and finance.

G. Brief Statement of the Financial Needs

Septic Sense will be initially funded by the three founders. Each founder will invest $2,000 for a total of $6,000. Our first sale of 50 Septic Sense units were manufactured and assembled by the founders. Manufacturing space, in phase 1, will be provided by Bolton Concrete. All other necessary capital funding will be generated within Septic Sense.

Detailed Business Plan

A. The Company and the Concept

Septic Sense provides a level-sensing device for septic tanks. The company's product trademark is Septic Sense. The Septic Sense device uses a new, innovative level-sensing technology to determine whether or not a septic tank is full. If the septic tank is full, the Septic Sense device indicates that the septic tank requires pumping.

The Septic Sense device went through three design iterations. First, capacitance technology was used. This technical approach did not produce the desired effect. The second design was to use a DC motor and attach to the motor a long metal spindle. This device measured the viscosity of the induced back EMF of the motor. After a safety review, this device was determined to be dangerous. The third design uses thermal technology. Proof of concept of this device has been performed. For further details on the final design, see "The Product" section on pages 531–532.

Septic Sense, the company, has the following vision, mission, goals, and values:

VISION:

Be a world-class leader in fluid/density-sensing technology for septic tanks.

MISSION:

To produce quality, reliable, environmentally conscious, customer-focused fluid/density-sensing technology for septic tanks.

GOALS:

Exceptional customer satisfaction
Quality, reliable products
Superior financial results
Inspired, innovative, and empowered employees
Implement continuous quality improvement for products and services

VALUES:

Customer first
Integrity in all we do
Respect for each other
Growth through innovation
Commitment to family

The primary customers of Septic Sense are septic tank manufacturers. There are 184 septic tank manufacturers across the United States and 17 septic tank manufacturers in Canada. Septic tank manufacturers usually supply septic tanks to a certain size market area surrounding their manufacturing facility. A local septic tank manufacturer, Bolton Concrete, Johnson City, Tennessee, sells and supplies septic tanks within approximately a 25-mile radius of Johnson City. The size of the septic tank manufacturer's market area is restricted due to the delivery cost of the septic tank. Furthermore, there is currently no barrier to entry into the septic tank manufacturing business. Small, home-based businesses can build septic tanks.

B. Potential Problems with Septic Tanks

Failing to pump the septic tank within the previously suggested guidelines will inevitably lead to serious problems with the proper functioning of the septic system. These problems range from backed-up lines to damaged or ruined leaching fields. Repairs of a septic system can cost tens of thousands of dollars.[2] The average cost of repairing a leaching field is $4 to $6 per square foot of field lines.

Experts agree that the most effective means for dealing with septic tank problems is to prevent them in the first place.[3] The recommended means of prevention is for homeowners to inspect their tanks regularly and have them pumped when necessary. Experts advise pumping or at least inspecting the septic tank every two years. The cost of pumping a tank can range anywhere from $150 to $300.

C. Level-Sensing Technology

Septic Sense, the device, was designed using a new level-sensing technology. This new level-sensing technology was developed by the founders of Septic Sense and provides a unique method for measuring the level of a septic tank. Other level-sensing technologies have proven limitations which prohibit their use in septic tanks. Specifically, float level-sensing devices can not be used in septic tanks because septic tanks are always full with water. Some level-sensing technologies are prone to fouling in a septic tank environment. Other level-sensing mechanisms are too cost prohibitive to be used in septic tanks. The Septic Sense device is both cost effective and operates successfully under the conditions of a septic tank environment. No similar device is presently on the market.

One in four households in the United States uses septic tanks as a means for waste disposal. Regular maintenance of backyard sewage systems is essential to avoid possible groundwater contamination and problems with the normal functioning of the septic tank. However, many homeowners neglect their septic systems. At this time, homeowners cannot easily, simply, and quickly determine whether or not their septic tanks must be pumped. To meet this need, the Septic Sense device was developed. This device determines the level of a septic tank and indicates whether or not the tank requires pumping.

D. Septic System Description and Pumping Requirements

A standard system is relatively simple and consists of: (1) a tank; (2) water feed lines (inlet and outlet); and (3) a leaching field. The septic tank is a box (concrete, plastic, metal, etc.) with two baffles, an inlet, and an outlet. Three different septic tank sizes are normally available: 800, 1,000, and 1,500 gallons. The tank is buried in the ground so the top is 18 to 24 inches below the surface. The inlet delivers the water to the tank and is positioned slightly higher than the outlet. The outlet transfers the outflow of the septic tank to the leaching field. In general, the leaching field consists of perforated pipe resting on gravel-filled beds. The gravel beds permit the water to drain into the underlying soil.

Together, the septic tank and leaching fields purify and decompose most of the household waste. However, some waste/sludge remains in the tank and accumulates over time. The sludge accumulates from the bottom of the tank. When the sludge reaches 12 inches from the outlet pipe, the septic tank must be pumped. A septic tank should also be pumped when the scum floating on top of the water in the tank reaches 3 inches from the outlet pipe.

E. The Product

Septic Sense is a device created in the fall of 1995 and designed to alleviate homeowners septic tank concerns/worries and to simplify the inspection process. The device indicates when a septic tank needs to be pumped. Septic Sense is a new, innovative, and unique product. A patent on the Septic Sense device is currently being pursued. In addition, the device has been sent to the National Sanitation Foundation (NSF) for Criteria C-9 certification.

The Septic Sense device is installed internal to the tank, with a remote indicator conveniently located for the homeowner's viewing. This device automatically monitors the septic tank's level on a monthly basis. An instant check can also be performed; a button permitting an immediate inspection of the tank's level is provided. The two indications used to signify when the tank requires pumping are an alarm/siren and a red light.

The Septic Sense system is a solid-state electronic device that uses convective heat-transfer characteristics to detect a transition of material (effluent). It consists of: (1) a probe, (2) circuitry, and (3) a display. The probe is composed of three temperature-sensing; 2-watt heaters. Two heaters are located above and below a reference heater. When the material the probe is immersed in is constant, all three heaters will heat to the same temperature. If effluent covers the upper, lower, or both temperature-sensing heaters, a delta temperature is created. The sensing circuit is composed of wein bridge-delta voltage circuit where the thermistors comprise each leg of the bridge. An instrumentation op-amp configuration (gain of 1), a differential op-amp (gain of 10), and an open-loop op-amp (used as a comparator) compose the signal conditioning circuit. The display is composed of a discrete indicator (LED) that is triggered by an opto-triac, controlled by the comparator circuit. Reset of the triac is accomplished by removing power from the circuit (shutting the power/test switch off). Additional features include: (1) a discrete indicator (LED) to verify that the tank is being tested, and (2) a discrete indicator (LED) to provide low-battery warning information. This circuit is comprised of a comparator with a voltage divider reference (5V source) and a voltage divided inverting input.

A fully functional prototype was developed, tested, and verified.

F. Market Entry and a Controlled Growth Strategy

Septic Sense sold 50 Septic Sense units to Bolton Concrete of Johnson City, Tennessee. Bolton Concrete agreed to purchase each Septic Sense unit for $195. The 50 units were manufactured and delivered in lots of ten. Manufacturing of each unit was accomplished through sweat labor of the founders. Bolton Concrete's space was used to manufacture and assemble each Septic Sense device. The total sales from this agreement were $9,750. These 50 units will be used as a pilot study for the Septic Sense device.

Septic Sense units are installed in conjunction with the installation of new septic systems. The manufacturing and distribution of the Septic Sense device will occur in three phases.

Phase 1 is 18 months long and involves selling the Septic Sense device to a local septic tank manufacturer, Bolton Concrete. Bolton Concrete has agreed to purchase the first 50 Septic Sense devices. Projected Septic Sense units sold in phase 1 are 1,290. Pricing of each Septic Sense unit is $195. The net profit on each device sold during phase 1 is $100.

Phase 2 is 24 months long and involves obtaining agreements similar to phase 1 with 16 septic tank manufacturers. Concentration will be placed on septic tank manufacturers within Tennessee and the surrounding states. Projected Septic Sense units sold in phase 2 are 18,000. Two capital investments will be required for phase 2. Pricing of each Septic Sense unit is $195. The net profit on each device sold during phase 2 is $100.

Phase 3 is 18 months long and involves obtaining agreements with 64 septic tank manufacturers. Projected Septic Sense units sold in phase 3 are 60,000. Two capital investments will be required for phase 3. Phase 3 distribution of Septic Sense devices will be on a national level. Pricing of each Septic Sense unit is $195. The net profit on each device sold during phase 3 is $100.

Marketing Plan

A. Overall Marketing Strategy

Our market strategy consists of three phases. In each phase, Septic Sense will be sold to septic tank manufacturers. Septic tank manufacturers will have to make only a minor adjustment in their manufacturing process to incorporate the Septic Sense device. This modification will be a 1-inch hole in the top of the septic tank. Bolton Concrete has agreed to modify its manufacturing process to incorporate the Septic Sense device.

In our initial phase, 50 units were sold to Bolton Concrete. These 50 units will be used as a pilot study and will establish credibility for our product within the septic tank industry.

In phase 2, we will market the Septic Sense product to other septic tank manufacturers through the tristate region (Tennessee, North Carolina, and Virginia). Agreements to sell the Septic Sense device with 16 regional septic tank manufacturers will be established. The introduction of the product statewide will give us a stronger segment of the market, which will lead to national exposure.

In phase 3, Septic Sense will be distributed nationally. Agreements to sell Septic Sense devices with 64 national septic tank manufacturers will be established.

B. Pricing

A price of $195 will be maintained for all three phases.

C. Sales Tactics

The sales tactics that will be used to market Septic Sense will be implemented at the point of the sale of the septic tank manufacturers. It is projected that manufacturers will realize a profit on each sale of this product and, therefore, have an incentive to offer it to each customer. This product will add value to the septic tank creating a more effective product, thus increasing customer satisfaction.

D. Service and Warranty Policies

Septic Sense will offer a five-year limited warranty on Septic Sense (the device). The warranty will only cover manufacturing defects and failures not resulting from customer action.

E. Advertising and Promotion

Septic Sense has no initial plans to advertise Septic Sense. Since the product is sold by the septic tank manufacturer to the customer, the purchaser will be made aware of the product when purchasing the septic tank. A pamphlet shall be created and distributed to the customer at point of purchase. Future advertising plans shall be determined during later phases. We expect to obtain a patent on the Septic Sense device, which will increase public awareness and the integrity of the product.

F. Distribution

In phase 1, there will be no distribution costs. The product will be made on the same site as the septic tank manufacturer.

If shipping is required, an inexpensive truck line shall be utilized. Further analysis of distribution will be performed as needed.

G. Desirability of Product

Our research has indicated there is no similar device on the market. The Septic Sense system adds value to homeowners by precluding septic system failure as a result of improper maintenance of septic systems.

H. Market Research

Although the customers of Septic Sense will be the septic tank manufacturers, the ultimate users will be the owners of new homes which require a septic tank. Our initial research indicates a desire for our product and a willingness to pay $200 for such a device. Our research also indicates that our device has the potential to save homeowners money and embarrassment due to septic system failure. The money spent on one unnecessary pumping will pay for the entire purchase price of Septic Sense. On average, septic tank pumping costs $259.

I. Ongoing Market Evaluation

Septic Sense plans to survey a portion of customers during each phase of production to ensure customer needs are being met or exceeded. In phase 1, we will be closely monitoring any problems that might become evident in the pilot study. This will ensure the ability to counteract any major problems early in our production phase.

In phase 2, we will focus on the service that Septic Sense provides. By doing this we will be able to assess the customers' satisfaction level with our product and see if they have any recommendations on how Septic Sense could be made to be a better product.

In phase 3, we will continue to monitor the product and customer satisfaction. By remaining customer focused, new product lines will be developed based on customer needs.

Manufacturing Plan

A. Basic Plan

Septic Sense plans to sell Septic Sense to a local concrete manufacturing company. During phase 1 of the production cycle, we will be using Bolton Concrete's existing facilities.

During the first production phase, we plan to manufacture 1,290 units for a local market extended over an 18-month period. Our production process is relatively simple. Exhibits 2 and 3 are the process flow diagrams of phases 1 and 2. Exhibit 4 on page 536 details the actual work flow. We will hire one hourly production worker. Joseph Kirkpatrick will also start as a salaried employee. Fixed investment required in manufacturing comes from Exhibit 5 on page 536.

During our phase 2 of production we plan to purchase a hot stamp machine for manufacturing our 55-inch pipe. We will lease a 1,500-square-foot facility at a rate of $4,500 per month. We will be hiring 13 hourly production workers at a rate of $8 per hour and adding Michael Reynolds and Karen Czuchry as salaried employees at $40,000 per year. Joseph Kirkpatrick will have his salary increased to $40,000 per year. We plan to penetrate a regional market, targeting 18,000 units during phase 2 over a 24-month period.

During phase 3 of production, we plan to penetrate a national market producing 60,000 units over an 18-month period. During this phase we will have two capital investments totaling $648,000 for facilities and $204,000 for equipment. We will be hiring 44 additional employees during phase 3.

During phase 3 of production, we plan to expand our market nationally.

Exhibit 2
Phase 1
Process Flow
for Septic Sense

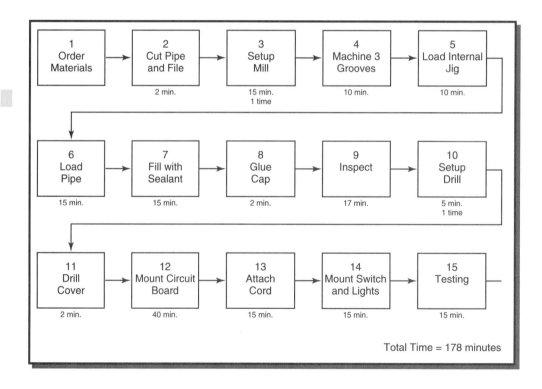

Total Time = 178 minutes

B. Research and Development

Much of the time and effort at Septic Sense during the past four-month period has been spent on research and product development.

All manufactured products listed in the Products section have been tested for ability to be manufactured; testing continues on these components.

Pilot testing indicates standard unit production will be approximately three hours per unit. Processes have been validated to ensure optimally cost-effective, quality product output.

Final tests were successful with regard to most evaluation criteria. Testing will continue through April 1996 at private facilities.

Volume testing will be accomplished by June 1996.

C. Production and Manufacturing

A key factor in the manufacturing process is testing the system. A system that doesn't work makes a very unsatisfied customer. Any rework or customer complaints could become expensive repairs at our cost.

Production and inventory control will be a key part of our manufacturing process. We will strive to develop and maintain a zero defect rate for our products. We will also have a supplier audit and incoming inspection policy to ensure an acceptable incoming product.

Ras/prefabricated materials, components, and subassemblies required for production have been identified and their prices negotiated (see Exhibit 6 on page 537).

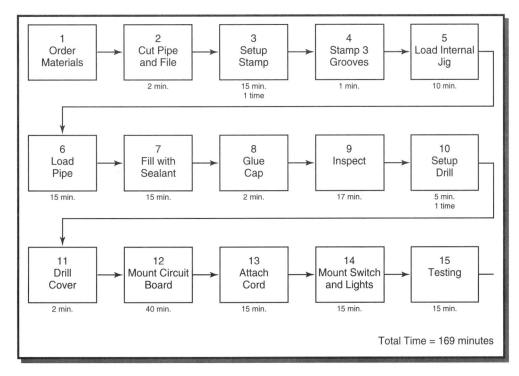

Exhibit 3
**Phase 2
Process Flow
for Septic Sense**

Exhibit 4
Septic Sense:
Work Flow

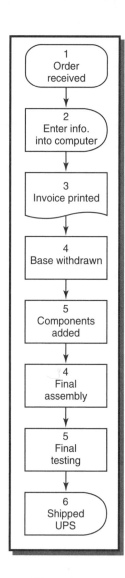

Exhibit 5
Fixed Investment

Fixed Investment	
(Phase 1)	
Sweat Labor	$0
(Phase 2a)	
Facility—1,500 square feet @ $3/square foot	$54,000
Equipment	$17,000
(Phase 2b)	
Facility—3,000 square feet @ $3/square foot	$108,000
Equipment	$34,000
Facility—6,000 square feet @ $3/square foot	$216,000
Equipment	$68,000
(Phase 3b)	
Facility—12,000 square feet @ $3/square foot	$432,000
Equipment	$136,000

Material	Part size or number	Cost	Quantity
55" PVC pipe	3/4" I.D. 1" O.D.	$1.07	1
5" PVC coupling	1/2" I.D. 3/4" O.D.	$0.19	1
90-degree PVC slip	3/4" I.D. 1" O.D.	$0.16	1
PVC cap	3/4" I. D.	$0.19	1
Silicon filling	TBD	$2.18	1
Metal box	TBD	$4.00	1
Circuit board	TBD	$7.00	1
10K Resistor	271-1335	$0.10	4
Thermistor	271-110	$0.99	2
1K Resistor	271-1321	$0.10	2
330 Resistor	271-1315	$0.10	2
100 Resistor	271-1311	$0.10	1
IM Resistor	271-059	$0.09	3
100K Resistor	271-1347	$0.10	1
220K Resistor	271-1350	$0.10	1
10-2W Resistor	271-080	$0.50	2
10K Potentiometer	271-343	$1.49	2
TBR Resistor	271-TBR	$0.10	1
470 mf Cap.	272-1018	$0.99	1
555 Timer	276-1723	$1.19	1
LM324 Quad	276-1711	$1.29	1
Opto-Triac	276-134	$1.99	1
5V-Reg.	276-1770	$1.49	1
100 mf Cap	272-1044	$1.19	1
SPST-Relay 5V	275-243	$2.99	1
Led	276-021	$0.50	2
Piezo	273-065	$2.99	1
9V-Power Supply	273-1651	$10.99	1
Switch Toggle	275-342	$2.99	1
Switch-P/B	TBD	$2.00	1
Interface Wiring	278-871	$0.20	25
Cement	TBD	$0.06	1
	Total Material Cost per Unit	$57.05	

Exhibit 6
List of Components

The Economics of the Business

A. Gross and Operating Margins

Gross margins for the business are approximately 40 percent in the first year, while the subsequent years will be approximately 50 percent. The industry average for Industrial Instruments for Measurement is 41.3 percent.[4]

B. Profit Potential and Durability

Net profit margin for the business is expected to remain stable over the five-year plan. The patent will protect potential and durability by creating a high barrier to competition. The net profit margin is about 27 percent after taxes.

C. Months to Breakeven

Breakeven will occur in the third month of production, or at unit number 31.

D. Months to Reach Positive Cash Flow

Positive cash flow shall occur in the sixth month. This is based on the projected cash flow activity.

E. Market Size and Trends

Septic Sense has the potential to obtain 100 percent of the market. Market size is limited by the following factors: education of consumers, cost/benefit, and the number of new homes built.

Market trends will be influenced by the prime lending rate, increase or decrease of sewer systems development, environmental concerns, and government regulations.

F. Competition and Competitive Edges

Septic Sense is a novel, innovative, and patented device that creates a barrier to competition.

Currently the competition is sewer systems and manual inspection (however, this method is seldom used, being unpleasant and involved).

G. Estimated Market Share and Sale

Projected market share and sales for each phase follow.

Phase 1	1,290 units	$251,550 in sales	24% of local market
Phase 2	18,000 units	$3.51 million in sales	25% of tristate market
Phase 3	60,000 units	$11.7 million in sales	29% of the U.S. and Canadian market

Financial Plan

A. Revenue Projections

The initial annual sales revenue projection was based on estimates of the size of potential markets at each phase of planned growth. The growth of Septic Sense will occur in three phases. This planned growth will allow for greater internally generated financing and, consequently, a safer financial situation.

Phase 1: Growth for phase 1 will be in three subphases. Total sales of subphase 1a was 50 units. This was the initial pilot study. Net sales of this subphase were $9,750. In subphase 1b, Septic Sense will target 13 percent of the local market. Based on 3,600 new septic systems per year, this will be total sales of 160 units. In subphase 1c, Septic Sense will attempt to extend its share to 40 percent of the local market. Again based on 3,600 new septic systems per year, total sales for subphase 1c will be 1,080 units.

Phase 2: Sales are expected to be 18,000 Septic Sense units over a two-year period. In phase 2, Septic Sense hopes to gain a 25 percent share of the tristate market area.

Phase 3: Sales are expected to be 60,000 units over an 18-month period. In phase 3, Septic Sense is targeting to earn a 29 percent of the national market.

B. Cost (Raw Materials, Labor, and Overhead)

RAW MATERIAL. The cost of raw material is determined by a cost evaluation of a working prototype. This cost is $57.05 with no price break for purchasing in volume. For further details, see appendix B.

LABOR. Labor costs are based on $8.00 per hour (personal experience of Joe Kirkpatrick). Using data supplied by the Social Security Administration and data derived from a Boeing pay stub, 17 percent is added to the base salary or wage, resulting in $10.62 per hour.

OVERHEAD. Overhead costs are based on *Valueline* industry information.

C. Sales and Management Costs

Joe Kirkpatrick will receive a salary of $30,000 in the first year of Septic Sense operations. His salary will be raised to $40,000 in the second year of Septic Sense operations. Karen Czuchry and Mike Reynolds will receive a salary of $40,000 during the second year of Septic Sense operations.

D. General and Administrative Costs

General and administrative costs are based on 8 percent of sales and on industry data.

E. Depreciation

Any assets are based on a ten-year straight-line depreciation using 3.385 percent.

F. Accounts Receivable

Accounts will be due on sale or net 30 (days).

G. Advertising

Advertising costs are not known since the channel of communication is not known. However, assumed costs are listed.

H. Equipment Costs

Milling Machine	$ 1,500.00
Band Saw	300.00
Drill Press	300.00
Total	$ 2,100.00
Other test equipment	15,500.00
Total	$17,600.00

Further phases are calculated by extending this amount in proportion to the production rate.

BUILDING LEASE. A local real estate office (Blue Chip Properties) indicated an amount of $3.00 per square foot for light industrial. A figure of 100 square feet per employee was used to calculate square footage required. This square footage was then doubled to account for manufacturing space and storage. A baseline calculation was determined for phase 2a and then extended in proportion to the production rate.

PHASE 2a:

(500 units) (12 months)/2,080 hours/year = 3 direct employees

(3 employees)(100 square feet per employee) = (600 square feet)(2) = 1,200 square feet

($3/square foot/month)(1,200 square feet) = $3,000

$4,500 was used as a contingency

I. Accounting and Legal

These expenses are absorbed and accounted for in the general and administrative costs.

Projected Financial Statements

Cash Flow Phase 1A							

AFTER TAX

	Startup	1	2	3	4	5	PHASE
Beginning Cash Balance	$6,000	$1,400	$2,311	$3,222	$4,133	$5,044	$6,000
Cash Receipts							
Total Sales	$0	$1,950	$1,950	$1,950	$1,950	$1,950	$9,750
Interest Income	$0	$0	$0	$0	$0	$0	$0
Total Cash Receipts	$0	$1,950	$1,950	$1,950	$1,950	$1,950	$9,750
Cash Disbursements							
Salaries and Labor	$0	$0	$0	$0	$0	$0	$0
Advertising	$200	$0	$0	$0	$0	$0	$200
Commissions	$0	$0	$0	$0	$0	$0	$0
Cost of Goods Sold (nonlabor)	$0	$570	$570	$570	$570	$570	$2,850
Other Disbursements	$0	$0	$0	$0	$0	$0	$0
Interest Expense	$0	$0	$0	$0	$0	$0	$0
Tax Payments	$0	$469	$469	$469	$469	$469	$2,345
Total Cash Disbursements	$200	$1,039	$1,039	$1,039	$1,039	$1,039	$5,395
Net Cash from Operations	($200)	$911	$911	$911	$911	$911	$4,355
Equipment Lease	$0	$0	$0	$0	$0	$0	$0
Incorporation Type S	$400	$0	$0	$0	$0	$0	$400
Patent	$4,000	$0	$0	$0	$0	$0	$4,000
Loan Repayment	$0	$0	$0	$0	$0	$0	$0
Sale of Stock	$0	$0	$0	$0	$0	$0	$0
Proceeds of Bank Loan	$0	$0	$0	$0	$0	$0	$0
Net Cash Balance	$1,400	$2,311	$3,222	$4,133	$5,044	$5,955	$5,955

Cash Flow Phase 1B

AFTER TAX

	6	7	8	9	PHASE 1B
Beginning Cash Balance	$5,955	$6,610	$7,372	$8,134	$5,955
Cash Receipts					
Total Sales ($195/unit)	$7,800	$7,800	$7,800	$7,800	$31,200
Interest Income	$0	$0	$0	$0	$0
Total Cash Receipts	$7,800	$7,800	$7,800	$7,800	$31,200
Cash Disbursements					
Salaries and Labor	$4,329	$4,329	$4,329	$4,329	$17,316
Advertising	$200	$0	$0	$0	$200
Commissions	$0	$0	$0	$0	$0
Cost of Goods Sold (nonlabor)	$2,280	$2,280	$2,280	$2,280	$9,120
Other Disbursements	$0	$0	$0	$0	$0
Interest Expense	$0	$0	$0	$0	$0
Tax Payments	$336	$429	$429	$429	$1,622
Total Cash Disbursements	$7,145	$7,038	$7,038	$7,038	$28,258
Net Cash from Operations	$655	$762	$762	$762	$2,942
Equipment Lease	$0	$0	$0	$0	$0
Incorporation Type S	$0	$0	$0	$0	$0
Patent	$0	$0	$0	$0	$0
Loan Repayment	$0	$0	$0	$0	$0
Sale of Stock	$0	$0	$0	$0	$0
Proceeds of Bank Loan	$0	$0	$0	$0	$0
Net Cash Balance	$6,610	$7,372	$8,134	$8,897	$8,897

Cash Flow Phase 1C

AFTER TAX

	10	11	12	13	14	15	16	17	18	PHASE 1C
Beginning Cash Balance	$8,897	$15,383	$22,529	$29,675	$36,821	$43,967	$51,113	$58,259	$65,405	$8,897
Cash Receipts										
Total Sales	$23,400	$23,400	$23,400	$23,400	$23,400	$23,400	$23,400	$23,400	$23,400	$210,600
Interest Income	$0	$0	$0	$0	$0	$0	$0	$0	$0	$0
Total Cash Receipts	$23,400	$23,400	$23,400	$23,400	$23,400	$23,400	$23,400	$23,400	$23,400	$210,600
Cash Disbursements										
Salaries and Labor	$5,733	$5,733	$5,733	$5,733	$5,733	$5,733	$5,733	$5,733	$5,733	$51,597
Advertising	$1,000	$0	$0	$0	$0	$0	$0	$0	$0	$1,000
Commissions	$0	$0	$0	$0	$0	$0	$0	$0	$0	$0
Cost of Goods Sold (nonlabor)	$6,840	$6,840	$6,840	$6,840	$6,840	$6,840	$6,840	$6,840	$6,840	$61,560
Other Disbursements	$0	$0	$0	$0	$0	$0	$0	$0	$0	$0
Interest Expense	$0	$0	$0	$0	$0	$0	$0	$0	$0	$0
Tax Payments	$3,341	$3,681	$3,681	$3,681	$3,681	$3,681	$3,681	$3,681	$3,681	$32,789
Total Cash Disbursements	$16,914	$16,254	$16,254	$16,254	$16,254	$16,254	$16,254	$16,254	$16,254	$146,946
Net Cash from Operations	$6,486	$7,146	$7,146	$7,146	$7,146	$7,146	$7,146	$7,146	$7,146	$63,654
Equipment Lease	$0	$0	$0	$0	$0	$0	$0	$0	$0	$0
Incorporation Type S	$0	$0	$0	$0	$0	$0	$0	$0	$0	$0
Patent	$0	$0	$0	$0	$0	$0	$0	$0	$0	$0
Loan Repayment	$0	$0	$0	$0	$0	$0	$0	$0	$0	$0
Sale of Stock	$0	$0	$0	$0	$0	$0	$0	$0	$0	$0
Proceeds of Bank Loan	$0	$0	$0	$0	$0	$0	$0	$0	$0	$0
Net Cash Balance	$15,383	$22,529	$29,675	$36,821	$43,967	$51,113	$58,259	$65,405	$72,551	$72,551

Cash Flow Phase 2A

AFTER TAX

	19	20	21	22	23
Beginning Cash Balance	$72,551	$81,752	$109,873	$137,994	$166,115
Cash Receipts					
Total Sales	$97,500	$97,500	$97,500	$97,500	$97,500
Interest Income	$0	$0	$0	$0	$0
Total Cash Receipts	$97,500	$97,500	$97,500	$97,500	$97,500
Cash Disbursements					
Salaries and Labor	$14,625	$14,625	$14,625	$14,625	$14,625
Advertising	$2,000	$0	$0	$0	$0
Commissions	$0	$0	$0	$0	$0
Cost of Goods Sold (90% Newark #113)	$25,650	$25,650	$25,650	$25,650	$25,650
Other Disbursements (G and A)	$7,800	$7,800	$7,800	$7,800	$7,800
Interest Expense	$0	$0	$0	$0	$0
Tax Payments	$16,124	$16,804	$16,804	$16,804	$16,804
Total Cash Disbursements	$66,199	$64,879	$64,879	$64,879	$64,879
Net Cash from Operations	$31,301	$32,621	$32,621	$32,621	$32,621
Lease Building	$4,500	$4,500	$4,500	$4,500	$4,500
Equipment/Test	$17,600	$0	$0	$0	$0
Patent	$0	$0	$0	$0	$0
Loan Repayment	$0	$0	$0	$0	$0
Sale of Stock	$0	$0	$0	$0	$0
Proceeds of Bank Loan	$0	$0	$0	$0	$0
Net Cash Balance	$81,752	$109,873	$137,994	$166,115	$194,236

24	25	26	27	28	29	30	PHASE 2A
$194,236	$222,357	$250,478	$278,599	$306,720	$334,841	$362,962	$72,551
$97,500	$97,500	$97,500	$97,500	$97,500	$97,500	$97,500	$1,170,000
$0	$0	$0	$0	$0	$0	$0	$0
$97,500	$97,500	$97,500	$97,500	$97,500	$97,500	$97,500	$1,170,000
$14,625	$14,625	$14,625	$14,625	$14,625	$14,625	$14,625	$175,500
$0	$0	$0	$0	$0	$0	$0	$2,000
$0	$0	$0	$0	$0	$0	$0	$0
$25,650	$25,650	$25,650	$25,650	$25,650	$25,650	$25,650	$307,800
$7,800	$7,800	$7,800	$7,800	$7,800	$7,800	$7,800	$93,600
$0	$0	$0	$0	$0	$0	$0	$0
$16,804	$16,804	$16,804	$16,804	$16,804	$16,804	$16,804	$200,968
$64,879	$64,879	$64,879	$64,879	$64,879	$64,879	$64,879	$779,868
$32,621	$32,621	$32,621	$32,621	$32,621	$32,621	$32,621	$390,132
$4,500	$4,500	$4,500	$4,500	$4,500	$4,500	$4,500	$54,000
$0	$0	$0	$0	$0	$0	$0	$17,600
$0	$0	$0	$0	$0	$0	$0	$0
$0	$0	$0	$0	$0	$0	$0	$0
$0	$0	$0	$0	$0	$0	$0	$0
$0	$0	$0	$0	$0	$0	$0	$0
$222,357	$250,478	$278,599	$306,720	$334,841	$362,962	$391,083	$391,083

Cash Flow Phase 2B

AFTER TAX

	31	32	33	34	35
Beginning Cash Balance	$391,083	$376,463	$428,843	$481,223	$533,603
Cash Receipts					
Total Sales	$195,000	$195,000	$195,000	$195,000	$195,000
Interest Income	$0	$0	$0	$0	$0
Total Cash Receipts	$195,000	$195,000	$195,000	$195,000	$195,000
Cash Disbursements					
Salaries and Labor	$35,100	$35,100	$35,100	$35,100	$35,100
Advertising	$50,000	$0	$0	$0	$0
Commissions	$0	$0	$0	$0	$0
Cost of Goods Sold (90% Newark #113)	$51,300	$51,300	$51,300	$51,300	$51,300
Other Disbursements (G and A)	$15,600	$15,600	$15,600	$15,600	$15,600
Interest Expense	$0	$0	$0	$0	$0
Tax Payments	$14,620	$31,620	$31,620	$31,620	$31,620
Total Cash Disbursements	$166,620	$133,620	$133,620	$133,620	$133,620
Net Cash from Operations	$28,380	$61,380	$61,380	$61,380	$61,380
Lease Building	$9,000	$9,000	$9,000	$9,000	$9,000
Equipment/Test	$34,000	$0	$0	$0	$0
Patent	$0	$0	$0	$0	$0
Loan Repayment	$0	$0	$0	$0	$0
Sale of Stock	$0	$0	$0	$0	$0
Proceeds of Bank Loan	$0	$0	$0	$0	$0
Net Cash Balance	$376,463	$428,843	$481,223	$533,603	$585,983

36	37	38	39	40	41	42	PHASE 2B
$585,983	$638,363	$690,743	$743,123	$795,503	$847,883	$900,263	$391,083
$195,000	$195,000	$195,000	$195,000	$195,000	$195,000	$195,000	$2,340,000
$0	$0	$0	$0	$0	$0	$0	$0
$195,000	$195,000	$195,000	$195,000	$195,000	$195,000	$195,000	$2,340,000
$35,100	$35,100	$35,100	$35,100	$35,100	$35,100	$35,100	$421,200
$0	$0	$0	$0	$0	$0	$0	$50,000
$0	$0	$0	$0	$0	$0	$0	$0
$51,300	$51,300	$51,300	$51,300	$51,300	$51,300	$51,300	$615,600
$15,600	$15,600	$15,600	$15,600	$15,600	$15,600	$15,600	$187,200
$0	$0	$0	$0	$0	$0	$0	$0
$31,620	$31,620	$31,620	$31,620	$31,620	$31,620	$31,620	$362,440
$133,620	$133,620	$133,620	$133,620	$133,620	$133,620	$133,620	$1,636,440
$61,380	$61,380	$61,380	$61,380	$61,380	$61,380	$61,380	$703,560
$9,000	$9,000	$9,000	$9,000	$9,000	$9,000	$9,000	$108,000
$0	$0	$0	$0	$0	$0	$0	$34,000
$0	$0	$0	$0	$0	$0	$0	$0
$0	$0	$0	$0	$0	$0	$0	$0
$0	$0	$0	$0	$0	$0	$0	$0
$0	$0	$0	$0	$0	$0	$0	$0
$638,363	$690,743	$743,123	$795,503	$847,883	$900,263	$952,643	$952,643

AFTER TAX

	43	44	45
Beginning Cash Balance	$952,643	$944,195	$1,036,747
Cash Receipts			
Total Sales	$390,000	$390,000	$390,000
Interest Income	$0	$0	$0
Total Cash Receipts	$390,000	$390,000	$390,000
Cash Disbursements			
Salaries and Labor	$61,425	$61,425	$61,425
Advertising	$50,000	$0	$0
Commissions	$0	$0	$0
Cost of Goods Sold (90% Newark #113)	$102,600	$102,600	$102,600
Other Disbursements (G and A)	$31,200	$31,200	$31,200
Interest Expense	$0	$0	$0
Tax Payments	$49,223	$66,223	$66,223
Total Cash Disbursements	$294,448	$261,448	$261,448
Net Cash from Operations	$95,552	$128,552	$128,552
Lease Building	$36,000	$36,000	$36,000
Equipment/Test	$68,000	$0	$0
Patent	$0	$0	$0
Loan Repayment	$0	$0	$0
Sale of Stock	$0	$0	$0
Proceeds of Bank Loan	$0	$0	$0
Net Cash Balance	$944,195	$1,036,747	$1,129,299

46	47	48	PHASE 3A
$1,129,299	$1,221,851	$1,314,403	$952,643
$390,000	$390,000	$390,000	$2,340,000
$0	$0	$0	$0
$390,000	$390,000	$390,000	$2,340,000
$61,425	$61,425	$61,425	$368,550
$0	$0	$0	$50,000
$0	$0	$0	$0
$102,600	$102,600	$102,600	$615,600
$31,200	$31,200	$31,200	$187,200
$0	$0	$0	$0
$66,223	$66,223	$66,223	$380,338
$261,448	$261,448	$261,448	$1,601,688
$128,552	$128,552	$128,552	$738,312
$36,000	$36,000	$36,000	$216,000
$0	$0	$0	$68,000
$0	$0	$0	$0
$0	$0	$0	$0
$0	$0	$0	$0
$0	$0	$0	$0
$1,221,851	$1,314,403	$1,406,955	$1,406,955

Cash Flow Phase 3B

AFTER TAX

	49	50	51	52	53
Beginning Cash Balance	$1,406,955	$1,431,894	$1,671,340	$1,910,786	$2,150,232
Cash Receipts					
Total Sales	$780,000	$780,000	$780,000	$780,000	$780,000
Interest Income	$0	$0	$0	$0	$0
Total Cash Receipts	$780,000	$780,000	$780,000	$780,000	$780,000
Cash Disbursements					
Salaries and Labor	$114,075	$114,075	$114,075	$114,075	$114,075
Advertising	$100,000	$0	$0	$0	$0
Commissions	$0	$0	$0	$0	$0
Cost of Goods Sold (90% Newark #113)	$205,200	$205,200	$205,200	$205,200	$205,200
Other Disbursements (G and A)	$62,333	$62,333	$62,333	$62,333	$62,333
Interest Expense	$0	$0	$0	$0	$0
Tax Payments	$101,453	$122,946	$122,946	$122,946	$122,946
Total Cash Disbursements	$583,061	$504,554	$504,554	$504,554	$504,554
Net Cash from Operations	$196,939	$275,446	$275,446	$275,446	$275,446
Lease Building	$36,000	$36,000	$36,000	$36,000	$36,000
Equipment/Test	$136,000	$0	$0	$0	$0
Patent	$0	$0	$0	$0	$0
Loan Repayment	$0	$0	$0	$0	$0
Sale of Stock	$0	$0	$0	$0	$0
Proceeds of Bank Loan	$0	$0	$0	$0	$0
Net Cash Balance	$1,431,894	$1,671,340	$1,910,786	$2,150,232	$2,389,678

	54	55	56	57	58	59	60	PHASE 3B
	$2,389,678	$2,629,124	$2,868,570	$3,108,016	$3,347,462	$3,586,908	$3,826,354	$1,406,955
	$780,000	$780,000	$780,000	$780,000	$780,000	$780,000	$780,000	$9,360,000
	$0	$0	$0	$0	$0	$0	$0	$0
	$780,000	$780,000	$780,000	$780,000	$780,000	$780,000	$780,000	$9,360,000
	$114,075	$114,075	$114,075	$114,075	$114,075	$114,075	$114,075	$1,368,900
	$0	$0	$0	$0	$0	$0	$0	$100,000
	$0	$0	$0	$0	$0	$0	$0	$0
	$205,200	$205,200	$205,200	$205,200	$205,200	$205,200	$205,200	$2,462,400
	$62,333	$62,333	$62,333	$62,333	$62,333	$62,333	$62,333	$747,996
	$0	$0	$0	$0	$0	$0	$0	$0
	$122,946	$122,946	$122,946	$122,946	$122,946	$122,946	$122,946	$1,453,859
	$504,554	$504,554	$504,554	$504,554	$504,554	$504,554	$504,554	$6,133,155
	$275,446	$275,446	$275,446	$275,446	$275,446	$275,446	$275,446	$3,226,845
	$36,000	$36,000	$36,000	$36,000	$36,000	$36,000	$36,000	$432,000
	$0	$0	$0	$0	$0	$0	$0	$136,000
	$0	$0	$0	$0	$0	$0	$0	$0
	$0	$0	$0	$0	$0	$0	$0	$0
	$0	$0	$0	$0	$0	$0	$0	$0
	$0	$0	$0	$0	$0	$0	$0	$0
	$2,629,124	$2,868,570	$3,108,016	$3,347,462	$3,586,908	$3,826,354	$4,065,800	$4,065,800

Breakeven Analysis—Phase 1

Cost Variables Fixed Costs	Optimistic −20%	Per Month Average Budgeted	Pessimistic 20%
Sales and Marketing	$0	$0	$0
Research and Development (Patent)	$4,000	$5,000	$6,000
Incorporation	$320	$400	$480
Depreciation	$0	$0	$0
(Other Fixed Costs)	$456	$570	$684
Total Fixed Costs	$4,776	$5,970	$7,164

Variable Costs	Optimistic −20%	Per Month Average Budgeted	Pessimistic 15%
Cost of Goods Sold	$0	$0	$0
(Other Variable Costs)	$0	$0	$0
Total Variable Costs	$0	$0	$0

Pricing and Unit Sales Variables	Optimistic 25%	Per Month Sales Estimate	Pessimistic −20%
Selling Price	$195.00	$195.00	$195.00
Number of Units Sold	13	10	8
Fixed Costs per Unit	$382.08	$597.00	$895.50
Variable Costs per Unit	$0	$0	$0
Breakeven Unit Volume	24	31	37
Units Over Breakeven Unit Volume	−12	−21	−29
Gross Profit per Unit	$195.00	$195.00	$195.00
Gross Profit (Over Breakeven)	($2,339.00)	($4,020.00)	($5,604.00)

Pro Forma Balance Sheet

	Year 1	Year 2	Year 3	Year 4	Year 5
Assets					
Current Assets					
Cash	$29,675	$222,357	$811,083	$1,406,955	$4,065,800
Investments	$0	$0	$0	$0	$0
Accounts Receivable	$0	$0	$0	$0	$0
Notes Receivable	$0	$0	$0	$0	$0
Inventory	$0	$0	$0	$0	$0
Total Current Assets	$29,675	$222,357	$811,083	$1,406,955	$4,065,800
Plant and Equipment					
Building	$0	$0	$0	$0	$0
Equipment (Capitalized Purchases)	$0	$17,600	$50,922	$116,962	$248,459
Leasehold Improvements	$0	$0	$0	$0	$0
Less Accumulated Depreciation	$0	$338	$1,960	$4,503	$9,565
Total Net Property and Equipment	$0	$17,262	$48,962	$112,459	$238,894
Other Assets	$0	$0	$0	$0	$0
Total Assets	$29,675	$239,619	$860,045	$1,519,414	$4,304,694
Liabilities and Owners' Equity					
Current Liabilities					
Short-Term Debt	$0	$0	$0	$0	$0
Accounts Payable	$0	$0	$0	$0	$0
Income Taxes Payable	$0	$0	$0	$0	$0
Accrued Liabilities	$0	$0	$0	$0	$0
Total Current Liabilities	$0	$0	$0	$0	$0
Long-Term Debt	$0	$0	$0	$0	$0
Total Liabilities	$0	$0	$0	$0	$0
Owner/Stockholders' Equity					
Common Stock	$0	$0	$0	$0	$0
Retained Earnings	$29,675	$239,619	$811,083	$1,406,955	$4,065,800
Less Cash Dividends	$0	$0	$0	$0	$0
Total Owners' Equity	$29,675	$239,619	$811,083	$1,406,955	$4,065,800
Total Liabilities and Equity	$29,675	$239,619	$811,083	$1,406,955	$4,065,800

Pro Forma Income Statement

	Year 1	Year 2	Year 3	Year 4	Year 5
Sales					
Septic Sense	$111,150	$725,400	$1,755,000	$3,510,000	$9,360,000
% of Total Sales	100%	100%	100%	100%	100%
Product/Service B	$0	$0	$0	$0	$0
% of Total Sales	0%	0%	0%	0%	0%
Product/Service C	$0	$0	$0	$0	$0
% of Total Sales	0%	0%	0%	0%	0%
Product/Service D	$0	$0	$0	$0	$0
% of Total Sales	0%	0%	0%	0%	0%
Product/Service E	$0	$0	$0	$0	$0
% of Total Sales	0%	0%	0%	0%	0%
Product/Service F	$0	$0	$0	$0	$0
% of Total Sales	0%	0%	0%	0%	0%
Product/Service G	$0	$0	$0	$0	$0
% of Total Sales	0%	0%	0%	0%	0%
Product/Service H	$0	$0	$0	$0	$0
% of Total Sales	0%	0%	0%	0%	0%
Total Sales	$111,150	$725,400	$1,755,000	$3,510,000	$9,360,000
Cost of Goods Sold					
Raw Materials	$32,490	$190,836	$461,700	$923,400	$2,462,400
% of Total Sales	29%	26%	26%	26%	26%
Labor	$34,515	$122,148	$298,350	$579,150	$1,368,900
% of Total Sales	31%	17%	17%	17%	15%
Overhead	$0	$46,800	$138,400	$280,800	$747,996
% of Total Sales	0%	6%	8%	8%	8%
Total Cost of Goods Sold	$67,005	$359,784	$898,450	$1,783,350	$4,579,296
Gross Profit	$44,145	$365,616	$856,550	$1,726,650	$4,780,704
Gross Margin	40%	50%	49%	49%	51%
Operating Expenses					
Sales and Marketing	$500	$3,000	$50,000	$100,000	$200,000
% of Total Sales	0%	0%	3%	3%	2%
Research and Development	$0	$0	$0	$0	$0
% of Total Sales	0%	0%	0%	0%	0%
G and A (Without Depreciation)	$0	$27,000	$81,000	$270,000	$432,000
% of Total Sales	0%	4%	5%	8%	5%
Depreciation	$0	$0	$0	$0	$0
% of Total Sales	0%	0%	0%	0%	0%
Total Operating Expenses	$500	$30,000	$131,000	$370,000	$632,000
% of Total Sales	0%	4%	7%	11%	7%

Pro Forma Income Statement, *Continued*					
	Year 1	**Year 2**	**Year 3**	**Year 4**	**Year 5**
Income from Operations	$43,645	$335,616	$725,550	$1,356,650	$4,148,704
% of Total Sales	39%	46%	41%	39%	44%
Interest Income	$736	$6,976	$23,434	$75,628	$146,662
Interest Expense	$0	$0	$0	$0	$0
Income Before Taxes	$44,381	$342,592	$748,984	$1,432,278	$4,295,366
Taxes on Income	$14,202	$122,230	$273,544	$570,058	$1,453,859
Net Income After Taxes	$30,179	$220,362	$475,440	$862,220	$2,841,507
% of Total Sales	27%	30%	27%	25%	30%

Management Team

A. *Personnel*

Septic Sense was founded in 1995 by Karen Czuchry, Joseph Kirkpatrick, and Michael Reynolds as part of ENTC—Innovative Entrepreneurship, a class within the Department of Technology at East Tennessee State University. The legal form of Septic Sense is a subchapter S corporation. The major advantage of an S corporation is that profits are not subject to double taxation and the personal assets of the founders are protected. Karen Czuchry was appointed president.

The founder and key managers of Septic Sense have combined experiences exceeding 20 years in various industries.

The strength of the Septic Sense's management team stems from the combined expertise in both management and technical areas.

The leadership and alignment characteristics of Septic Sense's management team have resulted in broad and flexible goal setting of excellence in customer satisfaction, quality and reliable products, and superior financial results.

Organization Chart

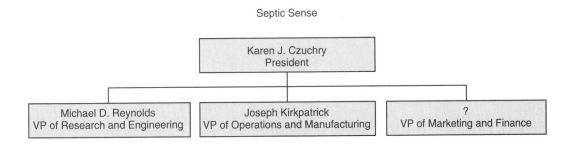

Karen Czuchry, President

B.S. Mathematics/Economics, Colby College
M.S. Computer Science, University of Tennessee

Ms. Czuchry's professional experience includes five years at Martin Marietta on a moderately high-profile computer applications project as project leader/manager. Ms. Czuchry is currently enrolled in a doctoral program at ETSU.

Joseph Kirkpatrick, Vice President—Operations/Manufacturing

B.S. Manufacturing Engineering Technology, East Tennessee State University.

Mr. Kirkpatrick has several years of experience in manufacturing and operations management. While completing his baccalaureate degree, he worked at several manufacturing companies including Morrell Motors of Tennessee and Dana Corporation. Mr. Kirkpatrick is currently working on his master's degree in technology at East Tennessee State University. He has also served as an ISO 9000 technician in a local manufacturing industry.

Michael Reynolds, Vice President—Research/Engineering

B.S. Electronic Engineering Technology, Central Washington University

Mr. Reynolds worked for Boeing for three years on the 747-400 program as a design engineer. From 1988 to 1993 he worked at Rogerson Aircraft as a senior engineer on the 737 auxiliary fuel system.

Mr. Reynolds is certified by the Federal Aviation Administration as an independent designated engineering representative (DER) for FAR25, systems and equipment for transport category aircraft. In 1993 he cofounded an aircraft wire harness fabrication company (Olympic Aero Services), which stilll operates in Port Angeles, Washington. Currently Mr. Reynolds is enrolled in a doctoral program at ETSU.

B. Major Responsibilities

Karen Czuchry, President: strategic planning, team development, and personnel management.

Joseph Kirkpatrick, Vice President—Operations/Manufacturing: perform service, manufacturing, raw materials management and allocation functions.

Michael Reynolds, Vice President—Research/Development: oversee product development, including quality control, physical distribution, product and packaging design, new-product development improvement, and improvements on existing products. Oversee research and development of new and existing products/ideas.

To be selected, Vice President—Marketing/Finance: manage market planning, advertising, public relations, sales promotion, merchandising, and facilitating staff services. Identify new markets and corporate scope and market research. Identify foreign markets. Manage working capital, including receivables, inventory, cash, and marketable securities. Perform financial forecasting, including capital budget, cash budget, pro forma financial statements, external financing requirements, and financial condition requirements.

C. Future Staffing

Septic Sense development team recognizes that additional staff is required to properly support marketing, sales, research, and support functions.

Currently, Septic Sense is composed of four people; two will be required during our first production phase. Septic Sense plans to expand to 65 employees during our third production phase over the next three years. Some of the areas in which we will need employment include:

Management	Maintenance Personnel
Sales	Field Service Technicians
Customer Relations	Marketing
Manufacturing	Administration

ENDNOTES

Chapter 1

1. Brian O'Reilly, "The New Face of Small Business," *Fortune*, May 2, 1994, p. 82.

2. Paul Reynolds, "What We Don't Know May Hurt Us," *Inc.*, September 1994, pp. 25–26.

3. John J. LaFalce, "Capitol Gains," *Entrepreneur,* May 1992, p. 82.

4. Howard H. Stevenson, "We Create Entrepreneurs," *Success*, September 1995, p. 51.

5. Gianna Jacobson, "Homeward Bound," *Success,* March 1996, pp. 12.

6. Charles Burck, "The Real World of the Entrepreneur," *Fortune,* April 5, 1993, p. 62.

7. David McClelland, *The Achieving Society* (Princeton, NJ: Van Nostrand, 1961), p. 16.

8. Paul Hawken, "A 'New Age' Look at Business," *U.S. News & World Report,* November 30, 1987, p. 51.

9. Martha E. Mangelsdorf, "Insider," *Inc.*, June 1988, p. 14.

10. Sabin Russell, "Being Your Own Boss in America," *Venture,* May 1984, p. 40.

11. Lisa Sanders, "It's Not That We're Greedy," *Forbes,* September 26, 1994, pp. 130–134.

12. Gayle Sato–Stodder, "Never Say Die," *Entrepreneur, D*ecember 1990, p. 95.

13. Bob Weinstein, "Success Secrets," *Business Start-Ups,* August 1995, p. 46.

14. Sato-Stodder,"Never Say Die," p. 93.

15. James C. Collins, "Sometimes a Great Notion," *Inc.*, July 1993, pp. 90–91; Andrew E. Serwer, "Lessons from America's Fastest–Growing Companies," *Fortune,* August 8, 1994, pp. 42–62.

16. Weinstein, "Success Secrets," pp. 47–48.

17. Ibid., p. 47.

18. John Case, "The Origins of Entrepreneurship," *Inc.*, June 1989, p. 52.

19. Michael Selz, "Young America Still Fosters Entrepreneurial Ambitions," *Wall Street Journal,* April 6, 1992, p. B2.

20. Kathleen Landis, "A New Spin on Outdoor Furniture," *In Business*, March/April 1996, pp. 32–33.

21. Kenneth Labich, "Kissing Off Corporate America," *Fortune*, February 20, 1995, p. 46.

22. Edward O. Welles, "How to Get Rich in America," *Inc.*, January 1993, pp. 50–56.

23. Selz, "Young America," p. B2.

24. Ronaleen R. Roha, "'Call Your Own Shots," *Kiplinger's Personal Finance Magazine,* June 1992, pp. 43–48.

25. Sato-Stodder, "Never Say Die," p. 94.

26. Jeremy Main, "A Golden Age for Entrepreneurs," *Fortune*, February 12, 1990, p. 126.

27. Kristen Von Kreisler–Bomben, "The Daddy Track," *Entrepreneur,* March 1990, p. 126.

28. Rafael J. Gerena, "How to Succeed in Business for $49," *Wall Street Journal*, June 12, 1995, p. A12.

29. Stephanie Barlow, "Making It," *Entrepreneur,* December 1992, pp. 103–106.

30. Albert G. Holzinger, "Reach New Markets," *Nation's Business,* December 1990, pp. 18–27; *The State of Small Business: A Report of the President,* (Washington, DC: U.S. Government Printing Office, 1990), p. 4.

31. Julie Ampareno Lopez, "Going Global," *Wall Street Journal,* October 16, 1992, p. R20.

32. Jeannette R. Scollard, "Who's the Boss?" *Entrepreneur*, March 1995, p. 292.

33. Janean Chun, "Blondie Ambition," *Entrepreneur*, March 1996, p. 40.

34. Sharon Nelton, "Women–Owned Firms Grow in Number and Importance," *Nation's Business*, April 1996, p. 7; Joline Godfrey, "Been There, Doing That," *Inc.*, March 1996, pp. 21–22.

35. Janean Chun, "Hear Them Roar," *Entrepreneur*, June 1995, pp. 10–11.

36. Lauren Picker, "The Key to My Success," *Parade*, April 24, 1996, pp. 4–5; Suzanne Oliver, "Seeds of Success," *Forbes*, August 15, 1994, pp. 98–102.

37. "Black Entrepreneurship in America," advertising supplement to *Wall Street Journal,* July 1994, p. 14.

38. Timothy Bates, "A New Kind of Business," *Inc.*, July 1994, pp. 23–24.

39. Joel Millman, "From Dakar to Detroit," *Forbes*, September 26, 1994, pp. 86–90.

40. Imran Husain, "After Hours," *Entrepreneur*, March 1995, pp. 230–233.

41. Guen Sublette, "Moon Lighting" *Business Start-Ups*, April 1995, pp. 34–38.

42. Jeanean Huber, "The Quiet Revolution," *Entrepreneur*, September 1993, pp. 77–81; Jeanean Huber, "Bright Lights, Small City," *Entrepreneur*, March 1994, pp. 102–109.

43. Barbara Marsh, "The Way It Works," *Wall Street Journal*, October 14, 1994, p. R8.

44. Huber, "The Quiet Revolution," p. 78.

45. Ibid., p. 77.

46. "Quickstats," *Home Business News Report*, Fall 1994, p. 1.

47. Bob Weinstein, "Spousal Support," *Business Start-Ups*, November 1995, pp. 74–79; G. Scott Budge, "Family Ties," *Sky*, March 1992, pp. 16–20; John L. Ward and Craig E. Aronoff, "Just What Is a Family Business?" *Nation's Business*, February 1990, pp. 32–33; Nancy Kercheval, "Business Grows with Family Tree," *The Times–Picayune*, November 12, 1989, pp. Gl, G4; Erik Calonius, "Blood and Money," *Newsweek*, Special Issue, pp. 82–84.

48. Erik Calonius, "Blood and Money," *Newsweek*, Special Issue, p. 82.

49. Brian Henson, "Setting the Stage," *Inc.*, June 1994, pp. 23–24.

50. Udayan Gupta, "And Business Makes Three: Couples Working Together," *Wall Street Journal*, February 26, 1990, p. B2.

51. Bob Weinstein, "For Better or Worse," *Your Company*, Spring 1992, pp. 28–31.

52. Echo M. Garrett, "And Business Makes Three," *Small Business Reports*, September 1993, pp. 27–31.

53. Bob Weinstein, "Spousal Support," *Business Start-Ups*, November 1995, pp.74–79.

54. Mark Musick, Gene Logsdon, and Jerome Goldstein, "Independent Cure for Overworked Americans," *In Business*, May/June 1992, pp. 28–30.

55. "Going Places," *Entrepreneur*, June 1994, p. 14.

56. Tom Ehrenfeld, "Out of the Blue," *Inc.*, July 1995, pp. 69–72.

57. O'Reilly, "The New Face of Small Business."

58. Donna Kato, "Changing Course, Burning Suits," *The Greenville News*, June 6, 1993, p. 1D.

59. O'Reilly, "The New Face of Small Business."

60. Kenneth Labich, "The New Low-Risk Entrepreneurs," *Fortune*, July 27, 1992, p. 84.

61. William J. Dennis Jr., *A Small Business Primer* (Washington, DC: The NFIB Foundation), 1993, p. 10.

62. Ibid; John Case, "The Wonderland Economy," *Inc.'s The State of Small Business 1995*, pp. 14–29.

63. Ingrid Abramovitch, "Gazelles Create Jobs," *Success*, September 1994, p. 8; Andrew Serwer, "Lessons from America' Fastest-Growing Companies," *Fortune*, August 8, 1994, p. 44; "Business Bulletin," *Wall Street Journal*, May 4, 1993, p. Al; "Where Good Jobs Grow," *Fortune*, June 14, 1993, p. 22.

64. Erskine Bowles, "Training Ground," *Entrepreneur*, March 1994, p. 168.

65. John Case, "The Wonderland Economy," *Inc.'s The State of Small Business 1995*, pp. 14–29.

66. John LaFalce, "The Driving Force," *Entrepreneur*, February 1990, pp. 161–166.

67. Stephanie Barlow, "What's Next?" *Entrepreneur*, March 1993, p. 126.

68. Case, "The Wonderland Economy."

69. Bruce G. Posner, "Why Companies Fail," *Inc.*, June 1993, p. 102.

70. Roy Hoopes, "Mind Your Own Business," *Modern Maturity*, February–March 1991, pp. 26–33.

71. Dave Kansas, "Don't Believe It," *Wall Street Journal*, October 15, 1993, p. R8.

72. Louise Lee, "A Company Failing From Too Much Success," *Wall Street Journal*, March 17, 1995, pp. B1–B2.

73. Burke, "The Real World of the Entrepreneur."

74. Eugene Carlson, "Spreading Your Wings," *The Wall Street Journal*, October 16, 1992, p. R2.

75. Carrie Dolan, "Entrepreneurs Often Fail as Managers," *Wall Street Journal*, May 15, 1989, p. Bl.

76. Sara Olkon, "Don't Even Think About It," *Wall Street Journal*, May 22, 1995, p. R12.

77 Joshua Hyatt, "Should You Start a Business?" *Inc.*, February 1992, p. 50.

78. Stephanie Barlow, "Hang On!" *Entrepreneur*, September 1992, p. 156.

79. James L. Bildner, "Hitting the Wall," *Inc.*, July 1995, p. 22.

80. Barbara Carton, "Help Wanted," *Wall Street Journal*, May 22, 1995, p. R10.

81. Kirsten Von Kriesler–Bomben, "The Obstacle Course," *Entrepreneur*, July 1990, p. 175.

Chapter 2

1. Ronald Henkoff, "How to Plan for 1995," *Fortune*, December 31, 1990, p. 70.

2. Alan W. Jackson, "It's All in the Plan," *Small Business Reports*, June 1994, pp. 38–43.

3. Les Burch, "Moving Away from 'Me–Too'" *Nation's Business*, August 1994, p.8.

4. Charles R. Doery, "It's warm, but not fuzzy," *Industry Week*, July 18, 1994, p. 7.

5. Margaret Kaeter, "Mission: Impossible?" *Business Ethics*, January/February 1995, p. 25.

6. Margaret Kaeter, "Old Twist on a New Business," *Business Ethics*, May/June 1995, p. 28.

7. Jacquelyn Lynn, "Single–Minded," *Entrepreneur*, January 1996, p. 97.

8. Kaeter, "Mission: Impossible?" pp. 24–25.

9. Sharon Nelton, "Putting the Purpose in Writing," *Nation's Business,* February 1994, p. 61.

10. Ibid, p. 61.

11. Kaeter, "Mission: Impossible?" p. 24.

12. Samantha Thompson, "It's not just a vacation, it's an adventure," *Upstate Business*, February 5, 1995, p. 5.

13. Sharon Nelton, "Beating Back the Competition," *Nation's Business*, September 1994, pp. 24–25.

14. Andrew Tanzer, "One Billion Potential Customers," *Forbes*, January 3, 1994, pp. 56–57.

15. Ellen Mahoney, "One Strike and You're Out!" *Cross Sections*, Spring 1995, pp. 26–27.

16. Aimee L. Stern, "Tracking Your Rivals," *Your Company*, Spring 1994, pp. 6–8.

17. Shari Caudron, "I Spy, You Spy," *Industry Week*, October 3, 1994, p. 36.

18. Michael E. Porter, *Competitive Strategy* (New York: Free Press, 1980), Chapter 2.

19. Matt Walsh, "Easy on the Popcorn," *Forbes*, September 20, 1994, pp. 126–127.

20. Sharon Nelton, "Beating Back the Competition," p. 22.

21. Andrew E. Serwer, "How to Reach the Major Leagues of Shopping," *Fortune*, August 7, 1995, p. 36.

22. Fleming Meeks, "Catering to Indulgent Parents," *Forbes*, October 23, 1995, pp. 148–155.

23. Edward O. Welles, "Lessons of a Bottom Feeder," *Inc.*, July 1994, pp. 54–62.

Chapter 3

1. Barbara Bucholz and Margaret Crane, "One–Man Bands," *Your Company*, Summer 1993, p. 24.

2. Ibid.

3. Jacquelyn Lynn, "Partnership Procedures," *Business Start-Ups*, June 1996, p. 73.

4. Frances Huffman, "Irreconcilable Differences," *Entrepreneur*, February 1992, p. 108.

5. Manuel Schiffres, "Partnerships with a Plus," *Changing Times*, October 1989. p. 49.

6. Chief Justice John Marshall, cited by Roger L. Miller and Gaylord A. Jentz, *Business Law Today* (St. Paul, MN: West Publishing Co., 1994), p. 632.

7. Jacquelyn Lynn, "Your Business Inc." *Business Start-Ups*, July 1996, p. 59.

8. Jane Easter Bahls, "Rethinking Inc.," *Entrepreneur*, August 1994, pp. 60–63; Barbara Marsh, "Suits Go After Personal Assets of Firm Owners," *Wall Street Journal*, August 13, 1993, pp. B1, B2.

9. Kylo-Patrick Hart, "Step 4: Decide Your Legal Structure," *Business Start-Ups*, August 1996, pp. 62–64.

10. Barbara Rudolph, "Franchising Is BIG Business for Small Business," *Your Company*, Spring 1992, p. 44.

11. Echo M. Garrett, "Job Creation," *Inc.*, December 1993, p. 151.

12. Lynn Beresford, "New Horizons," *Franchise and Business Opportunities 1996*, p. 4; Janean Huber, "Franchise Forecast," *Entrepreneur*, January 1993, p. 73.

13. Dan Fost and Susan Mitchell, "Small Stores with Big Names," *American Demographics*, November 1992, p. 52.

14. Meg Whittemore, "Changes Ahead for Franchising," *Nation's Business*, June 1990, p. 29.

15. Rudolph, "Franchising Is BIG Business," p. 46.

16. Gregory Matusky, "What Every Business Can Learn from Franchising," *Inc.*, January 1994, p. 91.

17. Jacqelyn Lynn, "Franchise Advantage," *Entrepreneur*, February 1995, p. 132.

18. Echo M. Garrett, "Reengineering the Franchise, " *Inc.*, December 1993, p. 148.

19. Kenneth Labich, "The New Low-Risk Entrepreneurs," *Fortune*, July 27, 1992, p. 84.

20. Lynn Beresford, "School Days," *Entrepreneur*, August 1995, p. 200.

21. Huber, "Franchise Forecast," p. 73.

22. Jacqelyn Lynn, "Franchise Advantage," *Entrepreneur*, February 1995, p. 136.

23. Andrew A. Caffey, "Franchises That Offer Creative Financing," *Business Start-Ups*, September 1996, pp. 62–68.

24. Jacquelyn Lynn, "Financing Your Franchise," *Business Start-Ups*, January 1996, p. 68.

25. Loren Gary, "In Search of the Perfect Franchise," advertising supplement, *Inc.*, April 1991.

26. Meg Whittemore, "The Franchise Search," *Nation's Business*, April 1993, p. 27.

27. Meg Whittemore and Carol Steinberg, "Venture's Guide to Franchising," *Venture*, July 1985, p. 75.

28. Jeffrey A. Tannenbaum, "Franchisees Balk at High Prices for Supplies from Franchisers," *Wall Street Journal*, July 5, 1995, pp. B1–B2.

29. Gregory Matusky, "The Franchise Hall of Fame," *Inc.*, April 1994, pp. 86–89.

30. Gregory Matusky, "What Every Business Can Learn From Franchising," *Inc.*, January 1994, p. 90.

31. Janean Chun, "Golden Rule?" *Entrepreneur*, April 1996, pp. 160–162.

32. David J. Kaufman, "The First Step," *Entrepreneur*, January 1992, pp. 90–97; Andrew A. Caffey, "Understanding the UFOC," *Entrepreneur*, January 1995, pp. 106–111; Lynn Beresford, "New Horizons," *Franchise & Business Opportunities 1996*, pp. 2–6.

33. Jeannie Ralston, "Before You Bet Your Buns," *Venture*, March 1988, p. 57.

34. Roberta Maynard, "Why Franchisers Look Abroad," *Nation's Business*, Otober 1995, pp. 65–72.

35. Jeffrey A. Tannenbaum, "Franchisers See a Future in East Bloc," *Wall Street Journal*, June 5, 1990, p. Bl.

36. Ibid., p. B2.

37. Scott Bernard Nelson, "Fill'er Up with a Big Mac and Fries," *Kiplinger's Personal Finance Magazine*, January 1996, p. 14.

38. Janean Huber, "Franchise Forecast," *Entrepreneur*, January 1993, p. 73.

39. Ibid.

40. Gary, "In Search of the Perfect Franchise."

41. Janean Huber, "What's Next?" *Entrepreneur*, September 1994, p. 149.

42. Roberta Maynard, "Why Franchisers Look Abroad," *Nation's Business*, October 1995, pp. 65–72.

43. Kevin McLaughlin, "A Welcome Addition," *Entrepreneur*, January 1990, p. 211.

44. Meg Whittemore, "Teaching Franchise Success," *Kiplinger's Personal Finance Magazine*, February 1996, pp. 82–84.

45. Lynn Beresford, "Seeing Double," *Entrepreneur*, October 1995, pp. 164–167.

46. Janean Huber, "What's Next?" p. 151

Chapter 4

1. Donna Fenn, "The Buyers," *Inc.*, June 1996, p. 48.

2. Joseph Anthony, "Maybe You Should Buy a Business," *Kiplinger's Personal Finance Magazine*, May 1993, pp. 83–87.

3. Fenn, "The Buyers," p. 48.

4. Hendrix F.C. Neimann, "Buying a Business," *Inc.*, February 1990, pp. 28–38.

5. Thomas Owens, "Growth Through Acquisition, " *Small Business Reports*, August 1990, p. 63.

6. Steven B. Kaufman, "Before You Buy, Be Careful," *Nation's Business*, March 1996, p. 45.

7. Erika Kotite, "Instant Business?" *Entrepreneur*, March 1994, p. 119.

8. John Case, "Buy Now—Avoid the Rush," *Inc.*, February 1991, p. 38.

9. Kaufman, "Before You Buy," p. 45.

10. Richard M. Rodnick, "Getting the Right Price for Your Firm," *Nation's Business*, March 1984, pp. 70–71.

11. David R. Evanson, "Know Your Worth," *Success*, June 1995, p. 22.

12. Christopher Caggiano, "The 8 Dumbest Ways to Try to Sell Your Company," *Inc.*, November 1994, pp. 73–79.

13. Janet Willen, "The Price Is Right," *Business News*, Summer 1995, p.12.

14. "Selling Your Business," Special Report no. 4, *The Business Owner*, November 1991, p. 8.

15. Bob Weinstein, "Cashing Out," *Business Start-Ups*, November 1995, p. 93.

16. Ibid.

17. Peter Nulty, "Smart Ways to Sell Your Business," *Fortune*, March 17, 1996, pp. 97–98.

18. Shannon P. Pratt, "Business Buyer's Valuation Guide," *In Business*, March–April 1987, p. 59.

19. Laura M. Litvan, "Selling Off, Staying On," *Nation's Business*, August 1995, pp. 29–30.

20. Peter Collins, "Cashing Out and Maintaining Control," *Small Business Reports*, December 1989, p. 28.

21. "More Business Owners May Be Selling Out," *Small Business Reports*, May 1990, p. 26.

22. "Problems with Foreign Owners," *Small Business Reports*, May 1991, p. 11.

23. "The Time Honored ESOP," *Inc.*, June 1991, p. 139.

Chapter 5

1. Dale D. Buss, "The Little Guys Strike Back," *Nation's Business*, July 1996, p. 19.

2. Paul Hughes, "Service Savvy," *Business Start-Ups*, January 1996, pp. 48–51.

3. Howard Dana Shaw, "Customer Care Checklist," *In Business*, September/October, 1987, p. 28.

4. David Altany, "Call Me Tom," *Industry Week*, January 22, 1990, p. 22.

5. Frances Huffman, "Search for Tomorrow," *Entrepreneur*, December 1993, pp. 94–95.

6. "Maid-to-Order for the Masses," *Kiplinger's Personal Finance Magazine*, January 1996, p. 16.

7. Roberta Maynard, "New Directions in Marketing" *Nation's Business*, July 1995, p. 26.

8. Carol Steinberg, "Target Selling," *Success*, May 1995, p. 79–83.

9. Laurel Toby, "The Customer's Always Right," *Your Company*, Spring 1995, p. 4.

10. Justin Martin, "Ignore Your Customer," *Fortune*, May 1, 1995, pp. 121–125.

11. Nancy L. Croft, "Smart Selling," *Nation's Business*, March 1988, pp. 51–52.

12. Ibid., p. 51.

13. Meg Whittemore, "Survival Tactics for Retailers," *Nation's Business*, June 1993, p. 23.

14. Jennifer deJong, "Turbocharging Customer Service," *Inc. Technology*, Number 2, 1995, pp. 35–39.

15. Stephen M. Silverman, "Retail Retold," *Inc. Technology*, Summer 1995, pp. 23–26.

16. Patricia Sellers, "Companies That Serve You Best," *Fortune*, May 31, 1993, p. 76.

17. Michael Collins, "Common–Sense Niche Marketing," *Small Business Reports*, September 1994, pp. 37–45.

18. Roberta Maynard, "Tailoring Products for a Niche of One," *Nation's Business*, November 1993, p. 40.

19. Leonard L. Berry, "Customer Service Solutions," *Success*, July/August 1995, pp. 90–95.

20. Faye Rice, "Making Generational Marketing Come of Age," *Fortune*, June 26, 1995, pp. 110–114.

21. R. Lee Sullivan, "Horse Sense Formula," *Forbes*, January 17, 1994, p. 91.

22. Meg Whittemore, "Retailing Looks to a New Century," *Nation's Business*, December 1994, p. 20.

23. Hughes,"Service Savvy," p.50.

24. Joshua Levine, "'Relationship Marketing,'" *Forbes*, December 20, 1993, p. 232.

25. Bradford McKee, "How Much Do You Really Value Your Customers?" *Nation's Business*, August 1993, p.8.

26. Hughes, "Service Savvy," p. 48.

27. Aimee L. Stern, "How to Build Customer Loyalty," *Your Company*, Spring 1995, p. 37.

28. "Deadly Game of Losing Customers," *In Business*, May 1988, p. 189.

29. Jim Campbell, "Good Customer Service Pays Off," *UP*, November 1988, pp. 12–13.

30. "Keeping Customers for Life," *Communication Briefings*, September 1990, p. 3.

31. Rahul Jacob, "Why Some Customers Are More Equal Than Others," *Fortune*, September 19, 1994, pp. 215–224.

32. Sellers, "Companies That Serve You Best," p. 75.

33. William A. Sherden, "The Tools of Retention," *Small Business Reports*, November 1994, pp. 43–47.

34. Stern, "How to Build Customer Loyalty," pp. 36–37.

35. "Be on the Lookout for Changes," *Communication Briefings*, October 1993, p. 4.

36. "Ways & Means," *Reader's Digest*, January 1993, p. 56.

37. Faye Rice, "How to Deal with Tougher Customers," *Fortune*, December 3, 1990, pp. 39–40.

38. Howard Rothman, "Quality's Link to Productivity," *Nation's Business*, February 1994, pp. 33–34.

39. Rahul Jacob, "TQM: More Than a Dying Fad," *Fortune*, October 18, 1993, p. 67.

40. Ibid.

41. Dave Zielinski, "Improving Service Doesn't Require a Big Investment," *Small Business Reports*, February 1991, p. 20.

42. Ibid.

43. Jo-Ann Johnston, "Waxing Philosophical," *Small Business Reports*, June 1994, pp. 14–19.

44. Bob Weinstein, "Bright Ideas," *Business Start-Ups*, August 1995, p. 57.

45. Alan Deutschman, "America's Fastest Risers," *Fortune*, October 7, 1991, p. 58.

46. Bob Weinstein, "Set in Stone," *Business Start-Ups*, October 1995, pp. 24–28.

47. "Hold That Price!" *Success*, May 1995, p. 25.

48. Ronald Henkoff, "Service Is Everybody's Business," *Fortune*, June 27, 1994, pp. 48–49.

49. "Keeping Customers for Life," *Communication Briefings*, September 1990, p. 3.

50. Mark Henricks, "Satisfaction Guaranteed," *Entrepreneur*, May 1991, p. 122.

51. Lore Croghan, "A Day in the Life of ...The Peabody Hotel," *FW*, November 21, 1995, pp. 58–60.

52. Jacquelyn Kynn, "Customers," *Business Start-Ups*, December 1995, p.12.

53. Joan Koob Cannie, "We Are the Champions," *Small Business Reports*, January 1993, pp. 31–41.

54. Ron Zemke and Dick Schaaf, "The Service Edge," *Small Business Reports*, July 1990, pp. 57–60.

55. Thomas A. Stewart, "After all you've done for your customers, why are they still NOT HAPPY?" *Fortune*, December 11, 1995, pp. 178–182.

56. Henkoff, "Service Is Everybody's Business," p. 49.

57. Berry, "Customer Service Solutions," pp. 90–94.

58. Hal Plotkin, "Dining a la Data," *Inc. Technology*, No. 4, 1995, pp. 85–86.

59. Zemke and Schaaf, "The Service Edge," p. 60.

60. Altany, "Call Me Tom," p. 14.

61. Brian Dumaine, "How Managers Can Succeed Through Speed," *Fortune*, February 13, 1989, pp. 54–59.

62. Mark Henricks, "Time Is Money," *Entrepreneur*, February 1993, p. 44.

63. Ibid.

64. Tom Stein, "Outsmarting the Giants," *Success*, May 1996, pp. 38–41.

65. Veronica Byrd and Brian L. Clark, "Increasing Your Net Profits," *Your Company*, June/July 1996, p. 24.

66. Wendy Taylor and Marty Jerome, "Internet Upstarts," *PC Computing*, August 1996, p. 63; Veronica Byrd and Brian L. Clark, "Increasing Your Net Profits," *Your Company*, June/July 1996, pp. 22–28.

67. John C. Dvorak, "Web Wake-up Call," *PC Computing*, August 1996, p. 59; Veronica Byrd and

Brian L. Clark, "Increasing Your Net Profits," *Your Company*, June/July 1996, pp. 22–28.

68. Andy Meisler, "Cast Your Internet Wide!" *Business News*, Spring 1996, pp. 14–18.

69. Byrd and Clark, "Increasing Your Net Profits," p. 27.

70. Steven Dickman, "Catching Customers on the Web," *Inc. Technology*, Summer 1995, p. 60.

71. Weinstein, "Set in Stone," p. 27.

72. Hughes, "Service Savvy," p. 50.

73. Lester A. Picker, "Selling to Women," *Your Company*, April/May 1996, pp. 32–38.

74. Roberta Maynard, "Rich Niches," *Nation's Business,* November 1993, pp. 39–42.

75. Stanley J. Winkelman, "Why Big-Name Stores Are Losing Out," *Fortune*, May 8, 1989, pp. 14–15.

76. Deanna Hodgin, "A War Baby Bounces Back in Trendy Style," *Insight*, April 1, 1991, p. 44.

77. Toddi Gutner Block, "Riding the Waves," *Forbes*, September 11, 1995, pp. 182–183.

78. Paul B. Brown, "The Eternal Second Act," *Inc.*, June 1988, pp. 119–120.

79. Marj Chandler, "Yuengling's Success Defies Convention," *Wall Street Journal*, August 26, 1993, pp. Bl, B8.

80. Weinstein, "Set in Stone," p. 27.

Chapter 6

1. Roberta Maynard, "The Lighter Side of Promotions," *Nation's Business*, July 1996, p. 48.

2. Meg Whittemore, "PR on a Shoestring," *Nation's Business*, January 1991, p. 31.

3. "Publicity Scores Over Ads," *Communication Briefings*, December 1994, p. 5

4. Lynn Beresford, "Going My Way?" *Entrepreneur*, February 1996, p. 32.

5. "Traits of Top Salespeople," *Small Business Reports*, December 1990, pp. 7–8.

6. Jaclyn Fierman, "The Death and Rebirth of the Salesman," *Fortune*, July 25, 1994, pp. 80–91.

7. "Most Salespeople Can't Sell," *Small Business Reports*, September 1990, p. 10.

8. "Prepare for Sales Calls," *Success*, May 1996, p. 25.

9. "Those Who Ask, Get," *The Competitive Advantage*, sample issue, p. 7.

10. "The Cost of a Sales Call," *Inc.*, May 1991, p. 86.

11. "Meeting Customer Needs," *In Business*, May/June 1989, p. 14.

12. "Business News," *Wall Street Journal*, July 13, 1995, p. A1.

13. Tom L. Brown, "Honesty Is the Best (PR) Policy," *Industry Week*, November 7, 1988, p. 13.

14. "Ad Suggestion from New Study," *Communication Briefings*, June 1995, p. 2.

15. *The Dynamics of Change in Markets and Media*, from a Magazine Publishers Association seminar, New York.

16. Janean Chun, "Going the Distance," *Entrepreneur*, June 1996, pp. 114–120.

17. Paul Hughes, "Winning Ways," *Entrepreneur*, February 1994, pp. 80–88.

18. "Why They Open Direct Mail," *Communication Briefings*, December 1993, p. 5.

19. Ernan Roman. "More for Your Money," *Inc.*, September 1992, p. 116.

20. Ibid.

21. Nancy Bader, "1-800-4-MO'BIZ," *Your Company*, Summer 1994, p. 4.

22. Ed Nanas, "Computer Diskettes," *Your Company*, Spring 1993, pp. 8–9.

23. Gillian Newson, "Interactive Marketing Is Driven to Succeed," *NewMedia*, June 1993, pp. 73–77; Kristin Davis, "Junk Mail Worthy of the Name," *Kiplinger's Personal Finance Magazine,* March 1993, pp. 56–61.

24. Jill H. Ellsworth, "Staking a Claim on the Internet," *Nation's Business*, January 1996, pp. 29–31.

25. Carol Steinberg, "Selling in Cyberspace," *Success*, May 1996, p. 77.

26. Ellsworth, "Staking a Claim on the Internet."

27. Cary Kimble, "The Inside Scoop on Outdoor Ads," *IB*, September/October 1990, pp. 14–17.

28. *The Big Outdoor* (New York: Institute of Outdoor Advertising), p. 15; "Outdoor Ads That Work Best," *Communication Briefings*, October 1993, p. 6.

29. *TAA Rate Directory of Transit Advertising* (New York: Transit Advertising Association), p. 2.

30. Geeta Dardick, "High Quality, High Success," *In Business*, January/February 1988, p. 39.

31. Bernie Ward, "Everything's the Medium," *Sky*, May 1989, pp. 96–110.

32. Randall Lane, "The Ultimate Sponsorship," *Forbes*, March 14, 1994, p. 106.

33. Carrie Dolan, "Putting on the Dog Just Comes Naturally in Fey Marin County," *Wall Street Journal*, September 20, 1985, p. 1.

34. Ronald Alsop, "To Share Shoppers, Companies Test Talking, Scented Displays," *Wall Street Journal*, June 12, 1986, p. 31.

35. Sue Clayton, "Handsome Prints," *Business Start-Ups*, October 1995, p. 30.

36. Shelby Meinhardt, "Put It in Print," *Entrepreneur*, January 1989, p. 54.

37. Clayton, "Handsome Prints," p. 32.

38. Ibid.

39. Meinhardt, "Put It in Print," p. 59.

40. Denise Osburn and Dawn Kopecki, "A Way to Stretch Ad Dollars," *Nation's Business*, May 1994, p. 68.

41. Ibid.

42. Jane Easter Bahls, "Ad It Up," *Entrepreneur*, December 1994, pp. 47–49.

43. Carol Rose Carey, "Cut Ad Costs Without Cutting Quality," *Inc.*, April 1982, pp. 108–110.

44. Ibid., p. 108.

45. Julie Catalano, "Extra!" *AdVentures*, May/June 1990, p. 13.

46. "Advertising Vehicles: Businesses Discover New Use for Old Cars," *The Greenville News*, June 19, 1993, p. 1D.

47. Sara Delano, "Give and You Shall Receive," *Inc.*, February 1983, p. 128.

48. Carolyn Z. Lawrence, "The Price Is Right," *Business Start-Ups*, February 1996, p. 64.

49. Ibid, p. 67.

50. Ibid, p. 6.

51. William Echilkson, "The Return of Luxury," *Fortune*, October 17, 1994, p. 18.

52. Joan Delaney, "Are Your Prices Too Low?" *Your Company*, Spring 1994, p. 4.

53. Bob Ortega, "When These Drinkers Crack Open a Cold One, It Can Cost $75," *Wall Street Journal*, August 18, 1995, pp. B1, B10.

54. Gayle Sato Stodder, "Paying the Price," *Entrepreneur*, October 1994, p. 54.

55. Mark Henricks, "War & Price," *Entrepreneur*, June 1995, p. 156.

56. Bob Weinstein, "Getting Carded," *Entrepreneur*, September 1995, pp. 76–80.

57. "Business Bulletin," *Wall Street Journal*, July 26, 1990, p. A1.

58. Richard J. Maturi, "Charging Ahead," *Entrepreneur*, July 1990, p. 56.

59. Weinstein, "Getting Carded," p. 76.

Chapter 7

1. Mary Baechler, "The Cash–Flow Quagmire," *Inc.*, October 1994, p. 25.

2. "Help! My Firm Is Hemorrhaging Cash," *Your Company*, April/May 1996, pp. 10–11.

3. Ibid.

4. Daniel Kehrer, "Big Ideas for Your Small Business," *Changing Times*, November 1989, p. 58.

5. William Bak, "I Owe, I Owe," *Entrepreneur*, October 1993, p. 56.

6. Jeannie Mandelker, "Put Numbers on Your Side," *Your Company*, Winter 1994, p. 33.

7. Douglas Bartholomew, "4 Common Financial Management Mistakes . . . And How to Avoid Them," *Your Company*, Fall 1991, p. 9.

8. Robert A. Mamis, "Money In, Money Out," *Inc.*, March 1993, p. 98.

9. Ibid.

10. Bartholomew, "4 Common Financial Management Mistakes," p. 9.

11. Phaedra Hise, "Paging for Cash Flow," *Inc.*, December 1995, p. 131.

12. Jill Andresky Fraser, "Monitoring Daily Cash Trends," *Inc.*, October 1992, p. 49.

13. William G. Shepherd, Jr., "Internal Financial Strategies," *Venture*, September 1985, p. 66.

14. David H. Bangs, *Financial Troubleshooting: An Action Plan for Money Management in the Small Business*, Dover, New Hampshire: Upstart Publishing Company, 1992, p. 61.

15. Richard G.P. McMahon and Scott Holmes, "Small Business Financial Management Practices in North America: A Literature Review," *Journal of Small Business Management*, April 1991, p. 21.

16. George Anders, "Truckers Trials: How One Firm Fights to Save Every Penny as Its Profits Plummet," *Wall Street Journal*, April 13, 1982, pp. 1, 22.

17. "Cash Flow/Cash Flow Management," *Small Business Reporter*, No. 9, 1982, p. 5.

18. William Bak, "Make 'Em Pay," *Entrepreneur*, November 1992, p. 64.

19. Michael Selz, "Big Customers' Late Bills Choke Small Suppliers," *Wall Street Journal*, June 22, 1994, p. B1.

20. McMahon and Holmes, "Small Business Financial Management Practices in North America," p. 21.

21. Roger Thompson, "Business Copes with the Recession," *Nation's Business*, January 1991, p. 21.

22. "The Check Isn't in the Mail," *Small Business Reports*, October 1991, p. 6.

23. Richard J. Maturi, "Collection Dues and Don'ts," *Entrepreneur*, January 1992, p. 326.

24. Frances Huffman, "Calling to Collect," *Entrepreneur*, September 1993, p. 50.

25. Thompson, "Business Copes with the Recession," p. 21.

26. Jim Carlton, "Tight Squeeze," *Wall Street Journal*, March 26, 1996, pp. A1, A6.

27. Jill Andresky Fraser, "A Confidence Game," *Inc.*, December 1989, p. 178.

28. Jill Andresky Fraser, "How to Get Paid," *Inc.*, March 1992, p. 105.

29. Shepherd, "Internal Financial Strategies," p. 68.

30. Stephanie Barlow, "Frozen Assets," *Entrepreneur*, September 1993, p. 53.

31. Roberta Maynard, "Can You Benefit from Barter?" *Nation's Business*, July 1994, p. 6.

32. "33 Ways to Increase Your Cash Flow and Manage Cash Balances," *The Business Owner*, February 1988, p. 8.

33. Mamis, "Money In, Money Out," p. 102.

34. Jeffrey Lant, "Cash Is King," *Small Business Reports*, May 1991, p. 49.

35. Ronaleen Roha, "How Bartering Saves Cash," *Kiplinger's Personal Finance Magazine*, February 1996, pp. 103–107.

36. Stephanie Barlow, "Trading Up," *Entrepreneur*, November 1991, pp. 167–172.

37. Maturi, "Collection Dues and Don'ts," p. 138.

38. Roha, "How Bartering Saves Cash," 103.

39. Janet L. Willen, "Should You Lease Office Equipment?" *Nation's Business*, May 1995, pp. 59–60.

40. Jack Wynn, "To Use But Not to Own," *Nation's Business*, January 1991, p. 38.

41. Michael Selz, "Many Small Businesses Are Sold on Leasing Equipment, " *Wall Street Journal*, October 27, 1993, p. B2.

42. William Bak, "Wise Buys," *Entrepreneur*, November 1993, p. 54.

43. Thompson, "Business Copes with the Recession," p. 20.

44. Ibid.

45. Bruce G. Posner, "Skipped–Payment Loans," *Inc.*, September 1992, p. 40.

46. "How to Win the Battle of Bad Checks," *Collection*, Fall 1990, p. 3.

47. Thompson, "Business Copes with the Recession," p. 21.

48. Jill Andresky Fraser, "Better Cash Management," *Inc.*, May 1993, p. 42.

49. Mamis, "Money In, Money Out," p. 103.

Chapter 8

1. Eileen Davis, "Dodging the Bullet," *Venture*, December 1988, p. 78.

2. "Odds and Ends," *Wall Street Journal*, July 25, 1990, p. Bl.

3. Richard G.P. McMahon and Scott Holmes, "Small Business Financial Management Practices in North America: A Literature Review," *Journal of Small Business Management*, April 1991, p. 21.

4. Daniel Kehrer, "Big Ideas for Your Small Business," *Changing Times*, November 1989, p. 57.

5. William Bak, "The Numbers Game," *Entrepreneur*, April 1993, p. 54.

6. Diedrich Von Soosten, "The Roots of Financial Destruction," *Industry Week*, April 5, 1993, pp. 33–34.

7. Richard Maturi, "Take Your Pulse," *Business Start-Ups*, January 1996, p. 72.

8. McMahon and Holmes, "Small Business Financial Management Practices in North America," p. 21.

9. Jill Andresky Fraser, "When Staffers Track Results," *Inc.*, October 1993, p. 42; Dan Callahan, "Everybody's an Accountant," *Business Ethics*, January/February 1994, p. 37.

10. "Putting Ratios to Work," *In Business*, December 1988, pp. 14–15.

11. Bak, "The Numbers Game," p. 57.

12. "Analyzing Creditworthiness," *Inc.*, November 1991, p. 196.

13. Jack Stack, "The Logic of Profit," *Inc.*, March 1996, p. 17.

14. Jill Andresky Fraser, "The No–Surprises Daily Money Watcher," *Inc.*, August 1995, pp. 73–74.

15. William F. Doescher, "Taking Stock," *Entrepreneur*, November 1994, p. 64.

16. Jeannie Mandelker, "Put Numbers on Your Side," *Your Company*, Winter 1994, p. 32.

17. Jack Egan, "Trump Plays His Biggest Ace," *U.S.News & World Report*, April 9, 1990, p. 41.

Chapter 9

1. Paul Hawken, "Money," *Growing a Business*, KQED, San Francisco, 1988.

2. Steve Marshall Cohen, "Calculated Risk," *Business Start-Ups*, January 1996, pp. 75–76.

3. Steve Marshall Cohen, "Money Rules," *Business Start-Ups*, July 1995, p. 79.

4. "Advice from the Great Ones," *Communication Briefings*, January 1992, p. 5.

5. Sandra Mardenfeld, "New World Order," *Business Start-Ups*, July 1996, pp. 60–64.

6. "Sales and Marketing," *Venturing*, Vermont Public Television, 1991.

7. Conversation with Charles Burke, CEO, Burke Financial Associates.

8. Ibid.

9. Steve Marshall Cohen, "Reality Check," *Business Start-Ups*, October 1995, pp. 74–75.

10. Roger Thompson, "Business Plans: Myth and Reality," *Nation's Business*, August 1988, p. 16.

Chapter 10

1. William Wetzel, Jr., "Needed: An Economic Policy for Angels," *In Business*, March/April 1993, p. 54.

2. Udayan Gupta, "The Right Fit," *Wall Street Journal*, May 22, 1995, p. R8.

3. Elizabeth Fenner, "How to Raise the Cash You Need, " *Money Guide*, Summer 1991, p.45.

4. Lee Berton, "Small Companies Try Avant-Garde Methods for Funds," *Wall Street Journal*, May 20, 1994, p.B2.

5. Sharon Nelton, "Capital Ideas for Financing," *Nation's Business*, September 1996, pp. 18–27.

6. Toni Mack, "They Stole My Baby," *Forbes*, February 12, 1996, pp. 90–91.

7. Fenner, "How to Raise The Cash You Need."

8. "Starting Up Without Borrowing," *In Business*, July/August 1988, p.48.

9. Alex Markels, "A Little Help from Their Friends," *Wall Street Journal*, May 22, 1995, p. R10.

10. Fenner, "How to Raise The Cash You Need."

11. Ibid.

12. Gianna Jacobson, "Capture an Angel," *Success*, November 1995, p. 46.

13. Gene Bylinsky, "Who Will Feed the Startups," *Fortune*, June 26, 1995, p. 102.

14. Gianna Jacobson, "Raise Money Now," *Success*, November 1995, pp. 39–50.

15. "Digging for Dollars," *Wall Street Journal*, February 24, 1989, p. R25.

16. Ibid.

17. Bruce G. Posner, "Talking to the Money Club," *Inc.*, June 1993, p. 39.

18. Bruce J. Blechman, "Step Right Up," *Entrepreneur*, June 1993, pp. 20–25.

19. Ellie Winninghoff, "Guardian Angels?" *Small Business Reports*, April 1993, pp. 30–39; Bruce G. Posner, "How to Finance Anything," *Inc.*, February 1993, pp. 54–68.

20. Nancy Scarlato, "Money," *Business Start-Ups*, December 1995, pp. 50–51; Gianna Jacobson, "Raise Money Now," *Success*, November 1995, pp. 39–50.

21. Mark Henricks, "Stand Your Ground," *Entrepreneur*, January 1993, p. 264.

22. Richard Florida, "What Start-Ups Don't Need Is Money," *Inc.*, April 1994, pp. 27–28.

23. Andrew Kruger, "America's Fastest Growing Company," *Fortune*, August 13, 1990, pp. 48–52.

24. Jenny C. McCune, "Get Global Cash," *Success*, December 1995, p. 16.

25. "You Can't Start Too Soon," *Inc.*, May 1995, p. 144.

26. "Venture Capitalists Take the Reins," *Small Business Reports*, April 1990, p. 23.

27. Anne B. Fisher, "Raising Capital for a New Venture," *Fortune*, June 13, 1994, p. 101.

28. "Equity Capital Sources Shift in the 90s," *In Business*, March/April 1990, p. 19.

29. Fisher, "Raising Capital for a New Venture."

30. David R. Evanson, "Tales of Caution in Going Public," *Nation's Business*, June 1996, p. 58.

31. "Planet Hollywood Stock Goes Public," *The Greenville News*, April 20, 1996, p. 13B.

32. Evanson, "Tales of Caution in Going Public."

33. Roberta Maynard, "Are You Ready to Go Public?" *Nation's Business*, January 1995, pp. 30–32.

34. Philip W.Taggart, Roy Alexander, and Robert M. Arnold, "Deciding Whether to Go Public," *Nation's Business*, May 1991, p.52.

35. Reena Aggarwal and Pietra Rivoli, "Evaluating the Costs of Raising Capital Through an Initial Public Offering," *Journal of Business Venturing*,Volume 6, 1991, pp. 351–361.

36. Jack and Hall Brill, "How Well Do IPOs Work?" *Wall Street Journal*,September 14, 1993, p.Cl.

37. Sara Calian, "Maternity-Wear IPO Has Pricing Problem," *Wall Street Journal*, September 14, 1993, p. Cl.

38. John R. Emswiller, "SCOR Funding Provides Short Form for Going Public," *Wall Street Journal*, January 21, 1992, p. B2.

39. Nelton, "Capital Ideas for Financing."

40. "Small Green Firms Use Direct Public Offerings," *In Business*, May/June 1996, p. 10; "A Fishy Success," *Business Ethics*, July/August 1996, p. 6.

41. "A Pitch for Private Equities," *Inc.*, December 1995, p. 126.

42. Mack, "They Stole My Baby."

43. Gianna Jacobson, "Find Your Fortune on the Internet," *Success*, November 1995, p.50.

44. Jenny C. McCune, "Raise Money on the Internet," *Success*, July/August 1995, p. 19.

45. Debra Phillips, "Northern Exposure," *Entrepreneur*, February 1996, p. 15.

46. Michelle L. Kezar, "Big Lending to Small Business," *Cross Sections*, Spring 1995, p. 28.

47. Ibid.

48. Rick Brooks, "Small Banks Lead the Way," *Wall Street Journal*, February 28, 1996, p. S3.

49. Daniel M. Clark, "Banks and Bankability," *Venture*, September 1989, p. 29.

50. J. Tol Broome Jr., "Credit on Call," *Nation's Business*, September 1995, p. 42.

51. *Inc.*, July 1990, p. 96.

52. Jill Andresky Fraser, "Rest Them (Or Be Told To)," *Inc.*, May 1994, p. 153.

53. Udayan Gupta, "Enterprise," *Wall Street Journal*, March 1, 1994, p. B2.

54. Teri Agins, "Asset–Based Lending to Firms Has Found Favor with Banks," *Wall Street Journal,* November 5, 1984, p. 35.

55. "Financing Small Business," *Small Business Reporter*, c3, p. 9.

56. Jill Andresky Fraser, "When Supplier Credit Helps Fuel Growth," *Inc.*, March 1995, p. 117.

57. Georgette Jasen, "Pros and Cons of Borrowing from Your Broker," *Wall Street Journal*, April 21, 1993, p. Cl.

58. Scott McMurray, "Personal Loans from Brokers Offer Low Rates," *Wall Street Journal*, January 7, 1986, p. 31.

59. Dawn Jopecki, "Good Reasons to Borrow from a Broker," *Kiplinger's Personal Financial Magazine*, August 1995, p. 37; Jill Bettner, "Brokers Begin Pushing Margin Loans—But Critics Say Borrowers Should Beware," *Wall Street Journal*, August 26, 1987, p. 19.

60. Bruce G. Posner, "Insurance Companies Move Into Smaller Deals," *Inc.*, October 1991, pp. 165–166.

61. Bruce G. Posner, "Tapping a Credit Union," *Inc.*, December 1992, p. 35.

62. Janean Chung, "Minority Rules," *Entrepreneur*, August 1995, p. 18.

63. Phil Adamsak, "Why SBLCs Are Eager to Lend," *Venture*, June 1984, p. 158.

64. Nelton, "Capital Ideas for Financing," pp. 18–27.

65. Joseph R. Mancuso, "The ABCs of Getting Money from the SBA," *Your Company*, June/July 1996, pp. 54–59.

66. Cythnia E. Griffin, "SBA Treasure Chest," *Business Start-Ups*, January 1996, pp. 38–41; Joseph R. Mancuso, "The ABCs of Getting Money from the SBA," *Your Company*, June/July 1996, pp. 54–59.; J. Tol Broome, "Less Hassle, More Loans," *Nation's Business*, August 1995, p.60; Meg Whittemore, "The Lowdown on Low Doc," *Nation's Business*, June 1995, p. 70.

67. Laura M. Litvan, "Some Rest for the Paperwork Weary," *Nation's Business*, June 1994, pp. 38–40; Robert W. Casey, "Getting Down to Business," *Your Company*, Summer 1994, pp. 30–33.

68. Veronica Byrd, "A Satisfied SBA Customer," *Your Company*, June/July 1996, p. 58.

69. Erika Kotite, "Fed Funds," *Enterprise*, February 1993, p. 122.

70. Nelton, "Capital Ideas for Financing."

71. Behind the Boom in Microloans," *Inc.*, April 1994, p. 114.

72. Erskine Bowles, "Bite–Sized Loans," *Entrepreneur*, December 1993, p. 152.

73. Philip Lader, "Techin' It to the Streets," *Entrepreneur*, June 1995, p. 176.

74. Ibid.

75. M. John Storey, "Triple Your Growth Power," *Success*, June 1996, p. 14.

76. Udayan Gupta and Brent Bowers, "States and Localities Help Small Firms Get New Capital," *Wall Street Journal*, April 23, 1992, p. B2.

77. Bruce J. Blechman, "The High Cost of Credit," *Entrepreneur*, January 1993, pp. 22–25.

78. Gianna Jacobson, "Cash Infusions," *Success*, June 1996, p. 16.

79. Gerri Detweiler, "Charge It," *Business Start-Ups*, January 1996, pp. 62–63.

80. Frances Huffman, "Financing," *Entrepreneur*, April 1993, pp. 196–199; "A New Complaint from Women," *Nation's Business*, May 1993, p. 74.

Chapter 11

1. Roberta Maynard, "A Growing Outlet for Small Firms, *Nation's Business*,, August 1996, pp. 45–48.

2. Karen Axelton, Janean Chun, Debra Philips, Cynthia E. Griffin, Heather Page, Lynn Beresford, and Holly Celeste Fisk, "30 Cities for Small Business," *Entrepreneur*, October 1996, pp. 120–138.

3. Andrew Kupfer, "The Champ of Cheap Clones," *Fortune*, September 23, 1991, pp. 115–120.

4. Bernard J. LaLonde, "New Frontiers in Store Location," *Supermarket Merchandising*, February 1963, p. 110.

5. Kylo-Patrick Hart, "Step 7: Choosing a Location," *Business Start-Ups*, November 1996, pp. 76–80.

6. Susan Greco, "Where the Shoppers Are," *Inc.* May 1995, p. 113.

7. Michael Totty, "'Power' Centers Lure Shoppers by Mixing Elements from Big Malls and Small Plazas," *Wall Street Journal*, December 27, 1988, p. B1.

8. Maynard, "A Growing Outlet for Small Firms."

9. International Council of Shopping Centers, New York (World Wide Web address: http://www.icsc.org/).

10. Maynard, "A Growing Outlet for Small Firms."

11. Laura Meyers, "Tough New Zoning Laws Threaten Activities of Home Businesses," *Your Company*, Fall 1995, pp. 8–9; Lynne Beresford, Janean Chun, Cynthia E. Griffin, Heather Page, and Debra Phillips, "Homeward Bound," *Entrepreneur*, September 1995,pp. 116–129.

12. Susan Gregory Thomas, "Home Offices That Really Do the Job," *U.S. News and World Report*, October 28, 1996, pp. 84–87.

13. The National Business Incubation Association, Athens, Ohio (World Wide Web address: http://www.nbia.org/).

14. Deborah L. Jacobs, "The Americans with Disabilities Act," *Your Company*, Summer 1994, pp. 10–12.

15. Mitchell Brill and Cheryl Parker, "Office Planning," *Small Business Reports*, December 1988, p. 36.

16. Heather Page, "Pedal to the Metal," *Entrepreneur*, August 1996, p. 15.

Chapter 12

1. Shawn Tully, "Purchasing's New Muscle," *Fortune*, February 20, 1995, p. 75–83.

2. Loretta Owens and Mark Henricks, "Quality Time," *Entrepreneur*, October 1995, p. 159.

3. Roberta Maynard, "A Company Is Turned Around Through Japanese Principles," *Nation's Business,* February 1996, p. 9.

4. "What Price Quality?" *Small Business Reports*, August 1990, p. 7.

5. Thomas M. Rohan, "Sermons Fall on Deaf Ears," *Industry Week,* November 20, 1989, pp. 35–36.

6. "Patience Pays Off," *Industry Week,* April 4, 1994, p. 9.

7. Owens and Henricks, "Quality Time," p. 158.

8. Michael Barrier, "Who Should Get How Much—and Why? *Nation's Business,* November 1995, pp. 58–59.

9. Mark Henricks, "80/20 Vision," *Entrepreneur*, April 1996, pp. 68–71.

10. Owens and Henricks, "Quality Time," p. 158

11. Roberta Maynard, "Striking the Right Match," *Nation's Business*, May 1996, pp. 18–28.

12. Robert Maynard, "The Power of Pooling," *Nation's Business*, March 1995, pp. 16–22.

13. Richard J. Maturi, "The One and Only," *Entrepreneur,* June 1993, p. 152.

14. Tully, "Purchasing's New Muscle," p. 76.

15. "Rarely Just in Time," *Small Business Reports,* April 1990, p. 12.

16. Jill Andresky Fraser, "Know Thy Inventory," *Inc.,* June 1996, p. 120.

17. Bob Weinstein, "Taking Stock," *Entrepreneur,* January 1995, p. 50.

18. Joshua Macht, "Are You Ready for Electronic Partnering?" *Inc. Technology*, Volume 4, 1995, pp. 43–51.

19. Laura Bird, "High–Tech Inventory System Coordinates Retailer's Clothes with Customer's Tastes," *Wall Street Journal*, June 12, 1996, pp. B1, B7.

20. John H. Sheridan, "Coherent," *Industry Week*, October 17, 1994, pp. 53–54.

21. Roberta Maynard, "The New Supplier Partnership: An Inside Story*," Nation's Business*, May 1996, p. 21.

Chapter 13

1. Max DePree, *Leadership Jazz*, Currency Doubleday, (New York: 1992), pp. 8–9.

2. Francis Huffman, "Taking the Lead," *Entrepreneur*, November 1993, p. 101.

3. Stratford Sherman, "How Tomorrow's Leaders Are Learning Their Stuff," *Fortune*, November 27, 1995 p. 102.

4. Bernard A. Nagle, "Wanted: A leader for the 21st century," *Industry Week*, November 20, 1995, p.29.

5. "Hiring Mistakes," *Practical Supervision*, November 1994, pp. 4–5.

6. Michael Barrier, "Hiring the Right People," *Nation's Business*, June 1996, pp. 18–27.

7. Richard J. Pinsker, "Hiring Winners," *Small Business Forum*, Fall 1994, pp. 66–84.

8. Barrier, "Hiring the Right People," p. 19.

9. Jim Johnson, "Take it from me: Write a Job Description," *Small Business Forum*, Fall 1994, pp. 10–11.

10. Barrier, "Hiring the Right People," p.21.

11. "Making the Most of Job Interviews," *Your Company*, Spring 1993, p. 6.

12. Michael Mercer, "Consider These Guidelines on Conducting Interviews," *Small Business Forum*, Fall 1994, pp. 11–14.

13. Greg Norred, "Weeding Out the Bad Apples," *Small Business Reports*, November 1993, pp. 58–61; Emma Fluker, "Checking Employee References," *Small Business Digest*, Premier Issue 1990, p. 7.

14. Bill Saporito, "Unsuit Yourself: Management Goes Informal," *Fortune*, September 20, 1993, p. 118.

15. John Case, "Corporate Culture," *Inc.*, November 1996, p. 45.

16. Ibid, pp. 42–53.

17. James L. Bildner, "Hitting the Wall," *Inc.*, July 1995, pp. 21–22.

18. Anna Brady, "Small Is as Small Does," *Journal of Business Strategy*, January/February 1996, pp. 44–52.

19. Ronald E. Merrill and Henry D. Sedgwick, "To Thine Own Self Be True," *Inc.*, August 1994, pp. 50–56.

20. Ibid, p. 56.

21. Robert McGarvey, "Joining Forces," *Entrepreneur*, September 1996, p. 83.

22. Brian Dumaine, "The Trouble with Teams," *Fortune*, September 5, 1994, p. 86.

23. McGarvey, "Joining Forces," pp. 80–83; "Whoa, Team," *Journal of Business Strategy*, January/February 1996, p. 8.

24. Mark Frohman and Perry Pascarella, "Don't Abdicate," *Industry Week*, November 6, 1995, p. 69.

25. McGarvey,"Joining Forces," p. 80.

26. Michael Selz, "Testing Self–Managed Work Teams, Entrepreneur Hopes to Lose Job," *Wall Street Journal*, January 11, 1994, p. B1; John Case, "The Open Book Revolution," *Inc.*, June 1995, pp. 26–43.

27. Brian S. Moskal, "Supervision (Or Lack Of It)," *Industry Week*, December 3, 1990. p. 56.

28. Michael Barrier, "Beyond the Suggestion Box," *Nation's Business*, July 1995, pp. 34–37.

29. Theodore B. Kinni, "The Empowered Workforce," *Industry Week*, September 19, 1994, p. 37.

30. Robert McGarvey, "More Power to Them," *Entrepreneur*, February 1995, p. 73.

31. David Maize, "Where It Pays to Have a Great Idea," *Reader's Digest*, June 1995, pp. 100–104.

32. Michael Barrier, "Beyond the Suggestion Box," *Nation's Business*, July 1995, p. 37.

33. John Case, "The Open–Book Revolution," *Inc.*, June 1995, pp. 26–43.

34. Jay Finnegan, "Pipe Dreams," *Inc.*, August 1994, pp. 64–70.

35. Michael Verespej, "A Workforce Revolution?" *Industry Week*, August 21, 1995, p. 23.

36. "Tips for Telecommuting," *Your Company*, Spring 1995, p. 2; Alice LaPlante, "Voluntary No More," *Forbes ASAP*, October 9, 1995, pp. 133–138.

37. "Tips for Telecommuting," *Your Company*, Spring 1995, p. 2.

38. Michael Barrier, "Improving Worker Performance," *Nation's Business*, September 1996, p. 30.

39. Harvey R. Meyer, "Linking Payday to Cash in Hand," *Nation's Business*, May 1996, pp. 36–38.

40. Shari Caudron, "Motivation? Money's Only No.2," *Industry Week*, November 15, 1993, p. 33.

41. Michael Barrier, "Improving Worker Performance," *Nation's Business*, September 1996, p. 28.

42. *Bits & Pieces*, July 21, 1994, p. 19.

43. Jennifer Pendleton, "Just Rewards," *Business News*, Spring 1994, pp. 30–32.

44. Donna Fenn, "Managing Generation X," *Inc.*, August 1996, p. 91; Roberta Maynard, "A Less–Stressed Work Force," *Nation's Business*, November 1996, pp. 50–51.

45. Alan Farnham, "Mary Kay's Lessons in Leadership," *Fortune*, September 20, 1993, pp. 68–77.

46. Robert McGarvey, "Bonus Points," *Entrepreneur*, July 1994, p. 74.

47. Ibid, pp. 74–77.

48. Jack Stack, "That Championship Season," *Inc.*, July 1996, p. 27.

49. Carla Goodman, "Destination: Success," *Business Start-Ups*, December 1996, p. 50.

50. Jack Stack, "The Logic of Profit," *Inc.*, March 1996, p. 17.

51. Ferdinand Fournies, "Why Performance Appraisals Don't Work," *Small Business Forum*, Winter 1993/1994, pp. 69–77.

52. Joan Delaney, "Rave Reviews," *Your Company*, Spring 1994, pp. 12–13.

53. Brian O'Reilly, "360 Feedback Can Change Your Life," *Fortune*, October 17, 1994, p. 93.

54. Vivian Marino, "Estate Planning Crucial for Family Business Survival," *Upstate Business*, October 13, 1996, pp. 4–5,16.

55. Ibid.

56. Ibid.

57. Ronaleen R. Roha, "Estate-Planning Solutions for Small Business Owners," *Kiplinger's Personal Finance Magazine*, August 1994, pp. 77–80

58. Marino, "Estate Planning Crucial for Family Business Survival," p. 4.

59. Patricia Schiff Estess, "Heir Raising," *Entrepreneur*, May 1996, pp. 80–82.

60. Marino, "Estate Planning Crucial for Family Business Survival."

61. Roha, "Estate-Planning Solutions for Small Business Owners."

62. Ibid.

Chapter 14

1. Amy Barrett, "It's a Small (Business) World," *Business Week*, April 17, 1995, pp. 96–101.

2. William Echikson, "Young Americans Go Abroad to Strike It Rich," *Fortune*, October 17, 1994, pp. 185–194.

3. "International Incentive," *Small Business Reports*, June 1992, p. 5.

4. Rob Norton, "Strategies for the New Export Boom," *Fortune*, August 22, 1994, p. 130.

5. Ted Miller, "Can America Compete in the Global Economy?" *Kiplinger's Personal Finance Magazine*, November 1991, p. 8.

6. Bernard Wysocki, Jr., "Going Global in the New World," *Wall Street Journal*, September 21, 1990, p. R3.

7. Preston Townley, "Global Business in the Next Decade," *Across the Board*, January/February 1990, p. 16.

8. Roger E. Axtell, *The Do's and Taboos of International Trade* (New York: John Wiley and Sons, 1994), p. 11.

9. Paul C. Hsu, "Profiting from a Global Mind-Set," *Nation's Business*, June 1994, p. 6.

10. Monci Jo Williams, "Rewriting the Export Rules," *Fortune*, April 23, 1990, p. 90.

11. Steven Taper, "From Main Street to Mexico City," *Cross Sections*, Fall 1995, p. 22.

12. "To Protect or Not to Protect," *FW*, June 1992, p. 56.

13. "Globesmanship," *Across The Board*, January/February 1990, p. 26.

14. Ibid.

15. "The Best Places to Do Business," *FW*, October 15, 1991, p. 26; *Breaking into the Trade Game: A Small Business Guide to Exporting*, (Washington, DC: U.S. Small Business Administration and AT&T, 1994), p. 11.

16. Michael Barrier, "Why Small Looms Large in the Global Economy," *Nation's Business*, February 1994, p. 9; Vivian Pospisil, "Global Paradox: Small is Powerful," *Industry Week*, July 18, 1994, p. 29.

17. Michael Barrier, "A Global Reach for Small Firms," *Nation's Business*, April 1994, p. 66.

18. Stephanie N. Mehta, "Artais Finds Smallness Isn't Handicap in Global Market," *Wall Street Journal*, June 23, 1994, p. B2.

19. Niklas von Daehne, "Ears to the Ground," *Success*, December 1995, p. 14.

20. Stephen J. Simurda, "Trade Secrets," *Entrepreneur*, May 1994, p. 99.

21. Jeremy Main, "Hot to Go Global—And Why," *Fortune*, August 28, 1989, p. 70.

22. Michael Self, "More Small Firms Are Turning to Trade Intermediaries," *Wall Street Journal*, February 2, 1993, p. B1.

23. Ibid.

24. "Reducing the Risk of Doing Business in China," *Nation's Business*, November 1994, p. 12.

25. Joseph E . Pattison, "Global Joint Ventures," *Overseas Business*, Winter 1990, p. 25.

26. Hal Plotkin, "In the China Shop," *Inc.* , September 1993, p. 108.

27. "Global Alliances," *Fortune* insert, pp. 67–82.

28. Jeffrey A. Tannenbaum, "Licensing May Be Quickest Route to Foreign Markets," *Wall Street Journal*, September 14, 1990, p. B2.

29. Gayle Sato Stodder, "Boxer Rebellion," *Entrepreneur*, August 1993, pp. 88–92.

30. Tannenbaum, "Licensing May Be Quickest Route to Foreign Markets."

31. *Breaking into the Trade Game: A Small Business Guide to Exporting* (Washington, DC: U.S. Small Business Administration and AT&T, 1994), p. 105.

32. Mary E. Tomzack, "Ripe New Markets," *Success*, April 1995, pp. 73–77.

33. Tara Parker-Pope, "Custom-Made," *Wall Street Journal*, September 26, 1996, p. R22.

34. Ibid.

35. Jeffrey A. Tannenbaum, "Franchisers See a Future in East Bloc," *Wall Street Journal*, June 5, 1990, p. B1.

36. Nathaniel Gilbert, "The Case for Countertrade," *Across The Board*, May 1992, pp. 43–45.

37. Axtell, "The Do's and Taboos of International Trade," p. 256.

38. Lourdes Lee Valeriano, "How Small Firms Can Get Free Help From Big Ones," W*all Street Journal*, July 30, 1991, p. B2.

39. Karin Moeller, "Top 10 Businesses for 1996," *Business Start-Ups*, January 1996, pp. 22–23.

40. Stephanie N. Mehta, "Small Companies Look to Cultivate Foreign Business," *Wall Street Journal,* July 7, 1994, p. B2.

41. Barrett, "It's a Small (Business) World," pp. 99–100.

42. Axtell, "The Do's and Taboos of International Trade," p. 10.

43. Hsu, "Profiting from a Global Mind-Set," p. 6.

44. Patricia M.Carey, "Growing Through Exports," *Your Company*, Fall 1994, p. 14.

45. Jeffrey A. Tannenbaum, "Among Fast-Growing Small Concerns, Exporters Expand the Most, Study Says," *Wall Street Journal*, June 19, 1996, p. B2.

46. Jan Alexander, "To Sell Well Overseas, Customize," *Your Company*, Fall 1995, p. 15.

47. Stephanie N.Mehta, "Small Companies Look to Cultivate Foreign Business," *Wall Street Journal,* July 7, 1994, p. B2.

48. Carter Henderson, "U.S. Small Business Heads Overseas," *In Business*, November/December 1995, pp. 18–21.

49. Christopher Knowlton, "The New Export Entrepreneurs," *Fortune*, June 6, 1988, p. 98

50. Alexander, "To Sell Well Overseas, Customize."

51. Jan Alexander, "How to Find an Overseas Distributor," *Your Company*, April/May 1996, pp. 52–54.

52. Stephanie Gruner, "Finding Overseas Agents," *Inc.*, May 1996, p. 108.

53. "The Pacific Rim on a Shoestring," *Inc.*, June 1991, pp. 122–123.

54. Philip Lader, "Export Ease," *Entrepreneur*, October 1995, p. 98.

55. John S. McClenahan, "Santec's European Connection," *Industry Week*, October 4, 1993, p. 30.

56. Echikson, "Young Ameicans Go Abroad to Strike It Rich," p. 190.

57. Stephen Kindel, "The New Corridors of Power," *FW*, March 5, 1991, p. 22.

58. Martha E. Mangelsdorf, "Unfair Trade," *Inc.*, April 1991, pp. 28–37.

59. Mark Robichaux, "Exporters Face Big Roadblocks at Home," *Wall Street Journal,* November 7, 1990, p. B1.

60. Ibid.

61. Walker E. Williams, "What Trade Laws Cost You," *Reader's Digest*, June 1993, pp. 197–202.

62. Christopher J. Chipelo, "Small U.S. Companies Take the Plunge into Japan's Market," *Wall Street Journal*, July 7, 1992, p. B2.

63. Jacob M. Schlesinger, "Tough Gamble," *Wall Street Journal*, May 11, 1993, pp. A1, A8.

64. Simurda,"Trade Secrets," p. 120.

65. Lawrence Van Gelder, "It Pays to Watch Words, Gestures While Abroad," *The Greenville News*, April 7, 1996, p. 8E.

66. Edward T. Hall, "The Silent Language of Overseas Business," *Harvard Business Review*, May–June 1960, pp. 5–14.

67. Ibid.

68. Roger E. Axtell, *Gestures: The Do's and Taboos of Body Language Around the World* (New York: John Wiley & Sons, Inc.) , 1991.

69. David A. Ricks, *Blunders in International Business* (Cambridge, MA: Blackwell Publishers, 1993), p. 5.

70. Stephanie Barlow, "Let's Make a Deal," *Entrepreneur*, May 1991, p. 40.

71. Barbara Pachter, When In Japan Don't Cross Your Legs," *Business Ethics*, March/April 1996, p. 50.

72. Michael J. Boskin, "Pass GATT Now," *Fortune*, December 12, 1994, p. 137; Louis S. Richman, "What's Next After GATT's Victory," *Fortune*, January 10, 1994, p. 66.

73. William Bak, "Triple Play," *Entrepreneur*, March 1994, p. 60.

74. Barrett, "It's a Small (Business) World."

75. John S. McClenahen, "Sound Thinking," *Industry Week*, May 3, 1993, p. 28.

76. Jeremy Main, "How To Go Global—And Why," *Fortune*, August 28, 1989, p. 70.

77. Ibid., pp. 70–76.

Chapter 15

1. "Thoughts on the Business of Life," *Forbes*, September 25, 1995, p. 248.

2. Jacquelyn Lynn, "A Matter of Principle," *Entrepreneur*, August 1995, p. 59.

3. William R. Holland, "Ethics in a Plain Manilla Envelope," *Industry Week*, March 18, 1996, p. 20.

4. Dale Kurschner, "5 Ways Ethical Busine$$ Creates Fatter Profit$," *Business Ethics*, March/April 1996, pp. 20–23.

5. Leah Ingram, "Doing Well by Doing Good," *Business News*, Spring 1995, pp. 14–18.

6. Ibid.

7. Gene Laczniak, "Business Ethics: A Manager's Primer," *Business*, January–February–March 1983, pp. 23–29; Jacquelyn Lynn, "A Matter of Principle," *Entrepreneur*, August 1995, p. 59.

8. Timothy Aeppel, "From License Plates to Fashion Plates," *Wall Street Journal*, September 21, 1994, pp. B1, B2.

9. Michael A. Verespej, "Trash to Cash," *Industry Week*, December 5, 1994, pp. 53–56.

10. Sharon Nelton, "Nurturing Diversity," *Nation's Business*, June 1995, pp. 25–27.

11. Ibid.

12. "Substance Abuse Still Top Problem," *Small Business Reports*, October 1991, p. 24.

13. David Warner, "The War on Drugs Wants You," *Nation's Business*, February 1996, pp. 54–55; Charles Carroll, "Five Point Plan Is a Blueprint for a Drug-free Workplace," *South Carolina Business Journal*, April 1996, p. 10.

14. Cynthia E. Griffin, "Crisis Control," *Entrepreneur*, August 1995, pp. 128–135.

15. Ira D. Singer, "AIDS Concerns for Business," *Nation's Business*, June 1989, pp. 75–77.

16. Philip Rutsohn and Donald Law, "Acquired Immune Deficiency Syndrome: A Small Business Dilemma," *Journal of Small Business Management*, January 1991, pp. 62–71.

17. Cindy Krischer Goodman, "Sexual Harassment Cases Growing More Frequent," *Upstate Business*, November 24, 1996, pp. 4–5.

18. Gary Schweikhart, "Sexual Harassment," *Business News*, Fall 1995, pp. 30–36.

19. Goodman, "Sexual Harassment Cases Growing More Frequent," p. 4.

20. Schweikhart, "Sexual Harassment."

21. William H. Miller, "More Than Just Making Money," *Industry Week*, August 21, 1995, p. 91.

22. Ingram, "Doing Well by Doing Good."

23. Marilyn Vos Savant, "Ask Marilyn," *Parade Magazine*, August 4, 1996, p. 6.

24. Jane Easter Bahls, "Truth or Dare," *Entrepreneur*, May 1995, pp. 66–69.

25. *Carbaugh* v. *Klick-Lewis, Inc.,* 561 A.2d 1248 (Supreme Ct, PA, 1989).

26. Citizens Against Law Abuse Web Page (http://pages.prodigy.com/cala/index61.htm).

27. Joan Szabo, "Protect Yourself Against Liability Lawsuits," *Your Company*, June/July 1996, pp. 14–15.

28. Citizens Against Law Abuse Web Page (http://pages.prodigy.com/cala/index61.htm).

29. Paula Mergerhagen, "Product Liability," *American Demographics*, June 1995, pp. 26–34.

30. Jeffrey F. Beatty and Susan S. Samuelson, *Business Law for a New Century*, Boston: Little, Brown and Company, 1996), p. 482.

31. Szabo, "Protect Yourself Against Liability Lawsuits."

32. Restatement (Second) of Torts, §402A (1).

33. "How to Protect What You Create," *In Business*, May/June 1996, p. 33.

Appendix

1. Rick Brooks, "Small Banks Lead the Way," *Wall Street Journal*, February 28, 1996, p. S3.

2. Ibid.

3. J. Romano, *The New York Times*, August 6, 1995, S9, p. R5(L).

4. *RMA Annual Statement Studies*, 1995, (Philiadelphia, PA: Robert Morris Associates, 1995), p. 204.

INDEX